# THE MODERN LAW OF CONTRACT

## Thirteenth Edition

# Richard Stone and James Devenney

Routledge
Taylor & Francis Group

LONDON AND NEW YORK

Thirteenth edition published in 2020
By Routledge
2 Park Square, Milton Park, Abingdon, Oxon OX14 4RN

and by Routledge
52 Vanderbilt Avenue, New York, NY 10017

*Routledge is an imprint of the Taylor & Francis Group, an informa business*

First edition published by Cavendish 2002
Twelfth edition published by Routledge 2017

*British Library Cataloguing-in-Publication Data*
A catalogue record for this book is available from the British Library

*Library of Congress Cataloging-in-Publication Data*
Names: Stone, Richard, 1951 March 7– author. | Devenney, James, author.
Title: The modern law of contract / Richard Stone and James Devenney.
Description: Thirteenth edition. | Milton Park, Abingdon, Oxon ; New York, NY : Routledge, [2019] | Includes bibliographical references and index.
Identifiers: LCCN 2019019689 | ISBN 9780367222857 (hbk) | ISBN 9780367222918 (pbk) | ISBN 9780429325199 (ebk)
Subjects: LCSH: Contracts—England.
Classification: LCC KD1554 .S758 2019 | DDC 346.4202—dc23
LC record available at https://lccn.loc.gov/2019019689

ISBN: 978-0-367-22285-7 (hbk)
ISBN: 978-0-367-22291-8 (pbk)
ISBN: 978-0-429-32519-9 (ebk)

Typeset in Helvetica
by Apex CoVantage, LLC

Visit the companion website: WWW.ROUTLEDGE.COM/CW/STONE

# Contents

# Detailed contents

# Preface

The aim of this book is to provide a comprehensive but readable account of what we have termed 'the modern law of contract'. By this we mean the law of contract as applied by the English and Welsh courts in the twenty-first century. This we see as being still rooted in the forms of the classical theory of contract (which is generally accepted as dating from the late nineteenth century), but with those forms increasingly being stretched to adapt to the modern world. The inadequacies of the classical model that are thus exposed have been the subject of much commentary and analysis, together with suggestions of better models that might be adopted. Understanding the modern law requires an awareness of these critical analyses and this we have attempted to provide throughout the text. What results is not, however, and is not intended to be, a radical re-reading of this area of law. A quick look at the chapter headings will show an overall structure that will be familiar to all contract lecturers. For the purposes of exposition, many familiar authorities have been used. Throughout, however, and in particular through the footnotes, we have tried to indicate ways in which the classical model of contract may be or is being challenged and developed, whether openly or surreptitiously. We hope that the result is a treatment of the law that is easy to follow (to the extent possible given the complexity of some areas) but that is also sufficiently rich to provide a challenge to more discerning readers. At the very least we hope that such readers will be encouraged to think about and explore new lines of thought on a variety of topics.

The previous editions have been well received by students and lecturers, and there are no major changes to the structure of this edition. The 'In focus' sections have been retained. These do not for the most part contain new material, but are designed to highlight some of the more discursive sections in each chapter, and to separate these more clearly from the straightforward exposition of the law. Diagrammatic summaries continue to appear at various points in every chapter to provide assistance to students who find visual representations easier to digest than plain text. 'Key cases' are highlighted. These are intended to be the cases that 'all students of contract law should know' on each topic. This is inevitably to some extent a personal selection, and no doubt other teachers will object that their favourite examples have been excluded. Many of the 'For thought' questions that appear in each chapter take the form of short hypothetical problems, giving them a more practical focus. They are still intended to stimulate students into thinking about issues for themselves, and developing a critical approach to the law – not simply accepting what judges and commentators say as the only possible answer to any particular question. For this reason, no answers are provided to these questions.

At the time of writing Brexit continues to generate much uncertainty and the text has been amended in appropriate places to reflect this. In terms of new case law, we have noted a large number of new Supreme Court decisions: *Brownlie v Four Seasons Holdings Inc* [2017] UKSC 80 (communication); *Rock Advertising Limited v MWB Business Exchange Centres Limited* [2018] UKSC 24 (enforceability); *Devani v Wells* [2019] UKSC 4 (agreement); *Lowick Rose LLP (in liquidation) v Swynson Ltd* [2017] UKSC 32 (privity of contract); *Playboy Club London Ltd v Banca Nazionale del Lavoro SpA* [2018] UKSC 43 (negligence); *Steel v NRAM Ltd (formerly NRAM Plc)* [2018] UKSC 13 (negligence); *Wood v Capita Insurance Services Limited* [2017] UKSC 24 (interpretation);

*James-Bowen v Comissioner of Police of the Metropolis* [2018] UKSC 40 (implied terms); *Prudential Assurance Co Ltd v Revenue and Customs Commissioners* [2018] UKSC 39 (mistake); *Impact Funding Solutions Ltd v Barrington Support Services Ltd* [2016] UKSC 57 (exclusion clauses); *Morris-Garner v One Step (Support) Ltd* [2018] UKSC 20 (damages); *Hughes-Holland v BPE Solicitors* [2017] UKSC 21 (damages); and *Fulton Shipping Inc of Panama v Globalia Business Travel S.A.U.* [2017] UKSC 43 (mitigation). Significant other new decisions include: *Bates v Post Office Ltd (No.3)* [2019] EWHC 606 (relational contracting); *Amey Birmingham Highways Ltd v Birmingham City Council* [2018] EWCA Civ 264 (relational contracting); *MSC Mediterranean Shipping Co SA v Cottonex Anstalt* [2016] EWCA Civ 789 (good faith); *Goodlife Foods Limited v Hall Fire Protection Limited* [2018] EWCA Civ 1371 (incorporation); *Persimmon Homes Ltd v Ove Arup and Partners Ltd* [2017] EWCA Civ 373 (construction); *First Tower Trustees Ltd, Intertrust Trustees Limited v CDS (Superstores International) Limited* [2018] EWCA Civ 1396 (non-reliance clauses); *African Export-Import Bank v Shebah Exploration and Production Co Ltd* [2017] EWCA Civ 845 (UCTA 1977); *Ashfaq v International Insurance Co of Hannover Plc* [2017] EWCA Civ 357 (meaning of consumer); *BV Nederlandse Industrie Van Eiprodukten v Rembrandt Enterprises Inc* [2018] EWHC 1857 (Comm) (misrepresentation); *Triple Seven MSN 27251 Ltd v Azman Air Services Ltd* [2018] EWHC 1348 (Comm) (mistake); *Al Nehayan v Kent* [2018] EWHC 333 (Comm) (duress); *Canary Wharf (BP4) T1 Ltd v European Medicines Agency* [2019] EWHC 335 (Ch) (frustration). Readers should note that as regards the use of the terms 'claimant' and 'plaintiff', we have continued the practice of previous editions, which is to use the label that will be found in the report of any particular case (which will depend on when the action was brought). Where the word is used generically, rather than in relation to a particular case, 'claimant' is used.

Although Richard, who is enjoying his retirement, was not involved in the production of this edition his work is still, of course, deeply embedded in this book. I would like to take this opportunity to acknowledge the wide and lasting contribution which Richard made to this area of law which has inspired so much of my own work. I would also like to thank Richard on behalf of the countless students who he helped develop over the years.

Finally, our thanks to our publishers, Routledge, and in particular Chloe James and Emily Kindleysides, for their patience and assistance in seeing this edition through to publication, and to my wife, Claire, for her support during the writing process. Special thanks also go to Mary Catherine Lucey of UCD, Ireland for all of her support over the last few years. I would like to dedicate this book to Norman Curtis and Cari Devenney.

The law is stated, as far as possible, as it stood on 1 January 2019 (although we were able to take account of some later developments).

*James Devenney*
*Reading*
April 2019

# Guide to using the book

*The Modern Law of Contract* is rich in features designed to support and reinforce your learning. This Guided Tour shows you how to make the most of your textbook by illustrating each of the features used by the authors.

## 7.1 OVERVIEW

This chapter deals with the situations wh
for breach of contract by including exclu
area governed by both common law and
in the latter half of the twentieth century a
law rules were developed earlier to deal v
parties. The common law is looked at firs

### Chapter overviews

These overviews are a brief introduction of the core themes and issues that you will encounter in each chapter.

### Diagrams

Visual learners are catered for via a series of diagrams and tables that help facilitate the understanding of concepts and interrelationships within key topics.

## For thought

*If you are invited to take part in a lott
written agreement as to how the prize i .*

### 'For thought'

'For thought' boxes encourage discussion on topical issues and help you to critique current law and reflect on how and in which direction it may develop in the future.

### 2.4.1 IN FOCUS: AGREEMEI
It has been argued by Collins th
courts are not actually looking f

> whether or not the negotiatio
> parties can reasonably supp
> it can be relied upon.[8]

### 'In focus'

The 'In focus' icon highlights sections that offer commentary on and critical evaluation of the law.

**Key case** RTS Flexible Systems Ltd v
(UK Production) (2010)

Facts: The parties were in negotiation i
work. Work started on the basis of a Let
intended that there should be a formal v
ment on many terms, including the pric
finalised or signed. On a preliminary issu

## Key cases

A variety of landmark cases are highlighted
in text boxes for ease of reference. The
facts and decisions are presented to help
you reach an understanding of how and
why the court reached the conclusion it
did.

### 3.16 SUMMARY OF KEY POINTS

- Promises can be enforceable wh
  by consideration, or where the d

- Consideration is the primary bas
  English law.

## Chapter summaries

The essential points and concepts covered
in each chapter are distilled into bulleted
summaries at the end of each chapter in
order to provide you with an at-a-glance
reference point for each topic.

### 11.12 FURTHER READING

- Auchmuty, R, 'The Rhetoric of Equa
  Chapter 3 in Mulcahy, L and Wheel
  Law, 2005, London: Glasshouse Pr

- Birks, P and Chin Nyuk Yin, 'On the

## Further reading

Selected further reading is included at the
end of each chapter to provide a pathway
for further study.

### COMPANION WEBSITE

Now visit the companion website to:

- Revise and consolidate your knowledge of Ille
  Choice Questions on this chapter

- Test your understanding of the chapter's key

## Companion website

Signposts to relevant material available
on the book's popular companion website
are included at the end of each chapter.

# Guide to the companion website

'An excellent resource, which will appeal to students; this is probably the best I have seen for any subject!'
**Valerie Humphreys,** *Deputy Head of School of Law, Birmingham City University*

Visit *The Modern Law of Contracts* companion website to discover a comprehensive range of resources designed to enhance the teaching and learning experience for both students and lecturers.

## For lecturers

A free suite of exclusive resources developed to help you to teach the law of contract.

## Testbank

Download a fully customisable bank of questions which test your students' understanding of contract law. These can be migrated to your university's Visual Learning Environment so that they can be customised and used to track student progress.

## Diagrams

Use diagrams from the text in your own lecture presentations with our PowerPoint slides.

# For students

## Multiple-choice questions

Test your progress by tackling a series of chapter-by-chapter multiple-choice questions. Each answer links you back to the text for further study.

## Glossary terms and flashcards

Look up the essential contract law terms in our handy online Glossary or check your knowledge with our interactive flashcards.

## Legal skills guide

Improve your essential legal skills with our practical guides to the important subjects in contract law, including 'Forming the agreement' and 'Remedies'.

## Questions and answers

Hone your writing skills by taking on a set of contract law essay and problem questions, and comparing your ideas with the authors' fully worked model answers.

## Explore further

Investigate contract law further with a series of chapter-by-chapter weblinks.

# Table of cases

# Legislation

# International legislation

# Introduction

## Contents

## 1.1 OVERVIEW

This chapter is divided into two broad sections.

In the first section there is a short introduction to the law of contract in England and Wales, giving an indication of some of the main issues that arise for discussion in subsequent chapters. The second section then undertakes a more thorough analysis of some of the theoretical issues that arise in discussing contract law.

In relation to contract theory, the order of treatment is:

- What is meant by the 'classical' law of contract? This refers to a body of rules generally developed by nineteenth-century cases and the first contract law textbook writers. It still has great influence in the modern law of contract.
- What is the 'subject matter' of contract law? Is it simply a matter of enforcing promises or is it concerned with regulating markets or facilitating trade? The idea of a 'voluntary agreement' seems to be at its heart.
- Should contracts be viewed as 'discrete' isolated events or, where appropriate, should they be viewed in the context of a continuing relationship between the parties? The work of Macneil, in particular, suggests that a 'relational' analysis is more satisfactory in many situations.
- How is 'contract' distinguished from other areas of law involving civil obligations, such as tort and restitution?
- How far is the law of contract governed by general principles, as opposed to specific rules applying to particular types of contract, such as sale of goods contracts, employment contracts, land contracts or credit contracts? It is argued that there is still some room for general principles, though the increasing divide between consumer and non-consumer contracts is arguably reducing the scope of such rules.
- What techniques for the analysis of contract can be adopted? Consideration is given to:
  - ☐ doctrinal analysis (focusing on cases and statutes);
  - ☐ socio-economic analysis (drawing on other disciplines to help explain the law); and
  - ☐ empirical research (investigating what happens in practice between contracting parties).
- What has been the influence of European Union law on contract law in England and Wales, and how will this be affected by 'Brexit'?

## 1.2 INTRODUCTION

The law of contract in England and Wales is a 'common law' subject. This means that most of its rules and principles are derived from case law and the application of the doctrine of precedent. There are, however, increasing areas that are affected by statutory provisions and, in particular, regulations in the area of consumer contracts that have origins in European Union law.

The rules forming the law of contract in England and Wales are generally, and subject to the intervention of statute, applicable to all contracts. The rules of contract formation, for example, apply to a contract to buy some vegetables in a supermarket as much as to a million-pound deal for the supply of goods and services between two multinational corporations. This universality can cause problems where very different types of contracts may have differing requirements, and do not fit easily into 'one size fits all' rules.

Contract law is, as is explained later in this chapter (1.5), concerned with the regulation of agreements and, in particular, agreements to exchange goods and services for money or other goods or services (or both). Contractual obligations are generally voluntarily assumed and on that basis it is distinguishable from the law of tort, which is broadly concerned with obligations that are imposed by the law (e.g. to avoid causing harm through negligence, such as through careless driving).

The following sections (1.2.1 to 1.2.6) highlight the main issues that arise in trying to regulate agreements and that are therefore dealt with in more detail in the subsequent chapters of this text.

### 1.2.1 FORMATION

If agreements are being analysed, the courts need to have some rules for determining when an agreement has been reached. For example, does an agreement need to be in writing? Contract law in England and Wales generally does not require formalities (such as writing) to establish a contract (although there are certain types of contract which are required to be in writing). Instead contract law in England and Wales considers what the parties said and did to determine if these words and actions, viewed objectively, indicate that they had reached an agreement. More specifically, the courts will normally look for an *offer* by one party that has been unequivocally *accepted* by the other party.

Problems in this area can arise when the parties are contracting at a distance by, for example, post or email. For example, delays in communications may mean that one party has had a change of mind by the time its message is received and there will then be difficult questions relating to when exactly a communication takes effect.

The issues relating to contract formation are dealt with in Chapter 2.

### 1.2.2 ENFORCEABILITY

Just because the parties have made an agreement, it does not necessarily follow that it is *legally enforceable* (a contract). Contract law in England and Wales has a number of methods for deciding whether an agreement is legally binding, the most important of which are the concept of 'consideration' and the requirement of an intention to create legal relations.

'Consideration' is a complex topic. It essentially involves a requirement that if an agreement is to be enforced by the courts, there must be an exchange (as opposed to, for example, a gift). In other words, both parties must be contributing something to the deal for it to be legally enforceable. For example, the contract may be for the transfer of goods in exchange for payment of a sum of money. In this case the payment of the money would be the 'consideration' for the transfer of the goods. If the goods were to be handed over without any payment being made or promised, this would be a gift and would fall outside the scope of the law of contract. The courts have developed extensive rules as to what does and does not constitute valid consideration.

In general, attempts to vary an existing agreement must also involve consideration if they are to be enforceable. In some limited circumstances a variation of an agreement may be enforceable without consideration, where the other party has reasonably relied on a promise that the variation will take place – this is dealt with by the doctrine of 'promissory estoppel'.

Finally, in relation to enforceability, just because there is an agreement and consideration, it does not necessarily follow that there is a legally enforceable agreement (a contract). There must also be an intention to create a legal enforceable agreement. A domestic agreement between, for example, a husband and wife under which the wife agrees to pay for certain bills in exchange for the husband paying for all the food shopping may have the characteristics of offer, acceptance and consideration, but is unlikely to be intended to be legally enforceable. Commercial agreements will, however, normally be taken to be intended to create a legal relationship.

Issues of enforceability are dealt with in Chapter 3 (consideration and promissory estoppel) and Chapter 4 (intention to create legal relations).

### 1.2.3 CONTENTS OF THE CONTRACT

Once an agreement has been made, disputes may arise as to what exactly its terms were intended to be. Even if the agreement is in writing, there may be arguments that it is not complete and that other terms should be read into it or implied. The courts are reluctant to add to agreements in this way but will do so in certain carefully defined situations. In some circumstances terms may also be implied by statute, for example the Sale of Goods Act 1979 or the Consumer Rights Act 2015.

There may also be arguments as to what particular terms of the contract were intended to mean. In such cases should the courts follow the literal meaning of the words if there is evidence that something else was actually intended? Currently the courts take the view that they should interpret terms of a contract in the light of all the factual circumstances and should not be tied to the literal meaning. This flexibility has its advantages, but can cause problems of uncertainty.

Particular types of clauses that can cause problems are the limitation or exclusion clause, whereby, for example, one party attempts to limit or exclude their liability if they break the contract. Such clauses may be entirely reasonable in many cases but the courts traditionally look at them very carefully, particularly where there is an imbalance in the bargaining power between the parties (as where a large business is attempting to exclude its liability to an individual consumer). They will want to be sure that the clause was properly incorporated into the contract (e.g. that the other party had appropriate notice) and that the clause does cover the situation that has arisen. In addition, most limitation and exclusion clauses will now be subject to statutory control in the form of the Unfair Contract Terms Act 1977 and the Consumer Rights Act 2015. These invalidate some types of exclusion, particularly in consumer contracts and make others enforceable only if they are found to be 'reasonable' or 'fair'. For example, even in non-consumer contracts attempts to exclude liability for death or personal injury caused by negligence will always be invalid; by contrast attempts to exclude liability for other losses caused by negligence in non-consumer contracts will only be valid if they are reasonable.

The terms of the contract are dealt with in Chapter 6 and exclusion clauses in Chapter 7.

### 1.2.4 REASONS FOR SETTING THE CONTRACT ASIDE

In some circumstances a contract that seems to have been validly formed will subsequently be set aside by the courts (or, in some circumstances, it will be declared never to have come into existence) because it is found to have some defect. The circumstances that can lead to this are sometimes referred to as 'vitiating factors'.

One example of a vitiating factor is where one party has been misled into making the contract by relying on a false statement by the other party – that is, the contract has been induced by a 'misrepresentation'. A misrepresentation, even if made innocently, can lead to the contract being set aside. If the misrepresentation was made fraudulently or negligently, then compensation can also be awarded. Misrepresentation is discussed fully in Chapter 8.

Sometimes a party will allege that they entered into the contract on the basis of a mistake and that it should therefore be set aside. The courts are generally reluctant to accept this argument but may declare the contract void (of no effect from the beginning) if the contract was always impossible to perform, for example because the contract relates to a cargo in a ship which, unknown to either party, had sunk before the contract was made. Where the other party is aware of the mistake (for example, where they have assumed a false identity in order to encourage the contract), the courts may be more receptive to arguments based on mistake but still impose fairly restrictive rules as to when the remedy will be available. Mistake is dealt with in Chapter 9.

Issuing threats of violence or other illegal conduct to induce the other party to make a contract will fall under the heading of duress. If proved, the courts may set the contract aside. The concept of duress has been expanded in recent case law to cover, for example, threats of economic action (e.g. to go on strike). As long as the threat involves inappropriate and illegitimate pressure on the other party, it is potentially 'duress'. This concept is dealt with in Chapter 10.

Related to the concept of duress is the concept of 'undue influence'. This concept can also cover overt threats but also more extensively regulates relational pressures where, for example, there is a relationship in which one party has influence over the other's decisions and uses that influence to persuade the person to enter into a contract. If inappropriate influence has been used, then the courts may not allow the contract to be enforced. Examples of situations where undue influence has been found in previous cases include in relation to the influence of a bank manager over an elderly customer, of a solicitor over a client and, in some cases, of a husband over a wife. Particular problems can arise where a husband (or wife) persuades his wife (or her husband) to use their home as security for a business loan from a bank. If the wife (or husband) later seeks to set her agreement with the bank aside on the basis of her husband's (or his wife's) undue influence, can she (or he) do so? The courts have struggled to find the appropriate balance between the creditor (bank) and the security (wife or husband) in such situations. The issues arising out of this area are dealt with in Chapter 11.

Clearly the courts would not enforce a contract to commit murder. But this is only a very clear example of a more general (and not entirely clear) rule that may render contracts which involve illegality, or are otherwise contrary to public policy, unenforceable or partially enforceable. Difficulties can arise where, for example, a contract is on the face of it legal but can only be performed by one or both parties acting illegally – for example, a contract to buy alcohol, where the seller's licence has expired. The rules in this area have not always been applied consistently and some of the case law became difficult to reconcile. Illegality is dealt with in Chapter 12.

## 1.2.5 FRUSTRATION

Sometimes a contract cannot be completed because of circumstances outside the control of either party. For example, the contract is to redecorate a house and between the making of the contract and performance starting, the house burns down. Where such an event happens, the contract may be said to be 'frustrated' and both parties may be absolved from future obligations. The main issues in this area relate to deciding what kind of circumstances are sufficiently serious to frustrate the contract and in sorting out the effects of frustration. The latter issue is affected by the provisions of the Law Reform (Frustrated Contracts) Act 1943.

Frustration is dealt with in Chapter 13.

## 1.2.6 PERFORMANCE, BREACH AND REMEDIES

If a party, for example, wishes to be paid for their performance of a contract, then they will generally need to show that they have completed the performance of their obligations under it. Issues may arise as to what constitutes complete performance and when the other party is entitled to withhold payment until further work is done.

Where a contract has been broken, the party not in breach may seek to terminate the contract. Whether this is possible may depend on the seriousness of the term broken – was it a major term of the contract? In all cases damages will be recoverable for losses that can be demonstrated to have been caused by the breach, subject, for example, to rules relating to 'remoteness' (was the loss one that could reasonably be expected to have followed from the breach) and 'mitigation' (did the party not in breach take all reasonable steps to limit the loss). Most contract damages will be for economic losses, including lost profits, but in some circumstances damages will be recoverable for non-pecuniary losses (for example, personal injury) including, exceptionally, disappointment and mental distress.

An order to perform a contract ('specific performance') is discretionary and will not generally be awarded in relation to straightforward commercial transactions, where the payment of damages will constitute an adequate remedy.

Performance, breach and remedies are dealt with in Chapters 14 and 15.

## 1.3 CONTRACT THEORY

The issues considered in the rest of this chapter are principally concerned with identifying the theoretical bases for the law of contract – including its nature and scope. There are a number of possible approaches to these issues.

It might be asked, for example, what relationships the courts currently regard as being within the scope of the law of contract. Answering this relatively easy question is, of course, of importance, particularly from the practical point of view of deciding how to deal with a dispute between A and B and whether the courts would be likely to treat it as a contract. The task would, however, be largely descriptive. If we want to go further and analyse the nature of contract or the contractual relationship, we will need to ask why some situations rather than others are dealt with as contractual, and try to find some rational basis for distinguishing between 'contract' and 'non-contract'. This is an issue that has been the subject of regular academic discussion over the last 50 years.[1] Moreover, even texts aimed at practitioners are unable to ignore it. *Chitty on Contracts*, the most well-established practitioners' text, has an introductory chapter dealing with the 'nature of contract'. Its more recently published rival, Furmston's *The Law of Contract*,[2] goes even further, including a lengthy first chapter on 'General Considerations' (written by Professor Roger Brownsword).[3]

Our starting point is the concept of the 'classical law of contract' which many would regard as still the dominant approach, certainly within the decisions of the courts on contractual issues.

## 1.4 THE CLASSICAL LAW OF CONTRACT

It is generally accepted in modern writings on the law of contract in England and Wales that during the latter half of the nineteenth century a concept of contract developed, together with an associated body of legal doctrine, which is now referred to as the 'classical law of contract'. This is not necessarily a matter of precise historical accuracy. As Wightman has pointed out,[4] the concept of the classical law of contract can be said to be 'invented' in two senses. First, although based on decisions of the courts, the synthesis of those decisions into a (more or less) coherent body of law was largely the work of the 'treatise writers',[5] whose work decided which cases would be given prominence and who encouraged the formulation of principles of general application to a wide range of transactions. Second, the recognition of the model of contract law that emerged from the latter part of the nineteenth century as 'classical', with the intention of using that model as the

---

1    See, for example, Macaulay, 1963; Gilmore, 1974; Simpson, 1975a; Macneil, 1978; Atiyah, 1979; Wightman, 1996; Collins, 2003; and Brownsword, 2006.

2    First published by Butterworths in 1999; now in 6th edn, 2017.

3    This chapter was published separately in the title *Contract Law: Themes for the Twenty-first Century*, 2000, London: Butterworths. It is now in its second edition, and cited here as 'Brownsword, 2006'. Unfortunately, the pagination is not the same in the two versions of the text. The references here are therefore to the page numbers in the second edition of Brownsword (i.e. Brownsword, 2006). Lord Steyn in the Preface to Furmston, 1999, commented that Brownsword's chapter 'examines the grand themes of our contract law in an impressive style. Nothing quite like it has ever been published in English law.'

4    Wightman, 1996, p 49. See also Brownsword, 2006, pp 46–50, and Swain, 2010. Chapter 5 of Wightman's book, entitled 'The Invention of Classical Contract', provides a useful summary of the development of the classical theory and its main elements. See also Chapter 1 in Beatson and Friedmann, 1995, especially pp 7–17.

5    For example, Powell, whose first edition appeared in 1790, and Anson, whose *Law of Contract* (designed for students) was first published in 1879.

basis for an argument that the requirements of 'modern' contract law were different and that adherence to the classical model was inhibiting its development, is largely the product of the work started by commentators writing in the 1970s.[6]

Whatever the accuracy of the precise historical origins of the classical theory, it is now generally accepted that it is centred on the concept of 'freedom of contract', probably as a reflection of the dominance in the nineteenth century of *laissez-faire* economic attitudes. At a time of the swift industrialisation and increasing commercialisation of society, the best way, so it was argued, of allowing wealth to develop was to let those involved in business regulate their own affairs, with the courts simply intervening to settle disputes. The parties to a contract will be governed by rational self-interest,[7] and giving effect to transactions that result from this will be to the benefit of both the parties and society.

'Freedom of contract' in this context has two main aspects.[8] The first is that it is the individual's choice whether or not to enter into a contract, and if so with whom – in other words, the freedom *to* contract, or 'party freedom'. The second is the freedom to decide on the content of the contractual obligations undertaken, or 'term freedom'. This allows parties to make unwise, and even 'unfair', bargains – it is their decision, and the courts will not generally intervene to protect them from their own foolishness.

The paradigmatic contract that emerges from the classical theory has the following characteristics:

(a)   It involves an 'exchange', so that each side is giving something in return for the other's promise. It is the existence of this mutuality (given effect through the doctrine of 'consideration')[9] that generally gives rise to enforceability.[10]

(b)   It is often based on an exchange of promises.

(c)   It is often executory. This means that the contract is formed, and obligations under it arise, before either side has performed any part of it.

(d)   The content of the contractual obligations is determined by deciding what the parties, objectively assessed, agreed at the time the contract was made. Later developments are of no significance.

(e)   Disputes about a contract can generally be determined by asking what the parties expressly or impliedly agreed in the contract itself. This is sometimes referred to as the 'will theory' of contract.

(f)   The transaction is viewed as being discrete, rather than being part of a continuing relationship.

(g)   The role of the court is to act as 'umpire' or 'arbiter', giving effect to the parties' agreement. In particular, it has no role in deciding whether or not the transaction is 'fair'.

There is probably also an underlying assumption that the parties are of equal bargaining power.

The type of contract that most closely fits the above paradigm is probably the commercial contract for the sale of goods, where the buyer and seller agree that at some agreed

---

6  See, in particular, Horwitz, 1974; Gilmore, 1974; Atiyah, 1979. Note that Horwitz's view of the historical development of contract was strongly challenged by Simpson, 1979.

7  In other words, each party will seek to organise and operate the contract in a way that produces the maximum 'utility' or benefit to that party.

8  Brownsword, 2006, pp 50–1. Brownsword also identifies 'sanctity of contract' – the fact that 'parties are to be held to the agreements that they have freely made': ibid, p 53. However, such a principle might apply even in the absence of party freedom and term freedom.

9  For which see Chapter 3.

10  This does not, however, take account of the role of the contract under seal, or deed, where no mutuality is required for a promise to be binding. See further on this, Chapter 3, 3.3.

date they will exchange the ownership of goods of a specified type for a specified sum of money. In practice, however, many contracts are not of this kind, and attempts to apply to them rules that were designed to be suitable for the paradigmatic case are likely to produce tensions and problems. Nevertheless, the classical theory of contract, and its model of the typical contract, can still be seen to cast its shadow over contract law in England and Wales. In the latter part of the twentieth century it was the subject of sustained attack by academic commentators and some judicial decisions can be seen to have moved, in practice at least, from the strict classical formulations. There is still, however, a reluctance to abandon them and it is frequently the case that the courts, when involved in a development away from the classical model, will continue to use language that suggests that they are being faithful to it.[11] The challenge for the student of the modern law of contract in England and Wales is to reconcile the fact that it is still rooted in classical theory, at least in the way in which its concepts are expressed, while at the same time developing away from it. This is the reason why this book has adopted a format and chapter division that is largely traditional. It is within this traditional framework that the courts continue to consider contract cases. The substance of many of their decisions, however, and virtually all the interventions of Parliament, are taking the law in new directions. The form may be 'classical' but the content is 'modern', and this tension must be kept in mind in considering all that follows.

With this background to the development of contract law in England and Wales in mind, we can now turn to the question of what exactly is meant by the 'law of contract'. What is its scope, and what are its boundaries?

## 1.5 THE SUBJECT MATTER OF CONTRACT LAW

What is the aim of the law of contract? This is a question to which, perhaps surprisingly, there is no clear and universally accepted answer. There are, however, several candidates for the basis of the legal enforceability of contractual obligations. This can be viewed, for example, as a means of:

(a)    enforcing promises; or
(b)    regulating the market in the provision of goods and services; or
(c)    facilitating exchanges (for example, of goods or services for money).

Any of these individually, or some combination of them, can be put forward as being at the root of the law of contract, but none of them is without difficulty.

As we have seen, the idea of the 'promise' is central to the classical law of contract and some modern commentators are happy to continue to regard this as its distinguishing feature. Burrows, for example, asserts that 'The law of contract is concerned with binding promises. It looks at what constitutes a binding promise and how such a promise is made; at the remedies for breach of such a promise; and at who is entitled to those remedies.'[12] There are, however, a number of limitations to an interpretation of contract based on promises. Although some contracts are clearly made by the exchange of promises – for example, 'I promise to build a house for you in accordance with these plans in exchange for your promising to pay me £100,000 on completion of the work' – there are many that

---

11 A particularly clear example of this is the Court of Appeal's decision in *Williams v Roffey Bros & Nicholls (Contractors) Ltd* [1991] 1 QB 1; [1990] 1 All ER 512, in which lip service was paid to the classical formulation of the doctrine of consideration, while in fact the decision departed significantly from it: see further, Chapter 3, 3.9.8.
12 Burrows, 1998, p 3: see, also, Fried, 2015.

do not easily fit this model. In particular, as has been pointed out judicially by Lord Wilberforce, many everyday transactions, such as buying goods in a shop or travelling by bus, do not do so without considerable strain.[13] They can be accommodated at best by taking the view that there is an *implicit* promise involved – for example, that the bus is travelling on the route indicated by its signboard. But in some situations it is arguably difficult to find even a promise of this kind. In the typical shop transaction, a person takes goods to a till and hands over money. The contract has the general effect of transferring the ownership of the goods from the seller to the buyer and of the money from the buyer to the seller. What promises are involved in a one-off transaction of this kind, which may well be conducted without any communication between the participants and indeed increasingly frequently by using a 'self-service' till? There may be some implicit promises, for example that the seller has the right to sell the goods and that they are of a satisfactory quality. However, since both these obligations are imposed by statute and cannot be avoided in a consumer contract,[14] it is not necessary to use the language of 'promises' to explain, at least, these aspects of the transaction.

Even in commercial transactions, as in the case in which Lord Wilberforce made the statement mentioned above, there are also some situations where contractual rights and liabilities are assumed to exist, but it is difficult to see that there has been any making of promises. The parties in the case that Lord Wilberforce was discussing assumed that stevedores unloading goods from a ship would have the benefit of an exemption clause contained in a contract between the owners of the goods and the carriers. No explicit promise of this kind was made to the stevedores, however. Indeed, in contracts of this type, the identity of the stevedores might well be unknown at the time the contract was entered into. The court resolved this effectively by 'imputing' a promise from the owners to the stevedores, via the agency of the carriers, that they would have the benefit of the clause.[15]

On the other hand, there are clearly some situations where promises *are* at the heart of the contractual obligation. Contracts for the purchase and sale of commodities on the futures market plainly depend on the assumption that promises will be kept or that, if broken, compensation will be payable. Another example is the doctrine of promissory estoppel,[16] which is based on the fact that it sometimes requires a person who makes a promise to be held to it, even though there is no consideration given for it.

The conclusion must be, therefore, as Brownsword has pointed out, that although it is possible to use 'promise' as a necessary definition of contract, this is only so if we include 'express, implicit and imputed promises'.[17] 'Promise' is not a sufficient condition, however, since there are situations in which clear and explicit promises are not enforced. In general, for example, promises that are neither supported by consideration nor contained in a deed will not generally be treated as binding on the promisor.[18] In other areas where apparently gratuitous promises have been held to be binding, such as in the case of *Williams v Roffey*

---

13 See Lord Wilberforce in *New Zealand Shipping Co Ltd v AM Satterthwaite & Co Ltd, The Eurymedon* [1975] AC 154, at p 167; [1974] 1 All ER 1015, at pp 1019–20.

14 See the Consumer Rights Act 2015, ss 9, 17 and 31, discussed in Chapter 6, 6.7, and Chapter 7, 7.8.

15 For further discussion of this case, see Chapter 5, 5.12.1.

16 See Chapter 3, 3.11.

17 Brownsword, 2006, pp 24–5.

18 See, for example, *Foakes v Beer* (1884) 9 App Cas 605 (Chapter 3, 3.13.1–3.13.3) and *Atlas Express Ltd v Kafco (Importers and Distributors) Ltd* [1989] QB 833; [1989] 1 All ER 641 (Chapter 10, 10.4.2). The main exception to this principle is to be found in the concept of promissory estoppel: *Central London Property Trust Ltd v High Trees House Ltd* [1947] KB 130; [1956] 1 All ER 256. Even here it should be noted that the gratuitous promise became unenforceable once the conditions which gave rise to its being made had disappeared (that is, the Second World War had come to an end). See further, Chapter 3, 3.11 and 3.13.3.

*Bros & Nicholls (Contractors) Ltd*,[19] the courts have been at pains to find 'consideration', even if this has involved 'stretching' this concept so as not to be seen to be departing from the orthodoxy that gratuitous promises are not binding.

Furthermore, there are agreements that appear to have all the hallmarks of the archetypal classical contract – that is, an exchange of promises and consideration – which will nevertheless not be treated as binding. This may arise where there is no 'intention to create legal relations'.[20] This may be because the arrangement has been made in a domestic context.[21] It can also arise, however, in a commercial context where it has been made clear that the agreement is 'binding in honour only'.[22] In both types of case, the courts are giving effect to what they see as being the intentions of the parties. This area, as an element in the formation of the contractual obligation, is discussed at length in Chapter 4. It is another indication, however, that a 'promise' is not in itself sufficient as a basis for identifying contractual obligations.

The second suggested candidate as the basis for modern contract law – market regulation – clearly has some force, in that part of what the courts do in developing and applying the law is to determine the limits of the free market. It does not, however, deal very satisfactorily with the situations where in fact the courts do not intervene to 'regulate' but simply give effect to what the parties themselves have agreed (or are deemed to have agreed) – even if the result may appear 'unfair' and provide no benefit to the general public.[23] The courts in such a situation will not hold back from enforcing a 'bad bargain'. Nevertheless, some commentators do see market regulation as being at the heart of contract law. Collins, for example, sees the 'social market' as being central to the modern law of contract.[24] He sees three themes – 'concern about unjustifiable domination, the equivalence of exchange, and the need to ensure co-operation' – as forming the core of his interpretation of the law of contract.[25] It might, of course, alternatively be argued that simply enforcing agreed obligations is to the general public benefit because it reduces transaction costs if the parties are aware that a clear agreement will be enforced, no matter that 'injustice' to one of the parties may result. This is the argument that 'certainty' in the law overall is preferable to 'fairness' on the facts of any particular case.

The third candidate identified above as a concept that might be said to be at the centre of contract is 'exchange', and this is at first sight an attractive proposition. Many of the transactions that we think of as involving a contract – for example, the purchase of goods or services – do involve 'exchange'. A person transfers the ownership of goods to another in exchange for the price; work is done in exchange for wages; a company agrees to license the use of a patented process in exchange for royalties. There are, however, situations that do not properly involve an exchange, but that are nevertheless essentially treated as contracts. First, there are those transfers of property that are effected by a formal deed. In this case, provided that the formalities of the deed are properly carried out, the transaction can be entirely gratuitous: nothing is required from the recipient to make the transaction legally binding. Such transactions are often regarded as being within the province of contract law, and therefore need to be accommodated within any definitional scheme intended to delineate its scope.

---

19  [1991] 1 QB 1; [1990] 1 All ER 512. This case is discussed in detail in Chapter 3, 3.9.9.

20  See Chapter 4.

21  For example, *Balfour v Balfour* [1919] 2 KB 571 – arrangement for a husband to provide financial support for his wife during the marriage (as opposed to following its break-up). See below, Chapter 4, 4.3.

22  For example, *Rose and Frank Co v JR Crompton and Bros Ltd* [1923] 2 KB 261. See below, Chapter 4, 4.4.

23  As arguably, for example, in *L'Estrange v F Graucob Ltd* [1934] 2 KB 394 – party held to an unread term in a signed contract. See, further, Chapter 7, 7.4.

24  Collins, 2003. See also Collins, 1999.

25  Collins, 2003, p 29. These themes are, in Collins' view, well illustrated by the case of *Schroeder Music Publishing Co Ltd v Macaulay* [1974] 3 All ER 616; [1974] 1 WLR 1308.

It might, perhaps, be possible to treat transfers by deed as being an example of cat-egorisation error, and to argue that they should be treated as *sui generis* and not part of the general law of contract. This would not solve the problem, however, since there are other situations that do not really involve any proper exchange that it would be much more difficult to 'hive off' in this way. As we will see later,[26] in informal contracts,[27] although the law of contract normally requires a degree of 'mutuality', so that something is being provided by each party to the agreement, the value of what is being provided is gener-ally irrelevant. Thus, suppose a rich aunt decides to make her favourite nephew, who is currently 19 years old, a gift of her Porsche on his twenty-first birthday. She could com-mit herself to this transaction by promising that she will transfer the car on the day of his birthday provided that he pays her one penny in exchange. The reality of this transaction is that she is making a gift of the car, and her nephew is providing nothing of real value in exchange. Nevertheless, the courts would treat this as a binding contract (subject to their being satisfied that there was an intention to create legal relations). The application of this approach in a more commercial context can be illustrated by the case of *Chappell & Co Ltd v Nestlé Co Ltd*,[28] where the provision of the wrappers from bars of chocolate was held to be part of the consideration for the supply of a gramophone record. This was the case even though the wrappers were worthless and were thrown away by the company when received. The transaction had the trappings of exchange but was in essence a 'free gift'. Nevertheless, it was treated as contractual.

The reason for this may relate to the fact that the courts are generally keen to adopt an approach that complies with the intention of the parties. If the parties have used the trap-pings of exchange to clothe a transaction that is in effect a gift, they may have done so in order to make their agreement legally enforceable without the trouble of using a deed. The courts should therefore be prepared to give effect to that intention and treat the transac-tion as a binding contract. Yet such an approach assumes that the parties are, to some extent, familiar with the intricacies of the law of contract in England and Wales.

## For thought

*Why do companies such as Nestlé want people to send in effectively worthless items, such as tokens or, in Nestlé's case, wrappers? What benefit is there to the company in such a promotion? Could this be sufficient to constitute consideration?*

We can, therefore, if we exclude contracts made by deed, argue for 'exchange' as being at the heart of contract. But here, similar to the way in which with the notion of 'promise' we needed to include implied, imputed and constructed promises, we will need to include 'sham' exchanges in order to make the approach work. And, if we do that, we may well feel that we have still not really got very near to the essence of what makes a 'contract'.

In the end, we may have to accept that we will not find a straightforward answer to the question of what contract 'is'. As Brownsword points out, finding an 'essential definition' (that is, identifying 'necessary and sufficient' elements) is more difficult than approaching it as a 'cluster concept (in which several elements are identified with the usage, but where no single set of these elements can be combined to represent the necessary and sufficient conditions

---

26  Chapter 3, 3.7.
27  That is those not created by deed.
28  [1960] AC 87; [1959] 2 All ER 701 – discussed further in Chapter 3, 3.7.1.

for correct usage)'.[29] This is accepted, but the view taken here is that, of the various possibilities for identifying the essence of contract, the concept of the 'voluntary exchange' is the one that comes nearest to doing the job. Although it must be recognised that this cannot be used as a comprehensive and universal definition, it provides a practical basis from which to embark on a discussion of the legal rules that surround the concept of the contract.

The function of contract law is therefore to facilitate exchanges. An important part of this is the allocation of 'risk'. One of the reasons why the parties will put their transaction into the form of a contract is that it provides a mechanism for enforcement of the way in which they have agreed to allocate the risks. In a consumer sale of goods contract, for example, the risk that the goods will be unsatisfactory is placed on the seller.[30] This will be reflected in the price charged. In more complex contracts there may be many more risks that the parties will allocate between them. They may well decide that in certain situations the liability for breach of contract will be excluded or limited;[31] the risk is therefore borne by the other party, who in some circumstances may then be moved to take out separate insurance against that eventuality occurring. The way in which such risks are allocated will again be likely to affect the price of the contract. The manner in which the rules of contract law interact with these allocations of risk will need to be kept in mind at various points in the following chapters.

### 1.5.1 VOLUNTARY TRANSACTIONS

The approach of this book is, therefore, as indicated in the previous section, that the subject matter of the law of contract comprises transactions under which people, essentially voluntarily, assume obligations towards each other,[32] in connection with the transfer of property (including money) or the provision of services. The transactions are only essentially voluntary, since people have little real choice whether or not to enter into some contracts, for example, contracts to buy food or to obtain work. Even where there is a real choice in this sense, for example, as regards a decision to buy a new television, there is likely to be little choice about the terms on which the contract can be made. Large retail organisations are rarely prepared to enter into bargaining with a consumer. Nevertheless, it is only in very rare situations, for example, the compulsory purchase of property by central or local government, that people are forced into a contract that is clearly against their will. Indeed, to the extent that a transaction is not in any way regulated by agreement between the parties, it may be argued that it is not properly categorised as a contract. In *Norweb plc v Dixon*,[33] for example, the view was taken that a particular supply of electricity to a consumer that was almost entirely regulated, both as to the creation of the relationship and its terms, by the Electricity Act 1989 could not be regarded as a contract. As a result, money owed by the consumer was not a 'contractual' debt. This decision was followed in *W v Essex CC*[34] in relation to a fostering agreement that was closely regulated by regulations made under the Children Act 1989. As Stuart-Smith LJ in the Court of Appeal commented:[35]

A contract is essentially an agreement that is freely entered into on terms that are freely negotiated. If there is a statutory obligation to enter into a form of agreement the terms of which are laid down, at any rate in their most important respects, there is no contract.

---

29  Brownsword, 2006, p 15.
30  Though this is now largely not a matter of choice but the result of the terms automatically included by the Consumer Rights Act 2015.
31  See Chapter 7.
32  Or allocate risks between each other.
33  [1995] 3 All ER 952.
34  [1999] Fam 90; [1998] 3 All ER 111 (reversed in part on other grounds: [2000] 2 WLR 601).
35  [1999] Fam 90 at p 113; [1998] 3 All ER 111 at p 128.

We may therefore use the definition at the beginning of this paragraph, in terms of voluntary transactions, as a broad indication of the situations with which we are concerned. The rules of contract law help to determine which transactions will be enforced by the courts and on what terms. They also provide a framework of remedies when contracts are broken.

Before leaving this point, it is important to remember that, to the extent that there is a 'general law of contract', it applies to all transactions within its scope. That is, the same general rules will apply to the purchase of a packet of sweets from a local newsagent as to a multi-million pound deal between large international corporations.

## 1.6 DISCRETE AND RELATIONAL TRANSACTIONS

As we have seen, the classical theory of contract law uses as part of its paradigmatic contract a 'one-off' transaction that is discrete and self-contained. It has been increasingly recognised, however, that many contracts are not of this kind but have a continuing or 'relational' aspect. The term 'relational' contracts was coined by Professor Ian Macneil, and his work on this area remains the most influential.[36]

What does 'relational' contract theory mean? One point of possible confusion in Macneil's work is the fact that, as he himself recognised,[37] he used 'relational' in two linked but distinct ways. First, he used it to refer to the fact that all contracts occur in the context of a 'social matrix'. At the minimum, even in relation to a contract that appears to be 'discrete', this matrix will require a common system of communication, a common recognition of a system of order, a mechanism for enforcement and, if we are talking about the majority of contracts, some system of money. In respect of most contracts, of course, the social matrix will be much more complex.[38] Macneil's view was that an understanding of this relational aspect of transactions is essential to their proper analysis, whether in terms of law or economics.

The second use of the term 'relational' refers to the fact that many contracts involve a continuing relationship between the parties, which will affect the way in which their contract operates.[39] An obvious example is an employment contract, but it also applies to commercial agreements that, for example, require the supply of goods or services over a period of time. A construction contract will be a 'relational' contract in this sense, as will any lease of property. Macneil gave as one example of a 'quite discrete' transaction 'a cash purchase of gasoline at a station on the New Jersey Turnpike by someone rarely travelling the road'.[40] Such a contract will become less discrete if, for example, payment is by cheque or credit card, or is charged to a business account, or the purchaser has chosen this particular filling station because of a wish to use a 'loyalty' card issued by a particular petrol distributor. Macneil uses the metaphor of the spectrum of contracts, with very 'discrete' contracts at one end, and very 'relational' contracts at the other. Because

---

36  The most accessible route into Macneil's writings is through the collection of extracts from his articles edited by Campbell and published in 2001. This is cited in this book as Campbell, 2001. It should be noted, however, that the extracts omit most of Macneil's footnotes, so that for a full appreciation of his work reference should be made to the original texts (see the comments in the Preface to Campbell, 2001).

37  Macneil, 2000; Campbell, 2001, p 379.

38  See, for example, Macneil's analysis of the relational aspects of the sale of bananas in a supermarket: Macneil, 2000; Campbell, 2001, pp 371–72.

39  Macneil has tried to avoid the confusion between the two uses of 'relational' by referring to the second use as dealing with 'intertwined' contracts (see Macneil, 1987). This has not been fully picked up by other writers, however, and the term 'relational' continues to be used to refer to both aspects of Macneil's theories.

40  Macneil, 1978; Campbell, 2001, p 189.

of the classical theory's focus on the discrete transaction, it has difficulty in coping with the more relational contracts. These may well require the obligations between the parties to be modified over time, to respond to changing circumstances. For example, an employer may need to change the ways in which its employees work to deal with additional orders that have been taken on; or a construction contract may need adjustment to take account of problems with the availability of materials. Classical theory, however, looking at all contracts as if they were discrete, expects everything to be sorted out in the original agreement and has great difficulty dealing with subsequent modifications. In reality, such situations are generally dealt with by co-operation between the parties in the form of negotiation, but classical theory offers little or no scope for the recognition of such a process. The response of the courts faced with trying to apply classical theory to such situations may be to develop 'exceptions', which in form leave the general principle intact, but in fact may serve to undermine it.[41]

This difficulty with dealing with contractual modification leads to a further important insight from Macneil's work concerning the limitations of classical theory. Macneil referred to this as the problem of 'presentiation'.[42] To presentiate is, according to the *Oxford English Dictionary*, to 'make or render present in place or time, to cause to be perceived or realised as present'.[43] In terms of the law of contract, Macneil used this to refer to the process whereby, under classical theory, every aspect of the contract is to be determined at the time at which it is formed, so that all future problems with the contract can be answered by simply asking 'what did the parties agree in the contract?' This 'presentiation' works tolerably well with relatively discrete transactions but the more a contract becomes 'relational', and the longer it lasts, the less likely it is that simply looking to the original agreement will provide satisfactory answers. One response of the English courts to this type of problem has been to make inventive use of the concept of the 'implied term'.[44] This enables the myth of presentiation to be maintained. A better response might be:[45]

> to develop an overall structure of contract law of greater applicability than now exists and to merge both the details and the structure of transactional contract law into that overall structure.

Macneil's suggestion is that classical theory's reliance on individual rational self-interest as the governing norm for contractual transactions should be replaced with 10 'common contract norms',[46] which will include 'flexibility'; there are also some separate norms applying according to whether the contract is more or less discrete or relational. The relational norms include 'preservation of the relation' and 'harmonization of relational

---

41  An obvious example of this process is the effect of the development of the doctrine of promissory estoppel in English law in the latter half of the twentieth century on the classical doctrine of consideration: see Chapter 3, 3.11.

42  See, in particular, Macneil, 1974; Campbell, 2001, p 182.

43  Macneil quotes this definition from the first edition of the OED: Macneil, 1974, p 589; Campbell, 2001, p 182. The second edition of the OED (1989) describes the word as 'rare'. The first use recorded is 1659, though, in the sense that Macneil uses it, the first example is 1689. Modern examples are largely taken from US law journals.

44  For which, see Chapter 6, 6.6.

45  Macneil, 1974; Campbell, 2001, p 187.

46  The 10 norms are: (1) role integrity; (2) reciprocity; (3) implementation of planning; (4) effectuation of consent; (5) flexibility; (6) contractual solidarity; (7) the restitution, reliance and expectation interests; (8) creation and restraint of power; (9) propriety of means; and (10) harmonisation with the social matrix: Macneil, 1982; Campbell, 2001, p 153.

conflict'.[47] Thus, the resolution of problems that arise in the course of a long-term, or relational, contract forms part of the norms underlying the contract, rather than having to be imposed on it, using tools more suited to discrete transactions.

Macneil's work has been influential on writings about contract law but has by no means received universal acceptance.[48] A number of recent cases have, however, referred explicitly to the contract under consideration in the case as 'relational' and used this concept as an explanation for the way in which the case is decided. These cases include *Yam Seng Pte Ltd v International Trade Corporation Ltd*[49] and *Bristol Groundschool Ltd v Intelligent Data Capture Ltd*.[50] These two cases will be discussed further in the context of 'good faith' in 1.11. The general approach in the rest of this text is to refer at the appropriate places to Macneil's work and how it might relate to the traditional and current approaches to particular issues. His exposure of the problems of presentation will be found to be particularly helpful at a number of points.

## 1.7 CONTRACT, TORT AND RESTITUTION

It is generally recognised that there are three main strands to the law of obligations in England and Wales – contract, tort and restitution. To what extent are these distinct, and is there any overlap between them?

As indicated above, the view taken here is that the province of contract law is the facilitation and enforcement of voluntary exchange transactions. The law of tort,[51] on the other hand, is generally concerned with imposition of standards of behaviour, irrespective of whether the behaviour is linked to a transaction or voluntarily undertaken. There is an overlap, however, in that the performance of a contract can involve a tort, giving rise to the possibility of dual liability. If, for example, during the course of the construction of a building the negligence of a builder leads to a wall collapsing and injuring a third party, the construction company may be liable in contract for the fact that the wall was defective and

---

47  Ibid, p 163.

48  For a full review see Vincent-Jones, 2001. Sceptical commentators include Eisenberg, 1995 and McKendrick, 1995b; see also Collins, 1996. Cf Lord Steyn in *Total Gas Marketing Ltd v Arco British Ltd* [1998] 2 Lloyd's Rep 209, p 218: '[This is] a contract of a type sometimes called a relational contract. But there are no special rules of interpretation applicable to such contracts.' Campbell, on the other hand, has argued that Macneil does not pursue the relational analysis far enough (Campbell, 1996).

49  [2013] EWHC 111 (QB) at [142]. See also *Bates v Post Office Ltd (No.3)* [2019] EWHC 606 (QB) at [725] where Fraser J stated: "What then, are the specific characteristics that are expected to be present in order to determine whether a contract between commercial parties ought to be considered a relational contract? I consider the following characteristics are relevant as to whether a contract is a relational one or not: 1. There must be no specific express terms in the contract that prevents a duty of good faith being implied into the contract. 2. The contract will be a long-term one, with the mutual intention of the parties being that there will be a long-term relationship. 3. The parties must intend that their respective roles be performed with integrity, and with fidelity to their bargain. 4. The parties will be committed to collaborating with one another in the performance of the contract. 5. The spirits and objectives of their venture may not be capable of being expressed exhaustively in a written contract. 6. They will each repose trust and confidence in one another, but of a different kind to that involved in fiduciary relationships. 7. The contract in question will involve a high degree of communication, co-operation and predictable performance based on mutual trust and confidence, and expectations of loyalty. 8. There may be a degree of significant investment by one party (or both) in the venture. This significant investment may be, in some cases, more accurately described as substantial financial commitment. 9. Exclusivity of the relationship may also be present."

50  [2014] EWHC 2145 (Ch) at [196]. See also the interesting discussion in *Amey Birmingham Highways Ltd v Birmingham City Council* [2018] EWCA Civ 264, discussed below at 6.2.

51  In discussions of the law of obligations it is not uncommon to use the term 'tort' to mean, in effect, the tort of negligence. It should not be forgotten, however, that tort encompasses a wider area than that including, for example, assault, nuisance, defamation and the interference with others' contractual rights.

**1. CONTRACT:**
Facilitation and enforcement of voluntary exchange transactions.
- Dual liability – performance of contract can involve a tort.
- Primary measure of damages = expectation interest, but can sometimes claim under reliance measure or restitution.

**2. TORT:**
Imposition of standards of behaviour.
- Damages – to put the claimant into the position he or she would have been in had the tort not occurred.
- Will include compensation for loss and damages, but generally not lost benefits.

Civil liability

**3. RESTITUTION:**
To prevent unjust enrichment. Provides the means to recover money which has been paid as a result of a mistake. Restitution is often used in situations where the parties have attempted to agree a contract that has for some reason failed. The aim of restitution is the return of property and the discharge of unjustified benefits.

Figure 1.1

also in tort to the injured party for the negligence in its construction. If the person injured is the other party to the contract, then there will be liability in both tort and contract to the same claimant.[52] The third element in the law of obligations – restitution – has been recognised much more recently as a separate head.[53] The aim of the law of restitution is broadly to prevent 'unjust enrichment'. Thus, where a person has been paid money as a result of a mistake, the law of restitution provides the means by which it may be recovered. There is no need for the situation to involve an exchange transaction, as in contract, or generally for the behaviour of the person who has been unjustly enriched to fall below an accepted standard, as in tort. Restitution has links with contract, however, in that it is not infrequently used in situations where the parties have been attempting to make a contract, but this has for some reason failed.

The difference between contract, tort and restitution is sometimes said to be based on the nature of the remedies available in relation to each, and in particular the measure of damages. Thus in contract the primary measure of damages is the 'expectation' interest, designed to put the claimant into the position as if the contract had been performed satisfactorily (so that benefits to be obtained from the contract, such as anticipated profits, can be recovered). Such damages can be described as forward-looking. In tort, on the other hand, the normal measure is, in broad terms, to put the claimant into the position he or

---

52 For a further possible example of dual liability in tort and contract see the area of negligent misstatements, dealt with in Chapter 8, 8.4.4.
53 See Chapter 15, 15.8.

she was in before the tort occurred. This will generally be backward-looking, compensating for actual loss and damage caused but generally not taking into account anticipated benefits under a contract.[54] In restitution, as indicated above, the object is the return of property and the disgorgement of unjustified benefits. Looking at the differences between the various strands of the law of obligations in terms of the remedies is, however, starting from the wrong end.

The basis of liability must be the foundation of the distinction between them, with the remedies that are available being a consequence of that liability. There is no absolute requirement, for example, that contract remedies should be centred on the expectation interest. Indeed, as will be seen in Chapter 15, it is possible in an action for breach of contract to recover damages on any of the three bases just mentioned – that is, expectation, the 'tort' measure (compensating for actual losses, rather than expected benefits)[55] or restitution.

## 1.8 A LAW OF CONTRACT OR LAW OF CONTRACTS?

Do we have a law of contract or a law of contracts? The premise of a contract text of this kind is that there is a sufficient body of general rules and principles that apply to all (or virtually all) contracts to say that there is a 'law of contract'. The counter-argument can be based on two grounds, both largely relating to developments in the area over the past 100 years.

First, it can be pointed out that there are many specific types of contract that are now the subject of quite detailed statutory regulation. Contracts of employment, consumer credit agreements and contracts for the sale of land, for example, all operate within elaborate statutory frameworks. Even the type of agreement that might be regarded as the archetypal contract – the exchange of goods for money – is governed by the Sale of Goods Act 1979, the Unfair Contract Terms Act 1977 and the Consumer Rights Act 2015. This dichotomy is reflected in the format of *Chitty on Contracts*, which appears in two volumes, one devoted to *General Principles*, the other to *Special Contracts*.

The consequences of this can be seen by looking at its effect on the way in which the novice law student learns about the law of contract. This in turn will affect the practitioner's understanding, and will eventually be likely to have an impact on the practical development of contractual doctrine as developed by the courts. The reality is that the contracts falling within 'specialist' areas are often treated for didactic purposes as being best dealt with separately from the general law. The LLB course, therefore, will typically have a contract law course, but also separate courses on employment law, land law, consumer law, commercial law, etc. The general contract law course will not have the time to deal in detail with the statutory regimes governing all the different types of contract, and will leave these to be dealt with by the specialist courses. Some of these specialist courses will be optional. The student who does not follow all of them will, therefore, have an incomplete picture of the rules and principles governing 'contracts'. More importantly, the student will be likely to retain the mental 'pigeon-holing' encouraged by this structure to his or her studies, and therefore be less likely to draw connections between different areas.

One response to this is to say that it does not matter. There is in reality a range of different types of contract, and there is no reason why the rules operating in one area should have any impact in another. A contrary view is to argue that the diversity should be

---

54  But see *East v Maurer* [1991] 2 All ER 733 for an example of a case where the tort measure took account of a certain type of lost profit. The case is discussed in Chapter 8, 8.4.3.
55  Generally referred to in this context as the 'reliance' interest.

embraced as adding vibrancy to the development of contractual principles. An attempt to adopt an inclusive approach has been put forward by Collins. Noting that the generality of the traditional approach made it 'increasingly irrelevant' to disputes governed by special rules, he puts forward an alternative:[56]

> In order to counter this incoherence and redundancy, the conception of contract law employed here focuses on the social context of market transactions, that is where people seek to acquire property or services by dealing with others.[57] Whilst acknowledging that the law regulates these transactions by classifying them into particular types, this conception of contract law seeks to understand the general principles and social policies which inform and guide the legal classifications and regulation.

This approach is based on the particular analysis of contract adopted by Collins, centred on the regulation of the market. This is not the analysis adopted here but, nevertheless, the discussion does adopt the view that developments in principle that derive from particular types of contract should not be ignored, but be regarded as enriching the general law with the possibility of cross-fertilisation to other areas where appropriate. Just one example will suffice here. There was a long-standing issue as to whether a serious breach of contract can ever have the effect of terminating that contract automatically, or whether there must always be a decision by the 'innocent' party whether or not to treat the contract as repudiated.[58] This has caused particular problems in the area of employment law.[59] One view might be to say that the fact that employment law has special requirements in this area means that a different set of rules should be held to apply to this category of contract. That is not the view adopted here. Nor was it the view of the Court of Appeal, which in *Gunton v Richmond-upon-Thames LBC* held that the rule as to termination was the same in employment contracts as in other contracts,[60] a view that has recently been confirmed by the Supreme Court in *Geys v Société Générale, London Branch*.[61] Although there clearly will be some issues on which particular types of contract need to have special provisions, this should be a situation of last resort. In general, the development of principles in one area should be seen as enlightening and informing their application in other areas, so that there is a continuing dialogue between the demands of special contracts and the development of general principles. To use another analogy, the general principles might be seen as the hub of a spoked wheel, with the special contracts ranged around the rim. The flow of ideas about the development of the law should be in both directions along the spokes; and moreover, an idea originating in one 'special contract' may flow into the hub (general principles) and then out along another spoke to inform the development of a different 'special contract'.

A slightly different divergence can also be observed as having an impact on the development of the law – that is, the difference between a consumer contract and a contract between businesses. There is no doubt that over the past 100 years both Parliament and the courts have seen an increasing need to protect the consumer against 'unfair' and 'unreasonable' terms in contracts drawn up by businesses. The consumer may suffer from ignorance (not understanding the effect of the terms being put forward) and lack of

---

56  Collins, 2003, p 10.
57  As Collins notes, this has the effect of tending to exclude market transactions establishing 'an economic organization such as a firm, a trade association or a partnership'.
58  This question is considered fully in Chapter 14, 14.6.1.
59  See, for example, *Hill v CA Parsons & Co Ltd* [1972] Ch 305; [1971] 3 All ER 1345 and *Sanders v EA Neale* [1974] ICR 565.
60  [1981] Ch 448.
61  [2012] UKSC 63.

bargaining power (there may be no real choice to contracting on the terms put forward). It was for this reason that in the exemption clause area the courts developed strict rules of incorporation and construction, and the doctrine of 'fundamental breach'.[62] In time this was supplemented by parliamentary intervention in the form of the Unfair Contract Terms Act 1977, and EU controls through the Unfair Terms in Consumer Contracts Regulations 1999[63] (now replaced by the Consumer Rights Act 2015). The often stated view is that the consumer is the 'weaker party' and therefore needs protection. But is this identification of the consumer for protection an indication that there are two distinct types of contract – the consumer contract and the business contract – or is it simply a question of degree? There may well be, and often are, contracts between businesses where there is also inequality in bargaining power and one party is significantly weaker than the other. The small business manufacturing a single product which has a major multinational as its sole or dominant purchaser may have no real choice about the terms on which it contracts.

The law has taken notice of this factor in various areas. As regards economic duress, for example, the case of *Atlas Express Ltd v Kafco (Importers and Distributors) Ltd*[64] turned in part on the fact that the defendant company would have been likely to go out of business if it had not agreed to the variation of contract put forward by the national carrier with which it was contracting. Although this is catered for in doctrinal terms by a principle expressed in general terms – that is, whether the party subject to the alleged duress had any realistic choice about complying[65] – this is a condition that is always most likely to be satisfied by a party that is in the weaker position in the contract. The related concept of undue influence, although frequently used in relation to 'non-business' contractors, can also be used in a business or quasi-business context. The defendant in *Lloyds Bank Ltd v Bundy*,[66] for example, was a farmer who had had regular dealings with the bank in relation to his farm business. Nevertheless, Mr Bundy's age and the fact that he, running a small business, had put his trust in the employees of the large corporation (the bank) meant that in the circumstances of the case he was entitled to escape from the agreement that he had made. In the area of exclusion of liability there is now a statutory divide, with consumers protected by the Consumer Rights Act 2015. Nevertheless the Unfair Contract Terms Act 1977 will continue to protect businesses in some circumstances where the attempt to exclude liability is 'unreasonable'.[67] Moreover, the tests of unreasonableness set out in Sched 2 to the Act[68] include the strength of the bargaining position of the business against which the clause is being applied, and the knowledge of the clause: in other words, the same factors as we noted above as justifying special treatment for consumers – 'ignorance' and lack of bargaining power.

The conclusion from all of this is that, although there is an increasing separation, there is no reason to divide consumer contracts from business contracts entirely and to hold that they are such different types of agreement that a different set of contractual principles should apply to each. It is quite possible for both to be contained within a general law of contract, which has sufficient flexibility to accommodate a range of differing 'power relationships'.

---

62 See Chapter 7, 7.5.3.

63 SI 1999/2083.

64 [1989] QB 833; [1989] 1 All ER 641 – see Chapter 10, 10.4.2.

65 As suggested by Lord Scarman in *Pao On v Lau Yiu Long* [1980] AC 614, p 635; [1979] 3 All ER 65, p 78 – see Chapter 10, 10.4.2.

66 [1975] QB 326; [1974] 3 All ER 757 – see Chapter 11, 11.5.

67 That is, it does not satisfy the 'requirement of reasonableness' in s 11.

68 Although on its face Sched 2 is only applicable to sale of goods cases, the Court of Appeal has made it clear that it may be used more generally – *Overseas Medical Supplies Ltd v Orient Transport Services Ltd* [1999] 2 Lloyd's Rep 273 (Chapter 7, 7.7.16).

**For thought**

*If it is thought that the operation of the free market produces the most efficient economy, does it make sense to try to regulate contracts between businesses on the basis of inequality of bargaining power?*

## 1.9 DIFFERENT APPROACHES TO ANALYSING CONTRACT

The approach in this book is, for the most part, to analyse the law of contract within its own terms. In other words, the concentration will be on analysing the relevant cases and statutes, examining how contractual principles have developed through them, and critically appraising the end result. This does not mean that issues of social and political context, or legal history, should be ignored. Consideration of such matters is often essential in making any full appraisal of the relevant legal rules. The initial focus, however, is on the law as it has emerged through decisions of the courts and legislation. This is sometimes referred to as 'doctrinal analysis' because it concentrates on legal doctrine.

### 1.9.1 ECONOMIC ANALYSIS

Other approaches are, of course, possible. Since contract is intimately linked with the commercial world, it is not surprising that attempts have been made to analyse it in terms of economics. At a basic level, it is clear that particular decisions about the content of the rules of contract can have a broader economic influence. To take a simple example, as regards consumer contracts it may be thought desirable that producers of goods should be strictly liable for the quality of what they sell. If they are to be liable, however, they may need to introduce strict quality control procedures and/or to take out insurance. The costs of either of these two measures will almost certainly be added to the price of the goods. In economic terms, therefore, the cost of greater consumer protection is higher prices. Economic analysis will also look at 'transaction costs' (which may lead to the conclusion that standard form contracts are more economically efficient than those that are individually negotiated), and 'adjudication costs' (which may suggest that it is more economically efficient to have fixed rules of law, rather than leave it to judges to resolve disputes 'on their merits'). To take an example from the law on exclusion clauses,[69] the decision of the House of Lords in the case of *Photo Production Ltd v Securicor Transport Ltd*,[70] upholding a very widely based clause excluding one of the parties from virtually all liability for breach of contract, might be analysed in economic terms as follows. First, it might be said to be based on an assumption that, as between two parties, freely negotiating, they will have allocated responsibilities and risks in the most efficient way, and so will have 'maximised wealth'. Second, the refusal of the court to interfere in a bargain of this kind may discourage others from litigating, and therefore have the overall beneficial economic effect of reducing transaction costs. There have also been attempts to root the foundations of contractual liability in economic theory. Much of this work has originated in the United States.[71] The approach is generally to try to analyse the rules of contract law in terms of their economic efficiency and consequences. It may be argued, for example, that there is a benefit to society in economic terms in allowing and facilitating voluntary exchanges of goods and services. Kronman and Posner use the example of the exchange of goods

69  For which, see Chapter 7.
70  [1980] AC 827; [1980] 1 All ER 556.
71  See, in particular, Kronman and Posner, 1979; Posner, 2014.

between A and B.[72] The goods are worth $100 to A, who owns them, but are worth $150 to B (presumably because of the use B can make of them). If A sells the goods to B for $125, this will be an exchange that will 'increase the wealth of society':[73]

> Before the exchange ... A had a good worth $100 to him and B had $125 in cash, a total of $225. After the exchange, A has $125 in cash and B has a good worth $150 to him, a total of $275. The exchange has increased the wealth of society by $50.

Kronman and Posner use the concept of the 'wealth-maximising' effect of voluntary exchanges as an argument for 'freedom of contract'. This conclusion has been the subject of strong challenges,[74] but the important point here is to note the *technique* rather than the conclusion. There is no doubt that analysing the economic effects of contract law is a valid method of appraisal and can lead to conclusions about how the law should best develop.

### 1.9.2 SOCIO-POLITICAL ANALYSIS

A further way of looking at the law of contract is from a socio-political standpoint. In fact, we all have some political assumptions in the background, even if we are looking at contract cases purely within their own terms. It is, for example, impossible to debate the merits of numerous contract principles without some notion of the value or otherwise of the idea of 'freedom of contract', which is, of course, a political concept. Some writers feel, however, that this political/ideological background, be it capitalist, Marxist or whatever, should be made explicit. For example, Collins, in the first edition of *The Law of Contract*, stated:[75]

> This book identifies the purpose of the law of contract as the channelling and regulation of market transactions according to ideals of social justice.

A more recent collection of writing has been based on feminist analysis.[76] One of the editors suggests that:[77]

> Nothing better embodies masculine abstract relations with each other than the model of the discrete contractual transaction with which the majority of the scholarship in the field remains concerned.

By contrast, she has a different approach:[78]

> My task then is not merely to undermine the understanding of voluntary obligations, suggested by the classical model, that continue to cast a shadow over developments in the field. That task has been undertaken by many others and is

---

72 Kronman and Posner, 1979, p 1.
73 Ibid. In this simple example, Kronman and Posner specifically exclude consideration of any adverse effects on third parties. If such effects were to be greater than the increase brought about by A and B's exchange, the transaction would no longer be economically 'efficient'.
74 See, for example, Atiyah, 1986, Chapter 7; Leff, 1974. Macneil argues that adherence to neo-classical economic theory in analysing contract ignores the relational aspect of contract, in that it tends to focus on discrete transactions: see above, 1.6.
75 Collins, 1986. This particular formulation does not appear in later editions of Collins' book, though his overall approach appears to remain the same.
76 Mulcahy and Wheeler, 2005.
77 Ibid, p 1.
78 Mulcahy and Wheeler, 2005, p 3.

well-documented. Instead, I seek to use this critique as a stepping stone to consider how feminist ideas around the notion of an ethic of care can contribute to the ambitious task of persuading lawyers to think differently about why people voluntarily bind themselves to an enforceable agreement with another.

Another approach is to try to identify the ideologies that underpin the decisions of the courts on contract issues. Adams and Brownsword, for example,[79] identify three competing ideologies that may be found in the cases. These are: (a) formalism; (b) consumer-welfarism; and (c) market-individualism. Thus, a court may be said to adopt a formalist approach if it feels obliged to follow rules established in earlier cases, even if it does not agree with them or feels that they do not produce the most satisfactory result on the facts before the court. The case of *Foakes v Beer*[80] may be said to be an example of this type of approach, at least as far as some members of the House of Lords were concerned in that they felt bound to follow what was regarded as an established rule that part payment of a debt could never discharge the debtor's liability for the balance, even if the creditor had promised to treat it as so doing. 'Consumer-welfarism', on the other hand, may operate where a court recognises that individuals may be in a weak position as regards dealings with large organisations, and that the rules of contract therefore need to be developed and applied so as to protect them. Examples of this type of approach would include *Carlill v Carbolic Smoke Ball Co*,[81] in which an advertiser was bound by a promise made to consumers who had relied on the advert, or the pre-1977 exclusion clause cases,[82] where the courts devised rules to prevent large organisations from imposing wide clauses exempting them from liability to people who bought their products and services.

The third approach identified by Adams and Brownsword – 'market-individualism' – gives freedom of contract the highest priority and leaves the parties to their bargain, even if it appears to operate harshly on one side. In this situation, the court adopts the role simply of 'referee', determining what obligations the parties must be taken to have agreed to, and then applying them to the situation. A case mentioned above in connection with the economic analysis, *Photo Production Ltd v Securicor Transport Ltd*, is a good example of the court adopting this approach.

### 1.9.3 EMPIRICAL RESEARCH

Finally, contract may be approached from the bottom rather than the top. In other words, instead of looking at decisions of the appellate courts and the rules that they have developed, the focus could be on how contract law operates in people's day-to-day lives. Does the existence of a particular set of contractual rules affect the way in which people behave? Do businesses have contractual principles in mind when they enter into agreements? When things go wrong, to what extent does the law influence the way in which disputes are resolved? There has been surprisingly little research on these issues, but such as there is suggests that the law of contract is of much less importance to business people than lawyers would like to think.[83] In particular, where parties to a long-standing business relationship find themselves in a dispute, the maintenance of their relationship is likely to be a much stronger influence over the way they resolve their differences than are the strict legal rights between the parties, as determined by the law of contract.

---

79  Adams and Brownsword, 2007, Chapter 8.
80  (1884) 9 App Cas 605 – discussed in Chapter 3, 3.13.2.
81  [1893] 1 QB 256 – discussed in Chapter 2, 2.7.8.
82  For which, see Chapter 7, 7.3–7.5.
83  See, in relation to the United States, the seminal work of Macaulay, 1963; and, in relation to this, England and Wales, Beale and Dugdale, 1975; Yates, 1982, pp 16–33 and Lewis, 1982.

### 1.9.4 WHICH APPROACH?

As has been indicated above, the approach taken here is primarily based on looking at legal materials within their own terms. At appropriate points throughout the book, however, aspects of one or more of the alternative approaches outlined above will be referred to, in order to produce a fuller understanding of the way in which the law has developed, or is likely to develop in the future.

## 1.10 INTERNATIONAL INFLUENCES

The common law of contract has tended to be insular in its outlook, though it has had a very significant international impact. The contract law of North America and much of the Commonwealth still derives many of its basic principles from the 'classical' English law of contract, which reached its developed form during the nineteenth century. Moreover, as these were its origins, the law in many of these overseas jurisdictions has continued to look to the decisions of the English courts as providing indicators for its own development. This has been so even when the last formal link, that is the existence of, for example, the Judicial Committee of the Privy Council as the final court of appeal, was severed. Until recently, however, the flow has tended to be in one direction, and courts in England and Wales have rarely paid much attention to developments in the law of contract in other parts of the common law world. The same has been largely true of the relationship between the common law and civil law jurisdictions.

One important exception to this has been in the area of international trade, where the demands of the commercial world for increased certainty, which is arguably most easily facilitated by increased uniformity, have led to the creation of international treaties. One of the most successful development of this kind was the establishment of the Hague-Visby Rules, applying to contracts for the carriage of goods by sea, which have achieved widespread acceptance.[84] The attempt to establish a similar regime for international sale of goods contracts, by the 1980 Vienna Convention,[85] has arguably been less successful[86] but the development of standard terms, which parties can choose whether or not to use, has increased the uniformity of contracts in the relevant areas.[87]

In more recent times the position has, to some extent, changed. There has first of all been an increased willingness among judges in England and Wales to recognise that authorities from other parts of the Commonwealth, and in particular from Australia, may be valuable in assisting the development of contractual principles in England and Wales. Second, there has been the impact of membership of the (now) European Union. Thirdly there has been the rapid growth in the ease of international telecommunications followed and assisted by the development of the internet and the World Wide Web.

All three of these developments are worth examining. As regards the influence of case law from other parts of the Commonwealth, this will be noted where appropriate throughout the rest of the text. The influence of the EU will be dealt with separately in 1.11.

---

84 They were enacted into the law of England and Wales by the Carriage of Goods by Sea Act 1971.

85 That is, the United Nations Convention on Contracts for the International Sale of Goods 1980.

86 It has not been ratified by the UK. For conflicting views among senior UK judges on the merits of mandatory attempts at unification in the commercial area, see the debate between Lord Hobhouse and Lord Steyn, discussed by Brownsword, 2006, pp 193–94.

87 For example, International Chamber of Commerce's INCOTERMS (for international sales) and the Federation International des Ingénieurs Conseils' contract templates (for international construction contracts). See also the Principles for International Commercial Contracts produced by the International Institution for the Unification of Private Law (UNIDROIT).

As regards the growth in telecommunications and the internet, the influence of these technological advances was seen first in the area of business contracting, dating in particular from the widespread adoption and use of telex machines and then faxes.[88] At its most basic this has required the courts to decide where contracts made by such devices are concluded.[89] Contracting by telex and fax has, however, largely been the preserve of businesses. The same is not the case as regards more recent telecommunications developments. In particular, the internet is seen as showing the future for much consumer shopping. The ability to access websites offering wide ranges of consumer products, and to order them 'online', is increasing all the time. In such transactions, the ease with which orders may be placed, and payment (by credit card) made, does not relate to the distance between the customer and the supplier. They may be in the same street or on opposite sides of the world. From the point of view of the customer, the information appearing on the screen and the manner in which the transaction proceeds will be the same whatever the location of the supplier. It becomes important, therefore, for the sake of developing consumer confidence, that there is clarity as to the law that applies to all such transactions. At the moment, the answer may well depend on the location of the supplier. It is not satisfactory, however, that the customer may be put in the uncertain position of not knowing what set of contractual rules will apply to the transaction. The assumption on the part of the customer may be that it will be the law of his or her own jurisdiction that will be relevant, whereas it may well be that of the jurisdiction where the supplier is located. Although in the short term this may be to the advantage of the supplier, in the long run, if the aim is to attract increasing trade in this form, customers will want rather greater security than this suggests. There will therefore be a strong motivation for making the rules applying to such transactions the same wherever the contract is made. This will, in turn, produce pressure for harmonisation and unification of laws across jurisdictions.

## 1.11 EUROPEAN INFLUENCE ON ENGLISH CONTRACT LAW

The influence of the EU on contract law in England and Wales can be seen most clearly in the directives that have required implementation in the UK. For example, the directive on commercial agents[90] was given effect by the Commercial Agents (Council Directive) Regulations 1993 (as amended),[91] and that on unfair terms in consumer contracts[92] by the Unfair Terms in Consumer Contracts Regulations 1999[93] (now replaced by the Consumer Rights Act 2015). More recently, the Consumer Rights Directive[94] has been implemented by, for example, the Consumer Contracts (Information, Cancellation and Additional Charges) Regulations 2013.[95] The Directive on electronic contracts[96] was implemented by the Electronic Commerce (EC Directive) Regulations 2002.[97] There have also been significant effects on employment contracts, particularly in relation to sex discrimination.

---

88  See, for example, *Entores v Miles Far East Corp* [1955] 2 QB 327; [1955] 2 All ER 493, discussed in Chapter 2, 2.12.11.
89  Cf. in *Brownlie v Four Seasons Holdings Inc* [2017] UKSC 80.
90  Directive 86/653/EEC.
91  SI 1993/3053.
92  Directive 93/13/EEC.
93  SI 1999/2083 – see Chapter 7, 7.8.
94  Directive 2011/83/EU.
95  SI 2013/3134 – discussed in Chapter 2, 2.14.
96  2000/31/EC.
97  SI 2002/2013 – see, further, Chapter 2, 2.12.13.

To some extent, for example, in the protection of consumers, the EU approach merely reflects concerns that exist independently in the law of England and Wales. This was illustrated by the overlap between the Unfair Contract Terms Act 1977 and the Unfair Terms in Consumer Contracts Regulations 1999, though this overlap has been removed by the Consumer Rights Act 2015. In other respects, however, the European Directives led to concepts novel to the law of England and Wales being incorporated. The most obvious example of this relates to the concept of 'good faith' in contracting. The common law has traditionally rejected any attempts to introduce a general obligation to contract 'in good faith'. The attempt by Lord Denning to introduce a concept of 'unconscionability' in *Lloyds Bank Ltd v Bundy*[98] was firmly rejected by his fellow judges,[99] and in *Walford v Miles*[100] the House of Lords, relying on the traditional English law rule that an 'agreement to agree' is unenforceable,[101] held that there could be no binding obligation to negotiate in good faith. Indeed, Lord Ackner felt that such an approach would be 'repugnant' to the adversarial position of the bargaining parties.[102]

Despite this judicial hostility, the concept of 'good faith' does now exist in some parts of the law of England and Wales. Both the Commercial Agents (Council Directive) Regulations 1993[103] and the Unfair Terms in Consumer Contracts Regulations 1999[104] (now replaced by the Consumer Rights Act 2015) following the wording of the directives on which they are based, imposed obligations of 'good faith' on the contracting parties. The reaction of the House of Lords to the introduction of this concept in the first case in which it was called upon to consider it was to give it flesh by regarding it as requiring fair and open dealing between the parties:[105]

> Openness requires that the terms should be expressed fully, clearly and legibly, containing no concealed pitfalls or traps ... Fair dealing requires that a supplier should not, whether deliberately or unconsciously, take advantage of the consumer's necessity, indigence, lack of experience, unfamiliarity with the subject matter of the contract, weak bargaining position.

As to whether the introduction of 'good faith' in these particular areas might lead to a greater willingness to adopt it more generally, as Brownsword has pointed out[106] there remains considerable scepticism about the concept.[107] He has suggested that the adoption of a good faith 'requirement', whereby a court 'simply acts on the standards of fair dealing that are already recognised in a particular contracting context',[108] is more likely than a good faith 'regime' that would attempt to prescribe 'the co-operative ground rules'.[109]

---

98  [1975] QB 326; [1974] 3 All ER 757. See also Chapter 11, 11.5 and 11.10.
99  In particular, by Lord Scarman in *National Westminster Bank v Morgan* [1985] AC 686; [1985] 1 All ER 821. He took a similar line in *Pao On v Lau Yiu Long* [1980] AC 614; [1979] 3 All ER 65.
100  [1992] 2 AC 128; [1992] 1 All ER 453.
101  *Courtney and Fairbairn Ltd v Tolaini Brothers (Hotels) Ltd* [1975] 1 WLR 297; *May and Butcher v R* [1934] 2 KB 17.
102  [1992] 2 AC 128 at p 138; [1992] 1 All ER 453 at p 460.
103  SI 1993/3053.
104  SI 1999/2083.
105  *Director General of Fair Trading v First National Bank plc* [2002] UKHL 52; [2002] 1 All ER 97, at [17] per Lord Bingham. Lord Steyn went further and suggested that the concept should not be limited to procedural fairness: ibid, [36] – [37]. The House of Lords was in this case concerned with the UTCCR 1994. For further discussion, see Chapter 7.
106  Brownsword, 2006, Chapter 6.
107  See, for example, Professor Bridge's characterisation of it as 'visceral justice', leading to impressionistic decision-making and undesirable uncertainty in commercial transactions: Bridge, 1999, p 140.
108  Brownsword, 2006, p 130.
109  Ibid.

This view may be seen to have been prescient, in that it is this type of approach that has been adopted in *Yam Seng Pte v International Trade Corp*[110] where Leggatt J attempted an analysis of the role of 'good faith' in the common law of contract, independent of any direct European influence. His view was that obligations to act 'in good faith' in relation to the performance of a contract could be based on implied terms that it must have been taken that the parties intended to be included in their contract. The precise extent of the obligation would depend on the context. For example, in a relational contract, it would be easier to imply a term of good faith co-operation in that such contracts will require:[111]

> a high degree of communication, cooperation and predictable performance based on mutual trust and confidence and involve expectations of loyalty which are not legislated for in the express terms of the contract but are implicit in the parties' understanding and necessary to give business efficacy to the arrangements.

The contract under consideration in the case, which related to an agreement between an English company and a Singaporean company for the distribution of toiletries branded in Manchester United colours, was of this type. More specifically, in relation to any ongoing contract it will be relatively easy to imply an obligation not to deliberately give false information to the other party (behaviour that occurs prior to the contract is controlled by the law on misrepresentation, see Chapter 8). He found a breach of this term in the actions of the English company.

This approach to 'good faith' is therefore dependent on context, and on implying terms that the parties must have been taken to have intended to underpin their agreement. If they do not wish to have such obligations, then they may specifically exclude them.[112]

Leggatt J's approach to good faith in *Yam Seng* was considered by the Court of Appeal in *Mid Essex Hospital Services NHS Trust v Compass Group UK and Ireland Ltd*,[113] where the contract contained a specific obligation to co-operate in good faith, which the trial judge found had been broken. The Court of Appeal disagreed, with Jackson LJ stating that 'there is no general doctrine of "good faith" in English contract law'.[114] More specifically, Beatson LJ, in approving Leggatt J's emphasis on 'context' when interpreting any implied good faith obligation, suggested that this approach should also apply to a specific obligation. In the present case he felt that the trial judge had given insufficient weight to specific provisions in other parts of the contract when finding that there had been a breach of the general good faith obligation. He warned against construing:[115]

> a general and potentially open-ended obligation such as an obligation to 'cooperate' or 'to act in good faith' as covering the same ground as other, more specific, provisions, lest it cut across those more specific provisions and any limitations in them.

The approach adopted by Leggatt J has also been applied by the High Court in *Bristol Groundschool Ltd v Intelligent Data Capture Ltd*. He noted that this approach had not been disapproved by the Court of Appeal in the *Mid Essex* case, and found that there was

---

110  [2013] EWHC 111 (QB).
111  Ibid, [142].
112  Ibid, [149].
113  [2013] EWCA Civ 200.
114  Ibid, [105].
115  Ibid, [154].

on the facts an obligation to act in good faith, at least in terms of acting 'honestly', defined as not engaging in 'conduct that would be regarded as "commercially unacceptable" by reasonable and honest people in the particular context involved'.[116]

It is arguable[117] that the English and Welsh courts are now edging towards an acceptance of a role for 'good faith' in contract law, particularly in relational contracts, and as long as it is based on what is reasonably to be expected in the context of the particular contract under consideration. Further consideration of the practical influence of such an approach will be considered further at appropriate places later in the text. The main point here is that a concept that has widespread acceptance in other European jurisdictions has begun to be accepted within the law of England and Wales.

A more far-reaching attempt to put forward general principles for a European law of contract was contained in the work of the Lando Commission. The approach of this group, which consisted of eminent lawyers from a number of European jurisdictions, was rather different from the piecemeal attempts at Europe-wide harmonisation at that point attempted by the institutions of the EU. These tended to be responses to areas where there was perceived to be a problem. The Lando approach, however, was to try to provide 'a bridge between the civil law and common law by providing rules to reconcile their differing legal philosophies'.[118] To this end, in 2000 it published a set of Principles of European Contract Law (PECL), together with commentary, divided into nine chapters, and covering most areas of contract, from formation to remedies.[119]

The work of the Lando Commission was absorbed into a European Union project aimed at producing a draft of a European Contract Law.[120] An Action Plan issued by the European Commission in 2003[121] proposed the development of a Common Frame of Reference (CFR) for European Contract Law, and this was followed in 2004 by a communication entitled *European Contract Law and the revision of the acquis: the way forward*.[122] This envisaged a structure for the CFR that would:[123]

> first set out common fundamental principles of contract law, including guidance on when exceptions to such fundamental principles could be required. Secondly, those fundamental principles would be supported by definitions of key concepts. Thirdly, these principles and definitions would be completed by model rules, forming the bulk of the CFR. A distinction between model rules applicable to contracts concluded between businesses or private persons and model rules applicable to contracts concluded between a business and a consumer could be envisaged.

---

116  [2014] EWHC 2145 (Ch).

117  Although compare *MSC Mediterranean Shipping Co SA v Cottonex Anstalt* [2016] EWCA Civ 789 at [45] where Moore-Bick LJ stated: "There is in my view a real danger that if a general principle of good faith were established it would be invoked as often to undermine as to support the terms in which the parties have reached agreement. The danger is not dissimilar to that posed by too liberal an approach to construction, against which the Supreme Court warned in *Arnold v Britton* [2015] UKSC 36, [2015] AC 1619." By contract in 2013 the Law Commission noted: "The test [of 'good faith' under the then Unfair Terms in Consumer Contracts Regulations 1999] is now more familiar to a UK audience, and has acquired a significant body of domestic and European case law to interpret it. It no longer appears to give rise to much confusion. We have been persuaded that the benefits of changing the formulation do not outweigh the risks of introducing new uncertainties" (Law Commission, 'Unfair Terms in Consumer Contracts: Advice to the Department for Business, Innovation and Skills' (March 2013) at 6.42).

118  Lando and Beale, 2000, p xxiii.

119  Lando and Beale, 2000.

120  A useful collection of essays on this development is to be found in Vogenauer and Weatherill, 2006.

121  COM(2003) 68 final.

122  COM(2004) 651 final.

123  Ibid, para 3.1.3.

As well as being used by the EU itself in framing legislation, it was also anticipated that the CFR could be used by national legislators:[124]

> when transposing EU directives in the area of contract law into national legislation. They could also draw on the CFR when enacting legislation on areas of contract law which are not regulated at Community level.

The paper also discussed the possible development of an optional instrument on European Contract Law, which would be available for parties to opt in to through a choice of law clause in their contract. The CFR project was taken forward by the European Commission, as part of a broader project aimed at the harmonisation of all private law, and in 2009 it published a Draft Common Frame of Reference (which draws extensively on the Principles of European Contract Law produced by the Lando Commission).[125] This was followed by a Green Paper on a European Contract Law,[126] which raised various possibilities for the status of any European Contract Law – from simple publication to the issue of a Regulation replacing national law with the European law. The UK Ministry of Justice opened a consultation on this in August 2010, and reported to the European Commission in February 2011.[127] The conclusion was that:

> there was insufficient evidence of a problem with the current arrangements to suggest that any of the options beyond the use of the [Common Frame of Reference] as a toolbox for legislators and the publication of the work of the Expert Groups would be proportionate and necessary. The Government could therefore only support only these options (1 and 2a of the Commission's Green Paper) and could not support any of the other options on the available evidence. It suggested that before any of the other options could be considered there would need to be a full and thorough analysis of the evidence and potential impacts.

Given this lukewarm response, further development in this area seemed unlikely.[128] This has now been reinforced as regards the UK by the decision in the referendum of 2016 to leave the European Union ('Brexit') although, at the time of writing, the precise nature and form of Brexit is subject to much uncertainty! In addition to there now being little prospect of English and Welsh contract law being subsumed into a European contract law, European Union Directives in this area will cease to need to be transposed in the UK post-Brexit (unless, perhaps, a condition of access to the Single Market required acceptance of European Union law relating to relevant transactions). On the other hand, it seems unlikely that there will be any wholesale move to repeal existing legislation in this area which has resulted from membership of the European Union.[129] The influence of European law will continue to be felt, particularly in the area of consumer transactions, even post-Brexit.

---

124  COM(2004) 651 final, para 2.1.2.
125  Von Bar, C, Clive, E and Schulte Nölke, H (eds), Principles, Definitions and Model Rules of European Private Law. Draft Common Frame of Reference (DCFR), 2009, Munich: Sellier.
126  COM(2010) 348 final.
127  Report on the UK Government Call for Evidence on the European Commission Consultation on Contract, Ministry of Justice, May 2011.
128  Indeed the proposal for an optional instrument, which had become the favoured option, was ultimately replaced by, for example, a proposal for a DIRECTIVE OF THE EUROPEAN PARLIAMENT AND OF THE COUNCIL on certain aspects concerning contracts for the online and other distance sales of goods (COM/2015/0635 final).
129  Compare HM Government, THE FUTURE RELATIONSHIP BETWEEN THE UNITED KINGDOM AND THE EUROPEAN UNION, Cm 9593 (July 2018) at [11]: "The UK and the EU would maintain a common rulebook for goods including agri-food, with the UK making an upfront choice to commit by treaty to ongoing harmonisation with EU rules on goods, covering only those necessary to provide for frictionless trade at the border. This common rulebook would be legislated for by the UK Parliament, as set out in detail in chapter 4."

## 1.12 FURTHER READING

### General

■ Adams, J and Brownsword, R, *Understanding Contract Law*, 5th edn, 2007, London: Sweet & Maxwell

■ Collins, H, *Regulating Contracts*, 1999, Oxford: Oxford University Press

■ Robertson, A (ed), *The Law of Obligations: Connections and Boundaries*, 2004, London: UCL Press

■ Smith, S A, *Atiyah's Introduction to the Law of Contract*, 6th edn, 2006, Oxford: Clarendon Press

### Theories of contract

■ Campbell, D (ed), *The Relational Theory of Contract: Selected Works of Ian Macneil*, 2001, London: Sweet & Maxwell

■ Campbell, D, Collins, H and Wightman, J (eds), *Implicit Dimensions of Contract*, 2003, Oxford: Hart Publishing

■ Gilmore, G, *The Death of Contract*, 1974, Columbus: Ohio State University Press

■ Macaulay, S, 'Non-contractual relations in business' (1963) 28 Am Sociological Rev 35

■ Smith, S A, *Contract Theory*, 2004, Oxford: Clarendon Press

■ Swain, W, 'The classical model of contract: the product of a revolution in legal thought?' (2010) 30 Legal Studies 513

### Socio-legal analysis

■ Beale, H and Dugdale, T, 'Contracts between businessmen' (1975) 2 Brit J Law & Society 45

### European influence

■ Twigg-Flessner, C (ed), *The Europeanisation of Contract Law*, 2nd edn, 2013, London: Routledge

■ Vogenauer, S and Weatherill, S, *The Harmonisation of European Contract Law*, 2006, Oxford: Hart Publishing

## COMPANION WEBSITE

*Now visit the companion website to:*

■ Revise and consolidate your knowledge of the basics of contract law by tackling a series of multiple-choice questions on this chapter

■ Test your understanding of the chapter's key terms by using the flashcard glossary

■ Explore the basics of contract law further by accessing a series of web links

# Forming the agreement

## Contents

## 2.1 OVERVIEW

'Agreement' is central to the law of contract in England and Wales. In most cases that are adjudicated, the court regards its role as giving effect to an agreement reached between the parties. The question of whether such an agreement has been formed is, therefore, a crucial one. This chapter is concerned with the mechanisms that the courts use to decide whether an agreement has been reached. The main areas covered are as follows:

- Formalities. To what extent does the law of England and Wales use formal mechanisms to decide whether an agreement has been reached? Generally, this will be where a 'deed' is used or where a statute requires formality, such as putting the agreement into writing, in relation to a particular type of contract.
- More generally there is no requirement of writing or other formality. The courts decide whether an agreement has been reached by looking at what the parties have said or done as indicators of whether they intended to make an agreement.
- The most common indicators will be a matching 'offer' and 'acceptance'. The identification of a matching offer and acceptance is the most common way for the courts to find that an agreement has been made.
- An offer must be distinguished from an invitation to treat, and an acceptance from a counter-offer.
- Particular problems arise in relation to the following:
  - ☐ Unilateral (as opposed to bilateral) contracts. The offer in a unilateral contract (for example, an offer of a reward for the return of property) may be made to the world and the acceptance usually takes the form of performing an action (for example, the return of the property).
  - ☐ The 'battle of the forms'. Where parties both try to contract on their own standard terms, and these are inconsistent, which should prevail?
  - ☐ Contracting at a distance. If the contract is made by letter, fax, email or over the web, when and where does it take effect? Special rules apply to posted acceptances, as opposed it seems to those communicated by telephone or electronically.
- Revocation of offers. An offer can generally be revoked at any time before it is accepted, provided that the revocation is communicated to the offeree.
- Certainty. The courts require an agreement to be sufficiently 'certain', and will not generally enforce an 'agreement to agree'.

## 2.2 INTRODUCTION

The main subject matter of this chapter is the means by which the courts decide whether parties have reached an agreement that is potentially one that the courts will enforce. A related set of questions are that of why and how the law of contract becomes engaged in dealing with the parties' transaction. There are several potential reasons. First, it might be the case that the courts will simply be responding to the wishes of the parties. In other words, the law is acting in a facilitative way. The parties have intentionally formulated their agreement as a contract and now wish to make use of the mechanism of the courts to resolve a dispute. They can choose not to use the courts if they wish, and indeed many commercial disputes are settled by alternative methods such as arbitration or mediation. Such methods will often also may make reference to the law of contract as it is thought it would be applied by the courts.

Another reason for the courts' involvement may, however, be where there is a dispute as to whether there is a contract at all. This might be because one of the parties disputes the fact of agreement, or wishes to argue that although there is an agreement, it is unenforceable. If the courts become involved, and again there is an element of choice in that one party must initiate an action by issuing a claim form, it may be against the wishes of one of the parties. That party will be arguing that there is no contract and that, therefore, the courts should not be involved at all. In this situation, the court is not acting in a purely facilitative way but may be holding that although at least one of the parties thought that it was not entering into a binding contract, in fact it did so, and therefore it is obliged to submit to the jurisdiction of the court. The extent to which parties can deliberately exclude an agreement from the jurisdiction of the court is considered further in Chapter 4, in connection with the requirement of 'intention to create legal relations', and Chapter 12 in relation to agreements contrary to public policy.

A third possibility that now exists is that a third party, who claims to be entitled to a benefit under a contract, may in some circumstances initiate an action against one or other of the contracting parties.[1] In theory, it is possible for this to arise in a situation where neither of the alleged contracting parties accepts that it has made a binding contract. The court, if it upholds the third party's claim in such circumstances, will in effect be overriding the wishes of the two parties who made the agreement. In doing so, it is likely to be acting to protect the reasonable expectations of the third party. To achieve this, it will hold that the parties have made a binding agreement, even though they dispute that they have done so.

In all these situations, however, the concept of an 'agreement' forms the basis of the court's intervention. As indicated in Chapter 1, this book takes as its subject matter the enforcement of agreements, entered into more or less voluntarily, concerning the transfer of goods or other property (permanently or temporarily) or the supply of services. That being so, it becomes important to identify when an agreement has been reached. There are two main ways in which this might be achieved. First, it might be done by identifying certain formal procedures, and deeming the following of those formalities as sufficient to establish that there was an agreement. Second, it might be done by trying to determine whether there was, at least objectively ascertained, a 'meeting of the minds' of the parties concerned. In practice, English law uses both approaches.

## 2.3 DEEDS AND OTHER FORMALITIES

The parties may decide to embed their transaction (whether or not it is an agreement) in a deed. This is a formal written document, signed and, traditionally, sealed (though this is no longer a requirement since the Law of Property (Miscellaneous Provisions) Act 1989). For present purposes, the existence of a deed will be regarded as indicating that there is a legally enforceable agreement. There are certain contracts where a deed is required (and these situations are considered further in Chapter 3), but the device can be used for any type of contract if the parties so wish. This type of formality should be distinguished from the situations where some special procedure is required *in addition to* the finding of an agreement. In these situations there may be an agreement but the courts will not be able to enforce it unless certain formalities have been complied with. Three examples will be mentioned here. First, by virtue of s 2(1) of the Law of Property (Miscellaneous Provisions) Act 1989, all contracts involving the sale, or other disposal, of an interest in land must be in writing and signed by the parties. The need for writing in relation to contracts

---

1    See the Contracts (Rights of Third Parties) Act 1999, discussed in detail in Chapter 5, 5.6.

concerning land is of long standing in the law of England and Wales, though prior to 1989 the requirement was only that the contract should be evidenced in writing, and signed by the person against whom it was to be enforced.[2] Although, in practice, the vast majority of such contracts were put into written form, this formulation left open the possibility of a verbal contract being evidenced by, for example, a letter signed by the relevant party. The 1989 amendment of this rule means that the agreement itself must be in writing and signed by both parties. The justification for the stricter rules that apply in relation to this type of contract is that contracts involving land are likely to be both complicated and valuable. Many commercial contracts, however, are also complex and valuable, yet there is no requirement of a written agreement (though, in practice, there is likely to be one). A second type of contract where there is a requirement of a certain degree of formality arises under the Consumer Credit Act 1974, which requires that contracts of hire purchase, and other credit transactions, should be in writing and signed.[3] This is a protective provision, designed to make sure that the individual consumer has written evidence of the agreement and has the opportunity to see all its terms. A similar protective procedure operates in relation to contracts of employment, though here the requirement is simply that the employee should receive a written statement of terms and conditions within a certain period of starting the job, rather than that the agreement itself should be in writing.[4]

A third situation where formality is required was the subject of consideration by the House of Lords in *Actionstrength Ltd v International Glass Engineering*.[5] The case concerned the requirement in s 4 of the Statute of Frauds 1677 that an agreement to guarantee the debt of a third party must, in order to be enforceable, be in writing and signed by the guarantor.

The claimant was a sub-contractor who had worked for the main contractor on a construction contract. When the main contractor became insolvent, the claimant sought to recover under an alleged oral guarantee of payment given by the party for whom the building was being constructed. In the Court of Appeal, it was held that the claimant could not succeed because an oral guarantee was unenforceable by virtue of s 4 of the 1677 Act.

In the House of Lords the claimant argued that, even if the Act applied, the defendant should not be allowed to rely on it, on the grounds that it would be unconscionable to do so. The claimant's argument was based on 'estoppel' – a concept that broadly, when it operates, prevents a party to an action relying on a point, where their words or behaviour have previously indicated that they would not rely on it. The defendant had allowed the claimant to run up the debt owed by the main contractor, knowing that it was relying on the guarantee. It was held that the effect of s 4 could not be overturned by an estoppel, at least not unless there had been, for example, a specific assurance that the statute would not be relied on.

---

2    Law of Property Act 1925, s 40. Cf the Statute of Frauds 1677, which required writing for various agreements, including contracts for the sale of goods to the value of more than £10.

3    In *Wilson v First County Trust Ltd* [2003] UKHL 40; [2003] 4 All ER 97, the Court of Appeal held that the then rigid statutory rule which rendered a consumer credit totally unenforceable if certain formalities had not been complied with was incompatible with the right to a fair trial under Art 6 of the ECHR. The House of Lords, however, reversed this decision, on the basis that the Human Rights Act 1998 did not apply to the contract in question (which was made prior to 2 October 2000), and because in any case the provisions were compatible with the ECHR. S 127 Consumer Credit Act 1974 was amended by the Consumer Credit Act 2006, Sched 4, para 1. This gives the courts more power to order enforcement in appropriate circumstances.

4    Employment Rights Act 1996, s 1.

5    [2003] 2 All ER 615. This case was endorsed in *Rock Advertising Limited v MWB Business Exchange Centres Limited* [2018] UKSC 24. In *MyBarrister Ltd v Hewetson* [2017] EWHC 2624 at [52] the learned judge stated: "… while the application of the statute to guarantees may be thought to be of questionable continuing value in current commercial circumstances, it represents the law and courts should not strive to find ways of getting round it by seeking somewhat artificial characterisations of obligations to take them outside its provisions".

The case emphasises the continuing importance of the Statute of Frauds in this area, and the need to ensure that any 'promise to answer for the debt, default or miscarriages of another' is put in writing.

## 2.4 GENERAL LACK OF FORMAL REQUIREMENT

In most cases, however, the law of England and Wales imposes no formal requirements and looks simply for an agreement between the parties. In other words, the contract generally does not have to be put into writing nor be signed, nor does any particular form of words have to be used. A purely verbal exchange can, in many cases, result in a binding contract. All that is needed is an agreement. This simple assertion, however, masks a considerable problem in identifying precisely what is meant by an agreement. This may seem easy enough: is it simply a question of identifying a 'meeting of the minds' between the parties at a particular point in time? That, however, is easier said than done. By the time two parties to a contract have arrived in court, they are clearly usually no longer of one mind. They may dispute whether there was ever an agreement between them at all or, while accepting that there was an agreement, they may disagree as to its terms. How are such disputes to be resolved? Clearly, there are difficulties in discovering as a matter of fact what was actually going on in the minds of the parties at the time of the alleged agreement (a subjective approach). Nor are the courts prepared to rely solely on what the parties now say was in their minds at that time (which would also be a 'subjective' approach), even if they are very convincing. Instead, the courts adopt what is primarily an 'objective' approach to deciding whether there was an agreement and, if so, what its terms were. This essentially means that they look at what was said and done between the parties from the point of view of the 'reasonable person' and try to decide what such a person would have thought was going on.

A further complication with regard to 'agreement' arises once parties start to contract over a distance – that is, not face to face. The particular problems relating to contracts made by post or other forms of distance communication are discussed later in this chapter.[6] Suffice it to say here that once this type of contracting is allowed, the idea that at any particular point in time there is a 'consensus ad idem', a 'meeting of the minds', becomes very difficult to sustain.[7] If there is a significant gap in time between an 'offer' and its 'acceptance', the likelihood is that in some cases the parties will not actually have been in (subjective) agreement at the point when the courts decide that a contract was formed.

###  2.4.1 IN FOCUS: AGREEMENT OR RELIANCE?

It has been argued by Collins that this approach means that the courts are not actually looking for agreements between the parties but:

> whether or not the negotiations and conduct have reached such a point that both parties can reasonably suppose that the other is committed to the contract so that it can be relied upon.[8]

In other words, it is behaviour justifying 'reasonable reliance' on the other party's commitment that the courts are in fact looking for, rather than 'agreement', whether looked at subjectively or objectively.[9] There is, however, not very much to choose between an

---

6   See below, 2.12.6.
7   Cf Gardner, 1992, p 171.
8   Collins, 2003, p 164.
9   Cf the approach of Steyn LJ in *Trentham Ltd v Archital Luxfer* [1993] 1 Lloyd's Rep 25, p 27 – discussed below, 2.11.5.

approach that uses the language of 'objective agreement' as opposed to that of 'reasonable reliance', and certainly little in the way of practical consequence. The former is what is used here, not least because it ties in more comfortably with the language used by the courts, which tends to focus on the presence or absence of 'agreement'. Provided that it is remembered that what is required is objective evidence of such agreement, rather than an actual 'meeting of the minds', this analysis will work satisfactorily, without giving a misleading picture of what is actually happening.

### 2.4.2 PROMISOR, PROMISEE AND DETACHED OBJECTIVITY

Although it is clear that an objective approach to agreement has to be adopted, as has been pointed out by McClintock and Howarth,[10] there are different types of objectivity. There is (a) 'promisor objectivity', where the court tries to decide what the reasonable promisor would have intended; (b) 'promisee objectivity', where the focus is on what the reasonable person being made a promise would have thought was intended; and (c) 'detached objectivity', which views what has happened through the eyes of an independent third party. In *Smith v Hughes*,[11] for example, where the dispute was over what type of oats the parties were contracting about, the test was said to be whether the party who wished to deny the contract acted so that 'a reasonable man would believe that he was assenting to the terms proposed by the other party': in other words, promisee objectivity. As we shall see, however, in subsequent chapters, the courts are not consistent as to which of these types of objectivity they use, changing between one and another as seems most appropriate in a particular case.

The use of the objective approach where there is a dispute as to whether the parties were ever in agreement is discussed further in Chapter 9, 9.5.1.

### 2.4.3 STATE OF MIND

The objective approach must, however, take account of all the evidence. Even if A has acted in a way that would reasonably cause B to assume a particular state of mind as regards an agreement, if B's behaviour, objectively viewed, indicates that such an assumption has not been made by B, the courts will take account of this. *The Hannah Blumenthal*,[12] for example, was a case concerning the sale of a ship, where the point at issue was whether the parties had agreed to abandon their dispute. The behaviour of the buyers was such that it would have been reasonable for the sellers to have believed that the action had been dropped. In fact, the sellers had continued to act (by seeking witnesses, etc.) in a way that indicated that they did not think the action had been dropped. This evidence of their actual response to the buyers' behaviour overrode the conclusion that the court might well have reached by applying a test based on an objectively reasonable response.[13]

### 2.5 THE EXTERNAL SIGNS OF AGREEMENT

As we have seen, the process by which the courts try to decide whether the parties have made an agreement does not necessarily involve looking for actual (subjective) agreement but rather focuses on the external signs of agreement. The classical theory of contract relied on a number of specific elements, which were regarded as both necessary and sufficient to identify an agreement that is intended to be legally binding. These were:

---

10  McClintock, 1988–91; Howarth, 1984.
11  (1871) LR 6 QB 597. This case is discussed further in Chapter 9, 9.5.3.
12  [1983] 1 All ER 34.
13  See, also, the similar case of *The Leonidas D* [1985] 1 WLR 925.

(a)    offer;
(b)    acceptance;
(c)    consideration; and
(d)    intention to create legal relations.

These four factors formed the classical basis for the identification of contracts in the law of England and Wales. As far as offer and acceptance are concerned, in the modern law the courts have, as will be noted below, at various times recognised the difficulty of analysing all contractual situations in terms of these concepts. Some attempts, with various degrees of success, have been made to apply a more general test of 'agreement'. This involves taking offer and acceptance as the normal basis for the creation of a contract, but recognising that not all contracts will be made in this way.[14]

The rest of this chapter explores the current approach in England and Wales to offer and acceptance in detail. Consideration is dealt with in Chapter 3 and intention to create legal relations in Chapter 4.

## 2.6 HISTORICAL BACKGROUND

The rules of 'offer' and 'acceptance', and their use as the basis for deciding whether there has been an agreement between contracting parties, derives, as with much of the classical law of contract, from late eighteenth-century and early nineteenth-century case law.[15]

## 2.7 OFFER

An offer may be defined as a definite indication by one person that he or she is prepared to contract with one or more others on certain terms, which are fixed, or capable of being fixed, at the time the offer is made. Thus the statement 'I will sell you 5,000 widgets for £1,000' is an offer, as is the statement 'I will buy from you 5,000 shares in X Ltd, at their closing price on the London Stock Exchange next Friday'. In the former case the terms are fixed by the offer itself; in the latter, they are capable of becoming fixed on Friday, according to the price of the shares at the close of business on the Stock Exchange. The offer may be made by words, conduct or a mixture of the two. The concept applies most easily to a situation such as that given in the above example where there are two parties communicating with each other about a commercial transaction. It fits less easily, as will be seen below, in many other everyday transactions, such as supermarket sales or those involving the advertisement of goods in a newspaper or magazine. What the courts are looking for is some behaviour that indicates a willingness to contract on particular terms. Once there is such an indication, all that is then required from the other person is a simple assent to the terms suggested, and an agreement will be formed. The 'indication of willingness' referred to above may take a number of forms – for example, the spoken word, a letter, a fax message, an email or an advertisement on a website. As long as it communicates to the potential acceptor or acceptors the basis on which the offeror is prepared to contract, then that is enough. It is not necessary for the offer itself to set out all the terms of the contract. The parties may have been negotiating over a period of time, and the offer may simply refer to terms appearing in earlier communications. That is quite acceptable, provided that it is clear what the terms are.

---

14 This is similar to the approach taken in the European Draft Common Frame of Reference – see Book II, Chapter 4, and in particular paragraphs II. – 4:101 and II. – 4:211.
15 See, in particular, *Adams v Lindsell* (1818) 1 B & Ald 681; 106 ER 250 – discussed in detail below, 2.12.6.

### 2.7.1 DISTINCTION FROM 'INVITATION TO TREAT'

As we have noted, the objective of looking for 'offer and acceptance' is to decide whether an agreement has been reached. It is important, therefore, that behaviour which may have some of the characteristics of an offer should not be treated as such if, viewed objectively, that was not what was intended. Once a statement or action is categorised as an offer, then the party who made the statement or did the action has put itself in the position where it can become legally bound by the other party accepting it. It must be clear, therefore, that the statement or action indicates an intention to be bound, without more. The courts have traditionally approached this issue by drawing a distinction between an offer and an 'invitation to treat'.

Sometimes a person will wish simply to open negotiations, rather than to make an offer that will lead immediately to an agreement on acceptance. If I wish to sell my car, for example, I may enquire if you are interested in buying it. This is clearly not an offer. Even if I indicate a price at which I am willing to sell, this may simply be an attempt to discover your interest, rather than committing me to particular terms. The courts refer to such a preliminary communication as an 'invitation to treat' or, even more archaically, as an 'invitation to chaffer'. The distinction between an offer and an invitation to treat is an important one but is not always easy to draw. Even where the parties appear to have reached agreement on the terms on which they are prepared to contract, the courts may decide that the language they have used is more appropriate to an invitation to treat than an offer.

This was the view taken in *Gibson v Manchester City Council*.[16]

---

**Key case** *Gibson v Manchester City Council* (1979)

Facts: Mr Gibson was a tenant of a house owned by Manchester City Council. The Council, which was at the time under the control of Conservative Party members, decided that it wished to give its tenants the opportunity to purchase the houses which they were renting. Mr Gibson wished to take advantage of this opportunity and started negotiations with the Council. He received a letter that indicated a price and that stated 'The Corporation may be prepared to sell the house to you' at that price. It also instructed Mr Gibson, if he wished to make 'a formal application', to complete a form and return it. This Mr Gibson did. At this point, local elections took place and control of the Council changed from the Conservative Party to the Labour Party. The new Labour Council immediately reversed the policy of the sale of council houses and refused to proceed with the sale to Mr Gibson. At first instance and in the Court of Appeal,[17] it was held that there was a binding contract, and that Mr Gibson could therefore enforce the sale. Lord Denning MR argued that it was not necessary to analyse the transaction in terms of offer and acceptance. He suggested that:

You should look at the correspondence as a whole and at the conduct of the parties and see from there whether the parties have come to an agreement on everything that was material. If by their correspondence and their conduct you can see an agreement on all material terms, which was intended thenceforward to be binding, then there is a binding contract in law even though all formalities have not been gone through.[18]

---

16  [1979] 1 All ER 972; [1979] 1 WLR 294.

17  [1978] 2 All ER 583.

18  Ibid, p 586. Ormrod LJ agreed with Lord Denning MR, but also held that an agreement could be found using the traditional offer and acceptance analysis. Lane LJ dissented.

Held: The House of Lords firmly rejected Lord Denning MR's approach. Despite the fact that all terms appeared to have been agreed between the parties, the House of Lords held that there was no contract. The language of the Council's letter to Mr Gibson was not sufficiently definite to amount to an offer. It was simply an invitation to treat. Mr Gibson had made an offer to buy but that had not been accepted.

### For thought

*If a person states that they 'are prepared to sell' property at a specified price (rather than 'may be prepared to sell'), would this constitute an offer capable of acceptance? Does the change of one word ('are' for 'may') make such a difference?*

The narrowness of the distinction being drawn can be seen by comparing this case with *Storer v Manchester City Council*,[19] where on very similar facts a contract was held to exist as Mr Storer had signed and returned a document entitled 'Agreement for Sale'. This document was deemed to be sufficiently definite to amount to an offer from the Council that Mr Storer had accepted. As regards the state of mind of the parties in the two cases, however, it is arguable that there was little difference. In both, each party had indicated a willingness to enter into the transaction and there was agreement on the price. The fact that the courts focus on the external signs, rather than the underlying agreement, however, led to the result being different in the two cases.

Finally, although the House of Lords in *Gibson* rejected Lord Denning MR's approach to finding agreement, a very similar approach has now been adopted in relation, at least, to certain situations arising in connection with commercial contracts that have been started without a formal agreement having been concluded. These cases are discussed below at 2.11.5.

### 2.7.2 IN FOCUS: THE POLITICAL CONTEXT

Before leaving these cases, it should be noted that there was potentially a political dimension to the decisions in *Storer* and *Gibson*. The question of the sale of council houses was at the time a very controversial political issue, with the Conservative Party strongly in favour and Labour vehemently opposed to it. In Manchester the local electors had decided to vote in a Labour Council and it might have been reasonable to assume that one of the reasons for this was opposition to the previous Conservative Council's approach to the sale of council houses. In such a situation, to decide strongly in favour of enforcing the sale of a council house (particularly since there were, apparently, 'hundreds' of other cases similar to that of Mr Gibson)[20] might have been seen as an intervention by the judges that would have the effect of disregarding the wishes of the electorate. Where the case was clear-cut (as in *Storer*), the courts would be obliged to respect the individual's vested rights; where there was ambiguity, however (as in *Gibson*), there would be an argument for deciding the case in a way that complied with the political decision indicated by the results of the election. There is, of course, no indication in the speeches in the House of Lords of any such political considerations having any effect on their Lordships' opinions. However, it has been strongly argued that judges can be influenced, consciously or

---

19 [1974] 3 All ER 824; [1974] 1 WLR 1403.

20 See Lord Diplock [1979] 3 All ER 972, p 973; [1979] 1 WLR 294, p 296. *The Guardian* in a front-page story on 9 March 1979, the day after the Lords' ruling, reported that there were 350 other sales that were affected by the Lords' ruling in Manchester alone, with doubts being raised about sales in other local authority areas.

unconsciously, by political matters,[21] and it is possible that this may have been a factor tipping the balance against Mr Gibson. In any case, the *Storer* and *Gibson* decisions are good examples of the fact that decisions on the law of contract operate in a social and political context, and their interrelationship with that context should not be ignored.

### 2.7.3 SELF-SERVICE DISPLAYS

Another area of difficulty arises in relation to the display of goods in a shop window, or on the shelves of a supermarket, or other shops where customers serve themselves. We commonly talk of such a situation as one in which the shop has the goods 'on offer'. This is especially true of attractive bargains, which may be labelled 'special offer'. Are these 'offers' in the technical sense for the purpose of the law of contract? The issue has been addressed in a number of criminal cases where the offence in question was based on there being a 'sale' or an 'offer for sale'. These cases are taken to establish the position under the law of contract, even though they were decided in a criminal law context. The Court of Appeal has more recently suggested that it is not appropriate to use contractual principles in defining the behaviour that constitutes a criminal offence, in this case relating to an offer to supply drugs.[22] This does not, however, affect the contractual rules deriving from older criminal cases where this was done. The first to consider is *Pharmaceutical Society of Great Britain v Boots Cash Chemists*.[23]

---

**Key case** *Pharmaceutical Society of Great Britain v Boots Cash Chemists* (1953)

Facts: Section 18(1) of the Pharmacy and Poisons Act 1933 made it an offence to sell certain medicines unless the sale was 'effected by, or under the supervision of, a registered pharmacist'. Boots introduced a system under which some of these medicines were made available to customers on a self-service basis. There was no supervision until the customer went to the cashier. At this point, a registered pharmacist would supervise the transaction and could intervene, if necessary. The Pharmaceutical Society claimed that this was an offence under s 18 because, it was argued, the sale was complete when the customer took an article from the shelves and put it into his or her basket.

Held: The Court of Appeal held against the Pharmaceutical Society. It decided that the sale was made at the cash desk, where the customer made an offer to buy, which could be accepted or rejected by the cashier. The reason for this decision was that it is clearly unacceptable to say that the contract is complete as soon as the goods are put into the basket because the customer may want to change his or her mind, and it is undoubtedly the intention of all concerned that this should be possible. The display of goods is therefore an invitation to treat and not an offer.

---

With respect to the Court of Appeal, the conclusion that was reached was not necessary to avoid the problem of the customer becoming committed too soon. It would have been quite possible to have said that the display of goods is an offer but that the customer does not accept that offer until presenting the goods to the cashier.[24] This analysis would,

---

21 See, in particular, Griffith, 2010.
22 *R v Karamjit Singh Dhillon* [2007] Crim LR 760. Cf the earlier comments on the unnecessary use of civil law concepts in a criminal context by Smith, 1972.
23 [1953] 1 QB 401; [1953] 1 All ER 482.
24 As was pointed out at the time by, for example, Williams, 1953. See also Unger, 1953. Montrose, 1955, however, prefers the analysis adopted in the *Boots* case, because it would be 'unfair' to hold the shopkeeper to a mistake in the pricing of goods.

of course, also have meant that the sale took place at the cash desk and that no offence was committed under s 18. Strictly speaking, therefore, the details of the Court of Appeal's analysis in this case as to what constitutes the offer, and what is the acceptance, may be regarded as *obiter*. It has, however, generally been accepted subsequently that the display of goods within a shop is an invitation to treat and not an offer.

### 2.7.4 IN FOCUS: THE SOCIAL AND ECONOMIC CONTEXT

The decision in this case was treated by the Court of Appeal very much as a 'technical' one on the law of contract. There were, however, several other broader issues that were involved in it. First, there was the issue of the degree of supervision necessary to protect the public in relation to the sale of certain types of pharmaceutical product. Second, there was the potential effect on the employment position of pharmacists – the self-service arrangement would probably have the effect of reducing the number of pharmacists that Boots, or other chemists adopting a self-service system, would need to employ. Third, there was the question of whether the law on formation of contracts was to be developed in a way that helped or hindered the growth of the self-service shop. On the first issue Somervell LJ emphasised that the substances concerned were not 'dangerous drugs'.[25] The implication is that the system of control operating under Boots' self-service scheme was sufficient to fulfil the objective of the 1933 Act in protecting the public. The second issue, the effect on pharmacists, was not addressed at all, even though this must have been one of the main reasons for the action being brought by the Pharmaceutical Society. Collins has suggested that the court may not have been impressed 'by the desire of the pharmacists to retain their restrictive practices',[26] but this does not appear from the judgments at all. As regards the final issue, the court noted that the self-service arrangement was a 'convenient' one for the customer.[27] It is also, of course, an efficient one for the shopkeeper, enabling the display of a wide range of goods with a relatively small number of staff. The self-service format has become so dominant in shops of all kinds today that it is important to remember that in the early 1950s it was only gradually being adopted. The decision in the *Boots* case, if it had gone the other way, would have hindered (though probably not halted) its development.[28] The Court of Appeal therefore can be seen by this decision to be making a contribution to the way in which the retail trade developed over the next 10 years.

### 2.7.5 SHOP WINDOW DISPLAYS

The slightly different issue of the shop window display was dealt with in *Fisher v Bell*.[29] The defendant displayed in his shop window a 'flick-knife' with the price attached. He was charged with an offence under s 1(1) of the Restriction of Offensive Weapons Act 1959, namely 'offering for sale' a 'flick-knife'. It was held by the Divisional Court that no offence had been committed because the display of the knife was an invitation to treat, not an offer.

Lord Parker had no doubt as to the contractual position:

> It is clear that according to the ordinary law of contract the display of an article with a price on it in a shop window is merely an invitation to treat. It is in no sense an offer for sale the acceptance of which constitutes a contract.[30]

No authority was cited for this proposition but the approach is certainly in line with that taken in the *Boots* case. There has never been any challenge to it and it must be taken

25  [1953] 1 QB 401, p 405.
26  Collins, 2003, p 172.
27  [1953] 1 QB 401, p 406; [1953] 1 All ER 482, p 484.
28  This was recognised by Romer LJ, ibid, p 408; p 485.
29  [1961] 1 QB 394; [1960] 3 All ER 731.
30  [1961] 1 QB 394, p 399; [1960] 3 All ER 731, p 733.

to represent the general law on this point. It was followed in *Mella v Monahan*,[31] where a charge of 'offering for sale' obscene articles, contrary to the Obscene Publications Act 1959, failed because the items were simply displayed in a shop window.

### 2.7.6 ISSUES OF PRINCIPLE

What are the principles lying behind the decisions in relation to self-service stores and shop window displays? In *Boots*, the court stressed the need for the shopper to be allowed a 'change of mind'. As we have seen, however, that does not necessarily require the offer to be made by the customer, just that the acceptance of the offer should be delayed beyond the point when the shopper may legitimately still be deciding whether to purchase. In any case, the argument cannot apply to the shop window cases. The customer who enters the shop will either say 'I want to buy that item displayed in your window', which could undoubtedly be treated as an acceptance, or 'I am interested in buying that item in your window; can I inspect it?' or 'can you tell me more about it?', which would simply be a stage in negotiation. There is no need, therefore, to protect the *customer* by making the shop window display simply an invitation to treat.

The most likely candidate as an alternative principle on which the decisions are based is freedom of contract. That freedom includes within it the principle that a person can choose with whom to contract – 'party freedom'.[32] On this analysis, the shop transaction needs to be analysed in a way that will allow the shopkeeper to say 'I do not want to do business with you'. This was the view expressed to counsel by Parke B in the nineteenth-century case of *Timothy v Simpson*.[33] There are two problems, however, with the modern law of contract allowing such freedom in these situations.

First, such freedom has the potential to be used in a discriminatory way.[34] Certain types of discrimination – on grounds, for example, of race, religion, sex, sexual orientation, age and disability[35] – have as a matter of social policy been made unlawful by statute.[36] To the extent, therefore, that the common law of contract still allows party freedom to operate in these areas, there is a tension between it and the statutory equality regime. A shopkeeper who discriminates on impermissible grounds in deciding with whom to contract is not forced by the common law to undertake the contractual obligation but may face an action under one of the relevant statutory provisions.

Second, application of the 'party freedom' principle leads to the conclusion that, as far as the law of contract is concerned, a shopkeeper is not bound by any price that is attached to goods displayed in the shop or in the window. He or she is entitled to say to the customer seeking to buy the item: 'That is a mistake. I am afraid the price is different.' Again, however, there may be a conflict with the statutory position. Such action on the part of the shopkeeper may constitute a criminal offence under the Consumer Protection from Unfair Trading Regulations 2008.[37] Regulation 5 prohibits the giving of misleading information as to the price of goods. An indication is 'misleading' if it leads the consumer to think that the price is less than in fact it is.[38] Thus, if a shop has a window display indicating that certain special packs of goods are on offer at a low price inside but in fact none of the special packs are available, an offence may have been committed. This was the situation

---

31  [1961] Crim LR 175.
32  See Brownsword, 2006, p 57.
33  (1834) 6 C & P 499, p 500.
34  See Beale, 1995a, p 190; Collins, 2003, p 33; Brownsword, 2006, p 57.
35  See the Equality Act 2010, which has largely consolidated all the previous legislation.
36  Note that the classic contract law did in fact also recognise some restriction on party freedom as regards common carriers and innkeepers – see *Halsbury's Laws*, Vol 5(1), para 441 and Vol 24, para 1113.
37  SI 2008/1277. Since October 2014 there is also the possiblity of private law remedies under Part 4A of the Regulations, as added by the Consumer Protection (Amendment) Regulations 2014, SI 2014/870.
38  Ibid, reg 5(2)(a) and (4).

in *Tesco Supermarkets Ltd v Nattrass*,[39] a case concerning s 11 of the then Trade Descriptions Act 1968, which was the predecessor to the current Regulations.

This means that, in practice, because of their awareness of the statutory position, and their wish to maintain good relationships with their customers, shops and other businesses are unlikely to insist on their strict contractual rights in situations of this kind. That being the case, the question arises as to whether the rule that it is the customer who makes the offer, and the shopkeeper who has the choice whether or not to accept it, might now be due for reconsideration.

### 2.7.7 ADVERTISEMENTS

Where goods or services are advertised, does this constitute an offer or an invitation to treat? It would be possible here for the law also to base its principles on 'party freedom': that is, a person putting forward an advertisement should not be taken to be waiving the right as to whom he or she chooses to contract with. In fact, however, the cases in this area generally show the courts adopting an approach based on pragmatism, rather than on the 'party freedom' principle. The answer to the question 'Is this advertisement an offer?' will generally be determined by the context in which the advertisement appears, and the practical consequences of treating it as either an offer or an invitation to treat.

Generally an advertisement, for example, on a hoarding, in a newspaper or on television will not be regarded as an offer. In *Harris v Nickerson*[40] the defendant had advertised that an auction of certain furniture was to take place on a certain day. The plaintiff travelled to the auction only to find that the items in which he was interested had, without notice, been withdrawn. He brought an action for breach of contract to recover his expenses in attending the advertised event. His claim was rejected by the Queen's Bench. The advertisement did not give rise to any contract that all the items mentioned would actually be put up for sale. To hold otherwise would, Blackburn J felt, be 'a startling proposition' and 'excessively inconvenient if carried out'. It would amount to saying that 'anyone who advertises a sale by publishing an advertisement becomes responsible to everybody who attends the sale for his cab hire or travelling expenses'.[41] In other words, the practical consequences of treating the advertisement as an offer would be such that it is highly unlikely that this is what the person placing the advert can have intended. Using an approach based on 'promisor objectivity',[42] it is concluded that the advertisement is nothing more than an invitation to treat.

It follows from this that these types of advertisement should be regarded simply as attempts to make the public aware of what is available. Such advertisements will often, in any case, not be specific enough to amount to an offer. Even where goods are clearly identified and a price specified, however, there may still not be an offer. A good example of this situation is another criminal law case, *Partridge v Crittenden*.[43]

---

**Key case** *Partridge v Crittenden* (1968)

Facts: The defendant put an advertisement in the 'classified' section of a periodical, advertising bramblefinches for sale at 25s each. He was charged under the Protection of Birds Act 1954 with 'offering for sale' a live wild bird, contrary to s 6(1).

---

39  [1972] AC 153; [1971] 2 All ER 127. Note that Tesco was found to have a defence under the statute.
40  (1873) LR 8 QB 286; (1873) 42 LJ QB 171.
41  (1873) LR 8 QB 286, p 288.
42  For which, see 2.4.2, above.
43  [1968] 2 All ER 421.

**Held:** It was held that he had committed no offence because the advert was an invitation to treat and not an offer. The court relied heavily on *Fisher v Bell*,[44] and appeared to feel that this kind of advertisement should be treated in the same way as the display of goods with a price attached. Lord Parker also argued that if it was an offer, this would mean that everyone who replied to the advertisement would be accepting it and would therefore be entitled to a bramblefinch. Assuming that the advertiser did not have an unlimited supply of bramblefinches, this could not be what he intended. The advertisement was only an invitation to treat.

This decision is in line with the concept of 'party freedom', in that it leaves the advertiser free to decide with whom to contract. In addition, the 'limited stock' argument seems to give a very strong ground to suggest that this advertisement, as will be the case with most advertisements for the sale of goods, was not intended to constitute an offer.[45] As with *Harris v Nickerson*, this is an analysis based on 'promisor objectivity', looking at what the reasonable advertiser would be taken to have meant by the advert.

This does not mean, however, that all advertisements will be treated as invitations to treat. If the guiding principle is promisor objectivity, rather than party freedom, then provided that the wording is clear and there are no problems of limited supply, there seems to be no reason why such an advertisement should not be an offer. If, for example, the advertiser in *Partridge v Crittenden* had said, '100 bramblefinches for sale. The first 100 replies enclosing 25s will secure a bird', then in all probability this would be construed as an offer. An advertisement of a similar kind was held to be an offer in the American case of *Lefkowitz v Great Minneapolis Surplus Stores*,[46] where the defendants published an advertisement in a newspaper stating: 'Saturday 9 am sharp; three brand new fur coats, worth to $100. First come first served, $1 each.' The plaintiff was one of the first three customers but the firm refused to sell him a coat because it said the offer was only open to women. The court held that the advertisement constituted an offer, which the plaintiff had accepted, and that he was therefore entitled to the coat.

## For thought

*If I publish an advertisement indicating that I will have three fur coats for sale at my shop on a particular date at a specified price, but do not say 'First come, first served', would this be an offer or an invitation to treat?*

Clearly in this case the court was rejecting any argument based on party freedom. In this context, any such freedom was waived by making such a specific offer to the general public, which did not indicate any intention by the advertiser to put limits on those who were entitled to take advantage of the bargain. The use of such an approach here arguably only serves to highlight the anomaly of the cases on shop sales discussed in the previous section.

---

44 [1961] 1 QB 394; [1960] 3 All ER 731 – discussed above, 2.7.5.

45 The Singapore High Court has doubted whether the limited stock argument should necessarily apply to web advertisements: *Chee Kin Keong v Digilandmall.com Pte Ltd* [2004] SGHC 71, [91] – [96]. This issue was not dealt with when the case went to the Singapore Court of Appeal.

46 (1957) 86 NW 2d 689.

### 2.7.8 *CARLILL V CARBOLIC SMOKE BALL CO*

In England the most famous case of an advertisement constituting an offer is *Carlill v Carbolic Smoke Ball Co*.[47]

---

**Key case** *Carlill v Carbolic Smoke Ball Co* (1893)

**Facts:** The manufacturers of a 'smoke ball' published an advertisement at the time of an influenza epidemic, proclaiming the virtues of their smoke ball for curing all kinds of ailments. In addition they stated that anybody who used one of their smoke balls as directed and then caught influenza, would be paid £100. Mrs Carlill, having bought and used a smoke ball but nevertheless having caught influenza, claimed £100 from the company. The company argued that the advertisement could not be taken to be an offer that could turn into a contract by acceptance. They claimed that the promise of £100 should be regarded as a 'mere puff', meaning it was of no contractual effect. There was, however, apparent evidence of serious intent on the part of the defendants. The advertisement had stated that '£1,000 is deposited with the Alliance Bank, showing our sincerity in this matter'. The defendants raised two further objections. First, they argued that the advertisement was widely distributed and that this was, therefore, not an offer made to anybody in particular. Second, the defendants said that Mrs Carlill should have given them notice of her acceptance.

**Held:** The court held in favour of Mrs Carlill. It took the view that the inclusion of the statement about the £1,000 deposit meant that reasonable people would treat the offer to pay £100 as one that was intended seriously, so that it could create a binding obligation in appropriate circumstances, such as those that had arisen. As to the wide distribution of the advert, the court did not regard this as a problem. Offers of reward (for example, for the return of a lost pet or for information leading to the conviction of a criminal) were generally in the same form and could be accepted by any person who fulfilled the condition. There was plenty of authority to support this, such as *Williams v Carwardine*.[48] Finally, as regards the fact that Mrs Carlill had not given notice of her acceptance, again the court, by analogy with the reward cases, held that the form of the advertisement could be taken to have waived the need for notification of acceptance, at least prior to the performance of the condition that entitled the plaintiff to claim. As Lindley LJ put it:[49]

> I ... think that the true view, in a case of this kind, is that the person who makes the offer shows by his language and from the nature of the transaction that he does not expect and does not require notice of the acceptance apart from notice of the performance.

---

47 [1893] 1 QB 256. Compare *Irvine v General Medical Council* [2017] EWHC 2038 (Admin) at [76] where Holroyde J stated: "Mr Stockinger was not able to identify any case law in support of his submission other than *Carlill*. His reliance on the decision in that case was in my view mistaken. It is important to note that in that case, the offer made by the Defendants' advertisement was addressed to the world at large, and was subject to no condition other than the requirement that the purchaser should use the product in the specified manner for the specified period. Here, in contrast, the professional organisations were inviting applications from registered medical practitioners, with a requirement that they provide specific details of their practice so that there could be a proper assessment of whether to accept the risk, and if so on what terms. The evidence in this case showed, in my view, that the submission of the completed application form and direct debit mandate was an offer by Mr Irvine to pay the subscription in return for the provision by the organisation of services by the professional organisation, including insurance, in accordance with their stated terms and conditions. The professional organisation could accept that offer, but was not obliged to do so."
48 (1833) 5 C & P 566 – see below, 2.12.17.
49 [1893] 1 QB 256, pp 262–63.

```
┌─────────────────────────────────────────────────────────┐
│     Distinction between an offer and invitation to treat  │
└─────────────────────────────────────────────────────────┘

              ┌───────────────────────────────┐
              │  Has the offeror made clear that│
              │  he/she intends to be bound on  │
              │  clearly specified terms as soon│
              │  as the other party accepts?    │
              └───────────────────────────────┘
               Yes                        No
```

| OFFER | INVITATION TO TREAT |
|---|---|
| e.g.: | e.g.: |
| ▪ Letter offering to sell specific goods at a specified price | ▪ Advertisement of goods for sale |
| ▪ Advertisement of a reward – e.g. *Carlill v Carbolic Smoke Ball Co* (1893) | ▪ Display of goods in shop – e.g. *Fisher v Bell* (1961) |
| ▪ Bid in an auction – Sale of Goods Act, s 57 | ▪ Tender document – e.g. *Spencer v Harding* (1870) |

Figure 2.1

The Smoke Ball Company cannot have expected that everyone who bought a smoke ball would get in touch with them. It was only those who, having used the ball, then contracted influenza who would do so.

This case, therefore, is authority for the propositions, first, that an advertisement can constitute an offer to 'the world' (that is, anyone who reads it) and, second, that it may, by the way in which it is stated, waive the need for communication of acceptance prior to a claim under it.

### 2.7.9 IN FOCUS: CONSUMER PROTECTION

The *Carlill* case has been viewed as giving a surprisingly broad scope to the situations that will fall within the law of contract.[50] Simpson has pointed out that there was much concern at the time about advertisements for dubious 'medicinal' products,[51] and this may have influenced the court towards finding liability. Nowadays, it would be expected that such situations would be more likely to be dealt with by legislation,[52] or by an agency such as the Advertising Standards Authority. This is certainly true of many advertising slogans (for example, 'Gillette – the Best a Man Can Get', 'The Best Hard Rock Album in the World ... Ever!') although a contractual action based on these particular slogans would

---

50  See, for example, the comments of Collins, 2003, p 4.

51  Simpson, 1985.

52  For example, the Consumer Protection from Unfair Trading Regulations 2008.

be very difficult! At the time of *Carlill*'s case, however, the consumer protection role had to be taken by the courts, even if this meant stretching contractual principles to provide a remedy.

## 2.8 UNILATERAL AND BILATERAL CONTRACTS

It should be noted that the offer in *Carlill*, was an offer of a particular kind, known in the law of England and Wales as an offer in a 'unilateral' (as opposed to a 'bilateral') contract. It will be convenient at this point to examine the difference between these two types of contract.

The typical model of the classic bilateral contract arises where A *promises* to sell goods to B in return for B *promising* to pay the purchase price. In this situation the contract is bilateral because as soon as these promises have been exchanged, there is a contract to which both are *bound*. In relation to services the same applies, so that an agreement between A and B that B will dig A's garden for £20 next Tuesday is a bilateral agreement. Suppose, however, that the arrangement is slightly different and that A says to B, 'If you decide to dig my garden next Tuesday, I will pay you £20 once it is completed.' B makes no commitment but says, 'I am not sure that I shall be able to, but if I do I shall be happy to take £20.' This arrangement is not bilateral. A has committed himself/herself to pay the £20 in certain circumstances but B has made no commitment at all. He/she is totally free to decide whether or not he/she wants to dig A's garden or not, and if he/she wakes up on Tuesday morning and decides that he/she just does not feel like doing so, there is nothing that A can do about it.[53] If, however, B does decide to go and do the work, this will be regarded as an acceptance of A's offer of £20 and the contract will be formed. Given its one-sided nature, therefore, this type of arrangement is known as a 'unilateral contract'. Another way of describing them is as 'if' contracts, in that it is possible to formulate the offer as a statement beginning with the word 'if', followed by the required action: for example, 'If you dig my garden, I will pay you £20.' Crucially the other party does not promise to carry out the requested act (dig the garden). On the other hand, the statement 'If you *promise to* dig my garden, I will pay you £20' would create a bilateral contract if the promise to do the digging was made. The arrangement in *Carlill* and arguably *Lefkowitz* were unilateral: 'If you *use* our smoke ball and catch influenza, we will pay you £100'; 'If you are the first person *to offer to buy* one of these coats, we will sell it to you for $1.' In each case, it is the performance of an action that creates the contract, not a promise to act.

The distinction between unilateral and bilateral contracts is important in relation to the areas of 'acceptance' and 'consideration', which are discussed further below.

## 2.9 TENDERS

Some confusion may arise as to what constitutes an offer when a person or, more probably, a company decides to put work out to tender, or seeks bids for certain goods. This means that potential contractors are invited to submit quotations or bids as the case may be. The invitation may be issued to the world or to specific parties. Generally such a request will amount simply to an invitation to treat and the person making it will be free to accept or reject any of the responses. In *Spencer v Harding*,[54] for example, it was held that the issue of a circular 'offering' stock for sale by tender was simply a 'proclamation'

---

53  See eg the comments of Longmore LJ in *Soulsbury v Soulsbury* [2007] EWCA Civ 969; [2008] 2 WLR 834 at [48] – [49].
54  (1870) LR 5 CP 561.

that the defendants were ready to negotiate for the sale of the goods and to receive offers for the purchase of them. There was no obligation to sell to the highest bidder or indeed to any bidder at all. The position may be different if the invitation indicates that the highest bid or, as appropriate, the lowest quotation will definitely be accepted. It may then be regarded as including an offer in a unilateral contract. The recipients of the invitation will not be bound to reply but, if they do, the one who submits the lowest quotation will be entitled to damages if they do not get the work or goods as the case might be. A similar situation arose in *Blackpool and Fylde Aero Club Ltd v Blackpool Borough Council*.[55] The Council had invited tenders for the operation of pleasure flights from an airfield. Tenders were to be placed in a designated box by a specified deadline. The plaintiff complied with this requirement but due to an oversight on the part of the defendant's employees, the plaintiff's tender was not removed from the box until the day after the deadline, and was accordingly marked as having arrived late. It was, therefore, ignored in the Council's deliberations as to who should be awarded the contract. The plaintiff succeeded in an action against the defendant, who appealed. The Court of Appeal noted that, in this type of situation, the inviter of tenders was in a strong position, as he/she could dictate the terms on which the tenders were to be made and the basis on which the selection of the successful one, if any, was to be made. There was nothing explicit in this case that indicated that all tenders meeting the deadline would be considered. Nevertheless:[56]

> in the context, a reasonable invitee would understand the invitation to be saying, quite clearly, that if he submitted a timely and conforming tender it would be considered, at least if any other such tender were considered.

By applying this test of 'promisee objectivity' to the circumstances, the court concluded that the defendant was in breach of an implicit unilateral contract, under which it promised that if a tender was received by the specified deadline, it would be given due consideration. The promise was not made explicitly, and indeed the defendant claimed that no such promise was intended,[57] but because it was reasonable for the plaintiff to have assumed that such a promise was implied, the court found that there was a contractual relationship obliging the defendant to consider all tenders fulfilling the terms of the invitation. A person inviting tenders arguably must therefore either explicitly state the terms on which responses will be considered, or be bound by the reasonable expectations of those who put in tenders.

This decision places some limits on the freedom of the party inviting tenders but these are limits that can be avoided by careful wording of the tender documentation. In *Warren v British Boxing Board of Control*,[58] for example, the Court held that the wording of the tender gave the Board absolute discretion as regards accepting any bid. Much more stringent controls currently exist over tendering in a range of public sector contracts as a result of EU directives on the issue, which have been implemented in the UK by various sets of regulations.[59]

The extent to which these specific controls over tendering will continue to apply post-Brexit is not entirely clear. Yet it is likely, however, that the kind of approach adopted will in any case continue to apply to public sector contracts, in that clear and transparent criteria

---

55  [1990] 3 All ER 25.

56  [1990] 3 All ER 25, p 31.

57  Brownsword uses this case as an example of the fact that an analysis of contract based on the making of express promises does not accord with the actual practice of the courts (Brownsword, 2006, pp 19–21).

58  [2014] EWHC 4913 (QB).

59  For example, the Public Contracts Regulations 2015, SI 2015/102, implementing the current EU Public Sector Procurement Directive (2014/24/EC).

for the awarding of such contracts will be regarded as 'good practice'. There is clearly also potential for such an approach to influence more generally the way in which tendering takes place. It would not be surprising if organisations that are required to use particular procedures in some areas of their activities found it convenient to use the same type of approach even if not constrained to do so by regulation. Such influences on business practice might in turn have an effect on the way in which the courts develop the general legal rules relating to tenders.

## 2.10 AUCTIONS

The Sale of Goods Act 1979 makes it clear that in relation to a sale of goods by auction, the bids constitute offers that are accepted by the fall of the hammer.[60] The same is also the case in relation to any other type of sale by auction.[61] The normal position will be that the auctioneer will be entitled to reject any of the bids made, and will not be obliged to sell to the highest bidder.

There are two situations, however, that require special consideration. The first is where the auction sale is stated, in an advertisement or in information given to a particular bidder, to be 'without reserve' (a reserve price in the minimum price set by the seller). This situation was first considered in the nineteenth-century case of *Warlow v Harrison*.[62] The plaintiff attended an auction of a horse that had been advertised as being 'without reserve'. He then discovered that the owner was being allowed to bid (thus in effect allowing the owner to set a price below which he would not sell). The plaintiff refused to continue bidding and sued the auctioneer. The Court of Exchequer held that, on the pleadings as entered, the plaintiff could not succeed but expressed the view that if the case had been pleaded correctly, he would have been entitled to succeed in an action for breach of contract against the auctioneer:[63]

> We think the auctioneer who puts the property up for sale upon such a condition pledges himself that the sale shall be without reserve; or, in other words, contracts that it shall be so; and that this contract is made with the highest *bona fide* bidder; and, in case of breach of it, that he has a right of action against the auctioneer.

Given the problem over the pleadings, the ruling in *Warlow v Harrison* was strictly *obiter*, but the principle stated was reconsidered and confirmed in *Barry v Heathcote Ball & Co (Commercial Auctions) Ltd*.[64]

**Key case** *Barry v Heathcote Ball & Co (Commercial Auctions) Ltd* (2001)

Facts: The claimant attended an auction to bid for two new machines which were being sold by Customs & Excise, who had instructed the auctioneer that the sale was to be 'without reserve'. The claimant had been told this by the auctioneer when viewing the machines. The machines were worth about £14,000 each. When they came up for sale there were no bids apart from one from the claimant, who bid £200 for each machine. The auctioneer refused to accept this and withdrew the machines from the

---

60  Sale of Goods Act 1979, s 57.
61  *Payne v Cave* (1789) 3 Term Rep 148.
62  (1859) 1 E & E 309; 29 LJ QB 14.
63  (1859) 1 E & E 309, pp 316–17; 29 LJ QB 14, p 15.
64  [2001] 1 All ER 944; [2000] 1 WLR 1962.

sale. They were subsequently sold privately for £750 each. The claimant sued the auctioneer for breach of contract. The trial judge held in his favour, on the basis of there being a collateral contract with the auctioneer to sell to the highest bidder. The claimant was awarded £27,600 damages. The defendant appealed.

Held: The Court of Appeal confirmed the decision of the trial judge. It followed the reasoning adopted by the court in *Warlow v Harrison*. An auctioneer who conducts a sale 'without reserve' is making a binding promise to sell to the highest bidder. It made no difference that in *Warlow v Harrison*, the identity of the seller was not disclosed, whereas here it was known. Moreover, the action of the auctioneer in this situation was tantamount to bidding on behalf of the seller, which is prohibited by s 57(4) of the Sale of Goods Act 1979. The claimant was entitled to recover the difference between what he had offered and the market price of the machines. The award of £27,600 damages was therefore also confirmed.

This case is a useful modern confirmation of the principle set out in *Warlow v Harrison*. In effect, the auctioneer is making an offer in a unilateral contract to all those who attend the auction along the lines of 'If you are the highest bidder for a particular lot, then I promise to accept your bid.' In *Warlow v Harrison*, the whole auction had been advertised as being 'without reserve'. Here the claimant had been told that this was the position as regard the particular lot in which he was interested. This made no difference to the principles to be applied.[65]

The second situation that requires further discussion is where a bidder tries to make a bid, the value of which is dependent on a bid made by another bidder. This may arise in a 'sealed bid' auction of the kind that was involved in *Harvela Investments v Royal Trust of Canada*.[66] In this case an invitation to two firms to submit sealed bids for a block of shares, together with a commitment to accept the highest offer, was treated as the equivalent of an auction sale. There was an obligation to sell to the highest bidder. This case was complicated, however, by the fact that one of the bids was what was described as a 'referential bid'. That is, it was in the form of 'C$2,100,000 or C$101,000 in excess of any other offer'. The House of Lords held that this bid was invalid and that the owner of the shares was obliged to sell to the other party, who had offered C$2,175,000.[67] It reached this conclusion by trying to identify the intentions of the firm issuing the invitation to bid from the quite detailed instructions issued to each potential bidder. From these, the House deduced that what the sellers had in mind was not a true auction (where a number of bidders make and adjust their bids in response to the bids being made by others) but a 'fixed bidding sale'. Lord Templeman noted three features of the invitation that he regarded as only being consistent with an intention to conduct a fixed bidding sale rather than an auction. First, the sellers specifically undertook to accept the highest bid. As we have seen, however, such an obligation can arise in relation to a straightforward auction, by means of a collateral contract with the auctioneer. It is hard to see this as conclusive, therefore. Lord Templeman took it, however, as also implying that the sellers were anxious to ensure

---

65  Note that the defendant in this case also queried whether there was any 'consideration' for the promise. As to this the court held that there was in the form of detriment to the bidder in that his offer can be accepted until withdrawn, and benefit to the auctioneer as the bidding is driven up. For further discussion of the doctrine of consideration, see Chapter 3.

66  [1986] 1 AC 207; [1985] 2 All ER 966.

67  Note that the Court of Appeal, while noting the practical difficulties involved, had come to the opposite conclusion, on the basis that bidders in making 'offers' were entitled to put them in whatever form they chose, in the absence of any express or implied term imposing restrictions: [1985] Ch 103; [1985] 1 All ER 261.

that a sale resulted from the exercise. If referential bids were allowed, there was clearly a possibility that this would not happen, because both bidders might submit a referential bid, and it would be impossible to determine who was the highest bidder. The second feature noted by Lord Templeman was that the invitation was issued to two prospective buyers alone. Again, it is difficult to see this as conclusive of the issue. It is quite possible to hold a straightforward auction with only two bidders. The third feature was that the bids were to be confidential and were to remain so until the time for submission of offers had lapsed. This is by far the most convincing reason why it should be assumed that the seller intended a fixed bidding sale rather than an auction. Confidentiality of the amount of a bid is clearly incompatible with an ordinary auction (though as Lord Templeman points out later in his speech, confidential bids combined with a requirement that each bidder states a maximum bid could work as a type of auction).

In the light of all these considerations, the House of Lords concluded that it was a fixed bidding sale that was intended and that referential bids should, therefore, be excluded. In effect, the House was here relying on 'promisor objectivity', in that its analysis is focused on what the reasonable 'inviter of bids' must be taken to have intended by the form in which the invitation to bid was framed. In terms of 'offer and acceptance' the inviter was entering into two unilateral contracts with the two bidders to the effect: 'If you submit the highest bid, then we promise to sell the shares to you.'[68]

The result in *Harvela* was clearly of considerable practical importance: if it had gone the other way, it would have made conducting sales by means of confidential bids much more difficult. It may well be, therefore, that considerations of the impact on commercial practice helped to push the House towards the conclusion it reached.[69]

## 2.11 ACCEPTANCE

The second stage of discovering whether or not an agreement has been reached, under classical contract theory, is to look for an acceptance that matches the offer that has been made.

No particular form of words is required for a valid acceptance. As has been explained above, an offer must be in a form whereby a simple assent to it is sufficient to lead to a contract being formed. It is in many cases, therefore, enough for an acceptance to take the form of the person to whom the offer has been made simply saying, 'Yes, I agree.' In some situations, however, particularly where there is a course of negotiations between the parties, it may become more difficult to determine precisely the point when the parties have exchanged a matching offer and acceptance. Unless they do match exactly, under the classical theory, there can be no contract. An 'offer' and an 'acceptance' must fit together like two pieces of a jigsaw puzzle. If they do not match, they will not slot together and the picture will be incomplete. At times, as we shall see, the courts in England and Wales have adopted a somewhat flexible approach to the need for a precise equivalence.[70] Nevertheless, once it is decided that there is a match, it is as if the two pieces of the jigsaw had been previously treated with 'superglue', for once in position it will be very hard, if not impossible, to pull them apart (although a statutory 'right of cancellation' is now available in many consumer contracts).[71]

---

68  This analysis appears most fully in the speech of Lord Diplock: [1986] 1 AC 206, p 224; [1985] 2 All ER 966, p 969. Note that here the offer in the unilateral contract was not implicit, but was explicitly made as part of the invitation to bid: ibid, p 229; p 973.
69  See, for example, Wheeler and Shaw, 1994, pp 229–30.
70  See, also, Collins, 2003, pp 166–68.
71  Discussed below, 2.14.

## 2.11.1 DISTINCTION FROM COUNTER-OFFER

Where parties are in negotiation, the response to an offer may be for the offeree to suggest slightly (or even substantially) different terms. Such a response will not, of course, be an acceptance, since it does not match the offer, but will be a 'counter-offer'. During lengthy negotiations, many such offers and counter-offers may be put on the table. Do they all remain there, available for acceptance at any stage? Or is only the last offer, or counteroffer, the one that can be accepted? This issue was addressed in the following case.

---

**Key case** *Hyde v Wrench* (1840)[72]

Facts: D offered to sell a farm to P for £1,000. P offered £900, which was rejected. P then purported to accept the offer to sell at £1,000. D refused to go through with the transaction and P brought an action for specific performance.

Held: The court held that a rejection of an offer in effect destroyed it. It could not later be accepted. Moreover, a counter-offer operated in the same way as a rejection. P's counter-offer of £900 therefore had the effect of rejecting and destroying D's original offer to sell at £1,000. P could not accept it. In effect, P's final communication had to be treated not as an acceptance but as a further offer to buy at £1,000, which D was free to accept or reject.

---

The answer to the question posed above, therefore, is that only the last offer submitted survives and is available for acceptance (if it has not been rejected or validly withdrawn). All earlier offers are destroyed by rejection or counter-offer. The courts have not been explicit about the reasons for this rule, but it may well be that it is intended to prevent the 'counter-offeror' having the best of both worlds – trying out a low counter-offer, while at the same time keeping the original offer available for acceptance.[73]

It should be noted, however, that the courts will not necessarily require exact precision, if it is clear that the parties were in agreement. An example of this approach can be found in the case of *Pars Technology Ltd v City Link Transport Holdings Ltd*,[74] where the parties were negotiating the contractual settlement of an earlier dispute. The defendant offered by letter of 7 February to pay £13,500 plus a refund of the carriage charges of £7.55 plus VAT. The claimant's letter of 12 February in response stated that the defendant's offer to pay £13,507.55 plus VAT was accepted. The defendant later claimed that this was not a valid acceptance because it stated that VAT was to be paid on the whole amount, rather than just on the carriage charge. The Court of Appeal agreed with the trial judge that the correspondence as a whole had to be considered and took the view that the claimant had merely been trying to restate the defendant's offer in a different way. The claimant's letter had clearly stated that the defendant's offer made in the letter of 7 February was being accepted. A contract had therefore been concluded on the terms stated in the defendant's offer letter. In essence the court adopted an objective approach based on what the reasonable person receiving the claimant's letter would have taken it to mean. Even though the defendant argued that that was not what he had understood by it, he was bound by the objective view. In fact, this may be an example of the court using 'third party objectivity'[75] – that is, what the reasonable third party looking at what passed between claimant and

---

72 (1840) 3 Beav 334.
73 See Atiyah, 1995, p 76.
74 [1999] EWCA Civ 1822.
75 See above, 2.4.2.

defendant would have taken to be the outcome. It may also have been that the court was unsympathetic in this case to what it saw as the defendant using a rather technical argument to escape from an arrangement that had clearly been agreed. This is behaviour that it would not wish to encourage because it wastes court time and adds unnecessary costs to litigation (bearing in mind that this contract was concerned with the conclusion of an earlier legal dispute). Although it has been confirmed that under the *Civil Procedure Rules* normal contractual principles applied to 'offers to settle' and their acceptance,[76] these should not be used in a way that will have the effect of unduly prolonging the settlement of litigation.

### 2.11.2 REQUEST FOR INFORMATION

In some situations, however, it may be quite difficult to determine whether a particular communication is a counter-offer or not. If, for example, a person offers to sell a television to another for £100, the potential buyer may ask whether cash is required or whether a cheque is acceptable. Such an inquiry is not a counter-offer. It is not suggesting alternative terms for the contract but attempting to clarify the way in which the contract will be performed and, in particular, whether a specific type of performance will be acceptable. The effect of an inquiry of this type was considered in *Stevenson, Jaques & Co v McLean*.[77] D wrote to P, offering to sell some iron at a particular price and saying that the offer would be kept open until the following Monday. On the Monday morning, P replied by telegram stating: 'Please wire whether you would accept 40 for delivery over two months, or if not, longest limit you could give.' D did not reply but sold the iron elsewhere. In the meantime, P sent a telegram accepting D's offer. P sued for breach of contract. D argued that P's first telegram was a counter-offer and that, therefore, the second telegram could not operate as an acceptance of D's offer. The court held that it was necessary to look at both the circumstances in which P's telegram was sent and the form that it took. As to the first aspect, the market in iron was very uncertain and it was not unreasonable for P to wish to clarify the position as to delivery. Moreover, as regards the form of the telegram, it did not say 'I offer 40 for delivery over two months' but was put as an inquiry. If it had been in the form of an offer, then *Hyde v Wrench* would have been applied, but since it was clearly only an inquiry, D's original offer still survived and P was entitled to accept it.

While the distinction being drawn here is clear, it is quite narrow. There is clearly scope in this type of situation for the courts to interpret communications in the way that appears to them best to do 'justice' between the parties.

### 2.11.3 BATTLE OF THE FORMS

One situation where it may become vital to decide whether a particular communication is a counter-offer or not is where there is what is frequently referred to as a 'battle of the forms'. This arises where two companies are in negotiation and, as part of their exchanges, they send each other standard contract forms. If the two sets of forms are incompatible, as is likely to be the case, what is the result? This is a not infrequent occurrence, probably because under the pressure of 'making a deal' the parties' attention is sometimes not focused explicitly on anything other than the most basic elements of the transaction.[78] How should the courts deal with it if a dispute then arises?

---

76 *Scammell v Dicker* [2001] 1 WLR 631; *Pitchmastic plc v Birse Construction Ltd* (2000) *The Times,* 21 June (QBD). Note, however, that there is an *obiter* suggestion in *Scammell v Dicker* that the rules as to the effect of rejection of an offer may not apply to those falling within Pt 36 of the CPR – see, also, Stone, 2001, p 23. See also *Rosario v Nadell Patisserie Ltd* [2010] EWHC 1886, where Tugendhat J applied a traditional offer/counter-offer approach to Pt 36 negotiations.

77 (1880) 5 QBD 346.

78 Beale and Dugdale, 1975, suggest in addition that contract planning is 'expensive'.

Figure 2.2

One possibility, if the contract is a fairly straightforward one such as a simple sale of goods, is that the court may be able to identify an offer and acceptance at an earlier stage of the negotiations, prior to the exchange of any forms. In such a case the contract may well not incorporate the standard terms of either party – it is likely to consist of simply the basic obligations, with all surrounding issues being determined by the general law of contract rather than any particular terms put forward by the parties. This was the situation in the Court of Appeal case of *Hertford Foods Ltd v Lidl UK GmbH*.[79] The claimant had tried to rely on a *force majeure* clause in its standard terms in order to excuse its non performance under a sale of goods contract. The Court of Appeal held that, in respect of the conflicting standard terms had been exchanged, neither set governed the contract. The court was able, however, to identify a prior oral agreement for the supply of the goods, which contained all the essential terms. The result was that the claimant's *force majeure* clause was of no effect,[80] the claimant was in breach and the defendant's counterclaim based on that breach was effective.

What if it is not possible to find an early offer and acceptance of this type? There are then three main possibilities:

(a)    the contract is made on the terms of the party whose form was put forward first;[81]
(b)    the contract is made on the terms of the party whose form was put forward last – the 'last shot' approach;
(c)    there is no contract at all, because the parties are not in agreement and there is no matching offer and acceptance.

---

79  [2001] EWCA Civ 938. The case is discussed by Ross, 2001. See also, for a similar result, *GHSP Inc v AB Electronic Ltd* [2010] EWHC 1828.

80  *Force majeure* clauses are discussed in Chapter 13.

81  This appears to have been the approach adopted by the judge at first instance in *Hertford Foods Ltd v Lidl UK GmbH* [2001] EWCA Civ 938.

Lord Denning MR suggested (in *Butler Machine Tool Co Ltd v Ex-Cell-O Corp (England) Ltd*)[82] that the first possibility might apply where the second set of terms (supplied by the offeree) is so different that the offeree 'ought not to be allowed to take advantage of the difference unless he draws it specifically to the attention of the other party'.[83] Subject to that, he also suggested, in the same case, that the second possibility would apply where the terms proposed were not objected to by the other party. Lord Denning MR's suggestions are, in fact, very much in line with the approach adopted in Art 19 of the Vienna Convention on International Sale of Goods, § 2–207 of the United States Uniform Commercial Code[84] and Art II. – 4:208 of the Draft Common Frame of Reference. The Draft Common Frame of Reference also deals with 'conflicting general standard terms' in Art II. – 4:209, providing that a contract will generally be formed on the basis of the common conditions. All of these approaches attempt to find a contract wherever possible. In contrast, the strict application of the classical offer and acceptance principles suggests that the third possible solution is the right answer, and that there is no contract at all. Nevertheless, there is a reluctance even in the courts of England and Wales to come to this conclusion because it will often be the case that the parties are willing, or indeed keen, to have a contract and will often have carried on their business as if such a contract had been validly made. If they are then told by the court that they have no contract at all, it may become very difficult to unscramble their respective rights and liabilities.[85]

### 2.11.4 THE TRADITIONAL VIEW

As it provides a good example of the way in which the courts in England and Wales have generally tackled the problem of the 'battle of the forms', it is worth looking in a little more detail at the case of *Butler Machine Tool Co Ltd v Ex-Cell-O Corp (England) Ltd*.[86]

---

**Key case** *Butler Machine Tool Co Ltd v Ex-Cell-O Corp (England) Ltd* (1979)

Facts: The buyers wished to purchase a machine for their business. On 23 May the sellers offered to sell them one for £75,535, with delivery in 10 months. The offer incorporated the sellers' standard terms, which were said to prevail over any terms in the buyers' order. It also contained a price variation clause, allowing the sellers to increase the price in certain situations. The buyers responded with an order on 27 May. This order incorporated the buyers' terms, which did not include a price variation clause. It also included a tear-off acknowledgment slip, stating: 'We accept your order on the Terms and Conditions stated therein.' The sellers signed and returned this acknowledgment, together with a covering letter, stating that delivery would be 'in accordance with our revised quotation of May 23'. There were no further relevant communications. When the sellers delivered the machine, they tried to enforce the price variation clause, but the buyers insisted that they were only obliged to pay £75,535. The trial judge upheld the sellers' claim but the buyers appealed.

Held: The Court of Appeal held unanimously in favour of the buyers. The sellers' original offer of 23 May was met with a counter-offer from the buyers, which, on the basis of *Hyde v Wrench*, destroyed the sellers' original offer. By completing and returning the

---

82  [1979] 1 All ER 965; [1979] 1 WLR 401.
83  Ibid, p 968; p 405.
84  Both of these are reproduced in Wheeler and Shaw, 1994, p 208.
85  This sort of situation will often fall to be dealt with by the law of 'quasi-contract' or 'restitution' – for which see Chapter 15.
86  [1979] 1 All ER 965; [1979] 1 WLR 401.

acknowledgment slip, the sellers were accepting this counter-offer, and their covering letter was thought not to be sufficiently specific so as to revive the detailed terms of the offer of 23 May. Although the original terms were referred to in that letter, it was, according to Bridge LJ, in language that was 'equivocal and wholly ineffective to override the plain and unequivocal terms of the printed acknowledgment of order'.[87]

### For thought

*If the covering letter had stated explicitly 'this contract is to be on the payment terms set out in our quotation of 23 May, including the price variation clause', would it have overridden the acknowledgment slip? If so, would it have been an acceptance? If not, what would it have been?*

Lord Denning MR would have liked to have decided for the buyers on the basis that the overall negotiations between the parties indicated that there was a contract, even if it was not possible to identify a clear matching offer and acceptance. He subsequently developed his argument for this method of identifying a contract in the Court of Appeal in *Gibson v Manchester City Council*,[88] where it was, however, fairly decisively rejected by the House of Lords. In *Butler*, he was also able to find a contract by the traditional 'offer/counter-offer' analysis. This was the line taken by the other members of the Court of Appeal. It was on this basis that the court was unanimous in holding that the buyers' terms should prevail.

The *Butler Machine Tool* case confirmed the courts' adherence to the traditional analysis in terms of looking for what objectively appears to be a matching offer and acceptance. It did little to resolve a true 'battle of the forms' such as might have arisen had there been no acknowledgment slip but simply an exchange of incompatible terms, followed by the manufacture and delivery of the machinery. In such a situation, a court that followed the traditional line might be forced to say that there was no contract. Other possibilities might be to argue that delivery, or taking delivery, of the machinery amounted to *acceptance by conduct*, or that the failure to respond to the last offer sent amounted to *acceptance by silence*. These two concepts are considered below. Further suggestions have subsequently been made, however, particularly in a more recent decision of the Supreme Court that, in certain situations, an approach similar to that advocated by Lord Denning MR might be adopted, and these need to be noted first.

### 2.11.5 SUBSEQUENT DEVELOPMENTS

In *Trentham Ltd v Archital Luxfer*,[89] the plaintiffs (Trentham) were the main contractors on a building contract. They entered into negotiations with the defendants (Archital) for sub-contracts to supply and install doors, windows, etc. The work was done, and paid for, but when the plaintiffs tried to recover a contribution from the defendants towards a penalty that the plaintiffs had had to pay under the main contract, the defendants denied that a binding contract had ever been formed. There had been exchanges of letters, and various telephone conversations, but there was no clear matching offer and acceptance. In particular, there was a dispute as to whose standard terms should govern the contract. The trial judge held that there was a contract, in that the defendants, in carrying out the

---

87  [1979] 1 All ER 965, p 971; [1979] 1 WLR 401, p 408.
88  [1978] 2 All ER 583; [1978] 1 WLR 520, CA.
89  [1993] 1 Lloyd's Rep 25.

work, had accepted Trentham's offer – in other words, acceptance by conduct.[90] The defendants appealed. The only full judgment was delivered by Steyn LJ, with whom the other two members of the court agreed. Steyn LJ agreed that there was a contract here. In reaching this conclusion, he started by stating four basic points that he considered relevant to the case:

(a)   The approach to the issue of contract formation is 'objective' and so does not take account of the 'subjective expectations and unexpressed mental reservations of the parties'.[91] In this case, the relevant yardstick was 'the reasonable expectations of sensible businessmen'.[92]

(b)   In the vast majority of cases, the coincidence of offer and acceptance represents the mechanism of contract formation but 'it is not necessarily so in the case of a contract alleged to have come into existence during and as a result of performance'.[93]

(c)   The fact that a contract is executed (that is, performance has taken place, as in this case), rather than executory, is of considerable importance – it will often preclude, for example, an argument that there was no intention to create legal relations, or that the contract is void for vagueness or uncertainty.

(d)   If a contract only comes into existence during and as a result of performance of the transaction, it will frequently be possible to hold that the contract impliedly and retrospectively covers pre-contractual performance.[94]

Applying these points to the case before him, Steyn LJ concluded that the judge had sufficient evidence before him to conclude that there was a binding contract. The parties had clearly intended to enter into a legal relationship. The contemporary exchanges, and the carrying out of what was agreed in those exchanges, support the view that there was a course of dealing that on Trentham's side created a right to performance of the work by Archital and on Archital's side created a right to be paid on an agreed basis. Thus, although the trial judge had found that there was offer and acceptance, Steyn LJ was of the view that, in any event:

in this fully executed transaction, a contract came into existence during performance even if it cannot be precisely analysed in terms of offer and acceptance.[95]

Moreover, even if the contract came into existence after part of the work had been carried out and paid for, it impliedly governed pre-contractual performance.

The two main points that this case raises are, first, the potential retrospective effect of a contract. This is of considerable importance in relation to major contracts, in particular construction contracts, where it is common for at least some work to take place before any formal agreement has been reached. This decision clearly recognises that such work will generally be governed by any later agreement that is entered into. The need to use restitutionary remedies will therefore be reduced.[96] The second issue, which is of more importance to the subject matter of this chapter, is the finding that contracts do not

---

90   As in *Brogden v Metropolitan Railway* (1877) 2 App Cas 666 – discussed further below, 2.12.1.

91   [1993] 1 Lloyd's Rep 25, p 27.

92   Ibid.

93   Ibid, citing *Brogden v Metropolitan Railway* (1887) 2 App Cas 666; *New Zealand Shipping Co Ltd v AM Satterthwaite & Co Ltd* [1975] AC 154 and *Gibson v Manchester City Council* [1979] 1 All ER 965; [1979] 1 WLR 401, none of which provides clear authority for the proposition.

94   [1993] 1 Lloyd's Rep 25, p 27, citing *Trollope & Colls v Atomic Power Construction Ltd* [1963] 1 WLR 333.

95   Ibid, pp 29–30.

96   Such remedies are discussed in Chapter 15.

necessarily have to be formed by means of a matching offer and acceptance. This unanimous finding by the Court of Appeal was difficult to reconcile, however, with the rejection by the House of Lords in *Gibson* of Lord Denning's similar attempt to weaken the dominance of 'offer and acceptance', and in the 14 years since the decision was reached there was little evidence of this approach being more widely adopted. It has now been given new impetus, however, by the Supreme Court decision in *RTS Flexible Systems Ltd v Molkerei Alois Müller Gmbh & Company KG (UK Production)*.

---

**Key case** *RTS Flexible Systems Ltd v Molkerei Alois Müller Gmbh & Company KG (UK Production)* (2010)

Facts: The parties were in negotiation in relation to supplying equipment and associated work. Work started on the basis of a letter of intent, which later expired. It was always intended that there should be a formal written contract but although there was agreement on many terms, including the price of £1,682,000, no written contract was ever finalised or signed. On a preliminary issue the trial judge held that there was a contract but simply to supply the equipment at the stated price: none of the other negotiated terms applied. The Court of Appeal held that there was no contract at all. The parties appealed to the Supreme Court.

Held: Looking at the overall communications and actions between the parties in relation to the project, there was a contract between them and it was intended to be governed by those terms that had been settled during the negotiations. The fact that as part of the draft agreement it was stated that no contract was to come into existence until a formal written agreement had been signed and exchanged had been superseded by subsequent events. The parties had clearly waived this requirement.

---

As with the *Trentham* case, this was a situation where much work on the project had taken place before the dispute arose, and the issue of what, if any, contract governed the agreement fell to be decided. As Lord Clarke pointed out, the case demonstrates 'the perils of beginning work without agreeing the precise basis upon which it is to be done. The moral of the story is to agree first and to start work later.'[97] In dealing with the main question, as to whether there was a contract, and if so on what terms, he summarised the principles to be applied as follows:[98]

> The general principles are not in doubt. Whether there is a binding contract between the parties and, if so, upon what terms depends upon what they have agreed. It depends not upon their subjective state of mind, but upon a consideration of what was communicated between them by words or conduct, and whether that leads objectively to a conclusion that they intended to create legal relations and had agreed upon all the terms which they regarded or the law requires as essential for the formation of legally binding relations.

Lord Clarke then proceeded to apply these principles to the facts without any reference to 'offer and acceptance'. He found that the behaviour of the parties, objectively

---

97 [2010] UKSC 14; [2010] 1 WLR 753 at [1]. For a fuller discussion of this case and its implications, see R Stone, 'Forming contracts without offer and acceptance, Lord Denning and the harmonisation of English contract law' [2012] WebJCLI.

98 Ibid, at [45]. This was followed by the Supreme Court in *Devani v Wells* [2019] UKSC 4.

viewed, indicated that they had intended to make an agreement on the terms referred to in their draft contract.

This looks very like the approach that Lord Denning MR had advocated in *Gibson v Manchester City Council* and *Butler Machine Tool v Ex-Cell-O*. It seems that it is now permissible to use this approach at least in situations where the parties have started work without coming to a complete agreement. The extent to which it has a wider application is open to question. It still seems likely that where the courts can identify an exchange of correspondence, they will stick with the more traditional approach. This was certainly the view of the Court of Appeal in *Tekdata Interconnections Ltd v Amphenol*,[99] which was decided shortly before the Supreme Court decision in *RTS Flexible Systems Ltd v Molkerei Alois Müller Gmbh & Company KG (UK Production)*. This concerned a sale of goods contract between companies that had been in a long-term (20-year) business relationship. Goods were ordered by the buyer on forms setting out its terms and conditions. The seller acknowledged the order, but stated that its own terms and conditions applied. The goods were then supplied and accepted by the buyer. The judge, looking at the overall relationship between the parties, held that the buyer's terms prevailed, relying in part on Lord Denning MR's statements in *Butler Machine Tool v Ex-Cell-O*. The Court of Appeal disagreed with this approach. It held that a straightforward offer and acceptance analysis should be used. On this basis, the seller's acknowledgment of the buyer's order was a counter-offer to supply the goods on its terms. This was accepted by the buyer when it took delivery of the goods. In other words, the contract was accepted by conduct. This type of acceptance is discussed in the following section.[100]

Despite the highly likely continued use of offer and acceptance, the approach taken in *RTS Flexible Systems* has been referred to in several subsequent cases. In particular, the statement of 'general principles' given by Lord Clarke, and quoted in the discussion of the case, above, has been accepted as the correct approach to adopt in deciding whether a contract has been formed.[101]

## 2.12 METHODS OF ACCEPTANCE

We now turn to examine in more detail the issues of acceptance by conduct and acceptance by silence. The adoption of an approach to identifying agreement based on a reasonable interpretation of behaviour (the 'objective' test) means that there is clearly potential for both these types of behaviour being considered adequate to indicate acceptance. In fact, however, they are not always regarded as providing sufficient evidence of acceptance and so the relevant case law needs to be analysed carefully.

### 2.12.1 ACCEPTANCE BY CONDUCT

In unilateral contracts, the acceptance will always be by conduct – using the smoke ball, digging the garden, etc. – though there are some problems as to exactly what conduct amounts to acceptance. These issues will be considered further later.[102] Can the same apply in bilateral contracts, so that they too can be accepted by conduct? In some everyday

---

99  [2009] EWCA Civ 1209; [2010] 2 All ER (Comm) 302.

100  For other examples of the courts using an offer and acceptance approach in battle of the forms cases, see: *Balmoral Group Ltd v Borealis (UK) Ltd* [2006] 2 CLC 220 and *Sterling Hydraulics Ltd v Dichtomatik Ltd* [2007] 1 Lloyd's Rep 8.

101  See, for example, *Air Studios (Lyndhurst) Ltd v Lombard North Central Plc* [2012] EWHC 3162 (QB), *Proton Energy Group SA v Orlen Lietuva* [2013] EWHC 2872 (Comm), *Williams v Jones* [2014] 2 WLUK 765 and *Devani v Wells* [2019] UKSC 4.

102  See below, 2.12.13.

situations, this would seem to be the case. In a shop transaction, for example, there may be no exchange of words between the customer and cashier. The customer may simply present the goods selected together with payment, constituting an offer to buy,[103] which will be accepted by the cashier taking the money and, generally, giving a receipt. Can there be acceptance by conduct in more complicated, commercial transactions? This issue was considered in *Brogden v Metropolitan Railway*.[104] The plaintiffs sent the defendants a draft agreement for the supply of a certain quantity of coal per week from 1 January 1872, at £1 per ton. The defendants completed the draft by adding the name of an arbitrator, signed it and returned it to the plaintiffs. This constituted an offer. The plaintiffs' manager, however, simply put the signed agreement into a drawer. There was no communication of acceptance by the plaintiffs. Coal was ordered and delivered on the terms specified in the contract for a period of time, until there was a dispute between the parties. The defendants then argued that there was no contract because the plaintiffs had never accepted their offer, as contained in the signed agreement they returned. The House of Lords confirmed that it was not enough that the plaintiffs should have decided to accept: there had to be some external manifestation of acceptance, of which the defendants were aware. In this case, however, that was supplied by the fact that the plaintiffs had subsequently placed orders. The defendants should therefore be taken to be bound by its terms.

This decision confirms that a bilateral contract may be accepted by conduct and there is no need for a verbal or written indication of acceptance. In *Brogden*, the 'external manifestation' of acceptance (that is, the placing of orders) was also a 'communication' to the other party. As we have seen in the previous section, this analysis continues to be accepted by the courts, with a more recent example being the Court of Appeal decision in *Tekdata Interconnections Ltd v Amphenol* (above, 2.11.5).

What is the position if there is conduct by one party that objectively indicates an intention to accept but the other party is unaware of it? It is to that issue that we now, in part, turn.

### 2.12.2 ACCEPTANCE BY SILENCE

In *Brogden v Metropolitan Railway*, as we have just seen, it was held that you cannot accept a contract simply by deciding that you are going to do so. There must be some external evidence that would lead a reasonable person to believe that your intention was to accept. Does that external evidence have to come to the attention of the other potential party to the contract, or is it enough that the parties were in agreement, objectively assessed, even if one side was in ignorance of it?

In some cases, the issue will be determined by the form of the offer. In unilateral contracts, for example, it has been recognised since *Carlill v Carbolic Smoke Ball Co*[105] that the offeror may waive the need for communication of acceptance. The court thought that it clearly could not have been intended that everyone who bought a smoke ball in reliance on the company's advertisement should be expected to tell the company of this. It would be perfectly possible, of course, for an offeror to require such notice but where an offer is made to the world, as in the *Carlill* case, or where a reward is offered for the return of property or the provision of information, the intention to waive such a requirement will easily be found.

### 2.12.3 ACCEPTANCE BY SILENCE IN BILATERAL CONTRACTS

In relation to bilateral contracts, the position is different. The leading authority is *Felthouse v Bindley*.[106]

---

103 Assuming that the approach adopted in *Pharmaceutical Society of Great Britain v Boots Cash Chemists* [1953] 1 QB 401; [1953] 1 All ER 482 is followed.
104 (1877) 2 App Cas 666.
105 [1893] 1 QB 256.
106 (1862) 11 CB(NS) 869; affirmed (1863) 1 NR 401.

**Key case** *Felthouse v Bindley* (1862)

Facts: An uncle was negotiating to buy a horse from his nephew. The uncle wrote to his nephew offering a particular sum and saying, 'If I hear no more about him, I consider the horse mine.' The nephew did not respond but told an auctioneer to remove this horse from a forthcoming auction. The auctioneer omitted to do so and the horse was sold to a third party. The uncle sued the auctioneer and the question arose as to whether the uncle had made a binding contract for the purchase of the horse.

Held: There was no contract because the nephew had never communicated his intention to accept his uncle's offer. It is true that he had taken an action (removing the horse from the auction) which objectively could be taken to have indicated his intention to accept but, because his uncle knew nothing of this at the time, it was not effective to complete the contract.

This case has long been taken to be authority for the proposition that silence cannot amount to acceptance, at least in bilateral contracts. It is by no means clear that the court intended to go this far. It is uncertain, for example, what the court's attitude would have been had it been the nephew, rather than the uncle, who was trying to enforce the contract. Nevertheless, later courts have taken the principle to be well established. In *The Leonidas D*,[107] for example, Robert Goff J commented:

> We have all been brought up to believe it to be axiomatic that acceptance of an offer cannot be inferred from silence, save in the most exceptional circumstances.[108]

No court has challenged the correctness of the general principle said to be established by *Felthouse v Bindley*, though commentators have doubted it.[109] In considering the analogous situation of acceptance of a repudiatory breach of contract, the House of Lords has suggested in *Vitol SA v Norelf Ltd*[110] that silence and inaction can be effective provided that they can be regarded as 'clear and unequivocal' and the other party has notice. If the same approach can be applied to acceptance of an offer, this will presumably fall within the 'exceptional circumstances' referred to by Robert Goff J. In most cases, however, silence by itself will inevitably be equivocal, in that it will be impossible to tell objectively whether the offeree has decided to accept or reject the offer.

The policy that may be said to lie behind the principle is that one potential contracting party should not be able to impose a contract on another by requiring the other to take some action in order not to be bound. It was felt that someone in the position of the nephew in *Felthouse v Bindley* should not be obliged to tell his uncle if he did not want to accept the offer. He should be entitled to do nothing, and not incur contractual obligations simply by inaction.

## 2.12.4 INERTIA SELLING

During the 1960s, a related problem arose out of the growing practice of what came to be known as 'inertia selling'. The seller in these transactions would send a person who was thought to be a potential buyer a copy of a book, for example, with a covering letter stating that, unless the book was returned within a certain time limit, the recipient would be assumed to want to keep it and would be obliged to pay the purchase price. As we have seen, on the basis of *Felthouse v Bindley*, no binding contract could arise in this way. But,

---

107  [1985] 2 All ER 796; [1985] 1 WLR 925.
108  [1985] 2 All ER 796, p 805; [1985] 1 WLR 925, p 937.
109  See, for example, Miller, 1972.
110  *Vitol SA v Norelf Ltd* [1996] 3 All ER 193 – discussed in more detail below, Chapter 14, 14.9.1.

of course, many people were ignorant of their rights under contract law and were led in this way to pay for items which they did not really want. In order to remedy this, the Unsolicited Goods and Services Act 1971 was passed, which allowed the recipient of unsolicited goods, in circumstances such as those outlined above, to treat them after a specified period of time as an unconditional gift, with all rights of the sender being extinguished. These provisions of this Act have now been largely replaced by reg 27M of the Consumer Protection from Unfair Trading Regulations 2008.[111] These enable the consumer to treat the goods as an unconditional gift as soon as they are received.

### 2.12.5 CONCLUSIONS ON 'SILENCE'

The basic rule, therefore, as derived from *Felthouse v Bindley* and reinforced by the Consumer Protection from Unfair Trading Regulations 2008, is that acceptance, whether by words or action, must be communicated to the offeror. It is clear, however, from the decision in *Carlill v Carbolic Smoke Ball Co*[112] that, in relation to certain types of unilateral contract, the offeror may waive the need for communication of acceptance. What is not clear is whether this can ever be done in a bilateral contract. While it clearly cannot be used as a means of imposing a contract on an unwilling offeree, should an offeree be able to enforce a contract against an offeror who has stated that he will presume acceptance from non-communication? To return to *Felthouse v Bindley*, for example, if the horse had not been sold to a third party, would the nephew have been able to hold his uncle to the promise to buy at the price he had specified? There are two arguments that might be raised against allowing this. The first is that it would run contrary to the principle of mutuality that generally underpins the law of contract. If A can sue B, then B ought to be able to sue A. This principle does not apply universally, however. In relation to contracts with minors, for example, there are situations in which the minor is allowed to enforce a contract, even though the adult with whom he or she has dealt would not be able to do so. Moreover, mutuality only operates to a limited extent in unilateral contracts. This objection is not therefore conclusive. The second argument against allowing the silent offeree to sue is a practical one. If there is no outward manifestation of acceptance, how does a court (or anyone else) know that it has occurred? In other words, silence fails the test of unequivocality referred to in *Vitol SA v Norelf Ltd*. The rule would have to require some objective evidence that the offeree had decided to accept. What would not be required, however, would be knowledge of this on the part of the offeror. Thus, again using the facts of *Felthouse v Bindley*, the nephew's removal of the horse from the auction could be regarded as an objective indication of his acceptance of his uncle's offer. The fact that the uncle was unaware of this should not preclude the nephew from enforcing the contract, since the uncle had, by the terms of his offer, waived the need for communication of acceptance. In conclusion, however, it must be stressed that while the above analysis does not directly contradict any existing authority, neither is there any authority that clearly supports it. The issue as to whether an offeror in a bilateral contract can ever be bound if he has waived the need for communication of acceptance remains open.

Other jurisdictions adopt a more relaxed approach to the question. The American Second Restatement, for example, provides in s 69 for silence to amount to acceptance in various situations including:

(b)    where the offeror has stated or given the offeree reason to understand that assent may be manifested by silence or inaction, and the offeree in remaining silent or inactive intends to accept the offer;

(c)    where because of previous dealings or otherwise, it is reasonable that the offeree should notify the offeror if he does not intend to accept.

---

111  SI 2008/1277.
112  [1893] 1 QB 256.

Application of the principle stated in (b) would be likely to lead to a different result if applied to the facts of *Felthouse v Bindley*. On the other hand, the European Draft Common Frame of Reference provides simply that 'silence or inactivity does not in itself amount to acceptance', thus following the traditional English view.[113]

## 2.12.6 ACCEPTANCE BY POST

A requirement of actual communication will not, however, answer all problems. In the modern world, communication can take many forms: through face-to-face conversations, telephone, letters, faxes or email. In some of these, there will be a delay between the sending of an acceptance and its coming to the attention of the offeror. The law of contract has to have rules, therefore, to make clear what is meant by 'communication'. A simple rule would be to state that no communication is effective until it is received and understood by the person to whom it is addressed. This is, in effect, the rule that applies to offers; though, as we shall see, there are some cases that suggest that it may be possible to accept an offer of which you are unaware.[114] These cases are of dubious authority, however, and can only possibly apply in very restricted circumstances. In any case, they simply suggest that in some situations, communication of an offer may not be necessary. Where communication of the offer is required, which is the case in virtually all situations, it is safe to say that communication means that the person to whom the offer is addressed is aware of it. Why should the position be any different as regards acceptances?

The problem first arose in relation to the post, where the delay is likely to be longest. Generally there will be a delay of at least 12 to 18 hours between the sending of an acceptance by post and its receipt by the addressee. Does the sender of the acceptance have to wait until it is certain that the letter has arrived before being sure that a contract has been made? The issue was considered in *Adams v Lindsell*.[115]

---

**Key case** *Adams v Lindsell* (1818)

Facts: The defendants sent a letter to the plaintiffs offering wool for sale and asking for a reply 'in course of post'. The letter was misdirected by the defendants and arrived later than would normally have been the case. The plaintiffs replied at once accepting but the defendants, having decided that because of the delay the plaintiffs were not going to accept, had already sold the wool elsewhere. The plaintiffs sued for breach of contract.

Held: The court decided that to require a posted acceptance to arrive at its destination before it could be effective would be impractical and inefficient. The acceptor would not be able to take any action on the contract until it had been confirmed that the acceptance had arrived. The court felt that this might result in each side waiting for confirmation of receipt of the last communication *ad infinitum*. This would not promote business efficacy. It would be much better if, as soon as the letter was posted, the acceptor could proceed on the basis that a contract had been made, and take action accordingly. The plaintiffs therefore succeeded: the defendants were in breach of contract.

---

The court, in coming to this conclusion, focused on the practicalities of doing business. It is quite possible that by the time the letter of acceptance arrives, the offeror has had a

---

113 Article II. – 4:204(2).
114 See below, 2.12.17.
115 (1818) 1 B & Ald 681; 106 ER 250.

change of mind and sent a withdrawal of the offer or made a contract with someone else (as happened in *Adams v Lindsell* itself). Nevertheless, because in the court's view the conduct of business would in general be better served by giving the offeree certainty in this situation, the postal rule was established.[116]

---

### For thought

*If you post me a letter, and then want to find out whether I have received it, how would you go about doing so? Would this have been possible at the date when Adams v Lindsell was decided?*

---

At times the justification of the postal rule has been argued to be based on agency – that is, that the Royal Mail was acting as agent for the offeror in receiving the acceptance from the offeree. But this analysis was strongly criticised in *Henthorn v Fraser*.[117] The Royal Mail is more obviously acting as agent for the offeree rather than the offeror and, in any case, if it is acting as agent at all, it would be more accurate to describe it as agent for the physical transfer of the acceptance letter, rather than the communication of its contents.

### 2.12.7 IN FOCUS: THE PENNY POST AND CONTRACT LAW

Gardner, adopting a 'critical legal studies' approach, has suggested that the real reasons for the way in which the postal rule developed are to be found in enthusiasm for the newly established 'penny post' (which began in 1840).[118] He also suggests that the cases on the topic at the end of the late nineteenth century should be looked at in the context of the widespread 'share offers' that were being made at the time. The courts applied the postal rules to stop people escaping from what they felt might be 'bad bargains' for the purchase of shares.[119] Neither of these explanations, however, can deal with the original statement of the rule in 1818, in *Adams v Lindsell*, which was 22 years before the introduction of the penny post, and 60 years before the 'share offer' cases. The arguments based around pragmatism and business efficiency remain the most convincing explanations for the rule's adoption.

### 2.12.8 LIMITATIONS ON THE POSTAL RULE

The rule that comes from *Adams v Lindsell* is thus that a posted acceptance is complete on posting. The offeror is, therefore, bound to a contract without necessarily being aware that this has happened. The same rule was applied to telegrams, where a similar, though shorter, delay in communication would occur.[120] As the rule is a rather unusual one, however, its limitations must be noted. First, it only applies to acceptances and not to any other type of communication that may pass between potential contracting parties. Offers, counter-offers, revocations of offers, etc., must all be properly communicated, even if sent

---

116 Evans, 1966, disputes whether this was the basis for the decision in *Adams v Lindsell* and indeed whether the case established the postal rule at all but concludes (p 561) that of all the reasons put forward justifying it, the one outlined in the text here is the only one which is 'wholly valid'.
117 [1892] 2 Ch 27 – see, in particular, the judgment of Kay LJ. Gardner, 1992, describes the case as 'exploding' the agency analysis.
118 Gardner, 1992.
119 See, for example, *Household Fire and Carriage Accident Insurance Co v Grant* (1879) 4 Ex D 216.
120 *Bruner v Moore* [1904] 1 Ch 305 (exercise of an option).

through the post or by telegram.[121] Second, it only applies where it was reasonable for the acceptance to be sent by post.[122] Clearly, where the offer was made by post, then, in the absence of any indication from the offeror to the contrary, it will certainly be reasonable to reply in the same form, and the postal rule will operate. Wherever the parties are communicating over a distance, it is also likely to be reasonable to use the post, even if the offer has been made in some other way. As Lord Herschell put it in *Henthorn v Fraser*:[123]

> Where the circumstances are such that it must have been within the contemplation of the parties that, according to the ordinary usages of mankind, the post might be used as a means of communicating the acceptance of an offer, the acceptance is complete as soon as it is posted.

In this case, the fact that the parties were based in towns some distance apart was held to make the use of the post reasonable, despite the fact that the offer had been hand-delivered.

The final limitation that must be noted is that the rule can always be displaced by the offeror. The offer itself may expressly, or possibly impliedly, require the acceptance to take a particular form. In *Quenerduaine v Cole*,[124] for example, it was held that an offer that was made by telegram impliedly required an equally speedy reply. A reply by post would not therefore take effect on posting. (There seems no reason, however, why it should not take effect at some point on arrival, provided that the offer was still open.) Any implication from the form of the offer should, of course, be looked at alongside the more general rule as to what is reasonable to expect, as set out in *Henthorn v Fraser*. If the offeror wants to be sure that the postal rule will not operate, this should be made explicit in the offer. In *Holwell Securities Ltd v Hughes*,[125] the offer required the acceptance (in fact, the exercise of an option) to be given by 'notice in writing' to the offeror. It was held that this formulation meant that the acceptance would only take effect when actually received by the offeror. The insertion of this phrase is all that is required, therefore, to displace the postal rule. Other language may, of course, be used, provided the intention is clear. The fact that the offeror has this power may be taken as justifying the fact that the postal rule can operate harshly on the offeror. If a party takes the risk of allowing the postal rule to operate, when it is within its power to displace it, then it should not be allowed to complain if it operates to its disadvantage.[126]

If, however, the postal rule is to operate, the fact that the acceptance is complete on posting has been taken to its logical limit. It does not matter that the letter is delayed in the post; the offeror is still bound. In *Household Fire and Carriage Accident Insurance Co v Grant*,[127] it was held that an acceptance that was entirely lost in the post, and never arrived at its destination, was still effective to create a contract.

## 2.12.9 ACCEPTANCE BY PRIVATE COURIER

The cases that have been discussed in the previous section were all concerned with the service provided by the Royal Mail. Recently, there has been a growth in the availability of various kinds of private courier service, which might also be used to deliver communications creating a contract. Does the postal rule apply to acceptances sent by such means?

---

121 *Byrne v van Tienhoven* (1880) 5 CPD 344.
122 *Henthorn v Fraser* [1892] 2 Ch 27.
123 Ibid, p 33.
124 (1883) 32 WR 185.
125 [1974] 1 All ER 161; [1974] 1 WLR 155.
126 See the comments of Collins, 2003, p 169.
127 (1879) 4 Ex D 216.

There is no conclusive authority on this point. There are two possible lines that the law might take. First, it might be argued that the reasons for applying the postal rule in *Adams v Lindsell* apply equally to communications via a private courier. The acceptor gives the letter to a private courier and thereby puts the acceptance out of his or her control. It would not be conducive to business efficiency to require the acceptor to wait for notification that the acceptance had been received before being able to take any action on the contract. Provided that it was reasonable for the acceptor to use the courier service, the acceptance should take effect as soon as it is given to the courier.

The second line of argument might resist the notion of extending the postal rule beyond its current application. It might well be said that communications have developed dramatically since 1818, when *Adams v Lindsell* was decided. Nowadays, if an acceptor wants to proceed quickly on the basis of a contract, where the acceptance has been given to a private courier, there is no need to wait a long time to receive confirmation that the acceptance has arrived. A telephone call to the offeror will enable the acceptor to find out very quickly whether this has happened or not. If the need for speed is even greater, then the acceptance could be sent by fax or email, with a request for confirmation by phone, fax or email, as soon as it has arrived.

It is difficult to predict which line of argument the courts would find more attractive. If the second approach were accepted, there would be a strong argument for saying that the postal rule itself should be reviewed. As will become apparent from the following section, there has been no move by the courts in recent years to extend the postal rule to other media, and this may be an indication of an acceptance that in the modern context, the *Adams v Lindsell* approach has much less to recommend it than it did at the time it was decided. Other jurisdictions have managed without such a rule, and the drafters of the European Draft Common Frame of Reference did not feel the need to include anything equivalent to it. While there have been no moves in the courts of England and Wales to overrule *Adams v Lindsell* or the case law flowing from it, it may well be that the tendency will be to limit its scope, and confine it strictly to the area of communications via the Royal Mail.

## 2.12.10 ACCEPTANCE BY ELECTRONIC COMMUNICATION

In the modern world, contracts may well be made by much more sophisticated means of communication than the post. Faxes and emails are widely used, in addition to letters and the telephone, as means of transmitting offers, counter-offers, acceptances and rejections. If one of these methods is used for an acceptance, when and where is it effective?

## 2.12.11 THE *ENTORES* APPROACH

The starting point for the law in this area is the case of *Entores v Miles Far East Corp*.[128] This was concerned with communications by telex machine. The 'telex' system involved a message being typed on a special machine attached to a phone line. On being received on the recipient's machine, the message would be typed out on a roll of paper. The system is now obsolete, having been overtaken by the fax and, more recently, email. The primary issue before the court in *Entores* was the question of where the acceptance took effect, if it was sent from a telex machine in one country and received on a telex machine in another country. The answer to this would affect the position as to which country's law governed the contract.

The leading judgment in the Court of Appeal was given by Denning LJ. His approach was to take as his starting point a very simple form of communication over a distance (albeit a rather unlikely one in factual terms), that is two people making a contract by shouting across a river. In this situation, he argued, there would be no contract unless and

---

128  [1955] 2 QB 327; [1955] 2 All ER 493.

until the acceptance was heard by the offeror. If, for example, an aeroplane flew overhead just as the acceptor was shouting his or her agreement, so that the offeror could not hear what was being said, there would be no contract. The acceptor would be expected to repeat the acceptance once the noise from the aeroplane had diminished. Taking this as his starting point, he argued by analogy that the same approach should apply to all contracts made by means of communication that are instantaneous or virtually instantaneous (as opposed to post or telegram, where there is a delay). On this basis, regarding telex as falling into the 'instantaneous' category, he held that the acceptance by telex took place where it was received, rather than where it was sent.

The same answer is generally presumed to apply to all other forms of more sophisticated electronic communication that can be said to be more or less instantaneous in their effect, and has in fact been held to apply to faxed acceptances.[129] Such acceptances will all take effect at the place where they are received. It is at least questionable, however, whether an analogy with a face-to-face conversation does really hold up when applied to faxes and emails. The only true instantaneous types of communication are face to face, by telephone or, possibly, by the kind of electronic message service where both participants are online at the same time. A fax can sit unread in somebody's in-tray for some time and an email may not be opened as soon as it arrives. In that respect, they are more analogous to posted communications, which may not be read until some time after they have been delivered to the addressee. This becomes even more important when the time that the acceptance takes effect is the crucial issue.[130] The fact that an extension of the postal rule was rejected in *Entores* is thus more easily explained on the basis of an unwillingness to allow that anomalous approach to be applied more widely, rather than a logical necessity, based on an analysis of the types of communication involved.

There is perhaps a slightly stronger analogy, at least as regards faxes, when the question of what happens when there are problems with the communication is considered. As we have seen, Denning LJ took the view that in instantaneous communications it is generally up to the person sending the communication to ensure that his or her message gets through. The sender will in most cases (as with the aeroplane flying overhead) be aware if there is a problem. If, however, the reason for failure to communicate is clearly the responsibility of the recipient, then the position will be different. Thus:[131]

> if the listener on the telephone does not catch the words of acceptance, but nevertheless does not trouble to ask for them to be repeated: or the ink on the teleprinter fails at the receiving end, but the clerk does not ask for the message to be repeated: so that the man who sends an acceptance reasonably believes that his message has been received. The offeror in such circumstances is clearly bound, because he will be estopped from saying that he did not receive the message of acceptance.

On the other hand:[132]

> if there should be a case where an offeror without any fault on his part does not receive the message of acceptance – yet the sender of it reasonably concludes that it has got home when it has not – then I think there is no contract.

The expectation is that, as with a personal or telephone conversation, both sender and recipient will know quickly if the communication has failed. That is most likely to be the

---

129  *JSC Zestafoni G Nikoladze Ferroalloy Plant v Ronly Holdings Ltd* [2004] EWHC 245 (Comm).
130  As discussed in the next section, 2.12.12.
131  [1955] 2 QB 327, p 333; [1955] 2 All ER 493, p 495.
132  [1955] 2 QB 327, p 333; [1955] 2 All ER 493, p 495.

case with a fax, where the sender will normally expect to receive a confirmation that the message has got through, and the reply may well be received in an office where those working near to the relevant machine will notice if there has been a failed attempt to send a message. They will then, presumably, try to communicate with the sender. This is not necessarily the case with email, however, where the intended recipient may have no immediate indication of a failed attempt to communicate, and the sender may well only receive a message saying that the email has not been delivered at some time later (if at all). Even as regards fax, there may be no instant response from the recipient where the message is sent out of office hours, or where the recipient does not notice that an attempt to communicate has been made, or where the relevant machine is not located in an area where a malfunction will be noticed quickly. Even in this respect, therefore, the categorisation of these types of communication as closely analogous to a personal conversation tends to break down. They are 'instantaneous' in the sense that the message is received at the recipient's premises almost immediately, but otherwise are more akin to postal communications than personal or telephone conversations. Once again, the conclusions in *Entores* as to the consequences of telex communication can be seen to be based more on what it is reasonable to expect in a business context than on the analogy with other types of communication, which Denning LJ used as the overt basis of his analysis.

Some doubt as to whether the offer and acceptance analysis on the *Entores* model is appropriate, even in relation to instantaneous communication, was raised by the High Court's decision in *Apple Corps Ltd v Apple Computer, Inc.*[133] A contract had been formed at the end of a long period of negotiation in the course of a transatlantic telephone call. There was some dispute as to who had said exactly what, and when. There was no doubt, however, that a contract had been concluded. The question was whether that contract had been made in England or the United States. The judge took the view that using a traditional 'offer and acceptance' analysis might well be 'extremely forced' and introduce a 'highly random element':[134]

> The offer and acceptance may well depend on who speaks first and who speaks second, which is likely to be largely a matter of chance in closing an agreement of this sort. It is very arguably a much more satisfactory analysis to say that the contract was made in both places at the same time.

The issue of what law was to govern the contract could not, therefore, be determined by answering the question of where the contract was formed. Other rules relating to jurisdiction would have to be used to decide this issue.

This was not the only basis on which the judge reached his decision in this case, so his views on this issue cannot be said to be definitively part of the *ratio*. Nevertheless, this approach, accepting that a contract resulting from complex negotiations can be made in two places at once, has subsequently been applied to email.[135] These decisions lend support to the view that issues of contract formation need to be decided by pragmatism, and what will work in practice, as much as by the application of strict legal rules. More recently in *Four Seasons Holdings Incorporated v Brownlie*[136] Lord Sumption (with whom Lord Hughes agreed) stated:

> This is the test which has for many years been applied where the contract was made by instantaneous exchanges, eg by telephone: see *Entores v Miles Far East Corpn*

---

133  [2004] EWHC 768; [2004] IL Pr 34.
134  [2004] EWHC 768; [2004] IL Pr 34, at [42].
135  *Conductive Inkjet Technology Ltd v Uni-Pixel Displays Inc* [2013] EWHC 2968 (ChD).
136  [2017] UKSC 80.

[1955] 2 QB 327 (CA). It differs from the test applied to contracts made by post, which are complete when and where the letter of acceptance is posted: *Adams v Lindsell* (1818) 1 B & Ald 681, *Dunlop v Higgins* (1848) 1 HLC 381. These rules were adopted for reasons of pragmatic convenience, and provide a perfectly serviceable test for determining whether a contract has been concluded at all. However, their deployment for the purpose of determining when or where a contract was made is not at all satisfactory. It depends on assumptions about the point at which an offer is accepted or deemed to be accepted, which are particularly arbitrary when the mode of communication used is instantaneous (or practically so). It also gives rise to serious practical difficulties. The analysis of an informal conversation in terms of invitation to treat, offer and acceptance will often be impossible without a recording or a total recall of the sequence of exchanges and the exact words used at each stage, in order to establish points which are unlikely to have been of any importance to either party at the time.[137]

Lady Hale (with whom Lords Wilson and Clarke agreed) stressed that it was not appropriate to reconsider *Entores* in the instance case.

## 2.12.12 TIME OF ACCEPTANCE

It is important to remember that, as noted above, the court in *Entores* was concerned with the *place* where the contract was made, rather than the precise *time* at which it was made.

As noted, the former issue may be important in international transactions in deciding which set of legal rules governs the contract. The case provides no direct authority on the issue of the time when a telexed acceptance takes effect. Clearly the postal rule cannot apply, since that is based on the acceptance taking effect as soon as it is out of the hands of the acceptor, whereas *Entores* usually requires it to have arrived at the offeror's address. Several possibilities are feasible. It could take effect only when it is actually read by the person to whom it is addressed; or when it is read by someone on behalf of the addressee (for example, an employee of the addressee); or when it is received on the addressee's fax machine, although not read by anyone; or when the acceptor would reasonably expect it to have been read.

Two cases subsequent to *Entores* considered this issue, again in relation to telexes. In *The Brimnes*,[138] the communication was not an acceptance but a notice of the withdrawal of a ship from a charterparty. It was held to be effective when it was 'received' on the charterers' telex machine during office hours, although it was not actually read until the following morning. In *Brinkibon Ltd v Stahag Stahl*,[139] the House of Lords was dealing with a situation virtually identical to that under consideration in *Entores*, and approved the approach taken there. The House refused to indicate whether the same rule should apply in all circumstances, for example where the message is sent out of office hours, or at night, in the expectation that it will be read at a later time, or where there is some fault with the recipient's machine of which the sender is unaware. As Lord Wilberforce put it:[140]

No universal rule can cover all such cases: they must be resolved by reference to the intentions of the parties, by sound business practice and in some cases by a judgment where the risks should lie.

---

137 Ibid at [16].
138 [1975] QB 929; [1974] 3 All ER 88.
139 [1983] 2 AC 34; [1982] 1 All ER 293.
140 Ibid, p 42; p 296.

Figure 2.3

This is not particularly helpful, though it goes some way to confirming the suggestion made above that the *Entores* rule is based more on the needs of business practice than on logical analysis. In so far as any general principle can be read into it, it would seem to be the last of those suggested above, that is, that the communication should take effect at the time when the acceptor could reasonably have expected it to be read. It is an approach that has subsequently been adopted in relation to a fax giving notice under a contract.[141] Similarly an email might well be said only to be communicated once the expected time for checking has passed (although, it seems, many of us are checking e-mail much more regularly these days!). A similar approach might also need to be used in relation to messages left on a telephone answering system: that is, the message should only be regarded as communicated once a reasonable time has elapsed to allow it to be heard by the offeror.

If this line is to be taken, it is clearly to the advantage of the acceptor, in that it allows an acceptance to be treated as effective although the offeror may be unaware of it (as is the case under the postal rule). As with *Adams v Lindsell*, the counter-argument to those who say that this gives the acceptor too much of an advantage would be that the courts have always made it clear that the offeror can specify and insist on a particular mode of acceptance. If actual communication is required, this should be spelled out in the offer. If this

---

141 *Mondial Shipping and Chartering BV v Astarte Shipping Ltd* [1995] Com LC 1011.

is not done, the acceptor must be allowed to proceed on the basis that the acceptance will be read at a time that could reasonably be expected in the normal course of events.

## 2.12.13 ACCEPTANCE IN INTERNET TRANSACTIONS

It seems that an ever-increasing amount of business is conducted over the internet, either by means of email or, particularly in the case of consumer transactions, via a website. In the latter case, the consumer may be actually receiving a product over the web (for example, downloading a piece of software or a film or music file) or placing an order for goods to be delivered by the post or courier service. How do the principles outlined above apply in these situations?

In relation to email, as has been assumed in the previous discussion, there seems little reason to distinguish between this form of communication and other types of 'instantaneous' communication such as telex or fax. That was the view of the judge in *Thomas v BPE Solicitors*,[142] where it was necessary to consider when an emailed acceptance took effect. He rejected any suggestion that the postal rule should apply, and followed the approach taken in *Brinkibon*. On this basis, on the facts of this particular case, he held that the email was sent during office hours and so would take effect as soon as it was received. Similarly in *Greenclose Ltd v NatWest Bank plc*[143] the judge held, again *obiter*, that the postal rule has no application to emails and that the phrase 'giving notice to' implied that the person to whom notice was being given must actually have seen the email – arrival in his inbox would not be sufficient.[144]

Although the judge decided the case on other grounds, so that this did not form part of the *ratio* of the case, it indicates the analysis that the courts are likely to apply. The contract will be formed at the earliest when the acceptance is received by the offeror's email system and is available to be read. At the latest, it should be regarded as complete when, depending on the circumstances, it is read or once the time has passed at which it would be reasonable to expect the acceptance to have been read. Since most email systems will return an error message to the sender if delivery has not been possible, there is arguably no real need here for any other procedure for acknowledgment of receipt.

As regards contracting via a website, some of the potential problems were indicated by events in September 1999 when a retailer was found to be indicating on its website that televisions were available for the price of £3.[145] This was a mistake: the price should have been £300. However, before it could be rectified, a large number of people had attempted to buy a television at the lower price. A crucial question was whether by responding to the information contained on the website these people were accepting an offer by the retailer', or were themselves making an offer to buy at that price. Given that the purchasers would have had to submit credit card details in order to pay for the goods, and the retailer would presumably have reserved the right not to accept these as satisfactory, the better view would seem to be that the purchasers were making the offer to buy. The advertisement of the televisions would thus be simply an invitation to treat. The seller would, subject to relevant consumer protection legislation, be free to accept or reject the offers from the potential purchasers. The contract would be made when the seller had acknowledged to the purchaser that his or her offer was accepted, either by means of a direct response on the website or by a subsequent email.

This area was also the subject of proposals from the European Commission, which subsequently issued a directive dealing with a range of issues on electronic commerce including

---

142 [2012] EWHC 306 (Ch).
143 [2014] EWHC 1156. See also *Kyte v Revenue and Customs Commissioners* [2018] EWHC 1146 (Ch) for a discussion of offer, acceptance, intention to create legal relations and contractual certainty in this context.
144 [2014] EWHC 1156 at [138] – [143].
145 See (1999) *The Times,* 21 September.

provisions relevant to the time of acceptance. The final version of the Directive on Electronic Commerce was adopted in June 2000 (Directive 2000/31/EC). Article 11 provides that:

Member States shall ensure, except when otherwise agreed by parties who are not consumers, that in cases where the recipient of the service places his order through technological means, the following principles apply:

–    *the service provider has to acknowledge receipt of the recipient's order without undue delay and by electronic means;*[146]
–    *the order and the acknowledgment of receipt are deemed to be received when the parties to whom they are addressed are able to access them.*

These provisions are much vaguer than earlier drafts, which seemed to assume that it is the owner of the website who will be making the offer and the purchaser who will be accepting it. Since, as we have seen, by far the most likely situation under the law of England and Wales is that the service provider will be seen as making an invitation to treat, with the purchaser making the offer, this would have meant that the requirements of the Directive would arguably have had very little impact. The final draft, however, seems apt to cover the situation where it is the customer who makes the offer. In such a situation, the law of England and Wales in any case requires the offer to be accepted before it is effective and this would seem to satisfy the need for an acknowledgment of the order. If the offer is made by the website owner, however, and accepted by the customer, the Directive will place an additional requirement on the website owner to acknowledge the acceptance. In all cases, however, the Directive makes the test of when a communication takes place the point at which it can be accessed by the recipient.

The Directive was implemented in the law of England and Wales by the Electronic Commerce (EC Directive) Regulations 2002,[147] the relevant sections of which came into force on 21 August 2002.

Regulation 11, entitled 'placing of the order', which deals with the matters covered by Art 11 of the Directive, states as follows:

11 (1) Unless parties who are not consumers have agreed otherwise, where the recipient of the service places his order through technological means, a service provider shall -
    (a)   acknowledge receipt of the order to the recipient of the service without undue delay and by electronic means; and
    (b)   make available to the recipient of the service appropriate, effective and accessible technical means allowing him to identify and correct input errors prior to the placing of the order.
(2) For the purposes of paragraph (1)(a) above -
    (a)   the order and the acknowledgment of receipt will be deemed to be received when the parties to whom they are addressed are able to access them; and
    (b)   the acknowledgment of receipt may take the form of the provision of the service paid for where that service is an information society service.
(3) The requirements of paragraph (1) above shall not apply to contracts concluded exclusively by exchange of electronic mail or by equivalent individual communications.

---

146  But this requirement does not apply where the contract is concluded exclusively by the exchange of email 'or by equivalent individual communications' (Art 11(3)).
147  SI 2002/2013.

The word 'order' in reg 11(1)(b) (though not necessarily in reg 11(1)(a)) means the contractual offer (reg 12).

The sanctions for non-compliance with reg 11(1)(a) gives a right to the customer to sue the service provider for damages for breach of statutory duty (reg 13). Non-compliance with reg 11(1)(b) gives the customer the right to rescind the contract (reg 15).

The wording of the Regulations seems consistent with the suggestion made above that it will generally be the customer who makes the offer. However, as noted above, reg 11(1)(b) requires the service provider to make available to the customer 'appropriate, effective and accessible technical means allowing him to identify and correct input errors prior to the placing of an order'. Regulation 12 then provides that 'order' in reg 11(1)(b) means 'the contractual offer'. The service provider will thus be able to argue that any screen that it displays in response to a customer's initial 'order' is simply fulfilling the requirements of reg 11(1)(b), and that reg 12 means that this must be taken as preceding 'the contractual offer'. The 'contractual offer' then becomes the customer's clicking of a button confirming that he or she is happy with the terms set out on the page; so, although the Regulations do not on their face purport to affect the rules of offer and acceptance, it is clearly arguable that they do lead to particular conclusions about the stage at which an offer is made.

If the customer makes the offer then the acceptance will come from the supplier. The Directive and Regulations give no indication as to when that will occur. In the absence of any other statement on the matter it would often be reasonable to argue that the acceptance takes place when the supplier acknowledges the customer's offer, either via a web page or by a confirmation email. In either case, on the basis of the analysis outlined above in relation to faxes, etc., it is likely that the acceptance will often take effect at the time when it would be reasonable for the supplier to assume that it will have been read. Where the transaction is taking place online, and the response to the customer's order is virtually instantaneous, then the contract may be made immediately, since it may be reasonable for the supplier to assume that the customer has remained online to await the confirmation of the acceptance or rejection of the offer to buy.

In some cases the supplier will attempt to clarify the position through its terms of business. The terms of one major supplier of goods via the internet state:

> When you place an order to purchase a product from [us], we will send you an e-mail confirming receipt of your order and containing the details of your order (the 'Order Confirmation E-mail'). The Order Confirmation E-mail is acknowledgement that we have received your order, and does not confirm acceptance of your offer to buy the product(s) ordered. We only accept your offer, and conclude the contract of sale for a product ordered by you, when we dispatch the product to you and send e-mail confirmation to you that we've dispatched the product to you (the 'Dispatch Confirmation E-mail').

This has the effect of delaying the point of acceptance to the time when the email confirming dispatch of the goods is sent.

## For thought

*Should suppliers be able to regulate the situation in this way to their own advantage? Is there a need for further controls over this type of contracting to protect consumers?*

**Rejection**
A rejection may be express or implied
A counter-offer is an implied rejection
Any attempt by the offeree to change the terms of an offer will constitute a counter-offer and will terminate the offer –
*Hyde v Wrench* [1840]
*Brogden v Metropolitan Railway* [1877]

**Termination of an offer**

**Revocation**
Offer can be revoked at any time before it is accepted – *Payne v Cave* [1789]
Revocation must be **communicated** to be effective – *Byrne v Van Tienhoven* [1880]
Revocation is effective through a reliable third party – *Dickinson v Dodds* [1876]
Revocation may be express or implied

**Lapse**
Offer may become incapable of acceptance because of lapse of time
If no time limit is specified, the offer will remain open for a reasonable time – *Ramsgate Hotel Co v Montefiore* [1866]
Death of the offeror [contract of personal nature]
Failure of a condition – *Financings Ltd v Stimson* [1962]

Figure 2.4

### 2.12.14 ACCEPTANCE IN UNILATERAL CONTRACTS

Particular difficulties arise in connection with acceptances in unilateral contracts. We have already seen that one of the broad characteristics of the unilateral contract is that the 'acceptance' occurs through the performance of an act, rather than the expression of agreement. It has also been noted that, in certain cases, the offeror in a unilateral contract may be taken to have waived the need for communication of the fact of acceptance.[148] Indeed, there may be an argument for saying that a unilateral contract does not really involve an agreement at all but rather simply a promise that becomes enforceable once a certain condition is fulfilled. This issue will be considered further once certain other difficulties with acceptance in unilateral contracts have been considered.

---

148  For example, *Carlill v Carbolic Smoke Ball Co* [1893] 1 QB 256.

There is, first, an issue as to when acceptance is complete. Is it when the acceptor starts to perform? Or when performance is complete? If I offer a prize of £100 for the first person to walk from the Town Hall in Leicester to Trafalgar Square in London during the month of February, do you accept this offer when you take your first step away from Leicester or only when you arrive at Trafalgar Square? An acceptor in a unilateral contract is generally, as we have noted, under no obligation to perform the requested act and so if you decide to give up halfway to London, I will have no claim against you for breach of contract. This was clearly the view of Longmore LJ in an *obiter* comment in *Soulsbury v Soulsbury*, where a wife had made a unilateral contract to the effect that if she did not sue for maintenance she would receive £100,000 on the death of her former husband. Longmore LJ said:

> This is a classic unilateral contract of the *Carlill v Carbolic Smoke Ball Co [1893] 1 QB 256* or the "walk to York" kind. Once the promisee acts on the promise by inhaling the smoke ball, by starting the walk to York or (as here) by not suing for the maintenance to which she was entitled, the promisor cannot revoke or withdraw his offer. But there is no obligation on the promisee to continue to inhale, to walk the whole way to York or to refrain from suing. It is just that if she inhales no more, gives up the walk to York or does sue for her maintenance, she is not entitled to claim the promised sum.

This would suggest that acceptance only occurs with complete performance. There are problems with this, however, in relation to the offeror's power to withdraw the offer. As will be seen below, the offeror is generally free to withdraw an offer at any point before it has been accepted. If, in a unilateral contract, acceptance means complete performance, then this *prima facie* means that the offeror would be able to back out at any point before performance was complete. So, to use the example given above, if you have started out to walk from Leicester to London and have managed two-thirds of the distance, I would be entitled to come up to you and say: 'I'm sorry, I have changed my mind. My offer of £100 is withdrawn.' *Prima facie* you would have no redress, despite the fact that you might be perfectly willing to continue the walk, because we would not at that stage have a contract. The possibility of withdrawal by notice in this type of contract was given judicial recognition in *Great Northern Railway Co v Witham*,[149] but the court did not on the facts need to decide whether, and in what circumstances, it might be allowed. In an American case, *Petterson v Pattberg*,[150] an Appeals Court took the view that a unilateral offer to allow a reduction on a mortgage if it was paid off before a particular date could be withdrawn at any time before tender of the payment was made. In that case Petterson had gone to Pattberg's house and announced that he had come to pay off the mortgage, but Pattberg had responded by indicating that the offer was withdrawn. It was held that he was entitled to do so.[151]

Such a result clearly has the potential to operate unfairly and there have, therefore, been attempts to argue that partial performance may at least in some circumstances prevent withdrawal by the offeror.

---

149 (1873) LR 9 CP 16.

150 (1928) 248 NY 86, 161 NE 428.

151 This conclusion has, however, subsequently been described as 'obsolete' (Traynor J, in *Drennan v Star Paving Company* (1958) 51 Cal 2d 409, 333 P 2d 757) because of s 45 of the 2nd Restatement, which facilitates a subsidiary promise in a unilateral offer to keep the offer open for the stated time, or a 'reasonable time', and that partial performance provides consideration for that promise.

**Key case** *Errington v Errington* (1952)[152]

Facts: A father had promised his son and daughter-in-law that if they paid off the mortgage on a house owned by the father, he would transfer it to them. The young couple started to make the required payments but made no promise that they would continue. This appeared to be, therefore, a unilateral contract. The father died and his representatives denied that there was any binding agreement in relation to the house. They argued that his offer could be withdrawn because there had not been full acceptance. Held: The Court of Appeal refused to accept that the offer could be withdrawn. Denning LJ recognised that this was a unilateral contract but nevertheless held that the offer could not be withdrawn:[153]

> The father's promise was a unilateral contract – a promise of the house in return for their act of paying the instalments. It could not be revoked by him once the couple entered on performance of the act, but it would cease to bind him if they left it incomplete and unperformed.

The reasons behind this conclusion are not made clear, other than that this was a fair result where the young couple had acted in reliance on the father's promise.[154] This approach has clear links with the idea of estoppel, of which, as we shall see, Denning LJ made inventive use in other areas,[155] but this concept was not raised directly in this case.

The approach taken by Denning LJ in *Errington* received support from the later Court of Appeal decision in *Daulia v Four Millbank Nominees Ltd*.[156] The parties were negotiating over the sale of some properties. The unilateral contract here was that the defendants promised the plaintiffs that if they produced a signed contract plus a banker's draft by 10 am the next morning, the defendants would go ahead with the sale to the plaintiffs. The plaintiffs did what was requested but the defendants refused to go through with the contract. In the course of his judgment, Goff LJ considered the question of when the offeror in a unilateral contract is entitled to withdraw that offer. He started by confirming that in general the offeror cannot be bound to a unilateral contract until the acceptor has provided full performance of the condition imposed. That general rule is, however, subject to an important qualification, namely:[157]

> that there must be an implied obligation on the part of the offeror not to prevent the condition becoming satisfied, which obligation it seems to me must arise as soon as the offeree starts to perform. Until then, the offeror can revoke the whole thing, but once the offeree has embarked on performance it is too late for the offeror to revoke his offer.

Goff LJ provided no authority for this proposition,[158] but it received the support of Buckley LJ. It was not, however, part of the *ratio* of the case, since the court decided against the plaintiffs on other grounds. It seems likely, nevertheless, that the approach taken by

---

152 [1952] 1 All ER 149.
153 [1952] 1 All ER 149, p 153.
154 This could be seen as adding support to arguments that the basis of contractual liability is 'reasonable reliance', rather than 'consideration' or 'promise' – see below, Chapter 3, 3.4 and 3.15.2.
155 See below, Chapter 3, 3.11.
156 [1978] 2 All ER 557.
157 Ibid, p 561.
158 Though it is similar to the position taken by the American 2nd Restatement – see note 156, above.

Denning LJ and Goff LJ in these two cases would be followed in similar circumstances. In *Soulsbury v Soulsbury* Longmore LJ seemed to take the view that this approach should apply generally to unilateral contacts where performance has started.[159]

## 2.12.15 IN FOCUS: AN EXCEPTION – OR AGENCY?

A case that might appear to cause difficulties for such a conclusion is the earlier House of Lords' decision in *Luxor (Eastbourne) Ltd v Cooper*.[160] This was a case in which a company wished to sell some cinemas, and Cooper agreed to act as agent and try to provide a purchaser, at a price of not less than £185,000. He was to be paid his commission (£10,000) 'on completion of the sale'. Cooper provided a willing purchaser but the company withdrew from the sale. The House of Lords refused to imply a term that the principal would not unreasonably prevent the completion of the transaction. The clause referred to payment 'on completion' and since that had not occurred, the agent was not entitled to his commission. This type of arrangement might well be treated as a bilateral contract[161] but the House of Lords took it to be unilateral. As Lord Russell put it, in this type of estate agency contract:[162]

> No obligation is imposed on the agent to do anything. The contracts are merely promises binding on the principal to pay a sum of money on the happening of a specified event, which involves the rendering of some service by the agent.

The question then became whether any term should be implied into the principal's promise to the effect that the principal would not refuse to complete the sale to a client introduced by the agent. The House of Lords refused to imply any such term, since there was no necessity to do so – necessity being the normal basis for the implication of terms at common law.[163] In effect, therefore, the House was saying that the principal could withdraw his offer at any time before the specified event occurred. Since the sale had not been completed, the event had not occurred and the agent was not entitled to the commission. The decision could be seen as the House upholding 'party freedom', in that the principal should be entitled to refuse to contract with whomever the agent produces.[164] It may well be, however, that, as Atiyah has argued,[165] an important aspect in reaching this decision was the House's view that risk was inherent in the role of the estate agent. The risk of the principal withdrawing his offer was just one more to put alongside all the others. The rewards of success were great. As Lord Russell pointed out, £10,000 was at the time equivalent to the annual salary of the Lord Chancellor. The risk was therefore worth taking. If that is the case, then it is probably best to view *Luxor v Cooper* as being a case of relevance primarily to the law of agency. Certainly it does not seem to have troubled the Court of Appeal in expressing apparently contradictory views about the possibility of withdrawing unilateral offers in *Errington v Errington* or *Daulia v Four Millbank Nominees*. Even as far as agents are concerned, it is important to remember that *Luxor v Cooper* turned on the precise wording of the promise made by the principal. As later cases have

---

159  [2007] EWCA Civ 969; [2008] 2 WLR 834, [49].

160  [1941] AC 108; [1941] 1 All ER 33.

161  As, indeed, the Court of Appeal had done – [1939] 4 All ER 411.

162  [1941] AC 108, pp 124–25; [1941] 1 All ER 33, p 44. The issues involved in treating the agency contract as unilateral rather than bilateral are fully discussed in Murdoch, 1975. Compare also *Devani v Wells* [2019] UKSC 4 where the triggering event was not expressly set out but the Supreme Court nevertheless felt that the triggering event would be clear to a reasonable person.

163  See Chapter 6, 6.6.4.

164  See, for example, the comments of Lord Wright [1941] AC 108, p 138: 'It would be strange if what was preliminary ... should control the freedom of the action of the principal in regard to the main transaction ....'

165  Atiyah, 1986, pp 204–05.

shown,[166] agents are quite able to protect their commission against the kind of withdrawal that took place in *Luxor v Cooper*, by making it payable on the production of a purchaser 'ready, willing and able' to purchase, rather than the completion of a sale.

In conclusion, despite the difficulties raised by *Luxor v Cooper*, it is still suggested that in some cases, where the offeror knows that the offeree is trying to perform, there will be an implied obligation on the offeror not to withdraw the offer, at least until a reasonable time for performance has been allowed.

### 2.12.16 POSITION IN 'REWARD' CONTRACTS

It may be significant, however, that in both *Errington* and *Daulia*, the offeror was aware that the other person had embarked upon performance. In such a situation it is arguably relatively easy to conclude that the offeror should sometimes be under an obligation not to withdraw – though whether such an obligation arises as an implication of the intention of the parties or is simply imposed by the courts is not clear.[167] On the other hand, where the offer, such as the offer of a reward or prize, is one that is made to the world, it is by no means certain that precisely the same approach should apply.[168] In the case, for example, of the offer of £100 for the return of a lost dog, it seems right that where a person is seen at the opposite end of the street bringing the dog home, the offeror should not be able to shout out a withdrawal of the reward. But suppose the offeror has run into financial problems since offering the reward and cannot now afford to pay it: must the offeror remain committed to keeping the offer open as regards anyone who has started looking for the dog, even if the offeror is unaware of this? It would seem reasonable in some circumstances that the offeror should be allowed, by giving notice in a reasonable manner (perhaps in the same way in which the offer was made), to withdraw the offer. It is an issue on which there is no clear authority in England and Wales, so it is not possible to say with any certainty what the approach of the courts would be, but it is submitted that the *Errington/Daulia* approach would not apply in all cases.

### 2.12.17 ACCEPTANCE IN IGNORANCE OF AN OFFER

It would seem logical that there can be no acceptance of an offer of which the person accepting was ignorant. Some problems have arisen, however, in relation to certain types of unilateral contract. Suppose a reward is offered for the return of a stolen bicycle belonging to A and posters are displayed advertising this fact. B, who has not seen any of the posters, finds the bicycle and, recognising it, returns it to A, its rightful owner. Can B claim the reward from A? There is one authority that suggests that he/she might be able to. That is *Gibbons v Proctor*,[169] where a police officer gave information for which a reward had been offered. At the time that he gave the information the officer was unaware of the reward, though he had learnt of it by the time the information reached the person who had offered the reward. It was held that the officer was entitled to claim the reward. This decision has not been followed in any later case, however, and must be regarded as being of doubtful authority. The better view seems to be that knowledge is necessary for an effective acceptance. This was accepted as being the case, though without any authority being cited, in the criminal law case of *Taylor v Allon*.[170]

---

166  *Christie, Owen & Davies Ltd v Rapacioli* [1974] 1 QB 781.
167  See the comments of Beale, 1995a, p 205.
168  Though Longmore LJ in *Soulsbury v Soulsbury* [2007] EWCA Civ 969; [2008] 2 WLR 834, [49] seems to assume that it should.
169  (1891) 64 LT 594.
170  [1966] 1 QB 304; [1965] 1 All ER 557. Compare also *Great Eastern Shipping Company Limited v Far East Chartering Limited, Binani Cement Limited* [2011] EWHC 1372 (Comm) at [47] where His Honour Judge Mackie QC stated: "The issue is an open one under English law and an important one. No decision on the

A slightly different issue arises where the person performing the act has previously known of the offer but is acting from different motives. In the Australian case of *R v Carke*,[171] it was held that a person who had known of the offer but was at the time acting purely out of consideration for his own danger, should be treated as acting in ignorance of the offer. On the other hand, in *Williams v Carwardine*,[172] it was held that acting out of mixed motives (in this case, to ease one's conscience), while at the same time having the reward in mind, did not preclude a valid acceptance of the offer.

It seems, therefore, that there needs to be at the very least awareness of the offer and, probably, that responding to it must at least be part of the reason for undertaking the relevant actions.

### 2.12.18 UNILATERAL CONTRACTS AND 'AGREEMENT'

Having examined the issues surrounding the question of acceptance in unilateral contracts, we can now return to the question of how well such contracts fit with the concept of an 'agreement'. Is a unilateral contract really anything more than a promise that becomes enforceable on the fulfilment of a condition? Not all such promises are enforceable, of course. A promise by a mother to pay her daughter £500 on her eighteenth birthday is probably not enforceable. It is only where the promisee does something at the request of the promisor that the relationship becomes 'contractual'. A promise by the Smoke Ball Company to pay Mrs Carlill £100 the next time she caught flu would not have been enforceable. It was only because the advertisement was aimed to encourage people to use the company's smoke ball and Mrs Carlill had done so that she became eligible for the reward. This aspect of the unilateral contract derives from the doctrine of 'consideration', which is discussed in Chapter 3. The question here is whether the mere fact that the promisee does something at the request of the promisor means that there is an 'agreement'. Although the promisee is responding to the promisor,[173] in 'reward' or 'advertisement' situations the promisor will usually know nothing of this until performance is complete. Is it accurate to say that the promisor has an agreement with the promisee in such a situation? The answer is that, as discussed in Chapter 1, we can fit this into the overall 'agreement' framework by accepting that some agreements will be 'implied' or 'imputed'.[174] As long as we are prepared to accept this 'fiction', then the unilateral contract can be treated as falling within the overall classical paradigm of a contract.

Much of the difficulty derives from the insistence by the courts that a unilateral contract must have an offer and acceptance in the same way as a bilateral contract. It might have been better if the courts, recognising that the unilateral contract was not the same as a bilateral contract, had devised a separate set of rules to deal with it. It is arguable that this is what has happened in practice, since a number of the cases involving unilateral contracts (for example, *Errington v Errington, Daulia v Four Millbank Nominees, Williams v Carwardine*) seem to involve the courts taking a decision based on pragmatism and 'fairness' rather than formal and logical application of the rules as they apply to bilateral contracts. It is perhaps an area where doctrine has been a hindrance rather than a help to the development of a coherent set of principles.

---

point is necessary if I am right on the owners' main case. It is not necessary for me to decide any questions of primary fact to enable the Court of Appeal to determine the point should the need arise. In those circumstances, particularly where there has been limited time for argument on the point, I do not propose to decide it."

171 (1927) 40 CLR 227.
172 (1833) 5 C & P 566. See also Mitchell and Phillips, 2002.
173 Even this may not be necessary, if *Gibbons v Proctor* (1891) 64 LT 594 is good law – see above, 2.12.17.
174 See Chapter 1, 1.5.

### 2.12.19 CROSS-OFFERS

A situation similar to the unilateral contract cases on 'accepting' a reward of which one is unaware can arise in a bilateral contract if there are matching 'cross-offers'. Suppose, for example, that two parties send each other a letter offering respectively to buy and to sell certain goods at a certain price. Suppose, also, that the two offers match precisely. Does this create a contract? If what the courts were concerned with was simply a 'meeting of the minds', the answer might well be 'yes'. In *Tinn v Hoffman*,[175] however, it was held that such an exchange does not result in a contract. The case is not conclusive on the general issue because on the facts there were differences between the two offers. It seems likely, however, that given the general enthusiasm of the courts to look for an 'exchange' of offer and acceptance, rather than simply general agreement, *Tinn v Hoffman* would be followed, and that cross-offers would not be regarded as forming a contract. In practice, it is very unlikely that any set of cross-offers would be identical, so the question is probably only of theoretical interest.

## 2.13 ACCEPTANCE AND THE TERMINATION OF AN OFFER

The general rule is that an offer can be revoked at any point before it is accepted,[176] although, as we have seen, that requires some modification in relation to unilateral contracts. In this section the focus will be entirely on bilateral contracts.

The general rule will apply despite the fact that the offeror may have promised to keep the offer open for a specified time.[177] The reason for this is that before there is an acceptance, there is no contract and, if there is no contract, then the offeror cannot be legally bound to a promise. If the offeree has paid for the time allowance in some way (that is, has given consideration for the promise to keep the offer open), as may well be the case with the exercise of an option, then it will be upheld. In the absence of this, however, there can be no complaint if the offer is withdrawn.

### For thought

*Suppose that Steve offers to sell Bella his car for £2,000. She needs time to raise the money before accepting and Steve says he will keep the offer open for a week. Three days later, without referring back to Bella, he sells the car to Tom for £2,000. Is this unfair to Bella? Why? What loss has she suffered by Steve's actions? Why should it make a difference if Bella had paid Steve £1 to keep the offer open?*

### 2.13.1 NEED FOR COMMUNICATION

Revocation of an offer must be communicated to be effective. This was implicit in the decision in *Byrne v van Tienhoven*[178] in which the withdrawal of an offer, which was sent by telegram, was held not to take effect until it was received. The *Adams v Lindsell*[179] postal rule does not apply to revocations of offers but there may still be difficulties as to what exactly amounts to communication and when a revocation takes effect. The

---

175  (1873) 29 LT 271.
176  *Payne v Cave* (1789) 3 Term Rep 148.
177  *Routledge v Grant* (1828) 4 Bing 653; 130 ER 920.
178  (1880) 5 CPD 344.
179  (1818) 1 B & Ald 681; 106 ER 250.

issues are much the same as those dealt with in the section on acceptance by electronic communication,[180] and are not discussed again here.

It is clear, however, that communication of revocation need not come directly from the offeror. Provided that the offeree is fully aware at the time of a purported acceptance that the offeror has decided not to proceed with the contract, the offer will be regarded as having been revoked and no acceptance will be possible. This was the position in the following case.

---

**Key case** *Dickinson v Dodds* (1876)[181]

Facts: On 10 June Dodds offered to sell a property to Dickinson, with the offer to be held over to 12 June. On 11 June, Dickinson was told by a third party that Dodds was negotiating with Allan for the sale of property that he had previously offered to the Dickinson. Dickinson tried to accept the offer on the afternoon of the 11 June and the morning of the 12 June, but Dodds had already sold to Allan before he was aware of Dickinson's acceptance. Dickinson sued for breach of contract.

Held: The Court of Appeal decided that acceptance was not possible because Dickinson knew that Dodds was no longer minded to sell the property to him 'as plainly and clearly as if [the defendant] had told him in so many words, "I withdraw the offer"'.[182] Dodds was not in breach because no contract had been formed with Dickinson.

---

The reasoning of, at least some, of the judges in this case was clearly influenced by the idea of there needing to be a (subjective) 'meeting of the minds' in order for there to be a contract. Despite the fact that this approach to identifying agreements no longer has any support, *Dickinson v Dodds* is still regarded as good authority for the more general proposition that an offeree cannot accept an offer where he or she has learnt from a reliable source that the offer has been withdrawn, even where that source was acting without the knowledge of the offeror.

### 2.13.2 METHODS OF REVOCATION

As well as being communicated expressly, an offer may be revoked by implication. We have seen that a rejection of an offer, or a counter-offer, automatically means that the offer is taken as being no longer available for acceptance.[183] In *Pickfords v Celestica*,[184] the Court of Appeal held that a second offer made to the same offeree will generally have the effect of impliedly revoking the first offer, though this might be otherwise if the offeree had, for example, requested a second offer based on an alternative pricing method, specifically for the purpose of making a choice between the two pricing methods.

An offer may also become incapable of acceptance because of lapse of time. If the offeror has specified a time within which acceptance must be received, any acceptance received outside that time limit generally cannot create a contract. At best, it will be a fresh offer, which may be accepted or rejected. If no time is specified, the offer will remain open for a reasonable time, which will be a matter of fact in each case. In *Ramsgate Victoria*

---

180 See above, 2.12.13.
181 (1876) 2 Ch D 463.
182 Ibid, p 472.
183 *Hyde v Wrench* (1840) 3 Beav 334; see above, 2.11.1.
184 [2003] EWCA Civ 1741.

*Hotel Co v Montefiore*,[185] it was held that a delay of five months meant that an attempt to accept an offer to buy shares was ineffective.[186]

### 2.13.3 REVOCATION AND TENDERS

The ability of an offeror to revoke an offer, even when it has been stated that it will remain open for a specified period, has the potential to cause difficulties in large-scale contracts, where a main contractor may tender for work using a price on the basis of offers received from sub-contractors. What is the position if the main contractor's tender is successful but the sub-contractor then says that the offer to do the work at the specified price is withdrawn? The application of the principles outlined above would lead to the conclusion that the sub-contractor is entitled to withdraw. Concern about the difficulties that this might cause for contractors led the Law Commission in 1975 to make some provisional proposals that in certain circumstances a promise to keep an offer open for a specified time should be binding, bringing the law of England and Wales into line with what the Law Commission found to be the position in other European jurisdictions (including Scotland) and under the Uniform Commercial Code in the United States.[187] A study of business practice in this country by Lewis, however,[188] found that the problem was not regarded as being as serious as the Law Commission had supposed. Moreover, even where difficulties of this kind arose, informal, rather than legal remedies were seen as being the better option. No further action has been taken on the Law Commission's suggestions.

### 2.14 RETRACTION OF ACCEPTANCE

As soon as an acceptance takes effect, a contract is made and both parties are bound. It would seem, then, that in the normal course of events, retraction or revocation of an acceptance will be impossible. This general rule has been modified, for example, in relation to certain types of consumer contracts, where it has been deemed desirable that the consumer should have a 'cooling-off' period following the formation of the contract, during which a change of mind is permitted. In these cases, a valid contract, in which offer and acceptance have been exchanged, can be set aside largely at the discretion of the consumer contractor. These rights were originally introduced piecemeal to deal with particular types of contract. An example of this type of provision may be found in s 67 of the Consumer Credit Act 1974. A broadly based exception is now to be found in the Consumer Contracts (Information, Cancellation and Additional Charges) Regulations 2013,[189] implementing the European Consumer Rights Directive.[190]

The relevant parts of the 2013 Regulations apply to contracts for the supply of goods or services to a consumer, made at a distance (e.g. by telephone, post or over the internet) or face to face but, for example, away from business premises (an 'off-premises' contract). There are exceptions to the application of the Regulations – for example, they do not apply to off-premises contracts worth less than £42.

Also excluded are most contracts involving the sale or disposition of interests in land, contracts relating to financial services, sales via an automated vending machine, auction sales, contracts for the supply of food, etc. 'intended for everyday consumption' supplied

---

185  (1866) LR 1 Ex 109.
186  See, also, *Manchester Diocesan Council for Education v Commercial and General Investments Ltd* [1969] 3 All ER 1593; [1970] 1 WLR 241.
187  Law Commission Working Paper No 60, 'Firm Offers'.
188  Lewis, 1982.
189  SI 2013/3134.
190  Directive 2011/83/EU.

to the consumer's residence by the trader though frequent and regular rounds, and 'the supply of accommodation, transport of goods, vehicle rental services, catering or services related to leisure activities, if the contract provides for a specific date or period of performance'. This final category means, for example, that booking a car hire over the internet, a hotel room by telephone or ordering a pizza to be delivered are not within the scope of the cancellation provisions.

Where the contract is within the scope of the Regulations, the cancellation provisions contained in regs 29–31 apply. These mean that the consumer will generally be able to cancel the contract by giving notice within 14 working days of receiving goods, or within 14 days of the making of a contract for services. If the supplier has not complied with the requirements for the supply of information on cancellation rights, the period will not start to run until the day after such information is received.[191] If the information is not given within 12 months, then the cancellation period extends to 12 months and 14 days.[192]

### 2.14.1 IN FOCUS: AN EXCEPTION OR A CHANGE IN THE COMMON LAW?

The effect of these Regulations is that there are a wide range of consumer contracts where the traditional contractual rule that an acceptance cannot be withdrawn effectively no longer applies. Does this pose a threat to the continuation of the traditional rule? Probably not. The rationale for the Regulations is the avoidance of the risk of consumers being treated unfairly. Although it is possible that a similar approach could be adopted in a business context, in situations of unequal bargaining power, it seems unlikely that this will happen in any expansive form. Indeed, the courts in England and Wales may well be less likely to consider doing this now that specific provision has been made to protect consumers. The argument would probably be that now that Parliament has intervened to deal with this area, the courts should not rush to depart from established principle in those areas not covered by such intervention. The assumption will be that Parliament intended that the normal rules should continue to apply outside the specified areas.

### 2.14.2 WITHDRAWAL BEFORE 'COMMUNICATION'?

There is one area, however, where the possibility of withdrawal from a seemingly binding agreement arises under classical contractual doctrine – that is in relation to situations where the law deems acceptance to take effect at a point in time before that at which it actually comes to the attention of the offeror. The most obvious example of this is the *Adams v Lindsell*[193] postal rule.[194] It may also apply, however, in relation to, for example, acceptances by telex, fax or email, which are received during office hours but not read until some time later, or messages left on a telephone answering machine. As we have seen, the law provides no clear answer to the question of when acceptance takes effect in such cases but if it is decided that the relevant time is when the acceptance is received on the offeror's machine, rather than when it is read, there is again a delay between acceptance and actual communication, which may lead to the possibility of a retraction. The rest of this section will discuss the issue in relation to posted acceptances but the principles should surely apply in the same way to any acceptance where there is a delay between the point in time when the law says that the acceptance takes effect (for example, on posting or being printed by the offeror's fax machine) and when it is read by the offeror.

---

191  Regulation 31(2).
192  Regulations 31(3).
193  (1818) 1 B & Ald 681; 106 ER 250.
194  See above, 2.12.6.

### 2.14.3 FORMALIST APPROACH

If a 'formalist' approach is taken to this issue,[195] attempting to apply the established principles 'logically', then the answer must be that no retraction of an acceptance is possible. The general rule that a contract is complete on acceptance should be applied. So even if the acceptor is able, for example, by telephoning the offeror to indicate that an acceptance that is in the post should be ignored, the offeror should be entitled to say: 'Too bad! Your acceptance took effect on posting, and we have a contract. If you fail to go through with it, you will be in breach.'

### 2.14.4 PURPOSIVE APPROACH

This is not the only possible approach, however. It might also be argued that the purpose of the postal rule is to provide a benefit to the acceptor. As we have seen, the main reason for the decision in *Adams v Lindsell* was that such a rule allowed the acceptor to proceed on the basis that a contract had been made and that this promoted business efficiency. If that is the case, it might be argued that it is a little odd to then apply the rule in a way that is to the acceptor's disadvantage. Moreover, if, as must be the case for there to be any possibility of retraction, we are considering a point in time at which the offeror is as yet unaware of the acceptance, how can there be any harm in allowing the acceptor to withdraw? The offeror cannot in any way have acted on the acceptance, and so can suffer no harm from its retraction. There seems little point in forcing people to go through with a contract, when one party no longer wishes to proceed and the other party is unaware of the fact that there is a contract at all.

### 2.14.5 UNFAIRNESS TO OFFEROR

To allow withdrawal is said by some to be too favourable to the acceptor. The example is given of an acceptance of an offer to buy shares or goods that have a greatly fluctuating market price. If retraction of acceptance is allowed, then it is said that this gives the acceptor the best of both worlds. The offer can be accepted by posting a letter, which will bind the offeror. Then, if before the acceptance is read, the market price falls below the contract price, the acceptor can avoid what has now become a bad bargain by telephoning a withdrawal.[196] This could be regarded as 'unfair'. In an argument that is the converse of the one put forward in the last paragraph, it is sometimes argued that the postal rule exists for the benefit of the acceptor. It is tipping the scales too far in the acceptor's favour, however, to allow the possibility of retraction as well: a possibility that is not available in any other situation.

### 2.14.6 GUIDANCE FROM AUTHORITY

Attempts to argue the case from first principles, then, may lead to different conclusions. Three possibilities have been outlined above, one in favour of allowing retraction, the other two against. This author's preferred view is the pragmatic one of allowing retraction but this is by no means widely accepted. Unfortunately, there is little help from case law either.

The only UK case to deal with the issue at all is *Countess of Dunmore v Alexander*.[197] This is a Scottish case, which on one reading appears to support the view that a posted acceptance can be retracted by speedier means. The case is not a strong authority, however, since it is not absolutely clear that the court considered that the communication that was withdrawn was an acceptance, rather than an offer. Two cases from other common

---

195  See Chapter 1, 1.9.2.
196  See, for example, Treitel, 2015, p 30. Hudson, 1966, sets out a variety of reasons why Treitel's view on this point should not be accepted.
197  (1830) 9 Shaw 190.

law jurisdictions suggest the opposite. In *Wenckheim v Arndt*[198] and *A to Z Bazaars (Pty) Ltd v Minister of Agriculture*,[199] it was held that the attempt to withdraw the acceptance was not effective.[200]

A court in England and Wales faced with this issue would be free to decide it without any clear guidance from authority. The answer that is given will depend on which of the various possibilities outlined above is the more attractive. It is not unlikely that the court's decision in a particular case will be influenced by what the court sees as the best way to achieve justice between the parties, rather than on any preference based on general principle.

## 2.15 CERTAINTY IN OFFER AND ACCEPTANCE

Even though the parties may have appeared to make an agreement by the exchange of a matching offer and acceptance, the courts may refuse to enforce it if there appears to be uncertainty about what has been agreed or if some important aspect of the agreement is left open to be decided later. In *Scammell v Ouston*,[201] for example, the parties had agreed to the supply of a lorry on 'hire purchase terms'. The House of Lords held that in the absence of any other evidence of the details of the hire purchase agreement (duration, number of instalments, etc.), this was too vague to be enforceable, and there was therefore no contract.[202]

This does not necessarily mean that all details of a contract must be finally settled in advance. It is not uncommon, for example, in relation to contracts for the supply of services for the precise amount to be paid to be left unspecified at the time of the agreement. If a car is left at a garage for repair, it may not be possible to determine at that stage exactly what the repair will cost because this may depend on what the mechanic finds once work has started. The car owner may well say something along the lines of, 'Do the work, but if it looks as though it will cost more than £150, please contact me before going ahead.' It surely cannot be doubted that there is a contract for repairs up to the value of £150. The court's view of this situation may be that there is in effect an agreement that the customer will pay a 'reasonable price' for the work that is done. What is a reasonable price is a question of fact, which can, if necessary, be determined by the courts. This approach has statutory force in relation to contracts between businesses by virtue of s 15 of the Supply of Goods and Services Act 1982, which states:

(1)  Where ... the consideration for a service is not determined by the contract, left to be determined in a manner agreed by the contract or determined by the course of dealing between the parties, there is an implied term that the party contracting will pay a reasonable charge.
(2)  What is a reasonable charge is a question of fact.

A similar approach applies to consumer contracts by virtue of s 51 of the Consumer Rights Act 2015. The same rule also operates in relation to goods by virtue of the similar provision contained in s 8(2) and (3) of the Sale of Goods Act 1979.

---

198  (1861–1902) 1 JR 73 (New Zealand).
199  (1974) (4) SA 392(C) (South Africa).
200  But cf to the contrary, *Dick v United States* (1949) 113 Ct Cl 94; 82 F Supp 326, discussed in Evans, 1966.
201  [1941] AC 251; [1941] 1 All ER 14.
202  Note that the Court of Appeal had agreed with the judge at first instance that there was sufficient information to find a complete and enforceable agreement: [1940] 1 All ER 59.

The possibility of the courts giving specific content to an apparently vague phrase can apply in other areas apart from the price to be paid for goods or services. In *Hillas v Arcos*,[203] for example, there was a contract to supply timber 'of fair specification'. It was held that in the context of the agreement, which was between parties who knew each other and the timber trade well, and taking account of the fact that there had been part performance, the phrase 'fair specification' must be capable of being given a meaning. The contract was therefore enforceable.

### 2.15.1 MEANINGLESS PHRASES

The decision in *Scammell v Ouston*[204] might be thought to open the door to an unscrupulous party to include some meaningless phrase in an agreement, which would then allow him or her to escape from the contract if he or she wished on the basis of uncertainty. To have such an effect, however, the phrase must relate to some significant aspect of the contract. If it can be deleted and still leave a perfectly workable agreement, the courts may ignore it. This was the position in *Nicolene v Simmonds*,[205] where the contractual documentation contained the statement 'we are in agreement that the usual conditions of acceptance apply'. Since there were no 'usual conditions', it was held that this was simply a meaningless phrase, which could be ignored. There was nothing left open that needed to be determined.

### 2.15.2 INCOMPLETE AGREEMENTS

If an agreement leaves undecided, and undeterminable, some important aspect of the contract, then the courts will not enforce it. This can arise where perfectly clear words are used, about the meaning of which there is no dispute, but which do not settle some significant part of the contractual terms. In *May and Butcher v R*,[206] for example, the agreement provided that the price and the date of payment, under a contract of sale, was to be 'agreed upon from time to time'. The House of Lords held that there was no contract. The parties had not left the price open – when, as we have seen, a 'reasonable price' would have been payable – they had specifically stated that they would agree in the future. The contract contained an arbitration clause but the House of Lords considered that this was only meant to be used in the event of disputes and could not be the means of determining basic obligations.

The traditional refusal to give effect to an 'agreement to agree' was followed in *Courtney and Fairbairn Ltd v Tolaini Brothers (Hotels) Ltd*.[207] In this case there had been negotiations concerning property development. The plaintiffs, the prospective developers, were in a position to raise finance for the defendants, who were the owners of the property that was to be developed. This they did, in the expectation of being awarded the development contract. In the event, this contract was given to another firm, using the finance arranged by the plaintiffs. The plaintiffs argued that they had a contract with the defendants under which it was promised that if the plaintiffs arranged the finance, they would be awarded the development contract. The Court of Appeal disagreed. The letter that was alleged to provide evidence of this contract talked about the 'negotiation of fair and reasonable sums' for the project, based on 'agreed estimates'. This, the court felt, was far too vague to form the basis of determining the price in a major construction contract. Nor could there be a 'contract to negotiate'. Again it would be too uncertain to have binding force:[208]

---

203 (1932) 147 LT 503.
204 See above, 2.15.
205 [1963] 1 QB 543; [1953] 1 All ER 822.
206 [1934] 2 KB 17.
207 [1975] 1 WLR 297.
208 That is they arguably adhered to the myth of 'presentation' – see Chapter 1, 1.6.

No court could estimate the damages because no one can tell whether the negotiations would be successful or would fall through; or if successful, what the result would be.

This conclusion was approved by the House of Lords in the following case.

**Key case** *Walford v Miles* (1992)[209]

Facts: The parties had reached agreement on the basic terms of the sale of a business. This was 'subject to contract'. The defendants, the vendors, separately agreed that they would cease negotiations with anyone else. Subsequently, however, they sold to a third party. The plaintiffs sought damages for breach of a collateral contract not to negotiate with anyone else, which they also contended implied a positive obligation on the defendants to negotiate in good faith with them.

Held: The House of Lords confirmed that there could not be a 'contract to negotiate'. The positive obligation alleged was therefore ruled out on the basis of the reasons given in *Courtney v Tolaini*. As regards the 'lock-out' agreement not to negotiate with anyone else, this was similarly unenforceable on grounds of uncertainty since it was for an unspecified time. It was not satisfactory to argue that it should continue for a 'reasonable time'. A reasonable time would only come to an end when negotiations broke down completely; thus, it would indirectly involve an obligation to negotiate in good faith, which the House had already rejected as too uncertain.

This decision has been the subject of considerable academic comment,[210] in part because it can be seen as the House of Lords turning its back on the concept of 'good faith' in contracts,[211] which is commonly part of the law in other jurisdictions.[212] It can be seen as asserting an individualist, adversarial approach to contract, which emphasises in particular 'party freedom'.[213] In doing so, it can be said to be ignoring the reality of business transactions, which commonly do not operate on this basis.

*Walford v Miles* did, however, leave open the possibility that a 'lock-out' agreement not to negotiate with anyone else, which is sufficiently limited in terms of time, might be enforceable. That this is indeed possible was confirmed by the Court of Appeal in *Pitt v PHH Asset Management Ltd*.[214] The parties were in negotiations over the sale of a property and the plaintiffs, the prospective purchasers, were concerned that the defendants would accept a higher offer from a third party. An agreement was arrived at under which, in return for the plaintiffs agreeing to exchange contracts within two weeks, the defendants agreed not to consider any further offers within that period. The defendants went back on this agreement and sold to the third party at a price above that which the plaintiffs had offered. The Court of Appeal held that, in this case, the 'lock-out' agreement was

---

209 [1992] 2 AC 128; [1992] 1 All ER 453.
210 See, for example, Brown, 1992; Buckley, 1993; Cumberbatch, 1992; Neill, 1992; Steyn, 1997, p 439. Lord Steyn expressed the hope that if the matter were to be raised again 'with the benefit of fuller argument ... the concept of good faith would not be rejected out of hand'. See also the discussion of 'good faith' in Chapter 1, 1.11.
211 See, for example, Brownsword, 2006, p 149.
212 See Chapter 1, 1.11.
213 See, for example, Cumberbatch, 1992, p 173.
214 [1993] 4 All ER 961; [1994] 1 WLR 327.

sufficiently specific to be binding, and the plaintiffs' action against the defendants for damages for breach of this agreement was therefore successful.

### 2.15.3 IN FOCUS: CONTRACTUAL PRINCIPLE VERSUS COMMERCIAL REALITY

This reluctance to allow for the kind of arrangement that the parties had put into their contract in *May and Butcher v R* can be seen as an example of the courts in England and Wales refusing to take account of the ongoing, relational nature of many contracts.[215] Instead, they expect all facets of the contract to be determined at the outset, and very little scope is allowed for the modification and development of obligations over its existence. The practice of the courts thus becomes divorced from the commercial reality of the business relationship of the parties. As was seen in Chapter 1,[216] some recent cases have started to take more account of the ongoing, or 'relational' nature of many contracts between businesses.

### 2.15.4 OBLIGATIONS DISTINGUISHED FROM 'MACHINERY'

The contract will not be regarded as incomplete if it provides a machinery for resolving an aspect that has been left uncertain. As we have seen, in relation to the price the courts will sometimes be prepared to assume that a 'reasonable price' was intended. They will also be prepared to give effect to an agreement where property is to be valued by an independent valuer, or where the price is to be determined by reference to the prevailing market price. In such situations, the contract provides a mechanism by which the uncertainty can be resolved.

In some cases, however, the courts have been prepared to stretch this principle rather further than might have been expected. In *Sudbrook Trading Estate v Eggleton*,[217] the price for the exercise of an option to purchase was to be determined by two valuers, one to be nominated by each party. One party refused to appoint a valuer and claimed that the agreement was therefore void for uncertainty. The House of Lords disagreed. The contract was not uncertain in that it provided a clear machinery by which the price was to be determined. This machinery was not, however, itself an essential term of the contract. It was simply a way of establishing a 'fair' price. If the machinery failed, then the court could substitute its own means of determining what was a fair price. This approach was relied on by the Court of Appeal in *Didymi Corp v Atlantic Lines and Navigation Co Inc.*[218] The agreement contained a provision under which the hire under a charter of a ship could in some circumstances be increased 'equitably' by an amount 'to be mutually agreed between the parties'. At first sight, this looks like an 'agreement to agree', which would be unenforceable. The court, however, following the lead given by *Sudbrook Trading Estate v Eggleton*, ruled that the reference to 'mutual agreement' was simply part of the 'inessential machinery' by which the hire was to be determined. The agreement was that the hire should be 'equitable', which meant 'fair and reasonable'. There was therefore no reason why the court should not determine this as a question of fact.[219]

---

215  Chapter 1, 1.6.
216  Chapter 1, 1.6.
217  [1982] 3 All ER 1. Compare *Manchester Ship Canal Co Ltd v Environment Agency* [2017] EWHC 1340 (QB).
218  [1987] 2 Lloyd's Rep 166, affirmed on appeal: [1988] 2 Lloyd's Rep. 108. See also *Re Malpass* [1985] Ch 42.
219  A similar approach was taken by the Court of Appeal in *Mamidoil-Jetoil Greek Petroleum Co SA v Okta Crude Refinery AD* [2001] EWCA CIV 406; [2001] 2 All ER Comm 193.

In *Gillatt v Sky Television Ltd*,[220] the Court of Appeal, while not disagreeing with the approach taken in the *Sudbrook Trading Estate* or *Didymi Corp* cases, held on the facts that the valuation clause under consideration was not merely a mechanism for dispute resolution. The clause provided that the claimant was entitled to 55 per cent of the open market value of certain shares, 'as determined by an independent chartered accountant'. This provision was distinguishable from the clauses in the earlier authorities because there was no objective meaning to be given to 'open market value' in that there were different bases on which shares could be valued. The reference to the independent accountant as the determiner of the value was, therefore, an essential element in that process, and not simply 'machinery'. Moreover, this was not a case where the mechanism for dispute resolution had broken down; under the contract either party could have taken steps towards the appointment of the valuer, but neither had chosen to do so. In these circumstances, the Court of Appeal agreed with the trial judge that the claimant was not entitled to any payment under the contract.

The question of whether a particular valuation provision is 'essential' to the determination of an amount to be made or simply 'machinery' will therefore depend on the precise wording of the clause and the context in which it operates. If it appears that there is no basis for determining the relevant value when essential procedures in the contract have not been followed, then the courts will still be prepared, even in a commercial context, to say that there is no agreement and therefore no binding obligation. The parties should not, therefore, rely on the courts coming to their rescue if they fail to follow the procedures that they have set out in their agreement. In some circumstances they will do so, but the determination of whether particular provisions are 'essential' or simply 'machinery' is sufficiently unpredictable that reliance on the court to intervene is a dangerous option.

The lack of coherence in this distinction suggests that the courts recognise the problems which the classical theory's insistence on 'presentation' brings,[221] but are reluctant to find a proper method of addressing them. They must adhere to the myth that the parties will have fully determined all future obligations at the moment of contracting, even when this clearly does not accord with the parties' actual intentions or the requirements of business. The result is the unsatisfactory and unhelpful distinction between 'obligations' and 'machinery'.

An incomplete agreement, which is not regarded as creating an enforceable contract, may nevertheless give rise to some legal obligations between the parties under the law of 'restitution'. This is discussed further in Chapter 15.

## 2.16 SUMMARY OF KEY POINTS

- Formality is not generally required in making a contract, just a matching offer and acceptance. Exceptions include contracts concerning land and some consumer credit agreements.

- An offer must be distinguished from an invitation to treat. Displays of goods and advertisements are usually invitations to treat.

- An acceptance to be effective must precisely match the offer. Introduction of new terms will constitute a 'counter-offer' rather than an acceptance.

---

220  [2000] 1 All ER Comm 461.
221  See Chapter 1, 1.6.

- Acceptance can be by words or conduct but must generally be communicated to the offeror. In some unilateral contracts (e.g. reward advertisements), the need for communication may be waived.

- Acceptance by post generally takes effect on posting. Acceptance by telephone or electronic means may take effect when the acceptance is received (though physical receipt, rather than being read, may be sufficient for communications in office hours).

- An offer can generally be withdrawn at any time before acceptance, even if the offeror has indicated that it will be left open for a particular time. Revocation must be communicated to the offeree.

- In some unilateral contracts, revocation may not be permitted once performance has started.

- If an agreement is uncertain on an important issue, or leaves it open to be decided, there may be no contract. An 'agreement to agree' is not a binding contract.

## 2.17 FURTHER READING

### Finding agreement
- Howarth, W, 'The meaning of objectivity in contract' (1984) 100 LQR 205

- McClintock, R, 'Objectivity in contract' (1988–91) 6 Auckland UL Rev 317

- Mitchell, C, 'Contracts and contract law: challenging the distinction between the "real" and "paper" deal' (2009) 29 OJLS 675

- Mitchell, P and Phillips, J, 'The contractual nexus: is reliance essential?' (2002) 22 OJLS 115

- Rawlings, R, 'The battle of the forms' (1979) 42 MLR 715

- Steyn, J, 'Contract law: fulfilling the reasonable expectations of honest men' (1997) 113 LQR 433

- Stone, R, 'Forming contracts without offer and acceptance, Lord Denning and the harmonisation of English contract law' [2012] WebJCLI

### The postal rule
- Evans, D M, 'The Anglo-American mailing rule' (1966) 15 ICLQ 553

- Gardner, S, 'Trashing with Trollope: A deconstruction of the postal rules' (1992) 12 OJLS 170

- Goodrich, P, 'The posthumous life of the postal rule: requiem and revival of *Adams v Lindsell*', Chapter 4 in Mulcahy, L and Wheeler, S, *Feminist Perspectives on Contract Law*, 2005, London: Glasshouse Press

Hudson, A H, 'Retraction of letters of acceptance' (1966) 82 LQR 169

Macdonald, E, 'Dispatching the dispatch rule? The postal rule, email, revocation and implied terms' (2013) 19(2) WebJCLI

## COMPANION WEBSITE

*Now visit the companion website to:*

Revise and consolidate your knowledge of Formation by tackling a series of multiple-choice questions on this chapter

Test your understanding of the chapter's key terms by using the flashcard glossary

Fine-tune your legal skills by reading our tips and suggestions for Formation problem questions

Explore Formation further by accessing a series of web links

# Consideration and other tests of enforceability

**Contents**

## 3.1 OVERVIEW

This chapter is concerned with the issue of the enforceability of promises. How does English law decide whether a promise is to be treated as enforceable by the courts? In investigating this question, the following topics will be considered:

- Deeds. These constitute a means of indicating an intention to make an enforceable promise through formal means – that is, putting the promise into a particular type of document.
- Consideration. The doctrine of 'consideration' is one of the hallmarks of English contract law. It means, in effect, that promises usually do not have to take any particular form, or be put in writing, but will be enforceable if there is mutuality in the agreement – both parties bring something to it. Within this doctrine it will be necessary to consider:
  - ☐ What constitutes 'consideration'? Does it have to have a monetary value?
  - ☐ What is meant by the requirement that consideration must be 'sufficient', though not necessarily 'adequate'?
  - ☐ Can an action already performed (past consideration) be consideration for a new promise? (Generally, it cannot.)
  - ☐ When will the performance of an existing duty constitute good consideration? The answer will depend on the type of duty.
- Promissory estoppel. This doctrine allows a promise unsupported by consideration to be, to some extent, enforced – generally in the context of the variation of an existing contract.
- Part payment of debts. Generally, part payment of a debt is not good consideration for the remission of the balance, unless promissory estoppel applies.
- Alternative tests of enforceability. Other jurisdictions may use 'reliance' as a test of enforceability alongside consideration. To date, English law has made limited use of this test.

## 3.2 INTRODUCTION

In the previous chapter, the factors that lead a court to conclude that there is sufficient 'agreement' for there to be a binding contract were discussed. In this chapter the focus is on the question of whether all agreements that meet the requirements set out in that chapter will be treated as *legally* binding. The answer is 'no' – agreement is a necessary but not sufficient condition for a binding legal agreement. The English courts have developed other tests to assess the enforceability of agreements. The principal one is the requirement of 'consideration' and analysis of this doctrine will form the bulk of this chapter.

In essence, the doctrine of consideration requires that both sides to the agreement bring something to the bargain – if the obligations are all on one side then there will be no 'consideration' and probably no contract. This requirement of consideration is a particular characteristic of the common law approach to contractual obligations – it is generally not found in the same form in jurisdictions whose contract law is not based on English law. It is not without its problems. There are difficulties in deciding, for example, whether doing, or promising to do, something that you are already obliged to do (e.g. under another contract, or as part of a public duty) can be good consideration. Problems also arise in the context of the variation of contracts. To what extent are parties who are involved in an ongoing contractual relationship able to create binding variations to that contract, for example, as a result of changed circumstances? English contract law does not make this process easy. It has also traditionally taken a very strict line on the issue of whether a creditor who promises to forgo the balance of a debt on receipt of part payment can be held to that promise.

In response to some of these problems, the English courts have developed an equitable concept that is now generally referred to as 'promissory estoppel'. This is a secondary test of the enforceability of a promise, which does not replace 'consideration' but operates in certain specific situations, particularly in relation to the variation of contracts and the part payment of debts, to mitigate the strict application of the common law doctrine. Some analysts of the concept of promissory estoppel go further and argue that it is simply an example of a more wide-ranging test of enforceability that should be regarded as sitting alongside or even replacing consideration. This argument might be based around the concept of 'reasonable reliance'. This approach has received more acceptance in other common law jurisdictions (e.g. the USA, Australia) than it has in the English courts. The issues raised by this analysis are discussed towards the end of this chapter.

The final route to enforceability discussed in this chapter is the 'deed'. This is a route based on the form of the agreement, rather than its content, and can operate to make one-sided agreements (such as the promise to make a gift) enforceable, even though there is no consideration for the promise.

These tests of enforceability are not necessarily conclusive of the issue, however. The courts may still insist on asking the question as to whether an agreement that contains offer, acceptance, and consideration, was actually intended to be legally binding. The discussion of this concept of 'intention to create legal relations' is left to Chapter 4.

The chapter starts with a discussion of 'deeds' and then looks at consideration, promissory estoppel and 'reasonable reliance'.

## 3.3 DEEDS

The 'deed' is a way of using a particular method to record an agreement and to give it enforceability. The agreement is put in writing and, traditionally, 'sealed' by the party or parties to be bound to it. The 'seal' could take the form of a wax seal, a seal 'embossed' onto the document by a special stamp, or simply the attachment of an adhesive paper seal (usually red).[1] Such contracts were also known as 'contracts under seal' (in contrast to 'simple contracts' that use 'consideration' as the test of enforceability).

The formal requirements for making a 'deed' are now contained in s 1 of the Law of Property (Miscellaneous Provisions) Act 1989.[2] There is no longer any requirement that the document should be sealed.[3] The document must, however, make it clear 'on its face' that it is intended to be a deed and it must be 'validly executed' by the person making it or the parties to it.[4] 'Valid execution' for an individual means that the document must be signed in the presence of a witness who attests to the signature.[5] In addition there is a requirement of delivery – the document must be 'delivered as a deed'.[6] For a company incorporated under the Companies Acts, the position is partly governed by ss

---

1   Indeed, it was probably sufficient for the document to indicate on its face that it was 'sealed', without the need for any physical 'sealing' – see *First National Securities Ltd v Jones* [1978] Ch 109; Law Commission, Working Paper No 93, paras 4.2–4.3.
2   This followed from the Law Commission Report No 163, *Deeds and Escrows*.
3   Section 1(1)(b); nor is there any limitation on the substances on which a deed may be written. At one time, deeds were traditionally written on parchment rather than paper.
4   Section 1(2).
5   Section 1(3)(a). It may also be signed at the relevant person's direction but it must still be in his presence and, in this case, in the presence of two witnesses who must each attest the signature.
6   Section 1(3)(b).

44 and 46 of the Companies Act 2006. The 'execution' of a document by a company can take effect either by the affixing of its common seal,[7] or by being signed by two authorised signatories or a director in the presence of a witness or attests the signature.[8] For a document executed by a company to be a deed, it simply needs to make clear on its face that this is what is intended by whoever created it.[9] It will take effect as a deed upon delivery but, unless a contrary intention is proved, it is presumed to be delivered upon being executed.[10] In *OTV Birwelco Ltd v Technical and General Guarantee Co Ltd*,[11] it was held that a deed was validly executed where a company had used its trading name rather than its registered name; nor did it render the deed unenforceable that the seal used was engraved with the trading name rather than the registered name (contrary to s 350 of the Companies Act 1985 – now replaced by s 45 of the Companies Act 2006). Non-compliance with this section rendered the company concerned liable to a fine but had no automatic effect on the validity of the deed.

If the parties to an agreement have taken the trouble to put it into the form of a deed, following the requirements laid down by s 1 of the 1989 Act (and s 44 of the Companies Act 2006), the courts will assume that it was their intention to create a legally binding agreement, and will not inquire into whether the other main test of enforceability (that is, 'consideration') is present. As will be seen below, the characteristic of the modern doctrine of consideration is that there is mutuality in the arrangement, with something being supplied by both parties to the agreement. This is not necessary in an agreement that is put into the form of a deed. Where, therefore, a transaction is 'one-sided' with only one party giving, and the other party receiving, all the benefit without providing anything in exchange, the deed is one certain way of making the arrangement enforceable.

### 3.3.1 IN FOCUS: PRACTICAL USE OF DEEDS

Deeds may be used even where the transaction is supported by consideration.[12] This has traditionally been done in relation to complex contracts in the engineering and construction industries. This is probably because, by virtue of the Limitation Act 1980, the period within which an action for breach of an obligation contained in a deed is 12 years,[13] whereas for a 'simple' contract it is only six years.[14] The longer period is clearly an advantage in a contract where problems may not become apparent for a number of years. The practice of 'sealing' a document is also still used, even though it is no longer necessary even for a company. It may in some circumstances serve to make it clear that the document is intended to be a 'deed'. It does not in itself, however, make the transactions concerned any more or less enforceable.

### 3.4 CONSIDERATION OR RELIANCE?

For agreements that are not made in the form of a deed, 'consideration' is generally used as the test of enforceability and it is to this that we now turn.

The doctrine of consideration is one of the characteristics of classical English contract law. This provides that no matter how much the parties to a 'simple contract' may wish

---

7 Section 44(1).
8 Section 44(2). The document should make it clear that it is being executed by the company.
9 Law of Property (Miscellaneous Provisions) Act 1989, s 1(2).
10 Companies Act 2006, s 46(2).
11 [2002] EWHC 2240 (TCC); [2002] 4 All ER 668.
12 Sometimes a contract must be made by deed to have full effect: see Law of Property Act 1925, ss 52 and 54(2).
13 Limitation Act 1980, s 8(1). See also *Liberty Partnership Ltd v Tancred* [2018] EWHC 2707.
14 Ibid, s 5.

it to be legally enforceable, it will not be so unless it contains 'consideration'. What does the word mean in this context? It is important to note that it does not have its ordinary, everyday meaning. It is used in a technical sense. Essentially, it refers to what one party to an agreement is giving, or promising, in exchange for what is being given or promised from the other side. So, for example, in a contract where A is selling B 10 bags of grain for £100, what is the consideration? A is transferring the ownership of the grain to B. In consideration of this, B is paying £100. Or, to look at it the other way round, B is paying A £100. In consideration for this, A is transferring to B the ownership of the grain. From this example it will be seen that there is consideration on both sides of the agreement. It is this mutuality that makes the agreement enforceable. If B simply agreed to pay A £100, or A simply agreed to give B the grain, there would be no contract. The transaction would be a gift and would broadly not be legally enforceable.

The history of the development of this doctrine is a matter of controversy. Some writers have argued that a study of the history of the English law of contract shows that 'consideration', when first referred to by the judges, meant simply a 'reason' for enforcing a promise.[15] According to this view, such 'reasons' could be wide-ranging. It was only in the late eighteenth century at the earliest,[16] and probably not until the production of the first contract textbooks in the second half of the nineteenth century,[17] that the doctrine of consideration came to be regarded as consisting of the fairly rigid set of rules that it is now generally regarded as comprising. The approach here is to deal with the doctrine as it currently appears to be but to keep in mind that there are alternative tests of contract enforceability. The main alternative is the concept of 'reasonable reliance'. This will be discussed more fully at the end of this chapter[18] but a brief outline will be given here, in order to put the discussion of consideration in a proper perspective.

The concept of reliance as the basis for enforceability is that it is actions, and reliance on those actions, that creates obligations, rather than an exchange of promises (as under the classical doctrine of consideration). Thus, the window cleaner who, having checked that you want your windows cleaned, then does the work, does so in reliance on the fact that you will pay for what has been done. This is suggested to be a more accurate way of analysing many contractual situations than in terms of the mutual exchanges of promises, which forms the paradigmatic contract under the classical model.[19] Once this principle is accepted, it then opens the door to enforcing agreements where there is nothing that the classical law would recognise as 'consideration', provided that there is 'reasonable reliance'. This is accepted to a greater or lesser extent by many common law jurisdictions,[20] but has only received limited support to date by the English courts – though some recent decisions purportedly based on 'consideration' can be argued to be more accurately concerned with 'reliance'.[21]

We will return towards the end of the chapter to consider further questions about the theoretical basis of consideration,[22] and whether it is developing in a way that may perhaps have links to its historical origins. At that point it will also be worth looking more generally at the question of whether consideration still retains its dominant position at the heart of the English law of contract, or whether the growth in situations where promises

---

15 See, for example, Simpson, 1975a, Chapters IV-VII, and in particular p 321; Atiyah, 1986, Chapter 8. This is discussed in more detail below, at 3.15.1.
16 See, for example, *Rann v Hughes* (1778) 7 Term Rep 350n; 4 Bro PC 27.
17 For example, Anson's *Law of Contract,* first published in 1879.
18 See below, 3.15.2.
19 See Chapter 1, 1.2.
20 For example, the United States, Australia, New Zealand and Canada – see below, 3.15.2.
21 For example, *Williams v Roffey Bros & Nicholls (Contractors) Ltd* [1991] 1 QB 1; [1990] 1 All ER 512 – discussed below, 3.9.9.
22 See below, 3.15.1.

may be enforceable in the absence of consideration means that its role needs further reassessment. In the meantime, in the discussion of consideration in the following sections, the tension between the classical theory and the more modern trends towards reliance-based liability needs to be kept in mind, and will be highlighted at various points.

## 3.5 BENEFIT AND DETRIMENT

It is sometimes said that consideration requires benefit and detriment. The often quoted, but not particularly helpful, definition of consideration contained in *Currie v Misa*[23] refers to these elements:

> A valuable consideration, in the sense of the law, may consist either in some right, interest, profit or benefit accruing to one party or some forbearance, detriment, loss or responsibility, given, suffered or undertaken by the other.

In other words, what is provided by way of consideration should be a benefit to the person receiving it or a detriment to the person giving it. Sometimes, both are present. For example, in the contract concerning the sale of grain discussed in the previous section, B is suffering a detriment by paying the £100, and A is gaining a benefit by receiving the £100. B is gaining a benefit in receiving the grain, A is suffering a detriment by losing it. In many cases, there will thus be both benefit and detriment involved but it is not necessary that this should be the case. Benefit to one party, or detriment to the other, will be enough. Suppose that A agrees to transfer the grain, if B pays £100 to charity. In this case, B's consideration in paying the £100 is a detriment to B, but, at least in one sense, not a benefit to A. Nevertheless, B's act is good consideration and there may be a contract. In theory, it is enough that the recipient of the consideration receives a benefit, without the giver suffering a detriment. It is difficult, however, to think of common practical examples of a situation of this kind, given that the traditional rule is that consideration must move from the promisee.

## 3.6 MUTUAL PROMISES

The discussion so far has been in terms of acts constituting consideration. It is quite clear, however, that a *promise* to act can in itself be consideration. Lord Dunedin, in *Dunlop Pneumatic Tyre Co Ltd v Selfridge & Co Ltd*,[24] for example, approved the following statement from Pollock, 1902 (emphasis added):

> An act or forbearance of the one party, *or the promise thereof*, is the price for which the promise of the other is bought, and the promise thus given for value is enforceable.

Suppose, then, continuing the example used above, that on Monday A promises that he will deliver and transfer the ownership of the grain to B on the following Friday; and B promises, again on Monday, that when it is delivered she will pay £100. There is no doubt that there is a contract as soon as these promises have been exchanged, so that if on Tuesday B decides that she does not want the grain and tries to back out of the agreement,

---

23 (1875) LR 10 Ex 153.
24 [1915] AC 847.

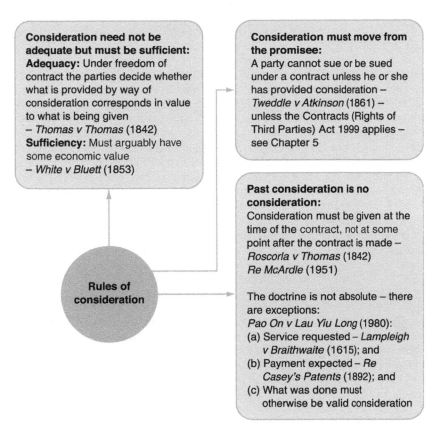

Figure 3.1

she will be in breach of contract. But where is the consideration? On each side, the giving of the promise is the consideration. A's promise to transfer the grain is consideration for B's promise to pay for it, and vice versa. The problem is that this does not fit easily with the idea of benefit and detriment. A's promise is only a benefit to B, and a detriment to A, if it is enforceable. But it will only be enforceable if it is a benefit or a detriment. The argument is circular, and cannot therefore explain why promises are accepted as good consideration.[25] There is no easy answer to this paradox,[26] but the undoubted acceptance by the courts of promises as good consideration casts some doubt on whether benefit and detriment can truly be said to be essential parts of the definition of consideration. It may be that the concept simply requires the performance of, or the promise to perform, some action that the other party would like to be done. This approach ignores the actual or potential detriment. Alternatively, if it is thought that the idea of benefit and detriment is too well established to be discarded, the test must arguably be restated so that consideration is provided where a person performs an act that will be a detriment to him or her or a benefit to the other party, or promises to perform such an act. On this analysis, benefit and detriment are not so much essential elements of consideration, as necessary consequences of its performance.

---

25  Cf Atiyah, 1986, p 191.
26  Though Treitel has suggested that an unenforceable promise may nevertheless constitute a benefit or detriment – Treitel, 1976.

## 3.7 CONSIDERATION NEED NOT BE 'ADEQUATE' BUT MUST BE 'SUFFICIENT'

The view that the element of 'mutuality' is the most important aspect of the doctrine of consideration is perhaps supported by the fact that the courts will not generally inquire into the 'adequacy' of consideration. 'Adequacy' means the question of whether what is provided by way of consideration corresponds in value to what it is being given for. This is to be distinguished from the question of whether consideration is 'sufficient', in the sense that what is being offered in exchange is recognised by the courts as being in law capable of amounting to consideration. This issue is discussed further below.

Looking first, however, at the question of adequacy, the reluctance of the courts to investigate this means, for example, that if I own a car valued at £20,000 and I agree to sell it to you for £1, the courts will treat this as a binding contract.[27] Your agreement to pay £1 provides sufficient consideration for my transfer of ownership of the car, even though it is totally 'inadequate' in terms of its relationship to the value of the car.

This aspect of consideration was confirmed in *Thomas v Thomas*.[28]

---

**Key case** *Thomas v Thomas* (1842)

Facts: The testator, Mr Thomas, before his death, expressed a wish that his wife should have for the rest of her life the house in which they had lived. After his death, his executors made an agreement with Mrs Thomas to this effect, expressed to be 'in consideration' of the testator's wishes. There was also an obligation on Mrs Thomas to pay £1 per year and to keep the house in repair. It was argued that there was no contract here because Mrs Thomas had provided no sufficient consideration.

Held: The statement that the agreement was 'in consideration' of the testator's wishes was not using 'consideration' in its technical contractual sense but was expressing the motive for making the agreement. The actual 'consideration' was the payment of £1 and the agreement to keep the house in repair. Either of these was clearly recognised as good consideration, even though the payment of £1 could in no way be regarded as anything approaching a commercial rent for the property.

---

This approach to the question of 'adequacy' may be seen as flowing from a 'freedom of contract' approach. The parties are regarded as being entitled to make their agreement in whatever form, and on whatever terms they wish. The fact that one of the parties appears to be making a bad bargain is no reason for the court's interference. They are presumed to be able to look after themselves, and it is only if there is some evidence of impropriety that the court will inquire further.[29] The mere fact that there is an apparent imbalance, even a very large one, in the value of what is being exchanged under the contract, will not normally in itself be the catalyst for such further inquiry. It might be thought that with the decline of the dominance of 'freedom of contract' during the twentieth century, this aspect

---

27  This assumes that there is no evidence of any improper behaviour on the part of the purchaser to induce the sale at such a low price, such as misrepresentation (see Chapter 8), duress (see Chapter 10) or the exercise of 'undue influence' (see Chapter 11).

28  (1842) 2 QB 851.

29  See note 27, above. Campbell has argued that the fact that there appear to be exceptions to the basic principle, in that adequacy *will* be relevant in raising suspicions of, for example, duress or undue influence, means that this basic principle of classical theory is 'metaphysical nonsense': Campbell, 1996, p 44.

of the doctrine of consideration might have also weakened, but there is no evidence of this from the case law.[30]

## 3.7.1 ECONOMIC VALUE

Turning to the question of the 'sufficiency' of consideration (that is, whether what is offered is *capable* of amounting to consideration), in coming to its conclusion in *Thomas v Thomas*, the court pointed out that consideration must be 'something which is of some value in the eye of the law'.[31] This has generally been interpreted to mean that it must have some economic value. Thus, the moral obligation which the executors might have felt, or been under, to comply with the testator's wishes would not have been sufficient to create consideration (perhaps in the form of a sense of relief in having been able to achieve the testator's wish). An example of the application of this principle may perhaps be found in the case of *White v Bluett*.[32] A father promised not to enforce a promissory note (that is, a document acknowledging a debt) against his son, provided that the son stopped complaining about the distribution of his father's property. It was held that this was not an enforceable agreement, because the son had not provided any consideration. As Pollock CB explained:[33]

> The son had no right to complain, for the father might make what distribution of his property he liked; and the son's abstaining from what he had no right to do can be no consideration.

The courts have not been consistent in this approach, however. In the American case of *Hamer v Sidway*,[34] a promise not to drink alcohol, smoke tobacco or swear was held to be good consideration, and in *Ward v Byham*[35] it was suggested that a promise to ensure that a child was happy could be good consideration.

Even in cases that have a more obvious commercial context, the requirement of economic value does not seem to have been applied very strictly. An example is *Chappell & Co v Nestlé Co Ltd*.[36]

---

**Key case** *Chappell & Co v Nestlé Co Ltd* (1960)

Facts: This case arose out of a 'special offer' of a familiar kind, from Nestlé, under which a person who sent in three wrappers from bars of their chocolate could buy a record, *Rockin' Shoes*, at a special price. For the purpose of the law of copyright, it was important to decide whether the chocolate wrappers were part of the consideration in the contract to buy the record.
Held: The House of Lords decided that the wrappers were part of the consideration, despite the fact that it was established that they were thrown away by Nestlé, and were thus of no direct value to them.

---

30  See, for example, *Chappell & Co Ltd v Nestlé Co Ltd* [1960] AC 87; [1959] 2 All ER 701 – discussed below, 3.7.1.
31  [1842] 2 QB 851, p 859 (per Patteson J).
32  (1853) 23 LJ Ex 36.
33  Ibid, p 37. If the son did actually comply with his father's request, there is an argument that a 'reliance'-based approach would allow the son to recover (subject only to the question of whether this was a situation where there was an intention to create legal obligations – for which, see Chapter 4).
34  (1891) 27 NE 256; 124 NY 538. This case may reflect the greater willingness of United States courts to accept 'reasonable reliance' as a basis for contractual liability – see below, 3.15.2.
35  [1956] 2 All ER 318.
36  [1960] AC 87; [1959] 2 All ER 701.

The only economic value in the wrappers that it is at all possible to discern is that they represented sales of chocolate bars, which was obviously the point of Nestlé's promotion. This is, however, very indirect, particularly as there was no necessity for the person who bought the chocolate to be the same as the person who sent the wrappers in. In contrast to this decision, the House of Lords held in *Lipkin Gorman v Karpnale Ltd*[37] that gambling chips, given in exchange for money by a gambling club to its customers, did not constitute valuable consideration. The case concerned an attempt to recover £154,693 of stolen money that had been received in good faith by the club from a member of the club. If 'good consideration' for the money had been given by the club, then the money could not be recovered by the true owner. What the club had given for the money were plastic chips that could be used for gambling, or to purchase refreshments in the club. Any chips not lost or spent could be reconverted to cash. This was not regarded by the House of Lords as providing consideration for the money but simply as a mechanism for enabling bets to be made without using cash. If the contract had been one for the straightforward purchase of the chips, then presumably the transfer of ownership of the chips to the member would have been good consideration, since the club presumably made such a contract when it bought the chips from the manufacturer or wholesaler. The fact that the amount of money paid by the member far exceeded the intrinsic value of the chips (that is, their value as pieces of coloured plastic, rather than as a means of gambling) would have been irrelevant under the principle discussed above relating to the adequacy of consideration. The conclusion that on the facts before the court the chips themselves were not consideration must, therefore, be regarded as being governed by the situation in which they were provided. The contractual relationship between the member and the club is probably best analysed in the way suggested by Lord Goff, who took the view that the transaction involved a unilateral contract under which the club issuing the chips agreed to accept them as bets or, indeed, in payment for other services provided by the club. The case should not be treated as giving any strong support to the view that consideration must have some economic value.

An example of the lengths to which the courts will sometimes go to identify consideration is *De La Bere v Pearson*.[38] The plaintiff had written to a newspaper that invited readers to write in for financial advice. Some of the readers' letters, together with the newspaper's financial editor's advice, were published. The plaintiff received and followed negligently given advice, which caused him loss. Since the tort of negligent misstatement was at the time unrecognised, the plaintiff had to frame his action in contract. But where was the consideration for the defendants' apparently gratuitous advice? The purchase of the newspaper was one possibility, but there was no evidence that this was done in order to receive advice. The only other possibility, which was favoured by the court, was that the plaintiff, by submitting a letter, had provided free copy that could be published. This was thought to be sufficient consideration for the provision of the advice, which it would be implied should be given with due care.

### For thought

*Loamshire Radio runs a programme called 'Health Check' which operates on the basis of listeners emailing or texting in questions about health problems, which are then answered on air. Is Loamshire Radio entering into a contract with its listeners? If so, does it need to issue disclaimers to protect itself?*

---

37  [1992] 2 AC 548. Compare *London Clubs Management Ltd v Revenue and Customs Commissioners* [2018] EWCA Civ 2210.
38  [1908] 1 KB 280.

*De La Bere v Pearson* is a case that might well be considered to be dealt with better by using 'reasonable reliance' as a basis for liability. If it was reasonable in all the circumstances for the plaintiff to rely on the defendant's advice, and he did so to his detriment, he should be able to recover compensation.[39] Such an approach would be more satisfactory than the technical arguments about consideration in which the court was obliged to indulge in applying the classical theory.

The sufficiency of consideration was considered in a different context in *Edmonds v Lawson*.[40] The Court of Appeal was considering whether there was a contract between a pupil barrister and her chambers in relation to pupillage. The problem was to identify what benefit the pupil would supply to her pupilmaster/mistress or to chambers during the pupillage. The court noted that the pupil was not obliged to do anything that was not conducive to her own professional development. Moreover, where work of real value was done by the pupil, whether for the pupilmaster/mistress or anyone else, there was a professional obligation to remunerate the pupil. This led the court to the conclusion that there was no contract between the pupil and pupilmaster/mistress, because of lack of consideration. It came to a different view, however, as to the relationship between the pupil and her chambers. Chambers have an incentive to attract talented pupils who may compete for tenancies (and thus further the development of the chambers). Even if they do not remain at the chambers (for example, by moving to another set, or working in the employed bar or overseas), there may be advantages in the relationships that will have been established. The conclusion was that:[41]

> On balance, we take the view that pupils such as the claimant provide consideration for the offer made by chambers ... by agreeing to enter into the close, important and potentially very productive relationship which pupillage involves.

The court was therefore prepared to accept the general benefits to chambers in the operation of a pupillage system as being sufficient to amount to consideration in relation to contracts with individual pupils, without defining with any precision the economic value of such benefits.

As these cases illustrate, the requirement of 'economic value' is not particularly strict. Indeed, in the overall pattern of decisions in this area, it is the case of *White v Bluett* (1853) that looks increasingly out of line. The flexibility that the courts have adopted in this area has led Treitel to refer to the concept of 'invented consideration'.[42] This arises where the courts 'regard an act or forbearance as the consideration for a promise even though it may not have been the object of the promisor to secure it'; or 'regard the possibility of some prejudice to the promisee as a detriment without regard to the question of whether it has in fact been suffered'.[43] This analysis has been strongly criticised by Atiyah as an artificial means of reconciling difficult decisions with 'orthodox' doctrine on the nature of consideration.[44] He argues that if something is treated by the courts as consideration, then it is consideration, and that Treitel's 'invented' consideration is in the end the same thing as ordinary consideration. If some cases do not, as a result, fit with orthodox doctrine, then it is the doctrine that needs adjusting.[45]

39 This, in effect, would now be likely to be the position under the tort of negligent misstatement – discussed in Chapter 8, 8.4.4.

40 [2000] 2 WLR 1091.

41 [2000] 2 WLR 1091, p 1101.

42 See Treitel, 1976, and also 2015, 3–009.

43 Ibid.

44 Atiyah, 1986, p 183.

45 Ibid. Atiyah, of course, argues for a broader concept of consideration anyway, as simply being a 'reason' for the enforcement of a promise or obligation. This is discussed further at 3.15.1.

As we have seen, the issue of the 'sufficiency' of consideration looks to the type, or characteristics, of the thing that has been done or promised, rather than to its value. In addition to the requirement of economic value, which as we have seen is applied very flexibly, there are two other issues that must be considered here. The first is the question of so-called 'past consideration'. The second is whether the performance of, or promise to perform, an existing duty can ever amount to consideration.

## 3.8 PAST CONSIDERATION IS NO CONSIDERATION

Consideration must be given at the time of the contract. It is not generally possible to use as consideration some act or forbearance that has taken place *prior* to the contract. Suppose that I take pity on my poverty-stricken niece and give her my old car. If the following week she wins £10,000 on the lottery and says she will now give me £500 out of her winnings as payment for the car, is that promise enforceable? English law says no, because I have provided no consideration for it. My transfer of the car was undertaken and completed without any thought of payment, and before my niece made her promise. This is 'past consideration' and so cannot be used to enforce an agreement. A case that applies this basic principle is *Roscorla v Thomas*.[46] The plaintiff had bought a horse from the defendant. The defendant then promised that the horse was 'sound and free from vice', which turned out to be untrue. The plaintiff was unable to sue on this promise, however, since he had provided no consideration for it. The sale was already complete before the promise was made.

A more recent example of the same approach is *Re McArdle*.[47]

### Key case *Re McArdle* (1951)

Facts: William McArdle left a house to his sons and daughter. One of the sons was living in the house, and he and his wife carried out various improvements to it. His wife then got each of his siblings to sign a document agreeing to contribute to the costs of the work. The document was worded in a way that read as though work was to be done and that, when it was completed, the other members of the family would make their contribution out of their share of William McArdle's estate.

Held: The document did not truly represent the facts. If it had done so, then, of course, it would have constituted a binding contract, but, as Jenkins LJ pointed out:[48]

> The true position was that, as the work had in fact all been done and nothing remained to be done ... at all, the consideration was a wholly past consideration, and therefore the beneficiaries' agreement for the repayment ... of the £488 out of the estate was *nudum pactum*, a promise with no consideration to support it.

This being so, the agreements to pay were unenforceable.

### 3.8.1 THE COMMON LAW EXCEPTIONS

The doctrine of past consideration is not an absolute one, however. The courts have always recognised certain situations where a promise made subsequent to the performance of

---

46  (1842) 3 QB 234.
47  [1951] Ch 669; [1951] 1 All ER 905.
48  Ibid, p 678; p 910.

an act may nevertheless be enforceable. The rules derived from various cases have now been restated as a threefold test by the Privy Council in *Pao On v Lau Yiu Long*.[49] Lord Scarman, delivering the opinion of the Privy Council, recognised that:[50]

> an act done before the giving of a promise to make a payment or to confer some other benefit can sometimes be consideration for the promise.

For the exception to apply, the following three conditions must be satisfied. First, the act must have been done at the promisor's request. This derives from the case of *Lampleigh v Braithwaite*,[51] where the defendant had asked the plaintiff to seek a pardon for him in relation to a criminal offence that he had committed. After the plaintiff had made considerable efforts to do this, the defendant promised him £100 for his trouble. It was held that the promise was enforceable. Second, the parties must have understood that the act was to be rewarded either by a payment or the conferment of some other benefit. In *Re Casey's Patents*,[52] the plaintiff had managed certain patents on behalf of the defendants. They then promised him a one-third share in consideration of the work that he had done. It was held that the plaintiff must always have assumed that his work was to be paid for in some way. The defendants' promise was simply a crystallisation of this reasonable expectation and was therefore enforceable.

Third, the payment, or conferment of other benefits, must have been legally enforceable had it been promised in advance. There is little that needs to be said about this. It simply means that the usual requirements for a binding agreement must apply.

The effect of these tests is that consideration will be valid to support a later promise, provided that all along there was an expectation of reward. It is very similar to the situation where goods or services are provided without the exact price being specified. As we have seen, the courts may enforce the payment of a reasonable sum for what has been provided. That is, in effect, also what they are doing in situations falling within the three tests outlined above. It is an example of the courts implementing what they see as having been the intention of the parties, taking an approach based on third party objectivity.[53]

It can also be argued that the whole common law doctrine of 'past consideration' could be dealt with more simply, and with very similar results, by an overall principle of 'reasonable reliance'. Thus, in *Re McArdle*, the son did the work before any promise was made by his siblings. He did not, therefore, act in reliance on their promises. By contrast, in *Lampleigh v Braithwaite* and *Re Casey's Patents*, the work was done in reliance on a promise or expectation of payment. The advantage of an analysis on these lines is that it involves one general principle governing all situations, rather than stating a general rule and then making it subject to exceptions. This is not, so far, however, the approach of the English courts, which prefer to adhere to at least the form of classical theory.

### 3.8.2 EXCEPTIONS UNDER STATUTE

Two statutory exceptions to the rule that past consideration is no consideration should be briefly noted. First, s 27 of the Bills of Exchange Act 1882 states:

> Valuable consideration for a bill [of exchange] may be constituted by (a) any consideration sufficient to support a simple contract, (b) an antecedent debt or liability.

---

49  [1980] AC 614; [1979] 3 All ER 65.
50  Ibid, p 628; p 74.
51  (1615) Hob 105; 80 ER 255.
52  [1892] 1 Ch 104.
53  For which, see Chapter 2, 2.4.1.

The inclusion of (b) indicates that an existing debt, which is not generally good consideration for a promise,[54] can be so where it is owed by a person receiving the benefit of a promise contained in a bill of exchange.

The second statutory exception is to be found in s 29(5) of the Limitation Act 1980, which provides that where a person liable or accountable for a debt[55] acknowledges it, the right 'shall be treated as having accrued on and not before the date of the acknowledgment'. The acknowledgment must be in writing and signed by the person making it.[56] The relevance of this provision to the current discussion is that if the acknowledgment is in the form of a promise,[57] it will have the effect of extending the limitation period for recovery of the debt, even though no fresh consideration has been given. The statute is thus in effect allowing 'past consideration' to support a new promise.

## 3.9 PERFORMANCE OF EXISTING DUTIES

Can the performance of, or the promise to perform, an act that a person is already under a legal obligation to carry out ever amount to consideration? Three possible types of existing obligation may exist, and they need to be considered separately. These are: first, where the obligation that is alleged to constitute consideration is already imposed by a separate *public* duty; second, where the same obligation already exists under a contract with a *third party*; and, third, where the same obligation already exists under a previous contract with the *same party* by whom the promise is now being made.

### 3.9.1 EXISTING DUTY IMPOSED BY LAW: PUBLIC POLICY

Where a person is doing something that is a duty imposed on them by some public obligation, there is a reluctance to allow this to be used as the basis of a contract. It would clearly be contrary to public policy if, for example, an official with the duty to issue licences to market traders was allowed to make enforceable agreements under which the official received personal payment for issuing such a licence. The possibilities for corruption are obvious. It would be equally unacceptable for the householder whose house is on fire to be bound by a promise of payment in return for putting out the fire made to a member of the fire brigade. The difficulty is in discerning whether the refusal to enforce such a contract is on the basis that it is vitiated as being contrary to public policy,[58] or because the consideration that has been provided is not valid. The case law provides no clear answer. The starting point is *Collins v Godefroy*.[59] In this case, a promise had been made to pay a witness, who was under an order to attend the court, six guineas for his trouble. It was held that this promise was unenforceable because there was no consideration for it. This seems to have been on the basis that the duty to attend was 'a duty imposed by law'.

In cases where the possibilities for extortion are less obvious, there has been a greater willingness to regard performance of an existing non-contractual legal duty as being good consideration, though it must be said that the clearest statements to that effect have come from one judge, that is Lord Denning. In *Ward v Byham*,[60] the duty was that of a mother

---

54  See, e.g., *Rodger v Comptoir d'Escompte de Paris* (1869) LR 2 CP 393.
55  Or other 'liquidated pecuniary claim'.
56  Limitation Act 1980, s 30(1).
57  It need not be so: *Surrendra Overseas Ltd v Government of Sri Lanka* [1977] 1 WLR 565, p 575.
58  This is discussed further in Chapter 12.
59  (1831) 1 B & Ald 950; 120 ER 241.
60  [1956] 2 All ER 318.

Figure 3.2

to look after her illegitimate child. The father promised to make payments, provided that the child was well looked after and happy, and was allowed to decide with whom she should live. Arguably only the looking after of the child could involve the provision of things of 'economic value' sufficient to amount to consideration but the mother was already obliged to do this. Lord Denning had no doubt that this could, nevertheless, be good consideration:[61]

> I have always thought that a promise to perform an existing duty, or the performance of it, should be regarded as good consideration, because it is a benefit to the person to whom it is given.

The other two members of the Court of Appeal were not as explicit as Lord Denning, and seem to have regarded the whole package of what the father asked for as amounting to good consideration. This clearly went beyond the mother's existing obligation, but, as has been pointed out,[62] arguably did not involve anything of extra economic value. So, on either basis, the decision raises difficulties as regards consideration. Lord Denning returned to the same point in *Williams v Williams*,[63] which concerned a promise by a husband to make regular payments to his wife, who had deserted him, in return for her promise to maintain herself 'out of the said weekly sum or otherwise'. The question arose as to whether this provided any consideration for the husband's promise, since a wife in

---

61 [1956] 2 All ER 318, p 319.
62 See above, 3.7.1.
63 [1957] 1 All ER 305.

desertion had no claim on her husband for maintenance and was in any case bound to support herself. Once again, Lord Denning commented:[64]

> a promise to perform an existing duty is, I think, sufficient consideration to support a promise, so long as there is nothing in the transaction which is contrary to the public interest.

Once again, the other members of the Court of Appeal managed to find in the wife's favour without such an explicit statement. What this quote from Lord Denning makes clear, however, is that he regards the rule against using an existing non-contractual duty as consideration as being based on the requirements of the public interest, which might arise in the examples using government officials of one kind or another. Where this element is not present, however, he is saying that an existing duty of this kind can provide good consideration.

The law on this issue remains uncertain but, in view of the position in relation to duties owed to third parties, and recent developments in relation to duties already owed under a contract with the other party (that is, in the case of *Williams v Roffey*), it seems likely that Lord Denning's approach would be followed. There does not seem to be any general hostility in English law to the argument that an existing duty can provide good consideration. In other words, performance of, or the promise to perform, an existing 'public' duty imposed by law can be good consideration, provided that there is no conflict with the public interest.[65]

### 3.9.2 PUBLIC DUTY: EXCEEDING THE DUTY

Whatever the correct answer to the above situation, it is clear that if what is promised or done goes beyond the existing duty imposed by law, then it can be regarded as good consideration. This applies whatever the nature of the duty, so that even as regards public officials, consideration may be provided by exceeding their statutory or other legal obligations. The point was confirmed in *Glasbrook Bros v Glamorgan CC*.[66]

---

**Key case** *Glasbrook Bros v Glamorgan CC* (1925)

Facts: In the course of a strike at a coal mine, the owners of the mine were concerned that certain workers who had the obligation of keeping the mines safe and in good repair should not be prevented from carrying out their duties. They sought the assistance of the police in this. The police suggested the provision of a mobile group, but the owners insisted that the officers should be billeted on the premises. For this, the owners promised to pay. Subsequently, however, they tried to deny any obligation to pay, claiming that the police were doing no more than fulfilling their legal obligation to keep the peace.

Held: The House of Lords held that the provision of the force billeted on the premises went beyond what the police were obliged to do. Viscount Cave LC accepted that if the police were simply taking the steps which they considered necessary to keep the peace, etc., members of the public, who already pay for these police services through taxation, could not be made to pay again. Nevertheless, if, at the request of a member of the public, the police provided services that went beyond what they (the police) reasonably considered necessary, this could provide good consideration for a promise of payment.

---

64  Ibid, p 307.
65  [1991] 1 QB 1; [1990] 1 All ER 512 – discussed below, at 3.9.8.
66  [1925] AC 270.

This rule is now generally accepted, so that wherever the performance of an act goes beyond the performer's public duty, it will be capable of providing consideration for a promise.

In relation to the police, however, the position is now dealt with largely by statute. Section 25(1) of the Police Act 1996 states:

> The chief officer of police of a police force may provide, at the request of any person, special police services at any premises or in any locality in the police area for which the force is maintained, subject to the payment to the local policing body of charges on such scales as may be determined by that body.

In *Harris v Sheffield Utd FC*,[67] which concerned the provision of policing for football matches, the court confirmed the approach taken in *Glasbrook*. Moreover, in applying the predecessor to s 25 of the Police Act 1996,[68] the Court of Appeal held that if a football club decided to hold matches and requested a police presence, such presence could constitute 'special police services' even though it did not go beyond what the police felt was necessary to maintain the peace. A 'request' for a police presence could be implied if police attendance was necessary to enable the club to conduct its matches safely. The football club was therefore held liable to pay for the services provided. If, however, the club disagrees with the police as to the level of policing required, and specifically asks for a lower level of attendance, there will be no implied request for the higher level of provision that the police may think appropriate. The club will only be liable to pay for the services that it actually requested. This was the view of the Court of Appeal in *Chief Constable for Greater Manchester v Wigan Athletic AFC Ltd*.[69] Moreover, the obligation to pay does not extend to policing on land not owned by or under the control of the organiser of the event: *Leeds United FC Ltd v Chief Constable of West Yorkshire*.[70]

It seems, therefore, that the holding of an 'event' to which the public are invited, but which cannot safely be allowed to go ahead without a police presence, will lay the organisers open to paying for 'special services'. To that extent, the position has gone beyond that which applied in *Glasbrook*, in that under the statute the police can receive payment even though they are only doing what they feel is necessary to keep the peace. This clearly applies to sporting events and entertainments (such as music festivals). There is some question as to whether it should apply to political rallies or demonstrations, although Balcombe LJ stated that, in his view, political events fell into a different category:[71]

> I do not accept that the cases are *in pari materia* and I do not consider that dismissal of this appeal poses any threat to the political freedoms which the citizen of this country enjoys.

Nevertheless, the effect of the interpretation of the statutory provisions adopted in *Harris* means that in certain circumstances the police can receive payment for doing no more than carrying out their duty to maintain public order.

---

67  [1987] 2 All ER 838. See also *Ipswich Town Football Club Co Ltd v Chief Constable of Suffolk* [2017] EWCA Civ 1484.

68  That is, Police Act 1964, s 15, which used the same wording as s 25 of the 1996 Act.

69  [2008] EWCA Civ 1449; [2009] WLR 1580, applying the decision in *Reading Festival Ltd v West Yorkshire Police Authority* [2006] EWCA Civ 524, [2006] 1 WLR 2005.

70  [2013] EWCA Civ 115; [2014] QB 168.

71  [1987] 2 All ER 838, p 850.

### 3.9.3 EXISTING CONTRACTUAL DUTY OWED TO THIRD PARTY

If a person is already bound to perform a particular act under a contract, can the performance of, or promise to perform, this act amount to good consideration for a contract with someone else? Suppose that A is contractually bound to deliver 5,000 widgets to B by 1 June. B is to use these widgets in producing items that he has contracted to supply to C. C therefore has an interest in A performing the contract for delivery to B on time, and promises A £5,000 if the goods are delivered to B by 1 June. Can A enforce this payment by C if the goods are delivered to B on the date required? Perhaps somewhat surprisingly, the courts have given a clear positive answer to this question. In other words, they have been quite happy to accept that doing something that forms part, or indeed the whole, of the consideration in one contract can perfectly well also be consideration in another contract.

The starting point is the case of *Shadwell v Shadwell*.[72]

---

**Key case** *Shadwell v Shadwell* (1860)

Facts: An uncle promised his nephew, who was about to get married, the sum of £150 a year until the nephew's annual income as a barrister reached 600 guineas. The uncle paid 12 instalments on this basis, but then he died and the payments ceased. The nephew sued the uncle's estate for the outstanding instalments, to which the defence was raised that the nephew had provided no consideration. The nephew put forward his going through with the marriage as consideration. At the time, a promise to marry was enforceable against the man making such a promise.[73]

Held: The majority of the court had no doubt that performance of the marriage contract could be used as consideration for the uncle's promise, on the basis that that promise was in effect an inducement to the nephew to go through with the marriage. Erle CJ recognised that there was some delicacy involved in categorising the nephew's marriage to the woman of his choice as a 'detriment' to him, but nevertheless considered that in financial terms it might well be. He put the issue in these terms:[74]

> ... do these facts shew a loss sustained by the plaintiff at his uncle's request? When I answer this in the affirmative, I am aware that a man's marriage with the woman of his choice is in one sense a boon, and in that sense the reverse of a loss: yet, as between the plaintiff and the party promising to supply an income to support the marriage, it may well be also a loss. The plaintiff may have made a most material change in his position, and induced the object of his affection to do the same, and may have incurred pecuniary liabilities resulting in embarrassments which would be in every sense a loss if the income which had been promised should be withheld.

Moreover, a marriage, while primarily affecting the parties to it, 'may be an object of interest to a near relative, and in that sense a benefit to him'. Thus, not only was going through with the marriage a 'detriment' to the nephew, it was also a 'benefit' to his uncle. On this basis, there was no doubt that it could constitute good consideration for the promise to pay the annuity.

---

72  (1860) 9 CBNS 159; 142 ER 62.
73  This is no longer the case as a result of the Law Reform (Miscellaneous Provisions) Act 1970, s 1.
74  (1860) 9 CBNS 159, p 173; 142 ER 62, p 68.

### 3.9.4 IN FOCUS: AN ALTERNATIVE VIEW OF SHADWELL

The dissenting judge in Shadwell, Byles J, was not convinced that the uncle's promise was made on the basis that it was in return for the nephew getting married. There is some force in this view of the facts,[75] and a possible construction of the case is that the majority of the court was 'inventing' consideration because it felt that the nephew had relied on his uncle's promise. If the nephew had organised his affairs on the basis that he would continue to receive the payment – a reliance reinforced by the fact that payments had been made regularly over 12 years – then it would be unfair to withdraw it.[76] Such an analysis is relevant to the general issue of 'reliance' as an alternative to consideration, as discussed at the end of this chapter. It is, however, the majority view in Shadwell v Shadwell that has been accepted by later courts, and the case is therefore taken as authority for the proposition that performance of a contractual obligation owed to a third party can be good consideration to found a contract with another promisor.

### 3.9.5 DUTY TO THIRD PARTY: COMMERCIAL APPLICATION

The approach taken in Shadwell v Shadwell was subsequently applied in a commercial context in Scotson v Pegg,[77] where it was held that the delivery of a cargo of coal to the defendant constituted good consideration, even though the plaintiff was already contractually bound to a third party to make such delivery. It was accepted as good law in the twentieth century by the Privy Council New Zealand Shipping Co Ltd v Satterthwaite, The Eurymedon.[78] Goods were being carried on a ship. The carriers contracted with a firm of stevedores to unload the ship. The consignees of the goods were taken to have promised the stevedores the benefit of an exclusion clause contained in the contract of carriage if the stevedores unloaded the goods. The Privy Council viewed the stevedores' performance of their unloading contract as being good consideration for this promise. As Lord Wilberforce said:[79]

> An agreement to do an act which the promisor is under an existing obligation to a third party to do, may quite well amount to consideration and does so in the present case: the promisee obtains the benefit of a direct obligation which he can enforce.

### 3.9.6 PERFORMANCE OR PROMISE?

In all three cases so far considered, it has been performance of the existing obligation that has constituted the consideration. Can a promise to perform an existing obligation also amount to consideration? Take the example used at the start of this section, where A is bound to deliver goods to B on 1 June, and C promises A £5,000 if he does so. We have seen that if A does deliver by the specified date, he will, on the basis of Shadwell v Shadwell and Scotson v Pegg, be able to recover the promised £5,000 from C. What if, however, A also promises to C that he will deliver by 1 June? In other words, the contract, instead of being unilateral ('If you deliver to B by 1 June, I promise to pay you £5,000') becomes bilateral ('In return for your promise to deliver to B by 1 June, I promise to pay you £5,000'). A promises to deliver by 1 June; C promises £5,000. Is A's promise to perform in a way to which he is already committed by his contract with B sufficient consideration for C's promise, so that, if A fails to deliver on time, C, as well as B, may sue A? The reference by Lord Reid in the quotation given above to 'an agreement to do an act' would suggest that a promise is sufficient, though the facts of The Eurymedon itself clearly

---

75  Which appears to have been accepted by Salmon LJ in Jones v Padavatton [1969] 2 All ER 616, p 621.
76  See the comments of Collins, 2003.
77  (1861) 6 H & N 295.
78  [1975] AC 154; [1974] 1 All ER 1015.
79  Ibid, p 168; p 1021.

involved a unilateral contract ('If you unload the goods, we promise you the benefit of the exclusion clause'). The issue was, however, addressed more directly by the Privy Council in *Pao On v Lau Yiu Long*,[80] where it was held that such a promise could be good consideration. Citing *The Eurymedon*, Lord Scarman simply stated:[81]

> Their Lordships do not doubt that a promise to perform, or the performance of, a pre-existing contractual obligation to a third party can be valid consideration.

Given the general approach to consideration, under which promises themselves can be good consideration, this decision is entirely consistent. The law on this point is, therefore, straightforward and simple. The fact that what is promised or performed is something that the promisor is already committed to do under a contract with someone else is irrelevant. Provided it has the other characteristics of valid consideration, it will be sufficient to make the new agreement enforceable.

### 3.9.7  EXISTING DUTY TO THE SAME PROMISOR

The issue of whether performance of an existing duty already owed to the other party can be good consideration is the most difficult one in this area. If there is a contract between A and B, and A then promises B additional money for the performance of the same contract, is this promise binding? It would seem that the general answer should be 'no'. It is normally considered that once a contract is made, its terms are fixed. Any variation, to be binding, must be mutual, in the sense of both sides offering something additional. If the promise is simply to carry out exactly the same performance for extra money, it is totally one-sided. It would amount to a rewriting of the contract, and so should be unenforceable.[82]

This approach was until 1990, and the case of *Williams v Roffey*,[83] taken to represent English law on this point. The authority was said to be the case of *Stilk v Myrick*.[84]

---

**Key case** *Stilk v Myrick* (1809)

Facts: The dispute in this case arose out of a contract between the crew of a ship and its owners. The crew had been employed to sail the ship from London to the Baltic and back. Part way through the voyage, some of the crew deserted. The captain promised that if the rest of the crew sailed the ship back without the missing crew, the wages of the deserters would be divided among those who remained. When the ship returned to London, the owners refused to honour this promise. A crew member sued to recover the promised money.

Held: The sailors could not recover. There was no consideration for the promise to pay the extra money, as the sailors were only doing what they were obliged to do under their existing contract – i.e. work the ship back to England.

---

The basis for the decision in *Stilk v Myrick* is not without controversy, not least because of the fact that it was reported in two rather different ways in the two published

---

80  [1980] AC 614; [1979] 3 All ER 65.

81  Ibid, p 632; p 76.

82  This illustrates the difficulty which the classical doctrine of consideration has in dealing with relational contracts, where the modification of obligations may well be necessary and expected: see Chapter 1, 1.6.

83  [1991] 1 QB 1; [1990] 1 All ER 512.

84  (1809) 2 Camp 317; 170 ER 1168; 6 Esp 129; 170 ER 851.

reports (that is, Campbell and Espinasse).[85] There was, for example, some suggestion that this decision was based on public policy, in that there was a risk in this type of situation of the crew 'blackmailing' the captain into promising extra wages to avoid being stranded. This had been the approach taken in the earlier, similar, case of *Harris v Watson*.[86] This issue, and the alternative views of *Stilk v Myrick*, is one to which we shall need to return later. For the moment, however, we will deal with the case in the way in which it has been traditionally treated as part of the 'classical' law of contract. This view of it (which is stated in the summary of the case above) has been based on the judgment of Lord Ellenborough, as reported by Campbell.[87] He seemed to base his decision on the lack of consideration, rather than public policy. The remaining crew were only promising to do what they were already obliged to do under their existing contract, and this could not be good consideration. The desertion of part of the crew was just part of the normal hazards of the voyage. Campbell's report records Lord Ellenborough's views in the following way:[88]

> There was no consideration for the ulterior pay promised to the mariners who remained with the ship. Before they sailed from London, they had undertaken to do all that they could under all the emergencies of the voyage. They had sold all their services till the voyage should be completed ... the desertion of a part of the crew is to be considered an emergency of the voyage as much as their death; and those who remain are bound by the terms of their original contract to exert themselves to the utmost to bring the ship in safely to her destined port.

It might have been otherwise if they had not contracted for the whole voyage, and had been free to leave at the time of the desertion, or if the captain had 'capriciously' dismissed part of the crew (rather than some sailors having deserted). Such circumstances would fall outside the normal hazards of the voyage. Thus, in either of these cases, the remaining crew might not have been compelled by the original contract to proceed with the voyage and would therefore have provided good consideration by agreeing to do so. On the facts that had actually occurred, however, they had not provided any consideration for the promise of extra money, and so could not recover it.

### 3.9.8 GOING BEYOND THE EXISTING DUTY

It is implicit in *Stilk v Myrick* that if the crew had gone beyond their existing duty, they would have provided good consideration. In addition to the examples given by Lord Ellenborough, the decision in *Hartley v Ponsonby*[89] suggests that a certain level of desertion may in fact give rise to a situation falling outside the normal hazards of the voyage. In this case, a ship that had started out with a crew of 36 had, at the time that the relevant promise was made to the plaintiff, only 19 left, of whom only four or five were able seamen. In this situation, it was held that the voyage had become so dangerous that it was unreasonable to require the crew to continue. In effect (though the decision does not use this terminology), the original contract with the plaintiff had been 'frustrated' (i.e. had become radically different from what was originally agreed),[90] and therefore a fresh contract on the

---

85  See, for example, Luther, 1999; Gilmore, 1974, pp 22–8.
86  (1791) Peake 102.
87  It has been suggested that *Williams v Roffey* can be distinguished on the basis that it involved a 'relational contract': Campbell, D, 'Good faith and the ubiquity of the "relational" contract' (2014) 77 MLR 475, at 478–80.
88  (1809) 2 Camp 317, p 319; 170 ER 1168, p 1169.
89  (1857) 7 E & B 872.
90  The doctrine of frustration is fully discussed in Chapter 13.

revised (more favourable) terms could be created. The performance of, or promise to perform, actions that are inside an existing duty cannot, however, amount to consideration.

### 3.9.9 A RE-CONSIDERATION: *WILLIAMS V ROFFEY*[91]

The true basis for the decision in *Stilk v Myrick* is not without dispute, not least because of
the differences noted above between the two published reports.[92] Nevertheless, the analysis outlined above (based mainly on Campbell's report) has been accepted and applied,
almost without question, in many cases.[93] In 1990, however, a decision of the Court of
Appeal cast some doubt on its scope and continued validity. The case was *Williams v Roffey Bros & Nicholls (Contractors) Ltd*.[94]

---

**Key case** *Williams v Roffey Bros & Nicholls (Contractors) Ltd* (1991)

Facts: The case concerned a contract to refurbish a block of flats. The defendants
were the main contractors for this work and had engaged the plaintiffs as subcontractors to carry out carpentry work. The agreed price for this was £20,000. Part way
through the contract, the plaintiffs got into financial difficulties, at least in part because
the contract price for the carpentry work was too low. The defendants were worried
that the plaintiffs would not complete the work on time or would stop work altogether.
There was a penalty clause in the main contract under which the defendants would
have been liable in the event of late completion. The defendants therefore promised
to pay the plaintiffs a further £10,300, at a rate of £575 for each flat completed. On
this basis, the plaintiffs continued to work on the flats, and completed a further eight.
Because, at this stage, it seemed that the defendants were going to default on their
promise of additional payments, the plaintiffs then ceased work, and subsequently
sued for the additional sums in relation to the eight completed flats. The county court
judge found for the plaintiffs, and the defendants appealed. They argued that since
the plaintiffs, in completing or promising to complete the work on the flats, were only
doing something they were already bound to do under the existing contract with the
defendants, they provided no new consideration.

Held: The Court of Appeal held that the promise to make the extra payments was enforceable. The agreement provided a 'practical benefit' to the defendants, in that it meant they
were less likely to have to pay under a penalty clause in the main contract relating to late
performance and avoided the trouble and expense of employing other carpenters.

---

In considering the defendants' argument that there was no consideration, Glidewell LJ
first outlined the benefits (as identified by counsel for the defendants) that accrued to the
defendants from the plaintiffs' continuation with the contract. These were:[95]

(i) seeking to ensure that the plaintiff continued work and did not stop in breach of
the sub-contract; (ii) avoiding the penalty for delay; and (iii) avoiding the trouble and
expense of engaging other people to complete the carpentry work.

---

91  [1991] 1 QB 1; [1990] 1 All ER 512.
92  See, for example, Luther, 1999; Gilmore, 1974, pp 22–8.
93  For example, *North Ocean Shipping Co Ltd v Hyundai Construction Co* [1979] QB 705; [1978] 3 All ER 1170;
    *Atlas Express v Kafco* [1989] QB 833; [1989] 1 All ER 641.
94  [1991] 1 QB 1; [1990] 1 All ER 512.
95  [1991] 1 QB 1, p 11; [1990] 1 All ER 512, p 518.

In the view of Glidewell LJ and the rest of the Court of Appeal, this was enough to support the defendant's promise to make the additional payments. In reaching this conclusion, all members of the court were at pains to stress that they were not suggesting that the principle in *Stilk v Myrick* was wrong, but that the present case could be distinguished from it.

---

**For thought**

*Sparks Electrics Ltd are doing work on the construction of a housing estate by Large Developments plc. They find that they have underpriced the contract, and go to Large Developments saying that they will stop work unless Large Developments agree to a 10% increase in the contract price. If Large Developments promise to pay the extra, will this be enforceable by Sparks, on the basis of Williams v Roffey? If not, how would you distinguish the cases?*

---

### 3.9.10 *WILLIAMS V ROFFEY*: EFFECT ON *STILK V MYRICK*[96]

The basis on which the court distinguished *Williams v Roffey* from *Stilk v Myrick* is not wholly clear from the judgments. Similar benefits to those identified could be said to have been present in *Stilk v Myrick*. For example, as a result of his promise, the captain did not have to seek replacement crew, avoided delays, and made sure the existing crew continued to work.[97] The main reason for distinguishing *Stilk v Myrick* seems in fact to have been related to the alternative, public policy basis for the decision mentioned above. In other words, the court regarded it as significant that there was in *Williams v Roffey* no question of improper pressure having been put on the defendants. Indeed, it was they who suggested the increased payments.[98]

The result is that the position as regards duties owed to the other contracting party are closely assimilated to the position in relation to duties owed to third parties. Thus, Glidewell LJ summarised the current state of the law as follows:[99]

> (i) if A has entered into a contract with B to do work for, or to supply goods or services to, B in return for payment by B; and (ii) at some stage before A has completely performed his obligations under the contract B has reason to doubt whether A will, or will be able to, complete his side of the bargain; and (iii) B thereupon promises A an additional payment in return for A's promise to perform his contractual obligations on time; and (iv) as a result of giving his promise B obtains in practice a benefit, or obviates a disbenefit; then (v) the benefit to B is capable of being consideration for B's promise, so that the promise will be legally binding.

*Williams v Roffey* is clearly very significant as regards defining the limits of valid consideration, and undoubtedly has the effect of widening those limits. Promises to perform existing obligations can now amount to consideration, even between contracting parties. Nevertheless, within these wider limits, consideration must still be found, as Russell LJ makes clear:[100]

> Consideration there must still be but, in my judgment, the courts nowadays should be more ready to find its existence so as to reflect the intention of the parties to

---

96 For further discussion of the potential implications of *Williams v Roffey,* see Halson, 1990; Hird and Blair, 1996.
97 See, also, *Lee v GEC Plessey Telecommunications* [1993] IRLR 383, discussed below.
98 [1991] 1 QB 1, p 10; [1990] 1 All ER 512, p 517.
99 [1991] 1 QB 1, p 16; [1990] 1 All ER 512, p 521.
100 Ibid, p 18; p 524.

the contract where the bargaining powers are not unequal and where the finding of consideration reflects the true intention of the parties.

This statement indicates the fact that despite the extensive intervention by Parliament to control various aspects of the contractual relationship in particular situations, where the courts are dealing with a business transaction between parties who are more or less equal, they still adhere to the classical principles of freedom of contract. The starting point is to decide what the parties have agreed, and what their intentions were. Once these have been identified, the courts will as far as possible give effect to them, unless there is a good reason for taking another approach. In *Williams v Roffey*, the courts were faced with what appeared to be a clear arrangement entered into voluntarily, and that in the end has the potential to be for the benefit of both parties. In such a situation, arguments taking a narrow view of the scope of the doctrine of consideration, which might allow one party to escape the effects of a promise, freely given, from which it had gained some advantage, were inappropriate and unnecessary.

The approach taken in *Williams v Roffey* has subsequently been applied in other decisions concerning commercial contracts – that is, *Anangel Atlas Compania Naviera SA v Ishikawajima-Harima Heavy Industries Co Ltd (No 2)*[101] and *Simon Container Machinery Ltd v Emba Machinery AB*.[102] In both cases, the avoidance of the other party withdrawing from a contract was held to be sufficient 'practical benefit' to provide consideration for a new promise designed to keep them 'on board'. In *Lee v GEC Plessey Telecommunications*,[103] *Williams v Roffey* was cited as supporting the view that, in the context of a contract of employment, employees provide sufficient consideration for an award of enhanced pay or redundancy terms by continuing to work under the contract. The abandoning by the employee of any argument that the pay should be even higher or the terms even more favourable means that 'the employer has secured a benefit and avoided a detriment'.[104] If this is taken at its face value, then it clearly consigns *Stilk v Myrick* to history. The seamen in accepting the offer of additional money and not continuing to bargain for more would be providing sufficient benefit to the employer and suffering sufficient detriment themselves to amount to consideration for the Master's promise. A subsequent reference to *Williams v Roffey* in the High Court, however, suggests a more sceptical approach. In *South Caribbean Trading Ltd v Trafigura Beheer BV*,[105] the claimant had only agreed to unload a cargo of oil on the basis that a letter of credit was extended by the defendants. One question was whether the unloading of the oil, which the claimants were already obliged to do, could constitute good consideration for the promise to extend the letter of credit. The judge found the existence of other consideration, but stated, *obiter*, that he would not have treated the promise to unload as good consideration. He noted that this would be contrary to the principle in *Stilk v Myrick*. As regards *Williams v Roffey*, he said:[106]

> But for the fact that *Williams v Roffey Bros* was a decision of the Court of Appeal, I would not have followed it. That decision is inconsistent with the long-standing rule that consideration, being the price of the promise sued upon, must move *from* the promisee.

He felt that the Court of Appeal in *Williams v Roffey* had relied too much on analogies with three-party situations, to which different considerations applied. Since, however, as he put

---

101 [1990] 2 Lloyd's Rep 526.
102 [1998] 2 Lloyd's Rep 429.
103 [1993] IRLR 383.
104 Ibid, p 389.
105 [2004] EWHC 2676; [2005] 1 Lloyd's Rep 128.
106 [2004] EWHC 2576; [2005] 1 Lloyd's Rep 128, para 107.

it, the case had 'not yet been held by the House of Lords to have been wrongly decided',[107] he would have needed to distinguish it. This he would have done on the basis that the claimants in this case had put pressure, analogous to economic duress, on the defendants to accept the variation in the contract. On that basis the case was different from *Williams v Roffey*. This view may or may not be significant. It is only the opinion of one High Court judge and, as we have seen, other judges have been prepared to follow and apply *Williams v Roffey*. Only the Supreme Court will be able to determine whether it was not rightly decided;[108] for the time being, it is binding on the lower courts.

Another response to *Williams v Roffey* and the subsequent cases is to suggest that, despite the fact that the decisions are put in the language of consideration, they are in fact examples of the courts basing contractual liability on reasonable reliance. In other words, the carpenters in *Williams v Roffey* had relied on the promise of extra money in completing the flats, and it was therefore right (in the absence of any suggestion of impropriety on their part in extracting the promise) that they should be able to recover this. The application of this principle to *Stilk v Myrick* would also lead to the seamen being able to recover, on the basis that their continued crewing of the ship was based on the promise of extra payment. The questions then become issues of fact: Was any improper pressure applied? Was there *in fact* any reliance?[109] Such issues are likely to be easier to determine than technical arguments based on what precisely constitutes consideration.

### 3.9.11 POSSIBLE LIMITATION ON *WILLIAMS V ROFFEY*

An area of uncertainty in relation to *Williams v Roffey* is whether it applies to a promise to accept less sum than is owed as a debt. In *Re Selectmove*,[110] the Court of Appeal seemed to suggest that it did not. Later decisions have, however, cast doubt on this.[111] The issue is discussed fully below at 3.13 in the context of the general law on part payment of debts.

## 3.10 CONSIDERATION AND THE VARIATION OF CONTRACTS

The above discussion leads conveniently into a review of the more general issue of the way in which the doctrine of consideration affects the freedom of parties to vary the obligations under a contract that they have entered into. This is an area where classical theory has considerable difficulty in coping with the 'relational' aspect of many contracts.[112]

### 3.10.1 NEED FOR ACCORD AND SATISFACTION

We have already referred to the general principle under classical theory that for a contract to be altered, there must be consideration. To use the language often adopted by the courts, 'accord and satisfaction' must be present: 'accord' meaning agreement and 'satisfaction' essentially consideration. The approach taken in *Stilk v Myrick*,[113] as redefined in *Williams v Roffey*,[114] fits into this general principle. The same approach applies where

---

107  [2004] EWHC 2576; [2005] 1 Lloyd's Rep 128, para 109.

108  Although the Supreme Court declined to rule on the correctness of *Williams v Roffey* in *Rock Advertising Ltd v MWB Business Exchange Centres Ltd* [2018] UKSC 24. See also *Dan Simantob v Yacob Shavleyan t/a Yacob's Gallery* [2018] EWHC 2005 (QB) at [127].

109  In other words, could it be shown that, as a matter of fact, the sailors did not rely on the promise, but would have continued to work in any case?

110  [1995] 2 All ER 534; [1995] 1 WLR 474.

111  Although compare *Rock Advertising Ltd v MWB Business Exchange Centres Ltd* [2018] UKSC 24 at [18], which is discussed below at 3.13.1.

112  See Chapter 1, 1.6.

113  (1809) 2 Camp 317; 170 ER 1168; 6 Esp 129; 170 ER 851.

114  [1991] 1 QB 1; [1990] 1 All ER 512.

a contract is brought to an end by mutual agreement. As long as there are outstanding obligations on both sides of the contract, the agreement to terminate will be binding. The foregoing of the existing rights under both sides of the contract will amount to good consideration for the promise to release the other party from his or her obligation.

### 3.10.2 THE CONCEPT OF 'WAIVER'

Over the years, however, this approach, though still applied where appropriate, has often been found in practice to be too restrictive. Why should parties who are on an equal footing and who wish to vary obligations under an existing contract, not be allowed to do so without worrying about the technicality of 'consideration'? Various concepts have been used to allow more flexibility, and to give some force to agreed variations, even where these are not supported by consideration.[115] One such is the concept of 'waiver'. Under this principle, a person who 'waives' (that is, promises not to enforce) certain rights under a contract for a period of time may be stopped from later insisting on performance in accordance with the letter of the contract. So, in *Hartley v Hymans*,[116] a seller requested to be allowed to make late delivery, and the buyer agreed to this. When the seller delivered, the buyer refused to accept. It was held that the seller was entitled to recover damages, despite the fact that delivery was outside the terms of the contract and that the buyer's promise to accept late delivery was unsupported by consideration. The buyer had waived the right to insist on delivery at a particular time and could not go back on that.

Waiver was used by the common law courts but was then taken over by the chancery courts, and is now almost exclusively an equitable concept. It is important to note that waiver may not be permanent in its effect. The person waiving the rights may do so for a fixed period of time, or may be able to revive the original right by giving notice. The latter was the case in *Charles Rickards Ltd v Oppenheim*.[117] The contract here was for the building of a car body to fit a Rolls-Royce chassis. The suppliers promised the buyer that they could fulfil the contract in 'six or, at the most, seven months'. The precise specification of the work to be done was agreed on 20 August 1947. The latest time for delivery, according to the suppliers' promise, was therefore 20 March 1948. The suppliers failed to meet this deadline, which was held to be a term of the original contract. The buyer, however, did not sue for breach of contract as soon as the date had passed, but continued to seek delivery. This was regarded as the buyer having waived the right to delivery at a particular time.

Although there was continued delay, the buyer would not have been able to refuse delivery if the car had been finished in April, May or June 1948. By the end of June, however, the buyer's patience ran out, and on 29 June 1948 he told the suppliers that unless the car was delivered by 25 July 1948, he would not accept it. The car was not in fact finished until 18 October 1948. The suppliers then sued for non-acceptance, on the basis of the buyer's waiver of the original term specifying a date for delivery. The Court of Appeal, however, did not accept that such a waiver was permanent in its effect. As Lord Denning put it:[118]

> It would be most unreasonable if, having been lenient and having waived the initial expressed time, [the buyer] should thereby have prevented himself from ever thereafter insisting on reasonably quick delivery. In my judgment, he was entitled to give a reasonable notice making time of the essence of the matter.

---

115 This, it may be suggested, illustrates the weakness of the classical doctrine of consideration: the more the exceptions mount, the less it can really be said to provide a coherent governing principle.
116 [1920] 3 KB 475.
117 [1950] 1 KB 616; [1950] 1 All ER 420.
118 Ibid, p 624; p 423.

On the facts, the notice of four weeks given on 29 June 1948 was reasonable and, once it had expired, the buyer – having waited many months for his car – was entitled to cancel the contract. A waiver of rights will, therefore, generally be capable of withdrawal on the giving of reasonable notice.

Looked at in this way, the concept of equitable waiver has clear links with the common law concept of estoppel. This is the rule whereby if A, a party to an action, has made a statement of fact on which the other party, B, has relied, A will not be allowed to deny that the original statement was untrue.[119] This rule applies only to statements of existing fact, however. In *Jorden v Money*,[120] an attempt was made to apply it to a promise not to enforce a debt. Mrs Jorden had made repeated statements that she would not enforce a bond for £1,200 issued by Money, which she held. On the basis of that assurance, Money married. He then sought a declaration from the courts that the debt had been abandoned. He succeeded at first instance, but the House of Lords took a different view. Lord Cranworth LC, having stated the general principles of the doctrine of estoppel, continued:[121]

> I think that that doctrine does not apply to a case where the representation is not a representation of fact, but a statement of something which the party intends or does not intend to do.

Whereas the former type of statement (representation of fact) may provide the basis of an enforceable estoppel, the latter type (statement as to future intentions) can only become enforceable by being made part of a contract. Mrs Jorden's statements were of the latter type and, therefore, since they had not been made as part of a contract, were not enforceable. This decision established, therefore, that the doctrine of estoppel in the strict sense had no application to promises.

### 3.10.3 IN FOCUS: AN ALTERNATIVE VIEW OF *JORDEN V MONEY*

Atiyah has argued forcefully that the orthodox view of *Jorden v Money* misunderstands what lay behind the reason why counsel argued it on the basis of estoppel rather than contract.[122] This was not that there was a lack of consideration for the promise not to enforce the debt. Atiyah argues that the marriage would have provided such consideration, since it was action taken in reliance on the promise (even though not requested by the promisor).[123] The problem was that, at the time, the Statute of Frauds 1677 required such a promise to be evidenced in writing. Since there was no writing available, the plaintiff tried to plead the case in estoppel rather than contract. The court, however, would not allow this to be used as a means of circumventing the requirements of the Statute of Frauds. To do so, as Atiyah points out, would have constituted a significant undermining of the statute – 'for it would have meant that any plaintiff who could show that he had altered his position in reliance on the defendant's promise could ignore the statute and rely on estoppel'.[124]

---

119 As will be seen from this description, estoppel is based on reliance. Waiver might also be said to be based on the fact that a person relies on the other party's promise not to enforce a particular contractual obligation.
120 (1854) 5 HL 185.
121 Ibid, p 214.
122 See Atiyah, 1986, at pp 234–38. The same point is made by Baker, 1979, p 27.
123 Cf *Shadwell v Shadwell* (1860) 9 CBNS 159; 142 ER 62 – see above, 3.9.3.
124 Atiyah, 1986, p 235.

### 3.10.4 THE ACCEPTED ANALYSIS

Even if *Jorden v Money* has been misunderstood (and not all commentators would agree with Atiyah),[125] it has been generally accepted in subsequent cases as establishing that estoppel can only be used in relation to statements of existing fact.[126] This means that simply because action was taken in reliance on a promise, this will not in itself generally render the promise enforceable. To mitigate the practical problems caused by this analysis, particularly where the parties are in agreement about wishing to vary the terms of a contract, in the last 70 years the courts have developed the concept of equitable waiver into a broader doctrine, generally referred to as 'promissory estoppel'.

## 3.11 THE DOCTRINE OF PROMISSORY ESTOPPEL

The modern law on this topic, which gives rise to situations in which a contract can in effect be varied without there being consideration, derives from *Central London Property Trust Ltd v High Trees House Ltd*.

---

**Key case** *Central London Property Trust Ltd v High Trees House Ltd* (1947)

Facts: The plaintiffs were the owners of a block of flats in London, which they rented to the defendants at a rent of £2,500 per annum. Following the outbreak of the Second World War in 1939, the defendants were unable to find sufficient tenants to take the flats, because of the large numbers of people leaving London. As a result, the plaintiffs agreed that, in the circumstances, the rent could be reduced by half, to £1,250 per annum. This arrangement continued until after the war ended in 1945, and the difficulty in letting the flats ceased. The plaintiffs then sought to return to the original terms of the agreement, and also queried whether they might not be entitled to claim the other half of the rent for the war years, since the promise to accept less was not supported by any consideration.

Held: Denning J confirmed that the plaintiffs were entitled to recover the full rent from the end of the war. Their promise to take less had clearly only been intended to last until that point. On the more general issue, however, he considered that the plaintiffs would not be able to recover the balance for the war years. The reason for this was that he thought that there was a general equitable principle whereby:[127]

> A promise intended to be binding, intended to be acted upon, and in fact acted on, is binding so far as its terms properly apply.

These conditions were satisfied on the facts of this case in relation to what had happened during the war years, and the plaintiffs were bound by their promise, which had been acted on by the defendants.

---

Denning's main authority for his analysis of the position relating to the war years was the 'equitable waiver' case of *Hughes v Metropolitan Railway*.[128] The defendant held a

---

125  See, for example, Treitel, 2015, 3–090.
126  See, for example, *Maddison v Alderson* (1883) 8 App Cas 467; *Argy Trading Development Co Ltd v Lapid* [1977] 1 WLR 444.
127  [1947] KB 130.
128  Ibid, p 136.

lease of certain houses from the plaintiff. The lease contained a covenant of repair within six months of being given notice. The plaintiff gave such notice. The defendant then suggested that a sale might be arranged, and said that it would defer carrying out any repairs until this had been discussed. Some negotiations took place, but they did not result in an agreement for the sale. The plaintiff then served notice to quit, on the basis of the defendant's failure to comply with the original notice to repair. It was held that the plaintiff was not entitled to do this. The effect of the notice had been suspended while the negotiations on the sale were taking place, and time did not start to run again until these had broken down. Lord Cairns stated the general principle in the following famous passage:[129]

> it is the first principle on which all Courts of Equity proceed, that if parties who have entered into definite and distinct terms involving certain legal results – certain penalties or legal forfeiture – afterwards by their own act or with their own consent enter upon a course of negotiation which has the effect of leading one of the parties to suppose that the strict rights arising under the contract will not be enforced, or will be kept in suspense, or held in abeyance, the person who otherwise might have enforced those rights will not be allowed to enforce them where it would be inequitable having regard to the dealings which have thus taken place between the parties.

Denning J, in *High Trees*, asserted that this general principle supported his view of the relationship between the parties in the case before him. His own statement of the general principle, as set out above, however, raised considerable controversy. First, taken at face value, it seemed to destroy the doctrine of consideration altogether.[130] Second, the application of the 'equitable waiver' approach to the facts of the case (that is, the nonpayment of rent) appeared to run counter to the House of Lords' decision in *Foakes v Beer*,[131] which stated that part payment of a debt can never be good satisfaction for the whole. Both of these objections, and their treatment in subsequent case law, must now be considered.

## 3.12 PROMISSORY ESTOPPEL AND CONSIDERATION

The first point to consider is whether the doctrine of promissory estoppel, as restated and developed by Lord Denning, does strike at the heart of the doctrine of consideration. The argument that it does is based on the fact that Lord Denning, in stating that 'a promise intended to be binding, intended to be acted upon, and in fact acted on, is binding so far as its terms properly apply',[132] was suggesting that all that was needed to make a promise enforceable is that the party to whom it was made has acted in reliance on it. In other words, it espouses a reliance-based theory of the enforceability of contracts. It, therefore, arguably becomes irrelevant whether the promisee has provided anything in exchange in terms of a benefit to the promisor or a detriment suffered at the promisor's request. As we have seen, the classical doctrine of consideration requires one or other of these as a condition of making a promise enforceable. If Lord Denning's statement is taken at face value, however, then it would mean that if A promises B £10,000, intending it to be a binding promise, and in reliance on this B decides to go out and buy a car, A would be bound to

---

129 (1877) 2 App Cas 439. He also cited *Birmingham and District Land v London and Northwestern Railway Co* (1888) 40 Ch D 268 and *Salisbury (Marquess) v Gilmore* [1942] 2 KB 38.
130 This may well have been his original intention, as he has indicated extra-judicially: Denning, 1979, pp 197–203, 223.
131 (1884) 9 App Cas 605.
132 [1947] KB 130, p 136.

Figure 3.3

the promise.[133] The classical doctrine of consideration would hold that B has not provided any consideration and that A is not therefore bound to pay the £10,000.

The question of whether the doctrine of consideration in its classical form does still survive and, if it does not, the extent to which the doctrine of promissory estoppel has contributed to its demise is one to which we shall return at the end of this chapter. At this stage, however, it is sufficient to note that the broad formulation of 'promissory estoppel' by Denning in *High Trees* has been limited by subsequent decisions. These cases establishing the borderlines of the doctrine can be viewed as supporting the view that it is simply an 'exception' to the general doctrine of consideration and does not strike at its roots.

There are five suggested limitations, of which four certainly apply: the status of the fifth is less clear.

### 3.12.1 THERE MUST BE AN EXISTING LEGAL RELATIONSHIP
It is suggested that promissory estoppel cannot exist in a vacuum: there must be an existing legal relationship between the parties that is purportedly altered by the promise of one of the parties. This was clearly the case in *High Trees* itself. It was concerned with the modification of the existing contractual rights between the landlord and tenants. This limitation may also be said to be exemplified by the following case.

---

133 A fully fledged reliance-based theory of enforceability would be likely to require B's reliance to be 'reasonable' – and perhaps foreseeable by A. See, further, below, 3.15.2.

**Key case** *Combe v Combe* (1951)[134]

Facts: In this case a husband and wife were getting divorced. Between the decree nisi and absolute, the husband agreed to pay his wife £100 per annum net of tax. The husband never paid any money and after seven years his former wife sued on the basis of his promise. Byrne J held that, while there was no consideration for the husband's promise, the wife could recover on the basis of the *High Trees* decision. The husband appealed. Held: The trial judge's decision was overturned by a Court of Appeal which included Lord Denning himself.[135] He commented that consideration remained 'a cardinal necessity of the formation of a contract, but not of its modification or discharge'.[136] If this is so, then it severely limits the doctrine's scope as a general challenge to the doctrine of consideration. Promissory estoppel is limited to the modification of existing legal relationships rather than to the establishment of new obligations.[137]

The existing relationship will generally be a contract. It seems, however, that this is not essential. The case of *Durham Fancy Goods Ltd v Michael Jackson (Fancy Goods) Ltd*[138] concerned a bill of exchange drawn by the plaintiffs on the defendants. The plaintiffs made an error by putting on the bill 'Accepted payable ... For and on behalf of M Jackson (Fancy Goods) Ltd', whereas the proper name of the company was 'Michael Jackson (Fancy Goods) Ltd'. A director of the defendant company signed his name on the bill and returned it,[139] without pointing out the error. When the bill was later dishonoured, the plaintiffs tried to enforce the bill against the director. It was claimed that he was personally liable by virtue of s 108 of the Companies Act 1948, which rendered a person who signs a bill liable if the proper name of the company does not appear on the bill. It was held that the director fell within s 108, because 'M Jackson' was not the same as 'Michael Jackson'. The plaintiffs were prevented from recovering from him, however, on the basis that their action in writing the words of acceptance on the bill (including the inaccurate name) amounted to a promise that 'acceptance in that form would be, or would be accepted by them as, a regular acceptance of the bill'.[140] This, in the view of Donaldson J, gave rise to a promissory estoppel, because it would be inequitable to allow the plaintiffs to enforce against the director personally. Such personal liability would not have arisen if the bill had been in the proper form. To the argument that promissory estoppel only arises where there is an existing contractual relationship, Donaldson J commented:[141]

[T]his does not seem to me to be essential, provided that there is a pre-existing legal relationship which could in certain circumstances give rise to liabilities and penalties. Such a relationship is created by (a) s 108 of the Companies Act 1948, (b) the fact that Mr Jackson was a director of Jacksons and (c) whatever contractual arrangement existed between the plaintiffs and Jacksons which led to the plaintiffs drawing a 90 day bill on Jacksons.

---

134 [1951] 2 KB 215; [1951] 1 All ER 767.
135 Part of the reason for the decision was the fact that promissory estoppel could only be used as a 'shield' rather than as a 'sword': this is discussed further below, 3.12.3.
136 [1951] 2 KB 215, p 220; [1951] 1 All ER 767, p 770.
137 But cf the Australian case of *Waltons Stores (Interstate) Ltd v Maher* (1988) 76 ALR 513, discussed below, 3.15.2.
138 [1968] 2 QB 839; [1968] 2 All ER 987.
139 The director's name was, in fact, Michael Jackson, and he was also secretary to the company.
140 [1968] 2 QB 839, at p 848; [1968] 2 All ER 987, p 991.
141 [1968] 2 QB 839, at p 848; [1968] 2 All ER 987, p 847; p 991.

In *Evenden v Guildford City FC*,[142] Lord Denning appeared to go further and, citing *Durham Fancy Goods Ltd v Michael Jackson (Fancy Goods) Ltd*, held that promissory estoppel could apply in a situation where it appears there was no existing legal relationship at all between the parties.[143] He was supported in this view by Browne LJ,[144] who was, however, also prepared to find for the plaintiff on the basis of a contractually binding promise.[145]

In *The Henrik Sif*,[146] Webster J took the view that the 'legal relationship' necessary as the background to a promissory estoppel could be found where:[147]

> two parties engaged in an exchange of correspondence in which one of them intends the correspondence to have legal effect in circumstances in which the other knows of that first party's intention and makes requests or purports to grant extensions of time which could only be of relevance to the first party if the correspondence between them affected their mutual rights and obligations.

This seems to amount to a kind of 'double-estoppel': the failure to correct a false impression about the parties' legal relationship leading to the context in which a promissory estoppel could operate.

To the extent that these cases suggest that promissory estoppel can apply even where there is no existing contract between the parties (within which consideration will have been provided), they add weight to the suggestion that the doctrine does have the effect of undermining the doctrine of consideration.

### 3.12.2 THERE MUST HAVE BEEN (DETRIMENTAL) RELIANCE

Under the normal rules for the creation of a contract, obligations may arise as soon as promises have been exchanged. There is no need for either side to have relied on the other's promise in order to be able to enforce it. In relation to promissory estoppel, however, the party trying to enforce the promise must have taken some action on it.

This simply means doing something as a result of it, for example, paying the lower rent, as in *High Trees*. In some cases, it has been suggested that the promisee must have suffered a detriment from such reliance but Lord Denning consistently denied that this is necessary.

In *WJ Alan & Co v El Nasr*,[148] for example, the dispute concerned a letter of credit, which had been opened in sterling rather than in Kenyan shillings, as specified by the contract. The other party had, however, drawn on this credit in relation to various transactions. The judge rejected the argument that this amounted to a binding waiver of the original terms as to currency because there was no evidence that the party for whose benefit the waiver would operate had acted 'to their detriment'. Lord Denning in the Court of Appeal refused to accept this as a necessary requirement for either waiver or promissory estoppel:[149]

---

142 [1975] QB 917. The actual decision in this case was overruled by the House of Lords in *Secretary of State for Employment v Globe Elastic Thread Co Ltd* [1980] A.C. 506.

143 It involved a representation made by a company which was about to become the employer of the plaintiff to the effect that his new employment would be treated as continuous from that which he was about to leave. This was important for the purpose of redundancy entitlement.

144 [1975] QB 917, p 926.

145 The third member of the Court of Appeal, Brightman J, also found for the plaintiff, on the basis that the statutory presumption of continuous employment under s 9 of the then Redundancy Payments Act 1965 could not be rebutted in the light of the statement made by the new employer.

146 [1982] 1 Lloyd's Rep 456.

147 Ibid, p 466. He relied to some extent on the comments of Robert Goff J in the first instance decision in *Amalgamated Investment & Property Co Ltd v Texas Commerce International Bank Ltd* [1981] 2 WLR 554.

148 [1972] 2 All ER 127.

149 [1972] 2 All ER 127, p 140.

I know that it has been suggested in some quarters that there must be detriment. But I can find no support for it in the authorities cited by the judge. The nearest approach to it is the statement of Viscount Simonds in the *Tool Metal* case that the other must have been led to 'alter his position'[150] ... But that only means that he must have been led to act differently from what he otherwise would have done. And, if you study the cases in which the doctrine has been applied, you will see that all that is required is that the one should have 'acted on the belief induced by the other party'. That is how Lord Cohen put it in the *Tool Metal* case, and is how I would put it myself.

Megaw LJ agreed that there had been a binding waiver, though without dealing with the specific point on 'detriment'. Stephenson LJ left open the question of whether 'any alteration of position' was sufficient but held that on the facts the party acting on the waiver had suffered a detriment anyway. Despite the fact that there is no absolutely clear authority on the issue, the current general view seems to be that action taken in reliance on the promise is enough, without the need for a specific detriment to be shown. This was confirmed by the Court of Appeal in *Collier v P & MJ Wright (Holdings) Ltd*.[151] The case involved a preliminary issue as to whether there was an arguable case for promissory estoppel. The court took the view that a debtor who makes a partial payment in response to a promise to forgo the rest of the debt has shown sufficient reliance to support an argument for promissory estoppel.

### 3.12.3 THE DOCTRINE CAN ONLY BE USED AS A 'SHIELD, NOT A SWORD'

The third limitation again derives from *Combe v Combe*,[152] the facts of which have been given above.[153] The Court of Appeal, including Lord Denning, thought that the attempt by the wife to use promissory estoppel to enforce her husband's promise was an inappropriate use of the doctrine. Promissory estoppel could not form the basis of a cause of action, and would generally only be available as a defence – 'as a shield, not a sword'.[154]

This limitation is clearly linked to the idea that the doctrine can only be used to modify existing relationships, rather than to create new ones. It does not mean, however, that promissory estoppel can only ever be used by a defendant and never by a claimant. For example, a landlord might promise to waive an obligation to repair that would otherwise fall on the tenant. Suppose that the landlord subsequently gives the tenant notice to quit for failing to carry out repairs. The tenant could then go to court, as claimant, to challenge the notice. Reliance would be placed on the landlord's promise as having modified the tenant's obligations. The principle stated in *Combe v Combe* would not prevent the tenant from bringing the action against the landlord.[155]

### 3.12.4 IT MUST BE INEQUITABLE FOR THE PROMISOR TO GO BACK ON THE PROMISE

Promissory estoppel is, as we have seen, derived from the concept of equitable waiver. Thus, as an equitable doctrine, its use is in the discretion of the courts, and even if the other elements for the applicability of it exist, it may still not be applied because it would

---

150 *Tool Metal Manufacturing Co v Tungsten Electric Co* [1955] 2 All ER 657 – discussed below, 3.12.5.
151 [2007] EWCA Civ 1329; [2008] 1 WLR 643. See also the commentary by Austen-Baker, 2008.
152 [1951] 2 KB 215; [1951] 1 All ER 767.
153 See above, 3.12.1.
154 [1951] 2 KB 215, p 224; [1951] 1 All ER 767, p 772. This phrase was apparently used by counsel for the defendant and adopted by Birkett LJ.
155 For further discussion of these issues, see Halson, 1999; Thompson, 1983.

be inequitable in the circumstances to do so. A clear example of the kind of situation where this would apply is the case of *D and C Builders v Rees*.[156]

---

**Key case** *D and C Builders v Rees* (1966)

Facts: The plaintiff builders had done work for the defendants and were owed nearly £500. After pressing for payment for some time, the plaintiff agreed to take £300 in satisfaction of the account. Mrs Rees, who knew that the plaintiffs were in financial difficulties, had told them that that was all they were likely to get. Despite their promise to accept the £300 (a promise for which there was no consideration), the builders then sought to recover the balance of the debt.

Held: Lord Denning, in the Court of Appeal, held that although there was clearly a promise here of a type which might raise promissory estoppel, the element of intimidation in the defendant's behaviour, knowingly taking advantage of the plaintiffs' circumstances, meant that it was not inequitable to allow the plaintiffs to go back on their promise. The other members of the Court of Appeal did not think it was even necessary to discuss the doctrine.[157]

---

**For thought**

*Better Painters have done some redecorating work for Jim at a price of £5,000, of which £3,000 is still owing. BP are aware that Jim is having difficulty finding the money. They know that if they reduce the price they can still make a profit, so they suggest to Jim that he pays £2,000 'in full settlement of your bill'. Would Better Painters be bound by this promise if Jim pays the £2,000, or could they still seek the other £1,000?*

---

The inequity in *D and C Builders* was fairly obvious. The concept of 'equitability' does not necessarily imply impropriety on the part of the promisee, however. In *The Post Chaser*,[158] the promise was made and withdrawn within a few days. Although the other side had relied on the promise, their position had not in fact been prejudiced by such reliance. It was not, therefore, inequitable to allow the promisor to withdraw the promise.

The question is thus not simply whether the promisee acted in reliance on the promise, but whether there was sufficient reliance to make it inequitable not to enforce the promise. Although Robert Goff J in *The Post Chaser* was clearly supportive of the view noted above that such 'reliance' does not require 'detriment', if there has been detriment then inequitability may be much easier to establish. In the absence of detriment, the court will probably look at the effect of allowing withdrawal of the promise. Would this have a significant adverse affect on the promisee, because of the way in which he or she has organised his affairs in the light of the promise? If not, then withdrawal is unlikely to be regarded as 'inequitable'.

---

156  [1966] 2 QB 617; [1965] 3 All ER 837.
157  It may be significant that the contract in this case was at the 'discrete' as opposed to the 'relational' end of Macneil's spectrum of contracts (see Chapter 1, 1.6). There was thus less need for provision for modification of obligations.
158  [1981] 2 Lloyd's Rep 695; [1982] 1 All ER 19.

### 3.12.5 THE DOCTRINE IS ONLY SUSPENSORY IN ITS EFFECT

Does the doctrine have a permanent or only a suspensory effect? This final limitation on promissory estoppel is the one about which there is most uncertainty. There is no doubt that in some circumstances a promissory estoppel will have a purely suspensory effect. In *Hughes v Metropolitan Railway*,[159] for example, the notice of obligation to repair was simply put in abeyance while the negotiations over a possible sale continued. It is also clear that in relation to some sorts of contract, the effect can be to both extinguish some rights and suspend others. This is what happened in *High Trees* itself. The right to receive the full rent during the war years was extinguished by the estoppel but because the promise was interpreted as having only been intended to be applicable during the war, once that was over the original terms of the lease automatically revived. So, to that extent, the effect was simply suspensory. Even if the promise is expressed to last indefinitely, it is likely that it will be able to be withdrawn (and thus be only suspensory in effect) by giving appropriate notice. In *Tool Metal Manufacturing Co v Tungsten Electric Co*,[160] for example, there was a promise to accept a reduced royalty in relation to the operation of some patents. It was held that the promisor could withdraw the promise by giving reasonable notice, from which point the original terms of the agreement would come back into operation. The House of Lords in fact held that the initiation of a previous, unsuccessful, action to escape from the promise constituted notice of withdrawal.

It is in relation to this type of continuing contract,[161] therefore, that promissory estoppel operates to both extinguish and suspend contractual rights. The obligations to make the higher payments during the period of the operation in both *High Trees* and the *Tool Metal* case were destroyed. The promisor was unable to recover the additional amounts for that period. The original terms were not in themselves extinguished, however, and could be reinstated for the future.

What is not clear is whether the doctrine of promissory estoppel could be used to extinguish, rather than suspend, an obligation that is not a continuing obligation. If, for example, the issue of inequitability had not arisen in *D and C Builders v Rees*,[162] would promissory estoppel have wiped out, or simply postponed, the payment of the balance? It seems clear that if the doctrine is to have any place at all in relation to this type of obligation, it must have the effect of extinguishing the right altogether. It would make no sense to say that Rees could rely on D and C Builders' promise to remit the balance of the debt, but that at any time the obligation to pay it could be revived by the giving of notice. This was the view of the Court of Appeal in *Collier v P & MJ Wright (Holdings) Ltd*.[163] The case concerned a partner who claimed that a creditor of a partnership had promised that the partner could discharge his liability by paying off his share (i.e. one third) of the partnership debts, rather than being liable, as would normally be the case, for the full amount owed by the partnership as a whole. On a preliminary issue, the Court of Appeal held that on these facts the partner had an arguable case for promissory estoppel, on the basis that by paying his share he had discharged his full debt to the creditor. The court relied heavily on Lord Denning's *obiter* view in *D & C Builders v Rees* that, in the absence of the inequitable behaviour of the debtor, promissory estoppel would have operated to discharge the debt.[164]

The conclusion must be, then, that it is not true to say that promissory estoppel can *only* operate in a suspensory way. The precise effect of promissory estoppel, in terms of

159 (1877) 2 App Cas 439 – discussed above, 3.11.
160 [1955] 2 All ER 657.
161 A 'relational' contract, in other words – see Chapter 1, 1.6.
162 [1966] 2 QB 617; [1965] 3 All ER 837.
163 [2007] EWCA Civ 1329; [2008] 1 WLR 643.
164 See also Austen-Baker, 2008.

whether it suspends or extinguishes rights, will depend on the nature of the promise and the type of contract to which it applies. If this is the case, then promissory estoppel is no different in this respect from a contractual modification that is supported by consideration. The precise effect of such a modification also depends on the terms in which it is expressed and the nature of the contract with which it is concerned. It would have been quite possible, for example, for an agreement of the type considered in *High Trees* to have been entered into on the basis that, during the war, the tenants would undertake additional responsibilities in respect of the maintenance of the property in return for the landlord accepting the reduced rent, thus providing consideration for the landlord's promise. As far as the obligation to pay the rent was concerned, the effect would have been the same as would occur through the application of promissory estoppel. The landlord's right to receive the full rent would have been extinguished during the war, but would have revived once peace had returned.

If this is right, then putting forward the suspensory nature of promissory estoppel as a basis for distinguishing it from the doctrine of consideration (and thus adding weight to the view that it does not 'undermine' consideration) does not look very convincing. In both cases, the issue of the suspension or extinction of rights depends on the nature of the promise and the surrounding circumstances. It does not, therefore, depend on whether or not consideration was given for the promise.

## 3.13 THE PART PAYMENT OF DEBTS

### 3.13.1 THE COMMON LAW POSITION

The common law has long recognised two particular situations where a promise to accept part payment of a debt can discharge the whole obligation. The first is where the payment is made by a third party. For example, in *Hirachand Punamchand v Temple*,[165] the debtor's father made a payment in relation to a promissory note which was accepted by the creditor in full settlement of the debt. It was held that the creditor could not subsequently sue the debtor for the balance. This followed a similar view taken in the earlier cases of *Welby v Drake*[166] and *Cooke v Lister*.[167]

Second, if a debtor owes money to several creditors, an agreement may be reached whereby each of them is to receive a proportion of the money owed (a 'composition agreement'). In that situation, none of the creditors will be allowed to sue the debtor to recover the full amount originally owed.[168]

Both of these two situations may be explained on the basis that the creditor should not be allowed to act in a way that would constitute a 'fraud' on the party who has made the part payment, but they do appear to be exceptions to the rule that part payment of a debt must be supported by consideration in order to make it enforceable.[169]

Apart from these special situations, however, the traditional common law position on the part payment of debts is to be found in *Pinnel's Case*,[170] as confirmed by the House of Lords in *Foakes v Beer*.[171] The rule is that part payment of a debt on the date on which it is

---

165  [1911] 2 KB 330.
166  (1825) 1 C & P 557.
167  (1863) CB(NS) 543.
168  *Good v Cheesman* (1831) 2 B & Ald 328.
169  For other possible explanations for these decisions, see Treitel, 2015, 3–108.
170  (1602) 5 Co Rep 117a; 77 ER 237.
171  (1884) 9 App Cas 605.

due can never be satisfaction for the full amount owed.[172] The creditor will still be able to recover the balance of the debt, unless the debtor can show that some consideration was supplied in return for the creditor's agreement to take the lesser sum. Thus, if payment is made early, or on the day but at a different place from that specified in the contract, the debt may be discharged. Equally, if the debtor provides goods or services, instead of cash, this, if accepted by the creditor, will discharge the debt fully, even if the value of what was supplied is less than the total amount owed: 'The gift of a horse, a hawk, or a robe, in satisfaction is good.'[173] Thus, the payment of £5 on the due date could not discharge a debt of £100 but if the debtor offered and the creditor accepted a book worth £5 in satisfaction, the creditor could not then claim the balance of £95. The justification for this rather odd rule is that the book must have been regarded by the creditor as more beneficial than money, otherwise it would not have been accepted and the court will not inquire further into the creditor's motives.

A question that has arisen more recently is whether the concept of consideration in this context can include the type of 'practical benefit' recognised by the Court of Appeal in the case of *Williams v Roffey*.[174] The initial answer seemed to be 'no', as indicated by the Court of Appeal in *Re Selectmove*.[175] The case concerned an assertion by a company that it had made a binding contract with the Inland Revenue under which it could, effectively, pay off its tax liabilities by instalments. The Inland Revenue argued that this agreement was not binding on them because the company provided no consideration for the agreement to accept instalments: it was only promising to do something (paying its debts) that it was already obliged to do. The Court of Appeal, while deciding the case in favour of the Inland Revenue on another point, considered whether *Williams v Roffey* could apply in this situation. The company argued that the arrangement was to the Inland Revenue's 'practical benefit' because it meant that the company could stay in business and therefore be more likely to meet its debts. The Court of Appeal, however, felt that this would be the case in relation to any agreement to pay by instalments. To treat this as providing consideration would be in direct conflict with the leading House of Lords decision on part payment of debts, that is *Foakes v Beer*, which had not even been cited in *Williams v Roffey*. The reversing of the decision in *Foakes v Beer* was a matter for the House of Lords (at the time – now the Supreme Court), or Parliament, and could not be undertaken by the Court of Appeal. At this point, therefore, it seemed, although the decision on this point was *obiter* in *Re Selectmove*, that the concept of a 'practical benefit' could not form part of the consideration provided for accepting part payment of a debt as full satisfaction. Subsequent decisions have, however, cast doubt on this.[176]

First, in *Re Sutton*[177] it was suggested that the provision of a 'practical benefit', in the form of getting third parties to contribute to the reduced sum that had been agreed with the creditor as settlement for the debt, could be sufficient to make the promise to accept the smaller sum enforceable. In a more recent decision, *MWB Business Exchange Centres*

---

172 It seems unlikely that a reliance-based approach would come up with any different general rule on this issue. It is difficult to see that a debtor who has made part payment has 'relied' on a promise to accept this in full satisfaction – unless, perhaps, the debtor has subsequently taken on other commitments on the basis that the original debt has been extinguished.

173 (1602) 5 Co Rep 117a; 77 ER 237.

174 [1991] 1 QB 1; [1990] 1 All ER 512, discussed fully above at 3.9.9.

175 [1995] 2 All ER 351; [1995] 1 WLR 474.

176 A similar unwillingness to restrict *Williams v Roffey* can be seen in Australia. In *Musumeci v Winadell Pty Ltd* (1994) 34 NSWLR 723, Santow J, while noting *Re Selectmove,* applied the *Williams v Roffey* approach to a promise to accept a reduction in the rent payable on a lease.

177 [2014] BPIR 1349.

*Ltd v Rock Advertising Ltd*,[178] however, the Court of Appeal went somewhat further. The case concerned a licence for the use of business premises. This was renegotiated to give use of larger premises at a higher fee, with the contract to run for one year from November 2011. By early 2012 it was clear that the defendants were in difficulties as regards meeting the new higher charge. The claimants subsequently purported to terminate the contract. The defendants argued that an agreement had been made in February 2012 under which the claimants agreed to accept reduced payments for a period, with the balance being made up with larger payments towards the end of the contract. The claimants denied that there was an agreement but claimed that it would in any case be unenforceable for want of consideration on the *Foakes v Beer* principle. The trial judge held that there was an agreement, and that there was sufficient consideration to make it enforceable. On appeal, the Court of Appeal upheld the trial judge's decision. It found that there was sufficient 'practical benefit' to the claimant in the arrangement agreed in February to amount to good consideration for the promise to accept less than was owed. Kitchin, LJ, with whom the other two members of the court concurred, noted the claimant's argument that, on the basis of *Re Selectmove* there was no room for the *Williams v Roffey* concept of 'practical benefit' in this situation, but suggested that this failed to take account of the judge's findings of fact, namely:[179]

> He was clearly of the view that the oral variation agreement would have a number of beneficial consequences for MWB. First, MWB would recover some of the arrears immediately and would have some hope of recovering them all in due course. But secondly and importantly, Rock would remain a licensee and continue to occupy the property with the result that it would not be left standing empty for some time at further loss to MWB.

There was no suggestion that MWB was under duress in reaching the agreement, and there was commercial advantage to both parties in relation to it. This went beyond the advantage of receiving a prompt, but incomplete, payment, which was ruled out as being consideration by *Foakes v Beer* and *Re Selectmove*.

Despite this insistence that its decision is consistent with both *Foakes v Beer* and *Re Selectmove* it is difficult to see this case as anything other than a significant limiting of the scope of those decisions, and extension of the scope of *Williams v Roffey*. The case was subsequently appealed to the Supreme Court[180] but the Supreme Court decided the case on other grounds with Lord Sumption stating:

> In *Williams v Roffey Bros & Nicholls (Contractors) Ltd* [1991] 1 QB 1, the Court of Appeal held that an expectation of commercial advantage was good consideration. The problem about this was that practical expectation of benefit was the very thing which the House of Lords held not to be adequate consideration in *Foakes v Beer* (1884) … There are arguable points of distinction, although the arguments are somewhat forced. A differently constituted Court of Appeal made these points in *In re Selectmove Ltd* [1995] 1 WLR 474, and declined to follow *Williams v Roffey*. The reality is that any decision on this point is likely to involve a re-examination of the decision in *Foakes v Beer*. It is probably ripe for re-examination. But if it is to be overruled or its effect substantially modified, it should be before an enlarged panel of the court and in a case where the decision would be more than obiter dictum.[181]

---

178  [2016] EWCA Civ 553.
179  Ibid. [47].
180  [2018] UKSC 24.
181  [2018] UKSC 24 at [18].

## 3.13.2 THE DECISION IN *FOAKES V BEER*

The rule in *Pinnel's Case* was strictly *obiter*, in that the debtor had paid early, and had therefore in any case provided sufficient consideration to discharge the whole debt but it was confirmed by the House of Lords in *Foakes v Beer*.

---

**Key case** *Foakes v Beer* (1884)

Facts: Dr Foakes owed Mrs Beer a sum of money in relation to a judgment debt. Mrs Beer agreed that Dr Foakes could pay this off in instalments. When he had done so, Mrs Beer sued to recover the interest on the debt, in relation to the delay in the completion of payment resulting from the payment by instalments.
Held: The House of Lords held that, even if Mrs Beer had promised to forgo the interest (which was by no means certain),[182] it was an unenforceable promise because Dr Foakes had provided no consideration for it. Part payment of a debt could not in itself extinguish the debt.

---

The Court of Appeal has confirmed in two cases in particular that this is still the standard position as regards part payment of debts.

The first is *Re Selectmove*,[183] which was discussed above;[184] the second is *Ferguson v Davies*.[185] In the latter case, the plaintiff started a county court action to recover a debt, originally stated at £486.50 but later increased to £1,745.79. The defendant, as part of his 'defence' in relation to these proceedings, sent the plaintiff a cheque for £150, sending letters to the plaintiff and the court indicating that while he admitted liability to this extent, the cheque was sent in full settlement of his dispute. The plaintiff, having sought advice from the county court, presented the cheque for payment but continued with his action. The trial judge held that by accepting the £150, the plaintiff had compromised his action by a binding 'accord and satisfaction'. The Court of Appeal disagreed. Henry LJ, with whom Aldous LJ agreed, did so on the basis that there was no consideration here for the plaintiff's alleged agreement to abandon his claim. This was not a situation where a claim for a disputed amount was settled by a compromise involving partial payment by the debtor (a common basis for the settlement of legal actions). On the contrary, the defendant had admitted liability for the £150 sent, and so was giving the plaintiff nothing that could amount to consideration for the plaintiff's alleged agreement to forgo any further claim. By his own admission, he was bound in law to pay the £150, so this payment merely constituted the settlement of an acknowledged debt, and could not serve as consideration for any other promise. The principles of *Foakes v Beer* and *D and C Builders v Rees*[186] applied, and the plaintiff was free to pursue his claim for the balance that he alleged was owed to him.

It should perhaps be noted that the other member of the Court of Appeal, Evans LJ, with whom Aldous LJ also agreed, decided the case on the different ground that, on the facts, there was no true 'accord', in that the defendant's letters could reasonably be interpreted as not being intended to assert that the £150 was sent as full settlement of all claims by the plaintiff. On the consideration issue, Evans LJ specifically indicated that he

---

182  Cf the comments of Gilmore, 1974, at pp 31–2.
183  [1995] 2 All ER 534.
184  See above, 3.9.11.
185  [1997] 1 All ER 315.
186  [1966] 2 QB 617; [1965] 3 All ER 837 – discussed above, 3.12.4.

was expressing no view. Nevertheless, there is no doubt that, in the light of these Court of Appeal decisions, the principles in *Pinnel's Case* and *Foakes v Beer* remain good law in relation to the payment of debts, though limited somewhat by the extension into this area of the principle of 'practical benefit' from *Williams v Roffey*, as discussed in the previous section (3.13.1).[187]

### 3.13.3  THE EFFECT OF PROMISSORY ESTOPPEL ON *FOAKES V BEER*

What is the effect, if any, of the doctrine of promissory estoppel on these principles? In this context, it is important to note that *Foakes v Beer* was decided in 1884, that is seven years after the 'waiver' case of *Hughes v Metropolitan Railway*[188] on which Denning J placed significant reliance in *Central London Property Trust v High Trees House*, in developing the principle now known as 'promissory estoppel'. *Hughes* was not even cited in *Foakes v Beer*. Given that three of the four members of the House of Lords who delivered speeches in *Foakes v Beer* expressed some unhappiness about the outcome to which they felt that the common law bound them,[189] so that they would gladly have accepted an escape route via the equitable doctrine of waiver if that had been available, it must be assumed that the approach taken in *Hughes* was considered to have no relevance to the situation of part payment of debts. This, then, was a further way in which Lord Denning's decision in *Central London Property Trust Ltd v High Trees House Ltd* broke new ground. The case was concerned, in effect, with the partial payment of a debt (that is, half the rent for the war years). Nevertheless, Lord Denning felt able to apply to it the *Hughes* principle of 'equitable waiver' and it seems now to be generally accepted that this doctrine, in its new guise of 'promissory estoppel', can mitigate the harshness of the rule in *Foakes v Beer*, in appropriate cases.[190] This is not to say that *Foakes v Beer* would definitely be decided differently if it came before the House of Lords again today. That would depend on what exactly Mrs Beer was found to have promised, whether Dr Foakes could be said to have relied on that promise and also on whether promissory estoppel can be applied to extinguish a 'one-off' debt as opposed to payment obligations under a continuing contract. As we have seen in the previous section, the Court of Appeal, in *Collier v P & MJ Wright (Holdings) Ltd*, has recently expressed the view that by making a part payment which a creditor has agreed to accept as discharging the debt, a debtor shows sufficient reliance to support an argument of promissory estoppel.[191] This decision was only on a preliminary issue, but it appears to support the view that promissory estoppel can completely discharge a 'one-off' debt, simply on the basis that the debtor has made the requested part payment. If that is the case, then the scope for the principle in *Foakes v Beer* has been considerably narrowed. It would only apply where there was no true agreement to accept the part payment as discharging the debt, or where it was not inequitable to allow the creditor to go back on the promise to remit the debt.[192]

---

187 See also *Dan Simantob v Yacob Shavleyan t/a Yacob's Gallery* [2018] EWHC 2005 (QB) at [127] where Kerr J stated: "It is not open to me to decide that *Williams v Roffey Bros* was wrong and must be taken to have been overruled. It is binding on me, just as In *Re Selectmove* is. Lord Sumption JSC [in *Rock Advertising Ltd v MWB Business Exchange Centres Ltd* [2018] UKSC 24] did not decide that either case was wrongly decided. However, *Williams v Roffey* was not a case of part payment of a debt, unlike *Selectmove*, but of extra payment in return for an existing obligation to perform services. The narrow reading of *Williams* in Peter Gibson LJ's judgment in *Selectmove* is also binding on me."

188 (1877) 2 App Cas 439.

189 See (1884) 9 App Cas 605, p 613 (Lord Selborne); p 622 (Lord Blackburn); p 630 (Lord Fitzgerald).

190 Note that an Australian court has gone further: in *Musumeci v Winadell Pty Ltd* (1994) 34 NSWLR 723, Santow J held that, following *Williams v Roffey* [1991] 1 QB 1, a promise to accept a reduced rent could amount to a binding variation of the contract, without the need to rely on promissory estoppel.

191 [2007] EWCA Civ 1329; [2008] 1 WLR 643.

192 See also Austen-Baker, 2008.

## 3.14 OTHER TYPES OF ESTOPPEL

Before leaving this area, we should also note two other types of estoppel that can have an effect on the operation of a contract. First, there is *estoppel by convention*. This may arise where the parties to an agreement have acted on the basis that some provision in the contract has a particular meaning. This type of estoppel will then operate to prevent one of the parties later trying to argue that the provision means something different. An example of its use is *Amalgamated Investment and Property Co Ltd* ['AIP'] *v Texas Commerce International Bank Ltd*[193] ['the Bank']. In this case, there was a contract of guarantee between AIP and the Bank. The guarantee was in respect of a loan made by the Bank to a firm called Amalgamated (New Providence) Property Ltd ('ANPP'), which was a subsidiary of AIP. The guarantee contained a promise by AIP to repay money 'owed to you' (that is, the Bank) by ANPP. In fact, ANPP had been lent the money not by the Bank direct, but by a specially created subsidiary of the Bank named 'Portsoken'. When AIP got into financial difficulties and went into liquidation, the liquidator sought a declaration to prevent the Bank using money that it owed to AIP under another transaction in order to discharge ANPP's debt. It was argued that the guarantee was not binding because it only referred to money owing to the Bank itself, whereas the money had actually been lent by Portsoken. There was no money owed to the Bank by ANPP to which the guarantee could attach. It was held, however, that all parties had acted on the basis that the wording of the guarantee referred to the money lent by Portsoken to ANPP and, on that basis, an estoppel by convention operated to prevent AIP arguing for a different meaning. Therefore, AIP's liquidator could not stop the Bank from using the money owed to AIP in the way it proposed.[194]

A more recent confirmation by the House of Lords of the concept of estoppel by convention is to be found in *Johnson v Gore Wood & Co*.[195] The majority of the House held that the compromise of an action by a company against a firm of solicitors did not preclude the managing director of the company subsequently bringing a personal action against the firm. This was not an 'abuse of process' because the House felt that the earlier negotiations were based on the assumption that a further proceeding by the managing director would be possible. This assumption operated as an 'estoppel by convention'.[196]

The second type of estoppel that needs to be noted is *proprietary estoppel*. This operates particularly in relation to rights in land. It also differs from promissory estoppel (though both are sometimes confusingly referred to as 'equitable estoppel') in that it may be used to found a cause of action. In other words, it can be used as a sword rather than a shield. An example of its use is *Crabb v Arun District Council*.[197] Mr Crabb owned a plot of land adjacent to a road. He decided to sell half of the plot to the Arun District Council (ADC). The ADC built a road along one edge of the piece of land that it had bought. Mr Crabb was allowed access to this road from a particular point on the land that he had retained. Mr Crabb then decided to sell another portion of this land. On the basis of a promise from the council that he would be allowed another access point onto its road, he sold the piece of land containing the first access point. The ADC, despite the fact that it had initially left a gap in its fencing at an appropriate point, then refused to allow the second access. The

---

193 [1982] QB 84; [1981] 3 All ER 577.
194 Note that the judgments of the Court of Appeal were not unanimous on the issue of whether the Bank could have sued on the promise in the guarantee (as opposed to using it as a defence to AIP's action): Eveleigh LJ took the view that it could not (see p 126), but Brandon LJ (on the facts, p 132) and Lord Denning MR (as a matter of principle, p 122) thought that it could.
195 [2001] 1 All ER 481.
196 Lord Goff preferred to regard the situation as one involving a 'promissory estoppel' – though this led him to the same conclusion as the majority: see [2001] 1 All ER 481, p 508.
197 [1975] 3 All ER 865.

result was that the piece of land that Mr Crabb had retained was completely blocked in, without any access from either the original road or the road built by the ADC. Mr Crabb brought an action to compel the ADC to grant him the second access point that had been promised. Although there was no consideration for this promise, Mr Crabb succeeded in his action. The words and actions of the ADC had led Mr Crabb to believe that he would have the second access point, and he had relied on this to his detriment in selling the piece of land containing the first access point. The Court of Appeal therefore allowed him to succeed on the basis of a proprietary estoppel.

## 3.15 ALTERNATIVE TESTS OF ENFORCEABILITY

As we have seen, the English courts, following classical theory, profess to use the existence of valid consideration as the test for the enforceability of simple contracts. It is said that, in effect, consideration is necessary to make an agreement binding. In particular, a promise unsupported by consideration cannot be enforced. As was noted at the start of this chapter, however,[198] this analysis is not universally accepted, even as an accurate description of what the courts actually do. Indeed, we have already seen that there is a breach in the standard approach via the concept of promissory estoppel and a probable weakening of it via the case of *Williams v Roffey*.[199]

### 3.15.1 WHAT DOES 'CONSIDERATION' REALLY MEAN?

One of the leading English sceptics in relation to the traditional analysis of the doctrine of consideration was Professor Atiyah. His views were set out, *inter alia*, in Chapter 8 of his *Essays on Contract*, entitled 'Consideration: a re-statement'.[200] Atiyah's view, which is supported by some legal historians,[201] was that 'consideration' originated simply as an indication of the need for a 'reason' for enforcing a promise or obligation, such as the fact that the promisee had given something to the promisor in expectation that the promise would be fulfilled. It became formalised, however, into a rigid set of rules, such as that there must be benefit and detriment, that past consideration is no consideration, that consideration must be of economic value, and that gratuitous promises will not generally be enforced.

In examining how these rules actually operate, however, Atiyah argued that they are not actually followed rigidly by the courts. For example, as regards the need for benefit/detriment, he cited *Chappell v Nestlé*[202] and *Hamer v Sidway*[203] as indicating that this is not necessary for a contract. Nor is it sufficient, in that contracts in which there is clearly benefit or detriment may still not be enforced, as we shall see in later chapters, because of considerations of illegality, duress or undue influence. In relation to the need for economic value, *Ward v Byham*[204] may be seen as an exception.

Moreover, the unenforceability of gratuitous promises is not applied where promissory estoppel operates. Atiyah argued that promissory estoppel, as expounded in *High Trees*, was a step in the right direction, following a wrong turning taken as a result of the

---

198 See above, 3.4.

199 [1991] 1 QB 1; [1990] 1 All ER 512. Compare *Chen v NG (British Virgin Islands)* [2017] UKPC 27.

200 Atiyah, 1986: this is in fact a revised version of an inaugural lecture delivered at the Australian National University, Canberra, in 1971 and published by the Australian National University Press in the same year. See also Atiyah, 1978, republished as Chapter 2 in Atiyah, 1986.

201 For example, Simpson, 1975a, Chapters IV–VII, and in particular p 321.

202 [1960] AC 87; [1959] 2 All ER 701 – discussed above, 3.7.1.

203 (1891) 27 NE 256; 124 NY 538 – discussed above, 3.7.1.

204 [1956] 2 All ER 318 – discussed above, 3.7.1.

misinterpretation of *Jorden v Money*[205] as an authority for the proposition that a statement of intention cannot give rise to an estoppel. As we have seen,[206] that case was actually decided as it was, according to Atiyah, because of the requirements of the Statute of Frauds 1677, which at the time required that a promise given in consideration of marriage (which was the situation in *Jorden v Money)* had to be proved by writing.

Because there was no writing, the case could not be pleaded in contract and was therefore pleaded as estoppel, but the court refused to allow this to be used as a means of circumventing the requirements of the Statute of Frauds 1677. *High Trees*, which recognised the enforceability of a statement of intention that had been relied on, should have shown the way forward, but was thrown off course by *Combe v Combe*.[207] The real reason for the decision in that case, Atiyah argued, was not the fact that the wife was trying to use promissory estoppel as a cause of action, but that justice was not on her side because she was earning more than her ex-husband. This was a reason (or consideration?) for not enforcing the husband's promise. But, in general, where there has been reasonable reliance on a promise, even if the promisee has not provided what we should recognise as 'consideration' in the technical sense, Atiyah was of the view that the promise should be enforceable. This concept of reliance would, he argued, be a more satisfactory way of determining the existence of contractual obligations, as opposed to the formalistic requirement of consideration, with all its technical limitations.

What Atiyah was in effect arguing is that we should return towards the original idea of 'consideration' as meaning a reason for enforcing a promise or acknowledging an obligation. This would be a much more flexible doctrine. The disadvantage, however, is that it would also be rather uncertain and unpredictable, and might depend too much on what the individual judge thinks amounts to a sufficient reason for enforcing a promise on a particular set of facts. One possible basis on which this might be done is by giving a greater status to the requirement of 'intention to create legal relations', to which we shall turn in the next chapter.

### 3.15.2 'RELIANCE' AS A TEST OF ENFORCEABILITY

It is at this point we must return to the issue raised at the beginning of this chapter,[208] that is the role of 'reliance' as an alternative to, or replacement for, consideration. One aspect of Atiyah's criticisms was his view that in fact 'reliance' provides a more accurate test of enforceability than the orthodox doctrine of consideration, which takes as its paradigm the mutual exchange of 'binding' promises.[209] Courts enforce promises where the promisee has relied on the promise and it would therefore be unfair to allow the promisor to escape from his or her commitment. This view was, for Atiyah, inaccurate both as a description of the typical contract and in the light of the way in which the courts deal with them. Many common transactions, such as booking holidays, making air reservations and ordering goods are not commonly discussed by the participants in terms of 'promises'.[210] It is actions, and reliance on actions, rather than the exchange of promises, which leads to the creation of obligations.[211] On this basis, if you deliver goods to me, on the basis that I will pay you for them, it is your action in transferring the goods to me that creates an enforceable obligation to pay. You have acted to your detriment in reliance on the fact that I will

---

205  (1854) 5 HL 185.

206  Above, 3.10.3.

207  [1951] 2 KB 215; [1951] 1 All ER 767 – above, 3.12.1; 3.12.3.

208  Above, 3.4.

209  This aspect of his theories about contract appeared at greatest length in Atiyah, 1986, Chapter 2. Cf also the arguments of Baker concerning 'reasonable expectation' as the basis of contractual liability: Baker, 1979.

210  Ibid, p 23.

211  Atiyah goes on to question whether the law *should* enforce purely executory agreements, where there has been no reliance by either party.

pay for the goods. The same is true of someone, for example, boarding a bus where there is a conductor rather than the obligation to pay on entry. It is unrealistic to talk about my action in terms of its containing an implied promise to pay the fare; rather it is my action in taking advantage of the bus service, and being carried on my journey, which creates the obligation to pay.

The notion of contractual obligations being based on reliance, rather than a bargained for exchange, is not peculiar to Professor Atiyah.[212] It has a long history in the United States.[213] Indeed, the American Restatement,[214] even in its first version published in 1932, recognised it as part of the law of obligations. In addition to s 75, which contained what we would regard as an orthodox definition of consideration based around the concept of 'bargain', it also included s 90,[215] which reads:

> A promise which the promisor should reasonably expect to induce action or forbear-ance of a definite and substantial character on the part of the promisee and which does induce such action or forbearance is binding if injustice can be avoided only by the enforcement of the promise.

As will be seen, this provides a test for the enforceability of promises based not on 'consideration' but on 'reliance', and this has remained a central part of the American law of contract. This demonstrates that the English law of contract does not need to make consideration its primary, if not sole, test of enforceability. Recent developments in Australia can be seen as indicating a similar trend away from consideration.

It will be noticed that the language which was used in s 90 of the American Restatement bears a considerable similarity to that used by Lord Denning in developing the doctrine of promissory estoppel.[216] That doctrine can indeed be seen as basing contractual obligations on reasonable reliance. Its limitation as a rival to consideration is, however, as we have seen, the reluctance of the English courts to accept that it can operate to create new obligations rather than to vary existing ones. The Australian courts have been bolder in taking that step, as shown by the case of *Waltons Stores (Interstate) Ltd v Maher*.[217] The case concerned the proposed lease of a piece of land as part of a development project. The owners of the land were led to believe that the prospective lessees would proceed with the transaction and that the necessary exchange of contracts would take place.[218] With that expectation they demolished an existing building on the land, in preparation for the construction of a new building to meet the lessees' requirements. In fact, the lessees had already decided not to proceed with the agreement. They failed to communicate this to the owners, even though they knew that the work on demolishing the building had started. Could the owners claim any compensation?

Although there appeared to be no contract between the parties, the High Court of Australia allowed the owners to succeed on the basis of estoppel. The court felt that the

---

212 A good review of the role of 'reliance' as a test of enforceability is to be found in Collins, 2003, Chapter 5.

213 For example, Fuller and Perdue, 1936.

214 Intended as a 'model' law for potential adoption by the individual states, but also as representing the current law as revealed by the cases.

215 The process by which these two, rather contradictory, sections dealing with the basis of contractual obligations came to co-exist in the same document is entertainingly described by Gilmore, 1974, pp 60–5. See the slightly different wording in the *Second Restatement on Contracts*.

216 See above, 3.11.

217 (1988) 164 CLR 387; 76 ALR 513. This case may be regarded as building on *Legione v Hateley* (1983) 152 CLR 406, where at least some members of the High Court of Australia had first accepted that promissory estoppel should be applicable in Australia to preclude the enforcement of rights, at least between parties to an existing contract.

218 A letter indicating this was sent by the lessees' solicitor.

lessees, having 'promised' that the contract would proceed, had acted 'unconscionably' in knowingly allowing the owners to carry on with their work, thereby incurring a detriment. The promise should therefore be enforced. In coming to this conclusion, Mason CJ and Wilson J made specific reference to s 90 of the American Restatement, thus providing the link with the way in which promissory estoppel has been used in that jurisdiction. Brennan J set out a six-point summary of the requirements for this type of estoppel:[219]

(1)    the plaintiff assumed or expected that a particular legal relationship exists between the plaintiff and the defendant or that a particular legal relationship will exist between them and, in the latter case, that the defendant is not free to withdraw from the expected legal relationship;
(2)    the defendant has induced the plaintiff to adopt that assumption or expectation;
(3)    the plaintiff acts or abstains from acting in reliance on the assumption or expectation;
(4)    the defendant knew or intended him to do so;
(5)    the plaintiff's action or inaction will occasion detriment if the assumption or expectation is not fulfilled; and
(6)    the defendant has failed to act to avoid that detriment whether by fulfilling the assumption or expectation or otherwise.

All these conditions were satisfied in the case, and so the owners (the plaintiffs) were entitled to succeed in their action.

*Waltons v Maher* has the effect of extending promissory estoppel to apply in a situation where it is being used to create a new cause of action. In other words, it is doing what the Court of Appeal refused to do in *Combe v Combe*.[220] It is thus, in effect, allowing 'detrimental reliance' as an alternative to consideration, provided that such reliance can be said to make it 'unconscionable' for the promisor to renege on the promise.

Subsequent decisions in Australia have accepted the principle applied in *Waltons'* case,[221] and similar developments can be seen in particular cases from New Zealand[222] and from Canada.[223] Taking into account also s 90 of the American Restatement, it would seem that in the common law world it is increasingly the approach taken by the English courts, in limiting the scope for enforcing agreements on the basis of reliance, that is out of line. It would not be surprising if the concept of promissory estoppel were soon to be developed in England in a way that would bring the law here more into step with the broader approach adopted elsewhere.[224] It seems, however, that any such development will have to be undertaken by the Supreme Court. That was the view of the Court of Appeal in *Baird Textile Holdings Ltd v Marks & Spencer plc*.[225] This was a preliminary hearing relating to an application to strike out the claimant's action. The claimant's case was based on Marks & Spencer's termination without notice of a long-standing arrangement under which it bought supplies from the claimant. The court held that the claimant had no realistic chance of arguing either that the arrangement amounted to a contract (because of lack

---

219  (1988) 164 CLR 387, p 428.
220  [1951] 2 KB 215; [1951] 1 All ER 767.
221  For example, *The Commonwealth of Australia v Verwayen* (1990) 170 CLR 394; *The Zhi Jiang Kou* [1991] 1 Lloyd's Rep 493.
222  For example, *Burbery Mortgage Finance and Savings Ltd v Hindsbank Holdings Ltd* [1989] 1 NZLR 356.
223  For example, *Gilbert Steel Ltd v University Construction Ltd* (1973) 36 DLR (3d) 496; *Litwin v Pan* (1986) 52 DLR (4th) 459.
224  For the contrary argument that promissory estoppel should be confined to the area with which it was primarily developed to deal, at least in England (that is, the modification of existing contracts), see Halson, 1999.
225  [2001] EWCA 274; [2002] 1 All ER (Comm) 737.

of certainty and of any evidence of an intention to create legal relations) or that Marks & Spencer should be 'estopped' from bringing it to an end without reasonable notice. The court was unanimous in the view that it would be necessary for the House of Lords to develop the law in the way suggested by the claimant.[226] Unless and until this happens, it cannot therefore be said that the doctrine of consideration has as yet been replaced by a reliance-based approach to enforceability, though the areas where 'exceptionally' the latter approach is allowed to be used has significantly increased over the last 70 years.

Before leaving this area, it should be noted that there may be a difference between 'consideration' and 'reliance'-based contracts in the area of remedies. This topic is discussed more fully in Chapter 15, but the issue will be outlined here. The traditional view is that the claimant who successfully argues that a contract has been broken is entitled to recover damages to compensate for the lost benefits that would have accrued had the contract been performed properly (the 'expectation interest'). This will be the standard (though not universal) approach where the contract is enforceable on the basis of the mutual exchange of consideration. Where contractual obligations are based on 'reliance', however, it is not certain that lost expectations will be compensated. This is reflected in the current wording of s 90 of the American Restatement, which states that 'The remedy granted for breach may be limited as justice requires.' Similarly, in Australia, it has been suggested that what is recoverable as a result of the breach of a promise that has been relied on, but that is not supported by consideration, is damages to compensate the claimant for losses incurred by reliance, rather than the benefits that might have accrued from full performance.[227] If this is the case, then it may be argued that, although reliance may provide an alternative test of the enforceability of a promise, full contractual liability (that is, liability that includes the obligation to compensate for expected benefits) only arises from an agreement based on the exchange of consideration.[228]

### 3.15.3 'PROMISE' AS A TEST OF ENFORCEABILITY

As has been pointed out earlier in this chapter,[229] there are difficulties in fitting a 'promise' within the normal definition of consideration as involving some detriment to the person providing the consideration or some benefit to the person to whom it is provided. Given, however, that (again as noted above) much of the classical law of contract is centred on the notion that an exchange of promises makes both enforceable, even while both are executory, it is not surprising to find that there have been attempts to argue that 'promises' rather than reliance should be regarded as providing the badge of enforceability. This involves arguing that the reason for enforcing a promise is the fact that the promisor has used this form of discourse. Thus, the focus is on what the promisor has done, rather than (as with the consideration and reliance analyses) on what the promisee has done in response to the promise. The fullest modern attempt to present this argument is to be found in the work of Charles Fried.[230]

Drawing on the work of earlier philosophers,[231] Fried argues that there is a moral obligation to keep a promise, independent of reliance by the promisee, or of utilitarian

---

226  Judge LJ, however, appeared rather more sympathetic to the claimant's argument than either of the other members of the court (the Vice-Chancellor, Sir Robert Andrew Morritt and Mance LJ).

227  *The Commonwealth of Australia v Verwayen* (1990) 170 CLR 394.

228  For an argument that the gap as far as remedies is concerned is less than might appear at first sight, see Collins, 2003, pp 89–90. Collins points out that a finding of an estoppel can lead to a requirement to complete a promised obligation in situations where the normal contractual remedy would only be damages.

229  Above, 3.6.

230  See Fried, 1981. For an argument for the enforcement of gratuitous promises based on an economic analysis, see Posner, 1977.

231  For example, Immanuel Kant.

arguments about the benefits that may flow from promise-keeping. Rather, the obligation to keep a promise 'is grounded in respect for individual autonomy and trust'.[232] More fully:[233]

> An individual is morally bound to keep his promises because he has intentionally invoked a convention whose function is to give grounds – moral grounds – for another to expect the promised performance. To renege is to abuse a confidence that he was free to invite or not, and which he intentionally did invite.

Part of Fried's argument for putting 'promise' at the centre of contract is that the doctrine of consideration is inadequate as a test of enforceability. He suggests that two principal elements of the doctrine are mutually inconsistent. One says that the law is not concerned with the adequacy of consideration.[234] This appears to support the idea that 'the free arrangements of rational persons should be respected'.[235] The second principle is that only where something is given in exchange for a promise should the promise be enforceable. This means that 'the free arrangements of rational persons',[236] which might include the making of binding gratuitous promises, can be frustrated by the doctrine of consideration. His conclusion is that an analysis based on promise provides a more coherent basis for enforceability. He recognises, however, that his approach does not accord with Anglo-American contract law as it currently operates: 'There are too many gaps in the common law enforcement of promises to permit so bold a statement.'[237] This mismatch between theory and reality has formed the basis of the criticisms of Fried's approach, with Professor Atiyah as one of the strongest sceptics.[238] Atiyah suggests that the gaps in the extent to which promises are actually enforced by the courts means that it is preferable to view promises as being *prima facie* binding rather than absolutely and conclusively binding'.[239] He continues:[240]

> Exchanges of benefits are likely to be in the interests of those who make them, and there is therefore a strong *prima facie* case for upholding them. Promises are likely to be relied upon and those who rely would suffer loss from breach: these too are *prima facie* good reasons for upholding the binding nature of a promise.

It is only fair to note, however, that Fried is aware of the limitations of his thesis. His conclusion, however, is that, although there are many gaps in the common law enforcement of promises:[241]

> the doctrine of consideration offers no coherent alternative basis for the force of contracts ... Along the way to this conclusion I have made or implied a number of qualifications to my thesis. The promise must be freely made and not unfair ... It must also have been made rationally, deliberately. The promisor must have been serious enough that subsequent legal enforcement was an aspect of what he should have contemplated at the time he promised.

---

232  Fried, 1981, p 16.
233  Ibid.
234  See above, 3.7.
235  Fried, 1981, p 35.
236  Ibid.
237  Ibid, pp 37–8.
238  See Atiyah, 1986, Chapter 6.
239  Ibid, p 148.
240  Ibid.
241  Fried, 1981, p 38.

Put like this, it is clear that any analysis of contract based on Fried's approach will need to put considerable weight on the question of whether the promisor *intended* (or, at least, should have realised that others would assume from his words and actions that he was intending) to bind himself legally. As we saw above,[242] this is also an issue in relation to attempts to give a broad definition to 'consideration'. The issue of intention to create legal relations, and its role in the formation of contract, is considered fully in the next chapter.

## 3.16 SUMMARY OF KEY POINTS

- Promises can be enforceable when they are contained in a deed, supported by consideration, or where the doctrine of promissory estoppel applies.

- Consideration is the primary basis on which promises are enforceable in English law.

- Consideration can take the form of an action, or a promise to act. It need not be 'adequate' (i.e. of equivalent value) but must be 'sufficient' (i.e. an act or promise of a type recognised by the law).

- Consideration generally needs to have some economic value, but there are some apparent exceptions to this.

- Past consideration is no consideration, except where there has been a prior request, and the situation is one in which payment would be expected.

- The performance of existing duties will sometimes be good consideration, i.e.:
  - □ where the duty is owed to a third party;
  - □ where the performance goes beyond what is required by the existing duty (either under law, or owed to another party);
  - □ where the performance results in a 'practical benefit' to the other contracting party (*Williams v Roffey* (1990)).

- Part payment of a debt will arguably never in itself be good consideration for a promise to discharge the debt, but may give rise to an issue of 'promissory estoppel'.

- A promise not to insist on strict rights under a contract will be binding where the doctrine of promissory estoppel applies. This can apply to a promise to accept part payment of a debt.

- Promissory estoppel applies where:
  - □ there is a variation of an existing legal relationship;
  - □ the promisee has relied on the promise;
  - □ it is used as a shield not a sword;
  - □ it would be inequitable to allow the promisor to go back on the promise.

- Some other common law jurisdictions (e.g. the USA, Australia) more readily accept 'reasonable reliance' as a basis for the enforceability of promises. English law does not do so as yet, other than in the context of promissory estoppel.

---

242 Above, 3.15.1.

## 3.17 FURTHER READING

### Consideration

- Adams, J and Brownsword, R, 'Contract, consideration and the critical path' (1990) 53 MLR 536

- Atiyah, P S, 'Contracts, promises and the law of obligations' (1978) 94 LQR 193

### Relational contracts

- Campbell, D, 'The relational constitution of the discrete contract', Chapter 3 in Campbell, D and Vincent-Jones, P (eds), *Contract and Economic Organisation*, 1996, Aldershot: Dartmouth

- Campbell, D, 'Good faith and the ubiquity of the relational contract' (2014) 77 MLR 475

### Promissory estoppel

- Austen-Baker, R, 'A strange sort of survival for *Pinnel's case: Collier v P & MJ Wright (Holdings) Ltd'* (2008) 71 MLR 611

- Halson, R, 'The offensive limits of promissory estoppel' (1999) LMCLQ 256

- O'Sullivan, J, 'In defence of *Foakes v Beer'* [1996] CLJ 219

- Thompson, M P, 'Representation to expectation: estoppel as a cause of action' (1983) 42 CLJ 257

### Existing obligations as consideration

- Halson, R, 'Sailors, sub-contractors and consideration' (1990) 106 LQR 183

- Hird, N J and Blair, A, 'Minding your own business – *Williams v Roffey* revisited' [1996] JBL 254

### Alternatives to consideration

- Atiyah, P S, 'Consideration: a re-statement', Chapter 8 in Atiyah, P S, *Essays on Contract*, 1986, Oxford: Clarendon Press

- Fried, C, *Contract as Promise*, 1981, Cambridge, Mass: Harvard University Press

- Treitel, G H, 'Consideration: a critical analysis of Professor Atiyah's fundamental restatement' (1976) 50 Australian LJ 439

## COMPANION WEBSITE

*Now visit the companion website to:*

- Revise and consolidate your knowledge of Consideration by tackling a series of multiple-choice questions on this chapter

- Test your understanding of the chapter's key terms by using the flashcard glossary

- Explore Consideration further by accessing a series of web links

# Intention to create legal relations

## Contents

### 4.1 OVERVIEW

There may be situations where, despite the identification of an agreement and consideration, the courts feel that an agreement should not be enforced because the parties did not intend that it should create legal relations. The main approach is based on two presumptions:

- If the agreement is a 'domestic' agreement, the courts will presume that it is not intended to be legally binding. It will be up to the party wishing to enforce to overturn that presumption.
- If the agreement is 'commercial', the courts will presume that it is intended to be legally binding. It will be up to the party wishing to escape from the agreement to prove that the presumption should be overturned.

The most frequent issues relate to the categorisation of the agreement (as domestic or commercial), and the evidence that is necessary to overturn the presumption.

There is also statutory control of the situation in relation to agreements between trade unions and employers, which are generally treated as unenforceable.

## 4.2 INTRODUCTION

In addition to the tests of the existence of a contract dealt with in the previous chapters, the courts will also sometimes inquire whether, despite the fact that offer, acceptance and consideration can be identified, the parties did really intend to create a legally binding relationship. In line with the traditional approach that the courts regard themselves simply as 'referees' or 'umpires' giving effect to the parties' intentions, it is only where the parties themselves have entered into an agreement that they intend to be legally binding that the courts will treat it as a contract. As with the tests of agreement and enforceability, the courts take an objective approach, looking at what the parties have said and done and the context in which they have been dealing with each other. This was confirmed by the Supreme Court in *RTS Flexible Systems Ltd v Molkerei Alois Muller*,[1] where Lord Clarke said (emphasis added):[2]

> Whether there is a binding contract between the parties and, if so, upon what terms depends upon what they have agreed. It depends not upon their subjective state of mind, but upon a consideration of what was communicated between them by words or conduct, and whether that leads objectively to a conclusion *that they intended to create legal relations* and had agreed upon all the terms which they regarded or the law requires as essential for the formation of legally binding relations.

### 4.2.1 IN FOCUS: HIDDEN POLICY CONSIDERATIONS?

Collins has suggested that the 'objective' approach may well not coincide with reality:[3]

> In cases where the issue is litigated, it seems likely that one party intended a legal agreement and the other wanted the agreement to be merely morally binding. This contradiction removes any possibility of justifying the limits of contracts on the basis of the joint intent of the parties. We are forced to the conclusion that the courts must rely upon hidden policy considerations when determining the intentions of the parties.

We are not necessarily, however, 'forced' to this conclusion. In many cases, rather than the parties having different intentions, they may not, at the time of entering into their agreement, have thought about the issue at all.[4] In such a situation the courts will adopt the approach, which they also adopt in other areas where there is later disagreement as to the parties' intentions at the time of contracting,[5] of asking what the reasonable person in the position of the parties would have been likely to intend.[6]

---

1   [2010] UKSC 14; [2010] 1 WLR 753.
2   Ibid, para [45]. Approved in *Devani v Wells* [2019] UKSC 4 at [17] *per* Lord Kitchin with whom Lord Wilson, Lord Carnwath and Lord Sumption agreed.
3   Collins, 2003, pp 104–05.
4   See, for example, the comments by Upjohn LJ in *Coward v Motor Insurers' Bureau* [1962] 1 All ER 531, p 536, and by Lord Cross in *Albert v Motor Insurers' Bureau* [1971] 2 All ER 1345, pp 1369–70.
5   See Chapter 2, 2.4.1.
6   Compare the European Draft Common Frame of Reference Article II. – 4:102.

Although this approach may be used as a device to bring 'policy' considerations into the law, it is also capable of acting as a means of coming to an 'objective' view in an area where the parties' evidence as to their respective states of mind is in conflict.

## 4.2.2 USE OF FORMALITY?

Another way of approaching the issue of 'intention' would be through formal requirements. It would be possible to require, for example, that an agreement, to be legally binding must be in writing and have within it a clause confirming that it is intended to be legally binding. In one particular situation, relating to the enforceability of collective agreements between trade unions and employers, this is precisely what has been required.[7] As has been explained in earlier chapters, however, generally the English law of contract does not require formalities. Verbal agreements are enforceable, and no particular forms of words are required. It can be argued, however, that the requirements of offer, acceptance and consideration, discussed in Chapters 2 and 3, may to a certain extent be regarded in themselves as indications of an intention to enter into a legally binding contract. If the parties have taken the trouble to specify their obligations in a way that makes them clear and unambiguous (as required by 'offer and acceptance'), and the agreement has the element of mutuality required by the doctrine of consideration, this may reassure a court that legal enforceability was intended. If, for example, a transaction that would otherwise appear as a gift has consideration introduced artificially, this may well be strong evidence of an intention to make a contract. The transfer of the ownership of a valuable painting, worth £50,000, which involves the recipient giving the supplier £1 in exchange, would fall into this category. There would be no point in the recipient giving the money unless the intention is to make the transaction of transfer into a contract, and the parties into 'seller' and 'buyer'. The introduction of consideration is in this case therefore evidence of an intention to create legal relations. Taking this approach to its logical conclusion, some have argued that there is no need for a separate heading of intention,[8] and this point will be discussed below.[9]

The generally accepted view, however, is that, although this analysis has some force, there are nevertheless some agreements that may have all the other characteristics of a contract but that are clearly not meant to be treated as legally binding. If the parties to an apparently binding commercial agreement specifically state that it is not to have legal consequences, surely the courts should pay attention to this? Certain domestic arrangements may also raise difficulties. If, for example, there is an agreement between a James and Claire that he will cook a meal for them both, in return for her providing the wine to go with it, this may involve an offer, acceptance and consideration, but no one would expect it to be regarded as legally binding. If she failed to turn up, he would not be able to sue for the cost of preparing the meal. Given, however, that no formalities are required, and that offer, acceptance and consideration can be identified, how are those agreements that are intended to be binding to be distinguished from those that are not? The evidence of the parties themselves is likely to be unreliable, so some other means of determining the issue must be found.

In fact, as we have noted above, English law operates on the basis of an 'objective' approach, based on what a reasonable person in the position of the parties would have been likely to have intended. This approach is assisted by the 'presumptions' as to intention, which differ according to whether the agreement is to be regarded as 'domestic' or 'commercial'. These two categories of agreement must therefore be looked at separately.[10]

---

7  See below 4.6. See also Trade Union and Labour Relations (Consolidation) Act 1992, s 179 – discussed, further, below, 4.5.

8  For example, Hepple, 1970.

9  See 4.6.

10  Unger (1983, pp 60–6), from a 'critical legal studies' perspective, suggests that the division between 'family' and 'commercial' agreements can be explained by the conflict between the principle of freedom to contract,

## 4.3 DOMESTIC AGREEMENTS

The leading case in this category is *Balfour v Balfour*.[11]

---

**Key case** *Balfour v Balfour* (1919)

Facts: There was an agreement between husband and wife, resulting from her inability (due to illness) to return with him to his place of work, in Ceylon. He agreed to pay her £30 per month while they were apart. Later, the marriage broke up and the wife sued the husband for his failure to make the promised payments.

Held: The Court of Appeal held that her action must fail. Two members of the court centred their decision on the lack of any consideration supplied by the wife. Atkin LJ, however, stressed that even if there were consideration, domestic arrangements of this kind are clearly not intended by the parties to be legally binding. He used the example of the husband who agrees to provide money for his wife in return for her 'maintenance of the household and children'.[12] If this was a contract, then each would be able to sue the other for failure to fulfil the promised obligation. As regards this possibility, Atkin LJ commented:[13]

> All I can say is that the small courts of this country would have to be multiplied one hundredfold if these arrangements were held to result in legal obligations. They are not sued upon, not because the parties are reluctant to enforce their legal rights when the agreement is broken, but because the parties, in the inception never intended that they should be sued upon. Agreements such as these are outside the realm of contracts altogether.

The onus was on the wife to establish a contract and she had failed to do so. Mr Balfour was not contractually bound to make the payments.

---

Atkin LJ's judgment is the one that has received most attention in subsequent case law and has been taken as establishing the position that in relation to domestic agreements there is a *presumption* that they are not intended to be legally binding.

There are two points to be noted here. First, the notion of the 'domestic' agreement should probably be taken as relating more to the subject matter than to the relationship between the parties. If, for example, a woman agrees to sell her car to her brother for £1,500, there seems little reason to deny this agreement the status of a contract and it should be presumed to be binding unless there is evidence to the contrary. A decision of the High Court, however, has cast some doubt on this. It suggests that there may be situations which fall into a sort of 'halfway house' between domestic and commercial, and that in this case the burden of overturning the presumption may be affected. In *Sadler v Reynolds*,[14] the alleged contract was between a journalist and a businessman. The journalist wanted to ghost-write the autobiography of the businessman, who had had a 'rags

---

and the counter-principle 'that the freedom to choose the contract partner will not be allowed to work in ways that subvert the communal aspects of social life'.

11 [1919] 2 KB 571.
12 Ibid, p 579.
13 Ibid.
14 [2005] EWHC 309.

to riches' life, involving more than one spell in prison. The two had become friendly, meeting socially, and the journalist alleged that there had been an oral contract for him to write the autobiography. The judge suggested that the agreement fell 'somewhere between an obviously commercial transaction and a social exchange'.[15] The onus was on the journalist to prove that there was an intention to create legal relations, 'albeit that the onus [was] a less heavy one than that which would be required to establish such an intent in the context of a purely social relationship'. The judge clearly viewed the nature of the relationship as more significant than the nature of the agreement, since at first sight an agreement to write a book would appear to be 'commercial', so that the burden of proving that it was not binding should have fallen on the businessman. The judge held, however, that it was up to the journalist to prove that it *was* binding. It follows that, as the cases already demonstrate, the presumption is not limited to relatives. An example of an agreement between friends is *Coward v Motor Insurers' Bureau*,[16] where an agreement between workmates to share the cost of transport to work was held not be legally binding.[17]

The second point to note is that, since the rule is simply based on a presumption, it will always be possible for that presumption to be rebutted (as indeed was the case in *Sadler v Reynolds*). In *Merritt v Merritt*,[18] for example, an arrangement between husband and wife similar to that agreed in *Balfour v Balfour*, but here made in the context of the break-up of the marriage, was held to be legally binding. Lord Denning distinguished *Balfour v Balfour* in the following terms:[19]

> The parties there [that is, in *Balfour v Balfour*] were living together in amity. In such cases, their domestic arrangements are ordinarily not intended to create legal relations. It is altogether different when the parties are not living in amity but are separated, or about to separate. They then bargain keenly. They do not rely on honourable understandings. They want everything cut and dried. It may safely be presumed that they intend to create legal relations.

The context in which the agreement was made was such therefore that although it *prima facie* concerned a domestic matter, the support of a wife by her husband, the presumption that it was not intended to be binding was rebutted.

The same principles apply to other 'domestic' agreements, as is shown by the following case, which involved an agreement that is of relevance to the increasing numbers of people involved in national lottery 'syndicates'.

---

**Key case** *Simpkins v Pays* (1955)[20]

Facts: Three women, the plaintiff, the defendant and the defendant's granddaughter, lived in the same house. They regularly entered a newspaper 'fashion' competition, which required the listing of eight items in order of merit. Each of the three women made a listing, and the three entries were submitted on one form. There was no fixed arrangement as to who paid the entry fee or the postage, but the form was submitted

---

15 Ibid, at [56].
16 [1963] 1 QB 259; [1962] 1 All ER 531.
17 Cf *Albert v Motor Insurers' Bureau* [1971] 2 All ER 1345, where, in relation to a very similar situation, Lord Cross (who alone dealt with the issue in the House of Lords) took the view that there was an intention to enter into a contract (despite the fact that it was unlikely that either party would have considered taking legal action to enforce it).
18 [1970] 2 All ER 760.
19 Ibid, pp 761–62. See also *Darke v Strout* [2003] EWCA Civ 176.
20 [1955] 3 All ER 10.

in the defendant's name. When one of the lines won £750, which was paid to the defendant, the plaintiff sued to recover a third share of this.

Held: The judge held that there was, on the evidence, an agreement to 'go shares' if one of the lines won,[21] and that this was intended to be legally binding.

The judge's reasons for coming to this conclusion are not very clear but seem to relate to the fact that there was a 'mutuality in the arrangement between the parties'. Having heard the evidence of the parties, he felt that their agreement went beyond the 'sort of rough and ready statement' made in family associations which would not be intended to be binding.[22] There was a clear understanding as to what would happen in the event of a win, and this agreement was meant to be enforceable.

**For thought**

*James decides to start a lottery syndicate with people working in his office. Harry, Radha and Emma all agree to take part. They each choose a set of numbers to be used, but James always buys the ticket. He usually collects the money from the others in advance, but sometimes they do not pay him until the following week. What steps would you advise the group to take to ensure that if one of the sets of numbers wins a prize they all get to share in the winnings?*

*Simpkins v Pays* needs to be contrasted with a more recent decision on similar facts. In *Wilson v Burnett*[23] three young women who worked together had attended a bingo session, at which one of them, Tania, had won a national prize of over £100,000. Her companions alleged that they had agreed, when deciding to have a night out at the bingo hall, that they would share any prize of over £10. The trial judge held against them. They appealed, on the basis that the judge's decision was not properly reasoned. The Court of Appeal, however, noted that the evidence for the agreement was not conclusive, and in particular was undermined by the fact that when Tania had won the local prize of £153 and they were waiting to hear the national result, her companions and others repeatedly asked if she was 'going to share'. In effect, the Court confirmed the judge's view that 'chat or talk' about sharing winnings had not 'crossed that line which exists between talk and "meaning business", or an intention to create a legal relationship'. This suggests that those who intend to share competition prizes would be well advised to make their agreement formal, since the presumption that social agreements are not intended to be legally binding will not necessarily be overturned as easily as it was in *Simpkins v Pays*.

All the surrounding circumstances need to be considered, as was stressed by Devlin J in *Parker v Clark*.[24] Here a young couple (the plaintiffs) agreed to live with older relatives (the defendants) and help look after them. In exchange, the plaintiffs were promised that the defendants' house and contents would be left to them. The

---

21  Ibid, p 12.
22  [1955] 3 All ER 10.
23  [2007] EWCA Civ 1170.
24  [1960] 1 All ER 93.

arrangement did not work out, and the plaintiffs, having moved out, sued for damages. Devlin J noted that:[25]

> a proposal between relatives to share a house, and a promise to make a bequest of it, may very well amount to no more than a family arrangement ... which the courts will not enforce.

On the other hand, it was possible for such an arrangement to be legally binding:[26]

> The question must, of course, depend on the intention of the parties, to be inferred from the language they use and from the circumstances in which they use it.

In this case, the fact that the plaintiffs had sold their own house in order to move in with the defendants suggested that this was intended to be a binding agreement. The presumption that there is no intention in domestic agreements was again held to be rebutted.

---

**For thought**

*Jack and Jill, who were renting a flat at the time, agreed to go and live with Jill's aunt, Bessie, because she wanted company after her husband died. Bessie promised to leave her house to Jack and Jill in her will. Would this promise be enforceable?*

---

Although the cases so far considered may suggest that it is relatively easy to see on which side of the dividing line an arrangement between relatives should fall, in some cases the decision may be very finely balanced. This is demonstrated by *Jones v Padavatton*,[27] where the four judges who considered the facts were divided 2:2 as to whether or not they indicated an intention to create legal relations. In this case, the alleged contract was between a mother and daughter. The mother, who lived in the West Indies, promised her daughter, who was at the time working in the United States, that if she (the daughter) would go to England to study for the Bar, she (the mother) would pay her $200 per month. The daughter agreed to this arrangement, which began in February 1962. In 1964, the mother bought a house in which the daughter was to live, supporting herself by letting out some of the rooms. This replaced the previous arrangement of monthly payments. In 1967, with her daughter still unsuccessful in the Bar examinations, the mother sought possession of the house. The daughter's defence was based on there being a contract between herself and her mother. The trial judge was convinced by the daughter's evidence to this effect, and held that there was a contract. On appeal, this view was supported by Salmon LJ, who felt that, among other things, neither party could have 'intended that if, after the daughter had been in London, say, for six months, the mother dishonoured her promise and left her daughter destitute, the daughter would have no legal redress'.[28] The other two members of the Court of Appeal disagreed. Fenton Atkinson LJ noted the vagueness of the arrangements, and the fact that in cross-examination the daughter had admitted that she had refused to see her

---

25  Ibid, p 100.
26  Ibid.
27  [1969] 2 All ER 616.
28  Ibid, p 622. He found, however, that the contract could not have been intended to last for more than five years, and so on that basis the mother was entitled to succeed in her action for possession.

mother when the latter had come to the house in London because 'a normal mother doesn't sue her daughter in court'.[29] In conclusion, his view was that:[30]

> At the time when the first arrangements were made, the mother and daughter were, and always had been, to use the daughter's own words, 'very close'. I am satisfied that neither party at that time intended to enter into a legally binding contract, either then or later when the house was bought. The daughter was prepared to trust the mother to honour her promise of support, just as the mother no doubt trusted the daughter to study for the Bar with diligence, and to get through her examinations as early as she could.

There was, therefore, never any contract between them, and the mother was entitled to succeed.[31]

This case perhaps serves to illustrate the importance of deciding whether the initial presumption is for or against there being a legal relationship. If there had been a presumption in favour of intention to create legal relations in *Jones v Padavatton*, which the mother had to rebut, it is not inconceivable that the result would have gone the other way. The fact that it was a 'domestic agreement' meant that the presumption went against there being an intention to be legally bound, and thus made it easier for the mother to succeed in her argument.

Finally, it should be noted that the question of whether or not, if the agreement is broken, the innocent party would in practice go to the courts to enforce it should not be regarded as being conclusive as to whether there was an intention to create legal relations. There are many minor commercial agreements (for example, the arrangement for newspapers to be delivered by a local newsagent) where the parties would be unlikely to consider it to be worth involving the courts to remedy a breach. Nevertheless, such agreements are clearly intended by the parties to affect their legal relations and to create binding obligations.[32] Moreover, even in relation to substantial commercial transactions, research has shown that parties often prefer to settle disputes in ways that do not involve recourse to lawyers.[33] This does not mean that they do not intend their agreements to be legally binding. As noted in *Jones v Padavatton*,[34] the fact that the parties would not be expected to sue each other may be relevant if such expectation is based on the relationship between the parties (for example, mother and daughter), but even then it cannot be conclusive.

## 4.4 COMMERCIAL AGREEMENTS

If the agreement is not a 'domestic' one, then it will be regarded as 'commercial'. This means the presumption is that the agreement is intended to be legally binding. It was

---

29  Ibid, p 625.

30  Ibid.

31  Danckwerts LJ delivered a judgment to the same effect, relying primarily on *Balfour v Balfour* [1919] 2 KB 571.

32  That is, in the example just given, on the part of the newsagent to deliver papers each day, and on the part of the customer to settle the bill at regular intervals. See also the comments of Lord Cross in *Albert v Motor Insurers' Bureau* [1971] 2 All ER 1345, p 1370, and Salmon LJ in *Jones v Padavatton* [1969] 2 All ER 616, p 622.

33  See, for example, Macaulay, 1963; Beale and Dugdale, 1975; Lewis, 1982.

34  [1969] 2 All ER 616.

confirmed in *Edmonds v Lawson*[35] that this could include an agreement that was primarily educational – as with the agreement between a pupil barrister and her chambers. The trouble taken by the chambers in selecting pupils and the importance to the pupil of obtaining a pupillage suggested that the arrangement was not intended to be binding in honour only. The fact that the relationship was also governed by the Bar Council's regulations, and that it was unlikely in practice that a chambers would sue a pupil who defaulted, did not prevent it from being intended to be legally binding.

In *Edwards v Skyways*,[36] Megaw J emphasised that there will be a heavy onus on a party to an ostensibly commercial agreement who wishes to argue that the presumption has been rebutted.

**Key case** *Edwards v Skyways* (1964)

Facts: The plaintiff was a pilot who had been made redundant. As part of the arrangements for this, he was offered and accepted a payment which was stated to be 'ex *gratia*'. The company then found that the terms that had been offered would be more expensive for it than it had realised, and denied that there was any legal obligation to make the payment.

Held: The judge held that 'ex *gratia*' did not mean 'not legally binding', but simply recognised that, prior to the offer being made, there had been no obligation to make such a payment. Once it had been made, however, and accepted as part of the redundancy arrangement, it was capable of being legally binding and there was no evidence to overturn the presumption that this should be the case. The pilot succeeded in his action.

A similar reluctance to overturn the presumption is shown by the House of Lords decision in *Esso Petroleum Ltd v Commissioners of Customs and Excise*.[37] This concerned a 'special offer' of a common type, under which garage owners offered a free 'World Cup Coin' to every purchaser of four gallons of petrol. The coins could be collected to make a set but had minimal intrinsic value. Promotional advertising will often be considered as a 'mere puff' and not intended to be legally binding. As discussed earlier, in relation to offer and acceptance, however, the case of *Carlill v Carbolic Smoke Ball Co*[38] shows that in appropriate circumstances it can be found to be intended to create a legal relationship, on the basis of a unilateral contract. Similarly, in the *Esso* case, the majority of the House of Lords held that there was a unilateral contract under which the garage proprietor was saying, 'If you buy four gallons of my petrol, I promise to give you one of these coins.' The minority (Viscount Dilhorne and Lord Russell) felt that there was, however, no intention to create legal relations. As Viscount Dilhorne put it, if this arrangement was held to be a contract:[39]

it would seem to exclude the possibility of any dealer ever making a free gift to any of his customers, however negligible its value, to promote his sales.

---

35 [2000] 2 WLR 1091.
36 [1964] 1 WLR 349. Compare *MacInnes v Gross* [2017] EWHC 46 (QB) where an 'agreement' over an informal dinner was held not to be intended to create legal relations.
37 [1976] 1 All ER 117.
38 [1893] 1 QB 256 – see above, 2.7.8.
39 [1976] 1 All ER 117, pp 120–21.

Moreover, he did 'not consider that the offer of a gift of a free coin is properly to be regarded as a business matter'. The majority, however, viewed what was being done as clearly a 'commercial' transaction. As Lord Simon commented:[40]

> Esso and the garage proprietors put the material out for their commercial advantage, and designed it to attract the custom of motorists. The whole transaction took place in the setting of business relations ... The coins may have been themselves of little intrinsic value; but all the evidence suggests that Esso contemplated that they would be attractive to motorists and that there would be a large commercial advantage to themselves from the scheme, an advantage in which the garage proprietors would share.

The decision thus emphasises the difficulty faced by a commercial organisation in avoiding legal liabilities in connection with any transaction that it enters into with a view to commercial advantage. The advantage here was indirect (neither Esso nor the garages benefited directly from the exchange of the coins for petrol), but was nevertheless sufficient (that is, in terms of the likely increased sales of petrol that would result) to bring the presumption of an intention to create legal relations into play.

## For thought

*The Daily Wail advertises that a DVD of music videos will be available as a 'free gift' inside the paper the following Saturday. When Ben buys his paper he finds that the DVD is missing. Could he sue the Daily Wail (rather than his newsagent) for this failure to supply the DVD?*

It is possible, however, by using sufficiently explicit wording, to rebut the presumption even in relation to a clearly commercial agreement. This is commonly done in relation to agreements relating to the sale of land that are generally stated to be 'subject to contract', even where a price has been agreed between the parties. This is intended to ensure that they are not binding until fully considered written contracts have been exchanged.[41] This approach is often also used in commercial contracts not concerned with land but the Supreme Court has recently indicated that this does not necessarily mean that it will be applied to prevent a contract arising if the parties' subsequent behaviour indicates that they have waived this requirement. In *RTS Flexible Systems Ltd v Molkerei Alois Müller GmbH & Co KG (UK Production)*, the parties had been negotiating a contract for the building and installation of machinery.[42] During the negotiations it was stated that the contract was not to become binding until signed by both parties. In fact, work started before negotiations were concluded, and the Supreme Court held that the behaviour of the parties indicated that they no longer intended to be bound by the requirement of a signed document. As Lord Clarke commented:[43]

> The price had been agreed, a significant amount of work had been carried out, agreement had been reached on 5 July and the subsequent agreement to vary the

---

40 [1976] 1 All ER 117, p 121.
41 Note also the formalities required for this type of contract by the Law of Property (Miscellaneous Provisions) Act 1989, s 2(1). See also the comments of Atiyah, 2006, pp 101–03.
42 [2010] UKSC 14; [2010] 1 WLR 753.
43 Ibid, para 86.

contract so that RTS agreed to provide line 1 before line 2 was reached without any suggestion that the variation was agreed subject to contract. The clear inference is that the parties had agreed to waive the subject to contract clause.... Any other conclusion makes no commercial sense.

In other words, the language used by the parties has to be looked at in the context of their overall relationship. If their behaviour indicates an intention to make a binding agreement, this may override any previous statements to the contrary.

An example of a successful attempt to exclude 'intention to create legal relations' in the commercial context is to be found in *Rose and Frank Co v Crompton Bros*.[44] This case was concerned with a continuing agency arrangement between two companies. The agreement contained within it an 'Honourable Pledge Clause', which specifically stated that it was not entered into as 'a formal or legal agreement' but was 'only a definite expression and record of the purpose and intention' of the parties. The parties 'honourably pledged' themselves to the agreement in the confidence 'that it will be carried through by each of the ... parties with mutual loyalty and friendly co-operation'.[45] The Court of Appeal held that this should not be regarded as creating a legally binding agreement. To hold otherwise would be to frustrate the clear intentions of the parties:[46]

> I can see no reason why, even in business matters, the parties should not intend to rely on each other's good faith and honour, and to exclude all idea of settling disputes by any outside intervention ... If they clearly express such an intention, I can see no reason in public policy why effect should not be given to their intention.

The House of Lords agreed with the Court of Appeal that the overall agency arrangement was not legally binding, and could therefore be terminated without notice. In relation to particular orders placed under the agreement, however, they preferred the dissenting view of Atkin LJ in the Court of Appeal that such orders were enforceable contracts of sale. The 'honour clause' applied only to the general framework agreement, and not to specific orders made under it. Once again, therefore, the presumption of legal enforceability prevails in relation to commercial dealings and the rejection of this by the parties is interpreted strictly so as to apply only in the limited circumstances to which the rejection most clearly applies.

'Honour clauses' have long been included on football pools' coupons, with the effect that the promoter is under no contractual obligation to pay winnings to a person who has submitted a coupon with a winning line ('the punter').[47] The Court of Appeal has also held that such a clause must be taken to apply to any agreement between the punter and a collector of coupons who then forwards them to the promoter. In *Halloway v Cuozzo*,[48] the collector had failed to forward the plaintiff's coupon, which contained a winning line. The Court of Appeal held that the collector had no contractual liability towards the punter. Moreover, the lack of intention to create legal relations also prevented the creation of a duty of care, so that there was no liability in the tort of negligence either.

Public policy arguments may also influence a decision as to whether there is intention to create legal relations. In *Robinson v HM Customs & Excise*,[49] the claimant was an informer for Customs and Excise. He tried to bring a contractual claim for the payment of reasonable remuneration and expenses. It was held, however, that there was no intention

---

44  [1925] AC 445.
45  [1925] AC 445, p 451.
46  [1923] 2 KB 261, p 288 (*per* Scrutton LJ).
47  *Jones v Vernons Pools* [1938] 2 All ER 626; *Appleson v H Littlewood Ltd* [1939] 1 All ER 464.
48  (1999) unreported, 9 February, CA.
49  (2000) *The Times*, 28 April.

to create legal relations in respect of the supply of information by the claimant. The payments were discretionary and dependent on results (for example, arrests, seizures of illicit goods) and there were reasons of public policy why the court could not become involved in inquiring into these matters.

At one time the courts took the view that there was no contract between a minister of religion and the church to which he or she belonged.[50] Although the arrangement might look like a contract of employment, it was regarded as not having this status because it was felt that the relationship had a spiritual basis rather than being intended to create legal relations. It therefore fell outside the 'commercial' presumption. This approach has now been rejected to some extent. The House of Lords in *Percy v Board of National Mission of the Church of Scotland*[51] took the view that the minister was able to bring a claim of sex discrimination against the church. This conclusion was based on a finding that the minister, while she might not have been engaged under a contract of employment, at least had a contract with the church in relation to the performance of certain duties for which she received payment and reimbursement of expenses. Subsequently the Court of Appeal in *The President of the Methodist Conference v Moore*[52] held that the previous suggestion that there was a rebuttable presumption against the relationship between a minister and church being intended to create enforceable legal obligations was to be regarded as having been rejected by the decision in *Percy*. In *Singh v The Members of the Management Committee of the Bristol Sikh Temple*[53] the same approach was applied in finding that a Granthi at a Sikh Temple had a contract with the management committee (although not a contract of employment). However, on appeal in *Moore*,[54] the Supreme Court held that the minister did not have a "contract of service" as her rights and duties came from the constitution of the Methodist Church rather than through contract. Lord Sumption (with whom Lord Wilson and Lord Carnwath agreed) stated:[55]

> It is clear from the judgments of the majority in *Percy* that the question whether a minister of religion serves under a contract of employment can no longer be answered simply by classifying the minister's occupation by type: office or employment, spiritual or secular. *Nor, in the generality of cases, can it be answered by reference to any presumption against the contractual character of the service of ministers of religion generally*: see, in particular, Baroness Hale at para 151. The primary considerations are the manner in which the minister was engaged, and the character of the rules or terms governing his or her service. But, as with all exercises in contractual construction, these documents and any other admissible evidence on the parties' intentions fall to be construed against their factual background. Part of that background is the fundamentally spiritual purpose of the functions of a minister of religion.

## 4.5 COLLECTIVE AGREEMENTS

Some problems of intention to create legal relations have arisen in the area of 'collective agreements'. By this is meant agreements between trade unions and employers, or

---

50  *President of the Methodist Church v Partitt* [1984] QB 368. See also *Davies v Presbyterian Church of Wales* [1986] 1 WLR 323 and *Diocese of Southwark v Coker* [1998] ICR 140.
51  [2005] UKHL 73; [2006] 2 AC 28.
52  [2011] EWCA Civ 1581.
53  UKEAT/0429/11/ZT, 14 February 2012.
54  *Moore v President of the Methodist Conference* [2013] UKSC 29.
55  At [10] (emphasis added). See also *Trustees of the Celestial Church of Christ, Edward Street Parish v Lawson* [2017] EWHC 97 (Ch).

Intention to Create Legal Relations

**BASIC PRINCIPLE:**

**Objective test: based on what a reasonable person would have intended**

The approach is based upon *rebuttable presumptions* which depend upon whether the agreement is 'domestic' or 'commercial'

**Domestic agreements:**
Presumption that agreements between family members will not usually be legally binding:
*Balfour v Balfour* (1919)

Presumption can be rebutted:
*Merritt v Merritt* (1970)
*Parker v Clark* (1960)

**Commercial agreements:**
Presumption that commercial agreements will be legally binding:
*Edwards v Skyways Ltd* (1964)

Can be rebutted if clear intention is stated:
*Rose & Frank Co v Crompton Bros* (1925)

**See also statutory intervention:** s 179 Trade Union & Labour Relations (Consolidation) Act 1992 – collective agreements presumed not to have been intended by parties to be legally enforceable unless in writing and expressly stated to be legally enforceable

Figure 4.1

employers' organisations, as to the terms and conditions of work of particular groups of employees. Each employee will have a binding contract of employment with the employer, but some of the terms of this agreement (for example, as to rates of pay) may specifically be stated to be subject to the current collective agreement between employer and trade union. What is the status of the collective agreement itself? It is clearly made in a commercial or business context, and therefore it would seem that there should be a presumption of legal enforceability.

The issue was considered by the High Court in *Ford Motor Co Ltd v AEF*.[56] Ford was seeking an injunction restraining the trade union from calling strike action by its members. Part of Ford's argument depended on establishing that the collective agreements that it had reached with the AEF were legally binding. In deciding this issue, Geoffrey Lane J took the view that it was necessary to look at the general context in which such agreements were made. An objective view of whether they were intended to be enforceable should take account of not only the wording of the agreements themselves and their nature, but also 'the climate of opinion voiced and evidence by the extra-judicial authorities'[57] (here, he had in mind the *Donovan Report* on industrial

---

56 [1969] 2 QB 303.
57 Ibid, pp 329–30.

relations that had recently been published,[58] and academic writing on the issue). Taking these matters into account:[59]

> Agreements such as these, composed largely of optimistic aspirations, present-ing grave practical problems of enforcement and reached against a background of opinion adverse to enforceability, are, in my judgment, not contracts in the legal sense and are not enforceable at law.

To make them legally binding would require 'clear and express provisions' to that effect.

This judgment seems to draw on a much wider range of factors than the other cases in this area in order to determine the issue. It is probably the case, however, that such an approach was a result of the particular sensitive context (that is, industrial relations) rather than being indicative of the way in which the issue should be dealt with more generally. The *Ford* decision should not, therefore, be regarded as indicating any general departure from the presumption of legal enforceability that attaches to agreements in the commer-cial area. As far as collective agreements themselves are concerned, the matter is now dealt with by statute. Section 179 of the Trade Union and Labour Relations (Consolidation) Act 1992 provides that collective agreements are 'conclusively presumed not to have been intended by the parties to be' legally enforceable. The only exception is where the agreement is in writing, and expressly stated to be legally enforceable. We thus have here a presumption against legal enforceability that is even stronger than that which operates in relation to domestic agreements. It cannot be rebutted by taking account of verbal state-ments, or by looking at the context, but only by a clear intention committed to writing. This, therefore, is one of the few occasions in which English law requires formality in the making of an agreement if it is to be legally enforceable.

## 4.6 IN FOCUS: IS A REQUIREMENT OF INTENTION NECESSARY?

At the beginning of this chapter, reference was made to the argument that the insistence on a requirement of intention, in addition to the other elements of validly formed contract (offer, acceptance, consideration), is unnecessary. This view has been taken by, for exam-ple, Hepple.[60] Hepple argues that the problems with this area derive largely from a failure to take account of the particular approach to consideration adopted by Atkin LJ in *Balfour v Balfour*.[61] He points out that, in defining consideration in terms of 'mutual promises' or as 'a benefit received by one party or a loss suffered by the other', Atkin LJ failed to add that the benefit or loss, or indeed the mutual promises, 'must be received as the price for the other'. Hepple argues that many domestic agreements may involve mutual promises, 'and yet not be ... contract[s] because the promise of the one party is not given as the price for the other'.[62] In other words, the concept of the *bargain* is central to the test of enforceability of contracts under English law and the vital elements in the identification of a bargain are offer, acceptance and consideration. These three elements should be treated *together* as indicating a *bargain*. Thus, an analysis that tries to separate out *agreement* (that is, offer and acceptance) from consideration is missing the point of why the courts started looking for evidence of these three elements in the first place:[63]

---

58  Cmnd 3623, 1968.
59  [1969] 2 QB 303, pp 330–31.
60  See Hepple, 1970.
61  [1919] 2 KB 571.
62  Hepple, 1970, p 128.
63  Ibid.

This separation of agreement from consideration ... has resulted in a fundamental point being overlooked. This is that the common law recognised at an early stage that usually parties do not define their intention to enter into legal relations. Consequently, the fact that they have cast their agreement into the form of bargain (offer, acceptance, consideration) provides an extremely practical test of that intention. This test of bargain renders superfluous any *additional* proof of intention.

Accordingly, Hepple regards the courts as falling into error in trying to identify an additional element of intention in cases such as *Ford Motor Co Ltd v AEF*.[64] This only results 'in the use of unnecessary legal fictions'.

The argument may be justified as according with the principle that the intention of the parties must be decided objectively. In other words, can the party who claims that he or she thought that the agreement was intended to be enforceable be said to have acted reasonably in this assumption?[65] The presumption would be that as long as offer, acceptance and consideration were present, and no specific statement had been made about enforceability, then it would be intended to be legally binding. Social and domestic agreements could still be excluded from enforceability either because no reasonable person expects them to be legally binding, and therefore an assumption that they are would be unreasonable, or because what is given in exchange in such agreements is not generally to be regarded as good consideration. In either case, no 'bargain' is created.

This line of argument is in effect introducing a rule of formality into the formation of contracts. The formal requirements become not writing, or signature, but 'offer', 'acceptance' and 'consideration'. The parties who go through the process of making an agreement that contains these elements will, in the absence of specific and explicit evidence to the contrary, be deemed to have made a 'bargain' and therefore a binding agreement. Although this has some attractions, it is submitted that it does not truly represent the English common law approach to contracts. This is based not only in relation to formation, but in many other areas as well, on the basis that the court is trying to give effect to the intention of the parties. This is the overriding concept, and the evidence that may go towards establishing whether any intention to create a legal relationship existed and, if so, what it was intended to be is subsidiary. For that reason, the courts legitimately remain concerned to establish the existence or absence of intention, even if other indicators of a binding agreement are present. The existence of the presumption of enforceability in commercial agreements does not contradict such an approach. It simply allows it to operate in a way that is efficient, and does not encourage the parties to an agreement to become involved in unnecessary disputes as to their supposed intentions.

## 4.7 SUMMARY OF KEY POINTS

- Intention to create legal relations in English contract law is determined by the use of presumptions.

- If the agreement is social or domestic it will be presumed to be not intended to be legally binding.

- If the agreement is commercial it will be presumed to be intended to be legally binding.

---

64  [1969] 1 WLR 339.
65  Cf European Draft Common Frame of Reference, Art II. – 4:102.

- It is possible to overturn both presumptions, but it is easier to do so in relation to social/domestic agreements, as opposed to commercial agreements.

- Collective agreements are only binding if in writing and expressed to be so.

## 4.8 FURTHER READING

- Allen, D, 'The gentleman's agreement in legal theory and in modern practice' [2000] Anglo-American Law Review 204

- Brown, I, 'The letter of comfort: placebo or promise?' [1990] JBL 281

- Freeman, M, 'Contracting in the haven: *Balfour v Balfour* revisited', in Halson, R (ed), *Exploring the Boundaries of Contract*, 1996, London: Dartmouth

- Hedley, S, 'Keeping contract in its place: *Balfour v Balfour* and the enforceability of informal agreements' (1985) OJLS 391

- Hepple, B, 'Intention to create legal relations' (1970) CLJ 122

- Unger, R, *The Critical Legal Studies Movement*, 1983, Cambridge, Mass: Harvard University Press, pp 60–66

## COMPANION WEBSITE

*Now visit the companion website to:*

- Revise and consolidate your knowledge of Intention by tackling a series of multiple-choice questions on this chapter

- Test your understanding of the chapter's key terms by using the flashcard glossary

- Explore Intention further by accessing a series of web links

# Privity

5

**Contents**

## 5.1 OVERVIEW

The doctrine of privity of contract states that generally only those who are parties to a contract can have rights or liabilities under it. The doctrine is well established in English law but also has a number of exceptions to it. In particular, the Contracts (Rights of Third Parties) Act 1999 means that there are situations where the parties can choose to sidestep the doctrine. The order of treatment here is:

- The origins of the doctrine. What are the reasons underlying the doctrine and how did it develop in English law?
- The Contracts (Rights of Third Parties) Act 1999. This is a major exception to the doctrine. It allows, in particular circumstances, the parties to a contract to create benefits that are legally enforceable by a third party.
- Common law devices to evade the doctrine. These include the following:
  - Damages on behalf of another. In some situations the courts will allow a party to a contract to recover damages for a loss *suffered by a third party* as a result of a breach of contract.
  - The trust of a promise. At times this device has been used to create third party rights although it has been used to a lesser extent in more recent times – and has probably been overtaken, in practical terms, by the 1999 Act.
  - Collateral contracts. In some situations the courts will find that there is in fact a 'collateral contract' with a third party, sitting alongside the main contract.
  - Tort of negligence. A third party to a contract has sometimes been allowed to use the tort of negligence to recover damages from a party in breach but recovery for pure economic loss has traditionally been very restricted.
- Statutory exceptions. There are some specific contracts (for example, certain types of insurance contract) where statutes give rights to third parties.
- Privity and exclusion clauses. Parties quite often purport to give the benefits of an exclusion clause to third parties and the courts have in some cases used agency concepts to enable these to be enforceable. The 1999 Act reduces the need for these devices to be used.
- Imposing burdens:
  - Restrictive covenants are used in land law to impose burdens on third party occupiers of land. Limited use of this approach has been made outside the land law context.
  - The tort of interference with contractual rights can be used to obtain an injunction to stop a third party encouraging a breach of contract.

## 5.2 INTRODUCTION

The essence of the doctrine of privity of contract is the idea that only those who are parties to a contract can have rights or liabilities under it. This doctrine has long been regarded as one of the fundamental characteristics of the English law of contract. The effect of it is that if the two parties to a contract agree that one of them will provide a benefit to a third party, the third party is generally unable to sue to enforce that agreement. Equally, should the parties agree that an obligation should be imposed on a third party, they will generally be unable to force the third party to undertake that obligation, even if he or she has previously agreed to do so.

The strict application of this doctrine and in particular the rule relating to benefits, has sometimes been found to be inconvenient in practice, and the courts have for a long time recognised a range of exceptions to it (e.g. the 'trust of a promise'), and sanctioned a variety of devices for avoiding its effect (e.g. allowing a party to recover damages on behalf of the third party or constructing a collateral contract). In addition, Parliament has given parties the opportunity to avoid a significant part of the doctrine by virtue of the Contracts (Rights of Third Parties) Act 1999. The basic principle is still, however, applied, as shown by the Court of Appeal's decision in *MacDonald Dickens & Macklin v Costello*.[1] Work had been done by builders for a company that failed to pay. The builder sought to recover compensation in the form of a restitutionary claim for unjust enrichment against the owners of the company. The court rejected this on the basis that the only contract was with the company and the owners were not parties to this. The restitutionary claim could not be used to circumvent the contractual arrangements.

The rule about non-imposition of burdens has fewer exceptions to it but restrictive covenants controlling the use to be made of land can bind non-parties, and in some cases tortious liability for interference with a contract has been used to circumvent the privity doctrine.

## 5.3 THE RATIONALE FOR THE DOCTRINE

Why has the English law of contract traditionally had such an attachment to the doctrine of privity? One, not entirely convincing, suggestion is that this stems from the classical paradigm of a contract as a two-party bargain formed through the will of the parties; it might be argued that it accordingly follows that only those two parties, whose dealings led to the creation of the contract, should be regarded as being able to enforce it or be sued under it. Yet even the classical law allowed for the possibility, in certain circumstances, for there to be multiparty contracts, for example, between members of a club or those entering a competition (and an analysis of such contracts in terms of offer and acceptance is often artificial).[2] Indeed, however many parties there are to a contract, why should a third party not be able to enforce the contract if that was the intention of the parties to the contract? It seems, therefore, that the doctrine cannot simply be explained on the basis that a contract is a bargain between two parties.

A related argument and one that, as we shall see, has often been put forward by the courts is that the doctrine of privity is based on the doctrine of consideration and, in particular, the rule that consideration must move from the promisee. This possibility is discussed in more detail below.

Whatever the technical arguments put forward, what, if any, policy reasons support the doctrine? What is it meant to achieve? There are two aspects to the doctrine, which need to be considered separately. First, there is the rule that the burden of a contract should not be placed on a third party. At first sight this seems like a rule that is clearly justifiable. To use an unlikely but striking example from Collins: 'It would plainly be a serious invasion of the liberty of the individual ... if the parties to a contract agreed that a third person should run a marathon.'[3] To make such an agreement enforceable, at least without the consent of the third party, would be an unjustifiable intrusion into personal freedom. There are other situations, however, where the answer may not be so clear-cut.

---

1   [2011] EWCA Civ 930. The court does not actually refer to 'privity' in its judgment – but it is clear that this is the underlying principle being applied.
2   See, for example, *Clarke v Dunraven* [1897] AC 59 – this is discussed further below, 5.4.2.
3   Collins, 2003, p 303.

Suppose, for example, that Anne owns a famous painting. Brian, the owner of a gallery, makes a contract with Anne for the loan of the painting for a special exhibition for three months. Brian spends a large amount of time and money promoting this exhibition, with Anne's painting being the central attraction. A week before the exhibition is to open Anne sells the painting to Claire. Should Claire be obliged to allow the painting to be used in Brian's exhibition? The doctrine of privity would say 'no'. Claire is not a party to the contract between Brian and Anne and so generally cannot be affected by obligations arising out of it. Brian is left with a remedy in damages against Anne, which may well be inadequate to recompense him,[4] and will not really make up for the fact that his exhibition has lost its central exhibit. It is arguably not clear why it would be unfair or unreasonable in such a situation to require Claire to honour Anne's commitment to lend the painting to Brian, particularly if Claire is aware of the commitment at the time when she buys the painting from Anne. As we shall see later in this chapter, the courts have struggled to find the best solution to this type of situation – wishing in some cases to require the third party to bear the burden of the obligation, while at the same time not undertaking a direct attack on the doctrine of privity.

Even in the area of the imposition of burdens, therefore, the rule that only a party can be affected by a contract is not necessarily appropriately applied in all situations. When we turn to the conferring of benefits, there seems to be even less justification for a strict doctrine of privity. If A and B have agreed that C should have a benefit under their contract, why should C not be able to enforce this? Suppose, for example, that Alison promises Bernard that she will pay £1,000 to Oxfam if Bernard gives up smoking for a year. This is a contract that (subject to the question of intention to create legal relations)[5] is clearly enforceable by Bernard. However, the charity that is to benefit will not at common law be allowed to enforce because it is not a party to the agreement. Treitel argues that the answer may lie with the doctrine of consideration:[6]

> A system of law which does not give a gratuitous promisee a right to enforce a promise may well be reluctant to give this right to a gratuitous beneficiary who is not even a promisee.

This argument is open to the objection, however, that what is really contrary to the doctrine of consideration is that a promise for which no consideration has been given should be enforceable.[7] In the example used above, consideration has been given for Alison's promise by Bernard. There could be no objection to Bernard seeking to enforce it (though his remedies might be limited).[8] If the charity were given a right to sue, Alison would be under no greater obligation than she already is as regards Bernard. She can obviously only be required to pay the money once, and there seems little reason why the charity should not be able to sue her directly for it. The justification becomes even less in a situation where the third party has acted in reliance on the promise; as we have seen in Chapter 3, reliance is increasingly used by the courts as the basis for enforcing promises between two parties and there seems little reason why this should not also apply in a tripartite relationship.

---

4    It is quite likely on the facts as given that only 'reliance' damages would be recoverable, the likely profits from the exhibition being too speculative: *Anglia Television Ltd v Reed* [1972] 1 QB 60. See the discussion of this case and related issues below, Chapter 15, 15.4.5.

5    See above, Chapter 4.

6    Treitel, 2015, p 621.

7    Cf Flannigan, 1987, p 577.

8    It is, *prima facie*, difficult to see what 'losses' he could recover for in an action for damages; he will undoubtedly have saved money through not smoking and his health may well have improved although compare Lord Griffiths' 'broad ground' in *Linden Gardens Ltd v Lenesta Sludge Disposals Ltd* [1993] 3 All ER 417, discussed below at 5.7. Nor is this a situation where an order for specific performance would normally be regarded as appropriate – on this, see Chapter 15, 15.9.4.

### 5.3.1 IN FOCUS: ARGUMENTS AGAINST PRIVITY

It seems, therefore, that the rationale for the doctrine of privity is by no means always clear and unanswerable. Moreover, there are several reasons why the doctrine may be said to be out of tune with the modern English law of contract. First, there is the weakening of the doctrine of consideration identified in the previous chapter with what constitutes consideration being, at least for the time being, greatly expanded by cases such as *Williams v Roffey*.[9] More importantly, there is the growth of the area of 'estoppel', with the associated idea of 'reliance' as a basis for the enforceability of promises attaining increasing importance. This would suggest that where a third party has relied on a promise made in a contract between two other parties, there may be good reason to regard the promise as enforceable by the third party.[10]

The second major reason why privity is out of tune with the modern law is that it does not accord with the reality of many commercial contracts. As Adams and Brownsword have pointed out,[11] many commercial transactions (such as those surrounding construction contracts) do not simply involve two parties entering into an agreement. They involve 'multiple linked contracts' that can be regarded as 'networks',[12] to which the traditional approach of the doctrine of privity is simply inappropriate and unhelpful. Adams and Brownsword have suggested that a 'network' of contracts, with a more relaxed approach to third party rights, would have the following characteristics:[13]

(a) there is a principal contract (or there are a number of principal contracts) within the set giving the set an overall objective;

(b) other contracts (secondary and tertiary contracts, and so on) are entered into an object of each of which is, directly or indirectly, to further the attainment of this overall objective; and

(c) the network of contractors expands until a sufficiency of contractors are obligated, whether to the parties to the principal contract, or to other contractors in the set, to attain the overall objective.

As well as construction contracts, Adams and Brownsword suggest that contracts for the carriage of goods and 'many credit and financing arrangements' fit this pattern. Within such a network, the interlocking obligations of contracts designed to achieve an overall objective is far from the classical paradigm of the two-party exchange of mutual promises or obligations and calls for a different regime from that which the traditional doctrine of privity has provided.

### 5.3.2 REFORM AT LAST

The doctrine had been ripe for reform for some time.[14] A significant amendment took place in 1999, by virtue of the Contracts (Rights of Third Parties) Act 1999. But this had to deal with the issue of the extent to which rights should be extended beyond the parties to the contract. As the Law Commission recognised, in its working paper on the subject published in 1991,[15] contracts can have far-reaching effects. It used the example of a

9 [1991] 1 QB 1; [1990] 1 All ER 512.
10 Cf the comments to this effect by Steyn LJ in *Darlington Borough Council v Wiltshier Northern Ltd* [1995] 3 All ER 895, p 904.
11 Adams and Brownsword, 1990b.
12 Ibid, p 27.
13 Ibid. See also Adams and Brownsword, 1995, p 149.
14 See, for example, the 1937 recommendations of the Law Revision Committee (Sixth Interim Report, 1937, Cmnd 5449).
15 In its Consultation Paper No 121, *Privity of Contract: Contracts for the Benefit of Third Parties,* 1991.

contract between a building company and a highway authority for the construction of a new road. The road may be intended for the benefit of all road users, but it would surely not be acceptable for them all to have a right of action, for example, in the event of delay in completion of the project.[16] It is this problem that Collins suggests provides the best rationale for having a doctrine of privity:[17]

> The most significant justification for the doctrine of privity thus boils down to the simple point that the law of contract must draw a line at some point to set the limits to the range of liability to third parties.

In other words, the doctrine is there to avoid there being indeterminate liability to an indeterminate number of people.[18] But this does not, of course, mean that the boundaries of liability have to be set as narrowly as they were under the traditional doctrine. A view can be taken as to the appropriate situations in which third parties should have rights (or even obligations) under a contract; provided that the limits are clearly defined, this should not cause problems for the law and is likely to be more effective in meeting the intentions of all concerned.[19]

The fact that the strict doctrine of privity as applied by the English courts is not necessary is illustrated by the fact that, although many common law jurisdictions have adopted it, a more relaxed view has long been taken in the United States.[20] Civil law jurisdictions have also not found it necessary to be as narrow as the English courts in determining who may enforce a contract. The European Draft Common Frame of Reference contains provisions very similar to those now to be found in the Contracts (Rights of Third Parties) Act 1999.[21]

It is the way in which the traditional doctrine deals with the conferring of benefits that has attracted the most criticism and it is this area in which, following recommendations to this effect from the Law Commission,[22] there has now been legislative intervention. The effect of the Contracts (Rights of Third Parties) Act 1999 is discussed in detail later in this chapter and we shall try to assess there whether the reform meets the objections that have been raised. Since the Act has not replaced the common law, however, we shall start by looking at the development of the common law doctrine.

## 5.4 DEVELOPMENT OF THE DOCTRINE

There are some decisions dating from the seventeenth century that allowed a third party beneficiary to enforce a promise but these pre-date the strict formulation of the doctrine of consideration. The modern law is generally taken to derive from the case of *Tweddle v Atkinson*.[23] This concerned an agreement reached between the fathers of a couple who were about to get married, under which the father of the bride was to pay £200 and the father of the groom £100 to the bridegroom, William Tweddle, the plaintiff. William sought

---

16  Ibid, paras 2.19, 5.9.
17  See Collins, 2003, p 317.
18  See Cardozo CJ, *Ultramares Corp v Touche* (1931) 174 NE 441, p 444.
19  The concept of the 'network contract', as defined by Adams and Brownsword and outlined above, would be one way of providing an extended limit without running the risk of indeterminate liability.
20  *Lawrence v Fox,* 20 NY 268 (1859). For a short overview of the US law on third party rights, see the Law Commission Consultation Paper 121, pp 151–55.
21  Art II. – 9:301.
22  Report No 242, *Privity of Contract: Contracts for the Benefit of Third Parties,* 1996, Cmnd 3329 – following on from Consultation Paper No 121, published in 1991.
23  (1861) 1 B & S 393; 121 ER 762.

to enforce his father-in-law's promise but it was held that he could not. The main justification appears to have been that it was necessary for there to be mutuality of obligations as between those enforcing a contract and having it enforced against them. As Crompton J put it:[24]

> It would be a monstrous proposition to say that a person was a party to the contract for the purpose of suing upon it for his own advantage, and not a party to it for the purpose of being sued.

It is not clear why this proposition should be thought to justify the strong epithet 'monstrous'. There are other situations in the law of contract where there is not mutuality of this kind and yet obligations are enforced. In certain situations, unilateral contracts will lack mutuality, as will some contracts made by minors. A better reason for the decision would seem to be that William Tweddle was not the person to whom the promise was made, even though it was intended for his benefit.[25] If he had been, it will be noted that it would have been quite possible for the court to have found that he had provided consideration for the promise. The agreement was clearly made in consideration of William's marriage and, as we saw in Chapter 3, 3.9.3 (in *Shadwell v Shadwell*,[26] decided just a year before *Tweddle v Atkinson*), going through with a marriage ceremony can be good consideration for a promise of payment. This again indicates that the doctrine of privity is properly regarded as separate from, though closely linked to, the doctrine of consideration.

### 5.4.1 AFFIRMATION BY THE HOUSE OF LORDS

*Tweddle v Atkinson* was a decision of the court of Queen's Bench but the principle it has been taken to have been based on was reaffirmed by the House of Lords in a commercial context in *Dunlop Pneumatic Tyre Co Ltd v Selfridge & Co Ltd*,[27] which concerned an attempt by Dunlop to control the price at which their tyres were sold to the public.

---

**Key case** *Dunlop Pneumatic Tyre Co Ltd v Selfridge & Co Ltd* (1915)

Facts: Dunlop had a contract with Dew & Co, wholesalers in motor accessories, under which, in exchange for a discount, Dew & Co agreed that in selling Dunlop's tyres to retailers it would not give a discount, unless the retailer agreed to sell at Dunlop's list price. Dunlop's objective was to prevent the tyres being sold to the public at a discount. Selfridge & Co entered into such an agreement with Dew & Co. Dunlop subsequently sought an injunction and damages against Selfridge & Co in relation to alleged breaches of this agreement.

Held: The House of Lords held that they could not succeed. The following passage from the speech of Viscount Haldane LC indicates the approach taken:[28]

> My Lords, in the law of England, certain principles are fundamental. One is that only a person who is a party to a contract can sue on it. Our law knows nothing of a *jus quaesitum tertio* arising by way of contract. Such a right may be conferred by way of property, as, for example, under a trust, but it cannot be conferred on a stranger to a contract as a right to enforce the contract *in personam*. A second

---

24  (1861) 1 B & S 393, p 398; 121 ER 762, p 764.
25  Cf the comments of Collins on 'autonomy' as a rationale for privity (Collins, 2003, p 314).
26  (1860) 9 CBNS 159; 142 ER 62.
27  [1915] AC 847.
28  Ibid, p 853.

> principle is that if a person with whom a contract not under seal has been made is to be able to enforce it, consideration must have been given by him to the promisor or to some other person at the promisor's request.
>
> On both grounds, Dunlop's action failed. It was not a party to the agreement between Dew and Selfridge and, moreover, had provided no consideration for Selfridge's promise not to sell below the list price.

Note also that although this was not raised as an issue in the case, Dunlop could not, of course, rely on the terms of its contract with Dew & Co, because Selfridge & Co was not a party to this contract.

### For thought

*Brown plc, a manufacturer, sells its goods to White Ltd, a wholesaler, under a contract that requires White to ensure that any retailers it sells to agree to only sell Brown's goods in their original packaging. White sells goods to Green, a retailer, who repackages the goods before selling them. Privity stops Brown plc from suing Green. Could Brown plc sue White Ltd in relation to this?*

The doctrine of privity of contract is not one for which the courts have always shown great affection,[29] but it was again reaffirmed by the House of Lords in 1968 in the case of *Beswick v Beswick*.[30] A nephew had bought his uncle's coal merchant's business, and had promised as part of the deal to pay his uncle £6.50 a week and then, when his uncle died, to pay his aunt (if she survived) £5 a week. After his uncle's death, the nephew refused to make the payments to his aunt and she sued. In the Court of Appeal, Lord Denning tried to open up a broad exception to the doctrine of privity by relying on s 56(1) of the Law of Property Act 1925, which states:

> A person may take an immediate or other interest in land or other property, or the benefit of any condition, right of entry, covenant or agreement over or respecting land or other property, although he may not be named as a party to the conveyance or other instrument.

Lord Denning's view (with which Danckwerts LJ agreed) was that this in effect abolished the doctrine of privity in relation to written contracts, and therefore allowed Mrs Beswick to sue her nephew on the promise made to her husband for her benefit.[31] The House of

---

29 See, for example, the comments of Lord Scarman in *Woodar Investment Development Ltd v Wimpey Construction (UK) Ltd* [1980] 1 All ER 571, p 591 and by Steyn LJ in *Darlington Borough Council v Wiltshier Northern Ltd* [1995] 3 All ER 895, pp 903–04: 'there is no doctrinal, logical or policy reason why the law should deny the effectiveness of a contract for the benefit of a third party where that is the expressed intention of the parties'. See, also, *Smith and Snipes Hall Farm Ltd v River Douglas Catchment Board* [1949] 2 KB 500; *Drive Yourself Hire Co (London) Ltd v Strutt* [1954] 1 QB 250.

30 [1968] AC 58.

31 Cf the *dicta* of Lord Denning in *Smith and Snipes Hall Farm Ltd v River Douglas Catchment Board* [1949] 2 KB 500, and *Drive Yourself Hire Company (London) Ltd v Strutt* [1954] 1 QB 250.

Lords rejected this argument, deciding that the history and context of s 56 meant that it should be interpreted as not intended to apply to a straightforward contractual situation such as that in *Beswick v Beswick*, although the exact scope of the section, perhaps, remains uncertain.[32] The case, therefore, fell to be dealt with under common law principles. The House accepted what Lord Reid referred to as the 'commonly held' view that where a contract between A and B contains an obligation to pay money to a third party, X, 'such a contract confers no right on X and X could not sue for the [money]'. In other words, the traditional doctrine of privity of contract applied and Mrs Beswick was therefore prevented from suing in her personal capacity. The House of Lords agreed, however, that as the administratrix of her husband's estate, she could take his place as a party to the contract with the nephew, and thus obtain an order for specific performance of the obligations contained in it. Thus, while affirming the doctrine of privity of contract, the House of Lords found a way to achieve what was clearly a just result.

### 5.4.2 A SPECIAL CASE: MULTIPARTY CONTRACTS

There is one particular situation that arguably does not fit neatly within the doctrine of privity contract, and that should be noted before moving on to consider the more general attempts that have been made to avoid the effects of the doctrine. This is the situation of the 'multiparty' contract.

As we have seen, the typical model of a contract is based on a two-party relationship. Nevertheless, there are situations that are clearly governed by contract but which do not fall into this pattern. Where each of a group of people contracts with one body, for example on joining a sports club, and agrees to abide by the body's rules, can one member enforce those rules against another? Or is the only contract between each member and the club itself? The issue was considered in *Clarke v Dunraven*.[33] The case concerned the participants in a race organised by a yacht club. There was a collision during the race, as a result of which the plaintiff's yacht sank.[34] The plaintiff sued the defendant, claiming damages based on provisions in the club rules. The defendant denied that there was any contractual relationship between him and the plaintiff. The House of Lords held that there was. The committee of the club had, in effect, made an offer to prospective entrants to the race to the effect that, if they wanted to take part in the race, they would have to abide by the conditions that the committee had laid down. One of the conditions must be deemed to be that (in the words of Lord Esher, in the Court of Appeal):[35]

> if you do sail [for a prize in a race], you must enter into an obligation with the owners of the yachts who are competing, which they at the same time enter into similarly with you, that if by a breach of any of our rules you do damage or injury to the owner of a competing yacht, you shall be liable to make good the damage you have so done.

There was, in other words, an obligation under a contract with the club's committee to enter into a contract with every other competitor. Applying this approach, the House of Lords held that there was a contract between all the competitors, which they had each entered into when they entered the race. The plaintiff was therefore entitled to succeed in his action, based on the obligation contained in the regulations governing the race to pay for damage caused by a breach of the rules of racing. Thus, in the example given above,

---

32  It more recently received a full consideration in *Amsprop Trading Ltd v Harris Distribution Ltd* [1997] 2 All ER 990.

33  [1897] AC 59.

34  It should be noted that under the modern law, this situation would be much more likely to be dealt with by the tort of negligence.

35  [1895] P 248, p 255.

each member of the sports club is in a contractual relationship, based on the rules of the club, with every other member.

Although the approach taken in *Clarke v Dunraven* has the potential to be applied to many situations involving clubs or competitions, it was not adopted by the Court of Appeal in *Ellesmere v Wallace*,[36] which concerned the recovery of entrance fees for a horse race.

### 5.4.3 IN FOCUS: ANOTHER PROBLEM

The *Clarke v Dunraven* analysis avoids any problems of privity but creates difficulties as regards offer and acceptance. Who exactly is making the offer and acceptance as between the first and last individuals to join? Any attempt to find a way around this, such as making the club the agent for the receipt of both offer and acceptance, is bound to look very artificial.

## 5.5 EVADING THE DOCTRINE

The current position as regards the doctrine of privity of contract is that, its status having been confirmed by *Beswick v Beswick*, there has not in recent years been any direct challenge in the courts. There have, however, been various attempts to evade the effects of the doctrine, some of which have been more successful than others. The whole area must, however, now be considered in the light of the Contracts (Rights of Third Parties) Act 1999. This has fundamentally changed the position in relation to the conferring of benefits. The order of treatment will, therefore, be to look first at the Act; then, briefly, at the various devices that have been used previously by the courts to confer benefits, and that may still be particularly relevant in situations to which the Act does not apply; and, finally, briefly at the common law rules relating to the imposition of burdens.[37]

## 5.6 THE CONTRACTS (RIGHTS OF THIRD PARTIES) ACT 1999

The Act received Royal Assent on 11 November 1999 and applies to contracts made on or after 11 May 2000. It also applies to contracts made between these two dates if the contract specifically states that the Act is to apply.[38]

The Act is based on the 1996 Law Commission Report No 242, *Privity of Contract: Contracts for the Benefit of Third Parties*.[39] In one respect, therefore, this may appear as a speedy response to an identified need for law reform. It should not be forgotten, however, that, over 60 years ago, a similar reform was recommended by the Law Revision Committee.[40]

### 5.6.1 THE MAIN EFFECT

The simplest reform would have been to say that third parties should be able to sue whenever a contract happens to benefit them. For reasons that were noted earlier,[41] the

---

36  [1929] 2 Ch 1. Since the fees went towards the prize for winning the race, to have found otherwise might have rendered the agreement unenforceable as a gaming and wagering contract within the then s 18 of the Gaming Act 1845. *Clarke v Dunraven* does not appear to have been cited in the case.

37  Note, also, that some aspects of the law of agency, in particular, the concept of the 'undisclosed principal', can be regarded as exceptions to the doctrine of privity of contract.

38  Section 10(2), (3).

39  Cmd 3329.

40  Sixth Interim Report, 1937, Cmd 5449.

41  Above, 5.2.

Law Commission rejected this as being unacceptably wide and potentially opening the floodgates to litigation. It should arguably only be where the contracting parties *intend* to confer a benefit on the third party that the right of action should arise. Even this would probably go too far, however. The Law Commission in its Consultation Paper which preceded the Report gave the example of a contract between a building company and a highway authority for the construction of a new road.[42] Although it is one of the objects of the contract, and therefore one of the intentions of the parties, that the road will potentially benefit all road users, it would not be acceptable to allow all such users to have a right of action, for example, in the event of delay in completion of the project. The range of potential third party claimants should be narrowed to those on whom the parties to the contract intend to confer an *enforceable legal obligation*.[43]

This objective is put into effect by s 1 of the Act, which states that:

(1)     ... a person who is not a party to a contract (a 'third party') may in his own right enforce a term of the contract if:
    (a)     the contract expressly provides that he may; or
    (b)     subject to sub-s (2), the term purports to confer a benefit on him.
(2)     Sub-section (1)(b) does not apply if on a proper construction of the contract it appears that the parties did not intend the term to be enforceable by the third party.

Sub-sections (1)(b) and (2) therefore operate to create a rebuttable presumption that if a contract appears to confer a benefit on a third party, such a benefit is intended to be legally enforceable by that third party. A court faced with a promisor who denies that such legal enforceability was intended will have to decide what the 'proper construction' of the contract is. This will presumably mean applying an objective test of what reasonable contracting parties would have thought was meant by the term or terms in question.

This analysis was adopted by the first reported case on the Act, *Nisshin Shipping Co Ltd v Cleaves & Co Ltd*,[44] and confirmed by the Court of Appeal in *Laemthong International Lines Company Ltd v Artis (The Laemthong Glory) (No 2)*.[45] The latter case concerned a letter of indemnity (LOI) issued by the receiver of goods to the charterer of the ship from which they had been unloaded. The ship was subsequently seized because another party alleged that it had a better claim to the goods. The shipowner sought to enforce the indemnity against the receiver. The Court of Appeal noted that one clause in the LOI referred to indemnifying the charterer's 'agents' and took the view that the shipowner could come within this. A further clause referred to providing indemnity in the event of the ship being arrested, and that benefit was one that could only benefit the shipowner. The clauses of the LOI therefore did purport to confer a benefit on the shipowner. Once this was established, the wording of the Act had the effect that the burden of proof was on the promisor (in this case the receiver) to show that there was no intention to give an enforceable right to the third party. The receivers tried to argue that the situation was analogous with the chain of contracts that exists, for example, when goods are sold from manufacturer to wholesaler to retailer, or as between a main contractor and sub-contractor in construction contracts, and which the Law Commission in its report that led to the 1999 Act had suggested should not be taken as creating third party rights. In this case the charterer had issued its own LOI to the shipowner but the court rejected the analogy with the 'chain' contracts. The situations referred to by the Law Commission were ones where established

---

42  Consultation Paper 121, paras 2.19, 5.9.
43  Report No 242.
44  [2003] EWHC 2602; [2004] 1 Lloyd's Rep 38.
45  [2005] 1 Lloyd's Rep 688.

commercial practice made it unlikely that third party rights would be intended. There was no comparable established practice in relation to LOIs. The receivers had failed to prove that the clauses were not intended to provide an enforceable benefit, and the shipowner was entitled to rely on them.

The fact that the burden of proof shifts in this way once a benefit is established means that care will need to be taken in drafting contracts. If the parties do not want a third party to be able to enforce any benefits under the contract, they will be well advised to say so in specific terms.[46]

Note, however, that the presumption in s 1(1)(b) relates to whether a benefit was intended to be enforceable, not to whether its terms provide for a relevant benefit. To meet the requirement of s 1(1)(b), it must be at least one of the *purposes* of the contract to confer a benefit on the third party, though it does not have to be the predominant purpose.[47] The mere fact that a third party will be better off if a contract is performed does not mean that the contract had the purpose of conferring a benefit on that party. Thus, the fact that a third party obtains an incidental benefit (as where an agent is authorised to receive money owed to the agent's principal, and is able to deduct its commission from this) is not enough to establish that a purpose of the contract was to benefit the third party.[48]

The intended third party beneficiary need not be in existence at the time of the contract, but must be expressly identified in the contract by name, or as a member of a class, or as answering a particular description.[49] Thus, unborn children, future spouses and companies that have not at the time been incorporated all have the potential to benefit. A contract between the partners of the firm – for example, that each of their spouses will in certain circumstances receive benefits from partnership property – will apply both to the spouses of those already married and any future spouses of those who at the time are single. Where, however, a contract for the transfer of a bathroom fitting business referred to the purchasing company 'settling the liabilities' of the company being bought, this was not specific enough to include liability to a customer who was dissatisfied with the work of the company being transferred.[50]

If the above conditions are satisfied, the third party will be able to enforce the term of the contract (subject to any other relevant terms of the contract)[51] in exactly the same way as a party to the contract, obtaining damages, injunctions or specific performance in the normal way.[52] If the term is an exclusion clause, the third party will be able to take advantage of the exclusion or limitation.[53]

---

46  It has been claimed that the Act has led to a 'proliferation' of clauses to this effect: Beale, Bishop and Furmston, 2001, p 1183.

47  *Prudential Assurance Co Ltd v Ayres* [2007] EWHC 775, [2007] 3 All ER 946 at [28]; reversed on different grounds by the Court of Appeal ([2008] EWCA Civ 52, [2008] 1 All ER 1266).

48  *Dolphin Maritime & Aviation Services Ltd v Sveriges Angfartygs Assurans Forening* [2009] EWHC 716; [2009] 1 CLC 460 at [74]ff.

49  Section 1(3). See *Starlight Shipping Co v Allianz Marine and Aviation Versicherungs AG* [2014] EWHC 3068 (Comm), in particular para [88], for a broad approach to s 1(3). In *Chudley & Others v Clydesdale Bank Plc (Trading as Yorkshire Bank)* [2019] EWCA Civ 344, Flaux LJ stated at [80]: "It may be said that it is somewhat serendipitous that the appellants can take the benefit of the contract contained in the PB LOI, given that they were unaware of its existence at the time of their investment and when they first sought to recover that investment in 2010. However, the appellants' claim is not reliance based (their negligent misstatement claim having failed at trial) but is for breach of contract and it is not a requirement of the 1999 Act that a third party who is entitled to the benefit of a contract was aware of the contract at the time it was made or at any particular time thereafter."

50  *Avraamides v Colwill* [2006] EWCA Civ 1533.

51  Section 1(4).

52  Section 1(5).

53  Section 1(6).

## 5.6.2 CHANGING THE AGREEMENT

An important issue that arises once third party rights are recognised in this way is the extent to which the parties to the contract should be free to change, or even cancel, their agreement. To some extent this is linked to the question of whether the third party has a legal right as soon as the contract is made or only at some later stage. Normally, of course, the parties to an agreement can change it in any way they wish, provided there is consideration for any such change.[54] Clearly, however, the right under s 1 would be of limited effect if the parties could at any time withdraw the promised benefit. At the same time, it would probably be restricting the normal freedom of the parties too greatly to prevent all possibility of such change. The Act deals with this situation by s 2.

The balance of s 2 lies in favour of the freedom of the contracting parties. Section 2(3) provides that they can include a clause in their agreement that removes the need for any consent by the third party to a variation, or which lays down different procedures for consent from those contained in the Act. If no such clause is included, however, the provisions of s 2(1) will operate. This provides that the parties may not rescind or vary the contract so as to extinguish or alter the third party's rights under it if one of three conditions is satisfied. These are that:

(a)     the third party has communicated to the promisor (by words or conduct) his assent to the relevant term (the 'postal rule' (see Chapter 2, 2.12.6 above) does not apply here – s 2(2)); or

(b)     the third party has relied on the term and the promisor is aware of this; or

(c)     the third party has relied on the term and the promisor could reasonably be expected to have foreseen that the third party would do so.

Where the situation is that the third party has relied on the promise, this reliance does not have to be detrimental. If, for example, T (the third party) has been promised £1,000 by A under a contract between A and B, the fact that T has, in reliance on that promise, bought goods at a bargain price, or has acquired shares that have subsequently doubled in value, will be enough to prevent A and B from cancelling the promise, provided that A knew or could reasonably be expected to have known that T had acted in reliance on the promise.

It is important to remember that these provisions relating to the ability of the parties to change the contract do not set out the requirements for the third party's right to arise. As soon as a contract is made that satisfies the requirement of s 1 of the Act, the third party acquires legal rights under it and may enforce the relevant term without having either assented to or relied on the promise. The significance of the provisions in s 2 is simply that once one of the events specified there has occurred, the promise may not be withdrawn or varied.

## 5.6.3 DEFENCES

The availability of defences is dealt with by s 3 of the Act. Unless the parties to the contract have agreed otherwise in the contract,[55] the promisor can raise against the third party any defences (including 'set-offs') that could have been raised against the promisee (that is, the other party to the contract). Thus, if the promisee has induced the contract by misrepresentation or duress, the promisor can use that as a defence to the action by the third party. Similarly, if goods are to be supplied by A to B, with B promising to pay the price to be paid to T, B could raise against T the fact that the goods were not of satisfactory quality

---

54 See above, Chapter 3, 3.9.6 and 3.10.1.
55 Section 3(5).

under s 14 of the Sale of Goods Act 1979. The main contracting parties may also agree that a set-off arising between them from unrelated dealings may nevertheless be used by the promisor against the third party. The Explanatory Notes to the Act suggest that this could arise where:

> P1 and P2 contract that P1 will pay P3 if P2 transfers his car to P1. P2 owes money under a wholly unrelated contract. P1 and P2 agree to an express term in the contract which provides that P1 can raise against a claim by P3 any matter which would have given P1 a defence or set-off to a claim by P2.

The promisor may also rely on defences, set-offs or counterclaims against the third party that arise from previous dealings between the promisor and the third party.[56] Thus, if T has induced A to contract with B on the basis of a misrepresentation, A may be able to rely on that as a defence to an action by T, whether or not it would have been available against B. Similarly, if A and B contract that A is to pay £1,000 to T, but T already owes A £500, that can be set off by A against any claim by T.

The effect of s 7(2) should also be noted in this context, since it provides additional protection for the promisor. If the third party is taking action for negligent performance of an obligation under the contract, s 2(2) of the Unfair Contract Terms Act 1977 (which restricts the ability of a party to limit liability for loss or damage, other than death or personal injury, caused by the party's negligence)[57] cannot be used to restrict the promisor's ability to rely on an exclusion clause.

Section 3(6) deals with the converse situation to those covered by s 3(2) – (5), that is where the third party seeks to rely on a term of the contract (the most obvious example being an exclusion clause) in an action brought against him. The sub-section provides that the third party will only be able to enforce the term if he/she could have done so if he had been a party to the contract.

### 5.6.4 PROTECTION FROM DOUBLE LIABILITY

The right of the promisee to enforce the contract is specifically preserved by s 4. In order that the promisor does not face being liable to both the promisee and the third party, however, s 5 provides that where the promisee has recovered compensation from the promisor in relation to a term falling within s 1 of the Act, this must be taken into account in any award subsequently made to the third party. The converse situation is not specifically dealt with but it must be presumed that the courts would not generally allow the promisee to recover where compensation has already been paid to the third party by the promisor.

### 5.6.5 EXCEPTIONS

Section 6 excludes certain types of contract from the provisions of the Act. These include:

(a)    contracts on a bill of exchange, promissory note or other negotiable instrument;[58]
(b)    contracts binding on a company and its members under s 33 of the Companies Act 2006;[59]

---

56  Section 3(4).
57  See Chapter 7, 7.7.
58  Section 6(1).
59  Section 6(2).

(c)    terms of a contract of employment, as against an employee;[60] and

(d)    contracts for the carriage of goods by sea,[61] or, if subject to an international transport convention, by road, rail or air.[62]

In relation to carriage contracts, however, the exception does not apply to reliance by a third party on an exclusion or limitation of liability contained in such a contract. The exclusion clause of the type considered in *The Eurymedon*[63] could therefore potentially now apply for the benefit of the stevedores without the need to rely on agency.

### 5.6.6 EFFECT OF THE ACT

The Contracts (Rights of Third Parties) Act 1999 has made significant changes to the way in which contracts can be enforced by third parties. For example, if applied to the facts of *Beswick v Beswick*,[64] the term in the contract between old Mr Beswick and his nephew purported to confer a benefit on Mrs Beswick, thus falling within s 1(1)(b) of the Act. It is likely that the court would construe this term as being intended to confer a legally enforceable benefit on her under s 1(2). She would therefore be able to sue the nephew in her personal capacity rather than only in her (fortuitous) capacity as administratrix of her husband's estate. Similarly, in the commercial context, in a case like *Woodar v Wimpey*,[65] there was a promise to pay part of the purchase price of a plot of land to a third party. The contract specifically identified the third party, and purported to confer a benefit on it. Again, assuming that the court construed this as being intended to confer a legally enforceable benefit, the third party could sue directly for the breach of the promise to pay. Other possible effects of the Act will be noted in discussing the cases dealt with in the rest of this chapter.

---

**For thought**

*Brown plc, a manufacturer, sells its goods to White Ltd, a wholesaler, under a contract that requires White Ltd to ensure that any retailers it sells to contract not to sell Brown plc's goods other than in their original packaging. White Ltd sells goods to Green, under such a contract, but Green repackages the goods before selling them. Would the 1999 Act allow Brown plc to sue Green?*

---

Not all commentators welcomed the Act. Stevens, for example, argued that the reform was unnecessary, given the developments in remedies available to the promisee.[66] Moreover, the Act runs the risk of creating uncertainty and has left the law in an 'incoherent state' doctrinally.[67] It must be remembered, however, that the main contracting parties are still in control. They can decide that the provisions of the new Act should not apply, and there will be nothing that

---

60   Section 6(3) – the same applies to 'workers' contracts' as against a worker (including a home worker), or a term of a relevant contract against an agency worker. Relevant definitions of employee and worker are those to be found in s 54 of the Minimum Wage Act 1998. For home worker, see s 35(2) of that Act, and for 'agency worker' see s 34. A 'relevant contract' is one dealing with work falling within s 34(1)(a) of the 1998 Act.

61   As defined in s 6(6).

62   For the appropriate convention, depending on the mode of transport, see s 6(8).

63   [1975] AC 154 – see below, 5.12.1.

64   [1968] AC 58 – see above, 5.4.1.

65   [1980] 1 WLR 277 – see below, 5.7.

66   Stevens, 2004, p 15.

67   Ibid.

the third party can do about it. They also have the freedom to change their minds, subject to the provisions restricting variation or cancellation. Where, however, the parties have decided that they wish to confer a benefit on a third party, and have put that clearly into their contract, the courts will be able to enforce their wishes directly, rather than having to rely on the range of, at times, rather strained devices that they have used in the past.

The extent to which these devices can be safely consigned to history is, however, not yet clear. Section 7(1) of the Act specifically states that the Act 'does not affect any right or remedy of a third party that exists or is available apart from this Act'. Moreover, as we have seen, the Act does not apply to all contracts. It is therefore still necessary to consider the ways in which the doctrine of privity of contract was circumvented prior to May 2000, since some of this law may prove to be of continued relevance.

## 5.7 DAMAGES ON BEHALF OF ANOTHER

It has been argued in some cases that where a contract is made by one person for the benefit of a third party, the contracting party should, in the event of breach, be able to recover damages from the other contracting party for the third party's loss. This was the approach taken by Lord Denning MR in *Jackson v Horizon Holidays*.[68] Mr Jackson had booked a holiday for himself and his family, which turned out to be a disaster. The hotel for which the booking was made had not been completed when the Jacksons arrived, and the alternative offered was of a very poor standard. The facilities did not match what had been promised, and the family found the food distasteful. There was no doubt that the defendants were in breach of contract. The trial judge awarded £1,100 damages but the defendants appealed against this as being excessive. The Court of Appeal upheld the award, with Lord Denning holding that Mr Jackson was entitled to recover damages on behalf of himself and the rest of his family. In particular, Lord Denning relied on the following quotation from Lush LJ in *Lloyd's v Harper*:[69]

> I consider it to be an established rule of law that where a contract is made with A for the benefit of B, A can sue on the contract for the benefit of B, and recover all that B could have recovered if the contract had been made with B himself.

Lord Denning felt that this indicated that where one person made a contract which was intended to benefit others, such as the father booking a family holiday, a host making a restaurant reservation for dinner or a vicar arranging a coach trip for the choir, and there was a breach of contract, the father, the host or the vicar should not only be able to recover lost expenses, but:[70]

> he should be able to recover for the discomfort, vexation and upset which the whole party have suffered by reason of the breach of contract, recompensing them accordingly out of what he recovers.

This had the potential of opening up a large hole in the doctrine of privity of contract, since all that a third party beneficiary would need to do would be to persuade the contracting party to sue in order to obtain the promised benefit or appropriate compensation. In *Woodar Investment Development Ltd v Wimpey Construction (UK) Ltd*,[71] the House of

---

68  [1975] 3 All ER 92; [1975] 1 WLR 1468.
69  (1880) 16 Ch D 290 at p 321.
70  [1975] 3 All ER 92, p 96; [1975] 1 WLR 1468 at p 1473.
71  [1980] 1 All ER 571; [1980] 1 WLR 277.

Lords rejected the idea that it was possible *generally* to circumvent the doctrine of privity of contract in this way. The actual decision in *Jackson* was accepted as being right, either (according to Lord Wilberforce) because it related to a special situation of a kind that perhaps calls for special treatment, such as ordering a meal in a restaurant, or hiring a taxi for a group, or, more generally, because, as James LJ had held in the Court of Appeal, Mr Jackson's damages could justifiably be increased to take account of the fact that the discomfort of the rest of the family was part of his loss, in that it contributed to his own bad experience. This did not constitute, however, any significant exception to the doctrine of privity of contract, and the more general basis on which Lord Denning had upheld the award of damages was specifically rejected. Lord Denning was held to have used the quotation from *Lloyd's v Harper*, on which he relied, out of context. As Lord Russell pointed out, Lush LJ was clearly concerned with the relationship between principal and agent, and it is to this situation alone that his statement should be taken to refer.

Despite this strong rejection of any *general* right to claim damages on behalf of a third party, in 1993 the House of Lords seemed to open the door again to claims of this kind.

**Key case** *Linden Gardens Ltd v Lenesta Sludge Disposals Ltd* (1993)[72]

Facts: This case concerned a building contract between a property company, P, and a construction company, C, in relation to a development containing shops, offices and flats. Before the building work was complete, P assigned its interests to T. The assignment was made without C's consent, and therefore was not effective to create a contractual relationship between T and C. Defects in the construction work were later discovered. The defective work had taken place after the assignment of the contract. P sued C but it was argued that P had suffered no loss because at the time of C's breach of contract, the property had already been assigned to T.

Held: The House of Lords held that P could recover substantial damages on behalf of T. The House drew an analogy with the law relating to the carriage of goods, where a consignor of goods was allowed to sue on the carriage contract even though ownership of the goods has been transferred to a third party.[73] It held that this was similarly a situation where a party to a contract was entitled to recover damages on behalf of another. Here, C knew that P was not going to occupy the premises itself, and therefore could foresee that any breaches would adversely impact on whoever acquired the premises from P. C should be liable for such losses, and P should be able to recover them on behalf of T.

This exception seemed to indicate some degree of retreat from *Woodar v Wimpey*. It was applied by the Court of Appeal in the subsequent cases of *Darlington BC v Wiltshier Northern Ltd*[74] and *Alfred McAlpine Construction Ltd v Panatown Ltd*.[75] The second of

---

72 [1993] 3 All ER 417.

73 *Dunlop v Lambert* (1839) 6 Cl & F 600; 7 ER 824, as interpreted in *The Albazero* [1976] 3 All ER 129. The House held that the limitation of *Dunlop v Lambert* laid down in *The Albazero* was confined to contracts for the carriage of goods under a bill of lading. Under such a contract it is established by statute that the consignee will be able to sue the carrier directly – the Carriage of Goods by Sea Act 1992. In *Sevylor Shipping and Trading Corp v Altfadul Company for Foods, Fruits & Livestock, Siat Societa Italiana Assicurazioni E Riassicurazioni S.P.A.* [2018] EWHC 629 (Comm) at [58] Andrew Baker J stated: "There may still be room for debate as to the precise ambit of the rule in *Dunlop v Lambert* as confined by *The Albazero*, but I do not need to resolve any such debate."

74 [1995] 3 All ER 895; [1995] 1 WLR 68.

75 [1998] EGCS 19; [1998] CLC 636.

these cases was appealed to the House of Lords,[76] however, which gave the opportunity for the House of Lords to reconsider the way in which the Court of Appeal had been developing the exception established in the *Linden Gardens* case.

The facts of the *Panatown* case were that M, a building contractor, entered into a contract with P to construct an office building and car park on land owned by U, a company within the same group of companies as P. The reason for this arrangement was that it (legitimately) avoided the payment of VAT. In addition to the main contract between P and M, there was also a 'duty of care deed' (DCD) executed between U and M, which gave U a right to sue M for negligent performance of its duties under the building contract. The DCD was expressed to be assignable to U's successors in title. When there were problems of alleged defective work and delay, P initiated arbitration proceedings under its contract with M. M sought to argue as a preliminary point that since P had no proprietary interest in the site, it had suffered no loss. It was this issue that the House of Lords had to consider.

The House was divided 3:2 on whether P was entitled to recover. There were two bases on which P argued that it should be able to do so. The first, so-called 'narrow ground', was based on *Dunlop v Lambert*,[77] as interpreted in *The Albazero*.[78] This principle was stated by Lord Diplock in [BT] *The Albazero* as follows:[79]

> in a commercial contract concerning goods where it is in the contemplation of the parties that the proprietary interests in the goods may be transferred from one owner to another after the contract has been entered into and before the breach which causes the loss or damage to the goods, an original party to the contract, if such be the intention of them both, is to be treated in law as having entered into the contract for the benefit of all persons who have or may acquire an interest in the goods before they are lost or damaged, and is entitled to recover by way of damages for breach of contract the actual loss sustained by those for whose benefit the contract is entered into.

Where this principle applies, the party recovering the damages is required to account for them to the third party who has suffered the loss. As we have seen, the House of Lords in the *Linden Gardens* case extended this approach from contracts concerning goods to those involving real property. Moreover, the Court of Appeal in *Darlington BC v Wiltshier Northern Ltd* held that it could apply even where the third party owned the property from the beginning, rather than it being transferred after the contract had been entered into. The justification for this principle, as an exception to the normal rule that a contracting party can only recover for his or her own loss, is that it should apply where otherwise the liability of the defaulting party would disappear into a legal 'black hole' – in that privity of contract would prevent the third party from suing, and the contracting party would only be able to recover nominal damages.[80]

The 'broader ground' argued by P was based on the speech of Lord Griffiths in the *Linden Gardens* case. This amounted to a more direct challenge to the assumption that a contracting party in this type of situation should only be able to recover nominal damages. Lord Griffiths gave an everyday example to show why that assumption should not always apply:[81]

---

76  [2001] AC 518. Reported as *Panatown Ltd v Alfred McAlpine Construction Ltd* [2000] 4 All ER 97.
77  (1839) 6 Cl & F 600; 7 ER 824 – though doubts were expressed as to whether this case had been properly understood by later courts – see, in particular, the speech of Lord Clyde.
78  [1976] 3 All ER 129.
79  Ibid, p 137.
80  See Steyn LJ in *Darlington BC v Wiltshier Northern Ltd* [1995] 1 WLR 68, p 79. Whether this 'black hole' actually exists has been a matter of debate among academic commentators: see, for example, Wallace, 1999, Unberath, 1999, Treitel, 1998b.
81  [1994] 1 AC 85 at p 96; [1993] 3 All ER 417 at p 421.

To take a common example, the matrimonial home is owned by the wife and the couple's remaining assets are owned by the husband and he is the sole earner. The house requires a new roof and the husband places a contract with the builder to carry out the work ... The builder fails to replace the roof properly and the husband has to call in and pay another builder to complete the work. Is it to be said that the husband has suffered no damage because he does not own the property? Such a result would in my view be absurd and the answer is that the husband has suffered loss because he did not receive the bargain for which he had contracted with the first builder and the measure of damages is the cost of securing the performance of that bargain by completing the roof repairs properly by the second builder.

Under this ground, P argued that the defective work by M caused loss to P, not just to U, because it had not received what it had contracted for. It should therefore be entitled to substantial damages related to the cost of remedying the defective work. It seems that if this ground applies, there is not necessarily any obligation on the successful claimant to use any damages recovered to remedy the defects – but the views of the Lords in *Panatown* were divided on this issue.

The majority of their Lordships in *Panatown* found that P should not be able to succeed because of the existence of the DCD. The fact that it had been specifically provided that the third party (U) should have a remedy against the builder (M) meant that there was no 'black hole' and therefore no need to apply the exception to the normal rule, even though the remedy available under the DCD was more limited than that which would be available in an action for breach of contract. In coming to this conclusion, the majority confirmed the existence of the 'narrow ground' exception, but expressed scepticism about whether the 'broader ground' was part of English law. The minority (Lords Goff and Millett) would have allowed P to recover on either ground.

The speeches in the *Panatown* case, while providing much fuel for further discussion, have not really helped to clarify the law in this area.[82] As the majority decision is based on the existence of the DCD, any comments on the more general principles will be able to be distinguished in a later case where no such deed exists. This leaves open the possibility that the views of the minority, that the 'broader ground' provides the better basis for the development of the law in this area, may still be adopted, despite the fact that the majority did not regard it with favour. However, some subsequent High Court cases, decided shortly after *Panatown*, seemed reluctant to apply the 'broader ground'.[83] By contrast the broad ground gained some support in *Lowick Rose LLP (in liquidation) v Swynson Ltd*[84] from Lord Sumption.[85]

It is possible, of course, that the availability of the power to confer rights directly on a third party under the Contracts (Rights of Third Parties) Act 1999 means that there will be less need to expand the situations where a contracting party can recover damages on behalf of a third party. Indeed, the fact that the parties can now make this specific provision for third party rights might lead the courts to return to a more restrictive line in this area, as suggested by *Woodar v Wimpey*. However, as Lord Goff pointed out in his

---

82 In *Lowick Rose LLP (in liquidation) v Swynson Ltd* [2017] UKSC 32 Lord Sumption was of the opinion that this exception could apply to other types of contract (indeed it was originally developed in the context of contracts of carriage) but it was still an exception to the general rule that a party to a contract can only claim in respect of its own loss. On the facts of *Lowick Rose LLP (in liquidation) v Swynson Ltd* (a case which involved a negligent report by accountants) Lord Sumption held that the exception did not apply as it was not part of the object of the contract to benefit the third party.

83 See, for example, *Rolls-Royce Power Engineering plc v Ricardo Consulting Engineers Ltd* [2003] EWHC 2871 (TCC) at [101]-[103]; *DRC Distribution Ltd v Ulva Ltd* [2007] EWHC 1716 at [69].

84 [2017] UKSC 32.

85 Ibid at [17] but cf. Lord Mance at [53].

speech in *Panatown*, the issue of what damages a contracting party can recover can be argued to be logically separate from the doctrine of privity.[86] If that approach is followed, then the existence of the 1999 Act, which is concerned with privity rather than damages, should not necessarily prevent further developments. Much will depend on how those in the relevant industries, in particular the construction industry, formulate their contracts in the future, and whether they decide to take advantage of the facility in the 1999 Act to give enforceable rights to third parties. If they do not, as some commentators have suggested,[87] this may leave the door open for further case law to develop the common law rules.

## 5.8 THE TRUST OF A PROMISE

The Chancery courts developed the concept of the 'trust' to deal with the situation where property was given to one person (the 'trustee') to look after and deal with for the benefit of another (the 'beneficiary'). Whereas the common law regarded the trustee as the legal owner of the property, and therefore as having a free hand to deal with it, in equity it was held that the trustee held the property for the beneficiary and, moreover, the beneficiary could take action to compel the trustee to act in the beneficiary's interest. This tripartite trust arrangement has obvious possibilities for the development of a way round the doctrine of privity of contract, and this was successfully attempted in *Les Affréteurs Réunis SA v Leopold Walford (London) Ltd*.[88] A contract for the hire of a ship (a 'time charterparty') included a clause promising a commission to the broker (Walford) who had arranged the contract. Walford was not a party to the contract but was held by the House of Lords to be able to sue to recover the commission, on the basis that the charterers, to whom the promise had been made, were trustees of this promise. The House of Lords was thus ruling that the trust concept could apply to a promise to pay money, as well as to a situation where property was transferred into the hands of the trustee. This opened up a potentially substantial exception to the doctrine of privity of contract. Later case law has, however, made the finding of the existence of a trust subject to some fairly strict requirements, which have limited the usefulness of the device. There must have been a definite intention to create a trust (Re *Schebsman*)[89] and, in looking for this, the court will expect to find a clear intention to benefit the third party *(Vandepitte v Preferred Accident Insurance)*,[90] which is intended to be irrevocable *(Re Sinclair's Life Policy)*.[91]

The trust of a promise is a true exception to the doctrine of privity of contract. The restrictions just outlined above mean, however, that it has limited application. Indeed, it was not even considered in *Beswick v Beswick*.[92] The principle has not been denied, however, and if an appropriate case arose again, no doubt the courts could apply it.[93] On the other hand, the situations where the trust device has been used are ones in which the parties could now generally achieve their objective much more easily by using the provisions of the Contracts (Rights of Third Parties) Act 1999.

---

86  [2000] 4 All ER 97, pp 119–20. See also Harris, Campbell and Halson, 2002, pp 80–1.
87  See, for example, Beale, Bishop and Furmston, 2001, p 1182.
88  [1919] AC 801.
89  [1944] Ch 83.
90  [1933] AC 70.
91  [1938] 1 Ch 799.
92  [1968] AC 58; [1967] 2 All ER 1197.
93  See, for example, the comments of Dillon and Waite LJJ in *Darlington BC v Wiltshier Northern* [1995] 3 All ER 895, pp 902–03, 908.

## 5.9 COLLATERAL CONTRACTS

A collateral contract generally takes the form of a unilateral contract under which one party says: 'If you enter into contract X, I will promise you Y.' The consideration for the promise is the entering into contract X. It is quite possible for such an agreement to be made between the two parties to contract X.[94] In a three-party situation, however, the construction of a collateral contract can be a means of evading the doctrine of privity of contract.

**Key case** *Shanklin Pier v Detel Products* (1951)[95]

Facts: The plaintiffs, who were the owners of a pier, were promised by the defendants, who were paint manufacturers, that the defendants' paint, if used to re-paint the pier, would last for seven years. As a result, the plaintiffs instructed the firm of painters who were undertaking the re-painting of the pier to purchase and use the defendants' paint. This they did but the paint only lasted three months. The plaintiffs sued the defendants in relation to the fact the paint had not lasted as promised. The defendants resisted on the basis that they had no contractual relationship with the plaintiffs. The plaintiffs, it was argued, had provided no consideration for the promise given by the defendants (the paint manufacturers). The only contract, it was argued, the defendants had made was to sell paint to the painters, and the plaintiffs were not a party to that agreement. Held: There was a collateral contract between the plaintiffs and the defendants, under which the defendants guaranteed the durability of the paint in return for the plaintiffs' promise to specify the defendants' paint to be used on the contract. The plaintiffs could recover for breach of this guarantee.

In other words, the consideration for the promise as to the paint's durability was the instruction by the plaintiffs to their painters to purchase the paint from the defendants.

**For thought**

*What would have been the position if the pier owners had relied on promotional material published by the paint manufacturers, rather than direct communication with them? Would the manufacturers have been making a promise in these circumstances?*

In this case, there was a particular 'main' contract in prospect, that is the purchase of the paint to re-paint the pier. This will usually be the case but the device can be used even where there is no such contract specified at the time of the promise. In *Wells (Merstham) Ltd v Buckland Sand and Silica Co Ltd*,[96] the plaintiffs, who were chrysanthemum growers, bought sand produced by the defendants from a third party on the basis of the defendants' assurances as to its iron oxide content. These assurances turned out to be unreliable and the plaintiffs sued the defendants for the resulting loss on the basis of a

---

94  See, for example, *Esso Petroleum Co v Mardon* [1976] QB 801; [1976] 2 All ER 5, discussed in Chapter 6, 6.4.2.
95  [1951] 2 KB 854; [1951] 2 All ER 471.
96  [1965] 2 QB 170; [1964] 1 All ER 41.

collateral contract. The court held that although at the time the assurance was given there was no specific main contract in contemplation, this did not matter as long as it could be said to be made *animus contrahendi*, that is, with a view to a contract being made shortly. The plaintiffs were entitled to succeed.

The collateral contract device is not, of course, a true exception to the doctrine of privity of contract (in the way that the trust is), because in the end the claimant and defendant are found to be the parties to a contract, albeit a collateral one. The way in which it has been used by the courts at times, however, has been clearly as a means of avoiding the doctrine of privity of contract, in that they have not been over-scrupulous in investigating whether the parties themselves thought that they were entering into a contract of the kind alleged or had any intention of doing so. It may well be that in the light of the Contracts (Rights of Third Parties) Act 1999, the courts will in future be less willing to find a collateral contract, given that the parties will now usually be able to achieve their objective of benefiting a third party more directly.

## 5.10 THE TORT OF NEGLIGENCE

Where a contract is performed negligently and this causes loss to a third party, can the third party bring an action in the tort of negligence? In certain circumstances the answer is clearly 'yes', particularly where the negligent performance has caused physical harm to the third party or his or her property. Suppose that A Ltd and B Ltd enter into a contract under which B Ltd is to transport goods owned by A Ltd from Leicester to London. B Ltd loads the goods negligently and in the course of the journey they fall from B's lorry onto C's car, injuring C and damaging her car. The negligent performance by B Ltd of the contract with A Ltd will probably render it liable for any damage to A Ltd's goods; B Ltd will also, however, probably be liable in the tort of negligence for the foreseeable losses suffered by C. This is not really any exception to the doctrine of privity of contract because C's remedy is not dependent on the fact that A Ltd and B Ltd have made a contract. The answer, as far as C is concerned, would be the same if B Ltd were transporting its own goods.

What if, however, there is a contractual relationship between C and A Ltd relating to the goods? Suppose, for example, the goods belong to C and that A Ltd has a contractual obligation to transport them to C's premises. A Ltd contracts with B Ltd to move the goods. Again, B Ltd loads the goods negligently and the goods are damaged in transit. In this situation, C may well be able to sue A Ltd for breach of contract and A Ltd, in turn, may be able to sue B Ltd. But can C sue B Ltd directly in tort? The answer would appear to be yes, provided that C was actually the owner of the goods at the time. B Ltd would normally owe a tortious duty of care towards C in relation to the goods.[97] This only applies, however, if C is the owner; lesser rights in relation to the goods (e.g. the right to have them delivered under a contract) will not be sufficient: see *The Aliakmon*.[98]

So far we have been concerned with cases of physical damage. Are there any situations in which the third party could sue for pure economic loss caused by negligence? The situations in which the law of tort has been prepared to allow recovery for economic loss have generally been very limited, but in *Junior Books Ltd v Veitchi Co Ltd*,[99] the House of Lords appeared to open up the area in a way which also constituted a potentially large

---

97 The existence of the duty will be established, of course, on the normal tortious principles as laid down in *Caparo Industries plc v Dickman* [1990] 2 AC 605 and *Robinson v Chief Constable of West Yorkshire Police* [2018] UKSC 4. Generally, where it is foreseeable that a negligent act will result in physical harm, there will be a duty but note *The Nicholas H* [1996] AC 211, in which it was held that in the particular circumstances of the case it was not 'just and reasonable' to impose a duty even where foreseeable physical harm had occurred.
98 [1986] AC 785.
99 [1983] 1 AC 520.

exception to the doctrine of privity of contract. The dispute concerned a floor that had been defectively laid and subsequently cracked. The floor was laid by a sub-contractor, who had been nominated by the owner of the building. There was no contract between the owner and the sub-contractor, and the only loss caused by the sub-contractor's negligence was economic; there was no physical damage to any of the owner's property. Nevertheless, the House of Lords held that the sub-contractor did owe a duty of care to the owner and that it could be liable in damages for the negligent manner in which it had laid the floor. The decision in *Junior Books* is now, however, considered to be highly anomalous, to be confined to its own facts, and not to be treated as laying down any principle of general application.[100] Moreover, the fact that the parties could now create a direct liability between the owner and the sub-contractor by virtue of the 1999 Act means that the *Junior Books* approach is no longer really needed.

There is a further group of cases where the tort of negligence does extend to pure economic loss, and has the potential to provide remedies to third parties where there has been a defective performance of a contract. These are concerned with the negligent carrying out of particular professional duties, often in the form of giving advice or opinions. The principles derive from *Hedley Byrne & Co v Heller & Partners*[101] as restated in *Caparo Industries plc v Dickman*[102] and then *Playboy Club London Ltd v Banca Nazionale del Lavoro SpA*[103] and *Steel v NRAM Ltd (formerly NRAM Plc)*.[104] Thus, in *Smith v Eric S Bush*,[105] the defendant surveyor had given a negligent valuation of a house that he had surveyed for a mortgage lender. This caused losses to the plaintiff, who had borrowed money from the mortgage lender in order to buy the house, and who had relied on the survey. There was no contractual relationship between the defendant and the plaintiff, though each of them had a contract with the mortgage lender. It was held that in the circumstances there was a duty of care owed by the surveyor to the plaintiff. It was clear that the surveyor was aware that the valuation was likely to be relied upon by the plaintiff as well as the mortgage lender.

A similar result was arrived at in *White v Jones*.[106] Here the defendant solicitor had failed to carry out his client's instructions to draw up a will. As a result, the intended beneficiaries of the client were disappointed and sued the solicitor for negligence. In this case there was a contract between the defendant and the client for the production of the will, but there was no contractual relationship between either of them and the disappointed beneficiaries. It was clear, however, that the contract for the will was intended to benefit the beneficiaries. The House of Lords was therefore prepared to find a duty of care owed by the solicitor to the beneficiaries. It was a significant factor in this conclusion that the estate of the client would not have been able to recover any substantial damages against the solicitor for breach of contract because it had not suffered any loss. A similar conclusion was reached in a subsequent 'disappointed beneficiary' case, *Carr-Glynn v Frearsons*,[107] so this appears to have become an established way of circumventing the doctrine of privity of contract and allowing a third party to obtain the intended benefit of a contract. In such cases the death of the testator would perhaps, in the absence of a remedy for the disappointed beneficiaries, make the holding of the solicitor to account less likely. Where this is not the case, the courts may be less likely to

---

100 *D and F Estates Ltd v Church Commissioners for England* [1989] AC 177. See also the criticisms in *Simaan General Contracting Co v Pilkington Glass Ltd (No 2)* [1988] QB 758.
101 [1963] 2 All ER 575. This case is discussed further in Chapter 8, in connection with the law relating to negligent misstatements that induce a contract: 8.4.4.
102 [1990] 2 AC 605.
103 [2018] UKSC 43.
104 [2018] UKSC 13.
105 [1990] 1 AC 831.
106 [1995] 2 AC 207; cf also *Ross v Caunters* [1980] Ch 287.
107 [1998] 4 All ER 225.

give a tortious remedy to a third party.[108] It is probably also significant that in this particular line of cases the courts have been prepared to use the tort of negligence to give the third party a remedy in situations involving a 'non-business' claimant. Where the three parties concerned are involved in a network of contractual business relationships, the courts may be much more reluctant to intervene since they will not wish to interfere with agreements as to liability that may have been carefully negotiated, in particular where such liabilities have been distributed on an understanding as to where the insurance obligations are to lie.

Finally, it is important to remember that even in those limited cases where tort provides a remedy, it is always going to be for the consequences of a *negligent act or omission*, and not simply for non performance.[109]

There is, therefore, some scope for the use of the tort of negligence as a means of avoiding the effects of privity of contract, but, as has been indicated, the circumstances in which this will apply are strictly limited.

There are, at least, two other situations where the law of tort may have an impact on situations involving the doctrine of privity of contract: these are where an exclusion clause purports to exclude a third party's liability; and where a third party is accused of interfering with the contractual position as between contracting parties. These are dealt with below at 5.12.2 and 5.14, respectively.

## 5.11 STATUTORY EXCEPTIONS

In a number of situations there has been statutory intervention to mitigate the effects of the doctrine of privity of contract. These are often connected with insurance and the need to make sure that the intended beneficiary under an insurance contract is enabled to enforce his or her rights. Examples include the Third Parties (Rights against Insurers) Act 2010, s 11 of the Married Women's Property Act 1882, s 148(7) of the Road Traffic Act 1988, and the Carriage of Goods by Sea Act 1992. These statutory exceptions are not generally affected by the Contracts (Rights of Third Parties) Act 1999.

## 5.12 PRIVITY AND EXCLUSION CLAUSES

One particular situation where the parties to a contract may wish to confer a benefit on a third party is in relation to exclusion clauses. Where some part of the contract is to be performed by employees or sub-contractors of one of the parties, that party may wish to extend the benefit of a clause excluding liability to such people. However, the doctrine of privity of contract *prima facie* stands in the way. The problem generally arises where some loss or damage has been caused by negligence. If it is the negligence of an employee of a contracting party, then that contracting party may well be protected, as far as breach of contract or vicarious liability in tort is concerned, by an exclusion clause. The employee will not be protected, however, and the injured party may decide to take action directly against him or her in tort, perhaps relying on the fact that the employer may well feel obliged to make good any damages awarded.

---

108 Cf *Goodwill v Pregnancy Advisory Service* [1996] 1 WLR 1397, concerning a failed vasectomy, where the partner of the supposedly sterilised man became pregnant. She was not able to sue in tort, but the man would have had an action in contract.

109 In this context, the failure of the solicitor in *White v Jones* to draw up the contract must be regarded as a 'negligent omission' rather than a deliberate refusal to perform.

Figure 5.1

---

**Key case** *Adler v Dickson* (1955)[110]

Facts: Mrs Adler was a passenger on a cruise. She was injured when she fell from the ship's gangplank, which had been negligently left unsecured. Her contract was with the shipping company but she sued the master and boatswain personally, alleging negligence. The contract contained a very broadly drawn exemption clause. The Court of Appeal held that the exemption clause only protected the company itself and not its employees, who were not parties to the contract with Mrs Adler. She was entitled to succeed in her tortious action against the individual employees.

Since in this case the company had made clear that it would reimburse any damages awarded against its employees, the decision had the effect of negating the benefit of the exclusion clause as regards the contracting party (that is, the company) as well. On the facts, this was probably justifiable, in that the clause had not purported to protect the employees.

If, however, a clause is specifically worded to have this extended effect, and there is evidence that both parties intended that it should do so, the *Adler v Dickson* approach

---

110 [1955] 1 QB 158; [1954] 3 All ER 397.

may have the effect of frustrating their intentions. The courts have therefore sought ways to avoid applying the doctrine of privity of contract in such situations. One possibility, where the claimant has specifically promised not to sue the third party, is for the promisee to intervene to seek a stay of the action. This was recognised as a possibility in *Gore v Van der Lann*,[111] where the plaintiff was injured boarding a bus and sued the bus conductor, rather than the corporation that ran the bus service. On the facts, however, there was no evidence of any contractual obligation on the part of the corporation to reimburse the conductor, and therefore no grounds for granting a stay of the action. A stay was granted on this basis, however, in *Snelling v Snelling*,[112] though this was not an exemption clause case. The plaintiff, the director of a company, had agreed with his fellow directors that if any of them resigned, they would forfeit the balance of a loan that each of them had made to the company. The plaintiff resigned, and sued to recover his loan from the company. The company was not a party to the agreement between the directors, but it was held that they could intervene to stop the plaintiff's action. Ormrod J held that it was a necessary implication of the agreement to forfeit the loan that the plaintiff would not sue the company for its recovery:[113]

> In my judgment, therefore, the second and third defendants have made out an unambiguous case and have shown that the interests of justice required that the plaintiff be not permitted to recover against the defendant company. It follows that this is a proper case in which to grant a stay of all further proceedings in the plaintiff's action against the company.

This principle could therefore be applied in an appropriate case to prevent an action against a third party who was purportedly protected by an exclusion clause, and therefore indirectly to give the third party the benefit of that clause. Its limitation, however, is that it is dependent on the willingness of the promisee to intervene on the third party's behalf. Other attempts to avoid the effects of privity in this type of situation have been more broadly based.

### For thought

*Brian makes a contract with Diggers Ltd under which it agrees to dig a large hole in Brian's garden, where Brian wants to create a fishpond. Fred, Diggers Ltd' employee, who is using a mechanical digger, negligently digs through an electrical cable, causing £7,000 worth of damage. Diggers Ltd' contract contains an exclusion clause, limiting its liability to £1,000, and purporting to exclude its employees' liability altogether. Would the Contract, (Rights of Third Parties) Act 1999 mean that Fred could claim the protection of this clause?*

### 5.12.1 VICARIOUS IMMUNITY

In *Elder, Dempster & Co v Paterson, Zochonis & Co*,[114] the House of Lords allowed shipowners to take the benefit of an exclusion clause (which was stated to apply to them) contained in a contract between the charterers of the ship and the owner of goods being carried on it. The *ratio* of the decision is not very clear, but one possible basis for it was a

---

111  [1967] 2 QB 31; [1967] 1 All ER 360.
112  [1973] 1 QB 87; [1972] 1 All ER 79.
113  Ibid, p 98; p 89.
114  [1924] AC 522.

principle of 'vicarious immunity', under which those who perform contracts on behalf of a contracting party can take the benefit of exclusion clauses contained in that contract. This analysis, which would constitute a major exception to the doctrine of privity, was, however, subsequently rejected by the House of Lords in *Scruttons Ltd v Midland Silicones Ltd*.[115] The House ruled that the third party stevedores in this case were unable to rely on an exclusion clause contained in a contract of carriage to which they were not parties. It recognised, however, that it might be possible in some situations for a contracting party to be regarded as the agent of someone who was involved in the performance of the contract, for the purpose of bringing them into a contractual nexus with the other party. Lord Reid identified four requirements that would need to be satisfied:[116]

> I can see a possibility of success of the agency argument if [first] the bill of lading makes it clear that the stevedore is intended to be protected by the provisions in it which limit liability; [secondly] the bill of lading makes it clear that the carrier ... is also contracting as agent for the stevedore that these provisions should apply to the stevedore; [thirdly] the carrier has authority from the stevedore to do that, or perhaps later ratification by the stevedore would suffice; and [fourthly] that any difficulties about consideration moving from the stevedore were overcome.

This possibility was developed by the Privy Council in *New Zealand Shipping Co v Satterthwaite & Co, The Eurymedon*.[117]

---

**Key case** *New Zealand Shipping Co v Satterthwaite & Co, The Eurymedon* (1975)

Facts: The case again concerned the liability of stevedores for the negligent unloading of a cargo. The contract of carriage contained a very detailed exclusion clause,[118] which, among other things, specifically stated that the carrier was to be regarded as acting as agent for any independent contractors carrying out any part of the contract, and that such contractors would have the benefit of the exclusion clause.

Held: The majority of the Privy Council found this clause sufficient to enable them to construct a contract between the owner of the goods and the stevedores. It was in the form of a unilateral contract, under which the owners said, 'If you agree to unload these goods, we will give you the benefit of the exclusion clause.' The carriers acted as the stevedores' agents for the receipt of this offer. The consideration provided was the unloading of the goods. The stevedores were, of course, bound to do this anyway under their contract with the carriers, but the performance of an existing contractual duty owed to a third party is generally regarded as perfectly good consideration.[119]

---

There is no doubt that the contract constructed in *The Eurymedon* was a 'fiction' in the sense that it is highly unlikely that any of the parties intended precisely such an arrangement as the Privy Council found to have existed. On the other hand, the result is clearly commercially convenient, since it is the clear desire and expectation of all concerned

---

115  [1962] AC 446; [1962] 1 All ER 1.
116  Ibid, p 474; p 10.
117  [1975] AC 154; [1974] 1 All ER 1015.
118  Commonly known as a 'Himalaya' clause, after the ship involved in *Adler v Dickson* [1955] 1 QB 158; [1954] 3 All ER 397.
119  See Chapter 3, 3.9.5.

in contracts of this kind that third parties who perform part of the contract should be able to take the benefit of any relevant exclusion clause. The decision has not, however, opened up a major exception to the doctrine of privity: indeed, like the collateral contract device, it is not really an exception at all, since the individual who initially looks like a non-contracting third party is found to be a party to a contract after all. The approach taken in *The Eurymedon* was applied again by the Privy Council in *The New York Star*,[120] and must now be regarded as an established principle, which can be applied wherever the wording of the clause and the relationships between the various parties make it appropriate.

In *The Mahkutai*,[121] however, the Privy Council, while recognising the general acceptance of *The Eurymedon* principles in relation to exemption clauses and third parties, refused to apply them on the facts. In this case, shipowners, who were not party to a contract for the carriage of goods entered into by a charterer of their ship, sought to rely on an exclusive jurisdiction clause contained in the bill of lading. The Privy Council noted, however, that the wording of the relevant clause limited its extension to sub-contractors to the benefit of 'exceptions, limitations, provisions, conditions and liberties'. The Privy Council interpreted this as being limited to terms 'inserted in the bill for the carrier's protection ... It cannot therefore extend to a *mutual* agreement, such as an exclusive jurisdiction clause.'[122]

### 5.12.2 IN FOCUS: COMMON LAW REFORM OF PRIVITY?

In reaching its conclusion in *The Mahkutai*, the Privy Council also noted the very technical nature of *The Eurymedon* analysis, involving fine points of contract and agency. It considered whether the time might have come to take a further step and to recognise the situations currently dealt with by this principle as involving 'a fully-fledged exception to the doctrine of privity of contract',[123] thus escaping from the technicalities. It concluded, however, that it was not appropriate in the present case to take such a step. Nevertheless, the question has been raised, and there would seem to be a clear invitation to counsel in subsequent cases to try to argue for a general exception to privity, rather than relying on the technical analysis in terms of agency and consideration.[124] The enactment of the Contracts (Rights of Third Parties) Act 1999 makes it much less likely, however, that this invitation will need to be taken up. The benefit of an exclusion clause can now be given to a third party quite straightforwardly, and the further development of the common law is therefore likely to prove unnecessary.

### 5.12.3 MODIFICATION OF THE DUTY OF CARE

An alternative way of giving negligent third parties the benefit of an exclusion clause has been recognised in some cases. This treats the contract as part of the context in which the negligence occurs, and therefore relevant to defining the defendant's duty of care. In *Southern Water Authority v Carey*,[125] the negligence of sub-contractors had caused the loss. The main contract contained an exclusion clause purporting to extend to the subcontractors, and stating that the main contractor contracted on their behalf. The agency argument, based on *The Eurymedon*, failed, however, because of the rule of agency that the principal (in this case the sub-contractors) for whom an agent acts must be identifiable at the time of the contract. That was not the case here. The judge

---

120  [1981] 1 WLR 138.
121  [1996] AC 650.
122  [1996] AC 650, p 666 (emphasis added).
123  Ibid, p 665.
124  Cf the approach of the Supreme Court of Canada in *London Drugs Ltd v Kuenhe & Nagel International Ltd* (1992) 97 DLR (4th) 261.
125  [1985] 2 All ER 1077.

nevertheless decided in favour of the sub-contractors, on the basis that the existence of the exclusion clause negated any duty of care owed by the sub-contractors to the plaintiff. In the absence of a duty of care, the tortious action must fail. The validity of this approach was subsequently confirmed by the Court of Appeal in *Norwich City Council v Harvey*.[126] Once again, the case concerned the negligence of sub-contractors, who in this case had set fire to the plaintiff's premises. The main contract, however, contained a clause placing the burden of insuring against fire on the plaintiff. In this context, the Court of Appeal took the view that the sub-contractors were not in breach of any duty of care. As May LJ put it:[127]

> I do not think that the mere fact that there is not strict privity between the employer and the sub-contractor should prevent the latter from relying on the clear basis on which all the parties contracted in relation to damage to the employer's building caused by fire, even when due to the negligence of the contractors or sub-contractors.

## 5.13 IMPOSING BURDENS: RESTRICTIVE COVENANTS

The exceptions and evasions of the doctrine of privity of contract that we have looked at so far have all been concerned with the recovery of a benefit by a third party. In this section we are concerned with the possibility of imposing a restriction on a third party's behaviour.

In land transactions, the seller of a piece of land will often wish to restrict the use to which the purchaser can put the land, particularly if the seller is retaining ownership of adjacent land. Of course, as between the original seller and purchaser this can be achieved by contract. But what about someone who buys from the original purchaser? Can that person be made subject to the restriction? In *Tulk v Moxhay*,[128] it was held that this could be the case in relation to land, provided that certain conditions were satisfied.

### 5.13.1 APPLICATION OUTSIDE LAND LAW

Land law has subsequently developed a complicated set of rules dealing with the enforceability of such 'restrictive covenants'. Outside the land law area, however, the courts have been reluctant to extend this exception to the privity of contract doctrine. In *Taddy v Sterious*,[129] the court refused to apply it to an attempt to restrict the price at which the plaintiff's goods were sold by a third party. The plaintiffs had attached a notice to the packets of tobacco that they manufactured indicating that they were supplied to retailers on condition that they were not sold below the stipulated price. Acceptance of the goods was deemed to be acceptance of these conditions and where the goods were bought from a wholesaler, the wholesaler was deemed to be the agent of the manufacturer. Despite this elaborate attempt to create an obligation that attached to the goods, in the same way as a covenant may attach to land, it was held that the defendant, who bought the goods from a wholesaler with full knowledge of the conditions, was nevertheless not bound by them. There have, however, been some cases concerned with shipping contracts where an approach analogous to the restrictive covenant has been used to bind a third party. In *De Mattos v Gibson*,[130] for example, the plaintiff had chartered a ship from its owner, C. C had then mortgaged the ship to G, who had notice

---

126  [1989] 1 All ER 1180.
127  [1989] 1 All ER 1180, p 1187.
128  (1848) 2 Ph 774; 41 ER 1143.
129  [1904] 1 Ch 354.
130  (1859) 4 D & J 276; 45 ER 108.

of the charter. When C ran into financial difficulties, G proposed to sell the ship. The plaintiff successfully obtained an injunction restraining G from acting in a way that was inconsistent with the charter. Knight Bruce LJ said that where a person had acquired property from another with knowledge of a prior binding contract as to the use of the property made with a third party:[131]

> the acquirer shall not, to the material damage of the third person, in opposition to the contract and inconsistently with it, use and employ the property in a manner not allowable to the giver or seller.

Moreover, he considered that the rule applied in the same way to both land and personal property. The same line was taken by the Privy Council in *Lord Strathcona SS Co v Dominion Coal Co*.[132] The plaintiffs had chartered a ship, which had subsequently been sold. It was held that the new owner, the defendant, could be restrained by injunction from using the ship in a way that would prevent the operation of the charter contract made by the previous owner. It was regarded as significant, however, that the new owner had been aware of the existence of the charter at the time that the ship was bought.

### 5.13.2 THE CURRENT POSITION

The further development of this exception to privity of contract was halted by the refusal of Diplock J (as he then was) in *Port Line Ltd v Ben Line Ltd*[133] to accept the earlier decisions as being correctly based on equitable principles analogous to the law relating to 'restrictive covenants'. He took the view that these cases could be more properly viewed as falling within the area where the law of tort could provide a remedy,[134] rather than as examples of a more general exception to the doctrine of privity of contract. This analysis was apparently accepted for the following 20 years but in 1979 Browne-Wilkinson J indicated that there might still be some life in the equitable, restrictive covenant approach outside the area of land law. In *Swiss Bank Corp v Lloyds Bank Ltd*,[135] a loan had been made to buy shares. The lender argued that the borrower was contractually bound to repay the loan and interest out of the proceeds of any dealings with the shares. This was said to be a specifically enforceable obligation. The shares were also subject to a charge by Lloyds Bank (presumably they had been put up as security for a loan). The lender alleged that Lloyds' rights over the shares were subject to the rights of the lender as set out in the original contract of loan. Browne-Wilkinson J held that the obligation to repay the loan out of dealings with the shares was specifically enforceable. This meant that the lender held an equitable interest in the shares, and that Lloyds' rights were subject to this obligation. The Court of Appeal and the House of Lords held that there was no specifically enforceable obligation of the kind alleged, but did not disagree with the judge's analysis of the relationship between the parties if there had been. It seems, therefore, that the equitable approach will still be available in certain appropriate cases. What will be needed is to show that the contract that is alleged to bind the third party has created an equitable interest in property falling within the scope of the contract. The third party will not then be allowed to act in a way that adversely affects this equitable interest. Nevertheless, although this demonstrates the theoretical availability of the 'restrictive covenant' approach in relation to personal property, the tortious action considered in the next section is more likely to work in practice.

---

131 (1859) 4 D & J 276; 45 ER 108, p 282; p 110.
132 [1926] AC 108.
133 [1958] 2 QB 146; [1958] 1 All ER 787.
134 See below, 5.14.
135 [1979] Ch 548; [1979] 2 All ER 853.

## 5.14 THE ROLE OF THE LAW OF TORT

The cases and principles discussed in this section are in many ways the proper concern of the law of tort. However, this is an area (of which there are several) in which the rigid division drawn between tort and contract is unhelpful. The particular tortious action that we need to consider is that of 'wrongful interference with contractual rights'. A person who knowingly and intentionally brings about a breach of contract between two others thereby commits a tort. Moreover, an injunction will generally be obtainable to prevent the interferer acting in this way. To this extent, it can be said that a third party is bound by the provisions of a contract between two other people.

The existence of this tort was recognised and applied in *Lumley v Gye*.[136] Lumley had engaged a singer, Johanna Wagner, to sing at a series of concerts at his theatre.[137] It was a provision of this contract that she should not sing elsewhere. The defendant, who knew of this, persuaded Ms Wagner to sing at his theatre. Lumley first obtained an injunction against Ms Wagner preventing her from breaking her contract in this way. Her response was to leave the jurisdiction, and to refuse to sing at either theatre. Lumley then sued Gye, and it was held that he would be entitled to recover damages if Gye had intentionally interfered with his contract with Wagner.[138] This remedy has also been held to be available where goods are sold subject to a restriction on their disposal. In *BMTA v Salvadori*,[139] the purchaser of a new car agreed not to sell it for a year without first offering it to the plaintiff. The defendant bought the car with knowledge of this restriction, and with the intention of evading its effects, and was again held liable in tort. This would be the way, therefore, in which, in the example given at the beginning of this chapter, the gallery owner might be able to recover compensation from the new owner of the painting.[140]

As has been noted above, this is an alternative way of analysing the outcome in cases such as *De Mattos v Gibson* and *Lord Strathcona SS Co v Dominion Coal Co*. It is, however, more limited than the 'restrictive covenant' approach. Such covenants may, in certain circumstances, bind even those who are unaware of them. The tort of interference with contract, on the other hand, requires knowledge on the part of the tortfeasor. It is generally only where he or she is aware of the other contract, and the fact that rights under it may be affected, that the tortious remedy will be available to restrain, or provide compensation for, the interference.

## 5.15 SUMMARY OF KEY POINTS

■ The essence of the doctrine of privity of contract is that only those who are parties to a contract can have rights or liabilities under it. It has links to the principle that consideration must move from the promisee.

---

136 (1853) 2 El & Bl 216; 118 ER 749.
137 The full story, together with a reconsideration of the legal issues raised by the case, can be found in Waddams, 2001.
138 Though when the action was re-heard on this basis the decision went against Lumley – see Waddams, 2001.
139 [1949] Ch 556.
140 See above, 5.3. It still does not give the gallery owner the right to insist on the painting being displayed – but the threat of legal action against the new owner might be enough to secure this outcome. It is perhaps more likely to do so than the existence of the contractual action for damages against the original owner.

■ The Contracts (Rights of Third Parties) Act 1999 enables the parties to a contract to create a benefit enforceable by a third party. This may be done specifically or implied from the wording of the contract.

■ The common law has developed various exceptions to, or means of avoiding the doctrine – these include:
  □ damages recoverable on behalf of another – mainly in 'consumer' contracts, but also in some commercial contexts;
  □ trust of a promise; and
  □ collateral contracts.

■ There are also some specific statutory exceptions, e.g. re insurance.

■ Exclusion clauses may benefit a third party by virtue of the 1999 Act, by using the principle of agency as in *The Eurymedon* (1975), or as a result of the modification of a negligence duty owed by the third party.

■ There are few exceptions to the ban on the imposition of burdens on third parties, but this may be possible for example:
  □ in land law (restrictive covenants); and
  □ in shipping contracts.

■ The tort of intentionally inducing a breach of contract may be used to restrict the actions of a person who is not a party to the contract.

## 5.16 FURTHER READING

### The nature of privity
■ Adams, J and Brownsword, R, 'Privity and the concept of a network contract' (1990) 10 Legal Studies 12

■ Flannigan, R, 'Privity – the end of an era (error)' (1987) 103 LQR 564

■ Smith, SA, 'Contracts for the benefit of third parties: in defence of the Third-Party Rule' (1997) OJLS 643

### Reform
■ Adams, J, Beyleveld, D and Brownsword, R, 'Privity of contract – the benefits and burdens of law reform' (1997) 60 MLR 238

■ Law Commission, *Privity of Contract: Contracts for the benefit of third parties*, Consultation Paper No 121, 1991

■ Law Revision Committee, Sixth Interim Report, 1937, Cmd 5449

### Contracts (Rights of Third Parties Act) 1999
■ Beale, H, 'A review of the Contracts (Rights of Third Parties) Act 1999', ch 11 in A Burrows and E Peel (eds), *Contract Formation and Parties*, 2010, Oxford: OUP

- Burrows, AS, 'The Contracts (Rights of Third Parties) Act and its implications for commercial contracts' [2000] LMCLQ 540

- Stevens, R, 'The Contracts (Rights of Third Parties) Act 1999' (2004) 120 LQR 292

**Imposing obligations on third parties**
- Waddams, S, 'Johanna Wagner and the rival opera houses' (2001) 117 LQR 431

## COMPANION WEBSITE

*Now visit the companion website to:*

- Revise and consolidate your knowledge of Privity by tackling a series of multiple-choice questions on this chapter

- Test your understanding of the chapter's key terms by using the flashcard glossary

- Explore Privity further by accessing a series of web links

# The contents of the contract

6

## Contents

## 6.1 OVERVIEW

Once the formation of a contract has been established, the next issue to deal with is the content of the contract. What are the parties' respective rights and obligations under the contract? In practice, this is an extremely important issue for the parties. This chapter deals with the approach of the courts to mapping the precise rights and obligations of the parties. In doing this, the following issues become relevant:

- Is a pre-contractual statement intended to be a term of the contract? This involves distinguishing between representations and terms, and identifying the factors, such as the importance of the issue, which help the courts to make a decision.
- Remedies for pre-contractual statements. Where a statement is not part of the main contract, the party to whom it was made may nevertheless have a remedy on the basis of a collateral contract or for misrepresentation.
- Express terms (terms put forward by one or more of the parties). The courts need to consider (for example):
  - ☐ if a term has been put forward in writing but not in a signed document, has it actually been incorporated into the contract?;
  - ☐ the precise meaning of a term – this will generally only arise where the term is ambiguous. Today the courts adopt a 'purposive' interpretation, taking account of the commercial context where appropriate.
- Implied terms (terms arising by implication). There are two main bases on which terms may be implied:
  - ☐ Common law. Courts will normally only imply terms which are 'necessary', or as a matter of policy in particular types of contract (for example, landlord and tenant).
  - ☐ Statute. The main examples of statutorily implied terms are those contained, for non-consumer contracts, in the Sale of Goods Act 1979, relating mainly to the quality of goods. For consumer contracts, similar terms are included in the relevant contract by virtue of the Consumer Rights Act 2015.
- Statutory controls. In relation to consumer contracts, the terms of an agreement must comply with the requirements of the Consumer Rights Act 2015 on 'unfair' terms.

## 6.2 INTRODUCTION

This chapter is concerned with the situation where the parties have fulfilled all the requirements for making a valid contract, as described in Chapters 2 to 4. It may then become necessary to determine exactly what the obligations are under the contract. Problems may arise in a number of ways. There may, perhaps, have been a lengthy period of pre-contractual negotiation, and it may not be clear which, if any, of the statements that were made at that stage were intended to form part of the contract. The contract may be in writing, and yet one of the parties may allege that it does not truly represent their intentions or there may be disagreement about the effect of the words used. In this case the job of the court will be to 'construct' the contract in order to decide what the language that it contains should be taken to mean. The task of 'interpreting' or 'constructing' the contract will be influenced by the surrounding circumstances.[1] Such a contextual approach arguably becomes easier if the courts adopt a 'relational' approach to construction.[2] This enables them to take a broad view of the commercial and personal factors surrounding the

---

1  Compare *Impact Funding Solutions Ltd v Barrington Support Services Ltd (formerly Lawyers at Work Ltd)* [2016] UKSC 57.
2  For which, see Chapter 1, 1.6. See also the interesting discussion in *Amey Birmingham Highways Ltd v Birmingham City Council* [2018] EWCA Civ 264 where Jackson LJ stated (at [93]): "Any relational contract of this character [the Court of Appeal were considering a private finance initiative contract with Birmingham City Council] is likely to be of massive length, containing many infelicities and oddities. Both parties should adopt a reasonable approach in accordance with what is obviously the long-term purpose of the contract. They should not be latching onto the infelicities and oddities, in order to disrupt the project and maximise their own gain."

agreement. The process of construing a written contract can also, in some circumstances, be constrained by statutory regulation.[3]

In other situations the contract may be purely verbal, in which case there may be a dispute as to what was said or promised, and by whom. The problems here are likely to be mainly evidential and so outside the scope of this book. Nevertheless, disputes as to the meaning of the agreement may arise here in a similar way to written contracts.

Some of the problems in deciding what the terms of a contract are may be resolved by the rules that the courts have developed to enable terms to be implied into a contract. Moreover, in certain situations, terms will be implied by statute, irrespective of the wishes or intentions of the parties.

The order of treatment adopted here is to look first at the question of pre-contractual statements, and the remedies that may be available for them. Second, the approach to express terms and their interpretation will be discussed. Finally, the rules relating to the implication of terms, both at common law and by statute, will be considered.

## 6.3 DISTINCTION BETWEEN REPRESENTATIONS AND TERMS

The importance of identifying those pre-contractual statements that do not form part of the contract arises from the question of the remedies that will be available in each case. If a statement amounts to a promise that forms part of a contract, then a person who breaks it will be liable for the full range of contractual remedies discussed in Chapter 15. In particular, the claimant will normally be entitled to damages that will compensate for any profits that may have been lost as a result of the broken promise. A statement that is not a term, however, and that turns out to be untrue, or that contains a promise that is broken, may still give rise to a remedy, but on a different and often more restricted basis. This is discussed in the next section (see below, 6.4) on remedies for pre-contractual statements.

Where there have been statements made prior to a contract, and there is then a dispute as to whether or not they were intended to form part of the contract, how do the courts resolve the issue? The courts' professed approach is (as in many other areas of contract law) to try to determine the intentions of the parties. Did they intend the statement to be contractually binding? In looking at this, the courts generally adopt an approach based on 'detached objectivity',[4] that is, asking what the reasonable third party would have taken the parties to have intended.[5]

In trying to identify the answer to this, there are a number of matters that will be considered. For example, the importance apparently attached to the statement by the claimant may be very significant, as in *Bannerman v White*.[6]

**Key case** *Bannerman v White* (1861)

Facts: A prospective buyer of hops had been assured that sulphur had not been used in their production. He had made it clear that he would not be interested in buying them if it had. After he had bought them, it turned out that sulphur had been used, and he wished to reject them. The seller argued that the statements about whether sulphur had been used were not part of the contract.

---

3   See, in particular, the Consumer Rights Act 2015 – discussed below, 6.7.
4   See Chapter 2, 2.4.2.
5   Which, of course, may not in the end correspond to what either party *really* intended – see, further, Chapter 9, 9.7.1.
6   (1861) 10 CBNS 844; 142 ER 685.

Held: The buyer was entitled to reject the hops for breach of contract. The undertaking that no sulphur had been used was a 'preliminary stipulation'.[7] If it had not been given, the purchaser would not have bothered to inquire about the price and would not have continued to negotiate towards a contract. The statement that sulphur had not been used was part of the contractual obligations.

Evidence, such as was given in this case, that the truth of a pre-contractual statement is a precondition of any binding agreement being reached will strongly support the view that it was intended to form part of the contract.[8]

In this case there was, in effect, a guarantee by the seller that sulphur had not been used, breach of which entitled the buyer to reject the goods. Even where the matter is of importance to the recipient of the statement, however, the maker will not be taken to have intended to guarantee its truth if it has been made clear that the truth should be verified independently. In *Ecay v Godfrey*,[9] for example, the seller of a boat made statements as to its condition, but also advised the buyer to have it surveyed. In this situation, it was clear that the seller could not be taken to have intended his statements to have formed part of the contract. The same principle will apply where such verification would normally be expected, even if it has not been actively encouraged. This will normally be the position, for example, in relation to the sale of houses, where a purchaser will generally be expected to commission an independent survey, rather than relying on the statements of the seller.

It would be possible, of course, to engage in a full-scale inquiry in each case as to the evidence of the parties' intentions. This would be time-consuming, however, and therefore not a very efficient way of proceeding. In practice, in situations where it is not clear that the pre-contractual statement amounted to a precondition for making the contract, the courts have developed three rather more specific tests, which they use as a means of determining whether it should be regarded as creating a contractual obligation. These tests tend to operate as presumptions of an intention as to whether the statement is part of the contract, which may, of course, be rebutted by other evidence suggesting the contrary intention. The tests focus on: (a) whether the contract was put into written form; (b) whether the claimant was relying on the skill and knowledge of the defendant; and (c) the lapse of time between the statement and the contract.

### 6.3.1 WAS THE CONTRACT PUT INTO WRITTEN FORM?

As we saw in Chapter 2, there is generally no need for a contract to be put into writing in order for it to be a valid agreement. On the other hand, if the parties have taken the trouble to commit their contract to writing, the courts will be reluctant to find that it does not contain all the terms that were important to either party. Moreover, if a written contract has been signed, the party who has done so may find it virtually impossible to depart from its express provisions.[10] This is linked to the 'parol evidence rule', by virtue of which the courts will be reluctant to accept oral evidence in order to add to the terms in what appears to be a complete written contract. The rule and the exceptions to it are further

---

7   (1861) 10 CBNS 844, p 860; 142 ER 685, p 692.
8   For a further example of this approach, see *Couchman v Hill* [1947] KB 554 – heifer warranted to be 'unserved' (that is, not in calf). The buyer had indicated that he would not bid for it if it was in calf. The apparently contrary decision in *Hopkins v Tanqueray* (1854) 15 CB 130 probably turns on the particular rules accepted to apply to the market where the sale took place.
9   (1947) 80 Lloyd's LR 286.
10  *L Estrange v Graucob* [1934] 2 KB 394. This case is discussed further in the context of exclusion clauses, in Chapter 7, 7.4.

discussed, later in this chapter, in the context of the identification of the express terms of a contract. This was part of the reason for the rejection of an alleged term (relating to the age of a motorcycle) in *Routledge v McKay*.[11] The purchaser of the motorcycle had prepared a 'written memorandum' at the time of the sale, but this was silent as to the age of the machine. The Court of Appeal was not prepared to say that this definitely precluded any term other than those specified in the memorandum, being part of the contract, but commented that:[12]

> as a matter of construction, it would be difficult to say that such an agreement was consistent with a warranty being given at the same time so as to be intended to form part of the bargain then made.

The rule is not an absolute one, however, and if the party can show that the term that was not included was of the utmost importance, then the courts may be prepared to allow it to be added. This is most likely to be the case where the written contract is in a standard form, rather than the result of individual negotiation. An example is *Evans & Son Ltd v Andrea Merzario Ltd*.[13] The plaintiffs had made a contract for the transport of machinery by sea. They had made it clear to the defendants that it was of great importance that the machinery should not be carried on deck. The defendants had given an oral assurance that the plaintiffs' machinery would be carried below deck. The printed standard conditions for the contract, however, allowed for freight to be carried on deck. The plaintiffs' machinery was carried on deck and was lost overboard. It was held by the Court of Appeal that in this case the verbal assurance took precedence over the written conditions. The statement that the plaintiffs' goods would be carried below deck was a contractual term, and the plaintiffs were entitled to succeed.

### 6.3.2 WAS THE CLAIMANT RELYING ON THE SKILL AND KNOWLEDGE OF THE DEFENDANT?

If there is an imbalance of skill and knowledge relating to the subject matter of the contract as between the claimant and defendant, this will be relevant in deciding whether an oral pre-contractual statement should be treated as a contractual term. The fact that the defendant is in a better position to be able to guarantee the truth of a statement will lend weight to its being regarded as part of the contract. If, on the other hand, it is the claimant who is the expert, then the reverse will be true.

Two cases concerning contracts for the sale of cars conveniently illustrate the two sides of this test. The first case to consider (though the later in time) is *Dick Bentley Productions Ltd v Harold Smith (Motors) Ltd*.[14] The plaintiff had bought a car from the defendants, relying on a pre-contractual statement as to its mileage, which later turned out to be untrue. The Court of Appeal held that the test to be applied was that of whether an intelligent bystander would reasonably infer from what was said or done that the statement was intended to be contractual (that is, 'detached objectivity').[15] Applying this test, the court came to the conclusion that the statement as to the mileage was a term of the contract, on the basis that the defendant was a car dealer who should be taken to have better knowledge of such matters than the plaintiff, who was not involved in the motor trade. In reaching this decision, the court distinguished the earlier case of *Oscar Chess Ltd v Williams*.[16]

---

11  [1954] 1 All ER 855; [1954] 1 WLR 615.
12  Ibid, p 859; p 622, per Lord Evershed MR.
13  [1976] 2 All ER 930; [1976] 1 WLR 1078.
14  [1965] 2 All ER 65.
15  For which, see Chapter 2, 2.4.2.
16  [1957] 1 All ER 325; [1957] 1 WLR 370.

### Key case *Oscar Chess Ltd v Williams* (1957)

Facts: The defendant was a private individual who had sold a car to a garage. Prior to the conclusion of the contract, the defendant had innocently told the garage that the date of the car was 1948, when in fact it had been first registered in 1939. The garage sued for breach of contract, arguing that the statement as to the age of the car was part of the contract.

Held: The Court of Appeal held that, on the basis of the fact that the plaintiffs here had the greater skill and knowledge of such matters, the statement should not be regarded as a term. The intelligent bystander, looking at all the circumstances, would not say that the seller intended to guarantee the age of the car. The seller was in no position to do so, since all he could rely on were the car's registration documents, and he had no means of determining whether they were accurate. The purchaser, on the other hand, being in the motor trade, could, for example, have taken the engine and chassis numbers and checked with the manufacturer.

Other cases where the greater skill and knowledge of the defendant has been relevant in giving contractual status to a pre-contractual statement include *Birch v Paramount Estates Ltd*[17] (developer stating that a house would be as good as the show house), *Schawel v Reade*[18] (owner selling a horse which he stated was 'perfectly sound') and *Harling v Eddy*[19] (owner selling a heifer stating that there was 'nothing wrong' with her).

It should be noted that a case such as *Bentley v Harold Smith*, if the facts recurred, may nowadays be dealt with as a negligent misrepresentation under s 2(1) of the Misrepresentation Act 1967. The remedy in damages for misrepresentations provided by this section was not, of course, available at the time.[20]

### 6.3.3 IN FOCUS: LIABILITY OF PRIVATE SELLERS

It is possible for a private seller of a car to be liable for a false statement as to its age, as is shown by *Beale v Taylor*[21] (discussed below, 6.6.12). Treitel sees this as inconsistent with *Oscar Chess v Williams* (which was not cited in *Beale v Taylor*).[22] But, as Halson points out, the seller in this case, while not in the motor trade, was in a better position than the buyer to know the age of the car, and in that respect the balance of knowledge was in favour of the seller.[23] It is also the case that *Beale v Taylor* turned on the interpretation and application of s 13 of the Sale of Goods Act 1893 (implied term as to compliance with description). This section was not mentioned in *Oscar Chess v Williams*, for reasons that are unclear.[24]

---

17  (1956) 16 EG 396.

18  [1913] 2 IR 64.

19  [1951] 2 KB 739; [1951] 2 All ER 212.

20  The Misrepresentation Act 1967 is dealt with in detail in Chapter 8.

21  [1967] 3 All ER 253.

22  Treitel, 2015, p 432.

23  Halson, 2013, p 286.

24  See Twigg-Flesner Canavan and MacQueen, 2016, p 124, where it is suggested that the reason may be that it would have been unreasonable for the car dealer in *Oscar Chess v Williams* to rely on the description of the car provided by the private seller. See also *Harlingdon & Leinster Enterprises v Christopher Hull Fine Art* [1991] 1 QB 564 discussed below at 6.6.12.

### 6.3.4 WAS THERE A SIGNIFICANT LAPSE OF TIME BETWEEN THE STATEMENT AND THE CONTRACT?

The courts generally consider that the closer in time that the statement was made to the conclusion of the contract, the more likely it is that it was a matter of importance to the claimant, and should therefore be treated as a contractual term. It is certainly true that if there is no significant gap, the statement may well be treated as being intended to be part of the contract, particularly if the agreement is not put into writing. It is by no means clear, however, that the mere existence of a delay should be regarded as in itself reducing the significance of the statement. Such delay may well have been caused by matters irrelevant to the statement, and the claimant may have felt that having settled the issue which the statement concerned, there was no need to re-state it at the time of the contract. Nevertheless, whatever the true significance of the delay, it is undoubtedly the case that as far as the courts are concerned it will weaken the claimant's case.

An example of the application of this test is the case of *Routledge v McKay*.[25] This concerned the sale of a motorbike. The defendant, who was selling the bike, had told the plaintiff that the date of the bike was 1942. In fact, it dated from 1930. A week elapsed between the defendant's statement and the making of the contract of sale (which was put into writing). It was held by the Court of Appeal that the defendant's statement was not a term of the contract. The decision may appear a little harsh, but it may be significant that application of both the other tests outlined above would have gone in favour of the defendant. Thus, the written agreement made no mention of the age of the bike, and neither party had any special skill or knowledge. Both were private individuals, and the defendant in making the statement had innocently relied on false information contained in the bike's registration document.[26]

---

**For thought**

*Geoff is thinking of buying Sarah's car. Sarah tells Geoff that the car is the '2 litre model'. In fact, as Sarah knows, the original engine has been replaced by a 1.6 litre version. Five days later Geoff agrees to buy the car. Can he argue that Sarah's statement as to the size of the engine has become part of his contract with her? If not, what would be the position if the time gap was three days?*

---

As this last case shows, it must be remembered that none of the tests discussed here is automatically conclusive of the issue. All may need to be considered and, if they point in different directions, weighed against each other. The ultimate question is whether the statement, viewed objectively, was intended to form part of the contract. All the other tests are simply matters that may provide guidance to the court in determining this issue.[27]

---

25 [1954] 1 All ER 855; [1954] 1 WLR 615.

26 In that respect, the case was therefore virtually identical to *Oscar Chess Ltd v Williams* [1957] 1 All ER 325; [1957] 1 WLR 370.

27 Of course, in reaching a conclusion on this issue, judges may well be influenced, consciously or unconsciously, by the question of where they feel that responsibility 'ought' to lie. This issue then ceases to be purely factual.

## 6.4 REMEDIES FOR PRE-CONTRACTUAL STATEMENTS

This section is concerned with the situation where the answer to the question raised in the previous section is that the statement is not a term of the (main) contract. What remedies, if any, are available to a person who has made a contract in reliance on such a statement? Although it may be argued that discussion of this issue is out of place in this chapter (since, by definition, such statements are not part of the 'contents of the contract'), it is nevertheless helpful to consider them briefly at this stage, in order to understand fully the importance of deciding whether a statement is part of the contract or not. It is only by considering the consequences of that decision that its significance can be properly appreciated.

There are three possible forms of action that must be considered: the action for misrepresentation, for breach of a collateral contract and for the tort of negligent misstatement.

### 6.4.1 MISREPRESENTATION

The common law and equity recognised two remedies for misrepresentation. Provided that there were no complicating factors, such as the involvement of third party rights, rescission of the contract was the main remedy for all types of misrepresentation. If the misrepresentation was made fraudulently, there was, in addition, the possibility of an action in tort for deceit, which would provide for the recovery of damages.[28] Both these remedies are still available in appropriate cases. In addition, however, there is now the possibility of an action for damages for so-called 'negligent misrepresentation' under s 2 of the Misrepresentation Act 1967.

For any of these remedies to be available, the statement must have been a representation in the strict sense. That is, it must have been a statement of existing fact, or of law,[29] not a statement of opinion,[30] or a promise to act in a particular way in the future. Thus, for example, a statement by a seller of a computer system that a 24-hour service facility will be provided is not a 'representation', but a promise. A statement that the system is ideal for a small business may well be a statement of opinion rather than fact.[31] However, a statement that the firm has already sold 1,000 similar systems, or that it has a team of six service engineers, are representations that, if untrue, may give the other party a remedy.

The statement must have induced the contract.[32] This rule, together with other aspects of the law relating to misrepresentations, is discussed in more detail in Chapter 8.

### 6.4.2 COLLATERAL CONTRACT

We have already encountered the concept of the collateral contract as a means of evading the doctrine of privity by bringing apparent third parties into a contractual relationship, as in *Shanklin Pier v Detel Products*.[33] As noted there, however, the collateral contract can also be used between parties who themselves subsequently enter into a main contract. The collateral contract will take the form of one party expressly, or impliedly, saying to the other, 'If you enter into the main contract, I will promise you X.' It can thus provide a remedy for pre-contractual statements that have not been incorporated into the main contract. It has the advantage over the remedies for misrepresentation in that it is not limited to statements of existing fact. A promise to act in a particular way is clearly covered.

---

28  *Derry v Peek* (1889) 14 App Cas 337.
29  See Chapter 8, 8.3.2 below.
30  *Bisset v Wilkinson* [1927] AC 177.
31  Unless it is based on facts which the maker of the statement knows to be untrue: *Smith v Land and House Property Corp* (1884) 28 Ch D 7.
32  *JEB Fasteners v Marks, Bloom & Co* [1983] 1 All ER 583.
33  [1951] 2 KB 854; [1951] 2 All ER 471; see Chapter 5, 5.9.

**Table 6.1** Pre-Contractual Statements: Term or Representation

|  | Yes: | No: |
|---|---|---|
| **Was the importance attached to the statement significant?** | The statement is likely to be a term if the contracting party has made it clear that he would not otherwise be interested in pursuing the contract in the absence of the specification: *Bannerman v White* (1861) | If the substance of the statement suggests that further verification is required, it is unlikely to be a term: *Ecay v Godfrey* (1947) If verification is discouraged the statement is likely to be a term: *Shawel v Reade* (1913) |
| **Was the contract put into written form?** | Where the parties have committed their statements to writing, they will be recognised as terms. By virtue of the parol evidence rule the courts are reluctant to accept later oral evidence to add to the terms in a complete written contract: *Routledge v McKay* (1954) | Where the term has not been included in a written contract, an exception can be made in standard form contracts where the term not included can be shown to have been of utmost importance: *Evans & Son Ltd v Andrea Merzario Ltd* (1976) |
| **Was the claimant relying on the skill and knowledge of the defendant?** | Where a statement is made by an expert in a particular area to a non-expert it is likely to be a term: *Dick Bentley Productions Ltd v Harold Smith (Motors) Ltd* (1965) | Where a statement is made by a non-expert to an expert in a particular area it is likely to amount to a representation: *Oscar Chess Ltd v Wiliams* (1957) |
| **Was there a significant lapse of time between the statement and the contract?** | A delay will not always be regarded as reducing the significance of the statement, but it can weaken the claimant's case: *Routledge v Mckay* (1954) | If there is no gap between the time that the statement was made and the conclusion of the contract, the statement is more likely to be a term |

Continuing the computer contract example used above, a statement that 'we will answer all service calls within six hours' could not be a misrepresentation, but could found an action for breach of a collateral contract. A statement of fact, or even opinion, may also give rise to a collateral contract, if it can be said that the maker of the statement was guaranteeing its truth.

An example of the use of a collateral contract in a two-party situation is *City of Westminster Properties v Mudd*.[34] A tenant had been in the practice of sleeping in the shop that he rented. When the lease was renewed, the landlord tried to insert a clause stating that the premises should not be used for lodging, dwelling or sleeping. The tenant objected, but was assured orally that if he signed the lease, he would be allowed to sleep there. In fact, probably due to an oversight, the new clause was omitted, but a provision containing an obligation only to use the premises for the purposes of trade remained. The landlord subsequently tried to rely on this clause to forfeit the lease, claiming that the tenant was in breach of it through sleeping on the premises. It was held that the tenant could rely on a collateral contract giving him the right to sleep on the premises, which, in effect, overrode the clause in the lease itself.

---

34 [1959] Ch 129; [1958] 2 All ER 733.

**Key case** *Esso Petroleum Co Ltd v Mardon* (1976)[35]

Facts: A representative of Esso had given a prospective tenant of a petrol station an estimate of the potential throughput, which was put at 200,000 gallons a year. This failed to take account of the fact that the local planning authority had required the petrol pumps to be sited on a side street, invisible from the main road. The tenant was dubious as to the accuracy of the estimate, but accepted it as being based on Esso's superior knowledge of the petrol retailing business. He entered into a lease, but the throughput never exceeded 78,000 gallons a year.

Held: The Court of Appeal held that the tenant was entitled to recover damages from Esso on the basis of a collateral contract. Although the estimate was an expression of opinion, rather than a statement of fact, or a promise as to the throughput that would be achieved, it contained the implied promise that it was made with reasonable care and skill. As Lord Denning commented:

> They [Esso] knew the facts. They knew the traffic in the town. They knew the throughput of comparable stations. They had much experience and expertise at their disposal. They were in a much better position than Mr Mardon to make a forecast. It seems to me that if such a person makes a forecast – intending that the other should act on it and he does act on it – it can well be interpreted as a warranty that the forecast is sound and reliable in the sense that they made it with reasonable care and skill.

The consideration for the promise that the estimate was made with due care and skill was Mr Mardon's agreement to enter into the lease. A contract collateral to the lease was thus created, and Mr Mardon was entitled to recover damages for Esso's breach of this contract.

### 6.4.3 LIMITATIONS OF THE 'COLLATERAL CONTRACT'

As will be seen from these examples, the collateral contract is a very flexible device. Its disadvantage, compared to the action for misrepresentation, is that it will only provide a remedy in damages, and will not allow the claimant the possibility of rescinding the main contract. Moreover, the level of damages that can be awarded may be more restricted than in the case of actions for deceit, or under s 2(1) of the Misrepresentation Act 1967.[36]

### 6.4.4 NEGLIGENT MISSTATEMENT

In 1963, the House of Lords confirmed that the tortious action for negligence could provide a remedy for negligent misstatements that have resulted in purely economic loss.[37] The development of the law in this area over the past 50 years or so has been complicated, as the courts have tried to decide exactly when a duty of care as regards

---

35 [1976] QB 801; [1976] 2 All ER 5. Note that Lord Denning also used the collateral contract analysis to find the defendants liable in *Evans & Son Ltd v Andrea Merzario Ltd* [1976] 1 WLR 1078, whereas (as noted above, at 6.3.1) the other members of the Court of Appeal found that the pre-contractual promise had been incorporated into the main contract. This shows that the approaches taken to finding liability for pre-contractual statements are not necessarily mutually exclusive.

36 See Chapter 8. The actions for deceit and under s 2(1) of the 1967 Act allow for recovery of *all* losses caused by the misrepresentation; in relation to a collateral contract, only losses that were in the reasonable contemplation of the parties at the time of the contract will be recoverable.

37 *Hedley Byrne & Co v Heller & Partners* [1964] AC 465; [1963] 2 All ER 575.

such statements can be said to arise. The subsequent trend, as shown by cases such as *Caparo Industries plc v Dickman*,[38] has been to limit strictly the number of 'special relationships' that can give rise to such a duty, though this has been softened to some extent by the later decisions in *Henderson v Merrett Syndicates Ltd*[39] and *White v Jones*.[40] There is little doubt, however, that a duty of this kind may arise between parties who subsequently enter into a contract. The possibility was recognised in *Esso v Mardon*, for example. In practice, however, the existence of the remedies under s 2(1) of the Misrepresentation Act 1967 means that it is not very likely to be needed in this situation.[41] The action under the 1967 Act has the advantage that the burden of proof as regards negligence is on the defendant (who effectively has to disprove it), and that more extensive damages are available. The only situation where it might be necessary for a party to a contract to look to the common law negligence action is where the statement is not a representation in the strict sense, and it is also impossible to construct a collateral contract.[42]

## 6.4.5 CONCLUSION ON PRE-CONTRACTUAL STATEMENTS

As we have seen, there is a variety of actions that may be available in relation to pre-contractual statements. There is nothing to stop a claimant relying on more than one, as was pointed out by Lord Denning in *Esso v Mardon*.[43] In an unusually frank (for a judge) recognition of the way in which lawyers manipulate legal concepts to achieve their desired result, he explained how, at a time when no damages were available for a non-fraudulent misrepresentation, other alternatives would be sought:[44]

> In order to escape from that rule, the pleader used to allege – I often did it myself – that the misrepresentation was fraudulent, or alternatively a collateral warranty. At the trial we nearly always succeeded on collateral warranty. We had to reckon, of course, with the *dictum* of Lord Moulton that 'such collateral contracts must from their nature be very rare'.[45] But more often than not the court elevated the innocent misrepresentation into a collateral warranty; and thereby did justice ... Besides that experience, there have been many cases since I have sat in this court where we have readily held a representation ... to be a warranty sounding in damages.

Nowadays, since damages for negligent misrepresentations are now available, the decision as to which action will be the most appropriate to press will depend mainly on the type of statement (is it a statement of fact?) and on the remedy that is being sought (is rescission of the contract required, or will damages be adequate?). If the statement cannot be constructed as being of fact, then collateral contract may be the best remedy to pursue. On the other hand, if rescission rather than damages is what is important, the contractual action for misrepresentation is the only one that will provide this.

---

38 [1990] 1 All ER 568.
39 [1995] 2 AC 145; [1994] 3 All ER 506.
40 [1995] 2 AC 207; [1995] 1 All ER 691. See also the speech of Lord Steyn in *Williams v Nature Life Ltd* [1998] 1 WLR 830, p 837, accepting 'assumption of responsibility' as the test for the existence of a duty. The approach taken in *White v Jones* to the identification of a duty of care was also applied by the Court of Appeal in *Gorham v British Telecommunications plc* [2000] 4 All ER 867. See, more recently, *Steel and another v NRAM Limited (formerly NRAM Plc) (Scotland)* [2018] UKSC 13.
41 See Chapter 8, 8.4.6.
42 The tortious remedy is discussed further in Chapter 8, 8.4.7.
43 [1976] QB 801; [1976] 2 All ER 5.
44 Ibid, p 817; p 13.
45 In *Heilbut, Symons & Co v Buckleton* [1913] AC 30, p 47.

## 6.5 EXPRESS TERMS

In this section, we are concerned with terms that have without doubt been put forward by one or other party as a term of the agreement. There may be disputes, however, as to whether the clause has been incorporated into the contract, as to its proper meaning, and as to the consequences of breaking it. In dealing with all these questions, the approach of the courts will again be professed to be that they are trying to determine the parties' intention, from an objective viewpoint. The focus under classical theory is on the time of the original agreement, with later developments being ignored.[46]

### 6.5.1 INCORPORATION

We have already discussed the rules that the courts adopt to decide whether pre-contractual statements should be regarded as having been incorporated into a contract. The situation under consideration here is slightly different: clauses that have been put forward by one or other of the parties as a term of the contract. The issues discussed in this section will often arise in relation to written clauses in a standard form which have not been signed. One party may object that a particular clause should not be regarded as being included in the contract because they were unaware of it for some reason and would have objected to it. The rules that operate in this area have mainly developed in relation to the incorporation of exclusion clauses, and detailed discussion of them will be left until Chapter 7. In appropriate cases, they can apply to other types of clause, however, as is shown by the case of *Interfoto Picture Library v Stiletto Visual Programmes*.[47]

---

**Key case** *Interfoto Picture Library v Stiletto Visual Programmes* (1988)

Facts: The defendants were an advertising agency. They needed some photographs for a presentation. On 5 March 1984, they contacted the plaintiffs, who ran a library of photographic transparencies, to see if they might have anything suitable. The plaintiffs sent round a packet of 47 transparencies, together with a delivery note. The transparencies were, however, apparently overlooked and not used. They were eventually returned on 2 April, that is, nearly a month after they had been received. The plaintiffs then claimed the sum of £3,783 from the defendants as a 'holding charge' for the transparencies. This was calculated in accordance with the terms laid down in the delivery note, which stated that, in relation to transparencies not returned within 14 days of receipt, a charge of £5 per day plus VAT would be made in respect of each transparency. The issue before the court was whether the terms of the delivery note formed part of a contract between the parties and, if so, whether the plaintiffs could enforce these terms against the defendants.

Held: The Court of Appeal held that the clause could not be enforced. It did so by reference to the case law on exclusion clauses and when they are deemed to have been incorporated into a contract. In particular, the court relied on *Parker v South Eastern Railway Co*,[48] and *Thornton v Shoe Lane Parking*.[49] *Parker* established the principle that, in order to rely on an exclusion clause in an unsigned contract, the defendant had to have taken reasonable steps to bring it to the attention of the claimant. *Thornton* added the gloss that the more unusual and onerous the clause, the more the defendant had

---

46 Whereas a 'relational' approach would allow later developments to be considered – see Macneil, 1978, and Chapter 1, 1.6.
47 [1988] QB 433; [1988] 1 All ER 348.
48 (1877) 2 CPD 416.
49 [1971] 2 QB 163; [1971] 1 All ER 686.

to do to draw it to the claimant's attention. The court saw no reason why this approach should not apply to the case before it. The clause was particularly, and unusually, onerous in its effect. The plaintiffs had done nothing to draw it to the defendants' attention. It should be regarded as not having been incorporated into the contract.

### 6.5.2 IN FOCUS: DO BUSINESSES NEED PROTECTING?

The approach taken in the *Interfoto* case is an unusual one in relation to a commercial agreement. This aspect of the rule of incorporation is perhaps more suited to use as a means of protecting consumers, particularly in relation to exclusion clauses. Where parties are contracting at arm's length, in a business context, it would more commonly be the case that the court would expect each party to take care over the obligations to which it was committing itself. If they agree to unfavourable terms, then that is their own fault. It is perhaps significant that the *Interfoto* decision has not so far led to many similar reported decisions. In *Kaye v Nu Skin UK Ltd*,[50] the High Court, dealing with a preliminary issues, held that the *Interfoto* approach could be relevant in a commercial contract between an individual, inexperienced business person and a franchise company, which contained a provision requiring mediation of any dispute to take place in Utah, USA. On the other hand, in a case involving the loss of transparencies, *Photolibrary Group Ltd v Burda Senator Verlag Gmbh*,[51] the *Interfoto* case was distinguished on the basis that there had been a course of dealing between the parties, and the terms used were ones that were common in the trade. In *AEG (UK) Ltd v Logic Resource Ltd*[52] a similar approach to that taken in *Interfoto* was adopted, but the majority Court of Appeal decision is strictly *obiter* on this point since it found that the clause was also unreasonable under the statutory test contained in the Unfair Contract Terms Act 1977.[53] Indeed, given the statutory control of exclusion and other clauses by this Act (and, indeed in the consumer sphere under Consumer Rights Act 2015),[54] there would seem to be little need to develop further a restrictive rule for incorporation under the common law.[55]

### 6.5.3 A MORE RELAXED APPROACH?

A move towards an arguably more relaxed approach to incorporation is exemplified by the Court of Appeal decision in *O'Brien v Mirror Group Newspapers*,[56] which was concerned with a consumer contract. The claim concerned a 'scratch card' game operated by the defendants, Mirror Newspapers. The claimant had obtained one of the scratch cards from a newspaper, from which it appeared that he would win £50,000 if this was the prize on a particular

---

50  [2009] EWHC 3509. However, in further proceedings in this matter HHJ Denyer QC ([2012] CTLC 69 at [43]-[59]) stated: 'I have to say that I find it slightly difficult to characterise an arbitration clause as being on its face unreasonable and/or extortionate. It is an extremely common clause in many commercial contracts.' See also [2012] EWCA Civ 1069. See also *Hawksford Trustees Jersey Limited v Halliwells LLP (In Liquidation)* [2015] EWHC 2996 (Ch) at [63] *per* HHJ Pelling QC.

51  [2008] EWHC 1343.

52  [1996] CLC 265 – the case is discussed in detail by Bradgate, 1997.

53  See Chapter 7, 7.6.

54  Also discussed in Chapter 7, 7.8.

55  As Hobhouse LJ pointed out in his dissent in *AEG (UK) Ltd v Logic Resource Ltd*, the *Interfoto* approach, unless strictly controlled, runs the risk of 'distorting the contractual relationship between the parties and the ordinary mechanisms of making contracts'. By contrast in *Goodlife Foods Limited v Hall Fire Protection Limited* [2018] EWCA Civ 1371 Coulson LJ stated (at [35]): "...I consider that these two principles (namely incorporation at common law on the one hand, and the reasonableness of any term incorporated pursuant to UCTA, on the other) are separate, and the questions to be decided in respect of each are distinct. There may be some overlap in the matters that fall to be considered under each principle, but that is all."

56  [2001] EWCA Civ 1279; [2002] CLC 33.

day, which could be discovered by ringing a particular telephone number. He rang the number and was told that the prize amount was £50,000, so he thought that he had won that amount. It then transpired that, because of an error, a large number of winning cards had been produced. The defendants therefore relied on rule 5 of the rules applying to the competition, which they claimed allowed them to draw lots between all the holders of the 'winning' cards to decide who won the £50,000. The claimant was not successful in this draw, and sued, claiming that rule 5 had not been incorporated into his contract with the defendants. The rules of the competition had been published in a number of newspapers, but did not appear every day. The Sunday paper from which the claimant had obtained his card stated 'FULL RULES AND HOW TO CLAIM SEE DAILY MIRROR'. The paper from which he obtained the number to ring to see if his card had 'won' stated 'Normal Mirror Group rules apply'. The claimant argued that this was insufficient for the rules to be incorporated into his contract.

The Court of Appeal agreed with the trial judge that a contract was made by an offer contained in the newspaper on the day the claimant telephoned the defendants, which the claimant accepted by making the telephone call. The trial judge thought that the claimant, who admitted buying a number of the relevant newspapers, must have seen the rules, or at least have been aware that there were rules applying to the competition. He did not feel that rule 5 was sufficiently unusual or onerous that the defendants ought to have done more to bring it to the attention of those who might play the scratch card game. The Court of Appeal agreed. As Hale LJ put it:[57]

> The offer and therefore the contract clearly incorporated the term 'Normal Mirror Group rules apply'. The words were there to be read and it makes no difference whether or not the claimant actually read or paid attention to them.
>
> The question, therefore, is whether those words, in the circumstances, were enough to incorporate the Rules, including Rule 5, into the contract.

Applying the approach taken in the *Interfoto* case, the test was whether the rules could be said to have been fairly and reasonably brought to the notice of the claimant. This depends on the nature of the contract and the nature of the term. In the view of Hale LJ, although rule 5 did turn an apparent winner into a loser, it could not by any normal use of language be called 'onerous' or 'outlandish'. It did not impose any extra burden upon the claimant, unlike the clause in *Interfoto*. It did not seek to absolve the defendant from liability for personal injuries negligently caused, unlike the clause in *Thornton v Shoe Lane Parking;* it merely deprived the claimant of a windfall for which he had done very little in return. He bought two newspapers and made a call to a premium rate number, which would have cost him a matter of pennies, not pounds. Nor was there any evidence that this type of rule was 'unusual' in this sort of competition. In any event, as Hale LJ concluded:[58]

> The words 'onerous or unusual' are not terms of art. They are simply one way of putting the general proposition that reasonable steps must be taken to draw the particular term in question to the notice of those who are to be bound by it and that more is required in relation to certain terms than to others depending on their effect. In the particular context of this particular game, I consider that the defendants did just enough to bring the Rules to the claimant's attention. There was a clear reference to rules on the face of the card he used. There was a clear reference to rules in the paper containing the offer of a telephone prize. There was evidence that those rules could be discovered either from the newspaper offices or from back issues of the paper. The claimant had been able to discover them when the problem arose.

---

57  Ibid, para 19.
58  [2001] EWCA Civ 1279; [2002] CLC 33, para 23.

Although the court had sympathy with the claimant, he was bound by the terms of the competition, and his claim failed. It would seem then that even in consumer contracts, there is no necessary requirement to take special steps to draw attention to a clause which may have the effect of disappointing the expectations of the unwary contractor.

## For thought

*What do you think the position would be if the consumer, unlike Mr O'Brien, had paid a significant sum for what he or she was expecting to obtain under the contract? Would the courts adopt a different approach?*

### 6.5.4 CONSTRUCTION

Even where there is no dispute as to whether a clause is incorporated, the parties may disagree as to what it was intended to mean. It will be necessary to try to construe the clause in order to give effect to it. The courts will adopt the approach of trying to assess objectively what the parties must be taken to have intended. Traditionally, in relation to a written contract, the parties are not be permitted to 'add to, vary or contradict that writing' *(Henderson v Arthur)*.[59] This rule is known as the 'parol evidence rule'. The Law Commission has doubted whether there is such a rule of law as the 'parol evidence rule' – regarding it as being essentially a circular statement, to the effect that when it is proved that a written document was intended to set out all the express terms of an agreement, other evidence of what was intended will not be admissible.[60] Nevertheless, as the Commission itself recognised, since the 'rule' has regularly been referred to by writers and judges, it provides a convenient shorthand for the approach to constructing contracts to which it applies.[61] The rule, whatever its precise status, thus makes it very important for the parties to ensure that any written document forming part of the contract is clear and explicit as to the obligations which are being imposed on each side. The parol evidence rule is not, however, unchallengeable, and there are certain established exceptions to it.

Exceptions to the parol evidence rule include the following:

(a) *Ambiguity*. Where a word or phrase contained in the written document is ambiguous, other evidence may be given as to what was actually intended, as in *Robertson v Jackson*.[62] The phrase in question was 'turn to deliver' in relation to the unloading of goods at a particular port. The contract did not on its face give any indication of when the ship's 'turn to deliver' would arise. The court was prepared to allow oral evidence as to the custom applying in that port. This exception must now be considered in the light of the overall approach to construction taken in recent cases, such as *Investors Compensation Scheme Ltd v West Bromwich Building Society*,[63] discussed in the next section.

(b) *Written agreement incomplete*. If either or both of the parties can show that the written agreement was not intended to contain all the terms of the contract, then oral or other extrinsic evidence may be used to fill it out. In *Allen v Pink*,[64] for example,

---

59 [1907] 1 KB 10.
60 See Law Commission Report No 154, 1986, para 2.7.
61 See also Wedderburn, 1959. Treitel does not accept the Commission's analysis of the rule as being 'circular' – see Treitel, 2015, p 234ff.
62 (1845) 2 CB 412.
63 [1998] 1 All ER 98.
64 (1838) 4 M & W 140.

the written document relating to the sale of a horse was little more than a receipt. It stated the price and the names of the parties, but contained no other terms. In the circumstances, the court was prepared to allow evidence of an oral promise as to the horse's behaviour in harness. This case was fairly clear. It will be more difficult where the written agreement contains some terms. The court will have to consider objectively whether it appears to be complete, or whether it is more likely that the parties intended it to be supplemented by other obligations. The insertion of a clause to the effect that 'this document contains all the terms of the contract' will presumably make it difficult to rebut the presumption that it is complete, and that any other evidence of additional terms should be excluded.[65]

(c)  *Custom*. Sometimes, a particular word or phrase is used in a particular trade, market or locality in a way that does not accord with its obvious meaning. In *Smith v Wilson*,[66] evidence was allowed to establish a local custom to the effect that the phrase '1,000 rabbits' meant '1,200 rabbits'. Custom may also be used to fill out an aspect of the contract on which the written document is silent. In *Hutton v Warren*,[67] a custom as to allowances to be given to an outgoing tenant for seeds and labour used in the last year of the tenancy was held to be incorporated into a lease which contained no such provision. Parke B commented that:[68]

It has long been settled that, in commercial transactions, extrinsic evidence of custom and usage is admissible to annex incidents to written contracts in matters with respect to which they are silent.

> This use of custom overlaps with the use of custom to imply terms; this is discussed further below. Custom may not be used, however, where it is clearly contradicted by the terms of the contract. Where, for example, a charter provided that the expenses of discharging a cargo should be borne by the charterer, it was not possible to override this by showing a custom that the expenses should be borne by the owner of the ship.[69]

(d)  *Starting or finishing date*. Extrinsic evidence may be used to establish the date on which a contract is intended to start to operate. In *Pym v Campbell*,[70] evidence was allowed as to an oral provision that the contract should not start to operate prior to the approval of a third party.

(e)  *Other exceptions*. Where it can be argued that a written document was intended simply to record earlier oral agreements, but fails to do so accurately, extrinsic evidence may be allowed to prove this, and thus to 'rectify' the written document.[71] The parol evidence rule may also be circumvented by showing the existence of a collateral contract. An example of this is the decision in *City of Westminster Properties v Mudd*,[72] which has been discussed above.[73] This is perhaps not a true

---

65  This is certainly the position as regards an 'entire agreement' clause, which generally has the effect of preventing reliance on any alleged collateral contract: *The Inntrepreneur Pub Co (GL) v East Crown Ltd* [2000] 2 Lloyd's Rep 611. However, in *Rock Advertising Ltd v MWB Business Exchange Centres Ltd* [2018] UKSC 24 Lord Sumption stated that such clauses would not prevent the enforceable of a truly independent collateral agreement with its own consideration. Similarly an entire agreement clause will not generally prevent the implication of terms in appropriate cases: *JN Hipwell and Son v Szurek* [2018] EWCA Civ 674.

66  (1832) 3 B & Ad 728.

67  (1836) 1 M & W 466; 150 ER 517.

68  (1836) 1 M & W 466, p 475; 150 ER 517, p 521.

69  *Palgrave, Brown & Son Ltd v SS Turid (Owners)* [1922] 1 AC 397.

70  (1856) 2 E & B 370.

71  The remedy of 'rectification' is discussed further in Chapter 9, 9.7.2.

72  [1959] Ch 129; [1958] 2 All ER 733.

73  At 6.4.2.

exception, since it concerns not the interpretation of one contract, but rather a decision as to the priority between two inconsistent contracts. Finally, as we have seen earlier,[74] a pre-contractual statement may become part of the contract if the courts feel that it related to something of great importance to one or other of the parties. This is perhaps best exemplified by the case of *Evans v Andrea Merzario*,[75] where the statement that the cargo would be carried below deck was held to override the provision in the written contract allowing it to be carried on deck.

### 6.5.5 'PURPOSIVE' OR 'COMMERCIAL' INTERPRETATION[76]

The approach of the courts to determining the meaning of an express term of a contract has been modified in recent years. Traditionally, it was said, particularly in relation to commercial agreements, that the courts used to apply a 'literal' approach,[77] subject only to the *contra proferentem* rule that any ambiguity would be interpreted against the person who put the clause forward.[78] The assumption was that contracting parties had an obligation to use the correct language to achieve their objectives, and that if they happened to have used words which bore a different meaning, the court would not look behind those words to discover their 'real' intentions.

This approach has now been clearly rejected. In *Prenn v Simmonds*,[79] Lord Wilberforce recognised that agreements may need to be placed in context to be properly understood:[80]

The time has long passed when agreements, even those under seal, were isolated from the matrix of facts in which they were set and interpreted purely on internal linguistic considerations.

Similarly, in *Reardon Smith Line v Hansen-Tangen*,[81] Lord Wilberforce again referred to the need for the court to place itself in the same 'factual matrix' to that of the parties when they made the contract.[82]

The modern approach has now been set out fully by Lord Hoffmann in *Investors Compensation Scheme Ltd v West Bromwich Building Society*.[83] He commented that 'almost all the old intellectual baggage of "legal" interpretation has been discarded' in favour of an approach which generally relies on 'the common sense principles by which any serious utterance would be interpreted in ordinary life'.[84] He then identified five relevant principles. First, he defined the overall approach in these terms:[85]

---

74 See 6.2 and 6.3 above.

75 [1976] 2 All ER 930; [1976] 1 WLR 1078.

76 See McMeel, 1998; Gee, 2001. McMeel argues that the modern approach is better categorised as 'commercial' rather than 'purposive'. He points to the decision in *Deutsche Genossenschaftsbank v Burnhope* [1996] 1 Lloyd's Rep 113 as illustrating the problems with 'unfocused purposive construction': McMeel, 1998, p 392.

77 Whether it is possible, in fact, ever to adopt a strict 'literal' approach, without paying any attention to the cultural background or other context in which language is used, is of course a matter open to debate.

78 The *contra proferentem* rule is discussed further in Chapter 7, in relation to exclusion clauses: 7.5.1.

79 [1971] 3 All ER 237. However, compare *Bominflot Bunkergesellschaft für Mineraloele mbH & Co KG v Petroplus Marketing AG* [2010] EWCA Civ 1145, discussed at Chapter 7, 7.5.2.

80 Ibid, p 239.

81 [1976] 2 Lloyd's Rep 621; [1976] 1 WLR 989.

82 Ibid, p 625; p 997.

83 [1998] 1 All ER 98.

84 Ibid, p 114. See also *The Law Society of Ireland v The Motor Insurers' Bureau of Ireland* [2017] IESC 31 at [13] where O'Donnell J in the Irish Supreme Court stated: "What might be described as the modern approach to interpretation probably owes something to a developing understanding of communication."

85 Ibid.

Interpretation is the ascertainment of the meaning which the document would convey to a reasonable person having all the background knowledge which would reasonably have been available to the parties in the situation they were in at the time of the contract.

Second, Lord Wilberforce's 'factual matrix' should be extended to include 'absolutely anything which would have affected the way in which the language of the document would have been understood by the reasonable man'.[86] Third, and as a restriction on the second principle, prior negotiations and expressions of subjective intent may only be used in an action for 'rectification'. Lord Hoffmann did not go into detail as to the reasons for this restriction, but Lord Wilberforce in *Prenn v Simmonds* dismissed such evidence as simply being 'unhelpful'.[87] Statements made during negotiations will frequently be made in a situation where the parties' positions are changing and are therefore not good evidence of the 'final' agreement. Moreover, statements about one party's objective may be 'dangerous', since there is no guarantee that this objective is accepted by the other side.[88] The reluctance to use negotiation statements, other than in relation to rectification, has been more recently confirmed by the House of Lords in *Chartbrook Ltd v Persimmon Homes Ltd*.[89] This does not, however, preclude consideration of evidence of the 'genesis' and the objectively determined 'aim' of the transaction.[90]

Lord Hoffmann's fourth principle is that 'the meaning which a document ... would convey to a reasonable man is not the same thing as the meaning of its words'. This is because the background may enable the reasonable person not only to resolve any ambiguity as to the meaning, but also to conclude that the parties must have used the wrong words or syntax.[91] As McMeel points out,[92] when Mrs Malaprop refers to a headstrong 'allegory' on the banks of the Nile,[93] no reasonable person would misunderstand her, because the context or 'background' makes it clear that she is intending to refer to an 'alligator'.[94]

The fifth and final principle identified by Lord Hoffmann recognises that, although there is a proper reluctance to accept that, particularly in formal documents, people have made linguistic mistakes, on the other hand:[95]

if one would nevertheless conclude from the background that something must have gone wrong with the language, the law does not require judges to attribute to the parties an intention which they plainly could not have had.

---

86 In *BNYMellon Corporate Trustee Services Limited v LBG Capital No 1 Plc* [2016] UKSC 29 Lord Neuberger (with whom Lord Mance and Lord Toulson agreed) stated that background regulatory documents from the Financial Services Authority could be taken into account in interpreting an agreement.

87 [1971] 3 All ER 237, p 240.

88 [1971] 3 All ER 237, p 241. See also the comments of the Court of Appeal in *P & S Platt Ltd v Crouch* [2003] EWCA Civ 1110; [2004] 1 P & CR 18, at paras 39 and 52–57 – applying the restrictive approach to a case concerned with s 62 of the Law of Property Act 1925. For discussion of this case, see Warwick, 2003.

89 [2009] UKHL 38; [2009] 1 AC 1101.

90 Ibid.

91 Lord Hoffmann here cites *Mannai Investment Co Ltd v Eagle Star Life Assurance Co Ltd* [1997] AC 749, where a tenant giving notice to terminate a lease that was stated to expire on *12* January was held to be effective, even though under the lease the date for termination would have been *13* January.

92 McMeel, 1998, p 390 – adopting and adapting an example used by Lord Hoffmann in *Mannai Investment Co Ltd v Eagle Star Life Assurance Co Ltd* [1997] AC 749, p 774.

93 Sheridan, *The Rivals,* Act III, Scene 3.

94 Although as McMeel (pedantically?) points out (McMeel, 1998, p 390), the creature would in fact be a 'crocodile' if it was on the Nile, since alligators are found in the Americas, rather than Africa.

95 [1998] 1 All ER 98, p 115.

The same point had been made previously by Lord Diplock:[96]

> if detailed semantic and syntactical analysis of words in a commercial contract are going to lead to a conclusion that flouts business common sense, it must be made to yield to business common sense.[97]

The approach embodied in Lord Hoffmann's five principles has the laudable aim of trying to ensure as far as possible that the agreed aims of contracting parties are not thwarted by an over-literal or blinkered approach by the courts. The court must pay attention to the surrounding context and, so far as it can be identified, the objective purpose of the agreement in deciding what the words of a written contract should be taken to 'mean'.[98]

It should not be thought, however, that these principles are necessarily easy to apply to actual cases, as is shown by the following case.

---

**Key case** *Bank of Credit and Commerce International SA v Ali* (2001)[99]

Facts: An agreement was made by employees as part of a redundancy arrangement that they would not pursue any further legal claims against their employers. It was later established, in other litigation,[100] that former employees of the company could claim 'stigma damages' as a result of their innocent association with an organisation that had been found to be carrying out its business in a corrupt and dishonest manner. The question in the present case was whether the agreement entered into by the claimants precluded them from pursuing an action for 'stigma damages'.

Held: The majority of the House of Lords held that, on its proper construction, the agreement should not be taken to cover a form of action which had not even been recognised as possible at the time the agreement was made. In coming to this conclusion, Lord Bingham, who gave the leading speech, referred specifically and approvingly to Lord Hoffmann's summary of the relevant principles in *Investors Compensation Scheme Ltd v West Bromwich Building Society*.[101] In other words, the 'factual matrix' of the situation in which the agreement was made, and the state of knowledge of the parties, led to the conclusion that the employees should not be precluded from seeking 'stigma damages'. Lord Hoffmann himself, however, was in a minority of one in the House of Lords in holding that the agreement should, on its proper construction, be held to preclude any action by the claimants.[102]

---

Both the majority and the minority in the above case purported to be operating on the same principles, and to be taking into account the context of the agreement. Nevertheless, they came to different conclusions. This suggests that the process of interpreting

---

96  In *Antaios Cia Naviera SA v Salen Redierna B, The Antaios* [1985] AC 191, p 201; [1984] 3 All ER 229, p 233.

97  A similar approach is to be found in *Schuler AG v Wickman Machine Tool Sales Ltd* [1974] AC 235; [1973] 2 All ER 39, in considering the question of whether a term is a 'condition' giving the right to repudiate for breach. See Chapter 14, 14.6.6.

98  For a discussion of issues of 'reasonable expectation', 'fairness' and 'good faith' which may be implicit in Lord Hoffmann's approach, see Brownsword, 2003.

99  [2001] 1 All ER 961.

100  *Malik v BCCI SA* [1998] AC 20; [1997] 3 All ER 1.

101  [1998] 1 All ER 98.

102  Indeed, he saw the approach of the majority as involving an 'artificial' approach to construction, out of line with modern trends.

contracts will continue to be a matter where there will be much scope for the particular opinions of individual judges, and that the modern 'contextual' approach will not be likely to lead to an increase in certainty, at least in the short term.

An example of the power of this approach to the construction of contracts is to be found in the decision of the House of Lords in *Chartbrook Ltd v Persimmon Homes Ltd*.[103]

---

**Key case** *Chartbrook Ltd v Persimmon Homes Ltd* (2009)

Facts: The contract concerned a housing and commercial development on land owned by the claimants. The dispute concerned the calculation of a 'balancing payment' to be made by the developer to the claimants, based on the extent to which the sale price of the residential properties exceeded what was expected at the time of the contract. The claimants calculated this as £4,484,862; the defendants calculated it as £897,051. The trial judge and a majority of the Court of Appeal held that the claimants' interpretation of the relevant clause reflected its clear meaning.

Held: The House of Lords held that while from a grammatical and syntactical point of view the interpretation adopted by the lower courts was the most obvious one, it did not make commercial sense in the context of the overall agreement. It would have meant a balancing payment being made in every case (in the absence of a catastrophic fall in the housing market). The interpretation suggested by the developer, and adopted by the dissenting judge in the Court of Appeal, was to be preferred.

---

In coming to this conclusion, Lord Hoffmann, who delivered the main judgment, while emphasising that it requires 'a strong case to persuade the court that something must have gone wrong with the language',[104] commented that:[105]

> To say ... that [the interpretation] requires 'rewriting', or that it "distorts the meaning and arithmetic of the definition" is only to say that it requires one to conclude that something has gone wrong with the language – not, in this case, with the meanings for words, but with the syntactical arrangement of those words. If, however, the context drives one to the conclusion that this must have happened, it is no answer that the interpretation does not reflect what the words would conventionally have been understood to mean.

While this approach allows the courts to do justice in particular cases, it adds to the uncertainty of interpreting contracts. In *Chartbrook v Persimmon* itself, three judges thought that the clause meant one thing, whereas six thought it meant something else. It is arguable that this will encourage litigation, which is undesirable. It might also have the effect of making those who draft contracts even more careful about the language used – which would be the preferable outcome.

Subsequently, in *Rainy Sky SA v Kookmin Bank*[106] the Supreme Court emphasised that where there are two possible constructions of a clause the courts should adopt the one that accords with 'commercial common sense'. In looking at the clause through the eyes of the reasonable third party the court should assume that that third party has knowledge

---

103 [2009] UKHL 38; [2009] 1 AC 1101.
104 Ibid, [15].
105 Ibid, [26].
106 [2011] UKSC 50, [2011] 1 WLR 2900.

of the commercial context in which the clause was intended to operate. It is not necessary for one interpretation of the clause to have an absurd or irrational result for the court to favour the other, if it seems to accord more clearly with what were likely to have been the commercial intentions of the parties at the time of the contract.

Similarly, in *Pink Floyd Music Ltd v EMI Records Ltd*,[107] a contract entered into in 1999 had covered the rights of the record company in publishing albums produced by the claimants. For example, one clause prohibited the release of separate tracks from an album as 'singles' without written permission from the claimants. Although online sales were not mentioned in the contract, the Court of Appeal concluded that the clause should cover distribution in digital form, as well as physical. This was in accordance with 'commercial common sense'. In subsequent cases the Court of Appeal has continued to advocate the purposive approach, often rejecting the more literal interpretation favoured by the trial judge – as in, for example, *Belfairs Management Ltd v Sutherland*,[108] and *Napier Park European Credit Opportunities Fund Ltd v Harbourmaster Pro-Rata CLO 2 BV*.[109]

By contrast in *Arnold v Britton*[110] Lord Neuberger (with whom Lord Sumption and Lord Hughes agreed) noted the limits of the use of business common sense:

> First, the reliance placed in some cases on commercial common sense and surrounding circumstances (eg in *Chartbrook*, paras 16–26) should not be invoked to undervalue the importance of the language of the provision which is to be construed. The exercise of interpreting a provision involves identifying what the parties meant through the eyes of a reasonable reader, and, save perhaps in a very unusual case, that meaning is most obviously to be gleaned from the language of the provision. Unlike commercial common sense and the surrounding circumstances, the parties have control over the language they use in a contract. And, again save perhaps in a very unusual case, the parties must have been specifically focussing on the issue covered by the provision when agreeing the wording of that provision.

Subsequently in *Wood v Capita Insurance Services Limited*[111] Lord Hodge (with whom Lord Neuberger, Lord Mance, Lord Clarke and Lord Sumption agreed) stated that *Arnold v Britton* was not a recalibration of *Rainy Sky*. In Lord Hodge's opinion, interpreting a contract is a unitary exercise where the court has to balance the language used (*Arnold v Britton*) with the implications of rival constructions (*Rainy Sky*). In determining the weight to be given to these factors, a court should consider the quality of the drafting and whether one party has actually just made a bad bargain.[112]

## 6.5.6 IN FOCUS: REWRITING THE AGREEMENT

An example of the kind of radical rewriting of the words of a contract that can result from the approach taken in *Chartbrook v Persimmon* is shown by the Court of Appeal's decision in *Prudential Assurance Co Ltd v Ayres*.[113] The case concerned a complex sequence of assignments of an underlease of a property, and the attempts to avoid liability attaching to the personal assets of the partners of a partnership which was one of the parties. A clause in a supplemental deed relating to this stated, *inter alia*:

---

107 [2010] EWCA Civ 1429.
108 [2013] EWCA Civ 185.
109 [2014] EWCA Civ 984.
110 [2015] UKSC 36 at [17]. See also *BP Gas Marketing Ltd v LA Societe Sonatrach* [2016] EWHC 2461 (Comm).
111 [2017] UKSC 24.
112 [2017] UKSC 24 at [9]-[11].
113 [2008] EWCA Civ 52; 2008 1 All ER 1266n.

**CLASSIFICATION OF TERMS**
**There are three categories of contractual term**

**CONDITION**

A fundamental term of the contract

Where a condition is breached, the claimant may sue for damages, terminate the contract, or take both of these options:

*Poussard v Spiers & Pond* (1876)

**WARRANTY**

A minor term of the contract

A contract will continue where a breach occurs

Where a breach of warranty occurs there is no right to terminate the contract. The claimant may sue for damages only:

*Bettini v Gye* (1876)

**INNOMINATE TERM**

The courts will look at the consequence of the breach in deciding what remedy is appropriate:

*Hong Kong Fir Shipping Co Ltd v Kawasaki Kisen Kaisha Ltd* [1962]

Figure 6.1

> Consequently, any recovery by the Landlord against the Tenant or any previous tenant under the Lease for any such default shall be limited to the assets of the Partnership ...

The defendant was a partner in a firm that was a previous tenant, but was not a party to this supplemental deed. He sought to claim protection under the clause, using the Contracts (Rights of Third Parties) Act 1999.[114] The trial judge, while finding this a surprising result, did not feel able to depart from the clear wording of the clause, which seemed to confer the protection sought on the defendant. The Court of Appeal disagreed. Taking account of the 'factual matrix' it was clear that it was only 'the Tenant' who was intended to have protection under this clause, including protection from action by former tenants. The clause should be read as if it said:

> Consequently a recovery by the Landlord *or any previous tenant* under the Lease against the Tenant for any such default shall be limited to the assets of the Partnership ...

Thus the *Investors'* approach allowed the Court of Appeal effectively to rewrite the agreement, despite the fact that its meaning appeared clear on its face.

---

114 For which see Chapter 5, 5.6.

### 6.5.7 CONDITIONS, WARRANTIES AND INNOMINATE TERMS

Not all terms within a contract are of equal importance. In a contract for the provision of a service, for example, terms specifying the dates on which the service is to be provided and the date for payment will be likely to be more important than, for example, a term requiring the supplier of the service to submit an annual account of the work done. The consequence of breach of one of the first two terms is probably going to be more serious than the latter, and may indeed result in the contract as a whole being terminated. The parties may attempt to give effect to such differences in the status of various contractual provisions by the way in which their agreement is drafted in respect of its 'express terms'. There is, in fact, a generally accepted hierarchy of terms, with 'conditions' being more important than 'warranties'. Use of these labels may well indicate an intention by the parties as to the relative status of the terms concerned, though any presumption to this effect may be rebutted by other evidence.[115]

As indicated above, the distinction between the status of terms is of most importance when the consequences of a breach are being considered. Breach of 'condition' may well lead to the other party having the right to treat the contract as being at an end as well as suing for damages. Breach of 'warranty' will probably only entitle the other party to claim damages. If no labels are used, and the term is difficult to classify, it may be regarded as an 'innominate' term, in relation to which the consequences of the particular breach that has occurred may determine whether the party not in breach has a right to bring it to an end.[116] The context in which the breach occurred will be important, as will its effect on the rest of the contract. The details of the rules that the courts apply in this area are, however, left until Chapter 14, which is concerned specifically with the issues of performance and breach. It is important, however, that the parties should have such issues in mind when drafting their agreement, so that if they wish they can include express terms dealing with the consequences of a breach of any particular obligation. They may also wish to agree in advance the amount of damages that will be recoverable in such circumstances. The principles governing such clauses, known as 'liquidated damages' clauses, are discussed in Chapter 15.

## 6.6 IMPLIED TERMS

The express terms of an agreement may not tell the complete story because in certain situations a term or terms may be 'implied' into a contract. This may arise from one or other of the parties to the agreement claiming that, although a particular term has not been set out explicitly either in words or writing, it should nevertheless be part of the contract. In addition, in some situations, a term will be implied because Parliament has by statute required that all contracts of a particular type should contain such a term.

The order of treatment here will be to look first at terms implied by the courts, which can be further divided into terms implied by custom, terms implied in fact and terms implied by law. Terms implied by statute will then be considered.[117]

### 6.6.1 TERMS IMPLIED BY THE COURTS

The general approach of the courts is that they are reluctant to imply terms. The parties are generally expected to take the trouble to set out the provisions of their agreement in full. A contract in which certain terms are implicit clearly gives great opportunities for dispute and the courts have been reluctant to give any encouragement to parties to try to escape from contractual obligations on the basis of some term that was not stated but that is now

---

115  *Schuler AG v Wickman Tool Sales Ltd* [1974] AC 235; [1973] 2 All ER 39 – see below, Chapter 14, 14.6.6.
116  *Hong Kong Fir Shipping Co v Kawasaki Kisen Kaisha Ltd* [1962] 2 QB 26; [1962] 1 All ER 474 – see below, Chapter 14, 14.6.8.
117  For a useful discussion of the justifications for the use of implied terms, see Collins, 2003, pp 245–46.

alleged to be of great significance. There are certain situations, however, where this reluctance is overcome, and terms are implied. When the courts do this, they run the risk of suggesting that all contractual issues can be resolved by deciding what the parties must have agreed at the time of the contract – that is, the myth of 'presentation'.[118] A 'relational' approach would recognise that not all issues can be solved in that way, in particular where a contract or a contractual relationship develops over time. This would allow a more flexible approach to the implication of terms to deal with particular situations.

The first basis on which the courts, applying the classical approach, will imply terms is where the implication of the term derives from a local or trade custom.

## 6.6.2  TERMS IMPLIED BY CUSTOM

Provided that there is sufficient evidence to establish the custom, the courts will be prepared to interpret the contract in the light of it. An early example is *Hutton v Warren*,[119] which has been discussed above at 6.5.4, in connection with the parol evidence rule. As will be remembered, a tenant claimed to be entitled, on quitting his tenancy, to an allowance for seed and labour. There was nothing in the lease to this effect, but the court accepted that this was a well-established local custom, and implied a term. A different kind of implication was suggested in *British Crane and Hire Corp Ltd v Ipswich Plant Hire Ltd*.[120] This concerned a contract for the hire of an earth-moving machine, together with a driver, and the issue was who was responsible for the cost of pulling it out of marshy land in which it had become stuck. One of the factors which the Court of Appeal regarded as relevant was that there was evidence that it was normal practice in the trade for liability to be placed on the hirer, rather than the owner, in such circumstances. Lord Denning commented:[121]

> The [hirers] themselves knew that firms in the plant hiring trade always imposed conditions in regard to the hiring of plant: and that their conditions were on much the same lines.

This, together with the fact that the hirers had previously contracted with the owners on such terms, led to the implication that liability should rest with the hirer. The issue is thus primarily one of fact. The person wishing to rely on the custom must produce convincing factual evidence of its existence and general acceptance. Assuming that there is sufficient evidence, the courts will imply a term to give it effect.

Such implication will not be possible, however, if the contract contains an express term that is inconsistent with the custom. In that case, the express term will prevail over the custom. In *Les Affréteurs Réunis SA v Leopold Walford (London) Ltd*,[122] there was evidence of a custom that a broker's commission was payable only in relation to hire that had been earned under a charter. The contract, however, provided that commission was payable on the signing of the charter. This specific term was held to indicate the parties' intention in relation to this issue. There was therefore no room for a term implied from custom.

---

### For thought

*If a party to a contract is unaware of a custom that may affect its interpretation, is it fair to allow that custom to operate? Should it only apply where both parties are aware of it?*

---

118  For which, see Chapter 1, 1.6.
119  (1836) 1 M & W 466; 150 ER 517.
120  [1975] QB 303.
121  Ibid, p 310.
122  [1919] AC 801.

### 6.6.3 TERMS IMPLIED IN FACT

The approach here is based on the attempt to determine the intention of the parties. The courts will imply a term if they consider that it represents the (objective) intention of the parties on a particular issue. In other words, the term is implied not as a matter of law, but on the basis that, as a matter of fact, this is what the parties had agreed, though the agreement was implicit rather than explicit. The courts will not easily, however, be convinced that such implication should take place. It is certainly not sufficient that a particular clause would appear to be 'reasonable'. Nor will a term necessarily be implied to deal with an eventuality that the parties had not anticipated:

> The question of implication arises when the instrument does not expressly provide for what is to happen when some event occurs. The most usual inference in such a case is that nothing is to happen. If the parties had intended something to happen, the instrument would have said so. Otherwise, the express provisions of the instrument are to continue to operate undisturbed. If the event has caused loss to one or other of the parties, the loss lies where it falls.[123]

Thus in *Crest Homes (South West) Ltd v Gloucestershire CC*,[124] where in a construction contract the local planning authority unexpectedly imposed conditions that entailed additional expense and a loss of profit for the builder, the Court of Appeal was not prepared, on the facts and without more, to imply a term that the defendant (that had performed its side of the bargain in accordance with the original contract) should bear any liability for these costs.[125] This also arguably shows the court being unwilling to use the concept of the implied term to deal with 'relational' aspects of contracts – which may require the modification of obligations to deal with changed circumstances.[126]

The correct approach to this type of implication has recently been reconsidered by the Privy Council in *Attorney General for Belize v Belize Telecom Ltd*[127] and the Supreme Court in *Marks and Spencer plc v BNP Paribas Securities Services Trust Company (Jersey) Ltd*.[128] The earlier case law will be considered first, however, before looking at these more recent decisions.

### 6.6.4 THE *MOORCOCK* TEST

The starting point for the law in this area is the case of *The Moorcock*.[129]

---

123  *Attorney General for Belize v Belize Telecom Ltd* [2009] UKPC; [2009] 1 WLR 1988 at [17] *per* Lord Hoffmann. Compare the historical approach in cases of frustration, discussed at 13.2.2. In *Bou-Simon v BGC Brokers LP* [2018] EWCA Civ 1525 the Court of Appeal warned of the dangers of hindsight in this process.

124  (1999) unreported, 22 June, CA.

125  Or in the words of Nourse LJ to 'fill up a gap which the parties have left unfilled'. The position might have been different if the term was a necessity – see 6.6.4ff.

126  See Macneil, 1978, and Chapter 1, 1.6.

127  [2009] UKPC 10; [2009] 1 WLR 1988.

128  [2015] UKSC 72. See also *Trump International Golf Club Scotland Limited and another v The Scottish Ministers (Scotland)* [2015] UKSC 74 at [35] *per* Lord Hodge (with whom Lord Neuberger, Lord Mance, Lord Reed and Lord Carnwath agreed): "Interpretation is not the same as the implication of terms. Interpretation of the words of a document is the precursor of implication. It forms the context in which the law may have to imply terms into a document, where the court concludes from its interpretation of the words used in the document that it must have been intended that the document would have a certain effect, although the words to give it that effect are absent. See the decision of the Privy Council in *Attorney General of Belize v Belize Telecom Ltd* [2009] 1 WLR 1988 per Lord Hoffmann at paras 16–24 as explained by this court in *Marks & Spencer plc v BNP Paribas Securities Trust Company (Jersey) Ltd* [2015] UKSC 71, per Lord Neuberger at paras 22–30."

129  (1889) 14 PD 64.

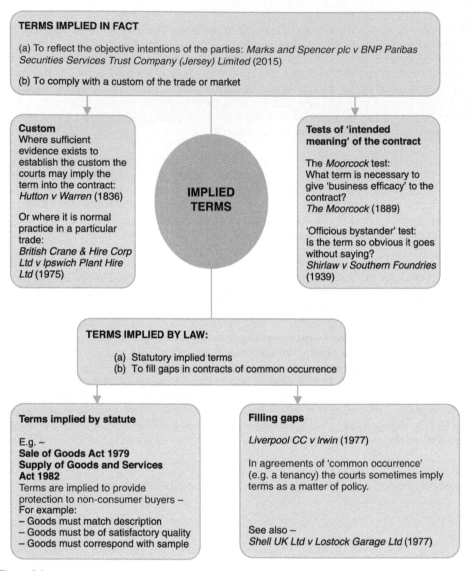

Figure 6.2

**Key case** *The Moorcock* (1889)

Facts: This case concerned a contract that involved the plaintiff's ship mooring at the defendant's wharf in the Thames. The Thames being a tidal river, at low tide the ship, as both parties knew would be the case, settled on the river bed. Unfortunately, the ship was damaged because of a ridge of hard ground beneath the mud of the river bed. The owner sued for breach of contract because the mooring was unsuitable, but there was no express term in the contract as to the suitability of the river bed for mooring a ship there.

Held: The Court of Appeal held that a term could, and should, be implied to the effect that the mooring was suitable. The reason for this was that without such a provision, the contract would have effectively been unworkable. It was implicit in the contract for the mooring of the ship that it would have to rest on the bottom of the river. Both parties must have contracted on the basis that it was safe to do so. On this basis, the court felt that it must have been the parties' intention that the owners of the wharf should warrant that the river bed was suitable for the purpose of the contract. Bowen LJ explained this reasoning as follows:

> Both parties knew that the jetty was let for the purpose of profit, and knew that it could only be used by the ship taking the ground and lying on the ground. They must have known, both of them, that unless the ground was safe the ship would be simply buying an opportunity of danger and buying no convenience at all, and that all consideration would fail unless the ground was safe. In fact, the business of the jetty could not be carried on unless, I do not say the ground was safe, it was supposed to be safe.

Note that the test being applied here is a stringent one. It is based not on the reasonable expectation of the owner of the ship, but rather on what is necessary in order to make the contract work at all. The fact that a contract might work better with a particular term implied would not be sufficient. *The Moorcock* can thus be characterised as having established a test of 'necessity' in relation to the implication of terms.[130]

### 6.6.5 THE 'OFFICIOUS BYSTANDER' TEST

The reason why necessity is a good test for the implication of terms is that it must be regarded as a sure guide as to what the parties intended. If a contract will not work without the inclusion of a particular term, it is a reasonable assumption that the parties intended that term to be included. The courts have been prepared, however, to consider other tests of intention. One of the tests used by the courts is that of the 'officious bystander'.[131] This derives from the case of *Shirlaw v Southern Foundries*.[132] MacKinnon LJ suggested that a term may be implied where it is so obvious that it 'goes without saying', so that:[133]

> if, while the parties were making their bargain, an officious bystander were to suggest some express provision for it in the agreement, they would testily suppress him with a common 'Oh, of course!'

The test is again a strict one, in that there will be relatively few provisions of such obviousness that they will satisfy the 'officious bystander' test. Moreover, it is not a particularly easy one to apply, as is perhaps shown by the fact that in *Shirlaw*'s case itself, there was considerable disagreement between members of the Court of Appeal and House of Lords as to what terms, if any, should be implied into a contract appointing the managing director of a company. Nor is it well suited to complex commercial transactions, in relation to which it may be difficult to formulate an appropriate question for the officious bystander to ask. A final difficulty is that in relation to terms other than those which are 'necessary' in the *Moorcock* sense, it may be difficult for a court, after the event, to establish what the

---

130 Collins, however, points out (2003, p 240) that, to the extent that this is based on identifying the objectives of the contract, the process may prove difficult because the parties may often disagree as to those objectives.
131 'Officious' means 'meddling' or being 'too forward in offering unwelcome or unwanted services' (The *Chambers Dictionary*).
132 [1939] 2 KB 206.
133 Ibid, p 227.

parties, at the time of the contract, would have (even objectively) agreed. If the matter is before the court, they are by definition in dispute, and identifying an obligation (which will inevitably favour one side of the agreement) to which they would clearly have said 'yes, of course that is included' may be very difficult.[134] Overall, the *Moorcock* test is probably the more satisfactory of the two.

The operation of both the *Moorcock* and the 'officious bystander' tests was considered by Gatehouse J in *Ashmore v Corp of Lloyd's* (*No* 2).[135] The case arose out the problems of Lloyd's 'names' who had made substantial losses out of insurance contracts. The plaintiffs were arguing that Lloyd's had a duty to alert names about matters of which Lloyd's became aware which might seriously affect their interests. One basis for the action was that the duty should be based on an implied term in the names' contracts with Lloyd's. Gatehouse J, however, was unable to find that either of the tests outlined above helped the plaintiffs. Looking first at the *Moorcock* test of business efficacy, many thousands of people had been or were names with Lloyd's under the same contractual arrangements as the plaintiffs. It could not be said that these contracts would not work without the suggested implied term.

As to the officious bystander, Gatehouse J found the suggested question too complicated to be answered by a simple 'yes'. The question was set out in this way by the plaintiffs:[136]

> If, at the Rota meeting to admit a new Member, an officious bystander interrupted the proceedings and said, 'You Lloyd's are asking this applicant to engage in a high risk business and, in effect, entrust his entire personal fortune to an underwriting agent approved by you with whom he is not to interfere, and whom you know he relies upon and is by the system you impose forced to rely on: [Question] what if something professionally discreditable is or becomes known to Lloyd's about the underwriting agent which might prejudice the member's underwriting interests, other than matters which in Lloyd's reasonable opinion are not capable of being seriously prejudicial to the member's underwriting interests, would you Lloyd's be obliged to take reasonable steps to alert the applicant, if thought necessary, in confidence, and tell the underwriting agent within a reasonable time thereafter what you have done?' Surely, the answer would be 'of course'.

On the contrary, the response of Lloyd's to such a complex question, thought Gatehouse J, would have been to refer the question to their lawyers, following which the most likely answer would have been an uncompromising 'no'.

Similarly, in *Wilson v Best Travel Ltd*,[137] the court refused to imply a term into a contract between a tour operator and holidaymaker that a hotel would be reasonably safe. Applying the officious bystander test, the judge did not think the tour operator would have said 'of course' to an inquiry as to whether such a term was included, given that the hotel was not under the operator's control.

These cases illustrate the reluctance of the courts to imply a term, and that the tests to be satisfied are applied quite strictly. There are, however, some recent examples of the courts being prepared to imply terms on the basis of what they thought that the parties must have intended. The first is *Griggs Group Ltd v Evans*,[138] which is an example of the use of the 'officious bystander' test to imply a term. The dispute was over whether the

---

134 Cf the comments of Collins (2003, p 240) on the fact that it is unlikely in many situations that the parties would be in agreement – the matter may indeed have been left out of the contract 'for fear of failure to reach agreement'.

135 [1992] 2 Lloyd's Rep 620.

136 [1992] 2 Lloyd's Rep 620, p 623.

137 [1993] 1 All ER 353.

138 [2005] FSR 31.

defendant retained the copyright in a logo that he had produced for the claimant, other than in relation to its use at the point of sale in the United Kingdom. The claimant alleged that it had acquired worldwide copyright in the contract under which the logo was produced. The contract was silent on the issue, so a term needed to be implied. Both the High Court and the Court of Appeal found in favour of the claimant. Jacob LJ commented:[139]

> If an officious bystander had asked at the time of the contract whether Mr Evans [the defendant] was going to retain the rights in the combined logo which could be used against the client by Mr Evans (or anyone to whom he sold the rights) anywhere in the world, other than in respect of point of sale material in the UK, the answer would surely have been 'of course not'. Mr Evans had no conceivable further interest in the work being created – indeed he surely would never have had the job at all if there had been a debate about this and he had asserted that that was to be the basis of his work.

In other words, in this case the 'officious bystander' test was conclusive, and led to the implication of a term that gave the claimant all the copyright in the work.

The second case is *Equitable Life Assurance Society v Hyman*,[140] where a more general approach to implication was adopted.

---

**Key case** *Equitable Life Assurance Society v Hyman* (2003)

Facts: The issue in this case was whether the life assurance society could decide to reduce the level of bonuses that certain of its policyholders would receive, in contravention of past practice and the expectations of the policyholders. The articles of association of the society, which governed the society's powers in relation to bonuses, gave the directors a very broad discretion, which seemed to allow them to make the reductions.
Held: The House of Lords held that a term should be implied into the articles to the effect that the society could not exercise its discretion under the articles so as to defeat the reasonable expectations of the parties, which included an expectation that the directors would not exercise their discretion in a way that prejudiced the rights of a particular group of policyholders. Lord Steyn confirmed that this term could be implied on the basis of the 'necessity': 'In my judgment an implication precluding the use of directors' discretion in this way is strictly necessary.'[141] As a result the court held in favour of the policyholders.

---

Despite the fact that the House of Lords in this case protests that its decision is based on 'necessity', the case seems to be an example of a rather more relaxed approach to the implication of a term 'in fact' than has been the case previously.[142] This trend may also be

---

139  Ibid, para 19.
140  [2000] 3 All ER 961.
141  [2000] 3 All ER 961, p 971.
142  Collins suggests (2003, pp 245–46) that neither the 'necessity' test nor the 'model contract' approach properly explain the reasons for implying terms. He suggests that the courts are in fact trying to achieve 'a fair and practical allocation of risks between the parties'. To the extent that he sees this as being based on the court's view of the 'reasonable expectations of the parties', the decision in *Equitable Life Assurance v Hyman* may be seen as recognising more explicitly than previously the true basis on which the courts decide that a term should be implied. Compare *Marks and Spencer plc v BNP Paribas Securities Services Trust Company (Jersey) Limited* [2015] UKSC 72, particularly at [21]. See also *Yam Seng Pte v International Trade Corporation Limited* [2013] EWHC 111 at [119]ff (an implied term, in fact, of good faith), above at 1.11.

seen to some extent in the more recent decision of the Privy Council in *Attorney General for Belize v Belize Telecom Ltd*.[143]

This case again concerned the interpretation of a company's articles of association, but the court made it clear that it considered the same approach should apply to the implication of terms into a contract. Lord Hoffmann delivered the judgment on behalf of the Privy Council and, perhaps not surprisingly, indicated that a similar approach should be adopted as he had advocated for the interpretation of contracts in *Investors Compensation Scheme Ltd v West Bromwich Building Society (No 1)*.[144] Essentially Lord Hoffmann regarded the implication of terms as an aspect of the construction of the contract. He stated the principle to be applied in implying terms as follows:[145]

> 16.... The court has no power to improve upon the instrument which it is called upon to construe, whether it be a contract, a statute or articles of association. It cannot introduce terms to make it fairer or more reasonable. It is concerned only to discover what the instrument means. However, that meaning is not necessarily or always what the authors or parties to the document would have intended. It is the meaning which the instrument would convey to a reasonable person having all the background knowledge which would reasonably be available to the audience to whom the instrument is addressed ...
>
> 21. It follows that in every case in which it is said that some provision ought to be implied in an instrument, the question for the court is whether such a provision would spell out in express words what the instrument, read against the relevant background, would reasonably be understood to mean.

In advocating this approach, Lord Hoffmann did not suggest that the tests of 'business efficacy' or 'the officious bystander' should be discarded. Rather, these tests should simply be seen as alternative ways of expressing the general principle set out in the above paragraphs.

More recently, however, in *Marks and Spencer plc v BNP Paribas Securities Services Trust Company (Jersey) Ltd*[146] Lord Neuberger (with whom Lord Sumption and Lord Hodge agreed) stated that Lord Hoffmann's 'observations [in *Attorney General of Belize v Belize Telecom Ltd* [2009] UKPC 10] should henceforth be treated as a characteristically inspired discussion rather than authoritative guidance on the law of implied terms'. Thus we revert back to previous tests and it is particularly noteworthy that Lord Neuberger regarded the 'business necessity and obviousness' tests as alternatives.[147]

This more flexible approach in cases such as *Equitable Life Assurance Society v Hyman* has been used to establish a principle that where a contract gives a discretion to one party (e.g. as to the payment of a bonus), there may be an implied term that that discretion must not be exercised in an 'arbitrary, irrational or capricious' way.[148] An example is *Paragon v Nash*,[149] which concerned the power to vary interest rates under a mortgage agreement.

---

143  [2009] UKPC 10; [2009] 1 WLR 1988.

144  See above para 6.5.5.

145  [2009] UKPC 10; [2009] 1 WLR 1988, para 16.

146  [2015] UKSC 72.

147  At [21].

148  Or the discretion may, depending on the terms of the contract, be fettered in some other way by an implied term: see, for example, *Property Alliance Group Limited v The Royal Bank of Scotland Plc* [2018] EWCA Civ 355 (where the discretion was fettered by requiring it to be exercised in accordance with a legitimate commercial interest).

149  [2001] EWCA Civ 1466. A similar approach was taken in *Horkulak v Cantor Fitzgerald International* [2004] EWCA Civ 1287, *Socimer International Bank Ltd v Standard Bank London Ltd* [2008] EWCA Civ 116 and *JML Direct Ltd v Freestat UK Ltd* [2010] EWCA Civ 34. *Paragon Finance* was more recently approved by

The Court of Appeal held that it was to be implied 'that the rates of interest would not be set dishonestly, for an improper purpose, capriciously or arbitrarily',[150] although, on the facts, there had been no breach of this term. There must be a genuine availability of discretion. If the contract itself contains detailed provisions as to how a power is to be exercised, there is no room for an implied term.[151]

### 6.6.6 TERMS IMPLIED BY LAW

The distinction between terms implied in fact and terms implied by law was well explained by Lord Denning in *Shell UK Ltd v Lostock Garage Ltd*.[152] The case concerned a contract under which a garage owner agreed to buy petrol exclusively from Shell. Subsequently, at a time when there was a petrol 'price war', the garage owner discovered that Shell was supplying other petrol stations in the area at a lower price. This was having a disastrous effect on his business. The garage owner was arguing that a term should be implied to the effect that Shell would not discriminate against him in the terms on which it supplied the petrol. The majority of the Court of Appeal (Bridge LJ dissenting) held that no such term could be implied. In coming to this conclusion, Lord Denning emphasised the difference between terms implied in fact, and those implied by law. As regards the first category, as we have seen, this involves deciding what the parties themselves would have put into the contract had they addressed themselves to the issue. Lord Denning thought that the required term could not be implied on this basis, because it was highly unlikely that Shell would have agreed to the inclusion of such a term if this had been requested by the garage owner. Terms implied by law, however, do not (directly) depend on determining the intention of the parties. The court in this case will imply a term as a necessary incident of a particular relationship.

Two conditions need to be satisfied before this can be done, however. First, the contract has to be of a sufficiently common type (for example, seller/buyer, owner/hirer, employer/employee, landlord/tenant) that it is possible to identify the typical obligations of such a contract. Second, generally the matter to which the implied term relates must be one which the parties have not in any way addressed in their contract.[153] There must be a clear gap to be filled. In *Shell v Lostock Garage*, the garage owner failed on the first test. Lord Denning was not prepared to hold that exclusive dealing contracts of this kind were sufficiently common that typical terms could be identified.

The distinction was recently explained by Baroness Hale in *Geys v Société Générale, London Branch* in the following way:[154]

> [I]t is important to distinguish between two different kinds of implied terms. First, there are those terms which are implied into a particular contract because, on its proper construction, the parties must have intended to include them ... Such terms are only implied where it is necessary to give business efficacy to the particular contract in question. Second, there are those terms which are implied into a class of contractual relationship, such as that between landlord and tenant or between

---

Lady Hale in *Braganza v BP Shipping Limited* [2015] UKSC 17. However, it is not the case that all instances of contractual discretion are subject to such an implied term: see *UBS AG v Rose Capital Ventures Ltd* [2018] EWHC 3137 (Ch) (a mortgagee's "absolute discretion" to require payment within three months was not tapered by such an implied term especially in the light of the duties which existed between a mortgagor and mortgagee in these circumstances).

150  [2001] EWCA Civ 1466, [36].
151  *Mid Essex Hospital Services NHS Trust v Compass Group UK & Ireland Ltd* [2013] EWCA Civ 200, [84] – [95].
152  [1977] 1 All ER 481.
153  Compare *Haywood v Newcastle upon Tyne Hospitals NHS Foundation Trust* [2018] UKSC 22.
154  [2012] UKSC 63, [55].

employer and employee, where the parties may have left a good deal unsaid, but the courts have implied the term as a necessary incident of the relationship concerned, unless the parties have expressly excluded it.

### 6.6.7 *LIVERPOOL CITY COUNCIL V IRWIN*

This type of implication of terms derives from the House of Lords' decision in *Liverpool City Council v Irwin*.[155]

---

**Key case** *Liverpool City Council v Irwin* (1977)

Facts: The contract in this case was a tenancy agreement in relation to a block of flats. The agreement said nothing about who was to be responsible for the maintenance of the common parts of the block and, in particular, the lifts and rubbish chutes. The tenants argued that a term should be implied that the City Council was responsible.
Held: The House of Lords held that it was possible to imply a term to the effect that the landlord should take reasonable steps to keep the common parts in repair.

---

It would clearly not have been possible to imply such a term using the *Moorcock* or the 'officious bystander' test. It would have been quite possible to have a workable tenancy agreement in which, for example, the responsibility for the common parts was shared among all the tenants of the block. An officious bystander suggesting that a term should be included imposing liability on the landlord alone would have been unlikely to have been considered to be stating the obvious, at least as far as the City Council was concerned. What the House was in effect doing was to say that:

(a)    the agreement was incomplete, in that it was mainly concerned with the tenant's obligations, and contained very little about those of the landlord;
(b)    it was an agreement of a type that was sufficiently common that the court could decide that certain terms would normally be expected to be found in it; and
(c)    the term implied was one that the House thought was reasonable in relation to the normal expectations of the obligations as between landlord and tenant.

Despite the fact that Lord Wilberforce insisted on referring to the test as one of 'necessity' rather than 'reasonableness', it is clear that in practice it is the latter word that indicates the approach being taken, once the preconditions for any implication in law have been met. In other words, if it is established that the agreement is one of 'common occurrence', and that it is 'incomplete', the courts will themselves decide what term should be implied in order to make the contract work 'reasonably' – meaning here 'as would commonly be expected in relation to a contract of this type'.[156]

An example of a term implied by law into an employment contract is to be found in *Malik v BCCI*.[157] The employee had worked for the Bank of Credit and Commerce International which collapsed in 1991, amidst allegations that the bank had operated in a corrupt and dishonest manner. The employee claimed that having worked for BCCI had adversely affected his future employment prospects. On a trial of a preliminary issue as to

---

155  [1977] AC 239.
156  Such an approach is likely to be most useful in respect of 'relational' contracts – see Macneil, 1978, and Chapter 1, 1.6.
157  [1998] AC 20; [1997] 3 All ER 1.

whether the employee had any cause of action, it was confirmed by the House of Lords that there should be implied into contracts of employment a mutual obligation of 'trust and confidence'. This obligation can be excluded or modified by the parties, but otherwise will operate as a 'default' clause in all contracts of employment. In this case, the implied term had not been amended by the parties, and was held to include the obligation that the employer should not:[158]

> Without reasonable and proper cause, conduct itself in a manner calculated and likely to destroy or seriously damage the relationship of confidence and trust between employer and employee.

Thus, the employee did have the basis for a cause of action against his former employer for the damage caused by the way it was alleged the business had been run.[159]

The possibility of implying a term in law was also raised in *Ashmore v Corp of Lloyd's (No 2)*[160] as an alternative to implication in fact. The plaintiff argued that there were many contracts in identical terms between 'names' and Lloyd's, and that therefore this was an appropriate situation in which to use the *Liverpool City Council v Irwin* approach. Gatehouse J disagreed. What was important was not the number of contracts; rather, there needed to be a broad category or type of relationship, even though within that type the detailed terms might vary on particular points. The fact that in this case each contract was in identical terms did not create a category, or genus, of contracts for which typical terms could be found. The plaintiff's attempt to imply a term by this means failed once again.

### 6.6.8 TERMS IMPLIED BY STATUTE

There are two reasons why it may be appropriate for Parliament to enact that certain provisions should be implied into all contracts of a particular type. One relates to efficiency. If it is virtually universal practice for certain terms to be used in particular contractual relationships, there is no need for the parties to state them specifically every time. In terms of economic analysis, there is a saving in 'transaction costs'. Rather than having to agree an appropriate wording on each occasion, the parties can rely on the statutory formulation as representing their obligations. In such a situation, however, there should be the possibility of the parties being able to agree to depart from the statutory wording, if they so wish.

The second reason why terms might need to be implied by statute is for the protection of one of the parties. It may be thought that a particular type of contractual relationship is likely to involve inequality of bargaining power, so that, unless protective provisions are implied, the weaker party may be forced into a very disadvantageous bargain. If this is the reason for the implication, then it may well be that the obligation to include the term should be absolute, without any possibility of it being excluded or amended in particular contracts.

### 6.6.9 IN FOCUS: IMPLIED TERMS VERSUS FREEDOM OF CONTRACT

Examples of both of the above bases for implying terms by statute can be found in the history of the implied terms as to quality under the Sale of Goods Acts. The original Sale of Goods Act (SGA) 1893 was intended to represent a codification of current commercial law and practice. Thus, the implied terms as to quality, contained in ss 13–15, were those that merchants of the time would have expected to appear in any contract for the sale of goods. This was an example of the first ground for implying terms, that is business efficiency. In line with this approach, s 55 of the SGA 1893 allowed the parties to agree to

---

158  Ibid, p 34.
159  Compare *James-Bowen v Comissioner of Police of the Metropolis* [2018] UKSC 40.
160  [1992] 2 Lloyd's Rep 620.

different terms as to quality, or to exclude them altogether, if they so wished. By the time of the enactment of the revised version of the SGA in 1979, however, the atmosphere had changed. The provisions as to quality had come to be regarded as important elements in the law of consumer protection (of course, the SGA 1979 originally applied to both consumer and non-consumer sales, a position that, as shown below,[161] has been fundamentally altered by the Consumer Rights Act 2015). The role of these terms was therefore at least in part to provide protection for the weaker party in a sale of goods contract. As a result, the Unfair Contract Terms Act (UCTA) 1977 initially made it impossible, in situations where the contract was made between a business and consumer, for the business to exclude the implied terms.[162] Even as between business parties, the exclusion would be (and still is) subject to a test of 'reasonableness'.

The implication of terms on a mandatory basis runs counter to the normal philosophy of classical English contract law, which is to make the intentions of the parties paramount. Here a clause may be imposed on the parties whether they like it or not. In such circumstances, even if they expressly agree that it is not to operate, the courts will usually be required to give effect to it. This is an area where there is clearly a tension between the 'classical' and 'modern' law.

### 6.6.10 IMPLIED TERMS UNDER THE SALE OF GOODS ACT[163]

Various terms are implied into all sale of goods contracts by virtue of ss 12–15 of the SGA 1979. In relation to consumer contracts, the terms in the SGA 1979 are no longer applicable and have been superseded by broadly similar provisions in the Consumer Rights Act 2015. These provisions are discussed below, at 6.7. The SGA 1979 implied terms will continue to apply to non-consumer contracts.[164]

The implied terms under the SGA 1979 are all labelled as 'conditions' or 'warranties'. Breach of a condition will generally give the innocent party the right to repudiate the contract as well as claiming damages, whereas breach of warranty will only give a right to damages.[165]

### 6.6.11 TITLE

Section 12 of the SGA 1979 is concerned with 'title' in the sense of the 'right to sell'. There is an implied condition in every sale of goods contract (including sales by private individuals) that the seller has this right 'at the time when property is to pass'. The condition will be broken if the goods belong to someone else, or if they cannot be sold without infringing another's rights, for example, in a trademark.[166] A breach of this condition will be regarded as constituting a 'total failure of consideration'. This has the potential to allow the purchaser to recover any money paid, even though use has been made of the goods transferred. In *Rowland v Divall*,[167] the plaintiff car dealer had bought a car from the defendant. The car had previously been stolen, but neither party was aware of this at the time. The plaintiff resold the car to a third party, from whom it was reclaimed, some months later, by the true owner's insurance company. The plaintiff had to repay the purchase price to the third party, and then sought to recover what he had paid to the defendant. Despite the

---

161  See 6.6.10ff.

162  See the UCTA 1977, s 6. Although UCTA 1977 no longer applies to consumer contracts, this approach is continued in the Consumer Rights Act 2015. For further discussion of both Acts, see Chapter 7.

163  The discussion of these terms is in outline only. For a full treatment see, for example, Twigg-Flesner, Canavan and MacQueen, 2016, or Bridge, 2009.

164  Similar provisions are to be found in the Supply of Goods and Services Act 1982, but these are not discussed here.

165  For further discussion of the distinction between 'conditions' and 'warranties', see Chapter 14, 14.6.5.

166  *Niblett v Confectioners' Materials* [1921] 3 KB 387.

167  [1923] 2 KB 500.

fact of the lapse of time, and the consequent reduction in the value of the car, which was demonstrated by the fact that the insurance company had in fact sold it back to the plaintiff at much less than the original contract price, the plaintiff was allowed to recover what he had paid to the defendant in full, on the basis of a total failure of consideration. The use that the plaintiff had made of the car was irrelevant. The essence of a sale of goods contract is not the use of the goods, but the transfer of ownership. The breach of s 12 meant that ownership had never been transferred, and the plaintiff was therefore entitled to recover all his money.

In *Rowland v Divall*, the plaintiff was a dealer who was primarily interested in the ability to resell the car. The same principle, however, applies to a private purchaser. In *Butterworth v Kingsway Motors*,[168] the plaintiff had bought a car that, unknown to him, was subject to a hire purchase agreement, and was reclaimed by the finance company nearly a year later. The plaintiff was allowed to recover the full purchase price from the defendant, notwithstanding the fact that the defendant was equally ignorant of the defect in title. The plaintiff thus had almost a year's free use of the car. This decision has been the subject of considerable criticism,[169] but has not as yet been overruled.

Section 12 also contains an implied warranty of quiet possession, and freedom from encumbrances.

## 6.6.12 DESCRIPTION

Section 13 says that where goods are sold by description, there is an implied condition that they will match the description. The description may come from the seller or the buyer, and can apply to specific as well as generic goods.[170] Section 13(3) makes it clear that selection by the buyer, as in a self-service shop, does not prevent the sale being by description. Virtually all sales will, as a result, be sales by description, unless the buyer indicates a particular article that he or she wishes to buy, without describing it in any way, and the article itself has no label or packaging containing a description. There must, however, be some reliance on the description by the buyer in order for s 13 to apply. *Harlingdon and Leinster Enterprises v Christopher Hull Fine Art Ltd*[171] concerned the sale of a painting that turned out not to be by the artist to whom it was attributed in the catalogue. It was found as a matter of fact that the buyer had not relied on this attribution, and therefore this was not a sale by description.[172]

It is important to distinguish statements as to *quality* from statements of description. To describe a car as 'new' is description; to say that it has 'good acceleration' is a statement of quality, and not within s 13. Statements in advertisements can, however, be regarded as part of the description, even if the goods have subsequently been inspected. In *Beale v Taylor*,[173] a car was advertised as a 1961 model. In fact, it was made of two halves welded together, only one of the halves dating from 1961. It was held that there was a breach of s 13.

Note that s 13 applies where the seller is a private individual, as well as to sales in the course of a business. Such private sales continue to be covered by s 13 after the Consumer Rights Act 2015 came into force.

---

168 [1954] 1 WLR 1286.
169 For example, Twigg-Flesner Canavan and MacQueen, 2016, pp 90–1.
170 *Varley v Whipp* [1900] 1 QB 513. Where particular items are identified at the time of the contract (for example, 'my Chippendale table'), they will be 'specific goods': SGA 1979, s 61. Where goods of a specified type are to be sold (for example, 10 tons of wheat), without any particular items being identified, they will be 'generic goods'.
171 [1990] 1 All ER 737.
172 It was significant in this case that the seller professed no specialist knowledge, whereas the buyer was an 'expert' in paintings of the relevant type.
173 [1967] 3 All ER 253. See also 6.3.3, and note 24, above.

### 6.6.13 SATISFACTORY QUALITY

Where a sale of goods contract is made in the course of business, s 14(2) implies a term of 'satisfactory quality'. The scope of the phrase 'in the course of business', which also applies to the implied term under s 14(3), was considered by the Court of Appeal in *Stevenson v Rogers*.[174] The case concerned the sale by a fisherman of his fishing boat. The court noted that the original wording of the relevant section in the Sale of Goods Act 1893 had limited liability to where the seller dealt 'in goods of that description'. This limitation had been removed, however, and did not appear in s 14 of the 1979 Act. The fact, therefore, that the fisherman was not regularly in the business of selling fishing boats did not prevent this being a sale 'in the course of business', so that the implied term under s 14(2) applied. In coming to this conclusion, the court held that the narrower interpretation of 'the course of a business' used by the Court of Appeal in *R and B Customs Brokers v UDT*[175] in relation to the UCTA 1977 should not be used in this context.

Where the requirement of 'satisfactory quality' applies, this means, according to s 14(2A):

> meet the standard that a reasonable person would regard as satisfactory, taking account of any description of the goods, the price (if relevant) and all other relevant circumstances.

This test of satisfactory quality was substituted for the previous test of 'merchantable quality' by the Sale and Supply of Goods Act 1994. The previous case law on s 14(2) is therefore only of limited assistance in the interpretation of this section. Section 14(2B), however, indicates some of the factors which will be relevant in applying the new test. These include the state and condition of the goods, and in particular their:

(a)    fitness for all the purposes for which goods of the kind in question are commonly supplied;
(b)    appearance and finish;
(c)    freedom from minor defects;
(d)    safety; and
(e)    durability.

The test refers to the expectations of a 'reasonable person' as to the quality of the goods. This was considered in *Bramhill v Edwards*.[176] The contract was for the purchase of a motor home that had been imported from the USA. The particular vehicle, which the buyer had inspected before purchase, was two inches wider than the maximum prescribed in the relevant United Kingdom regulations. There was evidence that the licensing authorities and insurers were 'turning a blind eye' to this issue, and that it was not causing significant problems for owners of such vehicles, many of which had been imported. The trial judge held that a reasonable person would have found the vehicle unsatisfactory. The Court of Appeal disagreed. The reasonable person should be taken to be aware of the relevant background facts – in this case, the significant number of imports, and the tolerant attitude of the authorities. On this basis, there was no breach of s 14(2).

Defects that have been brought to the buyer's attention prior to the contract, or that should have been revealed by any inspection actually undertaken by the buyer, will not make the goods of unsatisfactory quality (s 14(2C)). (This was a further basis on which the seller in *Bramhill v Edwards* succeeded.)

---

174  [1999] 1 All ER 613.
175  [1988] 1 All ER 847.
176  [2004] 2 Lloyd's Rep 653.

There seems no reason to doubt that the new test will, like the test of merchantability, include the containers in which the goods are supplied, and may also include instructions for use. If the goods are supplied in bulk, extraneous items which are concealed within them may render the goods unsatisfactory. In *Wilson v Rickett Cockerell Co*,[177] the presence of detonators in a bag of coal was held to make the coal unmerchantable.

Finally, it is important to note that the test of satisfactory quality does not relate to the particular use that the buyer has in mind (for which see s 14(3), below) but to the general standard of the goods. This is confirmed by the Court of Appeal decision in *Jewson Ltd v Boyhan*,[178] which is discussed below (see 6.6.15).

## 6.6.14 FITNESS FOR A PARTICULAR PURPOSE

If the buyer wants the goods for a particular purpose, and the seller is aware of this, then by virtue of s 14(3) there will, in all sales in the course of a business, be an implied term that the goods will be reasonably fit for that purpose, unless:

the circumstances show that the buyer does not rely, or that it is unreasonable for him to rely on the skill and judgment of the seller.

The section can apply even though the goods only have one purpose, in which case the seller will be taken to have notice of it,[179] but it will usually be more appropriate to use s 14(2) in such circumstances. Section 14(3) may need to be relied on, however, if there is something special about the circumstances in which the goods are to be used. In *Griffiths v Peter Conway*,[180] the plaintiff contracted dermatitis from wearing a Harris Tweed coat. This was brought about by the fact that the plaintiff had unusually sensitive skin. On the facts, this was not something that the seller knew, and so the claim under s 14(3) failed. If the seller had been aware, however, then the action under this section would have been the appropriate one, despite the fact that the coat had only one 'purpose', that is, to be worn.

---

### For thought

*Coats Ltd sells protective clothing made of a new fabric. It has recently been shown that 20 per cent of the population has some degree of allergic reaction to this fabric. Goff Ltd buys some of this protective clothing for its workforce from Coats Ltd and many of its workers suffer a severe allergic reaction to this fabric. Would Goff Ltd have a claim against Coats Ltd under s 14(3) of the SGA 1979?*

---

The same approach was used by the House of Lords in *Slater v Finning Ltd*.[181] A camshaft supplied by the defendant failed when used in an engine fitted to the plaintiff's fishing boat. Replacement camshafts supplied by the defendant also failed. The plaintiff sold the engine, with its latest replacement camshaft, and it was fitted to another fishing boat in which it was apparently used without problem. The judge found that the problem of the failure of the camshafts must have been caused by some unexplained idiosyncrasy of the plaintiff's fishing boat. There was therefore no breach of the implied condition of fitness for purpose. This conclusion

---

177 [1954] 1 QB 598.
178 [2003] EWCA Civ 1930.
179 *Preist v Last* [1903] 2 KB 148.
180 [1939] 1 All ER 685.
181 [1996] 3 All ER 398.

was confirmed by the House of Lords, which also made clear that where the problem arose from an abnormal or unusual situation not known to the seller, it was irrelevant for the purposes of s 14(3) whether or not this situation was known to the buyer.

A claim will not succeed under s 14(3) where the problems arise from the buyer's misunderstanding of instructions supplied with the goods. This was the view taken in *Wormell v RHM Agriculture (East) Ltd*.[182] This decision appears to accept, however, that defective instructions could lead to goods being found to be not fit for a particular purpose.

Once it is clear that the seller knew of the particular purpose, the burden is on the seller to show that there was no, or unreasonable, reliance. This is a hard test to satisfy, since the courts tend to favour the buyer, and have made it clear that partial reliance is sufficient to found an action.[183]

### 6.6.15 RELATIONSHIP BETWEEN S 14(2) AND S 14(3)

In *Jewson Ltd v Boyhan*,[184] the Court of Appeal emphasised the need to distinguish carefully between s 14(2) (satisfactory quality) and s 14(3) (fitness for a particular purpose). The defendant had supplied electric boilers for a flat conversion project. The boilers had the effect of reducing the energy efficiency rating of the flats and therefore made the flats more difficult to sell. The trial judge found the defendants in breach of both s 14(2) and s 14(3).

In allowing the defendant's appeal, the Court of Appeal held that s 14(2) was concerned with the intrinsic quality of what was supplied. Here the question under s 14(2) was whether the boilers were satisfactory as boilers for flats, ignoring the particular circumstances which gave rise to the problems in this case. The answer was 'yes', so there was no breach of s 14(2). As regards s 14(3), the important issue was whether the claimant had reasonably relied on the defendant's skill and judgment in supplying the boilers. The answer was 'yes' as regards the intrinsic quality of the boilers for heating flats, but 'no' as regards their suitability for these particular flats. On this issue, the defendant had insufficient information for it to be reasonable for the claimant to rely on them for this purpose. The defendant was therefore not liable under s 14(3) either.

### 6.6.16 SALE BY SAMPLE

Where there is a sale by sample there is an implied condition, by virtue of s 15:

(a)    that the bulk will correspond with the sample in quality;
(b)    [repealed];
(c)    that the goods will be free from any defect, making their quality unsatisfactory, which would not be apparent on reasonable examination of the sample.

This section does not seem to have given rise to any serious difficulties in application.

## 6.7 THE CONSUMER RIGHTS ACT 2015

For contracts to which the Consumer Rights Act 2015 (CRA 2015) applies, the implied terms outlined above cease to apply. These are sales where the buyer is an individual, not buying wholly or mainly in the course of a business, and the seller is a 'trader', i.e. a person acting for purposes relating to their trade, business, craft or profession.[185]

---

182  [1987] 3 All ER 75.
183  *Ashington Piggeries v Christopher Hill* [1972] AC 441.
184  [2003] EWCA Civ 1930.
185  CRA 2015, s 2.

**Table 6.2** Comparison of Sales of Goods Act sections and Consumer Rights Act sections

| Sale of Goods Act sections | Consumer Rights Act sections |
| --- | --- |
| 12 Right to sell | 17 Trader to have the right to supply goods |
| 13 Sale by description | 11 Goods to be as described |
| 14(2) Satisfactory quality | 9 Goods to be of satisfactory quality |
| 14(3) Fitness for particular purpose | 10 Goods to be fit for a particular purpose |
| 15 Sale by sample | 13 Goods to match sample |

Table 6.2 shows the equivalence between sections of the SGA 1979 and the CRA 2015:

In relation to the above provisions, the sections of the CRA 2015 generally repeat the wording of the equivalent SGA 1979 section, so that the substantive protection given to buyers in consumer contracts is essentially the same as under the SGA 1979. The CRA 2015 does not refer to 'implied terms' but states that the contract 'is to be treated as including' the relevant term – which in effect amounts to the same thing.

There are, however, some additional sections under the CRA 2015 that do not duplicate SGA 1979 provisions, two of which we will note at this point. First, under s 15 of the CRA 2015, if installation of goods by or on behalf of the trader forms part of the contract for their supply, an incorrect installation will mean that the goods will be treated as not conforming to the contract. Second, under s 16 of the CRA 2015, if the contract for the supply of goods includes digital content, then if the digital content does not conform to the contract, the goods will be treated as not conforming to the content.

Finally, it should be noted that the CRA 2015 refers throughout to the 'supply' of goods. This means that its provisions cover not only sale, but all other contracts under which goods are supplied, such as hire purchase, hire, or work and materials (e.g. in a contract to build a garage, the bricks and other materials will be 'supplied' for the purposes of the CRA 2015). The SGA 1979 deals only with sale, and other contracts under which goods are supplied are dealt with by similar implied terms set out in the Supply of Goods and Services Act 1982.

## 6.8 STATUTORY CONTROLS

As we have seen, the contents of the contract may be subject to statutory control, in that terms may be implied and exclusion of such terms may be prohibited by statute (for example, the SGA 1979; the UCTA 1977). A broader control of the contents of certain types of consumer contract appeared in the Unfair Terms in Consumer Contracts Regulations 1999.[186] These Regulations, until repealed by the Consumer Rights Act 2015, prohibited a wider range of contractual clauses than simply the exclusion clauses (albeit broadly interpreted) affected by the UCTA 1977. The provisions in the Regulations were replaced by the provisions of the CRA 2015 from 1 October 2015. These controls represent a further inroad into the traditional common law principle that the intention of the parties is paramount. Full discussion of these controls is left to Chapter 7. It is important to remember, however, that many clauses in consumer contracts will now be subject to a test of 'fairness'. This constitutes a very powerful control over the contents of consumer contracts. It enables the courts to abandon almost entirely any pretence that regulation is based on the intentions of the parties. What is 'fair' to the consumer will be the test,

---

186  SI 1999/2083.

which may well be decided by considering the consumer's reasonable expectations. This statutory framework means that the divide between the construction of contracts between businesses, and those between consumers, which has always to some extent existed, has grown considerably.

## 6.9 SUMMARY OF KEY POINTS

- The distinction between representations and terms is important because different remedies are available in relation to breach of a term as opposed to a misrepresentation.

- In deciding whether a pre-contractual statement has become part of the contract, the courts will look at:
  - ☐ the importance of the statement;
  - ☐ whether the contract was put into writing;
  - ☐ the relevant skill and knowledge of the parties; and
  - ☐ the lapse of time between the statement and the contract.

- Express terms must be incorporated. Specific notice may need to be given of very unusual terms.

- Where a contract is in writing, the courts will be reluctant to receive evidence that some other provision was intended to be included – the 'parol evidence' rule. Exceptions relate to the importance of the alleged term, custom and ambiguous terms.

- In interpreting terms, courts will not necessarily follow their literal meaning. They will be prepared to take into account the factual context. In commercial contracts a 'purposive' or 'commercial' approach to interpretation may be used.

- Terms may be implied by custom, as a question of fact or as a matter of law.

- Terms will only be implied as a question of fact where they are necessary for the contract, or by using the 'officious bystander' test.

- Terms will be implied in law by the courts into contracts of a common type (e.g. a lease, contract of employment) broadly as a matter of policy. The courts will imply a term that would reasonably be expected to be found in such a contract.

- Terms may be implied by statute – e.g. Sale of Goods Act 1979, Consumer Rights Act 2015.

## 6.10 FURTHER READING

### Incorporation of terms
- Law Commission, Report No 154, *Law of Contract: the Parol Evidence Rule*, 1986, Cmnd 9700

Mitchell, C, 'Leading a life of its own? The roles of reasonable expectation in contract law' (2003) 23 OJLS 639

Peden, E and Carter, J W, 'Incorporation of terms by signature: L'Estrange Rules!' (2005) 21 JCL 96

## Collateral contracts
Wedderburn, K W, 'Collateral Contracts' [1959] CLJ 58

## Implied terms
Phang, A, 'Implied terms, business efficacy and the officious bystander – a modern history' [1998b] JBL 1

Peel, E, 'Terms implied in fact' (2016) 132 LQR 531

## Interpretation of contracts
Brownsword, R, 'After *Investors:* interpretation, expectation and the implicit dimension of the "new contextualism"', Chapter 4 in Campbell, D, Collins, H, and Wightman, J (eds), *Implicit Dimensions of Contract*, 2003, Oxford: Hart Publishing

Gee, S, 'The interpretation of commercial contracts' (2001) 117 LQR 358

Havelock, R, 'The "unitary exercise" of contractual interpretation' (2017) 76 CLJ 486

McKendrick, E, 'The interpretation of contracts: Lord Hoffman's re-statement' in Worthington, S (ed), *Commercial Law and Commercial Practice*, 2003, Oxford: Hart Publishing, 139

McMeel, G, 'The rise of commercial construction in contract law' [1998] LMCLQ 382

Staughton, C, 'How do the courts interpret commercial contracts?' [1999] CLJ 303

## COMPANION WEBSITE

*Now visit the companion website to:*

Revise and consolidate your knowledge of Contents of the Contract by tackling a series of multiple-choice questions on this chapter

Test your understanding of the chapter's key terms by using the flashcard glossary

Explore Contents of the Contract further by accessing a series of web links

# Clauses excluding or limiting liability

7

**Contents**

## 7.1 OVERVIEW

This chapter deals primarily with situations where there is an attempt to exclude or limit liability for breach of contract (or for the tort of negligence) by including exclusion or limitation clauses in a contract. We will also consider more broadly 'unfair' terms in consumer contracts following the Consumer Rights Act (CRA) 2015. As such this chapter deals with an area governed by both common law and statute. The statutory provisions were developed in the latter half of the twentieth century and, overall, have tended to have a more protective stance in relation to consumers. The common law rules were developed earlier, broadly, to deal with imbalances in bargaining power between the parties. We examine the common law rules first, followed by the statutory rules:

- Common law:
  - ☐ Rules of incorporation. Was the clause part of the contract? Was appropriate notice of it given to the other party?
  - ☐ Rule of construction. Does the clause cover the breach that has occurred?
- Statute:
  - ☐ Unfair Contract Terms Act (UCTA) 1977. This statute renders some exclusion/limitation clauses ineffective (for example, clauses which attempt to exclude liability for death or personal injury caused by negligence). Other clauses are subject to a test of 'reasonableness'.
  - ☐ Originally UCTA 1977 had provisions regulating the use of, for example, exclusion/limitation clauses in consumer and non-consumer contracts. Nevertheless case law on the Act tended, for example, to allow businesses more freedom to exclude liability when contracting with each other than in contracts with consumers.
  - ☐ Following the Consumer Rights Act (CRA) 2015 there is a much clearer separation between consumer and non-consumer contracts: broadly the CRA 2015 regulates consumer contracts and, for present purposes, an amended UCTA 1977 regulates non-business contracts.
  - ☐ The CRA 2015 imposes a requirement of 'fairness' on many terms in consumer contracts. 'Good faith' is part of the test of fairness.

## 7.2 INTRODUCTION

It will often be the case that a contract will include a clause excluding the liability of one (or both) of the parties in the event of certain types of breach. The exclusion may be total, or may limit a party's liability to a specified sum of money. There may be nothing inherently objectionable about a clause of this kind. Provided that it has been included as a result of a clear voluntary agreement between the parties, it may simply indicate their decision as to where certain risks involved in the transaction should fall. If the contract involves the carriage of goods, for example, it may have been agreed that the owner should be responsible for insuring the goods while in transit. In that situation, it may be perfectly reasonable for the carrier to have very restricted liability for damage to the goods while they are being carried. The inclusion of the clause is simply an example of good contractual planning.[1]

### 7.2.1 IN FOCUS: EXCLUDING LIABILITY OR DEFINING OBLIGATIONS

It may be difficult, at times, to distinguish between a clause that limits/excludes liability and one that simply determines the obligations under the contract. Suppose, for example, that there is a contract for the regular servicing of a piece of machinery. The owner, O, is anxious that any replacement parts should be those made by the original manufacturer of the machine, M Ltd; the servicer, S, cannot guarantee that such parts will always be available. The situation might be dealt with in two ways. A clause might be inserted to say: 'S will use parts manufactured by M Ltd when available, but may substitute equivalent parts if necessary to complete a service within a reasonable time.' This would appear to define the obligations of S under the contract. Alternatively, the clause might say: 'S will use parts

---

1   See, for example, Yates, 1982, pp 11–33. See also *British Fermentation Products Ltd v Compare Reavell Ltd* [1998] BLR 352.

manufactured by M Ltd, but will not be liable for any loss arising from the use of equivalent parts, if this is necessary to complete a service within a reasonable time.' Here the clause is put in the form of a limitation/exclusion of the liability of S, but in effect it produces the same result as the previous version of the clause. It is often possible to rewrite a clause that, on its face, appears to limit liability for a breach of contract into one that defines the contracting parties' obligations.[2] If this is so, is there any need to treat 'exclusion clauses' as a special type of clause?[3] Could not all clauses simply be subject to the standard rules of incorporation and interpretation, which were discussed in Chapter 6? This has not been the traditional approach of the courts,[4] although the distinction between the two types of clause is blurred in relation to the statutory controls that now apply.[5] Indeed, the courts, however, have tended to view clauses that attempt to limit liability as a separate category, and have developed particular rules to deal with them.

### 7.2.2 UNEQUAL BARGAINING POWER

Part of the reason why the courts have thought it necessary to develop special rules for exclusion (and limitation) clauses is that many such clauses are not simply the product of good contractual planning between parties bargaining on an equal footing. Such clauses often appear in standard form contracts, which the other party has little choice as to whether to accept or not, and may give the party relying on them a very broad exemption from liability, both in tort and in contract.[6] When such clauses began to appear with some frequency in the nineteenth century, the courts devised ways of limiting their effectiveness. While the techniques adopted, as will be seen below, for the most part consisted of 'heightened' application of those used more generally for the purposes of constructing and interpreting contracts,[7] the courts clearly viewed exclusion/limitation clauses as a particular type of clause needing special treatment. This separation of exclusion/limitation clauses from the general run of contractual provisions, and in particular the distinction drawn between clauses that exclude/limit liability and those that define obligations, is understandable in the context of a general approach based on 'freedom of contract'. If the courts were saying on the one hand that parties should be free to determine their own contractual obligations, and that the question of whether the obligations undertaken were 'fair' or 'reasonable' was generally irrelevant, it would cause problems if, on the other hand, they were seen to be interfering in this contractual freedom. By treating exclusion clauses as distinct from clauses defining obligations, such interference could be seen as limited and designed to tackle a particular type of situation tangential to the central issue of the freedom of the parties to determine their obligations towards each other.

### 7.2.3 STATUTORY REGULATION

From the twentieth century, the fact that contracts at times needed regulation to achieve 'fairness' was acknowledged more directly and, moreover, Parliament intervened to add

---

2   The task is more difficult if the clause relates simply to consequential losses resulting from a breach, or is designed to put a financial 'cap' on liability, rather than removing it altogether. See also *Cremdean Properties v Nash* [1977] 2 EGLR 80 on the possible policy considerations against avoiding statutory regulation of exclusion clauses through clever drafting.

3   This argument has been put by, for example, Coote, 1964, Chapter 1, and Yates, 1982, pp 123–33.

4   See, for example, Beatson, J, Burrows, A and Cartwright, J (eds), *Anson's Law of Contract,* 30th edn, 2016, Oxford: OUP, p 211. Compare also *Impact Funding Solutions Ltd v Barrington Support Services Ltd (formerly Lawyers at Work Ltd)* [2016] UKSC 57.

5   For example, the Unfair Contract Terms Act 1977 – see below, 7.7.4.

6   Note that it is quite possible for an exclusion clause in a contract to restrict tortious liabilities, particularly for negligence occurring in the performance of the contract.

7   In particular, the rules relating to 'incorporation' and 'construction'. The doctrine of fundamental breach, while it lasted, was a technique developed more particularly to deal with exclusion clauses.

a statutory layer of controls on top of the common law rules (primarily the Unfair Contract Terms Act (UCTA) 1977, the (now repealed) Unfair Terms in Consumer Contracts Regulations (UTCCR) 1999[8] and now the Consumer Rights Act (CRA) 2015). These controls are not necessarily limited to clauses that are stated as excluding liability, and do extend to some extent to provisions that purport to define obligations. Despite the statutory interventions, the common law remains very important, not least because its rules apply to all contracts, whereas the UCTA 1977 and the CRA 2015 apply only in certain situations.

## 7.3 COMMON LAW RULES

The approach of the courts to exclusion and limitation clauses has not traditionally been to assess them directly on their merits. In other words, they have not said, 'We think this clause is unreasonable in its scope, or unfair in its operation, and therefore we will not give effect to it.' As has been noted above, such an approach would have run too directly counter to general ideas of 'freedom of contract', which were particularly important to the courts of the nineteenth century. So, instead, the courts developed and adapted formal rules relating to the determination of the contents of the contract and the scope of the clauses contained in it, which were used to indirectly police exclusion and limitation clauses (and, indeed, some other types of clause). The main rules used are those of 'incorporation' and 'construction', though we will also need to note the so-called 'doctrine of fundamental breach'.

## 7.4 INCORPORATION

A clause cannot be effective, at least in contract law, to exclude or limit liability if it is not part of the contract. The ways in which the courts determine the contents of a contract have been considered in the previous chapter. The rules discussed there, including the parol evidence rule and its exceptions, are also relevant to the decision as to whether an exclusion clause is part of the contract. It will almost always be the case that an exclusion or limitation clause will be in writing – though there is no principle that prevents a party stating an exclusion or limitation orally, as with any other contractual term. The first question will be often, therefore, whether that written term can be regarded as part of the contract. The courts have generally been concerned about the effect of exclusion or limitation clauses (particularly as regards consumers) and they have, therefore, in this context sometimes applied fairly strict rules as to the incorporation of terms. These rules are broadly based on the general principle that a party must have had reasonable notice of the exclusion clause or limitation clause at the time of the contract in order for it to be effective. If, however, the contract containing the clause has been signed by the claimant, the relevant rule is quite strict. In *L Estrange v Graucob*,[9] for example, the clause was in small print and very difficult to read, but because the contract had been signed, the clause was held to have been incorporated. Scrutton LJ stated:

> In cases in which the contract is contained in a railway ticket or other unsigned document, it is necessary to prove that an alleged party was aware, or ought to have been aware, of its terms and conditions. These cases have no application when the document has been signed. When a document containing contractual terms is signed, then, in the absence of fraud, or, I will add, misrepresentation, the party signing it is bound, and it is wholly immaterial whether he has read the document or not.

---

8   These Regulations replaced the Unfair Terms in Consumer Contracts Regulations 1994.
9   [1934] 2 KB 394.

This rule has been applied strictly by English courts.[10] The main exceptions relate to the situations referred to by Scrutton LJ in the above quotation – that is, where the signature has been induced by fraud or misrepresentation.[11] An example of the application of this principle is to be found in *Curtis v Chemical Cleaning and Dyeing Co Ltd*.[12] The plaintiff had taken a dress for cleaning. She was asked to sign a receipt containing a widely worded exemption clause. On querying this, she was told by the assistant that the clause meant that the defendants would not accept liability for damage to the beads and sequins with which the dress was trimmed. When it was returned, the dress had a stain on it. The defendants relied on the exclusion clause but the Court of Appeal held that the misrepresentation (albeit innocent) by the assistant of the scope of the clause overrode the fact that the plaintiff had signed the document.

A further possibility of challenge to a signature lies in the plea of *non est factum*, which is an argument that the party signing made a fundamental mistake about the nature of the document. This plea is rarely successful, however.[13] In general, when a person has signed the document, it is taken as conclusive evidence that the person has agreed to the contract and all its terms.[14]

Where the contract has not been signed, the court will be concerned with such matters as the time at which the clause was put forward, the steps that were taken to draw attention to it, the nature of the clause and the type of document in which it was contained. These matters will now be considered in turn.

## 7.4.1 RELEVANCE OF TIME

If a contract containing the clause has not been signed, then the *time* at which the clause is put forward will be important. If it is not put forward until after the contract has been made, then it clearly cannot be incorporated. Generally, the terms of the contract must be settled at the time of acceptance. This is, in effect, the same rule as was applied in *Roscorla v Thomas*,[15] preventing a promise made after the agreement from being enforced if no fresh consideration was given for it. In the same way, the promise by one party to give the other the benefit of an exclusion clause will generally be unenforceable if made after the formation of the contract. Thus, in *Olley v Marlborough Court Hotel*,[16] the plaintiff made the contract for the use of a hotel room at the reception desk. A clause purporting to exclude liability for lost luggage was

---

10  It has been strongly criticised by Spencer, who has argued that the rule was based on a misapplication of the parol evidence rule (see Chapter 6, 6.3.1) and the defence of *non est factum* (see 9.8): Spencer, 1973. He suggested that the claimant should not be bound by the clause where 'he did not mean to consent to the disputed term, and although he appeared to consent to it, the other party either caused or connived at his mistake': ibid, p 121. Compare *Coys of Kensington Automobiles Ltd v Pugliese* [2011] EWHC 655 at [40] *per* Ramsey J. The Ontario Court of Appeal took a less strict view than the English courts in *Tilden Rent-a-Car Co v Clendenning* (1978) 83 DLR (3d) 400, refusing to apply *LEstrange v Graucob* where the contract was made in a 'hurried, informal manner' and it was clear to the other party that the signatory had not read the contract. See also *Trigg v MI Movers International Transport Services Ltd* (1991) 84 DLR (4th) 504, applying the *Tilden* decision without reference to *L'Estrange v Graucob*.

11  For the law relating to the general effect of these on contractual obligations, see Chapter 8. Following the decision of the Supreme Court in *Autoclenz v Belcher* [2011] UKSC 41 a more flexible approach may be applied in employment contracts (see *Qantas Cabin Crew (UK) Ltd v Lopez* [2013] IRLR 43).

12  [1951] 1 KB 805.

13  It is discussed further in Chapter 9, at 9.8.

14  Collins (2003, p 234) has suggested that a distinction should perhaps be drawn between agreeing to the contractual obligation in general terms and agreeing to the particular provisions. As regards the latter, he suggests that the rules as to 'notice' dealt with in the next section should apply. There is no English case law to clearly support such an approach in this context, sensible though it might be. Compare, however, *Ocean Chemical Transport Inc v Exnor Craggs Ltd* [2000] I Lloyd's Rep 446 and *Woodeson v Credit Suisse (UK) Limited* [2018] EWCA Civ 1103.

15  (1842) 3 QB 234 – see above, Chapter 3, 3.8.

16  [1949] 1 KB 532. Note that the liability of a hotel owner for the loss of guests' property is now affected by the Hotel Proprietors Act 1956.

displayed in the room itself. It was held that this came too late to be incorporated into the contract.[17] The position might have been different if the plaintiff had been a regular user of the hotel and therefore as a result of a long and consistent 'course of dealing' could be said to have had prior notice of the clause.[18] The defendant might then be entitled to assume that the plaintiff had previously read the clause even if this was not in fact the case.

Incorporation by a 'course of dealing' was considered in *Kendall (Henry) & Sons v Lillico (William) & Sons Ltd*.[19] Here the contract was between buyers and sellers of animal feed. They had regularly contracted with each other on three or four occasions each month over a period of three years. On each occasion, a 'sold note' had been issued by the seller, which put responsibility for latent defects in the feed on the buyer. The buyer tried to argue that it did not know of this clause in the sold note. However, the House of Lords held that it was bound. A reasonable seller would assume that the buyer, having received more than 100 of these notes containing the clause, and having raised no objection to it, was agreeing to contract on the basis that it was part of the contract. Regularity is important, however, and *Kendall v Lillico* was distinguished in *Hollier v Rambler Motors*,[20] where there had only been three or four contracts over a period of five years. It was held that an exclusion clause contained in an invoice given to the plaintiff after the conclusion of an oral contract for car repairs was not incorporated into the contract. Inconsistency of procedure may also prevent incorporation. In *McCutcheon v MacBrayne*,[21] the plaintiff's agent had regularly shipped goods on the defendant's ship. On some occasions, he was required to sign a 'risk note' containing an exclusion clause; on other occasions, the contract was purely oral. The agent arranged for the carriage of the plaintiff's car that was lost as a result of the negligent navigation of the ship. No risk note had been signed and the House of Lords refused to accept that the exclusion clause could be incorporated from the agent's previous dealings. There was no consistent course of conduct sufficient to allow such an argument to succeed.

## 7.4.2 REQUIREMENT OF 'REASONABLE NOTICE'

More commonly the clause will be contained in a set of standard terms, which the other party will be given, or which are referred to, at the time of making the contract. In that situation, the key test is whether 'reasonable notice' of the clause has been given.

---

**Key case** *Parker v South Eastern Railway* (1877)[22]

Facts: The plaintiff had deposited a bag at a railway cloakroom. He was given a ticket in exchange. The front of the ticket, which contained a number and date, also said 'See back'. On the other side of the ticket were various clauses, including one excluding liability for goods exceeding the value of £10. The plaintiff's bag, worth £24.50, was lost. The jury found that the plaintiff had not read the ticket, nor was he under any obligation to do so. On that basis, the judge had directed that judgment should be given for the plaintiff. The defendant appealed.

---

17  See also *Thornton v Shoe Lane Parking* [1971] 2 QB 163; [1971] 1 All 686 – ticket from a machine – below, 7.4.3; and *Chapelton v Barry UDC* [1940] 1 KB 532; [1940] 1 All ER 356 – below, 7.4.5.

18  See in a non-exclusion clause context, *British Crane and Hire Corp Ltd v Ipswich Plant Hire Ltd* [1975] QB 303 – discussed in Chapter 6, 6.6.2.

19  [1969] 2 AC 31 – on appeal from *Hardwick Game Farm v Suffolk Agricultural Poultry Producers Association*. A useful summary of the relevant principles was recently given by Edwards-Stuart J in *Transformers & Rectifiers Ltd v Needs Ltd* [2015] EWHC 269 (TCC) at [42]ff.

20  [1972] 2 QB 71; [1972] 1 All ER 399.

21  [1964] 1 WLR 125.

22  (1877) 2 CPD 416.

Held: The Court of Appeal ordered a new trial, on the basis that the proper test was whether the defendants had given reasonable notice of the conditions contained on the ticket. The relevant principle was stated by Mellish LJ in the following terms:[23]

> I am of the opinion, therefore, that the proper direction to leave to the jury in these cases is that if the person receiving the ticket did not see or know that there was any writing on the ticket, he is not bound by the conditions; that if he knew there was writing, and knew or believed that the writing contained conditions, then he is bound by the conditions; that if he knew there was writing on the ticket, but did not know or believe that the writing contained conditions, nevertheless he would be bound, if the delivering of the ticket to him in such a manner that he could see there was writing upon it, was, in the opinion of the jury, reasonable notice that the writing contained conditions.

The test is therefore whether 'reasonable notice' of the clause has been given. The question of what constitutes reasonable notice is a question of fact. The standard to be applied is what is reasonable as regards the ordinary adult individual, capable of reading English.[24] Thus, in *Thompson v London, Midland and Scottish Railway*,[25] the fact that the plaintiff was illiterate did not help her. The position might be different, however, if the defendant had actual knowledge of the plaintiff's inability to read the terms and conditions. In such a case, the giving of reasonable notice might require rather more of the party wishing to rely on the clause. In *Thompson*, the Court of Appeal also held that stating on a ticket 'Issued subject to the conditions and regulations in the company's timetables and notices' was sufficient to draw the other party's attention to the existence of the terms, and thereby to incorporate them into the contract. This was so even though the timetable containing the relevant clause was not available for free, but had to be purchased from the company. This is perhaps at the limits of what could amount to reasonable notice,[26] but the principle remains that the contractual document itself does not need to set out the exclusion clause if it gives reasonable notice of the existence of the clause, and indicates where it can be read. What is reasonable will, of course, depend on all the circumstances. In *Thompson*, for example, the court placed some stress on the fact that the ticket was for a specially advertised excursion, at a particularly low price, and not for a regular service. There is some suggestion in the judgments, though the point is not made very clearly, that a different standard of notice might be required in relation to full-priced regular services. The point seems to be that special conditions, including the possibility of limited liability, were reasonably to be expected in relation to a cheap excursion, whereas there would not be the same level of expectation in relation to regular services.

## For thought

*Do you think the outcome of Thompson would (should) have been the same if the plaintiff had been blind, and carried a white stick?*

---

23  (1877) 2 CPD 416, p 423. The principle is stated in terms of the correct direction to a jury, since at that time it was common for civil cases to be heard before a jury.

24  (1877) 2 CPD 416, p 423.

25  [1930] 1 KB 41.

26  Indeed, Treitel (2015, p 267) suggests that the notice might not nowadays be regarded as sufficient.

### 7.4.3 INCORPORATION AND UNUSUAL EXCLUSIONS

The *Thompson* decision is clearly helpful to the defendant. More recently, the courts have tended to adopt an approach that requires an assessment of the nature of the clause alongside the amount of notice given. Thus, the more unusual or more onerous the exclusion clause, the greater the notice that will be expected to be given. In *Spurling v Bradshaw*,[27] for example, Lord Denning commented:[28]

> Some exclusion clauses I have seen would need to be printed in red ink on the face of the document with a red hand pointing to it before the notice could be held to be sufficient.

In *Thornton v Shoe Lane Parking Ltd*,[29] this approach was applied, so that a clause displayed on a notice inside a car park, containing extensive exclusions, was held not to be incorporated into a contract that was made by the purchase of a ticket from a machine. The Court of Appeal did not decide definitively the point at which the contract was made but it was probably when the customer accepted the car park owner's offer by driving up to the barrier, thus causing the machine to issue a ticket. If that was the case, then, applying the same principle as in *Olley v Marlborough Court Hotel*,[30] any conditions or reference to conditions contained on the ticket came too late – the contract was already made. It was not feasible, as would (at least theoretically) be possible if dealing with a human 'ticket issuer', for the recipient to inquire further about the conditions, or to reject the ticket. Even if the ticket could be a valid means of giving notice, however, or if the customer could be required to be put on inquiry by a notice at the entrance stating 'All cars parked at owner's risk', there was an issue about the degree of notice required. The exclusion clause in this case was very widely drawn, and purported to cover negligently caused personal injuries (which the plaintiff had in fact suffered). As a result, the court felt that the defendant needed to take more specific action to bring it to the attention of customers. In the view of Megaw LJ:[31]

> before it can be said that a condition of that sort, restrictive of statutory rights [that is, under the Occupiers' Liability Act 1957], has been fairly excluded there must be some clear indication which would lead an ordinary sensible person to realise, at or before the time of making the contract, that a term of that sort, relating to personal injury, was sought to be included.

In cases such as this, therefore, the nature and scope of the attempted exclusion become a relevant factor in relation to incorporation.

### 7.4.4 IN FOCUS: A COMMON LAW TEST OF 'REASONABLENESS'?

The approach taken in cases like *Thornton v Shoe Lane Parking* suggests that the issue is not solely procedural but is affected by the substance of the clause. We have seen that the same approach may be used in relation to other types of clause. Thus, in Chapter 6, it was noted that the same rule operated in *Interfoto Picture Library v Stiletto Visual Programmes*[32] to prevent the incorporation of a clause that was not an exclusion clause, but that was nevertheless exceptional, and unusually onerous.

---

27 [1956] 2 All ER 121.
28 Ibid, p 125.
29 [1971] 2 QB 163; [1971] 1 All ER 686.
30 [1949] 1 KB 532; [1949] 1 All ER 127 – above, 7.4.1.
31 [1971] 2 QB 163, p 173; [1971] 1 All ER 686, p 692.
32 [1989] QB 433; [1988] 1 All ER 348 – see 6.5.1.

Bradgate has argued that these cases, together with the Court of Appeal decision in *AEG (UK) Ltd v Logic Resource Ltd*,[33] have, in effect, created a common law test of the 'reasonableness' of exclusion clauses.[34] It is not clear, however, that they do go that far. If the person relying on the clause in each case had specifically drawn the other party's attention to it, in such a manner that actual notice was given, it seems likely that the courts would have held it to be incorporated and enforceable. The same would be likely to be true if the contract containing the clause had been signed.[35] It is only where there is reliance on 'reasonable notice', rather than actual knowledge, that the courts feel the need to consider the nature of the clause, and whether it is unusual. It is then still the reasonableness of the notice, rather than the reasonableness of the clause itself, that is the issue. The need for a common law test of substantive reasonableness is also unclear (as Bradgate recognised) given the statutory tests contained in the UCTA 1977, and now the CRA 2015.[36] In the *AEG* case, for example, the Court of Appeal also held the clause to be unreasonable under the 1977 Act. The existence of these statutory protections for the 'vulnerable' contracting party makes it less likely that the courts will expand the approach taken in *Thornton*, etc., into a more general test of the reasonableness of exclusion clauses.

## 7.4.5 NEED FOR A 'CONTRACTUAL' DOCUMENT

In order to be incorporated effectively, the exclusion clause must generally be contained, or referred to, in something that can be regarded as a contractual document. This is another aspect of the rule that reasonable notice must be given. Notice is unlikely to be regarded as reasonable if the clause appears in something that would not be expected to contain contractual terms.

---

**Key case** *Chapelton v Barry UDC* (1940)[37]

Facts: The plaintiff wished to hire a deckchair. He took a chair from a pile near a notice indicating the price and duration of hire, and requesting hirers to obtain a ticket from the attendant. The plaintiff obtained a ticket, but when he used the chair it collapsed, causing him injury. It was accepted that the collapse of the chair was due to the negligence of the defendant (Barry UDC), but the council argued that it was protected by a statement on the ticket that 'The council will not be liable for any accident or damage arising from hire of chair'.

Held: The Court of Appeal held that the ticket was a mere receipt. It was not a document on which the customer would expect to find contractual terms, and the exclusion clause printed on it was therefore not incorporated. The purpose of the ticket was simply to provide evidence for the hirer that he had discharged his obligation to pay for the chair. It was, the court felt, distinguishable from, for example, a railway ticket 'which contains upon it the terms upon which a railway company agrees to carry the passenger'.

---

33  [1996] CLC 265. Compare *Thinc Group v Armstrong* [2012] EWCA Civ 1227 at [27] *per* Rix LJ.
34  Bradgate, 1997. In *Goodlife Foods Ltd v Hall Fire Protection Ltd* [2018] EWCA Civ 1371 the Court of Appeal noted some of the differences in the language used in the relevant case law (extortionate, Draconian etc.) and also provided a reminder that exclusion clauses are not automatically onerous or unusual.
35  On the basis of *L'Estrange v Graucob* [1934] 2 KB 394 – above, 7.4. Compare *Do-Buy 925 Limited v National Westminster Bank Plc* [2010] EWHC 2862.
36  Both of which are discussed below, 7.7 and 7.8.
37  [1940] 1 KB 532; [1940] 1 All ER 356.

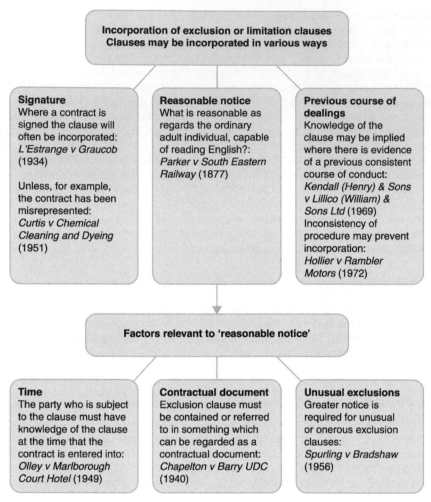

Figure 7.1

The plaintiff was entitled to recover for the council's breach of contract. The test of whether a document is deemed to be contractual or not will, presumably, depend on what information, terms, etc., the court thinks that a reasonable person would expect to find on it. In fact, in this case, the ticket was in any case provided too late, as it was held that the contract was formed when the deckchair was first taken for use, whereas the ticket was not handed over until after this had been done.[38]

## 7.5 CONSTRUCTION

Once it has been shown that a clause has been incorporated into the contract, the next issue is whether it covers the breach that has occurred. In other words, the wording of the

---

38 Thus applying the same principle as in *Olley v Marlborough Court Hotel* [1949] 1 KB 532; [1949] 1 All ER 127 – above, 7.4.1.

clause must be examined to see if it is apt to apply to the situation that has arisen. This is called the rule of 'construction' but might equally well be called the rule of 'interpretation'. The clause is being 'construed' or 'interpreted' to determine its scope.

## 7.5.1 CONTRA PROFERENTEM RULE

The rules of construction, like the rules for incorporation, are of general application, and can be used in relation to all clauses within a contract, not just exclusion or limitation clauses. The more general issues have been discussed in Chapter 6.[39] There has been much case law, however, involving the proper interpretation of exclusion and limitation clauses. In this context, the courts have traditionally taken a stricter approach to construction than elsewhere. The relevant rules of construction have been used as a means of limiting the effect of exclusion or limitation clauses, and a person wishing to avoid liability has often been required to be very precise in the use of language to achieve that aim. One aspect of this was the *contra proferentem* rule, whereby an exclusion or limitation clause was interpreted against the person putting it forward. Thus, in *Andrews v Singer*,[40] a clause excluding liability in relation to implied terms was ruled ineffective to exclude liability for breach of an express term. Similarly, in *Wallis, Son & Wells v Pratt*,[41] it was held that a clause stating that the suppliers of goods gave no 'warranty' in relation to them did not protect them from being liable for a breach of 'condition'.[42] Moreover, if there is ambiguity in the language used, this will be construed in the claimant's favour. Thus, it has been held that a reference in an insurance contract to excess 'loads' did not apply where a car was carrying more *passengers* than the number that it was constructed to carry.[43] It has also been held that the phrase 'consequential losses' does not cover direct losses flowing naturally from the breach, such as lost profits.[44]

Particular difficulty can arise where the defendant seeks to exclude liability for negligence in the performance of a contract. The principles to be applied here were at one time set out by the Privy Council in *Canada Steamship Lines Ltd v The King*.[45] The court was dealing with Canadian law, but the principles have been taken as applying to English law as well.[46] They were stated by Lord Morton as follows:

(1)     If the clause contains language that expressly exempts the person in whose favour it is made (hereafter called 'the *proferens*') from the consequence of the negligence of his own servants, effect must be given to that provision.

(2)     If there is no express reference to negligence, the court must consider whether the words used are wide enough, in their ordinary meaning, to cover negligence on the part of the servants of the *proferens*.

---

39  Above, 6.5.4.
40  [1934] 1 KB 17.
41  [1911] AC 394.
42  For the distinction between warranties and conditions, see Chapter 6, 6.5.7.
43  *Houghton v Trafalgar Insurance* [1954] 1 QB 247.
44  *Hotel Services Ltd v Hilton International Hotels (UK) Ltd* [2000] 1 All ER Comm 750, CA. This was in the context of a clause referring to 'indirect and consequential' losses. The court recognised that in other contexts, 'consequential' loss could be interpreted to cover direct losses; here, however, it should be interpreted together with 'indirect' and taken to refer only to losses falling within the second limb of the remoteness rule in *Hadley v Baxendale* (1854) 9 Exch 341; 156 ER 145 – for which, see Chapter 15, 15.6.2. This approach was followed in *McCain Foods GB Limited v ECO-TEC (Europe) Limited* [2011] EWHC 66 (TCC). Compare *Caledonia North Sea Ltd v London Bridge Engineering Ltd* [2002] UKHL 4 at [100] per Lord Hoffmann.
45  [1952] AC 192, p 208.
46  See, for example, *EE Caledonia Ltd v Orbit Valve plc* [1994] 1 WLR 1515; *Shell Chemical v P & O Tankers* [1995] 1 Lloyd's Rep 297; *Toomey v Eagle Star Insurance* [1995] 2 Lloyd's Rep 88 and *Monarch Airlines Ltd v London Luton Airport Ltd* [1997] CLC 698.

(3)    If the words used are wide enough for the above purpose, the court must then consider whether the 'head of damage may be based on some ground other than negligence'. The 'other' ground must not be so fanciful or remote that the *proferens* cannot be supposed to have desired protection against it; but subject to this qualification the existence of a possible head of damage other than negligence is fatal to the *proferens* even if the words used are *prima facie* wide enough to cover negligence on the part of his servants.

This approach is stated in terms of excluding liability for the acts of the defendant's 'servants' (that is, employees) but it will apply equally to the situation where the defendant is potentially directly liable for negligence.

As the first principle makes clear, if the drafter of a contract wishes to ensure that negligence liability is covered, the safest way is to say so explicitly. The use of the word 'negligence' is obviously sufficient but synonyms may also be enough. In *Monarch Airlines Ltd v London Luton Airport Ltd*,[47] for example, it was held that the phrase 'act, omission, neglect or default' was clearly intended to cover negligence.

This is relatively straightforward. It is when the drafter of the contract decides to use general words such as 'any loss howsoever caused' that difficulties start to arise.[48] In that situation, the second and third principles stated by Lord Morton come into play. A distinction then needs to be drawn between the situations where the defendant is liable only for negligence and situations where there is some other possible basis for liability. In the latter situation, the defendant will generally need to use words that specifically cover negligence in order to avoid liability. General words that purport to cover 'all liabilities' may well not be enough. If, for example, a bailee is strictly liable for the safety of the bailor's goods, a general clause excluding liability may be taken to attach to the strict liability and not to liability for negligence. Similarly, in *White v John Warwick*,[49] in a contract for the hire of a bicycle, a clause exempting the owners from liability for personal injuries was held to cover only breach of strict contractual liability as to the condition of the bicycle, and not injuries resulting from negligence in the fitting of the saddle.[50]

The position is different if the only basis of liability that exists is negligence liability. Then the implication of Lord Morton's second principle is that general words may be sufficient.[51] In *Alderslade v Hendon Laundry*,[52] the plaintiff had not received certain handkerchiefs that he had left with the defendant laundry. A clause in the contract stated: 'The maximum amount allowed for lost or damaged articles is 20 times the charge made for laundering.' Lord Greene MR took the view that as regards loss (as opposed to damage), the laundry could not be regarded as undertaking a strict obligation but only to take reasonable care of items (that is, not to be negligent). On that basis, the clause was apt to cover negligence liability. Salmon LJ in *Hollier v Rambler Motors*,[53] however, in discussing this case, took the view that it was the perception of the customer that was important:[54]

---

47  [1997] CLC 698.

48  It is not clear why some drafters of contracts do not explicitly refer to negligence. Maybe there is a feeling that the other party might be put off by such an explicit recognition of the possibility that their proposed contracting partner will not take reasonable care in the performance of the contract.

49  [1953] 2 All ER 1021.

50  Excluding liability for negligence giving rise to personal injury is now in any case prohibited by s 65 CRA 2015 (consumer cases) and s 2 of the UCTA 1977 (non-consumer cases): below, 7.7.5 and 7.8.

51  *Joseph Travers & Sons Ltd v Cooper* [1915] KB 73.

52  [1945] KB 189; [1945] 1 All ER 244.

53  [1972] 2 QB 71; [1972] 1 All ER 399. This case has been criticised by Barendt, 1972.

54  Ibid, p 79; p 405.

I think that the ordinary sensible housewife, or indeed anyone else who sends washing to the laundry, who saw that clause must have appreciated that almost always goods are lost or damaged because of the laundry's negligence, and, therefore, this clause could apply only to limit the liability of the laundry, when they were in fault or negligent.

This must be regarded as having modified the approach taken by the Court of Appeal in *Alderslade* itself. The position thus now seems to be that where the reasonable claimant would read a clause as covering negligence, the courts will be prepared to allow exclusion without any specific reference to negligence, or the use of a general phrase clearly including negligence.[55] In the end, it is a matter of attempting to assess the intentions and reasonable expectations of the parties.

---

**Key case** *Hollier v Rambler Motors* (1972)[56]

Facts: The plaintiff's car was at the defendant's premises when it was damaged by fire caused by the defendant's negligence. There was a clause in the contract that stated: 'The company is not responsible for damage caused by fire to customers' cars on the premises.' Held: The Court of Appeal took the view that customers would assume that this clause related to fires that arose without negligence on the part of the defendant (though as a matter of law there would in fact be no liability in such a case). The clause was not, in effect, an exclusion of liability but simply a 'warning' that the defendant was not, as a matter of law, liable for non-negligent fire damage. If the defendant wanted to exclude liability for negligence, this should have been done explicitly.

---

As the case shows, even where the only possible liability is for negligence, it is still better to use specific rather than general words.

The position as regards exclusion of liability for negligence was significantly affected by the UCTA 1977 and now the CRA 2015,[57] and this may mean that the above rules will be of less significance. Clauses purporting to exclude negligence may either be ineffective (if relating to death or personal injury)[58] or be subject to a requirement of 'reasonableness' (non-consumers) or 'fairness' (consumers).[59] In the consumer context the courts may well be reluctant to find that attempts to exclude liability for failing to take reasonable care in the performance of a contract are 'fair', even where the negligence is the fault of the defendant's employee rather than the defendant personally. However, as has been indicated above, the courts still make reference to Lord Morton's principles in the *Canada Steamship* case[60] albeit with a warning of the need to avoid artificial or strained approaches to construction.[61]

---

55  See *Rutter v Palmer* [1922] 2 KB 87 – garage in possession of the plaintiff's car with a view to selling it; clause stating 'Customers' cars are driven by your staff at customers' sole risk' was wide enough to cover negligence by the driver.

56  [1972] 2 QB 71; [1972] 1 All ER 399. Note that this case has been criticised by Barendt, 1972.

57  Below, 7.7.5 and 7.8.

58  See s 65 CRA 2015 (consumer cases) and s 2 of the UCTA 1977 (non-consumer cases): below, 7.7.5 and 7.8.

59  See s 2, UCTA 1977 and s 62 CRA 2015.

60  See, for example, *EE Caledonia Ltd v Orbit Valve plc* [1994] 1 WLR 1515; *Shell Chemical v P & O Tankers* [1995] 1 Lloyd's Rep 297; *Toomey v Eagle Star Insurance* [1995] 2 Lloyd's Rep 88; and *Monarch Airlines Ltd v London Luton Airport Ltd* [1997] CLC 698.

61  See *Persimmon Homes Ltd v Ove Arup and Partners Ltd* [2017] EWCA Civ 373.

## 7.5.2 RELAXATION OF THE RULES OF CONSTRUCTION

More generally, the existence of stricter statutory controls over exclusion and limitation clauses has encouraged the courts to take the line that there is no need for the rules of construction to be used in an artificial way in this context. In particular, the consumer and the standard form contract are dealt with by a combination of the CRA 2015 and the UCTA 1977.[62] Businesses negotiating at arm's length are generally expected to look after themselves. If they enter into contracts containing exclusion or limitation clauses, they must be presumed to know what they are doing. On at least three occasions since the passage of the UCTA 1977, the House of Lords has criticised an approach to the interpretation of exclusion/limitation clauses in commercial contracts that involved straining their plain meaning in order to limit their effect.[63] In *Photo Production Ltd v Securicor Transport Ltd*,[64] Lord Wilberforce commented that in the light of parliamentary intervention to protect consumers (by means of the UCTA 1977):[65]

> in commercial matters generally, when the parties are not of unequal bargaining power, and when risks are normally borne by insurance, not only is the case for judicial intervention undemonstrated, but there is everything to be said, and this seems to have been Parliament's intention, for leaving the parties free to apportion the risks as they think fit and for respecting their decisions.

Lord Diplock, agreeing with Lord Wilberforce, commented:[66]

> In commercial contracts negotiated between businessmen capable of looking after their own interests and of deciding how risks inherent in the performance of various kinds of contract can be most economically borne (generally by insurance), it is, in my view, wrong to place a strained construction on words in an exclusion clause which are clear and fairly susceptible of one meaning only.

Similarly, in *Ailsa Craig Fishing Co Ltd v Malvern Fishing Co Ltd*,[67] Lord Wilberforce again expressed the view (particularly in relation to clauses limiting liability, rather than excluding it altogether) that:[68]

> one must not strive to create ambiguities by strained construction, as I think the appellants have striven to do. The relevant words must be given, if possible, their natural, plain meaning.

Lord Fraser agreed that limitation clauses need not:[69]

> be judged by the specially exacting standards which are applied to exclusion and indemnity clauses ... It is enough ... that the clause must be clear and unambiguous.

---

62 Below, 7.7 and 7.8.
63 Compare *HIH Casualty & General Insurance Ltd v Chase Manhattan Bank* [2003] UKHL 6 at [11] where Lord Bingham warned against using Lord Morton's principles as a 'code'. The key is the intention of the parties: see also *Greenwich Millennium Village Ltd v Essex Services Group Plc* [2014] EWCA Civ 960. See also *Persimmon Homes Ltd v Ove Arup and Partners Ltd* [2017] EWCA Civ 373 and *Transocean Drilling UK Ltd v Providence Resources Plc* [2016] EWCA Civ 372.
64 [1980] AC 827; [1980] 1 All ER 556.
65 Ibid, p 843; p 561.
66 [1980] AC 827, p 851; [1980] 1 All ER 556, p 568.
67 [1983] 1 All ER 101.
68 [1983] 1 All ER 101, p 104.
69 Ibid, pp 105–06.

Finally, in *George Mitchell (Chesterhall) Ltd v Finney Lock Seeds Ltd*,[70] Lord Bridge reaffirmed the need for straightforward interpretation:[71]

> The relevant condition, read as a whole, unambiguously limits the appellants' liability to replacement of the seeds or refund of the price. It is only possible to read an ambiguity into it by the process of strained construction which was deprecated by Lord Diplock in the *Photo Production* case ... and by Lord Wilberforce in the *Ailsa Craig* case.

The interpretation of exclusion and limitation clauses particularly in commercial agreements should now also take into account the approach of Lord Hoffmann in *Investors Compensation Scheme Ltd v West Bromwich Building Society*,[72] as discussed in Chapter 6.[73] That this is the correct approach was confirmed by the Court of Appeal in *Keele University v Price Waterhouse*.[74] Indeed there has been some debate about the continuing existence of a *contra proferentem* rule in respect of exclusion clauses in commercial contracts[75] although, in cases of ambiguity, it can still probably be supported on the ground that "parties are not lightly to be taken to have intended to cut down the remedies which the law provides for breach of important contractual obligations without using clear words having that effect."[76]

By contrast, in *Bominflot Bunkergesellschaft für Mineraloele mbH & Co KG v Petroplus Marketing AG*,[77] the Court of Appeal followed *Wallis, Son & Wells v Pratt & Haynes*[78] despite the criticism of Professor Tettenborn[79] on the grounds that it represented a 'long established consensus'.[80]

---

### For thought

*Is it right that all commercial agreements should be approached in the way outlined? Doesn't the fact that the parties to a business contract may be of very different bargaining strength mean that in some circumstances a stricter approach to interpretation would be justified?*

---

### 7.5.3 IN FOCUS: FUNDAMENTAL BREACH

At one time, the view was taken by some courts, and in particular the Court of Appeal, that some breaches of contract were so serious that no exclusion clause could cover

---

70  [1983] 2 AC 803; [1983] 2 All ER 737.
71  Ibid, pp 814–15; p 742.
72  [1998] 1 All ER 98.
73  Above, 6.5.5.
74  [2004] EWCA Civ 583; [2004] PNLR 43. This case is also an example of the Court deciding not to consider the 'reasonableness' test under the UCTA 1977 because, on its true construction, the clause did not cover the loss for which the claimant sought to recover. In *McGee Group Ltd v Galliford Try Building Ltd* [2017] EWHC 87 (TCC) at [25] Coulson J stated: "...a clause which seeks to limit the liability of one party to a commercial contract, for some or all of the claims which may be made by the other party, should generally be treated as an element of the parties' wider allocation of benefit, risk and responsibility. No special rules apply to the construction or interpretation of such a clause although, in order to have the effect contended for by the party relying upon it, a clause limiting liability must be clear and unambiguous."
75  *Persimmon Homes Ltd v Ove Arup and Partners Ltd* [2017] EWCA Civ 373.
76  *Hut Group Ltd v Nobahar-Cookson* [2016] EWCA Civ 128 at [18] *per* Briggs LJ.
77  [2010] EWCA Civ 1145.
78  [1911] AC 394.
79  Tettenborn, 2009.
80  At [62].

them. This was expressed in the so-called doctrine of fundamental breach. This doctrine found its origins in shipping law where there was strong authority that if a ship 'deviated' from its agreed route, there could be no exclusion of liability in relation to events that occurred after the deviation, even though the deviation was not the cause of any loss that occurred.[81] Applied more generally to the law of contract, it took two forms. One was that there were certain terms within a contract that were so fundamental that there could not be an exclusion in respect of breach of them. Such might be the situation where the contract stipulated for the supply of peas, and beans were provided instead.[82] The supplier in such a case had departed so far from the basic contractual obligation that some courts felt that it could not be justifiable to allow the supplier to exclude liability. To do so would appear to make a mockery of the whole idea of a contractual obligation. If, for example, a person who had contracted to sell potatoes supplied the same weight of coal, it surely ought not to be ordinarily permissible to allow reliance on a broadly written exclusion clause that states 'the supplier may substitute any other goods for those specified in the contract'. The rules of incorporation and construction do not have any necessary effect on such a clause. The answer appeared to some to be to treat the promise to supply potatoes as a 'fundamental term'. Any breach of this term would provide a remedy to the other party irrespective of an exclusion clause.

Stated in this form, the doctrine had close links with the 'deviation' principle in shipping law, which similarly was concerned with the breach of a specific obligation regarded as being central to the contract. The second form of the doctrine of fundamental breach was different in that it looked not at the particular term that had been broken, but at the overall effects of the breach that had occurred: if the breach was so serious that it could be said to have destroyed the whole contract, then again exclusion of liability should not be possible. Two cases illustrate these two aspects of the doctrine: *Karsales v Wallis*[83] and *Harbutt's Plasticine Ltd v Wayne Tank and Pump Co Ltd*.[84] In *Karsales v Wallis* the contract was for the supply of a Buick car, which the plaintiff had inspected and found to be in good condition. When delivered (late at night), however, it had to be towed because it was incapable of self-propulsion. Among other things, the cylinder head had been removed, the valves had been burnt out and two of the pistons had been broken. The defendant purported to rely on a clause of the agreement that stated:

> No condition or warranty that the vehicle is roadworthy, or as to its age, condition or fitness for purpose is given by the owner or implied herein.

The county judge held for the defendant but the Court of Appeal reversed this. The majority of the Court (Lord Denning reached the same conclusion, but on slightly different grounds) held that what had been delivered was not, in effect, a 'car'. The defendant's 'performance' was totally different from that which had been contemplated by the contract (that is, the supply of a motor vehicle in working order). There was, therefore, a breach of a fundamental term of the agreement and the exclusion clause had no application.

In *Harbutt's Plasticine*, the contract involved the supply of pipework in the plaintiff's factory. The type of piping used was unsuitable and resulted in a fire that destroyed the whole of the plaintiff's factory. The obligation to supply piping that was fit for its purpose could clearly have been broken in various ways, not all of which would have led to serious

---

81 See, for example, *Joseph Thorley Ltd v Orchis SS Co Ltd* [1907] 1 KB 660. Compare *Dera Commercial Estate v Derya Inc* [2018] EWHC 1673 (Comm).

82 *Chanter v Hopkins* (1838) 3 M & W 252. See also *The Bow Cedar* [1980] 2 Lloyd's Rep 601 – contract for ground nut oil; goods supplied 50 per cent ground nut oil, 50 per cent soya bean oil.

83 [1956] 2 All ER 866.

84 [1970] 1 QB 447; [1970] 1 All ER 225.

damage to the plaintiff's premises. In this case, however, the consequences of the defendant's failure to meet its obligation in this respect were so serious that the Court of Appeal regarded it as a 'fundamental breach' of the contract, precluding any reliance on an exclusion clause.

These two Court of Appeal decisions illustrate that a 'fundamental breach' could occur either through the breach of a particularly important term, or through a breach that had the consequences of destroying the whole basis of the contract.

In arriving at its decision in *Harbutt's Plasticine*, however, the Court of Appeal had to deal with the views expressed by the House of Lords in *Suisse Atlantique Société d'Armemente SA v Rotterdamsche Kolen Centrale NV*.[85] The case concerned a charter that included provisions whereby, if there were delays, the charterers' liability was limited to paying $1,000 per day 'demurrage'. The owners attempted to argue that the charterers' breach was so serious that the demurrage clause should not apply and that they should be able to recover their full losses. The House of Lords rejected this and, in so doing, expressed strong disapproval of the argument that there was a substantive rule of law which meant that certain types of breach automatically prevented reliance on an exclusion clause. As Viscount Dilhorne commented:[86]

> In my view, it is not right to say that the law prohibits and nullifies a clause exempting or limiting liability for a fundamental breach or breach of a fundamental term. Such a rule of law would involve a restriction on freedom of contract and in the older cases I can find no trace of it.

As this quotation illustrates, the House was of the opinion that the parties should generally be allowed to determine their obligations and the effect of exclusion clauses in their contract. If there was a breach that appeared fundamental, then it was a question of trying to determine whether such a breach was intended to be covered by any exclusion clause. Of course, as Lord Wilberforce noted,[87] 'the courts are entitled to insist, as they do, that the more radical the breach, the clearer must be the language if it is to be covered', but the question is one of the proper construction of the clause and not a rule of law.

In *Harbutt's Plasticine*, the Court of Appeal attempted to distinguish *Suisse Atlantique* on the basis that in that case the parties had continued with the charter even after the alleged fundamental breach. The Court of Appeal therefore argued that the principles outlined by the House of Lords in *Suisse Atlantique* should apply only where there was an affirmation of the contract by the parties following the breach and not where the breach itself brought the contract to an end. In the latter type of situation, there should be no possibility of reliance on an exclusion clause. The difficulty with this argument was that it is a well-established principle in contract law that a breach never in itself brings a contract to an end.[88] The party not in breach usually has the option (if the breach is a serious one) of either (i) accepting the breach and terminating the contract, or (ii) affirming the contract and simply suing for damages. Suppose, for example, there is a contract for the sale of components that are to be supplied with certain fixing holes drilled in them. If, when delivered, the fixing holes are not there, this may amount to a breach of 'condition' by virtue of, where applicable, s 13 of the Sale of Goods Act 1979.[89] The buyer will have the right to accept the breach, reject the goods and sue for damages. Alternatively, however, the buyer may affirm the contract, accept the goods and simply sue for the cost of having the

---

85 [1967] 1 AC 361; [1966] 2 All ER 61.
86 [1967] 1 AC 361, p 392; [1966] 2 All ER 61, p 67.
87 [1967] 1 AC 361, p 432; [1966] 2 All ER 61, p 92.
88 This rule is discussed further in Chapter 14, 14.6.1.
89 See Chapter 6, 6.6.12.

holes drilled, and any other consequential losses. The Court of Appeal in *Harbutt's Plasticine* took the view that this did not apply to certain fundamental breaches of contract, which themselves brought the contract to an end, without the need for acceptance by the party not in breach. This view was, however, firmly rejected by the House of Lords in *Photo Production Ltd v Securicor Transport Ltd*,[90] which overruled *Harbutt's Plasticine* and finally disposed of the argument that certain types of fundamental breach could never be covered by an exclusion clause.[91]

### 7.5.4 ANY BREACH, NO MATTER HOW SERIOUS, MAY BE EXCLUDED

The decision of the House of Lords in *Photo Production v Securicor*[92] finally confirmed that in business-to-business contracts it was *possible* for liability for any breach to be excluded, no matter how serious, or what its effect on the contract.

---

**Key case** *Photo Production Ltd v Securicor Transport Ltd* (1980)

Facts: The plaintiffs owned a factory and engaged the defendants to provide security services, which included a night patrol. Unfortunately, one of the guards employed by the defendants to carry out these duties started a fire on the premises that got out of control and destroyed the entire factory. Thus, rather than protecting the plaintiffs' property as they had been contracted to do, the defendants could be said to have achieved the exact opposite. The contract, however, contained a very broadly worded exclusion clause, which, on its face, seemed to cover even the very serious breach of the agreement that had occurred. The Court of Appeal took the view that this could not protect the defendants. There had been a fundamental breach and the exclusion clause was ineffective.
Held: The House of Lords took this opportunity to state its position with no possible ambiguity. It ruled that there was no rule of law that a fundamental breach of contract prevented an exclusion clause from being effective. The so-called doctrine of fundamental breach was in fact no more than an aspect of the doctrine of construction. Of course, it was the case that the more serious the breach of contract, the clearer the words would need to be that would exclude liability for it. But, if two businesses had negotiated an agreement containing a clause that on its plain wording covered such a breach, there was no reason why the courts should not give effect to it. In the present case, the House, while noting the breadth of the exclusion clause, also noted that the plaintiffs were paying a very low rate for the defendants' services. It was therefore not unreasonable that the defendants should have a low level of liability. The *ratio* of the case was not, however, that the clause such as that under consideration could be enforced because it was reasonable in all the circumstances but because on its true construction it covered the breach.

---

The decision in *Photo Productions* is a strong affirmation of the 'freedom of contract' approach to commercial agreements and a rejection of an 'interventionist' role for the courts.

---

90  [1980] AC 827; [1980] 1 All ER 556.
91  See also s 9 of the UCTA 1977, which previously confirmed the position that exclusion clauses survive a breach of contract and can be given effect (subject to the other restrictions contained in the Act) whether or not the contract has been terminated as result of the breach. This provision has been repealed by the Consumer Rights Act 2015 apparently on the ground that it is no longer needed following the demise of the doctrine of fundamental breach: see Law Commission, *Unfair Terms in Contracts* (Law Com No 292, Scot Law Com No 199 (2005)) para.6.37.
92  [1980] AC 827; [1980] 1 All ER 556.

## 7.5.5 THE CURRENT POSITION

The demise of the doctrine of fundamental breach as a rule of law (and there has been no real attempt to revive it since the *Photo Production* decision) has to some extent simplified the law in this area. It may still be difficult to decide in particular cases, however, what to do where a breach effectively negates the whole purpose of the contract. It is a matter of looking at the precise wording of the exclusion clause and trying to determine the intentions of the parties in relation to it. The likelihood of exclusion being effective will decrease with the seriousness of the breach but it is now always a question of balance, rather than the application of a firm rule.

In considering where the balance is likely to be struck, some of the older case law may still be relevant in indicating the types of situation where the courts will require considerable convincing that the parties really did intend that a serious breach was intended to be covered by the exclusion clause. Some of the cases referred to above, such as *Karsales v Wallis*[93] and *Harbutt's Plasticine Ltd v Wayne Tank and Pump Co Ltd*,[94] may be relevant in this context. A decision to similar effect is *Pinnock Bros v Lewis and Peat Ltd*,[95] where the contract was for the supply of copra cake to be used as cattle feed. The cake was contaminated with castor beans and the cattle became ill. There was an exclusion clause expressed to cover liabilities for 'defects' in the goods. The court refused to apply the clause, holding that what was supplied was so contaminated that it could not be called 'copra cake' at all. On its proper construction, therefore, the clause referring to 'defects' was not apt to cover the situation.[96] In *Glynn v Margetson & Co*,[97] a bill of lading relating to a contract for the carriage of a cargo of oranges from Malaga to Liverpool contained a clause allowing considerable freedom (referring to most of Europe and the 'the coasts of Africa') in the route that could be taken 'for the purposes of delivering ... cargo ... or for any other purposes whatsoever'. The ship, having loaded the oranges, went to a port some 350 miles in the opposite direction from Liverpool to collect another load before proceeding to Liverpool. The oranges had deteriorated on arrival as a result of the prolonged voyage. The detour made here was strictly within the terms of the bill of lading,[98] but the House of Lords nevertheless held the carrier liable. It took the view that the clause in the bill of lading could not have been intended to allow the carrier to act in a way that was inconsistent with the 'main purpose' of the contract, that was to deliver the cargo from Malaga to Liverpool. Finally, in *Gibaud v Great Eastern Railway Co*,[99] the contract was for the storage of a bicycle in the cloakroom at a railway station. It was in fact left in the booking hall, from which it was stolen. The owner had been given a ticket that limited the railway's liability to £5. The Court of Appeal considered the argument that the defendant could not rely on the clause because the bicycle had not been kept in the cloakroom. It accepted, following *Lilley v Doubleday*[100] that where the bailee of goods had undertaken to store them in a particular warehouse but in fact stored them elsewhere, the benefit of an exclusion clause would be lost. The principle was that:[101]

> if you undertake to do a thing in a certain way, or to keep a thing in a certain place, with certain conditions protecting it, and have broken the contract by not doing the thing contracted for in the way contracted for, or not keeping the article in the place

---

93　[1956] 2 All ER 866.
94　[1970] 1 QB 447; [1970] 1 All ER 225.
95　[1923] 1 KB 690.
96　Note that the facts of this case would now fall within the scope of s 6 of the UCTA 1977 – see below, 7.7.19.
97　[1893] AC 351.
98　So this was not a 'deviation' case in the strict sense – see above, 7.5.3.
99　[1921] 2 KB 426.
100　(1881) 7 QBD 510.
101　[1921] 2 KB 426, p 435.

where you have contracted to keep it, you cannot rely on the conditions which were only intended to protect you if you carried out the contract in the way in which you had contracted to do it.

On the facts, however, it was held that there was no binding obligation to store the bicycle in the cloakroom, so that the railway company was able to take the benefit of the clause.

The courts are also likely to be reluctant to find that a clause allows a defendant to escape liability where there has been a deliberate breach of contract. Thus, in *Sze Hai Tong Bank Ltd v Rambler Cycle Co Ltd*,[102] the carrier delivered goods to a person who was known to have no authority to receive them,[103] and this resulted in a loss to the owner. The carrier attempted to rely on a clause in the bill of lading that stated that its liability ended once the goods were 'discharged' from the ship. The Privy Council held, however, that the clause could not have been intended to cover the carrier if the goods had simply been handed over to a passer-by. It must have been intended only to cover an authorised discharge, and not a deliberate delivery to an unauthorised recipient.[104] More recent confirmation of this approach to deliberate breaches is to be found in *Internet Broadcasting Corporation Ltd v Mar LLC*,[105] where the High Court suggested that:[106]

There is a presumption, which appears to be a strong presumption, against the exemption clause being construed so as to cover deliberate, repudiatory breach.

Very clear words would be needed to cover such a breach, and even then there would be reluctance to apply the literal meaning where to do so would defeat the 'main object' of the contract.[107]

## 7.6 STATUTORY CONTROLS

In many situations, the use of common law controls to indirectly 'police' exemption and limitation clauses, as discussed in the previous sections, has effectively been superseded by statutory controls contained in the Unfair Contract Terms Act (UCTA) 1977 and the Consumer Rights Act (CRA) 2015.[108] Although the issues of incorporation and construction are still important, it is more likely that the statutory provisions will determine the outcome of a case where the clause (a) is contained in a consumer contract, or (b) forms part of the defendant's written standard terms, or (c) purports to exclude liability for the defendant's negligence. Despite the fact that, strictly speaking, the common law rules are logically prior to any consideration of the statutory provisions – so that if a clause is not incorporated or does not cover the breach, it can have no effect at all and the statutory provisions are irrelevant – in practice, the statutory controls will often be considered first.

---

102 [1959] AC 576.
103 The person was in fact the buyer of the goods but the seller had not authorised delivery as was required by the contract. The buyer defaulted on payment for the goods.
104 The court also felt that the interpretation contended for by the carrier would fall foul of the 'main purpose' rule, as applied in *Glynn v Margetson & Co* [1893] AC 351, see above 7.5.5.
105 [2009] EWHC 844.
106 Ibid, at [33].
107 Ibid.
108 Which repealed, for contracts entered into from 1 October 2015, the Unfair Terms in Consumer Contracts Regulations 1999, SI 1999/2083: see Consumer Rights Act 2015 (Commencement No 3, Transitional Provisions, Savings and Consequential Amendments) Order 2015, SI 2015/1630.

That this is not necessarily the case, however, is demonstrated by the Court of Appeal decision in *Keele University v Price Waterhouse*,[109] where, having interpreted an exclusion clause in a way that meant that it did not cover the loss for which the claimant was seeking compensation, the court declined to consider the UCTA 1977, treating the question of reasonableness under that Act as 'moot'.[110]

Prior to the CRA 2015, UCTA 1977 had provisions dealing with both consumer and non-consumer contracts. This resulted in an overlap with the Unfair Terms in Consumer Contracts Regulations (UTCCR) 1999 (which only applied to consumer contracts):

> 3. As the law currently stands, there are two major pieces of legislation dealing with unfair contract terms. The Unfair Contract Terms Act 1977 sets out the traditional UK approach, while the Unfair Terms in Consumer Contracts Regulations 1999 implement the 1993 EU Directive. The two laws contain inconsistent and overlapping provisions, using different language and concepts to produce similar but not identical effects. A law that affects ordinary people in their everyday lives had been made unnecessarily complicated and difficult.[111]

In 2005, the Law Commission put forward proposals that would have resulted in the UCTA 1977 and the UTCCR 1999 being replaced by a new single piece of legislation.[112] Subsequently the Consumer Rights Act 2015 reformed a number of areas of consumer law including the law relating to unfair terms in consumer contracts. The work of the Law Commissions in this area was influential in shaping the CRA 2015, although not all of their recommendations made it into the CRA 2015 (for example, the recommendations in relation to 'unfair' terms and small businesses). Following the CRA 2015, which repealed the UTCCR 1999, there is a much clearer separation between consumer and non-consumer contracts: broadly the CRA 2015 regulates consumer contracts and, for present purposes, an amended UCTA 1977 regulates non-business contracts.

The CRA 2015 will be discussed in 7.8.

## 7.7 UNFAIR CONTRACT TERMS ACT 1977

The UCTA 1977 has had a very significant effect on the law relating to exclusion and limitation clauses. Where it applies, it is in many cases more significant in 'policing' exemption and limitation clauses than the common law rules. It must be remembered, however, that, in addition to now being focused on non-consumer contracts, the UCTA 1977 does not apply to all contracts. The first point for discussion here is, therefore, the precise scope of the Act.

### 7.7.1 SCOPE OF THE UCTA 1977
There are certain contracts, listed in Sched 1, which are not within the scope of ss 2–3 (which are some of the main protective provisions) at all. These include:[113]

(a)    contracts of insurance;
(b)    contracts concerning the creation or transfer of interests in land. This includes continuing covenants under a lease: *Electricity Supply Nominees v IAF Group*;[114]

---

109  [2004] EWCA Civ 583; [2004] PNLR 43.
110  [2004] EWCA Civ 583; [2004] PNLR 43, at [29].
111  Law Commission, *Unfair Terms in Contracts – Summary,* 2005, Law Com No 298, Scot Law Com, No 199, Cm 6464.
112  *Unfair Terms in Contracts,* Law Com No 292, Scot Law Com No 199, Cm 6464, 2005.
113  UCTA 1977, Sched 1, para 1.
114  [1993] 3 All ER 372.

(c)    contracts concerning the creation or transfer of intellectual property rights (copyright, patent, etc.);

(d)    contracts relating to the formation, dissolution or constitution of a company, partnership or unincorporated association;

(e)    contracts relating to the creation or transfer of securities; and

(f)    anything covered by EU Regulation 181/2011 on the rights of passengers in bus and coach transport.

The UCTA 1977 also has only limited application in relation to various types of shipping contract, including carriage of goods by sea.[115] In relation to contracts of employment, s 2(1) and (2) (which deal with exclusion of liability for negligence) do not apply other than in favour of an employee. It was suggested in *Brigden v American Express*[116] that an employee could potentially use s 3 of the Act against terms put forward by an employer (though on the facts the claim failed). This was specifically disapproved by the Court of Appeal in *Commerzbank AG v Keen*.[117] The court held that an employee did not contract with his or her employer 'as a consumer', and that the terms of employment were not standard terms of the employer's *business* (which in this case was the business of banking).

It is always advisable to check the provisions of Sched 1 in relation to contracts falling into the above categories.

### 7.7.2 'BUSINESS' LIABILITY

The next limitation on the scope of the UCTA 1977 which must be noted appears in s 1(3). This states that ss 2–7 apply only to:

business liability, that is, liability for breach of obligations or duties arising (a) from things done or to be done in the course of a business ... or (b) from the occupation of premises used for the business purposes of the occupier.[118]

In general, therefore, the non-business contractor is free to include exclusion and limitation clauses without their being controlled by the UCTA 1977.[119] In many situations, the test of whether obligations arise in the course of a 'business' will not give rise to problems but it is perhaps unfortunate that the Act does not contain a comprehensive definition of what is meant by 'business'.

### 7.7.3 MEANING OF 'BUSINESS'

Section 14 states that '"business" includes a profession and the activities of any government department or local or public authority'. This arguably seems to leave open the position of organisations such as charities or universities, which may engage in business activities but might not be thought to be contracting 'in the course of a business'.[120] The protective policy of the UCTA 1977 would suggest that such situations ought to be covered.

---

115 Contracts of marine salvage or towage, any charterparty of a ship or hovercraft, and any contract for the carriage of goods by ship or hovercraft are subject to s 2(1) (which deals with death or personal injury caused by negligence), but not to the other provisions of s 2, s 3 or s 7: UCTA 1977, Sched 1, para 2.

116 [2000] IRLR 94.

117 [2006] EWCA Civ 1536; [2006] 2 CLC 844. Discussed in *Alan Bates and Others v Post Office Limited* [2019] EWHC 606 (QB) at [1072]ff.

118 But note that where access is obtained to premises for recreational or educational purposes, any liability for loss or damage from the dangerous state of the premises is not 'business liability' unless granting access for such purposes falls within the business purposes of the occupier: UCTA, s 1(3)(b) as amended by the Occupiers' Liability Act 1984.

119 Though the scope of s 6, which deals with sale of goods contracts, is wider – see 7.7.16, below.

120 Though a publicly funded university might be treated as a 'public authority'.

## 7.7.4 DISCLAIMERS ETC

The final issue in relation to the scope of the UCTA 1977 concerns the types of clause that are covered. As was noted at the start of this chapter, in drawing up a contract it is possible to attempt to avoid liabilities in a number of ways. The most obvious is by a clause that states that in the event of a breach there will be no liability, or that it will be limited to a particular sum. It is also possible, however, to attempt to achieve the same objective by clauses that define the obligations arising under the contract restrictively ('disclaimers'), or make the enforcement of a liability subject to restrictive conditions (for example, 'all claims must be made within 48 hours of the conclusion of the contract'). Section 13 makes it clear that clauses of this kind that have the effect of excluding or restricting liability may be caught by the Act's provisions. Section 13 states:

(1)     To the extent that this Part of the Act prevents the exclusion or restriction of any liability, it also prevents:
  (a)     making the liability or its enforcement subject to restrictive or onerous conditions;
  (b)     excluding or restricting any right or remedy in respect of the liability, or subjecting a person to any prejudice in consequence of his pursuing any such right or remedy;
  (c)     excluding or restricting rules of evidence and procedure; and (to that extent) ss 2, 6 and 7 also prevent excluding or restricting liability by reference to terms and notices which exclude or restrict the relevant obligation or duty.
(2)     But an agreement in writing to submit present or future differences to arbitration is not to be treated under this Part of this Act as excluding or restricting any liability.

It should be noted that the final words of s 13(1), which deal with avoiding liability by the definition of contractual obligations,[121] do not apply to s 3. As will be seen below, the terms of s 3, which is concerned primarily with non-negligent contractual liability, are themselves wide enough to cover clauses that define obligations.

In *Smith v Eric S Bush*,[122] the House of Lords confirmed that s 13 can extend s 2 of the UCTA 1977 to a clause that is in the form of a disclaimer, which in this case was given by a surveyor providing a valuation of a property to the plaintiff via a building society. The valuation was stated to be given without any acceptance of responsibility as to its accuracy. This was held to be an 'exclusion clause' within the scope of the UCTA 1977, and to fall foul of its requirement of 'reasonableness'.[123] Similarly, in *Stewart Gill v Horatio Myer & Co Ltd*,[124] the Court of Appeal held that a clause restricting a right of set-off or counterclaim could be regarded as an exclusion clause, and therefore within the scope of the UCTA 1977.

---

121  These words have been criticised by Yates (1982, pp 75–81) in relation to their application to s 6 of the UCTA 1977 (for which, see below, 7.7.16), and more generally in terms of logical inconsistency.
122  [1990] AC 831; [1989] 2 All ER 514. Compare *I FE Fund SA v Goldman Sachs International* [2007] EWCA Civ 811, *Avrora Fine Arts Investment Ltd v Christie, Manson and Woods Ltd* [2012] EWHC 2198 at [136] – [146] *per* Newey J and *Carney v NM Rothschild and Sons Ltd* [2018] EWHC 958 (Comm). See also 8.5 where the important case of *First Tower Trustees Ltd, Intertrust Trustees Limited v CDS (Superstores International) Limited* [2018] EWCA Civ 1396 is discussed.
123  For which, see below, 7.7.10.
124  [1992] 2 All ER 257.

## 7.7.5 EXCLUSION OF NEGLIGENCE UNDER THE UCTA 1977

Section 2 of the UCTA 1977 is concerned with clauses that attempt to exclude or restrict business liability for 'negligence', which is defined for the purposes of the Act in s 1(1) to cover the breach:

(a)    of any obligation, arising from the express or implied terms of a contract, to take reasonable care or exercise reasonable skill in the performance of the contract;
(b)    of any common law duty to take reasonable care or exercise reasonable skill (but not any stricter duty); and
(c)    of the common duty of care imposed by the Occupiers' Liability Act 1957.

Thus, it applies to negligent performance of a contractual obligation to use reasonable care and skill (sub-s (2)(a)); the tort of negligence independent of any contract (sub-s (2)(b)); and the statutory duty of care imposed on occupiers towards lawful visitors (sub-s (2)(c)).

Section 2 states:

(1)    A person cannot by reference to any contract term or to a notice given to persons generally or to particular persons exclude or restrict his liability for death or personal injury resulting from negligence.
(2)    In the case of other loss or damage, a person cannot so exclude or restrict his liability for negligence except in so far as the term or notice satisfies the require-ment of reasonableness.
(3)    Where a contract term or notice purports to exclude or restrict liability for negli-gence a person's agreement to or awareness of it is not of itself to be taken as indicating his voluntary acceptance of such a risk.
(4)    This section does not apply to -
    (a)    a term in a consumer contract, or
    (b)    a notice to the extent that it is a consumer notice,
        (but see the provision made about such contracts and notices in sec-tions 62 and 65 of the Consumer Rights Act 2015).

The level of control imposed by s 2 thus depends on the consequences of the negli-gence. To the extent that the exclusion or limitation clause attempts to limit liability for death or personal injury resulting from negligence, it will be totally ineffective (s 2(1)). As regards any other types of loss or damage, the clause will be effective to the extent that the clause satisfies the 'requirement of reasonableness' set out in s 11 of the UCTA 1977.[125] It is interesting to consider what approach a court might take towards a clause that attempts to exclude or limit liability for all loss or damage (including death or per-sonal injury) resulting from negligence by the use of a general phrase such as 'no liability for any loss, injury or damage, howsoever caused'. Clearly, the clause will not be effec-tive in relation to death or personal injuries resulting from negligence. However, this does not mean that the clause is totally without effect. The Act does not invalidate a clause altogether simply because it attempts to exclude liability for personal injuries. It may be arguable, however, that the overall breadth of the clause makes it unreasonable even in relation to the other losses. The answer to this will depend on the precise interpretation of the requirement of reasonableness, and we will return to this issue in the context of that discussion.[126]

---

125  This is discussed further, below, 7.7.10.
126  Compare *Skipskredittforeningen v Emperor Navigation* [1997] CLC 1151.

## 7.7.6 STANDARD TERMS

Whereas s 2 is only concerned with the exclusion or limitation of negligence liability, s 3 covers all types of liability arising under a contract, including strict liability, but is limited in the types of contract which it affects. It states:

(1)    This section applies as between contracting parties where one of them deals on the other's written standard terms of business.

(2)    As against that party, the other cannot by reference to any contract term:
    (a)    when himself in breach of contract, exclude or restrict any liability of his in respect of the breach; or
    (b)    claim to be entitled:
        (i)    to render a contractual performance substantially different from that which was reasonably expected of him; or
        (ii)    in respect of the whole or any part of his contractual obligation, to render no performance at all, except in so far as (in all of the cases mentioned above in this sub-section) the contract term satisfies the requirement of reasonableness.

(3)    This section does not apply to a term in a consumer contract (but see the provision made about such contracts in section 62 of the Consumer Rights Act 2015).

The section is arguably directed at situations where there is often inequality of bargaining power and the claimant may have effectively been forced to accept a wide-ranging exclusion clause, which may operate unfairly. The section originally operated in relation to two types of contract. First, it covered consumer contracts. However, following the CRA 2015, s 3 no longer applies to consumer contracts. Today s 3 UCTA 1977 only applies to non-consumer contracts made on one party's 'written standard terms of business'.

## 7.7.7 STANDARD TERMS OF BUSINESS

One party's 'written standard terms of business' is not further defined but it is probably the case that the individual negotiation of some of the terms of the agreement will not necessarily prevent them from being 'standard'. In St *Albans City and District Council v International Computers Ltd*,[127] the Court of Appeal rejected an argument that the terms were not 'standard' because the contract had been preceded by negotiation and in *African Export-Import Bank v Shebah Exploration and Production Co Ltd*[128] the Court of Appeal held that a party could still be said to deal on the "other's written standard terms of business" if there had been insubstantial amendments to those terms. It has sometimes been suggested that in such cases the exclusion clause itself must remain part of the standard package although in *African Export-Import Bank v Shebah Exploration and Production Co Ltd* the Court of Appeal stated, in a slightly obscure way, that there was no requirement that there had to be negotiation in relation to the relevant exclusion clauses for s.3 to be inapplicable.[129] Regularity of use will suggest that terms are 'standard' but it is not necessary that they are *always* used by the party wishing to rely on them.[130] If the terms

---

127  [1996] 4 All ER 481.
128  [2017] EWCA Civ 845.
129  Ibid at [36].
130  *Chester Grosvenor Hotel v Alfred McAlpine Management Ltd* (1991) 56 BLR 115 and *African Export-Import Bank v Shebah Exploration and Production Co Ltd* [2017] EWCA Civ 845. More recently in *University of Wales v London College of Business Limited* [2015] EWHC 1280 (QB) at [93] HHJ Keyser QC stated: "I do not consider that the retention of a stock of forms is necessary; a set of terms may be both written and standard even if it is held on the computer and printed as and when necessary. Negotiation or even minor modification does not necessarily preclude the application of section 3; if it did, the effect of the section could be easily avoided."

are those of a trade association that are simply adopted by the mutual agreement of both parties, then presumably these will still be treated as 'standard terms' if they are regularly used by the party whom the clause concerned would benefit.

It is important to remember that this provision is not concerned directly with inequalities in bargaining power. It is likely in practice (because of the way in which the requirement of reasonableness operates) to benefit the weaker party more frequently but there is no reason in theory why it should not be relied on by a large corporation that happens to have made a contract on the basis of the standard terms of a much smaller and less powerful business.

### 7.7.8 EFFECT OF S 3

The effect of s 3 is that, in relation to any contract within its scope, any attempt to exclude or restrict liability by the non-consumer, or the party putting forward the standard terms, will be subject to the requirement of reasonableness (s 3(2)(a)). Moreover, s 3(2)(b) goes on to make it clear that this extends also to any contractual term by virtue of which such a party claims to be entitled:

(i)    to render a contractual performance substantially different from that which was reasonably to be expected of him; or

(ii)    in respect of the whole or any part of his contractual obligation, to render no performance at all ...

The point of the provisions in s 3(2)(b) is similar to that of s 13. It is trying to anticipate attempts to exclude liability indirectly by the use of clauses that define a party's obligations very restrictively. It would apply, for example, to a clause such as that used in *Karsales v Wallis*[131] purporting to allow the supplier of a 'car' to deliver something that was incapable of self-propulsion (though such a clause would probably also fall foul of the special provisions relating to sale of goods contracts), or to a clause allowing a party who had agreed to provide a cleaning service each month to miss several months in a row without penalty. Such clauses are permissible, but only to the extent that they satisfy the requirement of reasonableness. This arguably enables a court to distinguish clauses that are genuine and legitimate attempts to set out the parties' contractual obligations from those that are being used to escape any substantial liability at all. The test of legitimacy, as indicated by s 3(2)(b)(i) above, is likely to be the reasonable expectation of the other party.[132]

The precise scope of s 3(2)(b) was considered by the Court of Appeal in *Paragon Finance plc v Staunton*.[133] The claimant argued that a clause allowing the provider of a mortgage complete freedom to vary the interest payable should be regarded as subject to s 3(2)(b); in other words, if the clause could be used to permit the lender to charge an unexpectedly high interest rate, this would constitute 'a contractual performance different from that which was reasonably expected of him', and the clause could be declared 'unreasonable' under the UCTA 1977. The Court of Appeal rejected the claim, holding that the power to set the interest rate was not 'performance' of the contract in the sense meant by s 3(2)(b). In reaching this conclusion, the Court distinguished both *Timeload Ltd v British Telecommunications plc*[134] (power to terminate arbitrarily a contract for the use of a particular telephone number) and *Zockoll Group Ltd v Mercury Communications Ltd*[135] (power to withdraw a particular telephone number without giving reasons), where the court

---

131  [1956] 2 All ER 866 – see above, 7.5.3.

132  See also *AXA Sun Life Services Plc v Campbell Martin Ltd* [2011] EWCA Civ 133 at [50] *per* Stanley Burnton LJ. See also *Alan Bates and Others v Post Office Limited* [2019] EWHC 606 (QB).

133  [2002] 2 All ER 248.

134  [1995] EMLR 459.

135  [1999] EMLR 385.

had held that the terms concerned did potentially fall within the scope of s 3(2)(b). Both of those cases involved a positive obligation to provide something under the contract, which was not the case as regards the setting of the interest rate in *Paragon v Staunton*.

The overall effect of s 3 is that because the vast majority of exclusion clauses will be in either a consumer contract (under the Consumer Rights Act 2015) or one that is on standard terms, there will be very few situations in which an exclusion clause is not at least subject to the requirement of reasonableness. It gives the appeal courts the opportunity to indicate the acceptable limits of exclusion of liability, though as will be seen (see 7.7.9 to 7.7.14 below), it is not one that they have shown any great willingness to take.

### 7.7.9 THE REQUIREMENT OF REASONABLENESS

The test to be applied, where necessary, to determine whether a clause meets the requirement of reasonableness is set out in s 11 of the UCTA 1977. The central element of the test is stated in s 11(1) as being whether the clause was:

> a fair and reasonable one to be included having regard to the circumstances which were, or ought reasonably to have been, known to or in the contemplation of the parties when the contract was made.

This very general test imposes no very significant restrictions on the exercise of a court's discretion in relation to a clause, and therefore makes things difficult for the parties in terms of contractual planning. It may be very difficult to predict whether a particular clause is likely to fall foul of this test. A few guidelines to its operation can be found, however, both within the UCTA 1977 itself and from case law.

### 7.7.10 INTERPRETATION OF REASONABLENESS

Starting with the wording of s 11, it is clear that the point at which the clause should be assessed is when the contract was created and that the test is directed at the clause itself, not at any particular application of it. It is submitted that *obiter* statements to the contrary by the Court of Appeal in *Overseas Medical Supplies Ltd v Orient Transport Services Ltd*[136] (see 7.7.15 below) should be regarded with caution, as running against the clear wording of s 11. Thus, the issue should be whether the clause is one that, at the time at which the parties made the contract, could be regarded as fair and reasonable. Subsequent events should not be relevant in deciding this issue. In particular, the actual breach that has occurred and for which the clause is claimed to provide exclusion or limitation of liability should not, in theory, be considered. The strict reading of the section makes it clear that it is quite possible for a court to feel that it would be reasonable for the defendant to have excluded liability for the particular breach that has occurred, but that the clause is too widely worded to be reasonable, and should therefore fail. This is in line with a policy that aims to discourage the use of unnecessarily wide clauses, rather than simply trying to provide a just solution to individual disputes. The Court of Appeal in *Stewart Gill Ltd v Horatio Myer & Co Ltd*[137] confirmed that it is generally the reasonableness of a clause as a whole, rather than the part of it that is being relied on in the particular case, that must be considered.

Where, however, a clause contains two separate exclusions or limitations, and in particular if they are in two subclauses, it is appropriate to consider the reasonableness of each subclause individually.[138] This was confirmed by the Court of Appeal in *Regus (UK) Ltd v Epcot Solutions*.[139]

---

136 [1999] 2 Lloyd's Rep 273.
137 [1992] QB 600.
138 *Watford Electronics Ltd v Sanderson CFL Ltd* [2001] EWCA Civ 317; [2001] 1 All ER Comm 696.
139 [2008] EWCA Civ 361.

Figure 7.2

Where the clause is one that attempts to limit liability to a specific sum of money, rather than excluding it altogether, s 11(4) directs the court to take into account in assessing the reasonableness of the clause:

(a)   the resources which [the defendant] could expect to be available to him for the purpose of meeting the liability should it arise; and

(b)   how far it was open to him to cover himself by insurance.

This recognises that it may be quite reasonable for a contracting party who is impecunious, or is engaging in a particularly risky activity, to put a financial ceiling on liability.

Finally, s 11(5) states:

It is for those claiming that a contract term or notice satisfies the requirement of reasonableness to show that it does.

This makes it clear that the burden of proof as regards reasonableness lies on the party seeking to rely on the clause.

### 7.7.11 GUIDELINES IN SCHED 2

The only other part of the UCTA 1977 that provides guidance on the operation of the reasonableness test is Sched 2. The role of the schedule is indicated by s 11(2):

In determining for the purposes of s 6 or 7 above whether a contract term satisfies the requirement of reasonableness, regard shall be had in particular to the matters specified in Sched 2 to this Act; but this sub-section does not prevent the court or arbitrator from holding, in accordance with any rule of law, that a term which purports to exclude or restrict any relevant liability is not a term of the contract.

Strictly speaking, therefore, the 'guidelines' that it contains are to be used only in relation to exclusion clauses that attempt to limit liability for breach of the statutorily implied terms under sale of goods and hire purchase contracts. In practice, however, the considerations set out are likely to be regarded as relevant whenever reasonableness is in issue.[140] There are five factors listed, covering the following areas:

(a)    The relative strength of the bargaining position of the parties – in particular, did the claimant have any option about contracting with the defendant, or were there other means by which the claimant's requirements could have been met?

(b)    Whether the claimant received an inducement (for example, a discount) to agree to the term; could the same contract have been made with other persons without the exclusion clause?

(c)    Whether the claimant knew or ought reasonably to have known of the existence and extent of the term. (Note that there is a clear overlap here with the common law requirement of incorporation.)

(d)    Whether at the time of contract it was reasonable to expect that compliance would be practicable with any condition which, if not complied with, leads to the exclusion or restriction of liability.

(e)    Whether goods were manufactured, processed or adapted to the special order of the customer. (Note that this consideration is specifically linked to contracts for the supply of goods: put into general terms, it would require the court to consider whether the contract was specially negotiated to meet the claimant's requirements.)

The weight to be given to any of these considerations is left entirely to the discretion of the court. Moreover, since they are only 'guidelines', there is no obligation to look at them at all. It is unlikely, for example, that the Court of Appeal would overturn a judge's decision on the reasonableness issue simply because one of the above guidelines had not been considered, even in relation to a contract for the supply of goods. The list is not exhaustive, and other matters may be taken into consideration if the court feels that this is appropriate.

## 7.7.12 JUDICIAL APPROACH TO 'REASONABLENESS' – PRE-UCTA 1977

As far as the case law on 'reasonableness' is concerned, there are two House of Lords decisions that are particularly worth noting, one applying a test of reasonableness that pre-dated the UCTA 1977 and the other dealing with the UCTA 1977 itself.

The first case is *George Mitchell (Chesterhall) Ltd v Finney Lock Seeds Ltd*.[141] This concerned a contract for the sale of cabbage seed, which turned out not to match its description, with the result that the entire crop failed and the purchaser suffered a loss of £63,000. The contract contained a clause limiting the liability of the seller to the price of the seed, which was under £200. The clause was subject to the test of reasonableness (now superseded by the UCTA 1977) contained in s 55(4) of the Sale of Goods Act 1979,[142] which required the court to decide whether it was fair and reasonable to allow reliance on the clause. The trial judge and the Court of Appeal held that the clause did not

---

140 See, for example, *Overseas Medical Supplies Ltd v Orient Transport Services Ltd* [1999] 2 Lloyd's Rep 273 – discussed below, 7.7.15.

141 [1983] 2 AC 803; [1983] 2 All ER 737.

142 As set out in the 1979 Act, Sched 1, para 11.

on its true construction cover the breach. The House of Lords differed on the construction issue, holding that the wording was apt to cover the breach, and so had to go on to consider the question of reasonableness. The House emphasised that it was best on this issue, wherever possible, for the appeal courts to accept the judgment of the trial judge, who had the benefit of hearing all the witnesses.[143] Since that was not possible here, however, the House went on to determine the 'reasonableness' issue itself. It approached it as an exercise in 'balancing' various factors against each other. On the one hand, the clause was a common one in the trade, and had never been objected to by the National Union of Farmers. Moreover, the magnitude of the damage in proportion to the price of the goods sold also weighed in the defendants' favour. Lord Bridge, however, found three matters to put into the other side of the balance. First, the fact that the wrong seed was supplied was due to negligence (albeit of the defendants' sister company, rather than the defendants themselves). Second, the trial judge had found that the defendants would have been able to take out insurance against crop failure, without needing to increase the price of the seeds significantly. Third, and in Lord Bridge's view most importantly, there was evidence from a number of witnesses (including the chairman of the defendants) that it was general practice in the trade not to rely on this clause in cases like the one which the House was considering, but to negotiate more substantial compensation. As Lord Bridge put it:[144]

> This evidence indicates a clear recognition by seedsmen in general, and the [defendants] in particular, that reliance on the limitation of liability imposed by the relevant condition would not be fair and reasonable.

This indicates that where the courts are dealing with a common type of contract within a particular area of business activity, the practices of the trade or business are likely to be of considerable relevance. In addition, the fact that all the circumstances must be considered, and that the appeal courts are reluctant to interfere with decisions of the trial judge, means that it is not necessarily the case that because a particular exclusion clause has been found unreasonable in one situation, it will be precluded from use in others.[145] This element of uncertainty will pull in two directions. It will make those who wish to include exclusion clauses cautious, and may encourage them to word clauses narrowly and precisely. On the other hand, the claimant who wishes to challenge a clause may well be deterred by the fact that the outcome of such a challenge will be very unpredictable.

### 7.7.13 THE UCTA 1977 IN THE HOUSE OF LORDS

The second prominent House of Lords case which has discussed the concept of 'reasonableness' is *Smith v Eric S Bush*.[146] The case concerned a 'disclaimer' of liability for negligence put forward by a surveyor carrying out a valuation of a property for a building society, which was relied on by the purchaser of the property. Having decided that this disclaimer did constitute an exclusion clause, by virtue of s 13 of the UCTA 1977,[147] the

---

143  See the comments of the Court of Appeal to the same effect in *Phillips Products Ltd v Hyland* [1987] 2 All ER 620.

144  [1983] 2 AC 803, p 817; [1983] 2 All ER 737, p 744.

145  Compare *RÖHLIG (UK) Ltd v Rock Unique Ltd* [2011] EWCA Civ 18 at [23] where Moore-Bick LJ noted: "In principle the question must be considered separately in each case because the circumstances surrounding the contract may differ from case to case, but where a standard condition of this kind is involved I do not think that the court should be astute to draw fine distinctions between cases that in broad terms are very similar. It is important for those engaged in any commercial activity, whether as providers of goods or services or as customers, to know whether a particular clause will generally be regarded as reasonable in the context of contracts of a routine kind made between commercial parties."

146  [1990] 1 AC 831; [1989] 2 All ER 514.

147  See above, 7.7.4.

House then had to consider whether it satisfied the requirement of reasonableness. The factors that were considered relevant to this issue were set out most clearly in the speech of Lord Griffiths. He thought that there were four matters that should *always* be considered in deciding this issue. They were as follows:

(a) Were the parties of equal bargaining power? (This also appears in the guidelines in Sched 2 to the UCTA 1977.)

(b) In the case of advice, would it have been reasonably practicable to obtain the advice from an alternative source, taking into account considerations of costs and time? In this case, although the purchaser could have obtained another survey, it was relevant that the house was 'at the bottom end of the market', which made it less reasonable to expect the purchaser to pay for a second opinion.

(c) How difficult is the task being undertaken for which liability is being excluded? The more difficult or dangerous the undertaking, the more reasonable it may be to exclude liability.

(d) What are the practical consequences of the decision on reasonableness? For example, if the risk is one against which a defendant could quite easily have insured, but which will have very serious effects on a claimant who is required to bear the loss, this will suggest that exclusion is unreasonable. It might be otherwise if a finding of liability would 'open the floodgates' to claims.

With these considerations in mind and, in addition, the fact that this was an individual private house purchase, not a deal in relation to commercial property, the House decided that the disclaimer of liability did not meet the requirement of reasonableness.

### 7.7.14 INEQUALITY OF BARGAINING POWER

It is clear from the Sched 2 guidelines and the points made by the House of Lords in *Smith v Bush* that inequality of bargaining power is an important factor in deciding on the question of 'reasonableness'.[148] The existence of inequality does not, however, automatically render any exclusion unreasonable. This was illustrated by *Snookes v Jani-King (GB) Ltd*.[149] A clause in a franchise agreement stated that any proceedings relating to the agreement should 'be brought in a court of competent jurisdiction in London'. The claimant started proceedings in Swansea, and the defendants applied to strike out the claim on the basis that the Swansea court did not have jurisdiction. The claimant pleaded that the clause requiring claims to be brought in London was an unfair term under the UCTA 1977. The judge accepted that the clause was contained within the defendants' written standard terms and so potentially fell within s 3 of UCTA. He held, however, that the defendants had proved that the clause satisfied the test of reasonableness, taking into account the factors listed in Sched 2. Although the defendants were in the stronger bargaining position, this did not make the clause automatically unreasonable. The claimant had had plenty of time to object to the clause before signing the agreement and, since the claimant was based in Birmingham, a requirement to take action in London was not unduly onerous. It was not relevant that the defendants had not raised the clause in defending actions brought by other claimants. Overall the clause was reasonable.

### 7.7.15 'REASONABLENESS' IN THE COURT OF APPEAL

Several Court of Appeal decisions have involved a consideration of the test of reasonableness. Two of these, *Phillips Products Ltd v Hyland*[150] and *Thompson v T Lohan (Plant Hire)*

---

148  See also *Lloyd v Browning* [2013] EWCA Civ 1637.
149  [2006] ILPr 18.
150  [1987] 2 All ER 620.

*Ltd*,[151] involved differing interpretations of the same clause, but did not add significantly to the guidelines on how the test should be applied as indicated by the *George Mitchell v Finney Lock Seeds* and *Smith v Bush* decisions.

In *Phillips Products Ltd v Hyland*, however, Slade LJ noted, and followed, the injunction from Lord Bridge in *George Mitchell* that appeal courts should be very reluctant to interfere with the trial judge on this issue. Lord Bridge, having pointed out that the test of reasonableness involves a balancing of considerations, commented:[152]

> There will sometimes be room for a legitimate difference of judicial opinion as to what the answer should be, where it will be impossible to say that one view is demonstrably wrong, and the other demonstrably right. It must follow, in my view, that, when asked to review such a decision on appeal, the appellate court should treat the original decision with the utmost respect and refrain from interference with it unless satisfied that it proceeded on some erroneous principle or was plainly and obviously wrong.

With this in mind, Slade LJ concentrated his consideration of the first instance judgment on the issue of whether the judge had directed himself to the correct issues. Given that he appeared to have done so, and that his conclusion was not 'plainly or obviously wrong', the court did not feel it appropriate to interfere. It also followed from this approach, however, that:[153]

> our conclusion on the particular facts of this case should not be treated as a binding precedent in other cases where similar clauses fall to be considered but the evidence of the surrounding circumstances may be very different.

Subsequent Court of Appeal decisions have, however, given some further guidance as to factors that are relevant in applying the test. In *Schenkers Ltd v Overland Shoes Ltd*,[154] the clause was contained in the standard trading conditions of the British International Freight Association (BIFA). The Court of Appeal felt that it was relevant, particularly where the parties were of equal bargaining power, that the clause was one that was in common use and well known in the trade. It could therefore be taken to reflect a general view as to what was reasonable in the trade concerned. Although in *George Mitchell v Finney Lock* it had been found that there was an expectation in the trade that an exclusion clause that was in common use would not in practice be relied on, that had not been shown to be the case here. Although there was 'no ready or frequent resort to the clause', there was no evidence of a recognition in the trade that the clause was unreasonable.

The second case is *Overseas Medical Supplies Ltd v Orient Transport Services Ltd*,[155] which was also concerned with a clause (though a different one) contained in BIFA's standard trading conditions. The trial judge in this case held that the clause was unreasonable, and this was upheld by the Court of Appeal. In coming to that conclusion, Potter LJ outlined various factors that are relevant to the decision on reasonableness.[156] He pointed to eight relevant issues, namely: (1) the way in which the relevant conditions came into being (for example, whether they are part of the standard conditions used in a particular trade); (2) the guidelines in Sched 2 to the UCTA 1977 (even where the

---

151  [1987] 2 All ER 631.
152  [1983] 2 AC 803, p 816; [1983] 2 All ER 737, p 743.
153  [1987] 2 All ER 620, p 630.
154  [1998] 1 Lloyd's Rep 498.
155  [1999] 2 Lloyd's Rep 273.
156  Ibid, p 277.

contract is not concerned with sale of goods, and is not a consumer transaction); (3) in relation to equality of bargaining position, the question of whether the customer was obliged to use the services of the supplier and how far it would have been practical or convenient to go elsewhere; (4) the clause must be viewed as a whole, rather than taking any particular part of it in isolation. It must also be viewed 'against a breach of contract which is the subject matter of the present case' (but see the comment on this below); (5) the reality of the consent of the customer to the supplier's clause; (6) in cases of limitation, the size of the limit in comparison with other limits in widely used standard terms; (7) the availability of insurance (though this is by no means a decisive factor); and (8) the presence of a term allowing for an option to contract without the limitation clause but with an increase in price.

All of these factors are sensible ones for the court to consider. In relation to the second sentence of (4) above, however, which derives from *AEG Ltd v Logic Resource Ltd*,[157] it seems to be incompatible with the wording of s 11 of the UCTA 1977, which, as we have seen,[158] states that the test is whether the clause was a reasonable one to include in the contract having regard to the parties' state of knowledge at that time. The nature of the breach that has actually occurred ought therefore not to be relevant to the assessment of the reasonableness of the clause. The statement to the contrary by Potter LJ is clearly *obiter*, and it is submitted that it should not be relied upon pending further clarification by the appellate courts.

In both *Schenkers Ltd v Overland Shoes Ltd* and *Overseas Medical Supplies Ltd v Orient Transport Services Ltd*, the Court of Appeal again emphasised that the appeal courts should be reluctant to interfere with a decision on this issue by the trial judge, and in both cases upheld the first instance decision. Appealing decisions on 'reasonableness' may often turn out to be a fruitless exercise. In *Watford Electronics Ltd v Sanderson CFL Ltd*,[159] however, the Court of Appeal did intervene to find that a clause that the trial judge had regarded as unreasonable was in fact reasonable. Intervention was justified because the judge had misdirected himself on the proper basis for applying the reasonableness test; it was not, therefore, simply a disagreement on the result of applying the proper test, where intervention would presumably not generally be appropriate.

---

**Key case** *Watford Electronics Ltd v Sanderson CFL Ltd* (2001)

Facts: The contract was for the supply of computer software. It turned out not to function properly and caused the purchaser substantial losses. The supplier had included a clause excluding its liability for indirect and consequential losses, and limiting any compensation to a refund of the purchase price. The trial judge held that the supplier could not rely on these clauses because they failed the 'reasonableness' test. The supplier appealed.

Held: In deciding that these provisions were not unreasonable, the Court of Appeal took account of the fact that there had been considerable negotiation and the purchaser had, as a result, gained the inclusion of a 'best endeavours' clause; there was no significant difference in bargaining power between the parties; and the purchaser had used similar limitation clauses in its own contracts, thus indicating that it was aware of the fact that such clauses were used to allocate liabilities. Chadwick LJ concluded:[160]

---

157 [1996] CLC 265, CA.
158 See above, 7.7.10.
159 [2001] EWCA Civ 317; [2001] 1 All ER Comm 696.
160 [2001] EWCA Civ 317; [2001] 1 All ER Comm 696, para 55.

> Where experienced businessmen representing substantial companies of equal bargaining power negotiate an agreement, they may be taken to have had regard to the matters known to them. They should in my view be taken to be the best judge of the commercial fairness of the agreement which they have made; including the fairness of each of the terms in that agreement. They should be taken to be the best judge on the question whether the terms of the agreement are reasonable. The court should not assume that either is likely to commit his company to an agreement which he thinks is unfair, or which he thinks includes unreasonable terms. Unless satisfied that one party has, in effect, taken unfair advantage of the other – or that a term is so unreasonable that it cannot properly have been understood or considered – the court should not interfere.

This suggests a very 'hands-off' approach to the supervision of exclusion and limitation clauses in business contracts. A similar view was taken by the Court of Appeal in *Granville Oil & Chemicals Ltd v Davis Turner & Co Ltd*[161] in considering whether cl 30(B) of the British International Freight Association's Standard Trading Conditions met the requirement of 'reasonableness' under s 11 of the UCTA 1977. The clause required that if written notice of legal action was not given within nine months of the event giving rise to it, then the other party was discharged from liability. The judge had found that this clause was unreasonable, because he held that it could be used in relation to a situation where fraud was involved, and where the defendant had fraudulently concealed facts giving rise to the claim. The Court of Appeal disagreed. It held that the clause should not be interpreted to cover fraudulent behaviour and that it was therefore reasonable. The most interesting aspect of the judgment, however, is probably the final paragraph of the judgment of Tuckey LJ, in which he again confirmed the reluctance of the appeal courts to interfere in commercial agreements. He commented:

> I am pleased to reach this decision. The 1977 Act obviously plays a very important role in protecting vulnerable consumers from the effects of draconian contract terms. But I am less enthusiastic about its intrusion into contracts between commercial parties of equal bargaining strength, who should generally be considered capable of being able to make contracts of their choosing and expect to be bound by their terms.

Further confirmation of the Court of Appeal's reluctance to find clauses in commercial contracts unreasonable is to be found in *Regus (UK) Ltd v Epcot Solutions Ltd*.[162] The relevant clause stated that the defendants would not 'in any circumstances have any liability for loss of business, loss of profits, loss of anticipated savings, loss of or damage to data, third party claims, or any consequential loss'. The trial judge had found this unreasonable on the basis that it left the defendant with no liability whatsoever. The Court of Appeal disagreed. The clause would not be interpreted to cover breaches caused maliciously or fraudulently. Taking account of the fact that the contract had been freely negotiated, that the parties were of equal bargaining power, and that the claimants would probably have been in a better position to insure against the losses referred to in the clause than the defendants, the court concluded that the clause did satisfy the requirement of reasonableness.

---

161 [2003] EWCA Civ 570; [2003] 2 Lloyd's Rep 356.
162 [2008] EWCA Civ 361.

There seems, then, to be a general view at Court of Appeal level that intervention in commercial agreements on the basis of the UCTA 1977 should be a rare event. Two other recent cases show that trial judges nevertheless continue to be prepared to hold a clause unreasonable when they think that it is necessary to do so.

The Court of Appeal line was largely followed by the trial judge in *obiter* statements in *Sterling Hydraulics Ltd v Dichtomatik Ltd*.[163] The exclusion clause in a supply contract limited the supplier's liability to the contract price. This was reasonable given that the supplier was unaware of the precise purpose for which the product was to be used. A provision requiring claims based on hidden defects to be notified within a week of discovering the defect was, however, found to be unreasonable. An even more interventionist approach was taken in *Balmoral Group Ltd v Borealis (UK) Ltd*.[164] The contract was again one for the supply of goods, but the clause in this case had the effect of removing all liability on the part of the supplier for defects in the goods. The trial judge noted the comments in the *Granville Oil* case about the need to allow business parties to allocate their own risks, but held that this blanket exclusion of liability, judged at the time of the contract when the outcome of any breach would be uncertain, did not satisfy the requirement of reasonableness.

## For thought

*How should the courts decide when, exceptionally, to intervene in business contracts? Should they be looking primarily at the balance of power between the parties, or is it the scope of the clause that should be the determining factor in relation to 'reasonableness'?*

### 7.7.16 EXCLUSIONS OR RESTRICTIONS IN CONTRACTS FOR THE SUPPLY OF GOODS

Exclusion or restriction of the statutory implied terms in sale of goods contracts under the Sale of Goods Act (SGA) 1979[165] and their equivalent in hire purchase contracts under the Supply of Goods (Implied Terms) Act 1973 are currently governed by s 6 of the UCTA 1977. There is a total prohibition on the exclusion or restriction of liability for breach of the implied term as to title (s 12 of the 1979 Act and s 8 of the 1973 Act). For example, an individually negotiated provision in a contract between two businesses dealing on an equal footing that attempts to limit liability for breach of this implied term will nevertheless be treated as ineffective. Equally, although the Act is normally concerned only with 'business liability', s 6(4) of the UCTA 1977 extends the scope of s 6(1) to non-business contracts. If a contract between two private individuals contains an attempt to exclude s 12 of the 1979 Act or s 8 of the 1973 Act, this will also be ineffective. The broad scope of this provision can only be justified on the basis that the implied term as to title in contracts for the supply of goods is so fundamental that any attempt to exclude or limit liability in relation to it cannot be countenanced.

As regards the implied terms as to quality, there can be no exclusion or limitation of liability under s 13 SGA 1979 (description), s 14 SGA 1979 (satisfactory quality, fitness for particular purpose) or s 15 SGA 1979 (sample), or under the equivalent provisions in ss 9–11 of the 1973 Act unless it satisfies the 'requirement of reasonableness' under s 11.[166] The test of reasonableness also applies to an attempt to exclude the implied term as to

---

163  [2006] EWHC 2004, [2007] 1 Lloyd's Rep 8.
164  [2006] EWHC 2531, [2006] CLC 220.
165  For which, see Chapter 6, 6.6.10–6.6.16.
166  See above, 7.7.10.

description by a non-business supplier.[167] Terms similar to those implied by the SGA 1979 into sale of goods contracts are implied into other contracts under which the possession or ownership of goods passes by the Supply of Goods and Services Act 1982. This covers contracts of hire, and contracts for the supply or work and materials.[168] Section 7 of the UCTA 1977 applies similar restrictions on exclusion or restriction of liability for breach of these terms as are contained in s 6 in relation to sale of goods and hire purchase contracts. There can be no exclusion or restriction of liability for breach of an implied term as to title arising under s 2(1) of the 1982 Act. Where s 2(1) does not apply, any implied term as to the right to transfer ownership, possession or to guarantee quiet possession can only be excluded in so far as it satisfies the requirement of reasonableness.[169] As regards implied terms as to description, quality, fitness for purpose or compliance with sample, the position is the same as under s 6 – that is any clause must satisfy the requirement of reasonableness.[170]

### 7.7.17 EXCLUSION OF LIABILITY FOR MISREPRESENTATION

There are special provisions emanating from s 8 of the UCTA 1977 in relation to liability for misrepresentations. These are dealt with in Chapter 8.[171]

## 7.8 THE CONSUMER RIGHTS ACT 2015

From 1 July 1995, certain contracts have been subject to control deriving from the European Directive on Unfair Terms in Consumer Contracts.[172] The first set of Regulations was issued in 1994 (Unfair Terms in Consumer Contracts Regulations (UTCCR) 1994) but a revised set replaced these in 1999 (Unfair Terms in Consumer Contracts Regulations (UTCCR) 1999). More recently the UTCCR 1999 were repealed, subject to transitional arrangements, by the Consumer Rights Act 2015 (CRA 2015) and replaced by provisions contained (largely) in Part 2 of the CRA 2015. A number of the provisions in Part 2 of the CRA 2015 resemble those under the UTCCR 1999 but, as is allowed in the transposition of a minimum harmonisation directive, some extensions have been enacted. The Act also takes the opportunity to attempt to 'codify' an aspect of ECJ/ CJEU jurisprudence (see *Pannon GSM Zrt v Erzsé bet Sustikné Györfi*)[173] requiring in appropriate circumstances a court to consider 'unfairness' in proceedings of its own motion:

> 71 Duty of court to consider fairness of term
>
> (1) Subsection (2) applies to proceedings before a court which relate to a term of a consumer contract.
> (2) The court must consider whether the term is fair even if none of the parties to the proceedings has raised that issue or indicated that it intends to raise it.
> (3) But subsection (2) does not apply unless the court considers that it has before it sufficient legal and factual material to enable it to consider the fairness of the term.[174]

---

167 UCTA 1977, s 6(4). The implied terms in s 14 SGA 1979 only apply to sales in the course of a business.
168 For example, under a contract to build a wall, the ownership of the bricks will pass.
169 Section 7(3A) and (4).
170 Sections 7(1A).
171 See 8.5.
172 Directive 93/13/EC.
173 (C-243/08) [2009] ECR I-4713.
174 Compare *Cabot Financial UK Ltd v McGregor, Gardner and Brown* [2018] SAC (Civ) 12 on undefended actions.

### 7.8.1 APPLICATION OF PART 2 OF THE CRA 2015

By virtue of s 61, Part 2 of the CRA 2015 applies to contracts 'between a trader and a consumer'. The definition of a consumer for the purpose of Part 2 of the CRA 2015 is found in s 2(3), which states that a consumer 'means an individual acting for purposes that are wholly or mainly outside that individual's trade, business, craft or profession'.[175] Unlike the UCTA 1977, the CRA 2015 does not apply to business-to-business (B2B) contracts; and only a natural person, not a company, can be a consumer for the purpose of Part 2 of the CRA 2015 (the position as was otherwise under the pre-CRA 2015 version of UCTA 1977 (which had provisions relating to 'consumer' contracts): see *R and B Customs Brokers v* UDT).[176] The definition of a trader is found in s 2(2): 'a person acting for purposes relating to that person's trade, business, craft or profession, whether acting personally or through another person acting in the trader's name or on the trader's behalf'.

In one sense the CRA 2015 is broader than the UCTA 1977 in that it applies to a wide variety of contract terms, not just exclusion/limitation clauses. Moreover, in contrast to the UTCCR 1999, Part 2 of the CRA 2015 applies to both individually and non-individually negotiated terms; although the practical significance of this is unclear given that one would expect consumers to often deal of the other party's standard terms. Overall freedom of contract in relation to the content of consumer contracts has been significantly curtailed since 1995.[177]

On the other hand, s 73 provides that Part 2 of the CRA 2015 does not apply to contract terms inserted into the contract in compliance with a statutory or regulatory requirement or an international convention.[178] Nor does it apply to all types of contract.[179]

### 7.8.2 TERMS ATTACKED[180]

S 62(1) of the CRA 2015 provides that an 'unfair term' in a consumer contract 'shall not be binding on the consumer'. The test of 'unfairness' is contained in s 62(4):

> A term is unfair if, contrary to the requirement of good faith, it causes a significant imbalance in the parties' rights and obligations under the contract to the detriment of the consumer.

This definition, with its reference to 'good faith', reveals the European origins of this provision. Consumer law in England and Wales has no general concept of 'good faith' and so when the UTCCR 1994 (to which CRA 2015, s 62(4) can be traced) first came into force, there was debate about how the courts might treat this definition, and it was argued that they would concentrate on the questions of 'imbalance' and 'detriment', which were more familiar to them. The UTCCR 1994 contained a schedule setting out

---

175  In *Ashfaq v International Insurance Co of Hannover Plc* [2017] EWCA Civ 357 the Court of Appeal held that a person who, in addition to being a director of an information technology company, let out a property to students was not a consumer in respect of obtaining insurance for that property.

176  [1998] 1 All ER 847.

177  Although the CRA 2015 only has limited application to terms dealing with main subject matter and the price: s 64 – see below.

178  In *Jones v Roundlistic Ltd* [2018] EWCA Civ 2284 the Court of Appeal held that this meant statutory or regulatory provisions which prescribed the terms *and* the content of those terms.

179  See s 66(2) – it generally does not apply to employment contracts.

180  It is important to note that some terms (for example terms purporting to exclude liability for breach of some of the statutory terms included in contracts to supply goods between a trader and a seller) are prohibited outright. See s 62(8): '(8) This section does not affect the operation of – (a) section 31 (exclusion of liability: goods contracts), (b) section 47 (exclusion of liability: digital content contracts), (c) section 57 (exclusion of liability: services contracts), or (d) section 65 (exclusion of negligence liability).'

**Table 7.1** Comparison Table UCTA1977 and CRA 2015

| UCTA 1977 | CRA 2015 |
|---|---|
| Applies to non-consumer contracts | Applies to consumer contracts only |
| Applies to many types of term | Applies to many types of term |
| Some clauses are automatically made void and others are subject to the test of 'reasonableness' – s 11 UCTA1977 | Terms are subject to a test of 'unfairness' – CRA 2015, s 62(4) |

some factors that the court should have regard to in assessing the issue of good faith. These were:

(a) the strength of the bargaining position of the parties;
(b) whether the consumer had an inducement to agree to the term;
(c) whether the goods or services were sold or supplied to the special order of the consumer; and
(d) the extent to which the seller or supplier has dealt fairly and equitably with the consumer.

This list was not reproduced in the UTCCR 1999, although it was hard to believe, however, that the factors listed would not in practice have been amongst those that a court considered in assessing 'good faith'. S 62(5) provides:

Whether a term is fair is to be determined -

(a) taking into account the nature of the subject matter of the contract, and
(b) by reference to all the circumstances existing when the term was agreed and to all of the other terms of the contract or of any other contract on which it depends.

The first reported case on the UTCCR 1994, *Director General of Fair Trading v First National Bank plc*,[181] concerned a term in a loan agreement issued by a bank.

---

**Key case** *Director General of Fair Trading v First National Bank plc (2002)*

Facts: A loan agreement issued by the bank provided that if the consumer defaulted on an instalment, the full amount of the loan became payable. This is not unusual, but the term to which exception was taken, and about which the Director General received complaints, was to the effect that interest on the outstanding debt would remain payable even after a judgment of the court. Thus, a court might order the consumer to pay off the debt by specified instalments, but the effect of the contract was that interest would continue to accrue at the contractual rate while the instalments were being paid. The Director took legal action against the Bank, alleging that the term was in breach of the Unfair Terms in Consumer Contract Regulations 1994. The Court of Appeal concluded that the term created 'unfair surprise' and did not meet the requirement of 'good faith'. The Bank appealed to the House of Lords.

---

181 [2001] UKHL 52; [2002] 1 All ER 97.

Held: The House of Lords overturned the Court of Appeal's decision. Lord Bingham, with whom the other members of the House agreed, in interpreting what was Regulation 4(1) and is now essentially s 62 CRA 2015 (hence the continuing significance of this case), dealt with the requirements of 'significant imbalance' and 'good faith' separately. As regards the first factor he stated:[182]

The requirement of significant imbalance is met if a term is so weighted in favour of the supplier as to tilt the parties' rights and obligations under the contract significantly in his favour. This may be by the granting to the supplier of a beneficial option or discretion or power, or by the imposing on the consumer of a disadvantageous burden or risk or duty.

This test is concerned with the substance of the agreement, and requires consideration of the contract as a whole. 'Good faith', on the other hand, as far as Lord Bingham was concerned, seemed to be more concerned with procedural fairness:[183]

The requirement of good faith in this context is one of fair and open dealing. Openness requires that the terms should be expressed fully, clearly and legibly, containing no concealed pitfalls or traps. Appropriate prominence should be given to terms which might operate disadvantageously to the customer. Fair dealing requires that a supplier should not, whether deliberately or unconsciously, take advantage of the consumer's necessity, indigence, lack of experience, unfamiliarity with the subject matter of the contract, weak bargaining position, or any other factors listed in or analogous to those listed in Schedule 2 to the Regulations.

The test was therefore a composite one, 'covering both the making and the substance of the contract'. Applying the tests of 'significant imbalance' and 'good faith' to the clause before it, the House was unanimous that it did not contravene the Regulations. The provision for interest to be payable after judgment was not in itself unusual. The problems were created by the legislative framework, which restricted the power of the court to award interest when giving a creditor time to pay a debt by instalments, rather than by the contractual provision itself. It was the powers and procedures relating to the making of orders that needed to be addressed.[184]

Lord Steyn, while agreeing with Lord Bingham, took the view that 'good faith' was concerned with substance as well as procedure, and will therefore overlap with the test of 'significant imbalance':[185]

The examples given in Schedule 3 convincingly demonstrate that the argument of the bank that good faith is predominantly concerned with procedural defects in

---

182  Ibid, [17]; p 107.

183  Ibid, [17]; p 108.

184  In particular, there was a need to draw attention to the courts' powers under the Consumer Credit Act 1974, ss 129 and 136, which would allow it in appropriate circumstances to amend contractual provisions when making a 'time order' for the payment of a debt. This would allow the court to incorporate the recovery of interest into the calculation of instalment payments.

185  [2002] UKHL 52, paras 36–37; [2002] 1 All ER 97, p 113. Compare also *Du Plessis v Fontgary Leisure Parks Limited* [2012] EWCA Civ 409 and *Spreadex Ltd v Cochrane* [2012] EWHC 1290. More recently in *Cavendish Square Holding BV v Talal El Makdessi; ParkingEye Limited v Beavis* [2015] UKSC 67 Lord Neuberger and Lord Sumption: (with whom Lord Carnwath agreed) referred to a concept of 'legitimate interest' in finding that a parking fine was not unfair (the full facts are given at 15.7).

negotiating procedures cannot be sustained. Any purely procedural or even predominantly procedural interpretation of good faith must be rejected.

It is submitted that Lord Steyn's approach is preferable and more in accordance with the wording of the regulation, which makes 'significant imbalance' an element within an overall test of 'good faith'. The other members of the House, however, in concurring with Lord Bingham, expressed no specific view on the issue, so it must be taken that his analysis reflects the view of the majority. In practice, given that substantive issues are clearly raised by the 'significant imbalance' test, it probably does not matter in relation to these Regulations that 'good faith' is treated as primarily a procedural requirement. In other contexts, however, it might be important to give 'good faith' a role in considering the substantive effect of contractual provisions, rather than simply the procedures surrounding their adoption.

The CRA 2015 contain another type of guidance for the courts, which was also in the UTCCR 1994/1999 (in UTCCR 1994, Sched 3, as referred to by Lord Steyn in the passage quoted above, and in UTCCR 1999, Sched 2). This is contained in Sched 2 to the CRA 2015 and consists of an 'indicative and illustrative' list of terms that may be regarded as unfair. The inclusion of a term on the list does not necessarily mean that *any* clause of that type will be unfair: it will depend on the context in which it is put forward. Nor, on the other hand, is the list exhaustive. A clause of a type that does not appear in it may nevertheless be found to be unfair. The list contained in the Schedule is lengthy, and there is not space to reproduce it in full here. It contains some provisions that are familiar from the controls imposed by the UCTA 1977, such as clauses allowing the seller or supplier to provide inadequate performance, or a different product or service from that contracted for. Other provisions reflect the common law rules relating to exclusion clauses, such as the restriction on clauses with which the consumer had no real opportunity of becoming acquainted before the contract. In general, the list is concerned with clauses that allow the seller or supplier to impose on the consumer, for example, by allowing the seller or supplier to cancel the contract without notice, or giving the seller or supplier exclusive rights of interpretation, or requiring the consumer to pay disproportionately high compensation for a breach.

### For thought

*Is the test of 'unfairness' under the CRA 2015 significantly different in substance from the test of 'reasonableness' under UCTA?*

The UTCCR 1994/1999 did not apply to simply bad bargains. Nor were certain terms assessable for 'fairness'. For example, UTCCR 1999 regulation 6(2) (which could be traced to Art 4(2) of the relevant Directive) provided that clauses that defined the main subject matter of the contract, or concerned the adequacy of the price or remuneration for goods or services supplied, would not be assessed for 'fairness', provided they met the criterion of intelligibility.[186] The consumer who agreed to pay over the odds for goods or services would generally not have been helped by these Regulations. This limitation applied only to terms that fall within the wording of regulation 6(2) and the wider the interpretation of regulation 6(2), the fewer terms would have been subject to the test of 'unfairness' under

---

186  See below, 7.8.3.

UTCCR 1999. In *Director General of Fair Trading v First National Bank plc*[187] the House of Lords noted with approval the distinction drawn by Chitty between 'terms which express the substance of the bargain and "incidental" (if important) terms which surround them'.[188] Applying this approach, it held that a term in a credit agreement relating to interest payable after a judgment had been obtained against the debtor was 'ancillary' and not 'concerned with the adequacy of the bank's remuneration as against the services supplied'.[189] On that basis, the term was not within the scope of Regulation 6(2)[190] and the fairness of the clause had to be considered.

The approach taken in this case suggested that courts would take a narrow view of what was within the scope of regulation 6(2). A similarly narrow approach to the scope of regulation 6(2) was taken in *Bairstow Eves London Central Ltd v Smith*.[191] The High Court held that a provision whereby an estate agent's commission doubled from 1.5 per cent to 3 per cent in the event of late payment fell within the scope of the fairness provisions of the Regulations (and was found to be unfair). This was so, even though the format of the provision was to state that the standard commission was 3 per cent with a reduction for early payment.

By contrast, in *Office of Fair Trading v Abbey National plc*[192] the Supreme Court held that charges levied by banks on current accounts, including overdraft excess charges (payable when a customer exceeds an agreed overdraft or goes overdrawn without having arranged an overdraft), were part of the price for the banking services provided. As such they were within the scope of regulation 6(2) and so not susceptible to challenge by the Office of Fair Trading under the Regulations. In so doing, the Supreme Court expressed some caution on the distinction, which had been used in relation to regulation 6(2), between 'core' and 'ancillary' terms.[193] Overall the decision in *Office of Fair Trading v Abbey National plc* was met with some surprise;[194] in particular it might be argued that it risked applying the exclusion from the test of unfairness too widely. Indeed it was even suggested that the approach in this case could be contrary to EU Law:

> We think that the words of the judgment may be lulling some businesses into a false sense of security. There are other ways to interpret the judgment – and it could be overturned by the Court of Justice of the European Union (CJEU). The German Federal Supreme Court takes a different view on the UTD and has reviewed

---

187 [2002] UKHL 52; [2002] 1 All ER 97.

188 Ibid, para 11; p 105, quoting Chitty, 2004, para 15.025.

189 [2002] UKHL 52; [2002] 1 All ER 97.

190 Note that the House of Lords was in fact considering the 1994 version of the Regulations, where the relevant regulation was reg 4(2).

191 [2004] EWHC 263.

192 [2009] UKSC 6; [2010] 1 AC 696.

193 See, for example, [38] and [44] *per* Lord Walker.

194 Compare, in the context of gym membership, the judgment of Kitchen J in *Office of Fair Trading v Ashbourne Management Services Ltd* [2011] EWHC 1237 (Ch), which appears to have a different flavour: "This brings me to the final part of the analysis, namely whether this assessment of fairness relates to the definition of the main subject matter of the agreements. In my judgment it does not. The assessment does not relate to the meaning or description of the length of the minimum period, the facilities to which the member gains access or the monthly subscription which he has to pay; nor does it relate to the adequacy of the price as against the facilities provided. Instead it relates to the obligation upon members to pay monthly subscriptions for the minimum period when they have overestimated the use they will make of their memberships and failed to appreciate that unforeseen circumstances may make their continued use of a gym impractical or their memberships unaffordable. Put another way, it relates to the consequences to members of early termination in light of the minimum membership period. Accordingly I believe the assessment is not precluded by regulation 6(2)."

ancillary bank charges for fairness ... In a world of price comparison websites, there is increasing pressure on traders to advertise low headline prices, whilst earning their profits through other charges. Given this potential undermining of competition, the law should provide effective tools to prevent abuse ... The current uncertainty has the potential to damage businesses as well as consumers.[195]

The CRA 2015, s 64 now provides:

(1)    A term of a consumer contract may not be assessed for fairness under section 62 to the extent that -
    (a)    it specifies the main subject matter of the contract, or
    (b)    the assessment is of the appropriateness of the price payable under the contract by comparison with the goods, digital content or services supplied under it.
(2)    Subsection (1) excludes a term from an assessment under section 62 only if it is transparent and prominent.

In, at least, two respects this provision appears to reinforce aspects of *Office of Fair Trading v Abbey National Plc*. First, s 64(1)(b) clearly inclines to Lord Walker's view that only monetary payment terms are caught by Art 4(2) of the Directive. Secondly, s 64(2) states that '[s]ubsection (1) excludes a term from an assessment under section 62 only if it is transparent and prominent' which chimes with the analysis of *Office of Fair Trading v Foxtons*[196] by the Supreme Court in *Office of Fair Trading v Abbey National Plc*. Yet the bigger issue is whether the controversial reading of the exclusions from the test of unfairness in Art 4(2) of the Directive by the Supreme Court in *Office of Fair Trading v Abbey National Plc* should be used, notwithstanding Brexit, in relation to s 64(1)(b) of the CRA 2015.

The legislative history of s 64 suggests an intention that such an approach should be retained. More specifically s 64 can be traced back to the Law Commission's advice that the issues surrounding the impact of *Office of Fair Trading v Abbey National Plc* could be dealt with by the use of transparency and prominence requirements (rather than reverting to a previous interpretation of provisions transposing Art 4(2)).[197]

Leaving aside the concepts of transparency and prominence (which we shall return to below), this approach creates a number of problems. Indeed, as the Law Commission recognised, it is far from clear that such an approach is in conformity with EU law. Furthermore, subsequent judgments of the CJEU have cast more suspicion on the appropriateness of the approach in *Office of Fair Trading v Abbey National Plc*. For example in *Kásler v OTP Jelzálogbank Zrt*[198] the Court of Justice of the European Union (CJEU), in the context of a consumer credit agreement, held that a term that provided the exchange rate for the repayment of a loan in a foreign currency could be assessed for unfairness:

---

195  Law Commission, *Unfair Terms in Consumer Contracts: Advice to the Department for Business, Innovation and Skills* (2013) at s 11ff.
196  [2009] EWHC 1681.
197  Law Commission, *Unfair Terms in Consumer Contracts: Advice to the Department for Business, Innovation and Skills* (2013) at s 11ff. In *Casehub Limited v Wolf Cola Limited* [2017] EWHC 1169 (Ch) it was held, relying on *Office of Fair Trading v Abbey National plc*, that cancellation fees in respect of a 12 month cloud storage contract could not, as a result of s.64, be assessed for fairness if that meant assessing the appropriateness of the price in comparison with the services supplied. However, such clauses might have been challenged as unfair on other grounds.
198  (C-26/13) [2014] 2 All ER (Comm) 443.

in so far as it contains a pecuniary obligation for the consumer to pay, in repayment instalments of the loan, the difference between the selling rate of exchange and the buying rate of exchange of the foreign currency, cannot be considered as 'remuneration', the adequacy of which as consideration for a service supplied by the lender cannot be subject of an examination as regards unfairness under Article 4(2).[199]

Given the incomplete nature of the map left by the Supreme Court, it is not easy to compare the approach of the CJEU in *Kásler v OTP Jelzálogbank Zrt* with the approach in *Office of Fair Trading v Abbey National Plc*. Nevertheless the approach of the CJEU does appear to be more nuanced than the rather more blunt focus on monetary terms by the Supreme Court.

### 7.8.3 THE TRANSPARENCY REQUIREMENT

S 68 applies to all written terms (including terms excluded by s 64) and requires the trader to ensure that the terms are transparent. S 64(3) provides that '[a] term is transparent for the purposes of this Part if it is expressed in plain and intelligible language and (in the case of a written term) is legible.' The problem with the provision is that it does not explicitly prescribe any sanction for breach and therefore its status as a requirement remains unclear. Note, however, that the Competition and Markets Authority (CMA) guidance on Part 2 of the CRA 2015 draws a link between the unfairness test and the requirement of transparency:

> In order to achieve the openness required by good faith, terms should be 'expressed fully, clearly and legibly, containing no concealed pitfalls or traps. Appropriate prominence should be given to terms which might operate disadvantageously' to the consumer. Consumers should not be assumed necessarily to be able themselves to identify (particularly in longer contracts) terms which are important, or which may operate to their disadvantage or which would be likely to surprise them, if drawn to their attention ... openness is not enough on its own, since good faith relates to the content of terms as well as the way they are expressed. Fair dealing has been authoritatively said to require that, in drafting and using contract terms, a trader 'should not, whether deliberately or unconsciously, take advantage' of the consumers' circumstances to their detriment ... The CMA considers the CJEU's approach demonstrates that businesses need, in formulating their contract terms, not just to resist the temptation to take advantage, but actively to take the legitimate interests of the consumer into account.[200]

S 69 gives statutory effect to the common law *contra proferentem* rule:

(1)     If a term in a consumer contract, or a consumer notice, could have different meanings, the meaning that is most favourable to the consumer is to prevail.

(2)     Subsection (1) does not apply to the construction of a term or a notice in proceedings on an application for an injunction or interdict under paragraph 3 of Schedule 3.[201]

---

199  (C-26/13) [2014] 2 All ER (Comm) 443 at [59].

200  CMA, *Unfair contract terms guidance: Guidance on the unfair terms provisions in the Consumer Rights Act 2015* (July 2015) para 2.22ff. However, transparency (or the lack of transparency) is not conclusive: 'openness is not enough on its own, since good faith relates to the content of terms as well as the way they are expressed. Fair dealing has been authoritatively said to require that, in drafting and using contract terms, a trader "should not, whether deliberately or unconsciously, take advantage" of the consumers' circumstances to their detriment ... The CMA considers the CJEU's approach demonstrates that businesses need, in formulating their contract terms, not just to resist the temptation to take advantage, but actively to take the legitimate interests of the consumer into account' (CMA, *Unfair contract terms guidance: Guidance on the unfair terms provisions in the Consumer Rights Act 2015* (July 2015) para 2.23ff).

201  See also *A.J. Building & Plastering Ltd v Turner* [2013] EWHC 484 at [53] per HHJ Keyser QC.

Thus if a term is ambiguous in its meaning, it will be construed in favour of the consumer. In *County Homesearch Co (Thames & Chilterns) Ltd v Cowham*[202] the Court of Appeal refused to apply regulation 7(2), UTCCR 1999 (the forerunner of s 69). Longmore LJ stated:

> Mr Warwick had some difficulty in identifying the written term [regulation 7(2) was explicitly limited to written terms] in relation to which there was a doubt about its meaning. He first identified clause 3 but, read as a whole, there is no doubt about its meaning. He then identified clause 2 but that clause specifies the agent's obligation not the client's obligation to pay. He then said that the contract as a whole did not indicate clearly enough that the implied term was not to apply. This exposed his difficulty in relying on regulation 7(2). There has to be a written term as to which there is a doubt. The fact that it may be arguable whether a term should be implied (a fact I take for granted since permission to appeal has been given) does not mean that there is a doubt about the meaning of a written term.[203]

### 7.8.4 GENERAL SUPERVISION

In addition to the provisions noted above (e.g. s 62 and s 71 of the CRA 2015), the CRA 2015 sets out a framework for the public enforcement of Part 2 (as did the UTCCR 1994 and UTCCR 1999) by, for example, the CMA: see s 70. The relevant provisions are contained in Sched 3. This includes the power to apply for an injunction as well as more informal means.[204] The public enforcement provisions in the CRA 2015 are, in fact, part of a tapestry of public enforcement provisions relevant to the regulation of unfair terms. In addition to the provisions under the CRA 2015, it is possible at the time of writing to take public enforcement action under Part 8 of the Enterprise Act 2002 (which relates, in particular, to infringements of Community legislation and now provides for 'enhanced consumer measures')[205] and under the Consumer Protection from Unfair Trading Regulations 2008.

## 7.9 SUMMARY OF KEY POINTS

■   Exclusion and limitation clauses are, to some extent, controlled at common law by the rules of incorporation and construction.

■   For a clause to be incorporated into a contract: it must normally either be contained in a signed document or reasonable notice of it must have been given before or at the time of the contract. In relation to the latter method, the wider the clause, generally the more notice must be given; and the clause must be contained in a contractual document.

■   A course of dealing may also provide evidence of incorporation.

■   Exclusion and limitation clauses *may* be interpreted against the party seeking to rely on them (the *contra proferentem* rule). In particular, specific language will, generally, be needed to exclude liability for negligence.

---

202  [2008] 1 WLR 909.
203  [2008] 1 WLR 909 at [21].
204  On the effectiveness of which see Bright, 2000 and Wilkinson, 2000.
205  S 219A.

- The Unfair Contract Terms Act 1977 generally deals with attempts to exclude business liability in non-consumer contracts.
  - Under UCTA, liability for negligence causing death or personal injury can never be excluded or limited. Clauses limiting liability for other losses caused by negligence must satisfy the requirement of reasonableness.
  - Attempts to exclude or restrict the liability for breach of the implied terms in contracts for the supply of goods often must satisfy the requirement of reasonableness (although note the term implied by s 12 of the Sale of Goods Act 1979).
  - Other exclusion clauses in written standard terms will be subject to the requirement of reasonableness.
  - The requirement of reasonableness looks at such things as the bargaining strength of the parties, awareness of the clause, the ability to insure against the loss, and the opportunities to make the contract without the exclusion.
  - In this context (business-to-business contracts) the courts are very reluctant to find exclusion or limitation clauses to be unreasonable.

- The Consumer Rights Act 2015 subjects many terms in consumer contracts, other than those broadly defining the parties' principal obligations, to a requirement of fairness.

## 7.10 FURTHER READING

**Generally**

- Coote, B, *Exception Clauses*, 1964, London: Sweet & Maxwell

- Law Commission, *Unfair Terms in Contracts*, Law Com No 292, Cm 6464, 2005

- Yates, D, *Exclusion Clauses in Contracts*, 2nd edn, 1982, London: Sweet & Maxwell

**Common law policing of 'unfair' terms**

- Barendt, E, 'Exclusion clauses: incorporation and interpretation' (1972) 35 MLR 644

- Bradgate, R, 'Unreasonable standard terms' (1997) 60 MLR 582

- Spencer, J, 'Signature, consent and the rule in *LEstrange v Graucob*' (1973) 32 CLJ 104

**Statutory regulation**

- Adams, J and Brownsword, R, 'The Unfair Contract Terms Act: a decade of discretion' (1988) 104 LQR 94

- Beale, H, 'Unfair contracts in Britain and Europe' [1989] CLP 197

- Beale, H, 'Legislative control of fairness: the Directive on Unfair Terms in Consumer Contracts', in Beatson J and Friedmann, D (eds), *Good Faith and Fault in Contract Law*, 1995, Oxford: Clarendon

■    Collins, H, 'Good faith in European contract law' (1994) 14 OJLS 229

■    Devenney, J, 'Gordian knots in Europeanised private law: unfair terms, bank charges and political compromises' [2011] 62 NILQ 33

■    Devenney, J and Kenny, M, 'Unfair terms, surety transactions and European harmonisation: a crucible of Europeanised private law?' [2009] Conv 295

■    MacDonald, E, 'Unifying unfair terms legislation' (2004) 67 MLR 69

■    Palmer, N and Yates, D, 'The future of the Unfair Contract Terms Act 1977' (1981) 40 CLJ 108

■    Samuels, A, 'The Consumer Rights Act 2015' [2016] Journal of Business Law 159

## COMPANION WEBSITE

*Now visit the companion website to:*

■    Revise and consolidate your knowledge of Exclusion Clauses by tackling a series of multiple-choice questions on this chapter

■    Test your understanding of the chapter's key terms by using the flashcard glossary

■    Fine-tune your legal skills by reading our tips and suggestions for Exclusion Clauses problem questions

■    Explore Exclusion Clauses further by accessing a series of web links

# 8

# Misrepresentation

## Contents

## 8.1 OVERVIEW

The concept of misrepresentation is concerned with pre-contractual statements that induce a contract but turn out to be false. There may be contractual remedies for some false statements of this kind, perhaps through a collateral contract, but a claimant will often wish to rely on the remedies for misrepresentation. The following issues are important in deciding if remedies are available on this basis (and, if so, which remedies):

■ Definition. Broadly an actionable misrepresentation must be:
 ☐ made by one party to the other;
 ☐ a statement of existing fact or law;
 ☐ generally in the form of a positive statement, rather than silence. There are, however, a number of exceptions to this principle, for example when

circumstances change between the making of the statement and the making of the contract;

- □   something that in part, at least, induces the other party to make the contract.

- ■   Remedies for misrepresentation:
  - □   Rescission of the contract. This is the main remedy that is available for all types of misrepresentation, even if wholly innocent. Certain bars, such as lapse of time, or the intervention of third party rights, will prevent rescission being available.
  - □   Damages at common law. Damages are only available at common law if the maker of the statement has acted fraudulently, or been negligent in one of the situations where there is a duty of care (under the *Hedley Byrne v Heller* principle).
  - □   Damages under the Misrepresentation Act 1967, s 2(1). This is the most powerful remedy available, providing damages unless the maker of the misrepresentation can prove that there were reasonable grounds for him or her to believe in the truth of the statement.
- ■   Exclusion of liability for misrepresentation:
  - □   Exclusion of liability is governed by s 3 of the Misrepresentation Act 1967, which requires such clauses to satisfy the 'requirement of reasonableness'.
- ■   'Entire agreement' clauses may prevent contractual liability for pre-contractual statements but may not circumvent s 3 of the 1967 Act.

## 8.2 INTRODUCTION

This chapter and the next three deal with problems that may arise out of behaviour that takes place prior to a contract being formed. A party to a contract may, after a valid agreement has apparently been concluded, nevertheless decide that it has turned out not to be quite what was anticipated, or that the behaviour of the other party means that it should not be enforced. This may be the result of false information, a mistake as to some aspect of what was agreed, the imposition of threats, or the application of improper pressure. These situations are dealt with by the English law of contract by rules that are traditionally grouped under the headings 'misrepresentation', 'mistake', 'duress' and 'undue influence'. In such a situation, the party who is unhappy with the agreement may wish to escape from it altogether, or to seek compensation of some kind. This chapter discusses the rules relating to 'misrepresentation'. The other areas are covered in the subsequent chapters.

An issue central to the consideration of these areas is the level of responsibility placed on parties during negotiations. The European Draft Common Frame of Reference[1] dealt specifically with negotiations in Art II. – 3.301. This is headed 'Negotiations contrary to good faith and fair dealing' and contains the following four paragraphs:

1    A party is free to negotiate and is not liable for failure to reach an agreement.
2    A person who is engaged in negotiations has a duty to negotiate in accordance with good faith and fair dealing and not to break off negotiations contrary to the duty of good faith and fair dealing. This duty may not be excluded or limited by contract.

---

1   On which see Devenney and Kenny, 2015, pp 609–10.

3    A person who is in breach of the duty is liable for any loss caused to the other party by the breach.
4    It is contrary to good faith and fair dealing, in particular, for a party to enter into or continue negotiations with no real intention of reaching an agreement with the other party.

The article recognises that negotiation is an important part of contractual dealings, but that such negotiations do not always lead to a contract. There is nothing inherently wrong in negotiations breaking down. Parties should be allowed to explore the possibilities of making an agreement without the need to feel under any obligation to end up in a contract with each other. This view is also that taken by English contract law. The article goes further, however, and in paras 3 and 4 makes a party who, in negotiating, is not genuinely trying to reach an agreement liable for any losses that such behaviour may cause to the other party. This positive obligation is not recognised by English law and 'time-wasters' are free to back away from a contract without penalty. Similarly, para 2 of the article, which is probably the most significant provision, has the effect of placing a positive duty on parties to negotiate in accordance with principles of 'good faith and fair dealing'. There are two points of contrast here with English law. First, the article treats the negotiating process as a discrete entity, with liabilities arising irrespective of whether a contract is made. In general, under English law there is no liability for wrongdoing during negotiation unless the parties end up having made a contract.[2] Second, the duty is a positive one. In English law the duties in relation to negotiation are primarily negative.[3] That is, the law intervenes when a person has behaved in a way that leads to the breach of a particular individual rule;[4] in most contracts it does not impose an overriding, positive duty to act in good faith

## 8.2.1 IN FOCUS: SHOULD THERE BE AN OBLIGATION TO NEGOTIATE 'IN GOOD FAITH'?

The notion of positive obligations of 'good faith and fair dealing' in the performance of contractual obligations is common in other systems of law,[5] including some common law

---

2    The major exception to this is in relation to the tort of negligent misstatement, which is based on the existence of a 'duty of care' rather than the existence of a contract – see below, 8.4.4.
3    The idea of a specific obligation to negotiate in good faith was clearly rejected by the House of Lords in *Walford v Miles* [1992] 2 AC 128; [1992] 1 All ER 452 – see Chapter 2, 2.15.2. In *MSC Mediterranean Shipping Co SA v Cottonex Anstalt* [2016] EWCA Civ 789 at [45] where Moore-Bick LJ stated: 'There is in my view a real danger that if a general principle of good faith were established it would be invoked as often to undermine as to support the terms in which the parties have reached agreement. The danger is not dissimilar to that posed by too liberal an approach to construction, against which the Supreme Court warned in Arnold v Britton [2015] UKSC 36, [2015] AC 1619.' Compare, in the context of contractual discretions, *British Telecommunications plc v Telefónica O2 UK Ltd* [2014] UKSC 42 at [37] where Lord Sumption stated: 'As a general rule, the scope of a contractual discretion will depend on the nature of the discretion and the construction of the language conferring it. But it is well established that in the absence of very clear language to the contrary, a contractual discretion must be exercised in good faith and not arbitrarily or capriciously.' However, it is not the case that all instances of contractual discretion are subject to such an implied term: see *UBS AG v Rose Capital Ventures Ltd* [2018] EWHC 3137 (Ch) (a mortgagee's "absolute discretion" to require payment within three months was not tapered by such an implied term especially in the light of the duties which existed between a mortgagor and mortgagee in these circumstances).
    On *contractual* duties of good faith see, for example, *BP Gas Marketing Ltd v La Societe Sonatrach, Sonatrach Gas Marketing UK Limited* [2016] EWHC 2461 (Comm).
4    In *Interfoto Picture Library Ltd v Stiletto Visual Programmes Ltd* [1989] QB 433 at 439, Bingham LJ famously referred to the piecemeal approach of English Law in this regard.
5    See, for example, the discussion in *Yam Seng Pte Ltd v International Trade Corp Ltd* [2013] EWHC 111 (QB) at [124].

systems,[6] though they do not always extend to the negotiation stage. The concept had very limited recognition, however, under the classical law of contract.[7] It has, however, to some extent been introduced through the influence of European directives, such as those concerned with unfair terms in consumer contracts[8] or the rights of commercial agents.[9] The legislation giving effect to these directives have used the language of good faith, and the English courts are therefore having to get to grips with it;[10] and it is anticipated that many of those rules will be maintained post-Brexit.[11] Although, as indicated in Chapter 1,[12] there have been some recent, tentative, steps to recognise 'good faith' as part of the obligations in performing a contract, in relation to pre-contractual statements, which are the main concern of this chapter, the obligation is in general not to tell lies, rather than to tell the truth.

Why should this be the case? Why did the classical English law of contract not impose an obligation on contracting parties to be open with each other in negotiations, and to reveal all information which is relevant to their contract? In addition to some, justified or unjustified, concerns about uncertainty, two main answers may be given to this question. The first is that such a positive obligation would not have sat easily with the archetype of a contract that tended to form the basis of the classical analysis. This was of two business people, of equal bargaining power, negotiating at arm's length. In such a situation, the court's attitude, based on 'freedom of contract', is that they should as far as possible be left to their own devices. If one of the parties requires information prior to a contract, then that party should ask questions of the other party. If what is then said in response turns out to be untrue, then legal liability will follow, but if no such request for information has been made, then it is not the court's business to say to the silent party, 'You should have realised that this information would have been important to the other side, and you should therefore have disclosed it.'

The second answer is based on 'economic efficiency'. Information is valuable, and those in possession of it should not necessarily be required to disclose it. If, for example, a purchaser has spent money on extensive market research and is aware that there is a demand for a particular product in a particular market, it would not make economic sense (in a system based on capitalism and free trade) to require the disclosure of that information. The purchaser is enabled, by the use of the information, to buy goods at a price that is acceptable to the seller, and then resell them at a profit in the market that the purchaser has discovered. If the purchaser had to disclose the information to the seller in that situation, the point of having done the market research would be lost. In other words, disclosure would discourage entrepreneurial activity designed to increase economic activity, and thereby increase wealth.[13]

There is obviously some strength in this argument, but two notes of caution should be sounded. First, it is now recognised that it is not always legitimate to make use of

---

6 For an excellent discussion see *Yam Seng Pte Ltd v International Trade Corp Ltd* [2013] EWHC 111 (QB) at [125]ff.

7 For example, contracts of *uberrimae fidei* ('the utmost good faith') are the main exception – see below, 8.3.3.

8 As dealt with in Chapter 7, 7.8.

9 Commercial Agents (Council Directives) Regulations (1993).

10 See, for example, *Director General of Fair Trading v First National Bank plc* [2002] UKHL 52; [2002] 1 All ER 97, discussed in Chapter 7, 7.8.2.

11 Compare HM Government, THE FUTURE RELATIONSHIP BETWEEN THE UNITED KINGDOM AND THE EUROPEAN UNION, Cm 9593 (July 2018) at [11]: "The UK and the EU would maintain a common rulebook for goods including agri-food, with the UK making an upfront choice to commit by treaty to ongoing harmonisation with EU rules on goods, covering only those necessary to provide for frictionless trade at the border. This common rulebook would be legislated for by the UK Parliament, as set out in detail in chapter 4."

12 Chapter 1, at 1.11.

13 See, for example, Kronman, 1978, pp 13–25.

information that can be turned to economic advantage. In the area of share dealing, for example, the use of 'insider information' is now regarded as so undesirable that in certain circumstances to do so is treated as a criminal offence.[14] Second, the archetypal model does not, of course, conform to the reality of much contractual dealing. Most obviously, many, if not the majority, of contracts are made between parties who are unequal – most obviously when the contract is business to consumer, but also in many business-to-business contracts. Withholding information that disadvantages the weaker party in such a situation may well be regarded as unacceptable. Moreover, even where business contractors are more or less equal partners, it does not necessarily make economic sense to conceal information from the other side. Where the contract is a long-term, 'relational' one, or where it is expected that the two contracting parties will want to do business with each other in the future, acting in a way which the other side may see as 'taking an unfair advantage' is probably not a sensible policy.[15] Even where there is no such continuing relationship, it may not be advantageous to gain a reputation for sharp dealing, since this is likely to discourage other potential contractual partners. It is likely, therefore, that business practice will in fact be more open than might be assumed from a rigid application of the 'economic efficiency' model. If that is the case, and the courts are professing to operate commercial law in a way that reflects the way in which business people actually conduct their relationships, a greater recognition of the value of openness would be justifiable.

## 8.2.2 OTHER REMEDIES FOR PRE-CONTRACTUAL STATEMENTS

There are some situations where Parliament has intervened, generally in consumer contracts,[16] to impose an obligation of disclosure. A famous example was the requirement under the Consumer Credit Act 1974 that the interest charged for credit should be presented to the potential debtor in a standardised form (the 'APR'), which assisted in making comparisons between the terms offered by different lenders.[17] More recently the Consumer Contracts (Information, Cancellation and Additional Charges) Regulations 2013[18] require disclosure of various pieces of information in particular consumer contracts.[19] There are also some situations where, independent of any possible liability for misrepresentation, criminal liability is attached to making misleading statements to potential contractors.[20] These controls over pre-contractual statements are not discussed further here.

A further civil remedy for certain types of statement inducing a contract (that is, those which can be put into the form of a promise) may be available where the promise can be found to form part of a collateral unilateral contract, of the form 'If you enter into a contract with me, I promise you X'. This has been discussed in Chapters 5 and 6,[21] and is not considered further here.

---

14 See the Criminal Justice Act 1993, s 52.

15 See, for example, Macneil, 1978; Macaulay, 1963.

16 And often in response to the (then) requirements of European Union law.

17 See the Consumer Credit Act (CCA) 1974, s 44 (now repealed) and the Consumer Credit (Advertisements) Regulations 1989, SI 1989/1125, 2004/1484 and 2010/1970 (all repealed). Breach of the Regulations was a criminal offence: CCA 1974, s 167 (2). On the current regulation in this area see Beale, 2018, para 39–067.

18 SI 2003/3134.

19 For example, Regulation 9 deals with the information to be provided in "on-premises" contracts.

20 See, for example, the Consumer Protection from Unfair Trading Regulations 2008. Since October 2014 there is also the possibility of being able to 'unwind' the contract, claim a discount or claim (particular forms of) compensation under Part 4A of the Regulations, as added by the Consumer Protection (Amendment) Regulations 2014 (SI 2014/870). See Devenney (2016).

21 See 5.9 and 6.4.2.

## 8.3 DEFINITION OF MISREPRESENTATION

With the above background in mind, we can turn to the rules that are actually applied by the English courts in relation to pre-contractual statements, as encompassed in the law relating to 'misrepresentation'. The law here is based primarily on common law rules, but with statutory intervention in the form of the Misrepresentation Act 1967, mainly affecting the position as to remedies.

The law relating to misrepresentation is concerned with the situation in which a false statement induces a party to enter into a contract. It provides in certain circumstances for the party whose actions have been affected to escape from the contract or claim damages (or both). There are a number of possible actions. The contract may be rescinded under the common law. Damages may be recovered under the Misrepresentation Act 1967. The tort actions for deceit, or negligent misstatement,[22] may provide alternative bases for the recovery of damages.

The basic requirements that are necessary in order for there to be a contractual remedy for a misrepresentation are as follows. The false statement must have been made by one of the contracting parties to the other; it must be a statement of fact or law, not opinion; and the statement must have induced the other party to enter into the contract. These elements will be considered in turn.

### 8.3.1 STATEMENT BY ONE PARTY TO THE OTHER

Where a claimant is seeking to rescind a contract on the basis of a misrepresentation, or to recover damages under s 2 of the Misrepresentation Act 1967,[23] the normal rule is that the false statement must have been made by, or on behalf of,[24] the other contracting party. If a person has entered into a contract on the basis of a misrepresentation by a third party, this normally will have no effect on the contract, or on the person's legal relationship with the other contracting party. A person who buys shares in a company, on the basis of a third party's statement that it has just made a substantial profit, normally cannot undo the share purchase if the statement turns out to be untrue. In *Parallel Media LLC v Chamberlain*,[25] it was held that the fact that the defendant had verified statements in a document prepared by the claimant did not involve a misrepresentation, but rather the giving of a warranty.

This general principle has been affected, at least in certain circumstances, however, by the House of Lords' decision in *Barclays Bank v O'Brien*.[26] In this case, a husband made a misrepresentation to his wife as to the extent to which the matrimonial home was being used as security for his business debts. On the basis of this misrepresentation, the wife entered into a contract of guarantee with the bank, using the house as security. The House of Lords held that because the bank should have been aware of the risk of misrepresentation by the husband, but had taken no steps to encourage the wife to take independent legal advice, it could not enforce the contract of guarantee against her.[27] In effect, therefore, a misrepresentation made by a person who was not the other contracting

---

22  Under the principle first stated in *Hedley Byrne & Co Ltd v Heller & Partners Ltd* [1964] AC 465; [1963] 2 All ER 575 – see below, 8.4.4.

23  Below, 8.4.6.

24  For example, by an agent. A principal may be liable for false statements made by an agent even if these were made without actual authority.

25  [2014] EWHC 214 (QB).

26  [1994] 1 AC 180; [1993] 4 All ER 417.

27  The House of Lords specifically rejected any suggestion that the husband was acting as agent for the bank when making the false statement. For a warning against loosening this requirement in the internet age see: *Taberna Europe CDOII Plc v Selskabet (Formerly Roskilde Bank A/S) (In Bankruptcy)* [2016] EWCA Civ 1262.

party was being used to rescind the contract. This decision and subsequent case law are discussed in detail in Chapter 11.[28] There is no reason to expect it to result in a broad exception to the general principle stated above. It does open the door, however, to similar arguments in other circumstances where a party may reasonably expect a third party to make misrepresentations.[29]

If the claimant is simply seeking damages rather than rescission of the contract, the actions for deceit or negligent misstatement at common law may be available against the statement maker,[30] even if the statement was not made by or on behalf of the other party to the contract.

## 8.3.2 STATEMENT OF EXISTING FACT OR LAW

In relation to the actions for rescission, deceit or under the Misrepresentation Act 1967, the statement must be one of fact or law, not opinion.[31]

---

**Key case** *Bisset v Wilkinson* (1927)[32]

Facts: A farmer in New Zealand told the plaintiff, a prospective purchaser of his land, that it would support 2,000 sheep. The plaintiff bought the land but it failed to support 2,000 sheep. He sought to rescind the contract on the ground of misrepresentation.
Held: The Privy Council held that this was not a misrepresentation, even though it turned out to be inaccurate. Neither the farmer, nor anyone else, had at any point carried on sheep farming on the land, and the purchaser was aware of this. The farmer's view on the matter was no more than an expression of opinion, and not a statement of fact. Rescission was refused.

---

**For thought**

*Sam, a farmer, grows crops, mainly wheat and barley, on his land. He decides to sell three fields, which he has never used for crops. Fred, who is new to farming, is interested in buying Sam's fields. He intends to grow oil-seed rape in the fields, and asks Sam what sort of yield could be expected. Sam has only once grown oil-seed rape, and not in these fields. If he gives Fred an estimate of the likely yield which turns out to be inaccurate, will he be liable for misrepresentation?*

---

The courts have recognised three situations where a statement that appears to be one of opinion can nevertheless be treated as one of fact. First, the opinion must not be contradicted by other facts known to the person giving it. In *Smith v Land and House Property Corp*,[33] the statement that a tenant was 'most desirable', while on its face an opinion, was treated as a misrepresentation because the maker of the statement knew that the tenant had in fact been in arrears with his rent for some time. Second, where the statement of

---

28  See 11.8.3.
29  This is discussed further in Chapter 11 (see 11.8.1–11.8.5).
30  That is, under the *Hedley Byrne v Heller* principle – below, 8.4.4.
31  Under the *Hedley Byrne v Heller* type of action, a negligently given opinion can give rise to liability.
32  [1927] AC 177.
33  (1884) 28 Ch D 7.

> ## BASIC REQUIREMENTS OF MISREPRESENTATION

> ### 1. Statement by one party to the other.

> ### 2. Statement of existing fact. The statement must be one of fact or law, not opinion – *Bisset v Wilkinson* (1927). **Some exceptions exist:**
> - If the person making the statement was in a position to know the correct facts the opinion may be treated as a statement of fact – *Smith v Land and House Property Corp* (1884).
> - Where the statement of opinion comes from an expert it may be a statement of fact – *Esso Petroleum Co Ltd v Mardon* (1976).
> - A statement of opinion which is not genuinely held can be treated as a false statement of fact – *Edgington v Fitzmaurice* (1885).

> ### 3. Silence. There is no misrepresentation by silence. **Some exceptions exist:**
> - Where one party tells a half-truth – *Dimmock v Hallett* (1866).
> - If a true statement is made and a change of circumstances is not disclosed – *With v O'Flanagan* (1936).
> - Contracts of utmost good faith require the contracting party to disclose all relevant facts (e.g. traditionally insurance contracts).

> ### 4. Misrepresentation must induce the contract. The statement must have formed some part of the reason why the claimant entered into the contract – *JEB Fasteners Ltd v Bloom* (1983). But:
> - It does not have to be the sole reason – *Edgington v Fitzmaurice* (1885).
> - It does not matter if the party deceived has passed over a chance to discover the truth – *Redgrave v Hurd* (1881).

Figure 8.1

opinion comes from an 'expert', it may amount to a representation that the expert has based it on a proper consideration of all the relevant circumstances. In *Esso Petroleum Co Ltd v Mardon*,[34] a representative of Esso gave a view as to the likely throughput of petrol at a particular petrol station. In giving this estimate, however, the representative had overlooked the fact that the conditions imposed by the local planning authority meant that the petrol station would not have a frontage on the main road. The statement as to the likely throughput was clearly at one level an opinion. The Court of Appeal, however, took the view that in the circumstances it involved a representation that proper care had been taken in giving it, and that this was a statement of fact. Third, a statement of opinion that is not genuinely held can be treated as a false statement of fact in relation to the person's

---

34 [1976] QB 801; [1976] 2 All ER 5. See also Chapter 6, 6.4.2. Cf *Notts Patent Brick and Tile Co v Butler* (1866) 16 QBD 778 – a statement by a solicitor that he was 'not aware' of any restrictive covenants applying to a piece of land, when in fact he had not checked the position, was held to be a misrepresentation.

state of mind. This derives from the view expressed in *Edgington v Fitzmaurice*[35] that a statement of an intention to act in a particular way in the future may be interpreted as a statement of fact, if it is clear that the person making the statement did not, at that time, have any intention of so acting.

---

**Key case** *Edgington v Fitzmaurice* (1885)

Facts: A company prospectus, designed to attract subscribers, contained false statements about the uses to which the money raised would be put. It said that the funds raised would be used to make improvements to the business, by altering buildings, buying horses and vans, etc. In fact the real intention was to use the money to pay off existing debts.
Held: The Court of Appeal held that this statement of intention could be treated as a representation as to the directors' state of mind at the time that the prospectus was issued, and could thus be treated as a statement of fact. As Bowen LJ put it:[36]

> the state of a man's mind is as much a fact as the state of his digestion. It is true that it is very difficult to prove what the state of a man's mind at a particular time is, but if it can be ascertained it is as much a fact as anything else. A misrepresentation as to the state of a man's mind is, therefore, a misstatement of fact.

The directors, by misrepresenting their actual intentions, were making a false statement of fact.

---

A similar lack of belief in the truth of what is being said may also turn a statement of opinion into a misrepresentation. It is a false statement of the person's current state of mind.

It was traditionally thought that a false statement of law was not to be treated as a statement of fact for the purposes of misrepresentation.[37] This point has been reconsidered, however, in the light of the House of Lords' decision in *Kleinwort Benson Ltd v Lincoln City Council*.[38] Here the House overturned the long-held view that mistakes of law could not be used as the basis for an action for restitution of money paid. It had previously been thought that this was only available in relation to mistakes of fact. If the courts have here assimilated 'law' to 'fact', it seems that the same should apply to misrepresentations. This was the view taken by the High Court in *Pankhania v Hackney London Borough Council*,[39] in which the judge held that the 'misrepresentation of law' rule has not survived *Kleinwort*.[40] He took the view that:

> The distinction between fact and law in the context of relief from misrepresentation has no more underlying principle to it than it does in the context of relief from

---

35 (1885) 29 Ch D 459.
36 Ibid, p 482.
37 Unless, of course, the maker of the statement knew that the statement of law was false, in which case it would be a false representation as to the maker's state of mind about the accuracy of the statement of law (on the basis of *Edgington v Fitzmaurice*).
38 [1999] 2 AC 349. The case is discussed further in Chapter 15, 15.8.4. Compare *Prudential Assurance Co Ltd v Revenue and Customs Commissioners* [2018] UKSC 39 on some of the issues created by this case.
39 [2002] EWHC 2441.
40 Ibid, para 55. However, depending on the facts, it may be that a statement of law is only a statement of opinion: see *Bolt Burdon Solicitors v Tariq* [2016] EWHC 811 (QB).

mistake. Indeed, when the principles of mistake and misrepresentation are set side by side, there is a stronger case for granting relief against a party who has induced a mistaken belief as to law in another, than against one who has merely made the same mistake himself ... The survival of the 'misrepresentation of law' rule following the demise of the 'mistake of law' rule would be no more than a quixotic anachronism.

A misrepresentation can be made by actions as well as words. This is illustrated by the case of *Spice Girls Ltd v Aprilia World Service* BV.[41] Spice Girls Ltd, the company formed to promote the pop group, the Spice Girls, was in the process of making a contract for the promotion of Aprilia's scooters. Shortly before the contract was signed, the members of the group all took part in the filming of a commercial for Aprilia. At that time, they knew that one member of the group intended to leave, as she did shortly after the contract had been signed. The group's participation in the filming was held to amount to a representation that Spice Girls Ltd did not know and had no reasonable ground to believe that any of the existing members had at that time a declared intention to leave. This was untrue, and therefore the participation in the filming amounted to a misrepresentation by conduct.

### 8.3.3 MISREPRESENTATION BY SILENCE

In general, there is no misrepresentation by silence. Even where one party is aware that the other is contracting on the basis of a misunderstanding of some fact relating to the contract, there will generally be no liability. This is in line with the general approach outlined at the beginning of this chapter, that English law imposes a negative obligation not to tell falsehoods, rather than a positive obligation to tell the truth.

There are, however, some exceptions to this. First, the maker of the statement must not give only half the story on some aspect of the facts. Thus, in *Dimmock v Hallett*,[42] the statement that farms were fully let when, in fact, as the maker of the statement knew, the tenants had given notice to quit was capable of being a misrepresentation.[43] Second, if a true statement is made, but then circumstances change before the contract is concluded, making it false, a failure to disclose this will be treated as a misrepresentation.

---

**Key case** *With v O'Flanagan* (1936)[44]

Facts: A doctor was seeking to sell his practice. He told a prospective purchaser that the practice's income was £2,000 per annum. This was true at the time, but as a result of the vendor's illness the practice declined considerably over the next few months, so that by the time it was actually sold, its value had reduced significantly, and takings were averaging only £5 per week. The purchaser sought to rescind the contract.

Held: The Court of Appeal held that the failure to notify the purchaser of the fact that the earlier statement was no longer true amounted to a misrepresentation.[45] The purchaser was entitled to rescind the contract.

---

41 [2002] EMLR 27.
42 (1866) LR 2 Ch App 21.
43 This is similar to the situation where a statement of opinion can become a statement of fact because the maker is aware of facts making the opinion untrue: *Smith v Land and House Property Corp* (1884) 28 Ch D 7 – above, 8.3.2.
44 [1936] Ch 575. For discussion of this decision, see Bigwood, 2005.
45 This does not apply at common law, it seems, where the statement is one of intention, and the intention later changes: *Wales v Wadham* [1977] 1 WLR 199 – wife's statement during negotiations for a divorce settlement that she did not intend to remarry. Compare *Jenkins v Livesey* [1985] AC 424 and Treitel, 2015, p 481 for the position in relation to statutory proceedings for financial provision.

The third situation in which silence can constitute a misrepresentation is in relation to certain contracts that are treated as being 'of the utmost good faith' *(uberrimae fidei)*, and require the contracting party to disclose all relevant facts. Traditionally the most frequent type of contract falling into this category was a contract for insurance,[46] and there is case law in which this rule appeared to operate harshly against individual (as opposed to business) insurers. For example, in *Woolcutt v Sun Alliance and London Insurance Ltd*,[47] a policy for fire insurance on a house was invalidated because the insured had failed to disclose in a mortgage application, which indicated that the mortgagee would insure the property concerned, that he had been convicted of robbery some ten years previously. It is not immediately obvious why this fact was material. Caulfield J simply treated it as 'almost self-evident' that 'the criminal record of the assured can affect the moral hazard which the insurers have to assess'.[48] Inroads have been made by legislation into these principles. For example, section 2 of the Consumer Insurance (Disclosure and Representations) Act 2012 simply requires the consumer 'to take reasonable care not to make a misrepresentation to the insurer', though the section also provides that failing to comply with a request to amend or update the consumer's details can amount to a such a misrepresentation. To that extent, silence will continue to constitute a misrepresentation in relation to a consumer contract for insurance.[49]

A similar obligation of good faith disclosure applies to contracts establishing family settlements. Thus, in *Gordon v Gordon*,[50] a settlement was made on the presumption that an elder son was born outside marriage, and was therefore illegitimate. In fact, the younger son knew that his parents had been through a secret marriage ceremony prior to the birth of his elder brother. The fact that he had concealed this knowledge, which was clearly material, meant that the settlement had to be set aside.

Finally, there are some contracts that involve a fiduciary relationship, and this may entail a duty to disclose. In this category are to be found contracts between agent and principal,[51] solicitor and client, and a company and its promoters.[52] Other similar relationships that have a fiduciary character will be treated in the same way, and the list is not closed.

### 8.3.4 MISREPRESENTATION MUST INDUCE THE CONTRACT

It is not enough to give rise to a remedy for misrepresentation for the claimant to point to some false statement of fact made by the defendant prior to a contract that they have made. It must also be shown that that statement formed some part of the reason why the claimant entered into the agreement. In *JEB Fasteners Ltd v Bloom*,[53] for example, which was concerned with this issue of reliance in the context of an action for negligent misstatement at common law, it was established that the plaintiffs took over a business having seen inaccurate accounts prepared by the defendants. Their reason for taking over

---

46 In *Carter v Boehm* (1766) 3 Burr 1905, Lord Mansfield justified this approach to insurance contracts on the basis that they were based on 'speculation'.

47 [1978] 1 All ER 1253.

48 [1978] 1 All ER 1253, p 1257. As Collins points out (2003, p 210), if the insurer was concerned about previous criminal convictions it could have asked specific questions to this effect. The position was complicated by the fact that the insurance was effected via the mortgagee (a building society) so that there were no direct dealings between the assured and the insurer. The insurer could, however, presumably have required the building society to make relevant inquiries.

49 See also the Insurance Act 2015, s 21.

50 (1816–21) 3 Swans 400; 36 ER 910.

51 For example, *Armstrong v Jackson* [1917] 2 KB 822.

52 *Boardman v Phipps* [1967] 2 AC 46; [1966] 3 All ER 721.

53 [1983] 1 All ER 583. See also *BV Nederlandse Industrie Van Eiprodukten v Rembrandt Enterprises Inc* [2018] EWHC 1857 (Comm).

the business, however, was shown to have been the wish to secure the services of two directors. The accounts had not induced their action in taking over the business. Similarly, where the claimant has not relied on the statement, but has sought independent verification, there will not be sufficient reliance to found an action.[54]

On the other hand, it is not necessary for the misrepresentation to be the sole reason why the contract was entered into. In *Edgington v Fitzmaurice*,[55] the plaintiff was influenced not only by the prospectus, but also by his own mistaken belief that he would have a charge on the assets of the company. His action based on misrepresentation was nevertheless successful. Provided the misstatement was 'actively present to his mind when he decided to advance the money', then it was material. The test is, according to Bowen LJ:[56]

> what was the state of the plaintiff's mind, and if his mind was disturbed by the misstatement of the defendants, and such disturbance was in part the cause of what he did, the mere fact of his also making a mistake himself could make no difference.

Nor does it matter that the party deceived has spurned a chance to discover the truth. In *Redgrave v Hurd*,[57] false statements were made by the plaintiff about the income of his practice as a solicitor, on the strength of which the defendant had entered into a contract to buy the plaintiff's house and practice. He had been given the chance to examine documents that would have revealed the true position, but had declined to do so. This did not prevent his claim based on misrepresentation. This decision seems to have the effect of encouraging parties not to make full enquiries before entering into a contract. It is questionable whether this is an approach to contracting that the law should be supporting.

The principle adopted in *Redgrave v Hurd* will not be applied, however, where the true position was set out in the contract signed by the claimant. In *Peekay Intermark Ltd v Australia and New Zealand Banking Group Ltd*,[58] a representative of the defendant bank had described an investment opportunity to the claimant in general terms. Some days later the representative sent to the claimant the full terms and conditions of the investment. This contract contained provisions that made the investment more risky than it appeared from the initial broad description given by the representative. The claimant looked over the documents briefly, and initialled them, but did not read them in detail, assuming that they were in line with what he had been previously told. He subsequently sought damages under s 2(1) Misrepresentation Act 1967 on the basis of the representative's negligent misrepresentation of the terms. He succeeded at first instance, but on appeal, the Court of Appeal held for the defendant. It ruled that although the documents sent to the claimant did not correspond to the investment previously outlined by the representative, the defendants had not misrepresented the documents themselves. Since the claimant had looked at and signed these documents it was not then open to him to claim that he was induced to sign by an earlier misrepresentation.

It seems that if the statement is one on which a reasonable person would have relied, then there is a rebuttable presumption that the claimant did in fact rely on it. This was the view of the Court of Appeal in *Barton v County NatWest Ltd*.[59] Moreover, the presumption will not disappear simply as a result of the fact that the claimant has given evidence; the burden remains on the defendant to disprove it.

---

54  *Attwood v Small* (1838) 6 Cl & F 232. Compare *Hayward v Zurich Insurance Co Plc* [2016] UKSC 48 (suspicion that the representation was false).
55  (1885) 29 Ch D 459.
56  Ibid, p 483.
57  (1881) 20 Ch D 1.
58  [2006] 2 Lloyd's Rep 511.
59  [2002] 4 All ER 494 (note); [1999] Lloyd's Rep Bank 408, placing some reliance on the Australian case of *Australian Steel and Mining Corp Pty Ltd v Corben* [1974] 2 NSWLR 202.

The contrary position – that is, where it is claimed that the claimant did in fact rely on the statement, even though a reasonable person would not have done so – has also been given some consideration. In other words, does the reliance on the statement have to be 'reasonable' in order for it to be a material inducement to contract? This issue was considered in *Museprime Properties Ltd v Adhill Properties Ltd*.[60] Property owned by the defendant was sold by auction to the plaintiffs. There was an inaccurate statement in the auction particulars, which was reaffirmed by the auctioneer, to the effect that rent reviews of three leases to which the properties were subject had not been finalised. The plaintiffs sought to rescind the contract for misrepresentation. The defendants argued, as part of their case, that the misrepresentation was not material because no reasonable bidder would have allowed it to influence his bid. Scott J held (approving a passage to this effect in Goff and Jones, 1993)[61] that the materiality of the representation was not to be determined by whether a reasonable person would have been induced to contract. As long as the claimant was in *fact* induced, as was the case here, that was enough to entitle him to rescission. The reasonableness or otherwise of his or her behaviour was relevant only to the burden of proof: the less reasonable the inducement, the more difficult it would be for the claimant to convince the court that he or she had been affected by the misrepresentation.

The position is apparently different, however, in relation to insurance contracts. Where the case is one of non-disclosure in such a contract, the test is whether a reasonable insurer would have relied on the misrepresentation. This was the view of the House of Lords in *Pan Atlantic Insurance Co Ltd v Pine Top Insurance Co Ltd*.[62] Moreover in *Sharland v Sharland*[63] Lady Hale (with whom Lord Neuberger, Lord Clarke, Lord Wilson, Lord Sumption, Lord Reed and Lord Hodge agreed) *appeared* to accept a materiality requirement in relation to the general law of misrepresentation; although she was speaking in the (special) context of matrimonial consent orders.[64]

### 8.3.5 IN FOCUS: HOW UNREASONABLE CAN A PURCHASER BE?

It is difficult to be sure how far the general principle, if it survives *Sharland v Sharland*, that the reasonableness or otherwise of reliance on a misrepresentation is irrelevant, can be taken. Suppose, for example, I am selling my car and, prior to the contract, I tell the prospective purchaser that the car is amphibious and will go across water. Can the purchaser later claim against me because this ridiculous statement turns out to be untrue, as he has discovered now that the car is at the bottom of the river? Clearly, there may be difficulties of proving that there was reliance in fact, as noted above, but assuming that it is established that the statement was believed by the purchaser (for example, by the fact that he tried to drive across a river), the *Museprime* approach would give a remedy in misrepresentation. Would the courts go this far? Or would some degree of reasonable reliance be introduced, where, for example, no reasonable person would ever have believed the statement to be true?

The answer may lie in differentiating between 'reasonableness' for the purposes of materiality, and the reasonableness of a person's believing that the statement was true. The *Museprime* test can be seen as primarily concerned with the former type of 'reasonableness'. It is dealing with the question of whether a reasonable person would have regarded a statement of this type as containing information which would be a material

---

60  [1990] 2 EG 196; (1990) 61 P & CR 111.
61  Page 168.
62  [1995] AC 501. On the effect of the Consumer Insurance (Disclosure and Representations) Act 2012, see Beale, 2018, para 7–041.
63  [2015] UKSC 60 at [31] – [33].
64  Although compare *Taylor v Secretary of State for Business, Innovation and Skills* [2016] EWHC 1953 (Ch).

**Fraudulent misrepresentation**
Tort of deceit

*Derry v Peek* (1889) – Lord Herschell:
False representation must be proved 'to have been made knowingly; or without belief in its truth; or recklessly, careless whether it be true or false'

Negligence is insufficient – dishonesty on the part of the maker of the statement is required

**Negligent misstatement (common law)**
The courts have accepted the possibility of an action for negligent misstatement causing a pecuniary loss to be suffered by the other party:
*Hedley Byrne & Co Ltd v Heller & Partners Ltd* (1964)

For this remedy to be available a duty of care must be shown to exist between the maker of the statement and the person who acted upon it. There must be:
• reasonable foreseeability of reliance and harm
• sufficient proximity between the parties
It must be just and reasonable for the duty to be imposed:
*Caparo Industries plc v Dickman* (1990)
*Henderson v Merrett Syndicates Ltd* (1995)

**Types of misrepresentation**

**Negligent misrepresentation (statute)**
The Misrepresentation Act 1967 introduced a statutory remedy for negligent misrepresentation.
Where a false statement is made, the burden of proof shifts to the defendant to establish that there were reasonable grounds for believing the statement to be true.
The courts are strict on what will amount to reasonable grounds:
*Howard Marine Dredging Co Ltd v A Ogden & Sons (Excavations) Ltd* (1978)

**Innocent misrepresentation**
Misrepresentation which is neither fraudulent nor negligent – i.e. where a party has made a statement with an honest belief in its truth, and with reasonable grounds for that belief

Figure 8.2

factor in deciding whether to enter into the contract or not. In relation to the sale of a house, for example, a statement that a garden fence had been erected three years ago (when perhaps in fact it had been erected two years ago) might be seen as immaterial to the contract, so that the 'reasonable purchaser' would have been unlikely to have been induced to contract on the basis of it. The *Museprime* approach would say, however, that provided that the court believed that it was regarded as material by the particular purchaser, then it could be treated as a misrepresentation. The unreasonableness of that view would be irrelevant. On the other hand (as with the example of the allegedly amphibious car), if the statement, while about something that if true would undoubtedly be 'material' in that it would affect the value of what was being sold, is so far-fetched that no reasonable person would believe it, it may be that the courts would be more prepared to impose a test of reasonableness on the claimant. A distinction of this kind would make sense, but it cannot be said that it comes through clearly in the judgment in *Museprime*. That case seems to suggest that whether there was reliance on the statement is always simply a matter of proof, and that reasonableness only becomes relevant as part of the evidential process.

## 8.4 REMEDIES FOR MISREPRESENTATION

The remedies available for misrepresentation depend to some extent on the state of mind of the person making the false statement. If the statement is fraudulent, the remedies may be more extensive than if it is made negligently or innocently. There are remedies available under common law and equity and also under the Misrepresentation Act 1967.

### 8.4.1 RESCISSION

The principal remedy under English law for a misrepresentation was for a long time the rescission of the ensuing contract. This view of the effect of misrepresentation makes sense if the false statement is viewed as affecting the agreement between the parties. If the agreement has been reached on a false basis, then it is appropriate that it should be set aside. Moreover, once the agreement has been set aside there is then limited scope for the award of damages. This approach makes most sense if the dominant view of contractual obligations is, as it was under classical contract law, that they are based on a consensus between the parties (probably derived from the mutual exchange of promises). The growth of the idea of reliance as an important element in the definition of contractual obligations, however,[65] would suggest that the remedy for misrepresentation should be based on the extent to which reliance on the false statement has led to loss. This would mean the provision of compensatory damages playing a much more important role in the remedies available. That trend can be observed as having occurred during the latter half of the twentieth century, with both common law and statute providing for damages to be much more widely available as a remedy for misrepresentation. These developments are considered later in this chapter. This has not, however, been at the expense of the availability of rescission.

Rescission remains available in any situation where a misrepresentation has induced a contract, whether the false statement was fraudulent, negligent or wholly innocent.[66] The remedy allows the parties to be restored to their original positions. Thus, if the contract is one for the sale of goods, both the goods, and the price paid for them, must be returned. Prior to the Misrepresentation Act 1967, there could be no rescission for misrepresentation where either the false statement had become part of the contract or where the contract had been performed. This was changed by s 1 of the Misrepresentation Act 1967, which states:

> Where a person has entered into a contract after a misrepresentation has been made to him, and:

(a)    the misrepresentation has become a term of the contract; or
(b)    the contract has been performed;

> or both, then, if otherwise he would be entitled to rescind the contract without alleging fraud, he shall be so entitled, subject to the provisions of this Act, notwithstanding the matter mentioned in paras (a) and (b) of this section.

---

65  See Chapter 3, 3.15.2.
66  Although in certain circumstances the court now has a discretion under s 2(2) of the Misrepresentation Act 1967 to award damages in lieu of rescission for an innocent misrepresentation – see below, 8.4.8. See also the interesting case of *BV Nederlandse Industrie Van Eiprodukten v Rembrandt Enterprises Inc* [2018] EWHC 1857 (Comm) which involved the rescission of a revised contract with the consequence that the original contract was restored.

Figure 8.3

There are certain bars, however, to the availability of rescission. The remedy may be lost by:

- affirmation;
- lapse of time;
- impossibility of restitution; or
- adverse effect on third parties.

Looking first at 'affirmation', this arises where the party to whom the statement has been made, knowing or having discovered that the statement was false, nevertheless continues with the contract. In *Long v Lloyd*,[67] for example, a representation was made as to the fuel consumption of a lorry by the seller (the defendant). After buying the lorry, the plaintiff discovered that this statement was untrue, and that the lorry had various other defects. The defendant offered to contribute towards the cost of repairs. The plaintiff accepted this offer, and later sent the lorry on a long journey during which it broke down. He then tried to rescind the contract for misrepresentation. It was held that he had affirmed the contract with full knowledge of the false statement, and had therefore lost the right to rescind. The justification for this bar is presumably that if the claimant has continued with the contract, having knowledge of the misrepresentation, the statement cannot have been as material a factor in making the contract as is being alleged.

---

67 [1958] 2 All ER 402.

**For thought**

*Petra buys a van for her business from Steve. Steve tells her that the van has been serviced every year. When, a few days later, Petra checks the documentation given to her by Steve, she sees that the van has not been serviced for the past two years. She continues to use the van for three more days, at which point it breaks down, as a result of a serious oil leak, which would have been picked up if the van had been serviced. Will Petra be able to rescind the contract for misrepresentation?*

The second way in which the right to rescind may be lost is by lapse of time. In *Leaf v International Galleries*,[68] the purchaser of a picture stated to be by John Constable discovered, on trying to sell it some five years later, that this statement was false. His attempt to rescind for misrepresentation failed because of the lapse of time. This case was fairly clear. In other situations, it will be a matter for the court to consider in all the circumstances whether the lapse of time is sufficient to preclude rescission. It may be significant that in *Leaf v International Galleries*, Lord Denning drew an analogy with the rules relating to the acceptance of goods under the Sale of Goods Act 1893.[69] The case law on this issue used to suggest that a fairly short time from the contract, measured in days or weeks rather than years, would be sufficient to amount to 'acceptance' (and thereby prevent rejection for breach of contract).[70] Changes to the wording of the relevant section of the Sale of Goods Act 1979 have meant that more recent case law has adopted a more flexible approach to when a contract has been affirmed[71] and this, in turn, may require *Leaf* to be reconsidered.[72] The justification for this bar is less clear than that based on affirmation. Why should the fact that the claimant only discovers the falsity of the defendant's statement after a significant lapse of time mean that the right to rescind should be lost? If the misrepresentation was material, the claimant has still contracted on a false basis, and it is not clear why this falsity should not be regarded as allowing the claimant to say that the contract would never have been made had the truth been known. Of course, in some situations, if a contract has proceeded on a satisfactory basis for some time and the discovery of the misrepresentation is unlikely to make any practical difference, it may be justifiable to say that this is a situation equivalent to affirmation and the contract should stand. Once again, the basis would be that the statement was not in fact material to the contract. Alternatively, it might be argued that after a long lapse of time it is in practice difficult to undo a contract in a way that does not cause undue hardship to the other side. But this point is largely dealt with by the next bar, that is, where restitution is impossible. The bar based simply on lapse of time can probably be justified only on the basis that there is a desirability of certainty and finality in contractual relationships, and to have the possibility of rescission remaining open for years after the making of the contract would go against this. This bar remains, however, the one for which it is most difficult to find convincing justifications.

---

68 [1950] 2 KB 86; [1950] 1 All ER 693.

69 Now dealt with by the Sale of Goods Act 1979, s 35. Compare the Consumer Rights Act 2015, s 22.

70 See, for example, *Bernstein v Pamsons Motors (Golders Green) Ltd* [1987] 2 All ER 220. Compare *Truk (UK) Ltd v Tokmakidis GmbH* [2000] 1 Lloyd's Rep 543.

71 *Clegg v Olle Andersson* [2003] EWCA 320.

72 See *Salt v Stratstone Specialist Limited* [2015] EWCA Civ 745 at [34] where Longmore LJ stated: 'It must, moreover, be remembered that *Leaf* was decided well before the Misrepresentation Act was passed. It must be doubtful whether since the enactment of section 1 it is still good law that a representor should be in no worse position than if the representation had become a term of the contract, particularly if the representor takes no steps to prove that he was not negligent.' On wider limitation periods see *Riyait v Dawett* [2018] EWCA Civ 593.

The next bar arises where restitution is impossible. This may arise, for example, where goods have been destroyed, consumed or irretrievably mixed with others. In *Clarke v Dickson*,[73] Crompton J gave two colourful examples of this. In argument he commented: 'If you are fraudulently induced to buy a cake you may return it and get back the price; but you cannot both eat your cake and return your cake.'[74] In his judgment he gave the following example:[75]

> Take the case ... of a butcher buying live cattle, killing them and even selling the meat to his customers. If the rule of law were as the plaintiff contends, that butcher on discovering a fraud on the part of the grazier who sold him the cattle could rescind the contract and get back the whole price: but how could that be consistent with justice?

In *Clarke v Dickson* itself, the purchaser of shares in a company was unable to rescind the contract because he had:[76]

> changed the nature of the article: the shares he received were shares in a company on the cost book principle; the plaintiff offers to restore them after he has converted them into shares in a joint stock corporation.

Moreover, the company was at the time in the course of being wound up, so there was no chance of a profit being made from the shares. A simple decline in value will not, however, be sufficient to bar rescission.[77] The requirement of precise restitution has been applied less strictly in equity than under the common law. For example, the common law would not allow rescission where a lessee had gone into possession of the land leased, on the basis that once it had been occupied, precise restitution was impossible. Equity will allow rescission subject to rent being paid for the period of occupation.[78] In *Erlanger v New Sombrero Phosphate Co*,[79] the contract involved the purchase of a mine, which the buyer worked for a period before seeking to rescind. The court allowed rescission on the basis of a payment being made to cover the profits that the buyer had made and the deterioration in the mine. The approach of equity is to do what is 'practically just' even where precise restitution is impossible.[80]

The final bar arises where rescission would affect the rights of third parties. In some ways this is simply a further example of the bar based on impossibility of restitution. It constitutes a major limitation where goods obtained on the basis of a (probably fraudulent) misrepresentation have been sold on to an innocent third party. The courts will not, in such a situation, require the third party to disgorge the goods.[81] This has caused particular problems for claimants where there has been a misrepresentation as to the identity of a purchaser, which is relevant to creditworthiness. As a result, attempts have been made (generally unsuccessfully) to argue that such contracts are void for mistake.[82]

---

73  (1858) EB & E 148; 120 ER 463.
74  Ibid, p 152; p 465.
75  Ibid, p 155, p 466.
76  Ibid, p 154; p 466, per Erle J.
77  *Armstrong v Jackson* [1917] 2 KB 822; cf *Cheese v Thomas* [1994] 1 All ER 35, discussed in Chapter 11, 11.9.1.
78  *Hulton v Hulton* [1917] 1 KB 813.
79  (1878) App Cas 1218.
80  (1878) App Cas 1218, p 1279, per Lord Blackburn.
81  See, for example, *Phillips v Brooks* [1919] 2 KB 243; *Lewis v Averay* [1972] 2 All ER 229. The position is also affected by s 23 of the Sale of Goods Act 1979, which allows a buyer of goods who is in possession under a voidable title (which is the position where there has been a misrepresentation) to pass a good title to a third party who buys the goods in good faith.
82  See Chapter 9, 9.5.3 and 9.5.4.

## 8.4.2 OPERATION OF RESCISSION

A contract is not automatically rescinded as a result of a misrepresentation, even where none of the bars noted above apply. It is 'voidable' rather than 'void'. The choice of whether or not to rescind rests with the innocent party. Until that decision is made, the contract is treated as valid and enforceable. To rescind the contract, the innocent party will generally be expected to give notice of this to the other side. There is no particular form required as long as it is made clear the contract is being rescinded. Starting legal proceedings to have the contract set aside will constitute notice of rescission.[83]

It may well be, particularly where the misrepresentation was fraudulent, that the party making the false statement is no longer easily contactable. In that circumstance, there is authority that other reasonable steps that clearly indicate an intention to rescind may be enough. In *Car and Universal Finance Co Ltd v Caldwell*,[84] C, the owner of a car, sold it to N in return for a cheque, which was dishonoured. The giving of a cheque constitutes a representation that the drawer believes that it will be met when presented; if no such belief is held, it is a misrepresentation. As soon as the cheque was returned, C at once informed the police and the Automobile Association. It was held that this was sufficient to avoid the contract, in the circumstances. Since C had acted before N had managed to resell the car, the innocent third party who had later bought it had acquired no title. C could therefore recover the car.[85]

## 8.4.3 DAMAGES AT COMMON LAW

At common law, damages were traditionally only available in relation to fraudulent misrepresentations, under the tort of deceit. There is now the possibility of damages being recovered for negligent misstatements under the tort of negligence, as developed in *Hedley Byrne & Co Ltd v Heller & Partners Ltd*[86] and subsequent cases. These are discussed in the next section.[87]

The leading case on deceit is *Derry v Peek*.[88]

---

**Key case** *Derry v Peek* (1889)

Facts: A prospectus for a tram company indicated that it had the right to use steam power. The directors had assumed that the Board of Trade would give the necessary permission for this. In fact, the Board of Trade refused permission, and the company failed. The plaintiff had bought shares in reliance on the statement in the prospectus, and sought damages for the tort of deceit.

Held: The House of Lords held that for an action for deceit, it was necessary to show fraud. This meant, in the words of Lord Herschell, that a false representation must be proved to have been made:[89] '(1) knowingly; or (2) without belief in its truth; or (3) recklessly, careless whether it be true or false.' On the facts, the defendants were not liable because they honestly believed the truth of their statement in the prospectus. Statements made through 'want of care' were not fraudulent.

---

83 *Reese Silver Mining Co v Smith* (1869) LR 4 HL 64.
84 [1965] 1 QB 525; [1964] 1 All ER 290.
85 Treitel (2015, 9–088) doubts whether this rule should be extended beyond fraudulent misrepresentations, because of its harsh effect on the innocent third party. The Law Reform Committee for similar reasons recommended in 1966 that the decision in *Caldwell* should be reversed: 12th Report, Cmd 2958, para 16. Its practical effect has, however, been reduced by the decision in *Newtons of Wembley v Williams* [1965] 1 QB 560 that a fraudulent purchaser in possession can pass a good title by virtue of the Sale of Goods Act 1979, s 25.
86 [1964] AC 465; [1963] 2 All ER 575.
87 See 8.4.4.
88 (1889) 14 App Cas 337.
89 Ibid, p 374.

The requirements for deceit remain as set out in this case.[90] As can be seen, mere negligence is not enough – knowledge of the falsity or a reckless disregard for the truth is needed. In *Thomas Witter Ltd v TBP Industries Ltd*,[91] it was held that the 'recklessness' must be sufficiently serious to amount to fraud. This implies 'dishonesty' on the part of the maker of the statement.[92]

Once deceit is established, damages will be assessed according to the tortious measure, which aims to put the parties in the position they would have been in had the tort not occurred – that is, in this context, if the false statement had not been made.[93] This may not simply be a matter of restoring the parties to their pre-misrepresentation positions: in appropriate cases the court may also take account of benefits that the claimant has missed out on as a result of the misrepresentation.[94] Although the tortious measure is used, the damages for deceit may be more extensive than is usually the case in tort, since in *Doyle v Olby (Ironmongers) Ltd*[95] it was held that the defendant will be liable for all losses that can be shown to be the consequences of the false statement, without being limited by the normal rules of 'remoteness' (which would limit damages to those that were reasonably foreseeable by the defendant).[96] The justification for this rule seems to be a 'moral' one, based on the fact that the defendant who has deliberately or recklessly lied should not be allowed to place limits on the claimant's recovery of losses.[97] This is a clear departure from the normal approach towards damages in the civil law, which takes fair compensation for the claimant as the guiding principle. If the normal rule in tort is that fair compensation is limited by the foreseeability of the claimant's loss, why should this not apply to deceit? The state of mind of the defendant when making the statement has no effect on the claimant's losses. The wider measure of damages can only be seen as intended to punish the defendant for having acted deceitfully.[98]

The effect of this rule was demonstrated in the House of Lords' decision in *Smith and New Court Securities Ltd v Scrimgeour Vickers (Asset Management) Ltd*.[99] The case concerned the sale of a parcel of shares in F Ltd, owned by the defendants. They offered them to the plaintiffs, but fraudulently claimed that other bids had been received. This fraudulent misrepresentation led the plaintiffs to increase their offer from 78p per share to 82.25p per share. This offer was accepted, and the parcel of over 28 million shares was sold to the plaintiffs for just over £23m. It then transpired that F Ltd had been the victim of another unrelated fraud, and its share price plummeted. The plaintiffs resold the shares, suffering a loss of over £11m. The plaintiffs claimed this in damages from the defendants; the defendants claimed that they should be limited to the difference between the price they would have been prepared to pay without the misrepresentation (78p per share) and the contract price (82.25p per share). The defendants succeeded in the Court of Appeal, but the House of Lords held that the application of *Doyle v Olby* entitled the plaintiffs to recover their full losses. The plaintiffs would

---

90  There is no separate requirement of an 'intention to deceive'; all that is required is dishonesty or recklessness as to the truth, together with the intention that the other party should rely on the statement: *ECO3 Capital Ltd v Ludsin Overseas Ltd* [2013] EWCA Civ 413.

91  [1996] 2 All ER 573.

92  See *Standard Chartered Bank v Pakistan National Shipping Corp (No 2)* [2000] 1 Lloyd's Rep 218 (reversed in part on other grounds ([2002] UKHL 43)).

93  The contractual measure would aim to put them in the position they would have been in had the statement been true – see Chapter 15, 15.3. On the difficulties sometimes encountered in applying this measure see *Inter Export Llc v Townley* [2018] EWCA Civ 2068.

94  See, for example, *East v Maurer* [1991] 2 All ER 733, discussed below.

95  [1969] 2 QB 158; [1969] 2 All ER 119.

96  For further discussion of the rules of remoteness, see Chapter 15, 15.6.1.

97  See the comments of Lord Denning [1969] 2 QB 158, p 167; [1969] 2 All ER 119, p 122.

98  Or as enforcing 'the public policy of deterring deliberate wrongdoing': Hooley, 1991, p 550. See also Deveney, 2013.

99  [1996] 4 All ER 769.

not have made the contract but for the misrepresentation (the offer of 78p would not at the time have been acceptable to the defendants), and they were, therefore, as a result of the misrepresentation, 'locked into the property'. Their full consequential losses were therefore recoverable.

Attempting to put claimants into the position in which they would have ended up had the misrepresentation not been made may, in some circumstances, allow the recovery of certain types of lost profit. In *East v Maurer*[100] the false statement related to a hairdressing business that the plaintiff bought. The defendant had stated that he had no intention of opening another hairdressing shop in the area. This was untrue, and when he did open such a shop, the plaintiff sued for damages resulting from his loss of business. If the statement had been true, the plaintiff would have been likely to have made substantial profits from the business which he had bought. Such profits would only, however, be recoverable in an action for breach of contract, where 'expectation interests' are compensated.[101] On the other hand, if the statement had not been made, the plaintiff would probably have bought a different business, and would have made some (though not as extensive) profits from that. The court felt that these hypothetical profits should be recoverable. The action for fraudulent misrepresentation may thus come very close to providing the same level of damages as are available for breach of contract.

## 8.4.4 FALSE STATEMENTS AND THE TORT OF NEGLIGENCE

In certain situations, damages for the tort of negligence may be recoverable in relation to misstatements. The law governing this area derives from the House of Lords' decision in *Hedley Byrne & Co Ltd v Heller & Partners Ltd*.[102]

---

**Key case** *Hedley Byrne & Co Ltd v Heller & Partners Ltd* (1964)

Facts: The plaintiffs had asked their bank to give an opinion on the financial standing of another firm. The bank gave a positive report, and the plaintiffs entered into contracts with the firm. Shortly afterwards the firm went into liquidation, owing substantial sums to the plaintiffs. They sued the bank, alleging that the statements as to the financial status of the firm had been made negligently.

Held: The House of Lords held that the bank was protected by a 'without responsibility' disclaimer, which it had attached to its advice.[103] It held, however, that in the absence of this the bank would have been liable. The bank owed a duty of care to the plaintiff, and so could be liable for the consequences of negligent statements that caused economic loss.

---

This established the possibility, therefore, of taking action in the tort of negligence in relation to statements made without proper care which result in loss. For this to be available, however, a 'duty of care' must be shown to exist between the maker of the statement and the person who has acted on it. Much of the extensive subsequent case law on this area has been concerned with the question of when such a duty will arise, which, it has been suggested, depends on there being a 'special relationship' between

---

100 [1991] 2 All ER 733. Cf *Mortgage Express v Countrywide Surveyors Ltd* [2016] EWHC 1830 (Ch).
101 See Chapter 15, 15.4.1.
102 [1964] AC 465; [1963] 2 All ER 575.
103 The reasonableness of such a disclaimer may now have to be considered under s 2 of the UCTA 1977. See Chapter 7, 7.7.4, and the case of *Smith v Eric S Bush* [1990] 1 AC 831; [1989] 2 All ER 514.

the parties. At times, however, it seemed that all that was needed was that the maker of the statement could reasonably foresee that the person to whom the statement was made would rely on it, and would suffer loss if it turned out to be untrue.[104] The House of Lords' decision in *Caparo Industries plc v Dickman* severely restricted the circumstances in which such a duty will be found to exist, though this has been softened to some extent by the subsequent decisions in *Henderson v Merrett Syndicates Ltd*[105] and *White v Jones*.[106] The current position seems to be that, in addition to the reasonable foreseeability of reliance and harm, there must be sufficient 'proximity' between the parties, and that it must be just and reasonable for the duty to be imposed. *Henderson v Merrett* and *White v Jones* indicate that a voluntary assumption of responsibility by the maker of the statement will generally be sufficient to establish a duty.[107] The issue of proximity is the most difficult, but will normally be satisfied where the statement is made in a context in which the parties are anticipating that a contract will be made between them. It was held by the Court of Appeal in *Esso Petroleum Co Ltd v Mardon*[108] that a common law duty of care could arise in such a situation, and this was confirmed in the subsequent cases of *Gran Gelato Ltd v Richcliff (Group) Ltd*[109] and *Henderson v Merrett Syndicates Ltd*.[110]

Even where there is a duty, there also needs to be reliance on the statement. In *Hunt v Optima (Cambridge) Ltd*,[111] the claim was dismissed because documents containing the false statements were found not to have come into existence until after the contracts that they were said to have induced had been completed.

The need for the *Hedley Byrne* action for contracting parties was reduced by the enactment of the Misrepresentation Act 1967,[112] which for the first time introduced a remedy in damages for non-fraudulent misrepresentations. Nevertheless, there are still situations where it may be useful to plead common law negligence alongside, or as an alternative to, liability under the Act. One advantage of the *Hedley Byrne* action, for example, is that it applies to all types of statement, not just statements of fact. A negligently expressed opinion may therefore give rise to the possibility of action in tort, where an action in contract would not be available (because the statement is not one of fact), unless the claimant proved that the opinion was not genuinely held, or that the expresser of the opinion was aware of facts that rendered it untenable. In general, however, an action under s 2 of the Misrepresentation Act 1967 will be the preferred choice for the claimant because it offers, as will be seen below, advantages in terms of the burden of proof and the extent of damages which are recoverable.

### 8.4.5 INDEMNITY AT COMMON LAW

As has been indicated above, the primary remedy for misrepresentation at common law was rescission. There was also, however, in certain circumstances a right to claim an indemnity for expenses incurred, in addition to rescission. As is shown by *Whittington*

---

104  See, for example, *Anns v Merton London Borough Council* [1978] AC 728; [1977] 2 All ER 492.

105  [1995] 2 AC 145; [1994] 3 All ER 506. See also *Spring v Guardian Assurance plc* [1995] 2 AC 296; [1994] 3 All ER 129.

106  [1995] 2 AC 207. This case is discussed further in Chapter 5, 5.10.

107  This basis for a duty was recognised in *Hedley Byrne*. Some doubt was cast on it by *Caparo Industries plc v Dickman* but see now *Playboy Club London Ltd v Banca Nazionale del Lavoro SpA* [2018] UKSC 43 and *Steel v NRAM Ltd (formerly NRAM Plc)* [2018] UKSC 13.

108  [1976] QB 801; [1976] 2 All ER 5. The facts of this case have been given in Chapter 6, at 6.4.2.

109  [1992] Ch 560.

110  [1995] 2 AC 145; [1994] 3 All ER 506.

111  [2014] EWCA Civ 714.

112  See below, 8.4.6–8.5.

*v Seale-Hayne*,[113] however, such expenses must have been directly related to the obligations of the contract. The case concerned the lease of premises for poultry breeding, which the landlord had stated were in good sanitary condition. The lease included a covenant under which the tenant was obliged to effect certain repairs (in line with local authority requirements). In fact, the premises were not sanitary, and the plaintiffs decided to rescind for misrepresentation. They also claimed, in addition to a refund of the rent, compensation in relation to rates paid, repairs carried out, loss of stock, and medical and removal expenses. It was held that they could only recover the cost of the rates, and of repairs carried out under the covenant. These were obligations which arose directly from the contract, and were recoverable on an 'indemnity' basis. The other items came into the category of a claim for damages, and so were not recoverable. The test is whether the expenses or losses were necessarily incurred as a result of entering into the contract. Thus, the claim for an indemnity is very limited in scope.

The availability of an action for damages under the Misrepresentation Act 1967 means that the only situation nowadays when the claimant might wish to consider claiming for an indemnity is where the contract is being rescinded for a totally innocent, non-negligent, misrepresentation.

### 8.4.6 DAMAGES UNDER S 2(1) OF THE MISREPRESENTATION ACT 1967[114]

The Misrepresentation Act 1967 introduced a statutory remedy in damages (whether or not rescission is also granted) for what is commonly referred to as 'negligent misrepresentation'. In fact, s 2(1) does not use this phrase, but makes the remedy available where the person making the misrepresentation would have been liable to damages if it had been made fraudulently:

> Where a person has entered into a contract after a misrepresentation has been made to him by another party thereto and as a result thereof he has suffered loss, then, if the person making the misrepresentation would be liable to damages in respect thereof had the misrepresentation been made fraudulently, that person shall be so liable notwithstanding that the misrepresentation was not made fraudulently, unless he proves that he had reasonable grounds to believe and did believe up to the time the contract was made that the facts represented were true.

The test of what is a misrepresentation will be as set out earlier in this chapter. As will be noted from the final part of the section, this action is advantageous to the claimant in that, once it is established that a false statement was made, the burden of proof shifts to the defendant to establish that there were reasonable grounds for believing it to be true. Moreover, the courts seem to be prepared to be fairly strict as to what will be regarded as reasonable grounds.

---

113  (1900) 82 LT 49. See also *Newbigging v Adam* (1886) 34 Ch D 582 and (1888) LR 13 App Cas 308 – rescission of a partnership; indemnity against liabilities incurred while a partner.

114  S 2 of the Misrepresentation Act 1967 was amended by the Consumer Protection (Amendment) Regulations 2014 with a new s 2(4) providing: "This section does not entitle a person to be paid damages in respect of a misrepresentation if the person has a right to redress under Part 4A of the Consumer Protection from Unfair Trading Regulations 2008, SI 2008/1277, in respect of the conduct constituting the misrepresentation." From a consumer's point of view this restriction may be regarded as unfortunate given, as we shall examine below, the powerful nature of the remedy under s 2(1).

**Key case** *Howard Marine Dredging Co Ltd v A Ogden & Sons (Excavations) Ltd (1978)*[115]

Facts: A representative of the owner of a barge told a potential charterer that the capacity was about 1,600 tonnes. This figure was based on his memory of the relevant entry in the usually authoritative *Lloyd's Register*, which stated that the capacity was 1,800 tonnes. In fact, as was made clear in the ship's documents, the correct figure was much less, at only 1,055 tonnes. The charterers subsequently sought to claim damages under s 2(1) on the basis of this misrepresentation. The defendants claimed that the representative had had reasonable grounds for believing his statement to be true, since it came from the *Lloyd's Register*.

Held: The Court of Appeal held that the defendant had failed to prove that he had reasonable grounds for belief in the truth of the statement. Reliance on the *Lloyd's Register* was insufficient when the correct figure was in documentation in the owner's possession.

**For thought**

*Do you think the outcome of this case would have been any different if the representative had previously seen the correct figure, but no longer had the ship's documents available to him at the time when he relied on the Lloyd's Register?*

## 8.4.7 MEASURE OF DAMAGES UNDER S 2(1)

One difficulty that has arisen with s 2(1) is the measure of damages – should it be contractual or tortious? In *Watts v Spence*[116] there was some suggestion that it should be contractual. The Court of Appeal, however, in *Sharneyford v Edge*[117] ruled that it should be tortious. The issue was considered further in *Royscot Trust Ltd v Rogerson*.[118]

**Key case** *Royscot Trust Ltd v Rogerson* (1991)

Facts: A car dealer misrepresented to the plaintiff finance company the amount of a deposit paid by a customer in connection with a hire purchase agreement. The finance company would not have been prepared to lend as much as it did had it known of the true value of the deposit. The finance company suffered a loss when the customer defaulted on his payments, after having sold the car to an innocent third party (who obtained good title under the Hire Purchase Act 1964). In an action by the plaintiff against the dealer for non-fraudulent misrepresentation, the only dispute was as to the amount of damages payable. The measure used by the judge at first instance was supported by neither party in the appeal, so that the Court of Appeal effectively had to decide the matter *de novo*.

Held: The Court of Appeal confirmed that in an action for misrepresentation under s 2(1) of the Misrepresentation Act 1967, the correct measure of damages is tortious rather than contractual. Moreover, since the wording of s 2(1) makes liability conditional on the situation where 'the person making the misrepresentation would be liable to

---

115  [1978] QB 574.
116  [1976] Ch 165; [1975] 2 All ER 528.
117  [1987] Ch 305; [1987] 1 All ER 588.
118  [1991] 3 All ER 294.

damages in respect thereof had the misrepresentation been made fraudulently', damages should be assessed in the same way as for fraudulent misrepresentation. This meant that the defendant was liable for all losses flowing from the defendant's misrepresentation, as is the case with the tort of deceit,[119] and not simply for those losses that were reasonably foreseeable.

Although the wording of the section itself gives rise to the so-called 'fiction of fraud' alluded to in this case, the weight of academic opinion, as evidenced by all the leading contract textbooks, has been in favour of applying the negligence remoteness rules, because to apply the deceit rule would operate too harshly in a situation where the defendant has been negligent rather than deliberately fraudulent. The Court of Appeal in this case, however, was not prepared to be swayed by these arguments of policy. It found that s 2(1) aligned liability under it with liability for fraud. The wording of the section was clear and the court saw no reason to depart from its literal meaning.

The approach taken by the Court of Appeal in *Royscot* appeared to be treated with some scepticism by the House of Lords in *Smith New Court Securities Ltd v Scrimgeour Vickers (Asset Management) Ltd*,[120] but the issue was not directly before it, and so no final view was expressed. For the moment, at any rate, the 'fiction of fraud' analysis, unsatisfactory as it is, remains good law.

This presumably also means that, on the basis of *East v Maurer*,[121] certain types of lost profits may be recoverable in an action under s 2(1). The damages under s 2(1) may therefore be almost as extensive as for breach of contract, particularly since they are not restricted by any rule of remoteness. The result is that there seems to be little reason now why a person who enters into a contract on the basis of a misrepresentation should ever seek to establish deceit. The action under s 2(1) of the 1967 Act is much to be preferred since it places on the defendant the burden of proving not only that the statement was believed to be true, but also that there were reasonable grounds for such a belief. If no greater damages are recoverable by proving deceit, there seems little point in trying to do so.

### 8.4.8 IN FOCUS: WHY SHOULD NEGLIGENT MISREPRESENTATION BE TREATED IN THE SAME WAY AS FRAUD?

The analysis of s 2(1) in *Royscot v Rogerson* involved a very narrow view of statutory interpretation, which ignores the policy behind both the introduction of s 2(1) and the reason for the wide scope of damages in relation to deceit. The reason for enacting s 2(1) was to allow damages to be recovered for *negligent* misrepresentations leading to a contract, in the same way that *Hedley Byrne v Heller* had allowed a remedy for negligent misstatements in other contexts.[122] The policy behind the broader damages for deceit is to punish or deter deliberate wrongdoing. These two factors taken together suggest that it was unlikely to have been Parliament's intention to enact that more extensive damages should be available under s 2(1) than under the tort of negligence. Moreover, as has been pointed

---

119  *Doyle v Olby (Ironmongers) Ltd* [1969] 2 QB 158; [1969] 2 All ER 119 – see above, 8.4.3.

120  [1996] 4 All ER 769.

121  [1991] 2 All ER 733 – see above, 8.4.3. See also Poole and Devenney, 2007.

122  At the time that the Misrepresentation Act 1967 was enacted it was thought that *Hedley Byrne* would not apply as between contracting parties. This has now been shown to be incorrect: *Esso Petroleum Co Ltd v Mardon* [1976] QB 801; [1976] 2 All ER 5 – see above, 8.3.2. There may be differences in relation to limitation periods: see *Rizwan Hussain v Saleem Mukhtar* [2016] EWHC 424 (QB). On the availability of the defence of contributory negligence see *Taberna Europe CDO II Plc v Selskabet (Formerly Roskilde Bank A/S) (In Bankruptcy)* [2016] EWCA Civ 1262.

out by Hooley,[123] it is by no means clear that the literal meaning of the section is as clear as was suggested by the Court of Appeal. The phrase 'so liable' in s 2(1), rather than meaning 'liable in the same way as if the statement had been made fraudulently', could just as easily be interpreted to mean simply 'liable in damages'. If there is ambiguity, the court should be free to adopt a reading that accords with overall policy concerns. Interpreting the section in the way suggested by Hooley would have enabled the Court of Appeal to have applied the law in a way that was more in keeping with the overall objectives of the section, and would have left the wider range of damages to those cases where they are much more justifiable – that is, where the maker of the statement has deliberately lied, or at least has shown a reckless disregard for the truth.

### 8.4.9 DAMAGES UNDER S 2(2) OF THE MISREPRESENTATION ACT 1967

Section 2(2) of the Misrepresentation Act 1967 allows a court to award damages in lieu of rescission, whether or not they are also awarded under s 2(1). This power is to be exercised if the court is:

> of the opinion that it would be equitable to do so, having regard to the nature of the misrepresentation and the loss that would be caused by it if the contract were upheld, as well as to the loss that rescission would cause to the other party.

Since the power is stated to be in lieu of rescission, it has been presumed that it will be lost if the right to rescind has been lost, for example by lapse of time or the intervention of third party rights.[124] This was not accepted in *Thomas Witter Ltd v TBP Industries*,[125] in which it was suggested that the power to award damages was not dependent on the continued availability of the right to rescind, since this would be too restrictive an interpretation of the section. The judges in two subsequent cases have, however, not followed this line. In both *Floods of Queensferry Ltd v Shand Construction Ltd*[126] and *Government of Zanzibar v British Aerospace (Lancaster House) Ltd*,[127] the view was expressed that the availability of damages under s 2(2) is dependent on the right to rescind not having been lost. In the latter case, Judge Raymond Jack QC saw the purpose of s 2(2) as being to allow the court to award damages where, for some reason, this would be more equitable to the defendant than requiring or upholding rescission. Since the power was an alternative to rescission, it could not be used where rescission itself was not available. In that situation the claimant could still claim damages under s 2(1), though subject to the restriction that they were only available where the defendant had been negligent. The judge saw this as maintaining a correct balance between the remedies available for negligent and wholly innocent misrepresentation.[128] This view has recently been affirmed by the Court of Appeal in *Salt v Stratstone Specialist Ltd*.[129]

As regards the *measure* of damages under s 2(2), there is no binding authority, but some guidance has been provided by *obiter* statements in *William Sindall plc v Cambridgeshire County Council*.[130] Hoffmann and Evans LJJ agreed that the measure must be different from that applying under s 2(1). This must be so, given that s 2(3) recognises the possibility

---

123 Hooley, 1991.
124 See above, 8.4.1.
125 [1996] 2 All ER 573.
126 [2000] BLR 81.
127 [2000] 1 WLR 2333.
128 Beale (1995a and 1995b) has argued that there *should* be a power to award damages for non-negligent misrepresentation even where rescission is lost, in order to prevent the possibility of the unjust enrichment of the defendant, but doubts whether under the present wording of s 2(2) there is such a power.
129 [2015] EWCA Civ 745.
130 [1994] 3 All ER 932.

(or even likelihood) that damages under s 2(2) will be less than under s 2(1). Where, as in this case, the contract concerned the sale of property, the measure should simply be an amount that would compensate the plaintiff for the loss he had suffered on account of the property not being that which it was represented to be. As Evans LJ put it, it should be 'the difference in value between what the plaintiff was misled into believing he was acquiring, and the value of what he in fact received'.[131] The assessment should be made at the time of the contract, and subsequent losses caused by a fall in market value should not be taken into account. There is no suggestion in these statements that any account should be taken of consequential losses, and this is surely right. To compensate for these would go beyond replacing the value of the right to rescind, and is surely better left to be dealt with under s 2(1).[132]

## 8.5 EXCLUSION OF LIABILITY FOR MISREPRESENTATION

Section 3 of the Misrepresentation Act 1967, as amended by s 8 of the Unfair Contract Terms Act (UCTA) 1977, restricts the possibility of exclusion of liability for misrepresentation. It states:

If a contract contains a term which would exclude or restrict:
(a) *any liability to which a party to a contract may be subject by reason of any misrepresentation made by him before the contract was made; or*
(b) *any remedy available to another party to the contract by reason of such misrepresentation,*
that term shall be of no effect except in so far as it satisfies the requirement of reasonableness as stated in s 11(1) of the Unfair Contract Terms Act 1977; and it is for those claiming that the term satisfies that requirement to show that it does.

Under the Consumer Rights Act 2015, s 3 of the Misrepresentation Act 1967 will no longer apply to consumer contracts. Instead, clauses purporting to limit liability for misrepresentation in such contracts will be required to be 'fair', as defined in the Consumer Rights Act 2015. This concept is discussed further in Chapter 7, at 7.8. The rest of the discussion in this chapter is concerned with s 3 of the Misrepresentation Act 1967, which continue to apply to business-to-business contracts, even after the Consumer Rights Act 2015 is in force.

Under s 3 of the Misrepresentation Act 1967, any contract term that attempts to restrict[133] either liability for misrepresentation or any remedy available in relation to it will only be effective if it satisfies the requirement of reasonableness under s 11 of the UCTA 1977.[134] The fact that a clause is in common use will not prevent it from being found to be

---

131 Ibid, p 963.
132 See also the comments on this case by Beale, 1995a, approving the approach to s 2(2) based on 'difference in value' as at the time of the contract.
133 By contrast clauses which define obligations would generally not come within s.3. Compare, for example, *Impact Funding Solutions Ltd v Barrington Support Services Ltd* [2016] UKSC 57 at [36] per Lord Toulson: "If a decorator agrees to paint the outside woodwork of a house except the garage doors, no-one can seriously regard the words of exception as anything but a convenient way of defining the obligation; it would surely make no difference if the promise were to paint the outside woodwork with a clear proviso that the contractor was not obliged to paint the garage doors, or if there were a definition clause brought to the promisee's attention saying that 'outside woodwork' did not include the garage doors. Such provisions do not ... deprive the promisee of a right of a kind which social policy requires that he should enjoy, nor do they ... give the promisor the advantage of appearing to promise more than he is in fact promising." It is not always easy to distinguish such clauses from exclusion clauses, and the Courts are alive to the use of clever drafting to try to circumvent statutory regulation: see *Cremdean Properties v Nash* [1977] 2 EGLR 80.
134 For which, see Chapter 7, 7.7.9.

unreasonable. In *Walker v Boyle*,[135] the court considered a clause contained in a contract for the sale of property, which stated that 'no error, misstatement or omission in any preliminary answer concerning the property shall annul the sale'. Even though the clause in this case was one that was contained in the National Conditions of Sale, and commonly used by solicitors, this did not prevent the court from holding that it was unreasonable. It was also confirmed by the House of Lords in *HIH Casualty and General Insurance Ltd v Chase Manhattan Bank*[136] that a party generally cannot exclude liability for its own fraudulent misrepresentation (though it left open the possibility of excluding such liability where the statement was made by an agent, provided sufficiently explicit language was used).

There have been a number of cases on s 3 of the Act, relating to the question of the type of clause that is caught by this provision. In particular, what is its effect in relation to a clause which states that no representations have been made, or that no reliance is to be placed on any that are made?

In *Overbrooke Estates Ltd v Glencombe Properties Ltd*,[137] the conditions of sale at an auction contained the following clause: 'The vendors do not make or give and neither the Auctioneers nor any person in the employment of the Auctioneers has any authority to make or give any representation or warranty in relation to [the property].' The auctioneers, as agents for the vendors, told the prospective purchasers that there were no local authority schemes for the area in which the property was situated. The purchasers later discovered that it was likely to be included in a slum clearance scheme, and tried to withdraw from the contract. The vendors relied on the clause set out above; the purchasers claimed that this was an unreasonable limitation clause, caught by s 3 of the 1967 Act. The court held that the clause did not operate in this situation as a limitation of liability clause, but simply defined the authority of the vendor's agent. It was perfectly permissible for the vendors to do this. The purchasers were aware of the limitation of authority at the time they entered into the contract, and could not therefore use any statement by the agent to escape from it.

The *Overbrooke* decision did not make it clear what the approach would have been had the representation come directly from the vendors, rather than via their agents. In *Cremdean Properties Ltd v Nash*,[138] however, the Court of Appeal took the view that the scope of the earlier decision was limited to the situation of agency. The court was considering a clause in a contract for the sale of two properties that stated that the accuracy of the particulars supplied could not be guaranteed and that 'Any intending purchaser ... must satisfy himself by inspection or otherwise as to the correctness of each of the statements contained in these particulars.' It was suggested by the vendors that this did not amount to an attempt to exclude liability, but rather brought about a situation in which it was as if no representation had ever been made. The court firmly rejected this argument. Referring to the *Overbrooke* decision, Bridge LJ commented:

> It is one thing to say that s 3 [of the Misrepresentation Act 1967] does not inhibit a principal from publicly giving notice limiting the ostensible authority of his agents; it is quite another thing to say that a principal can circumvent the plainly intended effect of s 3 by a clause excluding his own liability for a representation which he has undoubtedly made.

Even if the vendor had explicitly said that, notwithstanding anything in the particulars, no misrepresentations within the meaning of the Misrepresentation Act 1967 were made, this

---

135 [1982] 1 WLR 495.
136 [2003] UKHL 6; [2003] 2 Lloyd's Rep 61.
137 [1974] 1 WLR 13355.
138 (1977) 244 EG 547.

would still have been treated by the court as an attempt to exclude liability falling within the scope of s 3. The same view was taken in *Inntrepreneur Estates (CPC) Ltd v Worth*,[139] where the clause stated that the lessee acknowledged that no reliance was placed on pre-contractual statements. Although on the facts it was held that there were no pre-contractual statements on which the lessee had relied, Laddie J stated that, if there had been, the clause would have fallen within the scope of s 3 and would have been treated as unreasonable.

Subsequent cases have followed the same line as in *Cremdean v Nash*, drawing a distinction between the effect of an 'entire agreement' clause on an action for breach of the main or collateral contract, and its effect on an action for misrepresentation. In *McGrath v Shah*,[140] it was held that a clause stating simply that 'This contract constitutes the entire contract between the parties, and may be varied ... only in writing under the hands of the parties or their solicitors' did not fall within the scope of s 3 of the Misrepresentation Act 1967. It was effective to prevent an argument that pre-contractual representations had become part of the contract. It did not, however, deal with actions for misrepresentation, and was not struck down by s 3.[141]

A similar analysis was adopted in *Thomas Witter Ltd v TBP Industries Ltd*.[142] The entire agreement clause was again held here to be ineffective in excluding liability for an action in misrepresentation, as opposed to a contractual action based on an allegation that a representation had become part of the contract. Nor was the second part of the clause effective. This purported to limit the pre-contractual statements that could be relied on in a misrepresentation action to those referred to in a schedule to the contract.[143] The clause might cause difficulties in establishing that some other representation had in fact been relied on, but if this could be shown, then an action could be based on it. Furthermore, Jacob J held, *obiter*, that even if these provisions did attempt to exclude liability for misrepresentation, they would be unreasonable under s 3 because their scope would be too wide, potentially extending to fraudulent misrepresentation.[144]

The position as to the relationship between entire agreements and the exclusion of liability for misrepresentation was usefully summarised by Lightman J in *Inntrepreneur Pub Co (GL) v East Crown Ltd*.[145] The clause in question had two parts. Clause 14.1 was an 'entire agreement' clause. Clause 14.2 stated that the tenants 'have not relied upon any advice or statement of the Company or its solicitors'.[146] Lightman J analysed the effect of these provisions as follows:[147]

An entire agreement provision does not preclude a claim in misrepresentation, for the denial of contractual force to a statement cannot affect the status of the statement of a misrepresentation. The same clause in an agreement may contain both an entire agreement provision and a further provision designed to exclude liability e.g. for misrepresentation or breach of duty. As an example, clause 14 in this case, after setting out in clause 14.1 the entire agreement clause, in clause 14.2 sets

---

139  [1996] 1 EGLR 84.

140  (1987) 57 P & CR 452.

141  The action in this case was not based on misrepresentation. The judge declined to express a view on the second half of the clause in question, which did explicitly refer to 'representations'.

142  [1996] 2 All ER 573.

143  This stated 'the Purchaser acknowledges that it has not been induced to enter into this Agreement by any representation or warranty other than statements contained or referred to in Schedule 6': ibid, p 595.

144  In coming to this conclusion, the judge emphasised that it was the potential scope of the clause that had to be considered when assessing reasonableness, rather than its application to the facts of the case before the court: ibid, p 598.

145  [2000] 2 Lloyd's LR 611.

146  Ibid, p 614.

147  Ibid.

out to exclude liability for misrepresentation and breach of duty. Whether this latter provision is legally effective for this purpose may turn on the question of its reasonableness as required by s 3 of the Misrepresentation Act 1967: see, e.g. *Inntrepreneur Estates (CPC) v Worth*. But ... s 3 has no application to an entire agreement clause defining where the contractual terms between the parties are to be found: see *McGrath v Shah*.

This clear statement was helpful, but only emphasised that the law in this area was based on fairly technical distinctions as to the precise effect of each particular clause. Subsequent cases at High Court level attempted to deal with this issue, but without providing any clearer guidance than emerged from the cases outlined above. In both *Peart Stevenson Associates Ltd v Holland*,[148] and *B Sky B Ltd v Enterprise Services UK Ltd*[149] the general approach appeared to be that if the defendant wished to avoid liability for misrepresentation via a 'non-reliance' clause, it would need to be clear that the claimant did genuinely intend to agree that there would be no reliance. In any case, it would be difficult, if not impossible, to avoid liability for fraudulent misrepresentations.

The issue was considered again by the Court of Appeal in *Springwell Navigation Corp v JP Morgan Chase Bank*,[150] and *Axa Sun Life Services plc v Campbell Martin*.[151] In the first case, a clause stating that '[A] has not relied on, and acknowledges that neither CMSCI nor CMIL has made, any representation or warranty with respect to the advisability of purchasing this note' was held to prevent (by estoppel) any claim based on misrepresentation. But in *Axa Sun Life* a clause that stated that 'this Agreement shall supersede any prior, promises, agreements, representations or Implications ... between you and us relating to the subject matter of this Agreement' was held not to preclude actions for misrepresentations of fact. These decisions have not taken matters much further.

Some clarity has been given to this area by the Court of Appeal decision in *First Tower Trustees Ltd, Intertrust Trustees Limited v CDS (Superstores International) Limited*.[152] Two substantive judgments were given in this case (Lewison and Leggatt LJJ with Sir Colin Rimer concurring with both judgments). The Court of Appeal accepted that some clauses may *define* the parties' obligations and that such clauses would not be subject to the s.3 Misrepresentation Act 1967.[153] The Court of Appeal also considered the principle of so-called "contractual estoppel" whereby "parties can bind themselves by contract to accept a particular state of affairs even if they know that state of affairs to be untrue".[154] In so doing, the following passage from the judgment of Aikens LJ in *Springwell Navigation Corp v JP Morgan Chase Bank* [2010] EWCA Civ 1221 was approved:[155]

If A and B enter into a contract then, unless there is some principle of law or statute to the contrary, they are entitled to agree what they like...[T]here is no legal principle that states that parties cannot agree to assume that a certain state of affairs is the case at the time the contract is concluded or has been so in the past, even if that is not the case, so that the contract is made upon the basis that the present or past facts are as stated and agreed by the parties.[156]

148  [2008] EWHC 1868, in particular paras 95–108.
149  [2010] BLR 267, in particular, paras 359–89.
150  [2010] EWCA Civ 1221.
151  [2011] EWCA Civ 133.
152  [2018] EWCA Civ 1396.
153  See [2018] EWCA Civ 1396 at [43] and [96].
154  See [2018] EWCA Civ 1396 at [47] and [97].
155  See [2018] EWCA Civ 1396 at [47].
156  [2010] EWCA Civ 1221 at [143].

However, that is not the end of the matter. A valid contractual estoppel may still be subject to, for example, s 3 of the Misrepresentation Act 1967.[157] Lewison LJ held:

> I would hold…that a clause which simply states (as clause 12.1 of the agreement for lease and clause 5.8 of the lease do) "that this lease has not been entered into in reliance wholly or partly on any statement or representation made by or on behalf of the landlord" is a contract term which would have the effect of excluding liability for misrepresentation; and consequently is subject to the test of reasonableness.

Leggatt LJ went even further:

> For the reasons I have given, as well as those given by Lewison LJ, I would hold that *whenever* a contracting party relies on the principle of contractual estoppel to argue that, by reason of a contract term, the other party to the contract is prevented from asserting a fact which is necessary to establish liability for a pre-contractual misrepresentation, the term falls within section 3 of the Misrepresentation Act 1967. Such a term is therefore of no effect except in so far as it satisfies the requirement of reasonableness as stated in section 11 of UCTA.[158]

## 8.6 SUMMARY OF KEY POINTS

- A misrepresentation is a false statement of fact or law made by one contracting party to the other which induces the contract. It can be made by words or actions.

- Statements of intention or opinion are not generally misrepresentations, unless they are not genuinely held, in which case they are misrepresentations of the state of mind of the person making the statement.

- Silence will not constitute a misrepresentation unless the contract is one of *uberrimae fidei*, or the maker of the statement fails to reveal the whole truth, or circumstances change between the making of the statement and the making of the contract.

- The misrepresentation need not be the only reason for making the contract, and the reliance on it may not need to be reasonable.

- Remedies for misrepresentation depend on whether it is made innocently, negligently or fraudulently.

- Rescission is in principle available for all types of misrepresentation, but can be lost through:
  - ☐ affirmation
  - ☐ lapse of time
  - ☐ impossibility of restitution.

---

157  See [2018] EWCA Civ 1396 at [66].
158  See [2018] EWCA Civ 1396 at [111] (emphasis added).

■ Damages are available for fraudulent misrepresentation (deceit), if the claimant proves that the statement was made with knowledge that it was untrue, or with a reckless disregard for the truth.

■ Damages may be available in the tort of negligence if the statement falls within the scope of the principles developed from the decision in *Hedley Byrne v Heller*.

■ Damages are available for negligent misstatements under s 2(1) of the Misrepresentation Act 1967. It is up to the person making the statement to prove that there were reasonable grounds for believing it to be true.

■ Under s 2(2) of the Misrepresentation Act 1967, damages may be awarded in lieu of rescission if the court feels that this is appropriate – but only where the remedy of rescission is still available.

■ Exclusions of liability for misrepresentation will only be effective if they satisfy the requirement of reasonableness under the Unfair Contract Terms Act 1977.

## 8.7 FURTHER READING

■ Allen, D, *Misrepresentation*, 1988, London: Sweet & Maxwell

■ Beale, H, 'Damages in lieu of rescission for misrepresentation' (1995a) 111 LQR 60

■ Beale, H, 'Points on misrepresentation' (1995b) 111 LQR 385

■ Bigwood, R, 'Pre-contractual misrepresentation and the limits of the principle in *With v O'Flanagan*' [2005] CLJ 94

■ Hooley, R, 'Damages and the Misrepresentation Act 1967' (1991) 107 LQR 547

## COMPANION WEBSITE

*Now visit the companion website to:*

■ Revise and consolidate your knowledge of Misrepresentation by tackling a series of multiple-choice questions on this chapter

■ Test your understanding of the chapter's key terms by using the flashcard glossary

■ Explore Misrepresentation further by accessing a series of web links

# 9

# Mistake

## Contents

## 9.1 OVERVIEW

This chapter deals with situations where an agreement is affected by a mistake on the part of one or both parties. The general approach of the English courts and the different categories of mistake are dealt with first. The main topics then discussed are as follows:

■ Mistakes nullifying agreement. This essentially deals with situations where the parties have reached agreement, but on the basis of an important (shared) mistake – such as the existence of the subject matter. Such mistakes may render the 'contract' void. Here the shared mistake must be:

- ☐    'fundamental', meaning performance is impossible or radically different from that which the parties had envisaged;
- ☐    but mistakes as to quality will not generally render the contract void.

▪ Mistakes negativing agreement. This type of mistake means that the parties were never in agreement. This may be because:

- ☐    they were at cross-purposes ('mutual mistake');
- ☐    one party was aware of the other's mistake ('unilateral mistake').

▪ Mistake as to the identity of the other party. This is generally a type of unilateral mistake and may render the 'contract' void. It is easier to establish an operative mistake of identity in contracts made at a distance (for example, by post) as opposed to those made face to face.

▪ In some circumstances the application of equitable principles may lead to:

- ☐    the refusal of specific performance;
- ☐    rectification of a written contract.

▪ *Non est factum*. This is essentially a plea that a person signed a document under a misapprehension as to its effect. It will only be effective where the mistake is fundamental, and the person signing it had not acted carelessly.

## 9.2 INTRODUCTION[1]

This chapter is concerned with the situations in which a putative contract may be regarded as never having come into existence, or may be brought to an end, as a result of a mistake by either or both of the parties. Although the overall theme is that of 'mistake', as will be seen, the situations that fall within this traditional categorisation are varied, and do not have any necessary conceptual unity. Moreover, they may have a considerable overlap or interaction with other areas of contract law – in particular, offer and acceptance, misrepresentation and frustration.[2]

The rules developed by the courts impose fairly heavy burdens on those arguing that a mistake that undermines the putative contract has been made. This is not surprising. It would not be satisfactory if a party to a contract could simply, by saying 'I'm sorry, I made a mistake', unstitch a complex agreement without any thought for the consequences for the other party, or any third parties who might be involved. To allow this to be done would be to strike at the purposes of the law of contract, which has as one of its main functions the provision of a structure within which people can organise their commercial relationships with a high degree of certainty. On the other hand, a fundamental principle of the English law of contract is that, as far as possible, the courts should give effect to the intentions of the parties. If either, or both, of the parties has genuinely made a mistake as to the nature of their contract, to enforce it may run counter to their intentions.[3] The courts do, therefore, recognise the possibility of

---

1    For a full history of the development of the concept of 'mistake' in English law, see Macmillan, 2010.

2    That is why in some texts one or more of the topics dealt with in this chapter are discussed in the context of the other rules to which they most closely relate. Smith (1994) has argued that 'there is no room for the application of a distinct doctrine of mistake, additional to the principles of the formation of the contract and of implied terms'.

3    The issue of how the parties' 'intentions' are determined by the courts, and in particular whether this is done by a 'subjective' or 'objective' approach, is a complex issue that is considered further below, 9.5.1. It is arguable that certain types of 'objective' approach may lead to the court deciding that what the parties 'intended' was something which in fact neither party had in mind: see, for example, Spencer, 1973.

mistakes affecting, or even destroying, contractual obligations that would otherwise arise. The power to intervene in this way is, however, used with considerable circumspection.

This general reluctance to allow mistakes to affect a contract does not, of course, prevent the parties themselves from agreeing that a mistake will allow the party who has made the mistake to rescind the contract. This is not unusual in relation to consumer contracts made with large chain stores. These organisations often feel able (presumably because of their volume of business and their strength of position in the market) to allow customers who have simply changed their minds to exchange or return goods even though they are in no way defective. As was noted in Chapter 2, there are also some statutory provisions that allow consumers a short period in which to change their minds about particular sorts of contract, particularly those involving 'distance contracts' or certain credit arrangements.[4] In such a situation, the consumer who realises that he or she has made a mistake of some kind in relation to the contract will be able to escape from it, usually provided that action is taken within the specified time limits. These arrangements are, however, exceptions to the general position under the common law, which will only allow a party to undo the agreement in a limited range of circumstances.

## 9.3 CATEGORIES OF MISTAKE

As noted above, there are various ways in which a party may make a mistake in relation to the contract. It may, for example, relate to the subject matter, the identity of the other contracting party or the specific terms of the contract. Three particular types of mistake may be identified. In the first, the parties are found to have reached agreement, but on the basis of an assumption as to the surrounding facts which turns out to be false (for example, the subject matter of the contract is in existence whereas, in fact, it has at the time of the agreement ceased to exist). The mistake may, following the House of Lords' decision in *Kleinwort Benson Ltd v Lincoln City Council*,[5] be one of law. This was confirmed by the Court of Appeal in *Brennan v Bolt Burdon*.[6] In this case a dispute had been settled on the basis of a ruling in a first instance decision that was then overturned on appeal. The claimant sought to set aside the settlement on the basis that it was based on a mistake of law. This argument succeeded in the High Court. The Court of Appeal set out the relevant approach in these terms:[7]

(1) As with any other contracts, compromises or consent orders may be vitiated by a common mistake of law. (2) It is initially a question of construction as to whether the alleged mistake has that consequence. (3) Whilst a general release executed in a prospective or nascent dispute requires clear language to justify an inference of an intention to surrender rights of which the releasor was unaware and could not have been aware ..., different considerations arise in relation to the compromise of litigation which the parties have agreed to settle on a give-and-take basis ... (4) For a common mistake of fact or law to vitiate a contract of any kind, it must render the performance of the contract impossible.

---

4   See, for example, the Consumer Contracts (Information, Cancellation and Additional Charges) Regulations 2013, SI 2013/3134 and the Consumer Credit Act 1974, s 67. For further discussion of this type of provision, see Chapter 2, 2.14.

5   [1999] 2 AC 349; [1998] 4 All ER 513.

6   [2004] EWCA Civ 1017; [2005] QB 303.

7   Ibid, at [17]. Compare *British Red Cross v Werry* [2017] EWHC 875 where a settlement agreement in respect of a claim under the Inheritance (Provision for Family and Dependants) Act 1975 was held to be void when it was subsequently discovered that the deceased had, in fact, left a will and the partner of the deceased had been left the property in question.

The question was, therefore, whether the courts below were correct to find that in this case there was a sufficient mistake of law to vitiate the agreement. The Court of Appeal found that there was not. A distinction can be drawn between situations where there is an unequivocal but mistaken view of the law, and where there is a doubt as to the law. The majority of the Court of Appeal felt that this case involved a doubt as to the law of service at the time the compromise agreement was made, rather than an unequivocal mistake. Moreover, the compromise agreement remained possible to perform. As a result, the appeal was allowed and the claimant was held to her compromise agreement.

This type of mistake, whether of fact or law, is the type of mistake referred to by Lord Atkin in *Bell v Lever Bros*[8] as a mistake that 'nullifies' consent.[9] There is here, in technical terms, a valid contract (in that it is formed by a matching offer and acceptance and supported by consideration), but it would, if put into effect, operate in a way that is fundamentally different from the parties' expectations.[10] The courts will therefore sometimes intervene to declare the contract void, and treat it as if it had never existed. This type of mistake has close links with the doctrine of 'frustration', which applies in situations where events *after* the formation of the contract (such as the destruction of the subject matter) fundamentally affect the nature of the agreement.[11]

The second and third types of mistake arise where the court finds that there is, in fact, a disagreement between the parties as to some important element of the contract. These are mistakes that Lord Atkin, in *Bell v Lever Bros*, referred to as 'negativing consent', in that they are said to operate to prevent a contract ever existing, because of the lack of agreement between the parties. Within this general category, however, two different situations must be distinguished. First, it may be that neither party is aware of the fact that the other is contracting on the basis of different assumptions as to the nature or terms of the agreement. They are at cross-purposes, but do not realise this until after the contract has apparently been agreed.[12] This situation relates to the issues discussed in Chapter 2, in that it can be questioned whether there was ever a matching offer and acceptance. The second type of situation where there may be a mistake 'negativing' agreement is where one party is aware of the mistake being made by the other, and indeed may even have encouraged it.[13] Where such encouragement has taken place, there is likely to be an overlap with misrepresentation; dissolution of the contract on the basis of mistake is then only likely to be sought where the remedies for misrepresentation would be inadequate.[14]

Although, as has been noted above, there is a lack of conceptual unity in this area, the theme that may be said to link these various situations is that of 'agreement failure'. There is an apparent agreement between the parties, but that agreement is either impossible to perform, or if performed would operate in a way that would be contrary to the expectations of at least one of the parties. Because this is the focus, there is little scope here for

---

8   [1932] AC 161.

9   It is also referred to by some writers as a 'common mistake' – see, for example, *Cheshire, Fifoot and Furmston's Law of Contract,* 2017, p 286.

10  Collins (2003, p 125) suggests that this type of mistake is better analysed as involving an implied condition precedent (for example, that the subject matter of the contract is still in existence) and that the failure of this condition renders the contract unenforceable. This is an attractive analysis, but does not represent the way in which the courts say they are dealing with the relevant cases.

11  See *Amalgamated Investment and Property Co Ltd v John Walker & Sons* [1976] 3 All ER 509, which was pleaded in both mistake and frustration. The doctrine of frustration is dealt with in Chapter 13.

12  *Cheshire, Fifoot and Furmston* call this 'mutual mistake', though this phrase is sometimes also, and confusingly, used to refer to what is here called a 'common mistake'.

13  This type of mistake is often referred to as a 'unilateral mistake'.

14  This is most likely to arise where one of the bars to rescission applies (see Chapter 8, 8.4.1) – such bars do not apply if the contract is found to be void for mistake.

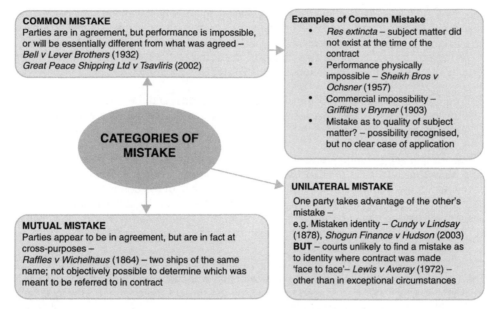

**COMMON MISTAKE**
Parties are in agreement, but performance is impossible, or will be essentially different from what was agreed –
*Bell v Lever Brothers* (1932)
*Great Peace Shipping Ltd v Tsavliris* (2002)

**Examples of Common Mistake**
- *Res extincta* – subject matter did not exist at the time of the contract
- Performance physically impossible – *Sheikh Bros v Ochsner* (1957)
- Commercial impossibility – *Griffiths v Brymer* (1903)
- Mistake as to quality of subject matter? – possibility recognised, but no clear case of application

**CATEGORIES OF MISTAKE**

**MUTUAL MISTAKE**
Parties appear to be in agreement, but are in fact at cross-purposes –
*Raffles v Wichelhaus* (1864) – two ships of the same name; not objectively possible to determine which was meant to be referred to in contract

**UNILATERAL MISTAKE**
One party takes advantage of the other's mistake –
e.g. Mistaken identity – *Cundy v Lindsay* (1878), *Shogun Finance v Hudson* (2003)
**BUT** – courts unlikely to find a mistake as to identity where contract was made 'face to face'– *Lewis v Averay* (1972) – other than in exceptional circumstances

Figure 9.1

reliance-based remedies. If a mistake is operative,[15] then the putative contract will be declared void or (possibly) voidable (in which case it might be set aside either in its entirety or on particular terms).[16] Damages are not awarded in relation to a contract that has been based on an operative mistake.[17]

## 9.4 MISTAKES NULLIFYING AGREEMENT ('COMMON MISTAKE')[18]

One of the clearest examples of operative mistake is where the parties have attempted to make a 'contract' about something that had ceased to exist at the time the contract is made.[19] If, for example, the contract concerns the hire of a specific boat that, unknown to either party, has been destroyed by fire the day before the contract was made, the agreement will usually be void for common mistake. The parties have reached agreement but that agreement is nullified by the fact that the subject matter no longer existed at the time of the agreement. This type of common mistake is sometimes referred to by the Latin tag of *res extincta*. An example from the cases is *Galloway v Galloway*.[20] The parties, who thought they

---

15 That is, sufficiently serious to justify the court's intervention.
16 This approach was adopted in some cases by the courts applying the rules of equity, but now seems to have been rejected – see below, 9.6. Alternatively, the court may use the mistake as the basis for a refusal to grant an order for specific performance.
17 Unless the mistake is the result of a misrepresentation – in which case damages may be recoverable on one of the bases outlined in Chapter 8. This will be an alternative, however, to setting the contract aside for mistake.
18 As to the history of this type of mistake, see Simpson, 1975b, pp 265–69. In *National Private Air Transport Co v Kaki* [2017] EWHC 1496 (Comm) the judge stressed that a party could not claim common mistake if there was no reasonable grounds for their mistaken belief.
19 Where the subject matter ceases to exist *after* the contract is made, the doctrine of frustration, which is dealt with in Chapter 13, might apply rather than mistake.
20 (1914) 30 TLR 531.

had been married to each other, made a separation agreement. It was then discovered that their supposed marriage was invalid because the husband's previous wife was still alive. As a result, the separation agreement was void and the 'husband' had no liability under it.

As regards contracts for the sale of goods, the common law rule is given statutory reinforcement by s 6 of the Sale of Goods Act (SGA) 1979. This states that:

> Where there is a contract for the sale of specific goods, and the goods without the knowledge of the seller have perished at the time when the contract is made, the contract is void.

The word 'perished' almost certainly encompasses more than simply physical destruction, as is shown by the pre-SGA 1893 case of *Couturier v Hastie*.[21] The contract in this case was for the purchase of a cargo of corn. At the time of the contract, the cargo had, because it was starting to deteriorate, been unloaded and sold to someone else. The purchaser was held to have no liability to pay the price. There are some doubts, however, as to the true basis for the decision in this case; these are referred to in 9.4.2.[22]

### 9.4.1 SUBJECT MATTER THAT NEVER EXISTED

The cases we have been considering deal with the situation where the subject matter *did* exist at one point, but has ceased to do so by the time of the contract. The position is more difficult where the subject matter has *never* existed. There seems no logical reason why the contract should not equally be void for mistake in such a case, but this was not the view of the High Court of Australia on the facts in *McRae v Commonwealth Disposals Commission*.[23] The Commission had invited tenders for a salvage operation in relation to an oil tanker, said to be 'lying on the Jourmand Reef'. The plaintiffs were awarded the contract, but on arrival found that neither the tanker nor the reef existed. The Commission claimed that the contract was void for mistake, and that they therefore had no liability. The court held, however, that there was a contract, in that the Commission had to be taken to have warranted the existence of the tanker. The plaintiffs were entitled to damages to compensate for their costs in putting together the abortive enterprise.

### 9.4.2 IN FOCUS: THE TRUE BASIS FOR THE DECISION IN *COUTURIER V HASTIE*

In reaching its conclusion in *McRae*, the court did not accept that the decision in *Couturier v Hastie* was truly based on 'mistake'. It was simply that the plaintiff's claim in that case, that the price was payable on production of the shipping documents, could not be upheld as being part of the contract. It is certainly true that the House of Lords in *Couturier v Hastie* never mentioned mistake as the basis for its decision. The case is perhaps in the end best regarded as an example of the kind of situation in which an operative mistake could occur, and that would now fall within s 6 of the SGA 1979, rather than as a direct authority on the issue.

---

**For thought**

*What do you think the outcome of McRae would have been if there had been a ship in the specified location, but it had already been salvaged by the time the Commission made the contract with McRae?*

---

21  (1856) 5 HLC 673. Section 6 of the 1893 Act, which was in the same terms as s 6 of the 1979 Act, was intended to give statutory effect to the principles applied in *Couturier v Hastie*.
22  For a thorough survey of the possible interpretations of the case, see Atiyah, 1957.
23  (1951) 84 CLR 377.

### 9.4.3 HAS THERE BEEN A PROMISE THAT THE SUBJECT MATTER EXISTS?

*McRae* can be taken to indicate a more general principle to the effect that where one of the parties has expressly or by implication promised that the subject matter exists, then mistake has no role to play where the subject matter does not exist as the other party can sue for breach of the promise. This could apply not only where the subject matter has never existed, but also where it did once exist and has been destroyed prior to the agreement. This makes particular sense where, as in *McRae*, one party can reasonably be taken to have superior knowledge about the existence of the subject matter. The other party may then *rely* on this superior knowledge in entering into the contract and it may well be appropriate that if that reliance turns out to be unjustified, damages should be recoverable. Simply setting the agreement aside because it has failed might not be sufficient in such circumstances.

There would be a difficulty, however, in applying this to contracts for the sale of goods. This is because s 6 of the SGA 1979 states that, in such a case, the contract is void. There is no express provision in the section for the parties to agree to the contrary and it is by no means clear that the courts would imply one.[24] There is no problem where the goods never existed because the use of the word 'perished' in s 6 implies that the goods did once exist: if they did not, then the section has no application. It would be odd, however, if the law drew such a clear distinction, simply in sale of goods cases, between the situation where the subject matter once existed and the situation where it never existed. There are several options. First, it might be said that the *McRae* approach *only* applies where the subject matter never existed. This would produce a workable rule, but it would be difficult to see any policy behind the distinction. Second, it might be argued that the word 'perished' in s 6 encompasses the situation where the goods never existed. This interpretation would lead to all sale of goods contracts being treated in the same way but differently from other contracts. However, it is again difficult to see any underlying policy that would justify the distinction. Third, it could be argued, as suggested by Atiyah,[25] that the courts should be prepared to interpret s 6 as not intended to apply whenever specific promises about the existence of the goods have been made. This would produce the most analytically satisfactory answer in that it would align all sale of goods contracts with the general rule. It probably also involves, however, the most adventurous statutory interpretation, and it is by no means certain that the courts would be willing to adopt it. The area therefore remains unclear. The approach adopted in *McRae*, however, seems sensible, and is in line with the modern law's recognition that disappointed reliance should generally be compensated. It makes sense for that approach to be adopted wherever possible, even if it does leave contracts for the sale of specific goods that have perished in an anomalous position.

### 9.4.4 IMPOSSIBILITY OF PERFORMANCE

An operative common mistake may also arise where, although the subject matter of the contract has not been destroyed, performance is, and always was, impossible. This may result from a physical impossibility, as in *Sheikh Bros v Ochsner*,[26] where land was not capable of growing the quantity of crop contracted for, or legal impossibility,[27] where the

---

24  At various points the Act states that the provisions of a section apply unless the parties agree otherwise: there is no statement of this kind in s 6. Nevertheless, Atiyah has argued that the effect of the section should be able to be overturned by a contrary intention of the parties: Atiyah, 1957, pp 348–49.

25  1957, pp 348–49. See also *Joseph Constantine SS Ltd v Imperial Smelting Corp* [1942] AC 154 at 184–86.

26  [1957] AC 136.

27  The case of *Cooper v Phibbs* (1867) LR 2 HL 149 is sometimes cited as an example of the application of this principle. In fact, the contract, which was to rent land in which the tenant already held a beneficial (though not legal) interest, was set aside by the House of Lords as being voidable in equity, rather than void at common law. This is indicated by the fact that terms were imposed on the rescission, which would not be possible if the contract were void at common law. As to the equitable remedies for mistake, see below, 9.6.

contract is to buy property which the purchaser already owned.[28] A contract based on a mistake of law will also fall into this category.[29] There is also one case, *Griffith v Brymer*,[30] where a contract was found void for what may be regarded as 'commercial impossibility'.[31] The contract was to hire a room to view an event which, at the time of the contract, had already been cancelled. Performance of the contract was physically and legally possible, but would have had no point.[32]

### 9.4.5 MISTAKE AS TO QUALITY

Can there be an operative common mistake where the parties are mistaken as to the quality of what they have contracted about? Suppose A sells B a table, both parties being under the impression that they are dealing with a valuable antique, whereas it subsequently turns out to be a fake. Can B claim that the contract should be treated as void on the basis of a common mistake?[33] The leading House of Lords authority is *Bell v Lever Bros*.[34]

---

**Key case** *Bell v Lever Bros* (1932)

Facts: The plaintiffs (Lever Bros) had reached an agreement for compensation with the defendant over the early termination of his contract of employment. This termination agreement was itself a contract, providing for the payment of £50,000. The plaintiffs then discovered that the defendant had previously behaved in a way (entering into secret deals for his personal benefit) that would have justified termination without compensation. They therefore argued that the compensation contract should be regarded as being void for mistake. At trial, although the jury found that the defendant had not been fraudulent, the judge held that the compensation agreement was void for mistake. The case was appealed to the House of Lords.

Held: The House of Lords was reluctant to allow a mistake as to the quality, or value, of what had been contracted for to be regarded as an operative mistake. As Lord Atkin put it:[35]

> In such a case, a mistake will not affect assent unless it is the mistake of both parties and is as to the existence of some quality which makes the thing without the quality essentially different from the thing as it was believed to be.

---

28  See Lord Atkin's statement to this effect in *Bell v Lever Bros Ltd* [1932] AC 161, p 218.
29  As indicated by *Brennan v Bolt Burdon* [2004] EWCA Civ 1017; [2005] QB 303 – discussed above, 9.3.
30  (1903) 19 TLR 434.
31  See Treitel, 2015, p 347.
32  There are a number of cases arising out of the same events as *Griffiths v Brymer* which, because the cancellation occurred *after* the contract had been made, were dealt with as cases of 'frustration' – see Chapter 13, 13.3.3.
33  This type of situation may, depending on the precise circumstances, be dealt with by the provisions of the SGA 1979 and, in particular, the implied term under s 13 that goods should match their description, as in *Nicholson and Venn v Smith-Marriott* (1947) 177 LT 189 although compare *Ashington Piggeries Ltd v Christopher Hill Ltd* [1972] AC 441. For discussion of s 13, see Chapter 6, 6.6.12. If A has made a statement about the nature of the table, there may also be the possibility of rescission or damages for misrepresentation.
34  [1932] AC 161. For a full discussion of the background to the case and the way in which it moved from being about the trustworthiness of managers to becoming a leading authority on 'mistake', see Macmillan, 2003.
35  [1932] AC 161, p 218.

This would not be the case in an example such as that of an antique that turns out to be a fake. Lord Atkin again commented:[36]

> A buys a picture from B: both A and B believe it to be the work of an old master, and high price is paid. It turns out to be a modern copy. A has no remedy in the absence of representation or warranty.

Applying this approach to the case before the House, the conclusion was that there was no operative mistake. The plaintiffs had obtained exactly what they had bargained for, that was, the release of the contract with the defendant. The fact that the plaintiffs could have achieved the same result without paying compensation by relying on the defendant's earlier conduct was immaterial.

This conclusion has sometimes been regarded as indicating that there can never be an operative mistake as to quality.[37] However, the decision does not go quite that far, as the first quotation from Lord Atkin above shows. He specifically recognised the possibility that a mistake is to quality, the absence of which makes the subject matter 'essentially different'. The difficulty is that if, as was held in *Bell v Lever Bros*, a mistake worth £50,000 does not make a contract essentially different, then what kind of mistake will do so? The fact that *Bell* did not shut the door on operative mistakes as to quality was, however, noted by Steyn J in *Associated Japanese Bank Ltd v Credit du Nord SA*.[38] He held that a contract of guarantee, which was given on the basis of the existence of certain packaging machines, was void at common law when it turned out the machines did not exist at all. B, as a means of raising capital, had entered into an arrangement with the plaintiff bank, under which the bank bought the four machines from B for £1,021,000. The bank then immediately leased the machines back to B. B, of course, had obligations to make payments under this lease to the plaintiff. These obligations were guaranteed by the defendant bank. B was unable to keep up the payments, and the plaintiff sought to enforce the guarantee against the defendant, by which time it had been discovered that the machines had never existed. This mistake, which had been made by both plaintiff and defendant, of course, had great significance for the guarantee. There is no doubt that the defendant would not have given the guarantee if it had known the truth. But was the guarantee rendered void by this mistake? Steyn J refused to accept that *Bell* precluded an argument based on common mistake as to quality. His view was that, on the facts, such a mistake was not operative in *Bell*, not least because it was by no means clear that Lever Bros would have acted any differently even if they had known the truth. It was open, therefore, to consider whether the mistake was operative in the case before him. It should be noted that this was not a case of *res extincta*, though it comes close. The machines were not the subject matter of the contract under consideration. The subject matter was in fact a contract in

---

36  Ibid, p 224.
37  The decision in *Bell v Lever Bros* has been described as possibly being 'the most unsatisfactory decision handed down by the House of Lords in modern times': Harris, Campbell and Halson, 2002, p 244. The criticism relates in part to the very limited scope for common mistake that was recognised by the House in this case. It is clear that it is not necessarily enough that the contract would not have been entered into if the true facts had been known: see *Triple Seven MSN 27251 Ltd v Azman Air Services Ltd* [2018] EWHC 1348 (Comm).
38  [1988] 3 All ER 902. For a detailed analysis of the relationship between this case and *Bell v Lever Bros*, see Treitel, 1988 and Smith, 1994.

relation to the machines the performance of which had been supported by a guarantee given by the defendant. Steyn J concluded:[39]

> For both parties, the guarantee of obligations under a lease with non-existent machines was essentially different from a guarantee of a lease with four machines which both parties at the time of the contract believed to exist.

The contract of guarantee was therefore void for common mistake at common law.[40] The position would therefore seem to be that some mistakes as to the quality, or value, of the subject matter of the contract can give rise to an operative mistake provided that the mistake has a sufficiently serious effect in relation to matters which are fundamental to the contract. There are *obiter* statements in *Nicholson and Venn v Smith-Marriott*,[41] where the mistake was as to the provenance of antique table linen, which would also support such a view, though equally, in *Leaf v International Galleries*,[42] where the mistake was as to whether a picture was painted by Constable, there are *obiter* statements that envisage a very limited role for this type of mistake. The fact that there are so few reported cases where it has been held that a common mistake is operative to avoid the contract at common law suggests that the latter view may well be correct.

This view is reinforced by the most recent reconsideration of the area by the Court of Appeal in *Great Peace Shipping Ltd v Tsavliris ('The Great Peace')*.[43]

---

**Key case** *Great Peace Shipping Ltd v Tsavliris ('The Great Peace')* (2002)

Facts: The contract concerned the charter of a ship, *The Great Peace*, to provide urgent assistance with a salvage operation. At the time of the contract both parties thought that the ship was about 35 miles from the salvage site. In fact it was about 410 miles away. When the charterer discovered this, it found another ship that was much closer and sought to avoid the contract for *The Great Peace* on the basis of common mistake. Held: The Court of Appeal held that the mistake was not sufficiently serious to render the contract void at common law – it would still have been possible for *The Great Peace* to render assistance at the salvage, even though at a later time than anticipated. The principles set out in *Bell v Lever Bros* were confirmed as indicating the correct approach to such issues. In coming to this conclusion, the Court of Appeal took the opportunity to review the whole basis for the doctrine of common mistake. It came to the view that it was properly regarded as being based not on any theory of terms to be implied into the contract but as a rule of law similar to that which operates in relation to the doctrine of frustration.[44] The court restated the requirements for common mistake in the following way (which it saw as consistent with *Bell v Lever Bros*):[45]

(i)     there must be a common assumption as to the existence of a state of affairs;

(ii)    there must be no warranty by either party that that state of affairs exists;

---

39  [1988] 3 All ER 902, p 913.
40  Treitel (1988, p 507) has suggested that *Bell v Lever Bros* exemplifies the application of the policy of respect for the sanctity of contract, whereas *Associated Bank* is based on the policy of giving effect to the reasonable expectations of honest men.
41  (1947) 177 LT 189.
42  [1950] 2 KB 86; [1950] 1 All ER 693. The case is discussed further in Chapter 8 at 8.4.1.
43  [2002] EWCA Civ 1407; [2002] 4 All ER 689.
44  Which is dealt with in Chapter 13.
45  [2002] EWCA Civ 1407; [2002] 4 All ER 689, para 76. See also *Dany Lions Ltd v Bristol Cars Ltd* [2013] EWHC 2997.

(iii)   the non-existence of the state of affairs must not be attributable to the fault of either party;

(iv)   the non-existence of the state of affairs must render performance of the contract impossible; and

(v)   the state of affairs may be the existence, or a vital attribute, of the consideration to be provided or the circumstance which must subsist if performance of the contractual adventure is to be possible.

Applying these principles to the facts of the case, there was no operative common mistake.

Point (ii) (and to some extent (iii)) of this analysis obviously deals with the situation that arose in *McRae v Commonwealth Disposals Commission*.[46] The reference to 'impossibility' in point (iv) must be read in the light of the analogies which the court was drawing with the doctrine of frustration. Under that doctrine, a contract may be discharged if performance has become impossible or 'radically different' from that which the parties intended. It would seem that such an approach should also apply in relation to mistake. That this is the view of the Court of Appeal in *The Great Peace* is confirmed by its treatment of mistakes as to quality. As will be seen, in point (v) it refers to a 'vital attribute' and this clearly extends the scope of the doctrine beyond physical non-existence of the subject matter. Moreover, the court approved the analysis of Steyn J in the *Associated Japanese Bank* case, in which he concluded that *Bell v Lever Bros* still left open the possibility of a mistake as to quality rendering a contract void where the mistake renders 'the subject matter of the contract essentially and radically different from the subject matter which the parties believed to exist'.[47] The Court of Appeal's specific approval of this passage, and of the conclusions reached by Steyn J on the facts of the *Associated Japanese Bank* case, confirm that mistakes as to quality may render a contract void, albeit very rarely.

On the facts that arose in *The Great Peace*, the Court of Appeal agreed with the trial judge that the mistake as to the position of the vessel was not sufficiently serious to render the contract void. In particular, when the true position of the vessel was discovered, the charterers did not cancel the contract until they had located another vessel that was nearer. The implication was that if no other such vessel had been located, they would have continued with the charter concerning *The Great Peace*. If that was the case, it was difficult to argue that the contract for *The Great Peace* was 'impossible' or even 'radically different' from that which the parties had intended.

## 9.4.6 EFFECT OF AN OPERATIVE COMMON MISTAKE

The effect of an operative common mistake at common law is to render the contract void *ab initio* (from the beginning). It is as if the contract had never existed and therefore, as far as is possible, all concerned must be returned to the position they were in before the contract was made. This applies equally to third parties, so that the innocent purchaser of goods which have been 'sold' under a void contract will be required to hand them back to the original owner. These powerful and far-reaching consequences perhaps explain

---

46  Above, 9.4.1.

47  [1988] 3 All ER 902, pp 912–13. On the difficulties of terminology in this area see *Triple Seven MSN 27251 Ltd v Azman Air Services Ltd* [2018] EWHC 1348 (Comm) and in *Swynson Ltd v Lowick Rose LLP (In Liquidation) (formerly Hurst Morrison Thomson LLP)* [2017] UKSC 32 where Lord Sumption refused to be drawn into this "controversy".

why the courts have shown a reluctance to extend the scope of common mistake too far, preferring to allow the flexible application of equitable remedies to pick up the pieces in many cases. The use of equity has, however, been significantly reduced since the Court of Appeal's decision in *The Great Peace*.[48]

## 9.5 MISTAKES NEGATIVING AGREEMENT

As indicated above, there are two categories of mistake that may have the effect of negativing agreement – that is the 'contract' fails because there never was an agreement between the parties. The first category is where neither side is aware of the fact that the other is contracting on a different basis. The lack of agreement is 'mutual'. The second category is where one party is aware of the other's mistake. Here the mistake is 'unilateral'. These two categories will be considered separately.

### 9.5.1 'MUTUAL MISTAKE'

'Mutual mistake' refers to the situation where the parties are at cross-purposes but neither side is aware of this when they purport to make a contract. The mistake may relate to the subject matter of the contract, or the identity of the other contracting party. If the mistake is sufficiently fundamental there will be no agreement between the parties, and therefore no contract, meaning any actions taken on the basis that there was a contract will have to be undone.

A classic example of a situation that might give rise to this kind of mistake is to be found in *Raffles v Wichelhaus*.[49]

---

**Key case** *Raffles v Wichelhaus* (1864)

Facts: The alleged contract was for the purchase of a cargo of cotton due to arrive in England on the ship *Peerless*, from Bombay. There were two ships of this name carrying cotton from Bombay, one of which left in October, the other in December.
Held: The plaintiff offered the December cargo for delivery but the defendant refused to accept this, claiming that he intended to buy the October cargo. The plaintiff tried to argue that the contract was simply for a certain quantity of cotton, and that the ship from which it was to be supplied was immaterial. The defendant, however, put his case in these terms:[50]

> There is nothing on the face of the contract to shew that any particular ship called the *Peerless* was meant; but the moment it appears that two ships called the *Peerless* were about to sail from Bombay there is a latent ambiguity, and parol evidence may be given for the purpose of shewing that the defendant meant one *Peerless*, and the plaintiff another. That being so, there was no *consensus ad idem*, and therefore no binding contract.

The court stopped argument at this point, and held for the defendant.

---

48  For the effect of this decision on the remedies available in equity to deal with mistake, see 9.6 below.
49  (1864) 2 H & C 906; 159 ER 375. The case has attracted much academic attention. For the historical context, see Simpson, 1989. For an argument that the commonly accepted interpretation of the case was 'invented' by Holmes, see Gilmore, 1974, pp 40–2. A similar view of the use of the case by English writers is taken by Macmillan, 2010, pp 186–90.
50  (1864) 2 H & C 906, pp 907–08; 159 ER 375, p 376. Contrast also *Chancery Client Partners Ltd v MRC 957 Ltd* [2016] EWHC 2142 (Ch).

There is, however, no report of any judgment in *Raffles v Wichelhaus*, so it is impossible to be certain of the exact basis of the decision. It is perhaps significant, however, that a few years later the case was cited by Hannen J in *Smith v Hughes* as authority for the proposition that:[51]

> if two persons enter into an apparent contract concerning a particular person or ship, and it turns out that each of them, misled by a similarity of name, had a different ship or person in his mind, no contract would exist between them.

Whatever the precise basis for the decision in *Raffles v Wichelhaus* itself, therefore, there seems no doubt that if the parties are at cross-purposes, a contract may be void for mutual mistake. This will, of course, only apply where there is a fundamental ambiguity in the contract and no objective means of resolving it.

This type of mistake raises a question which was discussed in Chapter 2 – that is, how do the courts decide what the parties intended? Clearly the intentions can only be inferred from the words and actions of the parties, rather than their actual states of mind. The approach is therefore primarily objective – what would a reasonable person viewing the actions and hearing the statements of the parties think that they intended? If, taking the objective view, there was agreement, then the contract will not be avoided for mutual mistake. As was noted in Chapter 2,[52] however, the objective valuation may be made from the point of view of one of the parties,[53] or from the point of view of an independent third party.[54] It seems that in the area of mutual mistake, the question of whether there is an agreement based on detached objectivity is going to be the crucial question. The facts of a mutual mistake case will often be such that both parties may be able to argue that they reasonably believed the other party to be intending to contract on a particular basis. Thus, in *Raffles v Wichelhaus*[55] the plaintiffs could have argued that they intended to sell the December cargo and reasonably believed that that was what they believed the defendants were intending to buy. Equally, the defendants could argue that they reasonably believed that the plaintiffs were intending to sell the October cargo. If the defendants' view had prevailed, it would have meant that there was a contract for sale of the October cargo, and the plaintiff was in breach of contract. This was not the outcome of the case, however.[56] It appears to have been the view of the court that there was no contract at all.

This will not necessarily be the outcome, however, if, from a point of view of detached objectivity, a third party would reasonably believe that the contract had been made on particular terms. Thus, in *Rose (Frederick E) (London) Ltd v William H Pim Jnr & Co Ltd*,[57] there was confusion between the parties as to whether they were contracting about 'horse-beans' or 'feveroles' (a particular type of horsebean). From the point of view of detached objectivity, however, the contract simply appeared to be for

---

51  (1871) LR 6 QB 597, p 609.
52  See Chapter 2, 2.4.2.
53  Promisor or promisee objectivity.
54  Detached objectivity.
55  Gilmore (1974, pp 35–40) argues that *Raffles v Wichelhaus* is in fact an example of the courts using a subjective approach to the question of whether there was agreement between the parties – there was no contract because there was no 'meeting of the minds'. He alleges that the modern 'interpretation' of the case derives solely from the writings of Holmes. See also Macmillan, 2010, pp 186–90 on the way in which the treatment of the case by English writers resulted in its acceptance as an authority on 'mutual mistake'.
56  At least in so far as it has been understood in *Smith v Hughes* and later cases.
57  [1953] 2 QB 450; [1953] 2 All ER 739.

'horsebeans', and that was how it was interpreted by the court.[58] This could not apply in *Raffles v Wichelhaus*, since a third party looking at what had passed between the parties would have been unable to determine which ship was intended. The only possibility in that case, therefore, was for the 'contract' to be treated as void, for failure of agreement.

### 9.5.2 IN FOCUS: DOES 'DETACHED OBJECTIVITY' RISK ABSURDITY?

Spencer has argued that the use of 'detached objectivity', which he labels the 'fly on the wall' approach, can lead to absurd results, as he felt that it did in *Rose v Pim*.[59] He gives the example of two people with little knowledge of English who contract for the sale and purchase of a 'bull', intending in fact to deal with a 'cow'. He suggests that the detached objectivity approach would lead to the contract being deemed to be one for a bull, which is not what either party intended. But this is to suggest that detached objectivity can be used in a way that ignores the context and the surrounding circumstances. In *Raffles v Wichelhaus*, for example, no doubt if there was evidence to show that the parties had in fact been in agreement about which ship was meant, then the contract would have been upheld, despite the fact that 'detached objectivity', applied in the absence of such additional information, would be unable to determine which ship was intended. The 'bull' and 'cow' example could surely take into account the understanding of these words as shared by the parties. In cases of mutual mistake, evidence that despite confusing language there was agreement will prevent the contract being declared void. In the absence of such agreement, the question to be asked is what would a reasonable third party, looking at what was said and done, think that the parties to the agreement intended. In *Raffles*, the confusion was such that it was not possible to give a definite answer to this question. A similar result occurred in *Scriven Bros v Hindley*,[60] where there was confusion as to the nature of two lots in an auction, one being 'hemp', the other being much less valuable 'tow'. The defendant, who had bid an unusually high price for the tow, in the mistaken belief that it was hemp, was allowed to negate the contract.[61]

### 9.5.3 THE LIMITS TO MUTUAL MISTAKE

In *Smith v Hughes*,[62] which again concerned an alleged mutual mistake in relation to the subject matter of the contract, a more restrictive view was taken as to what mistakes justify a finding that there was no agreement.

---

**Key case** *Smith v Hughes* (1871)

Facts: The plaintiff had offered to sell oats to the defendant, who trained horses. The defendant was shown a sample of oats and agreed to buy the whole quantity. When

---

58  The case was concerned with the possibility of the 'rectification' of a contract (and is discussed in that context below, 9.7.2). For a further example of a court's refusal to find a mutual mistake, using an 'objective' approach, see *NBTY Europe Ltd v Nutricia International BV* [2005] EWHC 734 Comm; [2005] 2 Lloyd's Rep 350.

59  Spencer, 1973. His criticism of *Rose v Pim* is based on the fact that both parties intended to deal in 'feveroles'. It is by no means clear, however, that that is an accurate view of the facts, since it seems that at the time of the contract neither party understood how feveroles differed from horsebeans.

60  [1913] 3 KB 564.

61  The case might now be categorised as one of 'unilateral mistake', since there was some evidence that the auctioneer realised that the bid was made on the basis of a mistake. At the time, however, it was not dealt with on this basis, the court finding that there was no contract simply on the basis that the parties were not *ad idem*.

62  (1871) LR 6 QB 597.

delivered, they turned out to be 'new' oats, which were of no use to the defendant. He sought to escape from the contract on the basis that he thought he was buying 'old' oats. There was a conflict of evidence as to whether the plaintiff had ever referred to the oats as 'old'. The trial judge directed the jury that if they thought that the defendant believed that he was contracting for old oats, they should give a verdict for the defendant, which they did. The plaintiff appealed.

Held: The Queen's Bench held that it was not enough that the defendant had made a mistake. To allow him to escape from the contract, it would be necessary to show that the defendant thought that it was a term of the contract that the oats were 'old', *and that the plaintiff was aware that the defendant thought this* (that is, a 'unilateral', rather than 'mutual', mistake). Looked at objectively, it appeared to be simply a contract for the sale of a specific parcel of oats, about which there was no ambiguity. The case was sent for retrial.

The approach here, therefore, as in general with issues as to the creation of an agreement, is to concentrate on what can be deduced objectively from what the parties have said or done, rather than to try to determine their precise state of mind at the time of the alleged agreement.

**For thought**

*What do you think the outcome of Smith v Hughes would have been if the defendant had, during pre-contractual discussion, indicated that he only used old oats in his business?*

### 9.5.4 'UNILATERAL MISTAKE'

'Unilateral mistake' refers to the situation where the agreement is 'negatived' (that is, prevented from coming into existence), because one party is aware that the other is mistaken about an aspect of the contract. In many situations involving unilateral mistake there will have been a misrepresentation that will provide the other party with a remedy. If there was no such misrepresentation, however, or the remedies available for misrepresentation are inadequate, there may be a remedy on the basis of a unilateral mistake. For this to be available, however, the mistake must be sufficiently important that, viewed objectively, it prevents there being an agreement. As we have seen, the court in *Smith v Hughes* thought that the result would have been different if the plaintiff had been aware that the defendant was acting on the basis of a mistake *as to a term of the contract*. For example, if the mistake, as in *Smith v Hughes*, relates to some quality of whatever constitutes the subject matter of the contract, it is not enough that A is aware that B has made some mistake about this quality; A must also realise that B regards A as having undertaken a contractual obligation that the subject matter has the quality concerned. As has been noted in the discussion of misrepresentation, the law of contract does not generally intervene simply because one party is more knowledgeable than the other.[63] Taking advantage of superior knowledge or information is seen as tending towards wealth creation in a capitalist economic context. The approach taken by English law is exemplified by the following

---

63 See Chapter 8, 8.2.

quotation from Rimer J in *Clarion Ltd v National Provident Institution*.[64] In considering the scope for the courts to intervene where one party is aware of another's mistake, he took the example of negotiations for a compromise of a legal action (though the approach suggested is clearly intended to be of wider application):[65]

> The compromise of litigation is a contractual exercise in which it is the commonest thing for each side to be aware of facts and matters of which it knows or at least suspects the other side is ignorant. If each side knew all that the other side knew then either no or only a very different compromise would be reached. In the negotiation of such compromises[66] the parties must be careful not to make any misrepresentations. But there is in my view no general duty imposed on them in the nature of a duty of disclosure. The negotiations are in the nature of an arm's length commercial bargain. Each party has to look after its own interests and neither owes a duty of care to the other. It would in my view be astonishing if, in the ordinary case, a defendant could later set aside a compromise merely because he had learnt ... that he had materially overpaid a claimant who, unbeknown to him but well known to the claimant's advisers, probably could not have proved his case at all.

It is, therefore, only where the party with the superior knowledge is seen as acting unfairly towards the other (for example, by inducing the other's misunderstanding through false statements) that the courts will intervene. This basis for intervention has clear links with the concept of 'good faith', which, as we have seen, operates in many other jurisdictions and was part of the European Draft Common Frame of Reference: Contract Law.[67]

An example of a situation where one party was not allowed to take advantage of a mistake made by the other is to be found in *Hartog v Colin and Shields*.[68] The contract was for the sale of hare skins. The price quoted by the seller was stated to be 'per pound'. This was a mistake, since the price should have been 'per piece'. The mistake meant that the skins appeared to be being offered at a price about two-thirds lower than intended by the seller. The normal practice in the trade is for skins to be sold by the piece. The buyers accepted the seller's offer in the terms stated, but the seller refused to supply on this basis, claiming that the buyers were trying to take unfair advantage of a genuine mistake. The court was of the view that the buyers were aware that a mistake had been made.[69] On this basis there was no contract, and the sellers did not have to supply at the price stated. This case fulfils the requirements set out in *Smith v Hughes*. The mistake was as to a term of the contract (the price of the goods) and the other party was aware that a mistake as to this term had been made.

### 9.5.5 MISTAKEN IDENTITY

Unilateral mistakes may arise in relation to any aspect of the contract. The majority of reported cases, however, concern mistakes as to the identity of the other contracting party. The traditional rule was that the mistake, to be operative, must have related to the

---

64 [2000] 2 All ER 265.

65 Ibid, p 281. He was commenting on issues raised by Young J in the Australian case of *EasyFind (NSW) Pty Ltd v Paterson* (1987) 11 NSWLR 98, p 106.

66 That is, in effect, 'contracts'.

67 See Article II. – 7:201 for the use of good faith in relation to mistake cases. See also Cartwright and SchmidtKessel 2013.

68 [1939] 3 All ER 566; see also *Centrovincial Estates plc v Merchant Investors Insurance Co Ltd* [1983] Com LR 158 and *Statoil ASA v Lewis Dreyfus Energy Sources LP* [2008] EWHC 2257 (Comm).

69 The case does not make it clear whether it is necessary to prove actual knowledge of the mistake, or simply that the party 'taking advantage' *should have been* aware of the mistake. The normal approach to deciding on issues as to the state of mind of a party would suggest that the test should be objective – that is, 'would a reasonable person in the position of this party have realised that a mistake had been made by the other side'.

*identity* of the person with whom you were contracting, not his or her *attributes*. This is a distinction that may be easier to state than to apply. Indeed, Lord Denning suggested in *Lewis v Averay* that it was a 'distinction without a difference':[70]

> A man's name is one of his attributes. It is also a key to his identity. If, then, he gives a false name, is it a mistake as to his identity? Or a mistake as to his attributes? These fine distinctions do no good to the law.

Nevertheless, it can be argued that the distinction may in some situations serve some purpose. Suppose, for example, I negotiate a contract for my shop to be opened by a particular film star and this is advertised widely. I will not be satisfied if the agency with whom I have made the contract sends either (a) someone with the same name as the film star, but with no other similar qualities, or (b) another film star, but not the one whose presence I have advertised. In such a case, the identity of the individual is of central importance to the contract. A misunderstanding on this matter should raise the possibility of the contract being void for mistake. On the other hand, in the majority of contractual situations, the identity of the party with whom one is contracting is not important. The concern is as to whether they will perform their obligations under the contract, not who they are. In particular, there is generally no reason to allow a person to back out of a contract simply for thinking mistakenly that the other party was wealthy and therefore creditworthy.

The courts have been more willing to treat mistakes of identity as operative where the contract has been made through the post, or via an agent, rather than in person. In *Boulton v Jones*,[71] for example, the defendant had sent an order to one 'Brocklehurst' with whom he had dealt regularly. Brocklehurst had, however, just transferred the business to his foreman, who fulfilled the order. The defendant resisted a claim for payment by the foreman on the basis that he had a 'set-off' against Brocklehurst, arising out of their previous dealings. The court accepted that the existence of this set-off made the identity of the other party of crucial importance to the defendant, and the 'contract' was therefore void.

This result may appear a little harsh to the plaintiff in *Boulton v Jones* who, while aware of the defendant's mistake, was not trying to take any unfair advantage. This was not the case, however, in *Cundy v Lindsay*.[72]

---

**Key case** *Cundy v Lindsay* (1878)

Facts: A fraudulent individual named Blenkarn placed large orders for handkerchiefs with the plaintiffs. Blenkarn was trading from Wood Street, and the plaintiffs thought that they were dealing with a reputable firm by the name of Blenkiron & Co, which also had its business in Wood Street. Blenkarn deliberately contributed to this mistake by the manner in which he signed his order. The goods were supplied on credit and sold on by Blenkarn to the defendant, who was an innocent third party.

Held: The House of Lords confirmed that there was no contract between the plaintiffs and Blenkarn. As Lord Cairns put it:[73]

> Of him [Blenkarn], they [the plaintiffs] knew nothing, and of him they never thought. With him they never intended to deal. Their minds never for an instant of

---

70 [1972] 1 QB 198, p 206. See also *Shogun Finance Ltd v Hudson* [2003] UKHL 62 at [5] per Lord Nicholls and [59] per Lord Millett.
71 (1857) 27 LJ Exch 117.
72 (1878) 3 App Cas 459.
73 (1878) 3 App Cas 459, p 465.

> time rested upon him, and as between him and them there was no consensus of mind which could lead to any agreement or any contract whatever.
>
> The contract was void for mistake as to the identity of the other contracting party.

As will be noted, the approach taken in *Cundy v Lindsay* introduces a rather more subjective element, concerned with the fact of agreement, than is usually the case in this area. Even from an objective point of view, however, the fact that the plaintiffs had addressed the orders, and other correspondence, to 'Messrs Blenkiron', indicated that they had been under a misapprehension about whom they were dealing with, and had not intended to contract with Blenkarn. The consequences of the decision, however, were serious for the innocent defendants, who had to return the handkerchiefs (for which they had paid) to the plaintiffs, and were left to seek compensation from the fraudulent Blenkarn. The continued authority of *Cundy v Lindsay* has been recently confirmed by the decision of the House of Lords in *Shogun Finance Ltd v Hudson*,[74] which is discussed below, in 9.5.6.

For the mistake as to identity to be operative, the mistaken party must be able to show who it was that was the intended contracting party. Thus, in *King's Norton Metal Co v Edridge, Merrett & Co*,[75] although once again a contract was induced by a fraudulent person (Wallis), who was pretending to be a firm called 'Hallam & Co', the contract was upheld. This was because 'Hallam & Co' was a pure invention, created by Wallis. There was no genuine firm of that name with whom the plaintiffs could have thought they were dealing. The mistake was therefore not one of identity, but of attributes. The plaintiffs thought that they were dealing with a firm, though in fact they were dealing with a private individual, Wallis.

### 9.5.6 CONTRACTS MADE 'FACE TO FACE'

It becomes much harder to argue that a unilateral mistake has taken place where the contract is made face to face or, as the courts often describe it, *inter praesentes*. The courts are reluctant to accept that you did not intend to contract with the person who is standing in front of you, even though you may have been under a misapprehension as to that person's identity, attributes or qualities. The importance of this distinction was demonstrated and reaffirmed in *Shogun Finance Ltd v Hudson*.[76] A person had pretended to be someone else for the purpose of obtaining a car on hire purchase terms. Although the negotiations relating to the transaction were with the car dealer, the written contract, in which the false name was given, was with the finance company. The majority of the House of Lords held that this was not a contract *inter praesentes*, and the finance company was allowed to avoid the contract on the basis of unilateral mistake.[77] They were clearly influenced in this conclusion by the fact that the finance company would only deal with a person whom, after carrying out checks, it deemed to be creditworthy – and this was the person named in the written contract, not the 'rogue' pretending to be that person. In addition, the contract was formed by the written documentation exchanged with the finance company, not by the dealer as

---

74 [2003] UKHL 62; [2004] 1 All ER 215. Though it should be noted that two members of the House (Lord Nicholls and Lord Millett) were of the view that *Cundy v Lindsay* should be overruled.

75 (1897) 14 TLR 98.

76 [2003] UKHL 62; [2004] 1 All ER 215.

77 This had the effect of preventing an innocent third party, who had bought the car from the 'rogue', from obtaining a good title. It meant that the finance company was able to avoid the protection normally given to private purchasers of cars which are sold in breach of a hire purchase agreement provided by the Hire Purchase Act 1964, s 27.

agent for the finance company. By contrast, the minority in the House of Lords felt that the decision in *Cundy v Lindsay*[78] should be overruled, and that the presumption outlined below, that one intends to contract with the person with whom one is dealing, should apply to contracts made in writing as well as those made in person. The majority's decision, however, means that the law continues to apply particular rules to contracts made face to face.

The starting point for consideration of the approach of English law to contracts *inter praesentes* is *Phillips v Brooks*.[79] In this case a person went into a jeweller's shop. He selected various valuable items, including a ring. As he was writing a cheque in payment, he said 'You see who I am, I am Sir George Bullough', giving an address in St James' Square. The plaintiff checked this information in a directory, and then allowed the man to take the ring with him. The cheque was dishonoured, and the man turned out not to be Sir George at all. He had in the meantime, however, passed the ring to the defendant, who had taken it in all innocence. The court held that the contract was with the person in the shop. The plaintiff had failed to establish that the identity of that person was a crucial element in the contract.

This approach was followed in *Lewis v Averay*.[80]

---

**Key case** *Lewis v Averay* (1972)

Facts: The plaintiff was a student, who had advertised his car for sale. The fraudulent party pretended to be Richard Greene, an actor famous at that time for playing Robin Hood in a television series. In support of his claim, the fraudulent party produced a 'pass' from Pinewood Film Studios that carried his photograph and an official stamp. Impressed, the plaintiff agreed to part with his car in return for a cheque, which subsequently proved to be worthless. By the time the cheque was dishonoured and the plaintiff had discovered the fraud, the car had been sold to the defendant, who had bought it in good faith, innocent of any deception. The perpetrator of the fraud having disappeared from the scene, the plaintiff sued the defendant in the tort of conversion for recovery of the car, or its value plus damages.

Held: It was held that the contract, while probably voidable for misrepresentation, was not void for mistake, so that the innocent third party who was now in possession of the car was entitled to retain it. Looking at the outward appearances of the transaction, it was simply a contract under which the plaintiff sold the car to the fraudulent purchaser. The identity of the purchaser was not an important factor. Since the plaintiff had not managed to avoid the contract before the car had been sold to an innocent third party, the contract had to stand.

---

It is difficult, however, to reconcile these two cases (*Phillips v Brooks* and *Lewis v Averay*) with the decision in *Ingram v Little*.[81] Here, the contract was, as in *Lewis v Averay*, for the sale of a car. It was owned by three women who lived together. A man calling himself Hutchinson answered their advertisement. He offered a sum that was acceptable to the women, but then produced a cheque book. The woman who was conducting the negotiations at that point indicated that in no circumstances would they accept payment by cheque. The man then gave a full name and an address. One of the other women then left the house to visit the post office and consult a telephone directory, which confirmed

---

78  (1878) 3 App Cas 459.
79  [1919] 2 KB 243.
80  [1972] 2 All ER 229.
81  [1961] 1 QB 31; [1960] 3 All ER 332.

that a person of that name lived at the address given. They then allowed him to take the car in exchange for the cheque. The man was not, however, Mr Hutchinson, and the cheque proved worthless. The women brought an action to recover the car from an innocent third party purchaser. The Court of Appeal confirmed the view of the trial judge that they should succeed. The response to the offer of a cheque, and the procedure of checking in the directory, indicated that the identity of the other contracting party was of the utmost importance, and the contract was therefore void for mistake.

The principle applied is the same in all three of the cases just discussed, that is the identity of the other contracting party must be sufficiently important to form part of the basis of the contract. It is difficult to see, however, that there really was that much difference in the situation in *Ingram v Little* to justify applying the principle differently from the way in which it was applied in *Phillips v Brooks* and *Lewis v Averay*. There have been attempts to explain the differences on the basis of the precise stage in the process when the contract was made. Thus, in *Phillips v Brooks*, it might be argued that the contract was made before there was any mention of 'Sir George Bullough',[82] whereas in *Ingram v Little* the plaintiffs were only prepared to contract once they had checked that a Mr Hutchinson did live at the address quoted. These arguments appear rather strained, however. The reality is that in all three cases the plaintiff was tricked into parting with property by the fraud of the other contracting party. They could not use the remedy of misrepresentation because the fraudulent party had already disposed of the property to an innocent third party by the time the fraud was discovered. The question was simply which of two 'innocent' parties should bear the loss caused by the fraud.

The general view seems to be that the approach taken in *Lewis v Averay* is in general to be preferred. The original owner may be marginally less 'innocent' than the third party because it is the owner's actions that have 'allowed' the fraud to be perpetrated.[83] Lewis could, for example, have insisted, notwithstanding the fact that he thought he was dealing with a famous actor, that the cheque should be cleared before possession of the car was surrendered. In that situation the 'fairest' result is to allow the loss to lie with the original owner. This result is also probably suggested by adopting the approach of 'detached objectivity'. What would a third party viewing the transaction reasonably think had occurred? Would they think that the seller was intending to deal with the person standing in front of them, or only with a particular named individual? All this suggests that *Ingram v Little* is the anomalous case, and that there is probably little point in engaging in protracted analysis to fit it into a coherent doctrine. Indeed, it does not appear to survive *Shogun*. However, the decision in *Ingram v Little* was not unanimous, since Lord Devlin dissented. In the course of his judgment, he expressed the view that it was unfortunate that the rules relating to mistake meant that if it was operative at common law, and the contract was void, it often meant that, as in *Ingram v Little*, one of two innocent parties had to suffer, and there was no good basis for choosing between them. He suggested that it would be better to have some system whereby the losses could be apportioned in such a case. This suggestion, which would be likely to produce a fairer result in many cases, has not, however, been taken up.[84] The current state of the law in this area was strongly criticised by the Court of Appeal and by the minority in the House of Lords in *Shogun Finance Ltd v Hudson*.[85] Lord Millett commented:[86]

---

82 This was the view taken by Viscount Haldane in *Lake v Simmons* [1927] AC 487, p 501, but does not really fit with the reported facts – see the comments of Treitel, 2015, pp 334–35.

83 There is no reason why such an argument should not equally apply to mistaken identity cases that involve fraud between parties who are not contracting face to face.

84 It was considered by the Law Reform Committee in 1966, but rejected as impractical: Twelfth Report, *Transfer of Title to Chattels,* Cmd 2958.

85 [2003] UKHL 62; [2004] 1 All ER 215.

86 Ibid, para 84.

## MISTAKEN IDENTITY

**Were the parties in each other's presence when the contract was made?**

NO                                   YES

Did the claimant intend to contract with another person other than the one with whom he has entered into a contract?

Yes                          No

The contract may be void if the claimant is mistaken as to the identity of the other party. The mistake must generally be with regard to identity and not attributes
*Cundy v Lindsay* (1878)
*Shogun Finance v Hudson* (2003)

It is highly unlikely that the courts will accept the argument that a party did not intend to contract with the person who was standing in front of him/her
*Philips v Brooks* (1919)
*Lewis v Averay* (1972)
But note the approach in the exceptional case of
*Ingram v Little* (1961), which probably did not survive *Shogun Finance v Hudson* (2003)

The contract will not be void if the claimant intended to contract with the person who has made the offer. The mistake may be in relation to offeror's attributes or creditworthiness, not his or her identity
*King's Norton Metal Co v Edridge Merrett & Co Ltd* (1897)

Figure 9.2

We cannot leave the law as it is. It is neither fair nor principled, and not all of the authorities can be reconciled; some, at least, must be overruled if it is to be extricated from the present quagmire.

Jackson has suggested that the judgments in *Ingram v Little* and *Lewis v Averay* reflect what is probably the general 'social evaluation' of the cases – that is, that while the plaintiffs in *Ingram v Little* were tricked out of their car, and were thereby 'defrauded', Lewis was simply 'fooled'.[87] He was the victim of his own stupidity. Jackson also suggested that this difference in approach is reflected in the language used by the judges in the two cases.

### For thought

(1)  Do you think the outcome of *Ingram v Little* would have been the same had the person defrauded been a young man rather than three elderly women?

(2)  What steps could Lewis have taken to put himself in the same position as the women in *Ingram v Little*?

---

87 Jackson, 1988.

It will be easier for a claimant to convince a court that the identity of the other party is important if the claimant has sought the person out. If you advertise goods to the general public, it may be difficult then to suggest that you really wanted to contract with one person in particular. If, however, you have gone to that person's place of business, specifically to enter into a contract, then the argument that the identity of the other party was important is likely to be much more convincing. This may be illustrated by *Hardman v Booth*.[88] The plaintiffs had approached a firm, Thomas Gandell & Sons. They dealt with Edward Gandell, a member of the family who they thought was acting for the firm, though in fact he was acting on his own account. He intercepted goods sent by the plaintiffs and sold them to the defendant. It was held that the plaintiffs never intended to deal with Edward, but only with the firm, and the contract was therefore void for mistake.

It may also be possible to rebut the presumption where the fraudulent party is deemed to have been contracted with on the basis that he or she was an agent for someone else, rather than contracting in his or her own right. This situation was considered in *Lake v Simmons*.[89] A woman went to a jeweller's shop and represented that she was the wife of VB. She asked to be allowed to take two pearl necklaces because VB was planning to purchase one for her and he wished to see them on approval. She was allowed by the plaintiff to take the necklaces. In fact she was not VB's wife, though she was living with him. Having received the necklaces, she absconded. The issue in the case was whether the plaintiff could recover from his insurance company. The decision turned primarily on the terms of the insurance policy and whether in giving the necklaces to the woman, the plaintiff could be said to have 'entrusted them to a customer'. If that were the case, the insurance company would not be liable. The House of Lords held that since the transaction was entered in the plaintiff's books as being with VB, the woman was not the 'customer' and the plaintiff could recover under his insurance policy. Viscount Haldane also suggested, however, that the plaintiff was only dealing with the woman as the wife of VB. Since the plaintiff was 'entirely deceived as to the identity of the person' with whom he was dealing, there was no *consensus ad idem*, and therefore no contract.[90] Identity was significant here, since if the woman were simply VB's agent, her own creditworthiness would be irrelevant, whereas if she were contracting on her own behalf, the plaintiff might well have been more reluctant to allow her to take goods without paying for them.[91]

The argument based on agency will not apply, however, if the 'agent' is a mere 'conduit' for the performance of a transaction. This was the view taken in *Citibank NA v Brown Shipley*,[92] where a rogue obtained foreign currency from Bank A by inducing Bank B to issue a draft on a genuine account. The draft was collected by the rogue, or his associate, from Bank B and presented to Bank A. Bank A rang Bank B to check that the draft was genuine, and having been assured that it was, delivered the foreign currency to the rogue. It was held that in this case the identity of the rogue was irrelevant to the transactions as between the two banks. It had not been established that it was 'fundamental' to them that the person who collected the draft from Bank B and presented it to Bank A 'was a particular person about whom they were mistaken, as opposed to a person whose attributes did not include authority from their customer [that is, the holder of the genuine account against which the draft was drawn] as they believed'.[93] An action against Bank A for conversion of the draft therefore failed.

---

88  (1863) 1 H & C 803.
89  [1927] AC 487.
90  Ibid, p 500.
91  A mistake which is simply as to creditworthiness would not, however, generally be sufficient to void the contract: see, for example, *Lewis v Averay*.
92  [1991] 2 All ER 690.
93  [1991] 2 All ER 690, p 702.

## 9.6 MISTAKE IN EQUITY

As we have seen, the common law rules for identifying an operative mistake are very restrictive. For about 50 years, at the end of the twentieth century, courts held that this restrictive approach could be mitigated by a broad equitable remedy of rescission. This would arise where a common mistake was not sufficiently fundamental for the contract to be set aside at common law, but was serious enough for equity to intervene. The starting point for this approach is generally agreed to have been Lord Denning's judgment in the Court of Appeal in *Solle v Butcher*.[94]

The (common) mistake in this case was as to whether the rent payable in relation to a particular property was subject to control under the Rent Restriction Acts. This was held not to be sufficiently serious to render the contract void. However, as Lord Denning put it:[95]

> A contract is also liable in equity to be set aside if the parties were under a common misapprehension either as to facts or as to their relative and respective rights, provided that the misapprehension was fundamental, and that the party seeking to set it aside was not himself at fault.

This made it clear that it was not every mistake which would give rise to equitable relief. It had to be 'fundamental' – but this seemed to be wide enough to include serious mistakes as to the quality or value of the subject matter of the contract.

The line taken by Lord Denning in *Solle v Butcher* was followed by the High Court and the Court of Appeal in a number of subsequent cases.[96] It was never really clear, however, why there should be two sets of rules dealing with the effect of (common) mistakes. Indeed, it is not clear why, if the rules of equity allowed a broader range of mistakes to attract relief, this approach was not applied in *Bell v Lever Bros*. None of the usual bars to equitable relief applied in that case, but the House of Lords in that case seemed to feel that the common law was all it was concerned with. In more recent cases, the courts struggled to explain the difference between mistakes that take effect in equity as opposed to at common law. The issue was considered by Evans LJ in *William Sindall plc v Cambridgeshire County Council*. His conclusion was that there must be:[97]

> a category of mistake which is 'fundamental', so as to permit the equitable remedy of rescission, which is wider than the kind of 'serious and radical' mistake which means that the contract is void and of no effect in law.

In trying to distinguish between them, he suggested that:

> The difference may be that the common law rule is limited to mistakes with regard to the subject matter of the contract, whilst equity can have regard to a wider and perhaps unlimited category of 'fundamental' mistake.

In the case before him, the mistake related to the existence of a sewer running across a piece of land sold for development. There was no mistake about the subject matter, which was the piece of land. The mistake as to the existence of the sewer could have been sufficiently serious to give rise to a right of rescission, but on the facts it

---

94 [1950] 1 KB 671; [1949] 2 All ER 1107.
95 Ibid, p 693; p 1120.
96 For example, *Grist v Bailey* [1967] Ch 532; *Magee v Pennine Insurance* [1969] 2 QB 507; *Nutt v Read* [2000] 32 HLR 761; *West Sussex Properties Ltd v Chichester DC* [2000] NPC 74.
97 [1994] 1 WLR 1016, p 1042.

was not. The additional cost raised by the existence of the sewer was no more than £20,000, which, on a contract where the sale price was over £5m, could not be said to be 'fundamental'.

The approach suggested by Evans LJ was reconsidered by Rimer J in *Clarion Ltd v National Provident Institution*.[98] He took the view, however, that mistake would only operate, in equity as in the common law, where the mistake was as to the terms of the contract or its subject matter, or as to the identity of the other contracting party. Noting the broader approach of Evans LJ in *William Sindall plc v Cambridgeshire County Council*, he rejected this as 'at most a somewhat tentative *obiter* comment',[99] and refused to develop it further. The rejection of Evans LJ's suggestion, however, made the distinction between common law and equitable mistake even more vague. Nevertheless it seemed to have been accepted since the decision of Steyn J in *Associated Japanese Bank (International) Ltd v Credit du Nord SA*[100] that common mistake is not limited to cases of *res extincta*, but that other mistakes, if sufficiently fundamental, may avoid a contract. If that is so, then what type of mistake is sufficiently fundamental to allow for relief in equity but not sufficiently fundamental to avoid the contract at common law?

The importance of this rather confused law on the scope of equitable mistake has, however, been significantly reduced by the decision of the Court of Appeal in *Great Peace Shipping Ltd v Tsavliris ('The Great Peace')*.[101] In this case, the facts of which have been given above,[102] the Court of Appeal reviewed the whole line of cases flowing from *Solle v Butcher*. Its conclusion was that *Solle v Butcher* was incorrectly decided. There is no general power to set aside contracts other than for a mistake which is operative at common law. As Lord Phillips put it, delivering the judgment of the court:[103]

> Our conclusion is that it is impossible to reconcile *Solle v Butcher* with *Bell v Lever Bros*. The jurisdiction asserted in the former case has not developed. It has been a fertile source of academic debate, but in practice it has given rise to a handful of cases that have merely emphasised the confusion of this area of our jurisprudence.

The result, it seems, is that the broad discretion to set aside a contract on terms no longer exists: the only remedies that equity can now employ to deal with mistakes where a contract is not void at common law are the refusal of specific performance and rectification, which are considered below.

Finally, it should be noted that, even in equity, the mistake must be made at the time of the contract. In *Amalgamated Investment and Property Co v John Walker & Sons*,[104] a property was listed as a building of special interest by the Department of the Environment. This placed serious restrictions on the ways in which it could be used, and reduced its value by £1.5m. This was clearly a mistake of the kind that might allow equitable relief, but unfortunately the 'listing' of the building had taken place two days after the contract for its sale had been concluded. The mistake was not operative at the time of the contract, and so there could be no relief on this basis either under common law or in equity.

---

98  [2000] 2 All ER 265.
99  [2000] 2 All ER 265, p 280.
100  [1988] 3 All ER 902.
101  [2002] EWCA Civ 1407; [2002] 4 All ER 689.
102  Above, 9.4.4.
103  [2002] EWCA Civ 1407; [2002] 4 All ER 689, at [157]. In *Pitt v Holt* [2013] UKSC 26 at [115] Lord Walker stated that *The Great Peace* had effectively overruled *Solle v Butcher*. However, it seems there is also an equitable jurisdiction to set aside gifts made as a result of a mistake (see *Van der Merwe v Goldman* [2016] EWHC 790 (Ch)).
104  [1976] 3 All ER 509.

## 9.7 FORMS OF EQUITABLE RELIEF

Once it is established that equity will take account of the mistake, what remedies are available? There are two: refusal of specific performance and rectification. As has been noted in the previous section, the remedy of rescission on terms, which was used for a time, has now been rejected by the Court of Appeal in *The Great Peace*. This was a very powerful remedy, in that it not only allowed the court to set a contract aside but also empowered it to impose conditions – so that in *Solle v Butcher* (discussed above, 9.6), for example, the lease was rescinded but on condition that the tenant could remain, provided that he paid rent at the maximum that the landlord could have asked for under the rent control legislation. Such a power was out of line with the classical reluctance of courts to intervene in the substance of contracts, and its rejection represents a return to a more traditional approach, as well as having the effect of decreasing uncertainty in this area.

### 9.7.1 REFUSAL OF SPECIFIC PERFORMANCE

As we will see in Chapter 15, the order of specific performance is a discretionary remedy. In deciding whether to order it, the court can take into account any hardship that might be caused by so doing. For example, the buyer of a painting that, between contract and performance, is discovered not to be by Constable, as had been thought, may well be able to resist specific performance (though there may still be a liability to pay compensatory damages). In *Malins v Freeman*,[105] where a buyer at an auction mistakenly bid for one lot, thinking that it was another, this mutual mistake was held to be sufficient to allow the buyer not to be made to go through with the contract. In contrast, in *Tamplin v James*,[106] where the defendant bid for an inn and shop, incorrectly thinking that a garden was included, the contract was enforced. The mistake as to the *extent* of the property was distinguishable from a case where the mistake was as to the identity of the property.

### 9.7.2 RECTIFICATION

Where an agreement is contained in a document that contains an inaccuracy, in the form of either an error or an omission, the equitable remedy of rectification may be granted. It is clearly available where both parties miss the error (a common mistake), or if one party knows of the other's mistake (a unilateral mistake). Thus, in *Roberts v Leicestershire County Council*,[107] a construction contract, which contained a completion date which was a year later than the contractors believed it to be, was rectified because there was clear evidence that representatives of the other party were well aware of the basis on which the contractors were undertaking the project. The position was similar in *Templiss Properties Ltd v Hyams*,[108] which concerned a lease where the intention had been that the rent should be exclusive of business rates, whereas it was expressed to be inclusive of such rates. Although in this case the tenant's solicitors were not aware of the mistake, it was shown that the tenant himself was aware and rectification was ordered. If the mistake is simply a mutual mistake, however, the courts will not grant rectification. A sufficiently serious mistake of this kind will allow the 'contract' to be declared void, of course, but rectification will not be available.[109]

It follows from this that if an oral agreement, though based on a mistake, is accurately reproduced in a subsequent document, rectification is not appropriate and will not be granted.

---

105  (1837) 2 Keen 25.
106  (1879) 15 Ch D 215.
107  [1961] Ch 555; [1961] 2 All ER 545. See also *Palo Alto Ltd v Alnor Estates Ltd* [2018] UKUT 231.
108  [1999] EGCS 60.
109  *Riverlate Properties Ltd v Paul* [1975] Ch 133; [1974] 2 All ER 656.

**Key case** *Rose (Frederick E) (London) Ltd v William H Pim Jnr & Co Ltd* (1953)[110]

Facts: The plaintiff had been asked by a third party to supply 'horsebeans described as feveroles'. The plaintiffs entered into a contract with the defendants under which the defendants agreed to sell the plaintiffs 500 tons of 'horsebeans'. Both plaintiffs and defendants thought that 'horsebeans' was just another name for 'feveroles'. In fact, feveroles are a higher quality horsebean. The defendants supplied ordinary horsebeans but these were unacceptable to the third party, who wanted feveroles. The plaintiffs sought to have their written contract with the defendants rectified to refer to feveroles. They would then be able to succeed in an action for supply of goods of the wrong description.

Held: The Court of Appeal held, however, that rectification was not possible:[111] 'Their agreement as expressed both orally and in writing, was for "horsebeans". That is all the sellers committed themselves to supply, and all they should be bound to.' Although there was a misapprehension underlying the contract (a 'common mistake', in other words), it was not a mistake about what the parties thought that they were agreeing. Objectively, it appeared to be a contract for horsebeans, and there was therefore no basis for providing the remedy of rectification.

In *Daventry District Council v Daventry & District Housing Ltd*[112] the Court of Appeal again emphasised the need for an objective approach in these situations. The question was what the parties objectively appeared to have agreed, not their subjective intentions. In this case there was a mistake about which of the parties was to pay for a deficit in the pension fund for employees whose employment was being transferred from the claimant to the defendant. The majority in the Court of Appeal thought that the knowledge of the chief negotiator for the defendant had to be attributed to it. Since he knew that the claimant understood that the defendant was to make up the deficit, and allowed a contract to be signed that stated the opposite, the contract should be rectified in line with the claimant's understanding, even though all those involved with the defendant, apart from the chief negotiator, had no awareness of the claimant's view.

### 9.7.3 BARS TO RECTIFICATION

Because this remedy is equitable and discretionary, it may be lost by virtue of lapse of time or the intervention of third party rights. If this is the case, the claimant will have to argue for common law mistake in order to obtain any remedy.

## 9.8 CONTRACTS SIGNED UNDER A MISTAKE

The courts are not inclined to be sympathetic towards people who put their names to contracts without reading or understanding them. In general, therefore, a person will be taken to have notice of, and to be bound by, all the provisions of a contract which has been signed, whether they have been read or not.[113] There are some exceptional circumstances, however, where the courts will allow a plea of *non est factum* – 'it is not my deed'. The mistake must be such that the document as a whole is 'radically different' from that

---

110  [1953] 2 QB 450; [1953] 2 All ER 739.
111  [1953] 2 QB 450; [1953] 2 All ER 739, p 462.
112  [2011] EWCA Civ 1153; [2012] 1 WLR 1333. See also Davies, 2016 and *NHS Commissioning Board v Silovsky* [2015] EWHC 3141 (Comm) and [2017] EWCA Civ 1389.
113  See *L'Estrange v Graucob* [1934] 2 KB 394, discussed above, Chapter 7, 7.4.

which the person thought he or she was signing. Moreover, the person must not have been 'careless' in signing the document. These principles are derived from the House of Lords' decision in *Saunders v Anglia Building Society*.[114]

## 9.8.1 AVAILABILITY OF THE PLEA

The result of these principles, and in particular the second one, is that the doctrine will rarely be available to literate adults of full capacity. The courts will, however, make the remedy available to those who are tricked into signing the contract and it may also operate to protect those who from 'defective education, illness, or innate incapacity'[115] fail to understand what they are signing.

A relatively recent (and fairly rare) example of the successful use of the plea is to be found in *Lloyds Bank plc v Waterhouse*.[116] Here, the defendant, who was illiterate, signed a guarantee regarding his son's future liabilities to the plaintiff bank. The father thought that this guarantee related solely to the son's purchase of a farm, whereas in fact it covered all the son's liabilities. The trial judge found that this did not amount to a fundamental difference and that the defendant had been careless in not having the document read to him. He gave judgment for the plaintiff. The defendant appealed.

The majority of the Court of Appeal regarded the mistake as to the extent of the guarantee as being sufficient to support the plea of *non est factum*. The evidence showed that the father would not have signed it if he had known its true nature, even though he was aware of the financial value of the guarantee. As to carelessness, although the bank was unaware of the defendant's illiteracy, and there was no suggestion of impropriety on its part, the defendant had clearly taken steps (by asking questions of the bank's officials) to ascertain his liability. The plea of *non est factum* was made out.

## 9.8.2 NATURE OF THE MISTAKE

At one time, the difference in the extent of the guarantee in the above case would not have been regarded as sufficient, as it was thought that the document had to be of a different 'character' for the defence to be available. That test was rejected, however, in *Saunders v Anglia Building Society*, in favour of the more broadly based question of whether the document was 'radically' or 'fundamentally' different.

---

**Key case** *Saunders v Anglia Building Society* (1971)

Facts: In this case, a 78-year-old widow, Mrs Gallie, wanted to enable her nephew to raise money on the security of her house. She knew that her nephew's business associate, Lee, was to collaborate in raising the money. Lee presented a document for her signature, and told her that it was a deed of gift of the house to her nephew. In fact it had the effect of assigning her interest in the house to Lee. The nephew colluded in this deception and witnessed his aunt's signature on the document. Their plan was for Lee to raise money on the house and then pay it in instalments to the nephew. The reason why Mrs Gallie had failed to read the document was that she had broken her reading glasses. She raised a plea of *non est factum*. This was successful at first instance, but overturned by the Court of Appeal. There was a further appeal to the House of Lords. Held: The House of Lords regarded Mrs Gallie's reason for failing to read the document as acceptable, and held that it did not amount to 'carelessness'. She failed, however, on the

---

114  [1971] AC 1004. The facts are given below at 9.8.2. The case also appears in some reports under the name *Gallie v Lee*. See also *CF Asset Finance Ltd v Okonji* [2014] EWCA Civ 870.
115  As Lord Reid put it in *Saunders v Anglia Building Society* [1971] AC 1004, p 1016.
116  [1990] Fam Law 23.

first test, relating to the nature of the document. Although it involved a different transaction from what she thought, the purpose of the assignment was, albeit indirectly, to provide financial assistance to her nephew. This is what she had wished to achieve by the deed of gift. The document was not, therefore, sufficiently different for the plea to succeed.

## For thought

*Do you think the outcome of this case would have been different if the woman had thought that she was signing a mortgage on the house, enabling her to raise money, rather than making a gift to her nephew? Would the document then have been 'radically different'?*

If the plea is successful, the transaction is void and unenforceable.

## 9.9  IN FOCUS: CONCLUSIONS ON 'MISTAKE'

The lack of coherence in English contract law in dealing with the issue of 'mistake' will be evident from the above discussion. Would it be possible to devise a set of principles to deal with mistakes that did not have these defects? One major improvement, which appears in the European Draft Common Frame of Reference, would be to treat mistakes as always rendering a contract 'voidable' rather than 'void'. This would allow much greater flexibility in dealing with the consequences of mistake. Moreover, it might be best if this applied to *all* categories of mistake (including 'mutual mistakes', which are not included within the scheme proposed by the Draft Common Frame of Reference). In other words, whenever the parties regard themselves as having made a contract,[117] but one of them subsequently raises the argument that it was founded on a mistake, the court should have the power to set the contract aside. In reaching the decision as to whether to do so, and if so on what terms, there are two main factors that ought to be considered. The first is whether the risk of the mistake was in fact dealt with by the contract – for example, did one party clearly agree to take the risk of the subject matter of the contract not existing?[118] The second is the extent of good faith reliance on the contract by the parties or third parties. One of the defects of the current finding that a contract is void for mistake is that, for example, in a common mistake situation, costs incurred towards performance are lost, even if these all fall on one side. A more flexible approach, based on voidability, would enable the court, if appropriate, to impose terms apportioning such losses between the parties.[119] Such a power should also be available in cases of unilateral mistake.[120] This is particularly important where the reliance of third parties on the fact that the original contract was valid needs proper consideration.[121] It may well be that in cases where a fraudulent contracting party has disappeared, the fact

---

117  Although this may appear to be a very subjective test, what is really important is whether the parties (or at least one of them) has *acted* in reliance on this supposed contract. If there has been no such reliance on either side, then there is no particular problem about setting the contract aside as if 'void' *ab initio*.

118  As, for example, in *McRae v Commonwealth Disposals Commission* (1951) 84 CLR 377 – discussed above, 9.4.1.

119  What is being suggested is something akin to the equitable power of rescission on terms used in cases such as *Solle v Butcher* [1950] 1 KB 671, but incorporating an even greater power to distribute losses.

120  The courts would, of course, still need to decide that the unilateral mistake went beyond making a 'bad bargain'.

121  It may be objected here that third parties in an *Ingram v Little* [1961] 1 QB 31 situation do not in fact 'rely' on the original contract. They are probably ignorant of that contract. What they are relying on is the fact that

of the third party's reliance should in general lead to the result most commonly arrived at in English law in relation to face-to-face contracts – that is, that the loss should fall entirely on the party to the original contract who has been the victim of the fraud. Nevertheless, it would be advantageous in relation to both face-to-face contracts, and those created without such interaction,[122] to allow the court the power to distribute losses, perhaps on a similar basis to that adopted in relation to frustrated contracts.[123]

It will be seen that the above suggestions are pragmatic rather than formalistic. They are based on the approach that where an agreement has failed as the result of a mistake (of whatever kind), the precise analysis of the nature of that agreement is in general of less importance than the practical consequences of its failure. Unless it is clear that one of the parties has undertaken the risk of the mistake being made, a flexible approach based on voidability is likely to lead to the most satisfactory results for all concerned.

## 9.10 SUMMARY OF KEY POINTS

- An operative mistake will have the effect of rendering a contract void, which will impact upon third party rights. It is therefore a very powerful concept that the courts use with care.

- Mistakes can be divided into those that nullify an agreement ('common mistake') and those that negative agreement ('mutual' and 'unilateral mistakes').

- Common mistakes that may be treated as nullifying the agreement are mistakes:
  - □ as to the existence of the subject matter (e.g. *res extincta*);
  - □ that make performance impossible – physically, legally or commercially.

- Mistakes as to quality will not generally be operative mistakes.

- Mutual mistakes arise where the parties are at cross-purposes. There is no agreement, and so no contract.

- Unilateral mistakes arise where one party is aware of the other's mistake as to a term of the contract. If the mistake is serious, the contract will be void.

- Unilateral mistakes as to identity may be operative where identity is of fundamental importance. It is much easier to establish an operative mistake as to identity when the parties do not contract face to face (*inter praesentes*).

- Equity provides only limited additional protection in relation to mistakes that are not operative at common law. Such mistakes may lead to:
  - □ the refusal of specific performance;
  - □ rectification of a document.

---

the person with whom they are dealing has good title to the property they are offering for sale. Nevertheless, this type of indirect reliance needs to be catered for.

122 The availability of more flexible powers would hopefully prevent arguments based on 'mistake' from leading to the circumvention of statutory provisions designed for the protection of consumers – as apparently happened in *Shogun Finance Ltd v Hudson*. This is surely unacceptable.

123 See the Law Reform (Frustrated Contracts) Act 1943 – discussed in Chapter 13. The precise methods used in that Act have not proved uncontroversial in their application and a clearer formula than the one used in that Act would be needed if the power to distribute were to be granted by statute, rather than being developed by the courts as part of their equitable remedies.

■ Contracts signed under a mistake might be dealt with by the plea of *non est factum*. Parties relying on this plea will need to show that the document was 'radically different' from what they thought they were signing, and that they had not been careless.

## 9.11 FURTHER READING

### Generally

■ Jackson, B, *Law, Fact and Narrative Coherence*, 1988, Liverpool: Deborah Charles

■ MacMillan, C, *Mistakes in Contract Law*, 2010, Oxford: Hart Publishing

■ Simpson, AWB, 'Innovation in nineteenth century contract law' (1975) 91 LQR 247

■ Simpson, AWB, 'Contracts for cotton to arrive: the case of the two ships *Peerless*' (1989) 11 Cardozo L Rev 287

■ Spencer, J, 'Signature, consent and the rule in *L'Estrange v Graucob* (1973) 32 CLJ 104

■ Treitel, G H, 'Mistake in contract' (1988) 104 LQR 501

### Common mistake

■ Chandler, A, Devenney, J and Poole, J, 'Common mistake: theoretical justification and remedial inflexibility' [2004] JBL 34

■ MacMillan, C, 'How temptation led to mistake: an explanation of *Bell v Lever Bros Ltd*' (2003) 119 LQR 625

■ Smith, J C, 'Contracts – mistake, frustration and implied terms' (1994) 110 LQR 400

### Unilateral mistake

■ Chandler, A and Devenney, J, 'Mistake as to identity and the threads of objectivity' (2004) 1 JOR 7

■ Hare, C, 'Identity mistakes: a missed opportunity' (2004) 67 MLR 993

■ MacMillan, C, 'Mistake as to identity clarified?' (2004) 120 LQR 369

## COMPANION WEBSITE

*Now visit the companion website to:*

■ Revise and consolidate your knowledge of Mistake by tackling a series of multiple-choice questions on this chapter

■ Test your understanding of the chapter's key terms by using the flashcard glossary

■ Explore Mistake further by accessing a series of web links.

# 10

# Duress

## Contents

## 10.1 OVERVIEW

This chapter deals with the position where one party alleges that he or she entered into the contract as a result of threats made, or pressure applied, by the other party. The questions that need to be considered are as follows:

- What type of threats or pressure will allow a party to escape from a contract? To what extent can threats, or pressure, other than of physical violence have this effect? The relevant question now seems to be whether there was illegitimate pressure.
- In what situations may 'economic duress' be sufficient to affect the contract? It is important here that the party alleging duress had no real alternative to compliance.

■ Can there be duress where there is a threat to perform an act that involves no breach of the criminal law or civil obligation (such as breach of contract)? The answer seems to be that there can be where, for example, the threat is being used for an improper purpose.

■ What are the remedies for duress? It renders a contract voidable but generally does not allow the recovery of damages.

## 10.2 INTRODUCTION

This chapter is concerned with situations in which an agreement that appears to be valid on its face is challenged because it is alleged that it is the product of improper pressure of some kind. This may, for example, take the form of threats of physical violence or 'economic' threats (such as to break a contract), which place pressure on the other party. In principle there seems to be no reason why there needs to be explicit threats. Suppose, for example, that a woman has been beaten by her husband in the past and is then asked by him to sell him her share in the matrimonial home at a gross undervalue. She agrees through fear of what he might do to her, even though he has made no threat to her on this occasion. It is difficult to argue that such a situation should not come within the scope of duress merely because the threat is implied rather than explicit.[1] In the past English courts might have dealt with such a situation under the closely related, but conceptually distinct,[2] category of 'undue influence' but there seems no reason why such situations might not also be treated as duress. Undue influence is dealt with in Chapter 11.

One of the problems with economic duress lies in establishing the boundaries of acceptable behaviour of this kind, since economic pressure clearly has a legitimate place within business dealings and this issue is explored below. If, however, the contract has been entered into as a result of *illegitimate* pressure, it is rendered voidable.[3] The courts may be regarded as intervening either because there is no true agreement between the parties, or simply because a person who has been led to make a contract as a result of the exertion of illegitimate pressure should be allowed to escape from it. The latter argument is probably the one that represents the most satisfactory analysis of the situation but there are many judicial statements that refer to duress 'vitiating' the consent of the threatened party. This is discussed further in the next section.

---

1   Compare the Australian case of *Farmers' Co-operative Executors and Trustees Ltd v Perks* (1989) 52 SASR 399, discussed in Birks and Chin, 1995, p 66, where it seems that the judge was prepared to find duress in circumstances similar to those given in the text. See also *Antonio v Antonio* [2010] EWHC 1199 where there was a history of intimidation between former husband and wife but the judge also found that there were specific threats leading to the agreement to transfer shares, which was set aside for duress. Note also *Borrelli v Ting* [2010] UKPC 21 where the Privy Council made a connection between duress and unconscionable conduct.

2   The distinction might be denied by, for example, those who argue that duress and undue influence can both be encompassed within a general doctrine of 'good faith' – see, for example, Adams and Brownsword, 1995, Chapter 7. For a link to 'good faith' see *Al Nehayan v Kent* [2018] EWHC 333 (Comm) at [187] where Leggatt LJ stated: "First, as the authorities have emphasised, the standard of unconscionability is a high one and it is only in cases where the demand made and means used to reinforce it are completely indefensible that the courts will intervene. Second, no apology is needed for intervening in such cases, as the enforcement of basic norms of commerce and of fair and honest dealing is an essential function of a system of commercial law."

3   There are statements by Lord Cross in *Barton v Armstrong* [1976] AC 104 suggesting that duress renders a contract void but the general view is that its effect is to make it voidable.

## 10.3 DURESS BY THREATS OF VIOLENCE OR OTHER COERCION

Although it is possible that a person could be physically forced to sign a contract by someone holding their arm and moving it, the most obvious form of duress is where a contract is brought about as a result of a threat of physical injury. A modern example is to be found in *Barton v Armstrong*,[4] where the managing director of a company was threatened with death if he did not arrange for his company to make a payment to, and buy shares from, the defendant. The Privy Council held that the contract could be set aside for duress.

Originally, the nature of the threats which would be treated as constituting duress was very limited; for example, threats in relation to goods were at one time held to be insufficient,[5] though even this rule was apparently subject to the exception that money paid under duress of goods could be recovered.[6] With the development of the concept of 'economic duress' (discussed below, at 10.4), however, a much broader view of the type of threats that can vitiate a contract has been taken.[7] The current approach would seem to be represented by the approach of the Privy Council in *Attorney General v R*.[8]

### Key case *Attorney General v R* (2003)

Facts: A former soldier had made arrangements with a publisher for them to publish an account of his involvement with the SAS in the Gulf War of 1991. This came to the attention of the British Government, and the Attorney General brought an action for breach of contract against the soldier, based on a 'confidentiality agreement' that the soldier had signed while still a member of the SAS. The soldier claimed that he had signed the agreement, restricting his ability to publish information about his experiences in the SAS, because if he had not he was threatened with being removed from the SAS (though remaining in the army). Such removal would normally only have taken place as a result of disciplinary action. The case originated in New Zealand, where the trial judge held in the soldier's favour. The New Zealand Court of Appeal reversed this decision. There was a further appeal to the Privy Council.

Held: The Privy Council dismissed the appeal. In doing so it identified the essential requirement of duress as being illegitimate pressure amounting to compulsion of the will of the victim. There was no doubt that the soldier was pressured into signing the agreement. Returning to his unit would have been regarded in the SAS as a public humiliation and he had no realistic alternative to compliance. The pressure was not, however, improper, as restricting unauthorised disclosures concerning military operations was a legitimate objective for the army. The confidentiality agreement was enforceable.

The decision was delivered by Lord Hoffmann: his starting point was the decision of the House of Lords in the 'economic duress' case, *Universe Tankships Inc of Monrovia v International Transport Workers' Federation*.[9] He noted that Lord Scarman had identified

---

4    [1976] AC 104. In *Holyoake v Candy* [2017] EWHC 3397 (Ch) the defendant sought to apply pressure by telling the claimant to think about his (the claimant's) pregnant wife. The court felt that this did not amount to a threat of violence.

5    *Skeate v Beale* (1840) 11 A & E 983.

6    *Astley v Reynolds* (1731) 2 Stra 915.

7    See, e.g., *Vantage Navigation Corp v Suhail and Saud Bahwan Building Materials (The 'Alev')* [1989] 1 Lloyd's Rep 138, where duress of goods was clearly accepted as being sufficient to render the contract voidable.

8    [2003] UKPC 22; [2003] EMLR 24.

9    [1983] 1 AC 366; [1982] 2 All ER 67 – discussed below, 10.4.1.

**Definition**
Physical threat or other illegitimate pressure being used for an improper objective which is sufficiently serious to vitiate the consent of the other party:
*Attorney General v R* (2003)

**Duress by physical threats of violence or other coercion**
Threat of personal injury:
*Barton v Armstrong* (1976)
To establish duress it should be established that the claimant entered into the contract at least partly as a result of illegitimate threats from the defendant

**DURESS**

**Remedies for duress**
Duress will render a contract voidable.
The remedy available is rescission.
There are certain bars to rescission.
Damages are not available for duress

**Economic duress**
The pressure applied must be improper commercial pressure:
*Occidental Worldwide Investment Corp v Skibs A/S Avanti, The Siboen & The Sibotre* (1976)

Threat of industrial action can amount to illegitimate pressure:
*Universe Tankships Inc of Monrovia v International Transport Workers' Federation, The Universe Sentinel* (1983)

Threat of breach of contract can amount to illegitimate pressure:
*Atlas Express Ltd v Kafco (Importers & Distributors) Ltd* (1989)

Figure 10.1

two elements to duress:[10] the first was pressure amounting to compulsion of the will of the victim; the second was the illegitimacy of that pressure. The first element was not in issue in the case, since it was accepted that for the soldier to be returned to a regular army unit would have been regarded in the SAS as a public humiliation. He had no practical alternative to compliance.

As regards the second element, this could be viewed from two aspects:

(a)    the nature of the pressure; and
(b)    the nature of the demand that the pressure is applied to support.

In relation to the 'nature of the pressure', where the threat was to carry out some unlawful act this would generally lead to the pressure being regarded as 'illegitimate'. It was not necessarily the case, however, that a threat of a lawful action would be legitimate. This is where the second aspect needs to be considered. This looks at what the person issuing the threat is trying to achieve. Was their objective a legitimate one? To illustrate the point, Lord Hoffmann quoted from Lord Atkin in *Thorne v Motor Trade Association*,[11] where he said:[12]

> The ordinary blackmailer normally threatens to do what he has a perfect right to do – namely communicate some compromising conduct to a person whose knowledge is likely to affect the person threatened ... What he has to justify is not the threat, but the demand of money.

---

10  Ibid, at [15].
11  [1937] AC 797.
12  Ibid, p 806.

**For thought**

*Bill reluctantly enters into a contract with a business rival, Salina, because Salina threatens to tell Bill's wife that he is having an affair with his PA. Could Bill escape from the contract on the grounds of duress?*

Applying this approach to the case before it, the Privy Council took the view that the threat was in itself lawful. The power to return to a regular unit could be exercised at the discretion of the relevant officers within the army. Was, then, the objective of the threat such that it rendered this lawful threat illegitimate? The trial judge had thought that it was, in that it was effectively a military order that purported to control R's conduct after he had left the service. The Court of Appeal and the Privy Council disagreed. R had not been issued with a command that created an obligation under military law; rather, he was faced with a choice that may have constituted 'overwhelming pressure', but was not an exercise by the Ministry of Defence of its legal powers over him. Since the objective of restricting unauthorised disclosures concerning military operations was in itself a legitimate objective, the plea of duress failed.

This broad approach to defining the limits of duress must be assumed to be the one that will be adopted by English courts in future (though, of course, as a decision of the Privy Council, *Attorney General v R* is only of persuasive authority – and since duress was not found, the more general statements could be treated as *obiter*). The case does not resolve all issues as to the nature of duress, however, and some of these are worth further consideration.

For example, the cases on duress are full of references to the claimant's will being 'overborne' (and this is echoed in the Privy Council's references to 'compulsion'). In most cases this will be an inaccurate description of what has happened. The claimant has not been forced to act as an automaton. The decision to make the contract has been taken as a matter of choice. It is simply that the threat that has led to that choice is regarded by the courts as illegitimate, and justifies allowing the party threatened to escape from the consequent contract.[13] The fact that this is the basis of the modern doctrine is illustrated by the fact that it was by no means certain in *Barton v Armstrong* that the threats that were made were the sole reason for the managing director's decision. The approach of the majority of the Privy Council in that case appears in the opinion of Lord Cross. He noted that, in relation to misrepresentation, there is no need to prove that the false statement was the sole reason for entering into the contract.[14] He then commented:[15]

> Their Lordships think that the same rule should apply in cases of duress and that if Armstrong's threats were 'a' reason for Barton's executing the deed he is entitled to relief even though he might well have entered into the contract if Armstrong had uttered no threats to influence him to do so.

If this is the case, then it clearly is inappropriate to talk of the will of the person subject to the threats being 'overborne'. The duress simply becomes a wrongful act of a similar

---

13 Nevertheless the language of 'overborne will' is sometimes still used in the relevant case law, sometimes as a convenient, although not particularly accurate, shorthand. See also Atiyah, 1982; Halson, 1991.
14 See Chapter 8, 8.3.4, above.
15 [1976] AC 104, p 119.

kind to a misrepresentation, which, if it has influenced the other party's decision to make a contract, provides a basis for that contract being voidable.[16]

This analysis suggests that the concept of duress focuses on the wrongfulness of the behaviour of the defendant rather than its effect on the claimant.[17] Not all commentators would accept that this necessarily follows from the rejection of the 'overborne will' approach to duress. Birks and Chin have pointed out that there are authorities that make it clear that duress may be used as a reason to set aside a transaction, notwithstanding the fact that the defendant has acted in good faith.[18] This, of course, raises questions of definition and the relationship between the concepts of good faith and illegitimate conduct. Nevertheless it is clear that the defendant's conduct is not a sufficient reason for treating a contract as voidable; the availability of the remedy also depends on the effect of the defendant's behaviour on the claimant. This point becomes more important once the categories of behaviour that can constitute duress are broadened. When the threats are of physical violence, it is easier to argue that criminality in itself justifies the court's intervention. When 'economic' and other threats are accepted as giving rise to the possibility of duress, the borderline between what is legitimate and illegitimate is narrow, and the likelihood of the threats being made in good faith increases. This leads to the conclusion that although, as indicated in *Barton v Armstrong*, the threats do not need to be the sole reason for the claimant's agreement to the contract, they do have to be *part* of that reason and, at least in relation to economic duress, perhaps a *significant* part of that reason, as suggested by Lord Goff in *Dimskal Shipping Co SA v International Transport Workers Federation, The Evia Luck*.[19] If a strong-willed claimant has shrugged off the threats, then a claim of duress will not be allowed, even if a reasonable claimant might have been affected by them.[20]

There are thus two questions to ask in relation to duress: (1) were the defendant's threats 'illegitimate', and (2) was the claimant's behaviour affected by them? Only if both

---

16  It seems also to be implicit in Lord Cross's opinion that there is not even any need for it to be proved that the threats were the major element in the decision. He certainly regards this as the case in relation to fraudulent misrepresentation, 'for in this field the court does not allow an examination into the relative importance of contributory causes' (ibid, p 118), and the whole tenor of his opinion is to align duress with fraud.

17  Note that in the following discussion, for ease of treatment, 'defendant' is used to indicate the party issuing the threat, and 'claimant' the party potentially affected by it, notwithstanding the fact that cases may involve the defendant seeking to prevent an action to enforce a contract on the basis that the claimant has used duress.

18  Birks and Chin, 1995, citing *Morgan v Palmer* (1824) 2 B & C 729 (money paid in order to pay a licence); *Maskell v Horner* [1915] 3 KB 106 (payment of tolls under threat of seizure of goods). Birks and Chin were mainly concerned with undue influence, rather than duress, but this does not affect the validity of the point being made. In *Universe Tankships Inc of Monrovia v International Transport Workers' Federation* [1982] 2 All ER 67, for example, the threat was to take industrial action that the union concerned thought was lawful: see below, 10.4.1. It may be, however, that if the threat is to do something otherwise lawful, 'bad faith' *will* usually be needed to turn it into duress: see *CTN Cash and Carry Ltd v Gallaher* [1994] 4 All ER 714 – discussed below, 10.4.3.

19  [1992] 2 AC 152, 165. For further discussion of this issue see R Stone and J Devenney, *Text, Cases and Materials on Contract Law,* (4th edn, London: Routledge 2017, 10.4.1.1.1). In *Al Nehayan v Kent* [2018] EWHC 333 (Comm) at [191] Leggatt LJ stated: "It is sometimes said to be a further requirement of economic duress that the claimant had no reasonable alternative to giving in to the illegitimate pressure. The alternative view, which is preferred in *Chitty on Contracts* (32nd Edn, 2015), vol 1, para 8–033, and was accepted by Christopher Clarke J in *Kolmar Group AG v Traxpo Enterprises Pvt Ltd* [2010] EWHC 113 (Comm) at para 92, is that the absence of any reasonable alternative is not an absolute requirement but rather is very strong evidence of whether the claimant was induced by the threat or other illegitimate pressure to enter into the contract. It is also, as it seems to me, a relevant factor in determining whether use of pressure was illegitimate in cases where the defendant has not acted or threatened to act unlawfully and the allegation of duress is based on exploitation of the claimant's situation to make an unjustified demand."

20  To this extent, the approach to duress is subjective.

are answered positively will the conditions arise for the contract to be set aside.[21] The claimant may have voluntarily entered into the contract, but would not have done so but for the threats of the defendant.[22]

### 10.3.1 IN FOCUS: CAN THERE BE DURESS IF THE CONTRACT WOULD HAVE BEEN MADE ANYWAY?

Lord Cross suggests, in the quotation above, that duress is available even if the contract would have been made without the threats. This arguably goes too far. Lord Cross accepts that there must be some causal link between the threats and the contract; it is difficult to understand how, if this is the case, the duress can be regarded as effective if the claimant would have made the contract even if the threats had not been made.[23] If we are to accept Lord Cross's suggestion, however, this would mean rewording the test suggested above (that is, 'The claimant may have voluntarily entered into the contract, but would not have done so but for the threats of the defendant') to, perhaps, read: 'The claimant may have voluntarily entered into the contract, but would not have done so *so readily* in the absence of the threats of the defendant.' Lord Scarman, on the other hand, has on more than one occasion emphasised that part of the test of whether duress was operative is whether the claimant had any real alternative but to submit.[24] This clearly implies that the contract would not have been made but for the threats, and this seems the more satisfactory approach.[25]

### 10.3.2 DIFFICULTIES OF LANGUAGE

The language used in talking of duress does not assist in clarifying these issues. First, the use of the word 'threat' carries pejorative overtones and suggests deliberate bad behaviour on the part of the defendant. The usage is understandable given the origins of duress in putting someone in fear of physical violence. What is, however, meant in the modern context is simply an indication from the defendant to the claimant that if the claimant does not enter into the contract, then the defendant will act in a particular way. The shorthand use of the word 'threat' must not be allowed to carry with it any necessary connotation of deliberate wrongdoing.

Second, 'improper' or 'illegitimate' are the adjectives most commonly used to qualify the defendant's behaviour. Once again these may carry the implication of wrongdoing by the defendant,[26] derived from the origins of duress. It would perhaps be more accurate

---

21 Smith (1997a) has argued that, in fact, there are two separate limbs to duress, namely 'operative wrongdoing' and 'impairment of consent', and that *either* of these may provide a basis for treating a contract as voidable.

22 An analogy might be drawn with the criminal law approach to consent in sexual offences: a person who agrees to have sexual intercourse because of threats that have been made may be found to have been raped. While the act of intercourse was 'voluntary', in that it was not brought about by physical force, it was not undertaken with consent – see, for example, *R v Olugboja* [1981] 3 All ER 443.

23 This might make sense if the rules relating to duress were being applied to punish the defendant or to discourage others from using threats in the future, rather than to provide relief for the claimant. This would, however, be contrary to the normal approach in contract, which normally takes as its primary concern the protection and compensation of the claimant.

24 See *Pao On v Lau Yiu Long* [1980] AC 614, p 635; *Universe Tankships Inc of Monrovia v International Transport Workers' Federation, The Universe Sentinel* [1983] 1 AC 366, p 400; [1982] 2 All ER 67, p 88.

25 In *Huyton SA v Peter Cremer GmbH & Co* [1999] CLC 230, Mance J suggested that Lord Cross's approach in *Barton v Armstrong* should be limited to cases involving threats of personal violence, whereas a stricter 'but for' test of causation should apply in cases of economic duress. This provides an explanation of the different approaches, but it is arguably unsatisfactory that duress should operate so differently depending on the type of threat involved. It can be argues that the better view is that Lord Cross's statement should not be followed.

26 'Improper' probably does so to a greater extent than 'illegitimate'.

to refer to behaviour that is 'inappropriate'. This allows account to be taken of the context in which the behaviour takes place – does it go beyond what a reasonable person would regard as acceptable in all the circumstances?

A reformulation of the test of duress using this language would be as follows. Did the claimant enter into the contract at least partly as a result of an indication of future behaviour by the defendant that put pressure on the claimant and was inappropriate in all the circumstances? No doubt, however, the more manageable formulation of 'Did the claimant enter into the contract at least partly as a result of illegitimate threats from the defendant?' will more likely, in practice, be used.

## 10.4 ECONOMIC DURESS

The broadening of the approach to what behaviour can constitute duress, as reflected in *Attorney General v R*,[27] perhaps means that it is no longer necessary to deal with 'economic duress' as a separate category. However, it was in this area that the courts really broadened the concept of duress, and so it is worth examining the development of the concept as a means of understanding how the law has developed to its current position.

The first recognition of economic duress as a basis for allowing a party to escape from a contract is probably to be found in the *obiter* statements of Kerr J in *Occidental Worldwide Investment Corp v Skibs A/S Avanti, The Siboen and The Sibotre*.[28] The case concerned a renegotiation of charters of two vessels, under the threat that otherwise the charterers would go out of business. In other words it was a threat that the contractual obligations under the charters would be broken. It was recognised that this could in some circumstances have amounted to duress sufficient to render the agreement voidable. On the facts, however, the other party had not agreed to the renegotiation under duress, but simply as a result of ordinary commercial pressures. In *North Ocean Shipping Co v Hyundai Construction, The Atlantic Baron*,[29] the devaluation of the dollar led to a demand for an increase in the price payable under a contract for the construction of a tanker. Mocatta J held that this did amount to duress:[30]

> The Yard were adamant in insisting on the increased price without having any legal justification for so doing and the owners realised that the Yard would not accept anything other than an unqualified agreement to the increase. The owners might have claimed damages in arbitration against the Yard with all the inherent uncertainties of litigation, but in view of the position of the Yard vis à vis [the owners'] relations with Shell[31] it would be unreasonable to hold that this is the course they should have taken: see *Astley v Reynolds* (1731) 2 Str 915. The owners made a very reasonable offer of arbitration coupled with security for any award in the Yard's favour that might be made, but this was refused. They then made their agreement, which can truly I think be said to have been made under compulsion.

There was duress because the defendants' threat to break their contract had no legal justification, and the plaintiffs had no realistic alternative but to submit if they wished to

---

27 [2003] UKPC 22; [2003] EMLR 24 – discussed above, 10.3.
28 [1976] 1 Lloyd's Rep 293, pp 335–36. Kerr J saw support for such an approach in the decision in *D and C Builders v Rees* [1966] 2 QB 617; [1965] 3 All ER 837 – discussed in Chapter 3, 3.12.4.
29 [1979] QB 705; [1978] 3 All ER 1170.
30 Ibid, p 719; pp 1182–83.
31 With whom the owners were negotiating for a lucrative contract for the charter of the tanker, once constructed.

preserve the chance of the charter to Shell. The plaintiffs had, however, delayed for eight months between the delivery of the tanker and the initiation of their claim. This delay meant that the right to rescind had been lost through lapse of time. These two cases therefore recognised the possibility of duress based on improper commercial pressure but did not in fact apply it to the facts before them. The difficulty with this test is the requirement that the pressure should be 'improper'. In commercial dealings, 'threats' may often be made as a means of encouraging the other party to contract – for example, 'If you don't agree to this contract we will take all our other business elsewhere', or 'we will not give you any discount on orders in the future', or 'we will provide these goods to your main competitor at a substantial discount'. All of these threats may have the effect of 'encouraging' the other party to contract, but they are not necessarily to be regarded as 'improper'. They are simply part of the rough and tumble of business life.[32] Where, then, is the line to be drawn?

It might be suggested that, at the very least, the threat should involve the commission of a tort, or a breach of contract – in other words, a threat to do an act that is, in the broadest sense, unlawful. Thus, the threat to encourage others not to fulfil their contracts with the victim (that is, the tort of 'inducing breach of contract'), or the threat to break other agreements that the party doing the threatening has with the victim, might give rise to the possibility of a plea of 'economic duress'. This test is satisfied in many of the cases where economic duress has been held to have occurred. On the other hand the decision of the Court of Appeal in *CTN Cash and Carry v Gallaher*[33] famously contains *obiter* statements to the effect that a threat to commit an entirely lawful act may nevertheless constitute duress. And, of course, in *Attorney General v R*, as we have seen,[34] the Privy Council has indicated that, in its view, threats can be 'illegitimate' as a result of their context, even if they are to do something lawful. *CTN Cash and Carry v Gallaher* is discussed further below (see 10.4.3).

## 10.4.1 INDUSTRIAL ACTION

The cases that have subsequently developed and applied the concept of economic duress have often been concerned with industrial action. A trade union threatens to encourage its members to break their contracts with a particular employer (for example, by going on strike or refusing to do certain work) unless the employer agrees to act in a certain way. To carry out the threatened action would (subject to the applicability of any protective trade union legislation) amount to the tort of inducement of breach of contract. This may well be regarded as going beyond legitimate pressure and thus amount to duress. For example, in *Universe Tankships Inc of Monrovia v International Transport Workers' Federation, The Universe Sentinel*,[35] the union 'blacked' a ship owned by the plaintiffs, by instructing its members not to deal with it, and therefore preventing it from leaving port. In order to escape from this, the owners, *inter alia*, made a payment to the union's welfare fund. They later brought an action to recover this as a payment made under duress. It was held that the threatened industrial action was unlawful under English law, and the payment was recoverable.

Subsequent changes in English employment law, extending the scope of unlawful industrial action, have had the effect of extending the scope of economic duress. This is shown by *Dimskal Shipping Co SA v International Transport Workers' Federation, The Evia Luck*,[36] which also confirmed that the question of whether the actions of a party amount

---

32  See also Collins, 2003, pp 155–57.
33  [1994] 4 All ER 714.
34  Above, 10.3.
35  [1983] 1 AC 366; [1982] 2 All ER 67.
36  [1992] 2 AC 152; [1991] 4 All ER 871.

to economic duress must be judged by English law, not the law of the country where the actions took place.

> **Key case** *Dimskal Shipping Co SA v International Transport Workers' Federation, The Evia Luck* (1992)
>
> Facts: The International Transport Workers Federation (a trade union) had, through industrial action, persuaded the respondent shipping company to agree to contracts involving the payment of large sums of money in respect of back pay to its crew. This was to bring the respondent's terms of employment in line with those approved by the ITF. The respondents sought to have these contracts, which were expressed to be governed by English law, avoided for duress. The judge at first instance refused, since the actions of the ITF were legal where they took place (in Sweden). The Court of Appeal overturned this judgment, and the ITF appealed to the House of Lords.
> Held: The issue of what amounted to duress had to be determined by English rather than Swedish law. Since the actions of the ITF would have been unlawful under English employment law, the respondents were entitled to avoid the contracts made as a result of them, on the basis of economic duress.

### 10.4.2 BREACH OF CONTRACT

Where the unlawful action threatened is simply a breach of contract, rather than a tort, it may be more difficult to identify the boundaries of legitimate pressure. Some assistance is provided by the opinion of Lord Scarman in the Privy Council case of *Pao On v Lau Yiu Long*.[37] In this case, the plaintiff had threatened not to proceed with a contract for the sale of shares, unless the other side agreed to a renegotiation of certain subsidiary arrangements. The defendant agreed, but, when the plaintiff later tried to enforce these arrangements, claimed that they had been extracted by duress and were therefore voidable. Lord Scarman identified the following factors as being relevant to whether a person acted voluntarily, or not, and therefore under duress:[38]

> it is material to inquire whether the person alleged to have been coerced did or did not protest; whether, at the time he was allegedly coerced into making the contract, he did or did not have an alternative course open to him such as an adequate legal remedy; whether he was independently advised; and whether after entering into the contract he took steps to avoid it.

On the facts of the case, the claim for duress failed because the defendant had had an alternative course open: that is, he had an adequate legal remedy in an action for specific performance in relation to the original agreement. Lord Scarman referred to this test again in *Universe Tankships Inc of Monrovia v International Transport Workers' Federation, The Universe Sentinel*, where he referred to the victim having 'no practical choice but to submit to the duress'.[39]

A clear example of a person being faced with no alternative but to comply, in a case not concerned with industrial action, is to be found in *Atlas Express Ltd v Kafco (Importers and Distributors) Ltd*.[40] The defendants, Kafco, were a small manufacturing company

---

37  [1980] AC 614; [1979] 3 All ER 65.
38  [1980] AC 614, p 635; [1979] 3 All ER 65, p 78.
39  [1983] 1 AC 366, p 400; [1982] 2 All ER 67, p 88.
40  [1989] QB 833; [1989] 1 All ER 641.

who had a very valuable contract with Woolworths, a store with branches throughout the country. Kafco employed Atlas, a national firm of carriers, to make deliveries to Woolworths. Atlas found that they had, through their own miscalculation of the quantities of Kafco's goods that could be carried on their lorries at one time, entered into the contract on un-economic terms. They told Kafco that they must agree to an increase in the charge for carriage, or else Atlas would not make the deliveries. Kafco could not risk being in breach of their contract with Woolworths, and so agreed to the increased charge, under protest. When Atlas brought an action to recover the increased charges, Kafco resisted on the grounds of duress. The court accepted the argument that losing the contract with Woolworths, or being sued by them, would have been so disastrous for Kafco that they had no real alternative but to go along with Atlas's suggestion. An action for damages against Atlas for breach of the original contract would not have been able to provide compensation sufficient to counteract the effects of the destruction of their business relationship with Woolworths. Kafco were not obliged to pay the additional carriage costs.

## For thought

*QuickCo Carriers plc have a five-year contract to deliver Sampson's honey to Tesda, a national supermarket chain. QuickCo threaten to stop deliveries under this contract unless Sampson agrees to a 15 per cent increase in the price. At the time, Sampson has just received an approach from another supermarket chain about buying his honey. If Sampson agrees to QuickCo's demand, could he later claim that this was voidable for duress?*

A similar situation arose in the earlier case of *B & S Contracts and Design Ltd v Victor Green Publications Ltd*.[41] There was a contract for the erection of exhibition stands. An industrial dispute arose a week before the exhibition between the constructor of the stands and its employees. The constructor sought a contribution of £4,500 from the defendants, who had let out the stands to exhibitors, to assist in settling the dispute with the employees. This was paid and the contract was performed. The defendants then deducted the £4,500 when paying the contract price. The constructor sued to recover this sum. It was held by the Court of Appeal that the payment of £4,500 was made under duress and was not enforceable. The defendants had no other way out of what would have been a disastrous situation, because of its effect on the exhibition, and they were entitled to treat the payment as being forced out of them by economic duress. Legal action against the constructor in this situation would not have been adequate, because of the time pressure. The failure of the exhibition would have had consequences for the defendants going beyond anything that would have been recoverable in damages from the constructor. A major component of economic duress thus seems to be that the action threatened leaves the person threatened with no realistic alternative to compliance.

Situations involving a threat to break a contract unless a further payment is made can, of course, raise issues of consideration. Under the doctrine in *Stilk v Myrick*,[42] the threatening party can be argued to be providing no consideration for a promise to make the additional payment. This indeed was regarded as an additional ground for the defendants'

---

41  [1984] ICR 419.
42  (1809) 2 Camp 317; 170 ER 1168; 6 Esp 129; 170 ER 851 – see Chapter 3, 3.9.6.

success in *Atlas Express v Kafco*. Tucker J, after lengthy discussion of economic duress, concluded his judgment with the terse comment:[43]

> In any event, I find that there was no consideration for the new agreement. The plaintiffs were already obliged to deliver the defendants' goods at the rates agreed under the terms of the original agreement. There was no consideration for the increased minimum charge.

The scope for the use of this means of dealing with cases of economic duress involving the modification of existing contracts has, of course, been significantly reduced by the Court of Appeal's decision in *Williams v Roffey Bros & Nicholls (Contractors) Ltd*.[44] The recognition that the 'practical benefit' of obtaining the timely performance of an existing obligation may amount to good consideration for a new promise means that in 'duress' situations, consideration may be found. The claimant will probably have agreed to make the additional payment (or whatever else is required) in order to avoid unfavourable consequences that would flow from the defendant's threatened actions. Avoiding those consequences will be likely to be regarded as a 'practical benefit' and therefore good consideration. The result is that duress becomes of increased importance in dealing with this type of situation.[45]

### 10.4.3 MUST THE THREAT BE OF AN UNLAWFUL ACT?

The examples of duress so far considered have all involved an act that is in some respects a breach of law. It involves a crime, or a tort, or a breach of contract. Is this a necessary characteristic for duress and, in particular, economic duress, to be operative?

---

**Key case** *CTN Cash and Carry v Gallaher* (1994)[46]

**Facts:** The threat in this case was to withdraw credit from the other party, and to insist on cash for goods supplied. The circumstances in which this occurred were that the plaintiffs had ordered from the defendants cigarettes to the value of £17,000. These had, as a result of the defendants' mistake, been delivered to the wrong warehouse, in a different town. It was arranged that the defendants would collect them and transport them to the right warehouse. Before this could be done, however, there was a burglary at the warehouse to which the cigarettes had been wrongly delivered, and they were stolen. The defendants believed, mistakenly as a matter of law, that the cigarettes were at the plaintiffs' risk when they were stolen. They therefore insisted that the plaintiffs should pay for them, backing this up with the threat to withdraw credit. The plaintiffs reluctantly paid, but then brought an action to recover the £17,000 on the basis that it had been paid under duress.

**Held:** The Court of Appeal found that, on the facts, there was no economic duress, partly because the 'threat' was issued in good faith.[47] Although the defendants

---

43  [1989] QB 833, p 841; [1989] 1 All ER 641, p 646.
44  [1991] 1 QB 1; [1990] 1 All ER 512 – see Chapter 3, 3.9.7.
45  Atiyah (1995, p 273) has suggested, however, that in a situation where the courts find that there were good commercial reasons for accepting a variation (and thus that there was consideration), it may be difficult to argue that the acceptance was forced by 'duress'.
46  [1994] 4 All ER 714. See also *Times Travel (UK) Ltd v Pakistan International Airlines Corp* [2017] EWHC 1367 (Ch).
47  It has been noted earlier that 'bad faith' is not generally a necessary requirement for duress – above, 10.3. Where, however, there is no other 'unlawfulness', it may well be that it becomes a much more relevant factor. See also *Chaggar v Chaggar* [2018] EWHC 1203 (QB).

might have been regarded as abusing their position as the monopoly supplier of certain very popular brands of cigarettes, they were in this case genuinely under the impression that their claim for payment was legitimate. Moreover, as Steyn LJ commented:[48]

> an extension [of the categories of duress] capable of covering the present case, involving 'lawful act duress' in a commercial context in pursuit of a *bona fide* claim, would be a radical one with far-reaching implications. It would introduce a substantial and undesirable element of uncertainty in the commercial bargaining process.

The court did not accept, however, that the fact that what was threatened was perfectly lawful, and would not have involved the supplier in any breach of contract, was in itself fatal to a claim. It thought that it was possible, in appropriate circumstances, for a threat to commit an entirely lawful act to amount to duress.

In coming to its conclusion in *CTN Cash & Carry v Gallaher*, the Court of Appeal noted with approval the opinion of Professor Birks that it ought not to be the case that 'those who devise outrageous but technically lawful means of compulsion must always escape restitution'.[49] The Court of Appeal's statements on this issue are, of course, *obiter*, but they are supported by the views (also strictly *obiter*) of the Privy Council in *Attorney General v R*,[50] and in *Borelli v Ting*.[51] In the latter case the threat was to oppose a scheme for liquidating a company unless there was an agreement not to investigate suspected prior misconduct by the former chairman. As such, they indicate a possible further extension of the concept of economic duress. Whether it is a desirable or necessary extension is open to doubt. The problems of drawing the line between legitimate pressure and economic duress will become even more difficult if a requirement of 'unlawfulness' is rejected. The arguments for and against such a development in the law are very similar to those that apply in relation to whether the courts should adopt a general principle that 'unconscionable' agreements are unenforceable. This is discussed in Chapter 11, 11.10.

## 10.5 REMEDIES FOR DURESS

The remedy that the victim of duress will be seeking is to escape from the agreement that has resulted from the duress – in other words, rescission. As has been noted in relation to mistake and misrepresentation,[52] however, rescission may be lost through affirmation of

---

48 [1994] 4 All ER 714, p 719.
49 Birks, 1989, p 177. In relation to blackmail, in *Al Nehayan v Kent* [2018] EWHC 333 (Comm) at [188] Leggatt LJ stated: "It does seem to me, however, that the test suggested in *Chitty on Contracts* could be made more precise by transposing into objective requirements the elements of the offence of blackmail. On this basis a demand coupled with a threat to commit a lawful act will be regarded as illegitimate if (a) the defendant has no reasonable grounds for making the demand and (b) the threat would not be considered by reasonable and honest people to be a proper means of reinforcing the demand."
50 [2003] UKPC 22; [2003] EMLR 24 – discussed above, 10.3.
51 [2010] UKPC 21. See also *Progress Bulk Carriers Ltd v Tube City IMS LLC* [2012] EWHC 273 (Comm) where in addition it was suggested that a previous breach of contract could provide the necessary 'unlawfulness'.
52 See Chapter 9, 9.7.2 and Chapter 8, 8.4.1 above.

the contract, lapse of time[53] or the intervention of third party rights. It might also be that, as in relation to misrepresentation, the person claiming duress should be in a position to make restitution of any property transferred for rescission to be available. This point has been reviewed by the Court of Appeal.

---

**Key case** *Halpern v Halpern* (2007)[54]

Facts: The parties had been engaged in a dispute over an inheritance. This was then settled on the basis of a compromise agreement. When the claimants sought damages for breach of this agreement, the defendants alleged that it had been entered into under duress. Certain documents had been destroyed as part of the compromise agreement. The High Court held, as a preliminary issue, that since these documents could not be restored to the claimants, the right to rescind the agreement for duress had been lost. The defendants appealed.

Held: The Court of Appeal adopted a more flexible approach to the issue. The Court noted that in relation to undue influence the House of Lords in *Erlanger v New Sombrero Phosphate Co* (1878) 3 App Cas 1218 had held that the courts may do 'what is practically just, though it cannot restore the parties precisely to the state they were in before the contract'. In other words, in some cases some monetary compensation may be a substitute for counter-restitution. The Court of Appeal thought that the same approach should apply to duress, so that the exact result will depend on the circumstances of the particular case. In relation to the case before it, Carnwath LJ commented that it would be surprising if, assuming the defendants could establish improper pressure, the courts would not provide a suitable remedy. However, 'The form of the remedy, whether equitable or tortious, is a matter which cannot sensibly be decided until the facts are known, not only as to the nature and effect of the improper pressure, but also as to the identity and significance of the documents destroyed.'[55] These matters would have to be determined at trial.

---

Damages are not available for duress *per se*, even where the contract is not rescinded.[56] This reflects the origins of duress in the idea that there was no binding agreement because of the lack of true consent. If that conceptual basis for duress no longer retains its dominance, however, there is little reason why damages resulting from the duress should not be recoverable, on a 'reliance' basis, as they are now for most categories of misrepresentation.

## 10.6 SUMMARY OF KEY POINTS

■    Duress involves a threat towards or pressure upon another person, which induces that person to enter into a contract. Traditionally the threats needed to be of physical

---

53  See, for example, *North Ocean Shipping Co v Hyundai Construction, The Atlantic Baron* [1979] QB 705; [1978] 3 All ER 1170; above, 10.4.
54  [2007] EWCA Civ 291; [2001] 3 All ER 478.
55  [2007] EWCA Civ 291; [2001] 3 All ER 478, para 76.
56  Compare *Al Nehayan v Kent* [2018] EWHC 333 (Comm) at [224]ff.

violence but the modern law recognises any threat involving illegitimate pressure (including economic pressure) as potentially involving 'duress'.

- A contract made under duress is voidable (not void).

- In relation to economic duress, the threat will normally be to do something unlawful, such as breach a contract or commit a tort (such as inducing breach of contract). Case law suggests that a threat to do something lawful *could* constitute illegitimate pressure.

- Courts will look to see whether the person to whom the threat was made was effectively compelled to comply. Relevant issues will be:
  - did the person object at the time?
  - was there any real alternative to compliance?
  - was there independent legal advice?
  - how quickly did the person act to avoid the contract?

- The remedy for duress is rescission of the contract. This may be granted even if the victim of the duress cannot make precise restitution.

- Damages are not available for duress *per se*.

## 10.7 FURTHER READING

### Theories of duress
- Bigwood, R, *Exploitative Contracts*, 2003, Oxford: Oxford University Press

- Birks, P and Chin Nyuk Yin, 'On the nature of undue influence' (1995), Chapter 3 in Beatson, J and Friedmann, D (eds), *Good Faith and Fault in Contract Law*, 1995, Oxford: Clarendon Press

- Smith, S A, 'Contracting under pressure: a theory of duress' (1997) CLJ 343

- Smith, S A, *Atiyah's Introduction to the Law of Contract*, 6th edn, 2006, Oxford: Clarendon Press, Chapter 11

### Economic duress
- Atiyah, P S, 'Economic duress and the overborne will' (1982) 98 LQR 197

- Devenney, J, 'A pack of unruly dogs: unconscionable bargains, lawful act (economic duress) and clogs of the equity of redemption' [2002] JBL 539

- Halson, R, 'Opportunism, economic duress and contractual modifications' (1991) 107 LQR 649

- Nolan, D, 'Economic duress and the availability of a reasonable alternative' [2000] RLR 105

## COMPANION WEBSITE

*Now visit the companion website to:*

■   Revise and consolidate your knowledge of Duress by tackling a series of multiple-choice questions on this chapter

■   Test your understanding of the chapter's key terms by using the flashcard glossary

■   Explore Duress further by accessing a series of web links

# Undue influence

## Contents

## 11.1 OVERVIEW

Undue influence is an equitable concept that supplements the common law vitiating factor of duress. It operates largely through the application of presumptions. The following aspects are discussed in this chapter:

- The underlying principles. When does influence become 'undue'? Imbalance of power between the parties is an important element in identifying undue influence.
- Actual undue influence. If there is direct evidence that a party agreed to a contract under the influence of improper pressure at that time, this will constitute actual undue influence. Such evidence is, however, rare.
- Presumed undue influence. A relationship of influence will be established where:
    - the parties are in one of a number of recognised relationships (for example, solicitor – client); the presumption of *influence* is in these circumstances irrebuttable;
    - the relationship between the parties has developed in a way that one party can be shown to have a sufficient degree of influence over the other party (sometimes referred to as one party dominating the other); this type of presumption of *influence* may be rebutted by evidence to the contrary.
- Presumed undue influence and disadvantageous transactions. Where a contract between parties in a relationship of *influence* clearly operates to the disadvantage of the weaker party, then *undue* influence will be presumed. It will be up to the alleged influencer to rebut this presumption of *undue* influence (for example by demonstrating that the other party entered into the contract with a full appreciation of what was involved (for example, after receiving independent legal advice)).
- Effects. A contract entered into on the basis of actual or presumed influence is voidable. The usual bars to rescission apply (for example, lapse of time, third party rights). Damages are generally not available.
- Third parties. Where, for example, a debtor has persuaded a person to act as surety or guarantor, the creditor will be put on notice whenever the relationship between debtor and surety is non-commercial (for example, husband persuading wife to use the family home as security for business debts). In that situation:
    - the creditor will be affected by any undue influence used by the debtor; the transaction may be voidable on that basis;
    - the creditor can protect itself by insisting that the surety receives legal advice before entering into the transaction.
- Unconscionability. English law recognises no general concept of unconscionability.

## 11.2 INTRODUCTION

Duress, as discussed in the previous chapter, is essentially a common law concept. Alongside it must be placed the (wider) equitable doctrine of 'undue influence'. This operates to release parties from contracts that they have entered into,[1] not only as a result of improper threats but also as a result of being 'influenced' by the other party, whether deliberately or not.[2]

One of the main difficulties with undue influence, as with duress, is to find the limits of legitimate persuasion. If it were impermissible to seek to persuade, cajole or otherwise encourage people to enter into agreements, then sales representatives would all be out of a job. 'Influence' in itself is perfectly acceptable: it is only when it becomes 'undue' that the law will intervene. Clarity in deciding when that has occurred is not assisted by the fact that the word 'undue' has two potential meanings. It can be used to indicate some

---

1   The concept can also be used to set aside gifts or bequests.
2   Though references to the 'abuse' of influence in the most recent House of Lords decision on the area suggest the need for some deliberation (that is, *Royal Bank of Scotland v Etridge (No 2)* [2001] UKHL 44; [2001] 4 All ER 449), the development of the concept does not seem to require this.

impropriety on the part of the influencer (even if the 'wrongdoing' on the part of the part of the influencer was not deliberate). The influence is 'undue' because an imbalance of power between the parties has been used illegitimately by the influencer. Alternatively, the word can be used simply to indicate that the level of influence is at such a level that the influenced party has lost autonomy in deciding whether to enter into a contract. The point has been recognised in the High Court of Australia, where 'undue' was given the second meaning, and undue influence distinguished from unconscionable conduct. As Deane J put it:[3]

> Undue influence, like common law duress, looks to the quality of the consent or assent of the weaker party ... Unconscionable dealing looks to the conduct of the stronger party in attempting to enforce, or retain the benefit of a dealing with a person under a special disability in circumstances where it is not consistent with equity or good conscience that he should do so.

English courts, however, have tended to emphasise the 'wrongdoing' of the stronger party in undue influence cases, though it cannot be said that their approach is consistent, and there are undue influence cases that indicate that such 'wrongdoing' is not an essential element.[4] The issue is whether the concept is 'claimant-focused' and/or 'defendant-focused'.[5] If it is claimant-focused, then what matters is whether the claimant acted autonomously in entering into the contract; if it is defendant-focused, then what matters is whether the defendant has taken advantage of the claimant's weaker position. As suggested above, the English courts have not consistently applied one approach or the other, and this adds to the uncertainty about the precise scope of the concept. The most recent House of Lords decision, *Royal Bank of Scotland v Etridge (No 2)*,[6] adopts what is primarily a defendant-focused analysis, based on whether there has been 'abuse' of a position of influence, and this seems to be the dominant approach.[7]

How, then, do the courts decide when influence has overstepped the limits of acceptability and become 'undue'? The focus of undue influence in English law is, broadly, on particular relationships between the parties (either continuing, or in relation to a particular transaction) that may lead to an inequality between them. The starting point for the law's analysis is therefore not the substance of the transaction, but the process by which it came about. Was this the result of an underlying relationship of influence between the parties? An initial task is therefore to identify which relationships the law regards as giving rise to this inequality. Once they have been identified, then further questions will arise as to how the doctrine applies to them.

### 11.2.1 IN FOCUS: SCOPE OF UNDUE INFLUENCE

The precise scope of the concept of undue influence may be due for reconsideration. At present, there are authorities that are treated as being concerned with undue influence, largely because of the limited scope given to duress at the time they were decided. In *Williams v Bayley*,[8] for example, the plaintiff had agreed to give a mortgage over his colliery as

---

3   *Commercial Bank of Australia Ltd v Amadio* (1983) 151 CLR 447, p 474.
4   For example, *Allcard v Skinner* (1887) 36 Ch D 145, where the defendant was the lady superior of a religious order. See also Birks and Chin, 1995, where the argument for the adoption of the approach taken in *Commercial Bank of Australia v Amadio* is strongly made.
5   The 'claimant' here being the person influenced and the 'defendant' the alleged 'influencer' – see the corresponding discussion in relation to duress, in Chapter 10, 10.3.
6   [2001] UKHL 44; [2001] 4 All ER 449.
7   See, in particular, the speech of Lord Hobhouse. See also the Court of Appeal decision in *UCB Corporate Services Ltd v Williams* [2002] EWCA Civ 555; [2002] 3 FCR 448.
8   (1866) LR 1 HL 200.

security for debts incurred by his son, who had forged his father's signature on promissory notes. The creditors had threatened that the son would be prosecuted if the mortgage was not given.[9] The agreement was set aside as being obtained by undue influence. Similarly, in *Mutual Finance Ltd v John Wetton & Sons Ltd*,[10] implied, though not explicit, threats to prosecute a member of a family company in relation to a forged guarantee led to the company giving a new guarantee.[11] This was again set aside on the basis of undue influence. Both these cases involve 'pressure' being placed on a party in much the same way as occurs with duress. It is possible that the expansion in the type of threats that are now treated as potentially giving rise to duress[12] would mean that they would be put in that category. There is a strong argument that all these situations, involving pressure resulting from express or implied threats, might be usefully re-categorised as 'duress', leaving 'undue influence' to deal with more surreptitious forms of influence (such as relationships where one party has lost autonomy because of his or her relationship with the 'influencer').[13] At the moment, the courts have generally not been prepared to take such a step.

### 11.2.2 THE MODERN LAW OF UNDUE INFLUENCE

The whole area of undue influence has twice in the last 25 or so years been given a thorough examination by the House of Lords – in 1993, in *Barclays Bank plc v O'Brien*,[14] and in 2001, in *Royal Bank of Scotland v Etridge (No 2)*.[15] Between these two decisions there were many Court of Appeal decisions, mainly concerned with the situation where a bank is infected by the undue influence of a husband who has persuaded his wife to use the matrimonial home as security for a business loan. Most of this case law is, following *Etridge*, of historical interest only, but one or two of the decisions are worthy of note. The main focus in the rest of this chapter will, however, be on the views of the House of Lords as expressed in *O'Brien* and *Etridge*.

In the leading speech in *O'Brien*, Lord Browne-Wilkinson adopted the analysis of the Court of Appeal in *Bank of Credit and Commerce International SA v Aboody*[16] to the effect that there are two main categories of undue influence, the second of which must be divided into two further separate sub-categories. The categories were actual undue influence (described as 'Class 1') and presumed undue influence (described as 'Class 2'). Presumed undue influence was then sub-divided into influence arising from certain relationships (such as solicitor – client, doctor – patient) which, on one reading of *O'Brien*, would always give rise to a presumption of undue influence ('Class 2A') and influence arising from other relationships that have developed into relationships of "trust and confidence" which, on one reading of *O'Brien*, would also give rise to a presumption of undue influence ('Class 2B'). These divisions have subsequently been used in many cases. The House of Lords took the view, however, in *Royal Bank of Scotland v Etridge (No 2)*[17] that,

---

9   It is not clear from the facts as reported whether specific threats were ever made by the creditors, but the House of Lords took the view that all concerned must have acted on the basis that this is what they were suggesting would happen if the father did not agree to the mortgage.

10  [1937] 2 All ER 657.

11  The forgery was committed by one of the Wetton sons; the other, in agreeing that the company should give the guarantee, was also concerned about the effects on his father's precarious health if his brother were prosecuted for forgery.

12  For which, see Chapter 10. See also *Al Nehayan v Kent* [2018] EWHC 333 (Comm) at [184] where these cases seem to have, in effect, be regarded as duress cases.

13  This argument is fully developed by Birks and Chin (1995), who suggest that all 'pressure' cases should be dealt with as duress. By contrast, Cope (1985) has suggested that all cases of duress should be treated as undue influence.

14  [1994] 1 AC 180; [1993] 4 All ER 417.

15  [2001] UKHL 44; [2001] 4 All ER 449.

16  [1990] 1 QB 923; [1992] 4 All ER 955.

17  [2001] UKHL 44; [2001] 4 All ER 449.

while there is a distinction between 'actual' and 'presumed' influence, it should not operate quite as suggested by the categorisation adopted in *O'Brien* and that, in particular, the concept of Class 2B influence is open to misinterpretation.[18]

The concept of 'actual undue influence' will be considered first, followed by 'presumed undue influence', and the review of this area by the House of Lords in *Etridge*.

## 11.3 ACTUAL UNDUE INFLUENCE

In relation to actual undue influence, the claimant must prove, on the balance of probabilities, that in relation to a particular transaction, the defendant used undue influence. There is no need for there to be a previous history of such influence. It can operate for the first time in connection with the transaction that is disputed. An example of this type of influence is to be found in *BCCI v Aboody*.[19] Mrs Aboody was 20 years younger than her husband. She had married him when she was 17. For many years, she signed documents relating to her husband's business, of which she was nominally a director, without reading them or questioning her husband about them. On the occasion that gave rise to the litigation, she had signed a number of guarantees and charges relating to the matrimonial home, in order to support loans by the bank to the business. She had taken no independent advice, though the bank's solicitor had at one meeting attempted to encourage her to take legal advice. During that meeting, Mr Aboody, in a state of some agitation, came into the room and, through arguing with the solicitor, managed to reduce his wife to tears. It was held that although Mr Aboody had not acted with any improper motive, he had unduly influenced his wife. He had concealed relevant matters from her, and his bullying manner had led her to sign without giving proper detached consideration to her own interests, simply because she wanted peace.

The Court of Appeal in this case, following *dicta* of Lord Scarman in *National Westminster Bank plc v Morgan*,[20] held that Mrs Aboody's claim to set aside the transaction nevertheless failed because it was not to her 'manifest disadvantage'. The loans that she was guaranteeing had, in fact, given the company a reasonably good chance of surviving, in which case the potential benefits to Mrs Aboody would have been substantial. The risks involved did not, therefore, clearly outweigh the benefits. The House of Lords, in *CIBC Mortgages plc v Pitt*,[21] subsequently indicated, however, that it is not a requirement in cases of actual undue influence that the transaction is disadvantageous to the victim. If similar facts were to recur, therefore, a person in the position of Mrs Aboody would be likely to succeed in having the transactions set aside. A person is entitled to have a contract set aside if they have been bullied into making it, notwithstanding that they may receive some benefit from it.

Where actual undue influence is proved it is not necessary for the claimant to prove that the transaction would not have been entered into but for the improper influence. This was the view of the Court of Appeal in *UCB Corporate Services Ltd v Williams*.[22] The position is analogous to that applying to misrepresentation or duress: as long as the influence was one factor in making the decision to enter into the transaction, that is sufficient.[23]

---

18 'It is not a useful forensic tool': ibid, [107]; p 483, per Lord Hobhouse.
19 [1990] 1 QB 923; [1992] 4 All ER 955.
20 [1985] AC 686; [1985] 1 All ER 821.
21 [1994] AC 200; [1993] 4 All ER 433.
22 [2002] EWCA Civ 555; [2002] 3 FCR 448, not following statements apparently to the contrary by the Court of Appeal in *BCCI v Aboody,* since these were regarded as inconsistent with the House of Lords' view of *Aboody,* as expressed in *CIBC Mortgages v Pitt: see* [85] – [91].
23 For a consideration of some of the problems with this position in the context of duress that may apply equally to undue influence, see Chapter 10, 10.3.

## 11.4 PRESUMED INFLUENCE: RECOGNISED RELATIONSHIPS

Under the *O'Brien* analysis there were certain relationships that were, it seemed, presumed to give rise to undue influence. The current position as set out by the House of Lords in *Etridge* is that such relationships give rise to a presumption of influence but not necessarily undue influence. They are relationships 'where one party is legally presumed to repose trust and confidence in the other'.[24] As Lord Nicholls put it:[25]

> The law has adopted a sternly protective attitude towards certain types of relationship in which one party acquires influence over another who is vulnerable and dependent ... In these cases the law presumes, irrebuttably, that one party had influence over the other. The complainant need not prove he actually reposed trust and confidence in the other party. It is sufficient for him to prove the existence of the type of relationship.

The relationships that fall into this category include parent/minor child,[26] guardian/ward,[27] trustee/beneficiary,[28] doctor/patient,[29] solicitor/client[30] and religious adviser/disciple.[31] It does not include husband/wife.[32] The relationships are those where it is assumed that one person has placed trust and confidence in another, and so is liable to act on that other's suggestions without seeking independent advice. Other relationships (other than husband/wife) that have these characteristics could possibly be added to the list in the future.

---

**Key case** *Allcard v Skinner* (1887)[33]

Facts: The plaintiff had entered a religious order of St Mary at the Cross, and had taken vows of poverty, chastity and obedience. The defendant was the lady superior of the order. Over a period of eight years during which she was a member of the order, the plaintiff gave property to the value of £7,000 to the defendant, most of which was spent on the purposes of the order. The plaintiff left the order, and some six years later sought to recover her property, on the basis that it was given to the order under undue influence.

Held: The property was *prima facie* recoverable as having been given under the undue influence of membership of the order, which required obedience to the defendant. This was so even though no direct pressure had been placed on the plaintiff. The influence was presumed from the relationship itself. The plaintiff's action to recover her property did not succeed, however, because of the delay between leaving the order and bringing the action (six years). This lapse of time operated as a bar to recovery.

---

24 [2001] UKHL 44; [2001] 4 All ER 449, at [104].
25 Ibid, [18].
26 *Bainbrigge v Browne* (1881) Ch D 188.
27 *Hylton v Hylton* (1754) 2 Ves Sen 547.
28 *Ellis v Barker* (1871) 7 Ch App 104.
29 *Radcliffe v Price* (1902) 18 TLR 466.
30 *Wright v Carter* [1903] 1 Ch 27.
31 *Allcard v Skinner* (1887) 36 Ch D 145.
32 *National Westminster Bank plc v Morgan* [1985] AC 686; [1985] 1 All ER 821.
33 (1887) 36 Ch D 145.

**For thought**

*What advice would you give to a religious group that requires its members to obey the orders of its leaders in order to protect itself from having to return any property that members may donate to it?*

Once there is a relationship from which influence is presumed, in what circumstances can the court conclude that the influence was 'undue', under the approach in *Etridge*?[34] This is where the concept that was previously referred to as 'manifest disadvantage' becomes relevant. Lord Nicholls referred back to the statement by Lindley LJ in *Allcard v Skinner*, which was cited by Lord Scarman in developing the concept of 'manifest disadvantage' in *National Westminster Bank plc v Morgan*. Lindley LJ pointed out that a small gift made to a person falling within one of the presumed categories of influence would not be enough in itself to put the transaction aside:[35]

> But if the gift is so large as not to be reasonably accounted for on the ground of friendship, relationship, charity, or other ordinary motives on which ordinary men act, the burden is upon the donee to support the gift.

Following this principle, Lord Nicholls pointed out that it would be absurd if every minor transaction between those in a relationship of presumed influence was also presumed to have been brought about by the exercise of *undue* influence:[36]

> The law would be out of touch with everyday life if the presumption were to apply to every Christmas or birthday gift by a child to a parent, or to an agreement whereby a client or patient agrees to be responsible for the reasonable fees of his legal or medical advisor ... So something more is needed before the law reverses the burden of proof, something which calls for an explanation. When that something more is present, the greater the disadvantage to the vulnerable person, the more cogent must be the explanation before the presumption will be regarded as rebutted.

What is being looked for is a transaction that 'failing proof to the contrary, is explicable only on the basis that it has been procured by undue influence'.[37] In other words, it is not the sort of transaction that the vulnerable person would have entered into in the normal course of events. Lord Hobhouse gives the example of a solicitor buying a client's property at a significant undervalue.[38] The fact that a transaction provides no benefit to the vulnerable person will be evidence supporting the suggestion of undue influence. Thus, once there is a relationship falling within one of the categories of automatically presumed influence, and a transaction that is not of a kind forming one of the normal incidents of such a relationship, there will be an inference of undue influence. It will then be up to the alleged influencer to show that the other party acted without being affected by such influence. The easiest way to do this is likely to be to show that the claimant received independent legal

---

34  Other than by proving actual undue influence, which would defeat the point of having a presumption of influence at all.

35  (1887) 36 Ch D 145, p 185.

36  [2001] UKHL 44; [2001] 4 All ER 449 at [24]. See the similar comments of Lord Hobhouse at [104] and Lord Scott at [156].

37  [2001] UKHL 44; [2001] 4 All ER 449 at [30].

38  Ibid, at [104].

advice before entering into the transaction, though the Privy Council in *Attorney General v R* did not think that this was necessarily conclusive.[39] The adequacy of the advice to protect the influenced party may need to be considered.[40] It is certainly not sufficient for the alleged influencer simply to show that there had been no 'wrongdoing' on his or her part.[41]

## 11.5 PRESUMED INFLUENCE: OTHER RELATIONSHIPS

Even where a relationship does not fall into one of the categories listed in the previous section, it may *in fact* have developed in a way that indicates that one person is in a 'dominant' position over the other. The 'dominated' person will be likely in such a situation to act on the advice, recommendation or orders of the other, without seeking any independent advice and without properly considering the consequences of his or her actions. The fact that the claimant, for example, placed trust and confidence in the defendant in relation to the management of the claimant's financial affairs will have to be proved by evidence.[42] If that is done, then a disadvantageous transaction entered into by the claimant may constitute *prima facie* evidence that the trust and confidence of the claimant has been abused. The burden of proof will shift to the defendant to produce evidence to counter this inference. If no such evidence is produced, the court will be entitled to conclude that the transaction was in fact brought about by the exercise of undue influence.[43] In other words, the issue is the inferences that the court is entitled to draw from the evidence before it and where the burden of proof lies in relation to that evidence.

Probably the majority of the reported cases that have been regarded as falling under this category of undue influence, based on an established relationship of trust and confidence, concern a husband and wife. For example, in *Hewett v First Plus Financial Group plc*[44] it was held that a wife had placed sufficient trust and confidence in her husband that the fact that he had concealed an ongoing affair with another woman from her amounted to undue influence, on the basis that he was accordingly in breach of his duty of fairness and candour to her, in relation to her agreement to a mortgage of the family home. Marriage is not essential for such a relationship of trust and confidence. In *Leeder v Stevens*[45] the Court of Appeal held that a relevant relationship had arisen between a married man and a woman with whom he had had what the court called 'a loving relationship' over a period of 10 years. A transaction in which she had transferred to him a half share in her house, valued at £70,000, in return for a payment of £5,000 was set aside. This case emphasised the strength of the presumptions. The trial judge had found no evidence of actual coercion at the time of the transaction. The Court of Appeal held that this was irrelevant. Once the relationship was established, and there was a transaction that called for explanation, then it was up to the man to prove that the woman had entered into the transaction with full appreciation of its consequences and having been properly advised.

---

39  [2003] UKPC 22; [2003] EMLR 24, at [23].

40  See the comments of Mummery LJ in *Pesticcio v Huet* [2004] EWCA Civ 372; [2004] WTRLR 699, at [23]. See also *Paull v Paull* [2018] EWHC 2520 (Ch).

41  *Hammond v Osborn* [2002] EWCA Civ 885; [2002] WTLR 1125 – applied in *Pesticcio v Huet* [2004] EWCA Civ 372; [2004] WTLR 699.

42  In *Etridge* Lord Scott was prepared to accept, however, that little or no evidence will be needed to establish a reciprocal relationship of trust and confidence between husband and wife living together (see [159]), although he also suggests that undue influence is an unlikely, though possible, explanation for a wife's agreement to act as surety for her husband's business debts (see [162]).

43  See *Etridge*: Lord Nicholls at [14]; Lord Hobhouse, at [106] – [107]; Lord Scott at [161]. All three suggest that an analogy with the tortious concept of *res ipsa loquitur* may be helpful.

44  [2010] EWCA Civ 312; [2010] 2 P & CR 22.

45  [2005] EWCA Civ 50; 149 SJLB 112.

Situations of trust do not only arise in the context of sexual or other intimate relationships, as is shown by *Attorney General v R*,[46] where the Privy Council recognised that a relationship between a soldier and his regiment could be such as to give rise to a presumption of influence. Another example is *Lloyds Bank Ltd v Bundy*.[47]

---

**Key case** *Lloyds Bank Ltd v Bundy* (1975)

Facts: Mr Bundy was an elderly farmer. He had provided a guarantee and a charge over his house to support the debts of his son's business. He was visited by his son and the assistant manager of the bank. The assistant manager told Mr Bundy that the bank could not continue to support the son's business without further security. Mr Bundy then, without seeking any other advice, increased the guarantee and charge to £11,000. When the bank, in enforcing the charge, subsequently sought possession of the house, Mr Bundy pleaded undue influence.

Held: The court took the view that the existence of long-standing relations between the Bundy family and the bank was important. Although the visit when the charge was increased was the first occasion on which this particular assistant manager had met Mr Bundy, he was, as Sir Eric Sachs put it, 'the last of a relevant chain of those who over the years had earned or inherited' Mr Bundy's trust and confidence.[48] The charge over the house was obviously risky given the precarious state of the son's business. There was no evidence that the risks had been properly explained to Mr Bundy by the assistant manager, and therefore Mr Bundy could not have come to an informed judgment on his actions. The charge was set aside on the basis of undue influence.[49]

---

Although the period of time over which a relationship has developed is clearly relevant to deciding whether trust and confidence has arisen, it need not be all that long. In *Goldsworthy v Brickell*,[50] for example, where the relationship existed between an elderly farmer and his neighbour, it had only been for a few months that the plaintiff had been relying on the defendant. Nevertheless, it was held that the relationship involved sufficient trust and confidence for a disadvantageous transaction to require explanation. In the absence of evidence that the elderly farmer had exercised an independent and informed judgment, the relevant transaction was set aside.

In *Credit Lyonnais Bank Nederland NV v Burch*,[51] it was held that a relationship of trust and confidence could arise between an employer and a junior employee. The employee had acted as babysitter for the employer, and had visited his family at weekends and on holidays abroad. She had agreed to her house being used as collateral for the employer's business overdraft. The transaction was set aside on the basis of undue influence.

---

46 [2003] UKPC 22; [2003] EMLR 24.
47 [1975] QB 326; [1974] 3 All ER 757.
48 Contrast the House of Lords' view in *National Westminster Bank plc v Morgan* [1985] 1 All ER 821, where it was held that there was no relationship of trust and confidence between a bank manager and a wife who had executed a charge over the matrimonial home. Although the manager had visited her at home to obtain her signature, the relationship did not go beyond the normal business relationship of banker and customer.
49 The judgments in this case make reference to 'presumptions' of abuse of influence that would need reconsideration in the light of *Etridge*. It is not suggested, however, that the *Etridge* approach would lead to a different conclusion on the facts.
50 [1987] 1 All ER 853.
51 [1997] 1 All ER 144.

### 11.5.1  IN FOCUS: CAN THE NATURE OF TRANSACTION ESTABLISH 'INFLUENCE'?

It was held by Millett LJ in the Court of Appeal in *Credit Lyonnais Bank Nederland NV v Burch* that a presumption of influence between two people in a relationship that was 'easily capable of developing into a relationship of trust and confidence' could be established by the 'nature of the transaction' that had been entered into.[52] If 'the transaction is so extravagantly improvident that it is virtually inexplicable on any other basis', then 'the inference will be readily drawn'.[53] This use of the substance of the transaction as an element in establishing a presumption of influence was unusual. The other *pre-Etridge* cases in this area operated on the basis of establishing the presumption from the way in which the relationship has developed, before looking at the position in relation to the transaction under consideration. As will be seen below, the disadvantageous nature of the transaction has generally been used as a basis for deciding whether or not relief should be granted, once a presumption of influence has been made. Millett LJ's approach was not specifically followed by the other members of the Court of Appeal, though Swinton Thomas LJ stated in general terms that he agreed with Millett LJ's reasons for his decision.[54] This aspect of *Burch* was not considered by the House of Lords in *Etridge*, though the outcome of the case was clearly approved by Lord Nicholls.[55] Millett LJ's analysis, however, would not seem to comfortably fit with the *Etridge* approach. This would look at the relationship between the employer and employee to see if trust and confidence had developed. If it had, then the disadvantageous and risky nature of the transaction that the employee had entered into would raise an inference that the trust and confidence had been 'abused'. The employer would then need to produce evidence to contradict that inference. If, on the other hand, there was no evidence of a relationship of trust and confidence, no inferences would be drawn from the disadvantageous nature of the transaction, and the employee would need to produce specific evidence of undue influence in order to have it set aside. There is no suggestion in the House of Lords' speeches in *Etridge* that the nature of the transaction can be used to establish a relationship of trust and confidence. Thus, if the employee had entered into a disadvantageous transaction simply because she thought it was a good way of currying favour with the boss, perhaps enhancing her prospects of promotion, there would be no scope for a finding of undue influence.

## 11.6  RELEVANCE OF THE DISADVANTAGEOUS NATURE OF THE TRANSACTION

The *Burch* case, discussed above, raises the question of the extent to which the risky or disadvantageous nature of a transaction is a part of the consideration of whether there was undue influence. *Etridge* has changed the focus on this issue but to understand where the law has got to, it will be helpful to look at a little of the history.

The concept that a transaction must be to the 'manifest disadvantage' of the claimant in order for it to be set aside for some types of undue influence derives from the speech of Lord Scarman in *National Westminster Bank plc v Morgan*.[56] Here, Mrs Morgan had

---

52  Ibid, p 154.

53  Ibid, p 155.

54  For an enthusiastic response to *Burch* as a welcome development in the law controlling substantively unfair transactions, as opposed to simply procedural unfairness, see Chen-Wishart, 1997. For a more sceptical reception see Tjio, 1997.

55  [2001] UKHL 44; [2001] 4 All ER 449 at [83], [89].

56  [1985] AC 686; [1985] 1 All ER 821. Lord Scarman was adopting and adapting an approach taken by Lindley LJ in *Allcard v Skinner* (1887) 36 Ch D 145, p 185.

agreed to a legal charge over the matrimonial home as part of an attempt to refinance debts that had arisen from her husband's business. She had been visited at home by the bank manager and had thereupon signed the charge. Lord Scarman, with whom the rest of the House agreed, held that her attempt to have the charge set aside for undue influence failed for two reasons. First, the bank manager's visit was very short (only about 15 minutes in total), and there was no history of reliance as in *Lloyds Bank v Bundy*. Second, for the presumption to arise, the transaction had to be to the 'manifest disadvantage' of Mrs Morgan. This was not the case here. The charge 'meant for her the rescue of her home on the terms sought by her: a short term loan at a commercial rate of interest'.[57] Thus, although any transaction that puts a person's home at risk must in one sense be regarded as 'disadvantageous', this could not be sufficient on its own to render a contract voidable. If it were, every mortgage agreement would have to be so regarded. In looking for disadvantage, it was necessary to consider the context in which the transaction took place. If it was clear, as it seemed to be in *Morgan*, that the risks involved were, as far as the claimant was concerned, worth running in order to obtain the potential benefits of the transaction and there was no other indication of unfairness, then the courts should be quite prepared to enforce it. As has been noted above, some of Lord Scarman's comments in *Morgan* were interpreted by the Court of Appeal in *BCCI v Aboody*[58] as applying the requirement of manifest disadvantage to situations of actual, rather than presumed, influence. This interpretation was firmly rejected by the House of Lords in *CIBC Mortgages plc v Pitt*.[59] At the same time, Lord Browne-Wilkinson expressed some concern over the need for the requirement even in cases of presumed undue influence.[60] The Court of Appeal in *Etridge* reaffirmed that it was necessary,[61] but in *Barclays Bank v Coleman*[62] suggested that the disadvantage that needed to be shown did not have to be 'large or even medium-sized', provided that it was 'clear and obvious and more than *de minimis*'.[63]

Prior to the House of Lords' decision in *Etridge*, therefore, the position was that in cases of presumed undue influence, there was a requirement that the transaction should be to the manifest disadvantage of the claimant before it would be set aside. No such requirement existed in relation to actual undue influence. What exactly was meant by 'manifest disadvantage' was, however, becoming increasingly obscure, with *obiter* statements in the House of Lords and in the Court of Appeal suggesting that it might not be necessary at all. The decision of the House of Lords in *Etridge* has not changed the position in relation to actual undue influence. If such influence is established, then the court should set the agreement aside irrespective of whether it was to the actual or potential benefit of the claimant. This must be based on the policy view that it is unacceptable for the courts to enforce any transaction where it has been demonstrated that the actions of one party have led to it being entered into without the free, informed consent of the other. The approach is similar to that taken in relation to a totally innocent misrepresentation, where a party is allowed to rescind without showing that the misrepresentation has caused any loss.[64]

---

57 [1985] AC 686, p 703; [1985] 1 All ER 821, p 826.

58 [1990] 1 QB 923.

59 [1994] 1 AC 200; [1993] 4 All ER 433.

60 He saw it as being potentially in conflict with the approach taken in 'abuse of confidence' cases such as *Demerara Bauxite Co Ltd v Hubbard* [1923] AC 673, where, on grounds of public policy (that is, the need to protect those to whom fiduciaries owe duties as a class from exploitation), the burden is on the fiduciary to prove that a transaction was advantageous to the claimant: ibid, p 209; pp 439–40.

61 *Royal Bank of Scotland v Etridge (No 2)* [1998] 4 All ER 705. The court was, of course, bound by the House of Lords' decision in *National Westminster Bank plc v Morgan*.

62 [2001] QB 20; [2000] 1 All ER 385.

63 Ibid, p 33; p 400.

64 See Chapter 8, 8.4.1.

In relation to situations where there is presumed influence, either from a recognised 'special relationship' or because a particular relationship of trust and confidence has been established, then, as indicated above,[65] the nature of the transaction becomes relevant in considering whether the court may draw any inferences of undue influence from that relationship. The phrase 'manifest disadvantage' should not be used,[66] and it is certainly not the case that the claimant has to prove such disadvantage to establish that there was undue influence in such a case. The relevance of the nature of the transaction is evidential.[67] If it is shown to be of a kind that calls for explanation (for example, because it benefits the defendant without providing any comparable benefit for the claimant), then this will impose a burden on the defendant to show that it was not in fact obtained by undue influence, that is, essentially an abuse of the relationship of trust and confidence.

Lord Nicholls and Lord Scott both indicated that they did not regard the fact that a wife acts as surety for her husband's business debts as in itself being sufficient to give rise to an inference that influence has been abused. As Lord Nicholls put it:[68]

> I do not think that, *in the ordinary course*, a guarantee of the character I have mentioned [that is, the guarantee by a wife of her husband's business debts] is to be regarded as a transaction which, failing proof to the contrary, is explicable only on the basis that it has been procured by the exercise of undue influence by the husband. Wives frequently enter into such transactions. There are good and sufficient reasons why they are willing to do so,[69] despite the risks involved for them and their families ... They may be anxious, perhaps exceedingly so. But this is a far cry from saying that such transactions as a class are to be regarded as *prima facie* evidence of the exercise of undue influence by husbands.
>
> I have emphasised the phrase 'in the ordinary course'. There will be cases where a wife's signature of a guarantee or a charge of her share in the matrimonial home does call for explanation.[70] Nothing I have said is directed at such a case.

Lord Hobhouse seemed prepared to regard the fact that a wife acts as surety for her husband's business debts as more readily raising an inference calling for an explanation by the husband – for example, that he has taken account of her interests, dealt fairly with her, and made sure that she entered into the obligation freely and with knowledge of the true facts.[71] It is likely, however, that the approach taken by Lord Nicholls and Lord Scott, with whom Lord Bingham concurred, will be the one that is followed.

The conclusion of all this is that 'manifest disadvantage' is no longer a part of the law relating to undue influence; the nature of the transaction may, however, in cases where influence is presumed, provide evidence that will put the burden on the defendant to show that the influence was not abused.

---

65  See 11.4–11.5.

66  Though it was in *Leeder v Stevens* [2005] EWCA Civ 50, at [14].

67  As Lord Scott comments, 'the nature of the transaction, its inexplicability by reference to the normal motives by which people act, may, and usually will, constitute important evidential material': [2001] UKHL 44; [2001] 4 All ER 449 at [155].

68  At [30] (emphasis in original); cf Lord Scott's comments at [159].

69  For example, because the husband's business may be the source of the family income: see [28].

70  It may be that the kind of situation in mind here is that referred to by Lord Hobhouse when, in the context of the actions to be taken by a creditor, he commented that 'A loan application backed by a viable business plan or to acquire a worthwhile asset is very different from a loan to postpone the collapse of an already failing business or to refinance with additional security loans which have fallen into arrears. The former would not aggravate the risk; the latter most certainly would do so': see [109].

71  See [106].

## 11.7 SUMMARY OF CURRENT POSITION ON PRESUMED UNDUE INFLUENCE

The current law is based on the House of Lords' decision in *Royal Bank of Scotland plc v Etridge (No 2)*, and all earlier case law must be considered in the light of this.

**Key case Royal** *Bank of Scotland plc v Etridge (No 2)* (2002)

Facts: The case concerned eight conjoined appeals. Each appeal arose out of a transaction in which a wife charged her interest in her home in favour of a bank as security for her husband's business debts. Seven of the claims involved an allegation of undue influence by the husband for which the bank should be held responsible. The House of Lords took the opportunity to set out the principles to be applied in cases of alleged undue influence.

Held: The House of Lords held that it was always up to the party alleging undue influence to prove it. In some cases, however, evidential presumptions will be applied, so that the burden will shift to the other party to disprove the presumption of undue influence. An evidential presumption of influence (though not necessarily undue influence) will arise in relation to certain recognised relationships – i.e. solicitor/client, doctor/patient, parent/child, religious leader/follower. In relation to such relationships the presumption is irrebuttable. In relation to other relationships, such as husband and wife, evidence that the relationship was one of 'trust and confidence' will be needed. If this is established, it will be presumed that one party exercised influence over the other. Wherever there was a relationship in which influence was proved or presumed, then, if the transaction is one that required some explanation (e.g. a sale of property at an undervalue), *undue* influence will be presumed. It will be up to the party presumed to have used the undue influence to prove that this was not the case.

The case also dealt with the implications for banks where undue influence by a third party was alleged. This is dealt with below, at 11.8.

## 11.8 UNDUE INFLUENCE AND THIRD PARTIES

The majority of reported cases on undue influence over the past 25 years have been concerned with the effect on a transaction of undue influence by a third party. Specifically, where one party to a transaction is giving to the other a guarantee of a third party's debts, what is the effect of undue influence by the third party debtor on the guarantor? A common situation of this kind, as will have been discerned from the earlier discussion, is where a wife is guaranteeing a husband's business debts and using her property, most commonly her share in the matrimonial home, as security. In such a situation, if the husband's actions amount to undue influence, does this affect the wife's transaction with the creditor? The husband is generally not a party to that transaction, and so the standard answer under the doctrine of privity would be 'no'. Nevertheless, in some situations of this kind (not necessarily involving husband and wife), the courts have been prepared to find that the transaction with the creditor can be set aside.

The problem that faces the court, particularly in the husband and wife cases, is that small businesses regularly depend on the use of the owner's house as collateral for loans

Figure 11.1

from banks and other suppliers of finance. There is a need for some protection of vulnerable parties in this situation but the rules should not become so strict that they lead to an unwillingness on the part of the banks to lend money. That would have a deleterious effect on small businesses and on the economy. This issue is considered further (see 11.8.5 and 11.8.6) in connection with the steps that a bank is now required to take in order to protect itself against the risk of the transaction being set aside on the ground of undue influence or other impropriety.

Prior to the House of Lords' decision in *Barclays Bank v O'Brien*,[72] there was some uncertainty as to the way in which the 'privity' problem should be dealt with, where the debtor has influenced the guarantor to enter into the transaction with the creditor. Two main possibilities were canvassed, namely agency[73] and a 'special equity' protecting wives.[74]

The House of Lords was not inclined to adopt either of these analyses.

---

**Key case** *Barclays Bank v O'Brien* (1994)

Facts: Mr O'Brien persuaded his wife to sign a guarantee in relation to an overdraft facility provided by a bank, using the jointly owned matrimonial home as security. He had told her that the security was limited to £60,000, whereas in fact it was for £130,000. The employee of the bank who presented the documents for the wife's signature failed to follow a superior's instructions to explain the transaction, and to suggest that the wife took independent legal advice if she had any doubts about it. The papers were presented to the wife, open at the place for signature, and she did not read them before signing. When the bank tried to enforce the security, Mrs O'Brien claimed that she was only bound, at most, up to the £60,000 that her husband had told her was the limit of the liability. It was found by the Court of Appeal, and not disputed in the House of Lords, that Mrs O'Brien was an intelligent and independent-minded woman, who had not been unduly influenced by her husband. The case, therefore, turned on her husband's misrepresentation of the extent of the liability, and whether this affected the bank. Although the case is therefore not strictly one that is concerned with undue influence, it was accepted in both the Court of Appeal and the House of Lords that the same principles should apply irrespective of whether the wife was claiming that it was her husband's undue influence, or his misrepresentation, that had led her to enter into the transaction.[75] The case was eventually appealed to the House of Lords.

Held: The House of Lords held that the proper approach to cases where a third party's misrepresentation or undue influence was relied on to set aside a contract with a creditor was to look at the question of whether the creditor had, or should have had, 'notice' of the misrepresentation or undue influence. In this case it felt that Barclays Bank should have been aware of the risk of Mr O'Brien's misrepresentation and had failed to ensure that Mrs O'Brien had been protected by receiving independent legal advice. Mrs O'Brien was entitled to rescind her agreement with the Bank on the basis of her husband's misrepresentation.[76]

---

72 [1994] 1 AC 180; [1993] 4 All ER 417.
73 *Kings North Trust Ltd v Bell* [1986] 1 All ER 423.
74 See e.g. the judgment of Scott LJ in the Court of Appeal in *Barclays Bank v O'Brien:* [1993] QB 109; [1992] 4 All ER 983.
75 Subsequent cases have followed this treatment of undue influence and misrepresentation as distinct but analogous concepts for these purposes. There are, however, some points in the speech of Lord Hobhouse in the more recent House of Lords decision *(Royal Bank of Scotland plc v Etridge (No 2)* [2001] UKHL 44; [2001] 4 All ER 449), which appear to suggest that misrepresentation (and duress) might be treated as a species of undue influence: see [103]. The other speeches, however, maintain the traditional distinction, and it is submitted that this approach is to be preferred. It may be, however, that there is in some cases an overlap: see *UCB Services Ltd v Williams* [2002] EWCA Civ 555; [2002] 3 FCR 448,at [86].
76 Note that where the underlying vitiating factor is misrepresentation, there must be a misrepresentation for these principles to apply – an honest (even if negligent) statement of opinion will not be enough: *RBS v Chandra* [2011] EWCA Civ 192.

Lord Browne-Wilkinson, who gave the only substantive speech in the House of Lords, found that the law in this area had developed 'in an artificial way, giving rise to artificial distinctions and conflicting decisions'. As a result, he sought to 'restate the law in a form which is principled, reflects the current requirements of society and provides as much certainty as possible'.[77]

### 11.8.1 THE DOCTRINE OF NOTICE

The basis on which he felt able to do this was by a proper application of the doctrine of 'notice', which he felt lies at the heart of equity. Where, for example, it is necessary to decide between the conflicting rights of two innocent parties, the issue may well be determined by asking whether the holder of the later right had actual or constructive notice of the earlier right. Looking first at the position of wives, Lord Browne-Wilkinson felt that the fact that many wives placed confidence and trust in their husbands in relation to their financial affairs, and that the informality of business dealings between spouses raised a substantial risk of misrepresentation, meant that creditors should in certain circumstances be put on inquiry. These circumstances arose where:[78]

(a)    the transaction is on the face of it not to the financial advantage of the wife; and
(b)    there is substantial risk in transactions of that kind that, in procuring the wife to act as surety, the husband has committed a legal or equitable wrong that entitles the wife to set aside the transaction.

The creditor who ignores the risk, and does not take steps to ensure that the wife is acting with fully informed agreement and consent, will be deemed to have constructive notice of the wife's rights, as against her husband, to set aside the transaction on the basis of misrepresentation or undue influence.

**For thought**

*Suppose that in Barclay's Bank v O'Brien the Bank's employee had actually followed instructions and had explained the transaction to her, and suggested that she should take independent legal advice if she had any doubts about it. Would this have meant that Mrs O'Brien, if she still went ahead with the agreement, would not have been able to set it aside?*

### 11.8.2 RELATIONSHIPS COVERED

Turning to the broader application of these principles, Lord Browne-Wilkinson saw no reason to confine them to wives. The special position of wives is not based on that status as such, but because of the emotional and sexual ties that may arise from the marriage relationship. Such ties may exist between other cohabitees, both heterosexual and homosexual, whether married or not. Moreover, the principles will also apply to any situation where the creditor is aware that the surety places trust and confidence in the debtor.[79] The further development of this area in *Royal Bank of Scotland v Etridge*[80] means that

---

77 [1994] 1 AC 180, pp 198–99; [1993] 4 All ER 417, pp 431–32.
78 Ibid, p 196; p 429.
79 As in *Avon Finance Co Ltd v Bridger* [1985] 2 All ER 581 – son and elderly parents.
80 [2001] UKHL 44; [2001] 4 All ER 449.

the creditor will be put on notice of the risk of undue influence wherever the relationship between the debtor and surety is non-commercial. This is discussed further below (11.8.6).

### 11.8.3 APPLICATION OF THE DOCTRINE OF NOTICE

Where the creditor is put on notice of the risk of undue influence, Lord Browne-Wilkinson outlined the following factors that will lead to the obligation being unenforceable:[81]

(a) There must be undue influence, misrepresentation or some other legal wrong by the principal debtor.
(b) The creditor will have constructive notice of such a wrong, and the surety's right to set aside the transaction, unless the creditor has taken reasonable steps to be satisfied that the surety entered into the obligation freely and with knowledge of the true facts.
(c) The creditor will normally be regarded as taking such steps by (1) warning the surety (not in the presence of the principal debtor) of the amount of the potential liability and the risks involved; and (2) advising the surety to take independent legal advice.

Applying these guidelines to the facts of the case (which now need to be considered alongside the further development of the area in *Royal Bank of Scotland v Etridge (No 2)* – discussed below at 11.8.6), Lord Browne-Wilkinson concluded that Mrs O'Brien, having been misled by her husband and not having received proper advice from the bank, was entitled to set aside the legal charge on the matrimonial home.

### 11.8.4 APPLICATION OF THE DOCTRINE OF NOTICE TO ACTUAL UNDUE INFLUENCE

*Barclays Bank v O'Brien* was, as we have seen, dealt with not as a case of undue influence but of misrepresentation. On the same day as it gave its opinion on this case, the House of Lords also ruled on another husband and wife case, which was agreed to have involved actual undue influence: *CIBC Mortgages plc v Pitt*.[82] Mrs Pitt sought to set aside a mortgage over the matrimonial home granted by the plaintiffs on the basis that she had been induced to agree to it by the undue influence of her husband. She was unaware of the amount of the mortgage (which was £150,000), though she was aware that her husband was borrowing money to finance share dealings. The trial judge found that Mr Pitt had not been acting as the creditor's agent, but that he had exercised actual undue influence over Mrs Pitt in persuading her to sign the mortgage. Moreover, the judge ruled that the mortgage agreement was to Mrs Pitt's manifest disadvantage. Nevertheless, he rejected Mrs Pitt's claim, because he held that the 'special equity' applying to wives only operated where the wife was standing surety, and not to a situation where there was a joint advance to both husband and wife by way of a loan. The Court of Appeal rejected Mrs Pitt's appeal, on the basis that the transaction was not to her manifest disadvantage. Mrs Pitt appealed to the House of Lords.

Lord Browne-Wilkinson again gave the leading speech. He, of course, applied the same approach as had been taken in *Barclays Bank v O'Brien* in relation to the effect of Mr Pitt's behaviour on the contractual relationship between Mrs Pitt and the creditor – that is, an approach based on notice. Before considering this, however, Lord Browne-Wilkinson ruled that the requirement of 'manifest disadvantage' did not apply to cases

---

81  [1994] 1 AC 180, pp 198–99; [1993] 4 All ER 417, pp 431–32.
82  [1994] 1 AC 200; [1993] 4 All ER 433.

of actual undue influence.[83] Mrs Pitt would, therefore, have been able to set aside the transaction as against Mr Pitt. As far as the creditor was concerned, however, it had no direct knowledge of the influence Mr Pitt had exercised. Should it be regarded as having constructive notice? The House of Lords thought not. To the creditor, it appeared to be a straight-forward mortgage transaction:[84]

> There was nothing to indicate to the [creditor] that this was anything other than a normal advance to a husband and wife for their joint benefit.

The situation of a joint advance could be distinguished from one involving a surety, because in the latter case:[85]

> there is not only the possibility of undue influence having been exercised but there is also the increased risk of it having in fact been exercised because, at least on its face, the guarantee by a wife of her husband's debts is not for her financial benefit. It is the combination of these two factors that puts the creditor on inquiry.

The emphasis in these cases is now on actual, or constructive, notice.

### 11.8.5 CONSEQUENCES FOR CREDITORS

The House of Lords' decision in *Barclays Bank v O'Brien* placed a burden on creditors to ensure that they took the steps outlined above where there is a risk of undue influence. In terms of the contractual principle, the case opened another fairly broad exception to the doctrine of privity, in that the actions of a third party are allowed to affect the relationship between creditor and surety. It should be noted, however, that if the bank's own procedures had been followed by its employees in this case, the requirements laid down by the House of Lords would have been fulfilled. It does not seem, then, that the House of Lords' approach placed unreasonable burdens on creditors, particularly those large organisations that will have standard procedures for dealing with such situations. The safest approach would have been to ensure that any private individual standing as surety is advised along the lines suggested by the House of Lords in *O'Brien*.

A number of Court of Appeal decisions subsequent to *O'Brien*, however, indicated that the courts might be prepared to accept something less than this. The whole area became rather uncertain, but was thoroughly reconsidered by the House of Lords in *Royal Bank of Scotland plc v Etridge (No 2)*.

### 11.8.6 *ROYAL BANK OF SCOTLAND V ETRIDGE (NO 2)*

At the start of his speech in *Royal Bank of Scotland v Etridge (No 2)*, Lord Bingham referred to the social and economic context in which cases of this type operate. The general policy of striking the balance between the protection of the guarantor on the one hand, and the creditor on the other, clearly informs the approach taken by the rest of the House to setting out the practical guidelines that should govern the practice of creditors and legal advisers. Lord Bingham put it in these terms:[86]

> The transactions which give rise to these appeals are commonplace but of great social and economic importance. It is important that a wife (or anyone in like

---

83  As has been noted above, the phrase 'manifest disadvantage' has now in any case been rejected as unhelpful in any situation of undue influence: *Royal Bank of Scotland v Etridge (No 2)* [2001] UKHL 44; [2001] 4 All ER 449.
84  [1994] 1 AC 200, p 211; [1993] 4 All ER 433, p 441.
85  Ibid.
86  [2001] UKHL 44; [2001] 4 All ER 449, at [44].

**Essentials of the doctrine**

Creditors will be put on
inquiry whenever they have
actual or constructive notice
that there is a risk that the
debtor (e.g. the husband) may
have acted improperly in
relation to the person providing
security (e.g. the wife), by
misrepresentation or the use of
undue influence:
*Barclays Bank v O'Brien*
(1994)

**Constructive notice** will arise
wherever the relationship
between the debtor and the
surety is 'non-commercial':
*RBS v Etridge (No 2)* (2001)

**Undue influence – doctrine of notice**

**Practical consequences**

Practical steps to be taken
by creditors when **put on
inquiry**:
*Royal Bank of Scotland v
Etridge* (2001):
1. Explain need for
independent
advice
2. Creditor should provide
the solicitor with all
necessary information
3. Creditor should inform
solicitor if it believes that the
surety is not acting freely
4. Creditor should seek
written confirmation from the
surety's solicitor that the
implications of the
transaction and the nature of
the documents have been
properly explained

Figure 11.2

position) should not charge her interest in the matrimonial home to secure the borrowing of her husband (or anyone in a like position) without fully understanding the nature and effect of the proposed transaction and that the decision is hers, to agree or not to agree. It is important that lenders should feel able to advance money, in run-of-the-mill cases with no abnormal features, on the security of the wife's interest in the matrimonial home in reasonable confidence that, if appropriate procedures have been followed in obtaining the security, it will be enforceable if the need for enforcement arises. The law must afford both parties a measure of protection. It cannot prescribe a code which will be proof against error, misunderstanding or mishap. But it can indicate minimum requirements which, if met, will reduce the risk of error, misunderstanding or mishap to an acceptable level. The paramount need in this field is that these minimum requirements should be clear, simple and practically operable.

The practical steps that banks should take in situations of this type in order to try to achieve Lord Bingham's objectives were considered in some detail by three members of the House of Lords in *Etridge* – Lord Nicholls, Lord Hobhouse and Lord Scott. There are some differences in their approaches, but the speech of Lord Nicholls was approved by the two other members of the court (Lord Bingham and Lord Clyde), and what follows is based on his guidelines.

The first issue is to decide when a bank or other creditor is 'put on inquiry' that there may be a danger of undue influence or misrepresentation, so that steps need to be taken to ensure that the bank is not affected by any impropriety. There is no doubt that this will occur whenever a wife stands surety for her husband's debts. The difficulty is to decide which other relationships, assuming the bank is aware of them, will have the same effect. Should it apply only to sexual or family relationships, or to those falling within the category where the law presumes influence? The Court of Appeal had already stepped outside these categories in the *Burch* case (employer/employee). Lord Nicholls considered the possibilities in [82] – [89] of his speech.[87] His conclusion was that 'there is no rational cut-off point with certain types of relationship being susceptible to the *O'Brien* principle and others not'.[88] Therefore, 'the only practical way forward is to regard banks as "put on inquiry" in every case where the relationship between the surety and the debtor is noncommercial'. The threshold was set at a low point,[89] but the burden on the bank is 'modest'.[90] It was right that the broader scope of the *O'Brien* principle indicated by the *Burch* decision should be developed into the more general principle of the bank being put on inquiry in all cases of a non-commercial surety. Such a principle is 'workable ... simple, coherent and eminently desirable'.[91]

Once the bank is put on inquiry, what steps does it need to protect its position, so that it will not be affected by any impropriety on the part of the debtor? Lord Browne-Wilkinson in *O'Brien* had, as noted above, suggested that representatives of the bank should see the guarantor separately, and explain the transaction and its risks. Lord Nicholls recognised the understandable reluctance of banks to do this.[92] It runs the risk that there will later be allegations that oral assurances were given by the bank's representative to the effect, for example, that the bank would continue to support the business, or would not call in its loan. Lengthy litigation may well follow as to what exactly was said and when. Banks much prefer, therefore, that the transaction should be explained by an independent adviser, generally a solicitor.

Given that it was acceptable that banks should adopt this course, what steps should they take? Lord Nicholls identified four stages in the process.[93] First, the bank must communicate directly with the wife to check whom she wishes to use as a solicitor.[94] This communication should indicate the reasons why the bank is encouraging her to take legal advice – that is, that she will not later be able to dispute that she is bound by the documents she has signed. She should also be told that the solicitor may be the same one as is acting for her husband in the transaction. The bank must not proceed with the transaction until the wife has responded to this communication. Second, once a solicitor has been nominated, the bank must provide that solicitor with the financial information necessary to enable the solicitor to advise the wife properly. To the extent that this involves information supplied to the bank in confidence by the husband, his permission will be required in order to disclose it. If that permission is not forthcoming, the bank should not proceed with the transaction. Third, if the bank has suspicions that the wife has been misled, or is not acting freely, these must be communicated to the wife's solicitor. Fourth, the bank will require from the wife's solicitor a written confirmation that the nature of the documents she is being asked to sign and the practical implications of them have been fully explained to her.

Three other issues need to be considered. First, why is it satisfactory for the solicitor to be acting for the husband and the wife (as indicated by stage one, above)? Second, what should the content of the solicitor's advice be? Third, if the solicitor does not carry out the responsibilities properly, what are the wife's remedies?

As to the common situation where the solicitor acts for both the husband and wife, Lord Nicholls considered the obvious arguments against this, such as the fact that the wife

87  [2001] 4 All ER 449, pp 474–76.

88  Ibid, at [87].

89  Lord Hobhouse acknowledged this, but noted that it has the practical advantage 'that it assists banks to put in place procedures which do not require an exercise of judgment by their officials': ibid, at [108].

90  Ibid, at [87].

91  Ibid, at [89]. Auchmuty (2005, pp 70–1) has argued that this approach tends to veil the significance of gender in the way in which undue influence arises in heterosexual relationships.

92  Ibid, at [55].

93  At [79]. As will be seen, the third stage will not apply in all cases.

94  Although these stages apply to any situation in which a creditor is put on inquiry, Lord Nicholls explained them in terms of a 'bank' and a 'wife' (the most common example), and that terminology is adopted here.

may be inhibited in dealing with a solicitor who is also acting for her husband, and that the wife's interests may, even unconsciously, rank lower in the solicitor's priorities than those of the husband, the 'primary' client.[95] He also considered the arguments in favour of just one solicitor being used, such as the reduction in costs, the fact that the wife may already know and be more comfortable with the 'family' solicitor as opposed to a stranger, and that a solicitor who has had previous dealings with the family may be better placed to give advice.[96] His conclusion was that 'the latter factors are more weighty than the former', and that therefore there should be no bar to the wife's legal adviser being the same person as the husband's.[97] The wife is, of course, free to choose another solicitor, and the husband's solicitor will need to think carefully as to whether there is any conflict of interest that would mean that the wife should be advised by someone else.[98] If, however, the husband's solicitor does act for the wife, then in advising her the solicitor is acting *for her alone*. This brings us to the second question: what should be the content of the solicitor's advice?

Lord Nicholls went into some detail on this issue, because of his view that 'the quality of the legal advice is the most disturbing feature' of some of the appeals that were before the House in *Etridge*.[99] What he had to say applies whether the solicitor is acting for both husband and wife, or solely for the wife. The solicitor must initially explain why the giving of advice is necessary, that is primarily to provide protection for the bank, and confirm that the wife wishes the solicitor to act for her.

Assuming that the wife wishes the solicitor to act for her, there must be a face-to-face meeting between the solicitor and the wife in the absence of the husband. The solicitor should explain the transaction and its implications in 'suitably non-technical language'.[100] The 'core minimum' of the solicitor's advice in performing this task is summarised by Lord Nicholls in four points.[101]

(a)    The nature of the documents the wife is being asked to sign must be explained, together with their consequences, such as the risk of the loss of the matrimonial home.

(b)    The seriousness of the risks must be pointed out. This will include discussion of the purpose of the proposed facility, and the sums involved, including the amount of the wife's liability. The solicitor must discuss the wife's financial means, and ensure that she understands the value of the property being made subject to charge. The possibility of the facility being increased without reference to the wife should be dealt with. The question of whether either the husband or wife has other assets that might be used to make repayments, should the business fail, should be explored. All of these factors relate to the seriousness of the risks.

(c)    The solicitor should make it clear that the decision to give the guarantee or not is the wife's and hers alone.

(d)    The solicitor should check that the wife wishes to proceed. She should be asked whether she wishes the solicitor to negotiate further on her behalf, or whether she is content for the solicitor to write to the bank confirming that he has explained the documents and their practical consequences to her. The solicitor must not give any confirmation to the bank without the wife's specific authority.

---

95  [2001] UKHL 44; [2001] 4 All ER 449, at [72].
96  Ibid, at [73].
97  Ibid, at [74].
98  The solicitor should also withdraw if, having agreed to act for the wife, it subsequently becomes clear that there is a real risk of any advice being inhibited by a conflict of interest or duty: ibid.
99  The case involved eight conjoined appeals.
100 [2001] UKHL 44; [2001] 4 All ER 449, at [66].
101 Ibid, at [65].

These guidelines focus on ensuring that the wife is fully informed of the nature of the transaction into which she is entering. Lord Hobhouse, however, while agreeing with Lord Nicholls' 'core minimum', emphasised that 'comprehension' does not mean the same thing as 'lack of undue influence':[102]

> Comprehension is essential for any legal documents of this complexity and obscurity. But for the purpose of negativing undue influence it is necessary to be satisfied that the agreement was, also, given freely in knowledge of the true facts. It must be remembered that the equitable doctrine of undue influence has been created for the protection of those who are *sui juris* and competent to undertake legal obligations but are nevertheless vulnerable and liable to have their will unduly influenced. It is their weakness that is being protected, not their inability to comprehend.

Lord Hobhouse was satisfied that Lord Nicholls' guidelines were sufficient to provide the necessary protection. He disagreed, however, with what he saw as being the view of Lord Scott, that belief on the part of a lender that the wife has understood the nature and effect of the transaction is sufficient to exonerate the lender.[103]

The final issue considered by Lord Nicholls was the position where the solicitor has failed to act in accordance with guidelines, and the wife is thereby prejudiced. Counsel for some of the wives involved in the cases in *Etridge* argued that the bank should take responsibility for the solicitor's failures, as if the solicitor were acting as an agent for the bank. Lord Nicholls rejected this. Provided that the bank has acted as outlined by Lord Nicholls, and has received a certificate from the solicitor confirming that the wife has been advised as required, this should be sufficient to protect the bank.[104] Only in the exceptional case where the bank for some reason has cause to suspect that the wife has not properly been advised will it lose its protection. Otherwise, the wife who has not been advised properly will be left to her remedy in damages against the solicitor for negligent performance of their contract, or for the tort of professional negligence.

The procedures set out in this case by which the banks can obtain protection apply to all surety transactions entered into in the future. For those that were entered into previously, the bank will ordinarily be protected if a solicitor acting for the wife has confirmed that the wife has had brought home to her the risks she was running, even if the precise steps set out in *Etridge* have not been followed.[105] In either case, it cannot be said that any onerous burden is being placed on the banks or other creditors. It is clear that the major banks have for some time had internal procedures designed to take account of the risks involved in this type of transaction, and to try to ensure that wives or other vulnerable parties are properly advised.[106] The continuing flow of cases indicates, however, either that these procedures are not being applied properly, or that they (and by implication those suggested in *Etridge)* are inadequate to deal with the social problem raised by the issue of homes being used as security for business debts.[107] The approach of the courts, despite *O'Brien* being seen as a victory for wives, is heavily balanced in favour of the creditor, as is indicated by the fact that only one of the appeals in *Etridge* which involved the

---

102  Ibid, at [111].
103  [2001] 4 All ER 449, p 470.
104  Ibid, [75] – [78].
105  Ibid, at [80].
106  See, for example, the procedures of the National Westminster Bank set out by Lord Hobhouse in *Etridge:* ibid, at [117] – [118]. As Lord Hobhouse pointed out, these may go further than the requirements set out by Lord Nicholls.
107  For a useful discussion of these and related issues from a feminist perspective, see Auchmuty, 2005. She argues for a greater recognition of the role of gender as an element in the way in which undue influence occurs in heterosexual relationships.

substantive issue of whether the wife could escape the effect of the transaction went in favour of the wife.[108] It is not clear that the courts have yet managed to find a satisfactory balance between the need to protect those vulnerable to undue influence, and the need to ensure that banks and other financial institutions remain willing to lend money to small businesses in situations where domestic property may provide the only realistic security.

### 11.8.7 IN FOCUS: PRACTICAL APPLICATION

Even under the approach recommended in *RBS v Etridge* it is questionable whether the courts have really taken on board the problem for a proposed surety, who is for example expecting to continue to live with the debtor, in refusing to provide a guarantee. Even if the surety has received independent advice, taking a decision that will be likely to lead to the collapse of the debtor's business will be very difficult, and will inevitably impose severe strains on the relationship. It is hard to see the decision as ever being 'free': on the other hand, it would clearly be unacceptable if all such transactions could be set aside at the choice of the surety. Although it is very difficult to strike the right balance, it is arguable that the law is still too favourable to the creditor and debtor.

## 11.9 REMEDIES FOR UNDUE INFLUENCE

The primary remedy for undue influence in cases such as those discussed in the previous section is the refusal of the courts to enforce the agreement against the person influenced. In other words, that person will often be in the position of defendant, and will use the alleged influence to escape from obligations.

In some cases, however, rescission may be sought,[109] and the usual limitations on this remedy (such as lapse of time, involvement of third party rights and impossibility of restitution) will apply.[110]

Where rescission is ordered, the whole transaction will be set aside.[111] In *TSB Bank plc v Camfield*,[112] the creditor tried to argue that even if it had constructive notice of the debtor's misrepresentation of the extent of the transaction to his wife, the wife had been prepared to undertake some risk. In this case, she had been willing to go ahead with a transaction that put the matrimonial home at risk to the extent of £15,000, whereas in fact liability was unlimited. The bank argued that she should still be liable for £15,000. The Court of Appeal rejected this. The test was what would the wife have done had she known the truth? The answer was clearly that she would not have entered into the transaction at all. Therefore, the right result was for the whole transaction to be rescinded.

A slightly different situation arose in *Dunbar Bank plc v Nadeem*.[113] Here the wife had not previously had any legal interest in the matrimonial home, which was held by her husband on a long lease. As part of a loan transaction, using the home as security, however, she acquired a beneficial interest in half of the property. When the husband defaulted on the

---

108 That is, *Bank of Scotland v Bennett*. In that case the appeal succeeded because the bank had failed to give the full information relevant to the transaction to the solicitor who advised the wife. Some of the appeals involved cases where the action had been struck out before trial: here the Court of Appeal was inclined to the view that there should be a full hearing, without expressing any view on the merits of the wife's claim.
109 As, for example, in *Allcard v Skinner* (1887) 36 Ch D 145.
110 As with misrepresentation – see Chapter 8, 8.4.1.
111 The position may be different where there are two distinct parts to the transaction in relation to only one of which there is a finding of undue influence: *Barclays Bank plc v Caplan* [1998] FLR 532. Here C had been properly advised in relation to an original charge and guarantee, but not in relation to a subsequent side letter extending the guarantee.
112 [1995] 1 All ER 951.
113 [1998] 3 All ER 876.

loan repayments, the bank sought to enforce its charge over the property. The wife claimed undue influence. The trial judge held in her favour, but also ruled that simply setting aside the charge would leave her unjustly enriched, as she would have acquired an interest in the property without having to contribute to the purchase. He therefore made the rescission of the charge conditional on her repaying to the bank one half of the loan plus interest. The Court of Appeal held that this was not the correct approach. In fact, the Court of Appeal decided that the transaction should not be set aside at all, because it was not manifestly disadvantageous to the wife, and the husband had not taken any unfair advantage of her. But, if there had been undue influence, it was suggested (though of course this was *obiter*) that the correct approach would have been for the wife to give up her interest in the property (which would then have reverted to her husband). She would be released from any personal liability on the loans made to her husband, but would not have acquired any unfair benefit. Of course, this would mean that she would still not have been able to resist the bank's claim for possession of the property, which was her main objective.

### 11.9.1 CHANGE IN VALUE OF PROPERTY

Where restitution is ordered, however, but the value of property has changed, it may be difficult to find the just result as to who should get what. This problem arose in *Cheese v Thomas*.[114] C, the plaintiff, and his great-nephew, T, the defendant, had bought a house for £83,000, C contributing £43,000, and T providing £40,000, by means of a mortgage for that amount. The house was in T's name, and C accepted that it would belong to T exclusively after C's death, but, in the meantime, it was agreed that C was to be entitled to have sole use of the house for the rest of his life. C became worried that T was not keeping up the mortgage repayments, and sought to withdraw from the arrangement. The trial judge ruled that the agreement could be set aside for undue influence. The issue before the Court of Appeal was the amount of money that C should receive, since the house had been sold for £55,400, that is a loss of over £27,500. Should he recover his full £43,000 or only, as the judge held, the appropriate proportion of the selling price? The Court of Appeal upheld the judge's view. The basic principle in applying a restitutionary remedy was that the parties were to be restored as closely as possible to the position they were in before the transaction was entered into. In general, if a claimant was able to return to the defendant property that had been transferred under the transaction, it did not matter that the property had meanwhile fallen in value. This case was different, however. The plaintiff had paid the defendant £43,000 not outright, but as part of a purchase price of a house in which both would have rights. Each had contributed a sum of money to buying a house in which each was to have an interest. In that situation, the appropriate course was for the loss in the value of the house to be shared. This was even more so where, as the judge had held, the personal conduct of the defendant was not open to criticism, in that he had acted as an 'innocent fiduciary', rather than in any morally reprehensible way.

This case was clearly a difficult one in which to do justice between the parties. It is not entirely convincing, however, on the need to depart from the basic principle of full restitution of cash paid for property, which would be the normal rule. It is not clear why the fact that the parties both had a continuing interest in the property should make such a difference. If the property had increased in value, would the plaintiff have been entitled to a share in that profit? The logical answer must be 'yes'.

### 11.9.2 SUBSEQUENT TRANSACTIONS

Where a contract is found to be voidable for undue influence, then a substitute transaction, particularly if entered into as a condition of discharging the first transaction, will be similarly voidable. This was the position in *Yorkshire Bank plc v Tinsley*.[115] A mortgage

---

114  [1994] 1 All ER 35.
115  [2004] 3 All ER 463.

used to secure a husband's business debts was held to be voidable by the wife because of her husband's undue influence, of which the bank had constructive notice. When the husband and wife divorced, a substitute mortgage was entered into by the wife in relation to a smaller property, but the bank required the security for the business debts to continue to apply to this property. When the bank sought to enforce the security, it was held that the wife was entitled to avoid the mortgage on the basis of undue influence. This decision was confirmed by the Court of Appeal.

## 11.10 UNCONSCIONABILITY AND INEQUALITY OF BARGAINING POWER[116]

Does the approach of the courts to the issues of duress and undue influence simply reflect a general reluctance to enforce transactions that are so unfair as to be regarded as 'unconscionable'? Is this the underlying principle in these cases?

In *Lloyds Bank Ltd v Bundy*,[117] Lord Denning based his decision in favour of Mr Bundy on a broader principle than that adopted by the other members of the Court of Appeal. He identified this as 'inequality of bargaining power'. By virtue of this, he claimed:

> English law gives relief to one who, without independent advice, enters into a contract on terms which are very unfair or transfers property for a consideration which is grossly inadequate, when his bargaining power is grievously impaired by his own needs or desires, or by his own ignorance or infirmity, coupled with undue influences or pressure brought to bear on him by or for the benefit of the other.

As will be seen, this identifies, alongside the unequal bargaining power, the nature of the transaction, and its substantive fairness, as an important element in the decision to set an agreement aside. In contrast, the general approach towards undue influence and duress cases is that if the influence or duress is proved, the question of whether the transaction was beneficial to the influenced party is of no particular significance. Even in cases of presumed influence, the fact that the transaction is disadvantageous is, after the House of Lords' decision in *Royal Bank of Scotland plc v Etridge (No 2)*,[118] simply a matter of evidence, which may lead to the need for an explanation, rather than being a specific element in the concept of undue influence. Lord Denning's statement therefore probably comes as close as any English judge has done to recognising a general principle of 'unconscionability'. His approach has not been followed, however, and indeed was specifically disapproved by Lord Scarman in *National Westminster Bank v Morgan*,[119] who felt that the fact that Parliament had intervened to deal with many situations of unequal bargaining power (for example, by the Consumer Credit Act 1974 and the Supply of Goods and Services Act 1982) meant that the courts should be reluctant to assume the burden of formulating further restrictions. The closest that the courts have come in the plethora of cases that have followed *Barclays Bank v O'Brien* to recognising 'unconscionability' as a ground for intervention is in *Credit Lyonnais Bank Nederland NV v Burch*.[120] Though this case and, in particular, the judgment of Millett LJ can be seen as giving some support to an approach similar to that taken by Lord Denning in *Lloyds Bank v Bundy*, the case can also be fitted

---

116 For a compact and useful survey of the English approach to this area, see Brownsword, 2006, Chapter 3.

117 [1975] QB 326; [1974] 3 All ER 757.

118 [2001] UKHL 44; [2001] 4 All ER 449.

119 [1985] AC 686; [1985] 1 All ER 821. He took a similar line in *Pao On v Lau Yiu Long* [1980] AC 614; [1979] 3 All ER 65.

120 [1997] 1 All ER 144, discussed above at 11.5. See, in particular, the judgment of Nourse LJ.

within the orthodox general principles applying to undue influence, and it has not led to any significant change of direction in later cases.

The English law relating to both duress and undue influence is still, therefore, primarily concerned with procedural rather than substantive fairness.[121] Unconscionability would, some would argue, require it to focus more directly on the nature of the contract itself, rather than the events that led to it being formed. Moreover, the intervention has been piecemeal, dealing with situations of fraud, duress and undue influence separately, rather than as part of an overall principle.[122] A further example is the principle applied in *Cresswell v Potter*.[123] In this case the court applied a power used by the Chancery courts in the nineteenth century to set aside a transaction 'where a purchase is made from a poor and ignorant man at a considerable undervalue, the vendor having no independent advice'.[124] In *Cresswell v Potter*, Megarry J took 'poor' to mean 'a member of the lower income group' and 'ignorant' to mean 'less highly educated'. The plaintiff in the case was a telephonist, with little understanding of conveyancing transactions and documentation, and was found by the judge to meet the relevant criteria. She had received no independent advice. Her conveyance to her husband, who had left her, of her half-share in the matrimonial home, in exchange for her release from liability under the mortgage,[125] was set aside. There has, however, been little use of this principle,[126] and it cannot be said to afford more than an exceptional additional ground for setting a transaction aside on grounds of unconscionability.[127]

---

### For thought

*Jack is 25. He left school at 16, having failed all his GCSEs, and has never worked. He has just won £10,000 on the lottery. Bill, a friend from school, persuades Jack to use this money to buy 1,000 shares in Bill's company. An objective valuation of these shares would value them at not more than £1 each. Could Jack claim to set this transaction aside on the basis of the Cresswell v Potter principle? Would it make any difference if Jack had passed A-level qualifications, or if the transaction was the straightforward purchase of a car, which Bill has overvalued?*

---

### 11.10.1 IN FOCUS: POSITION ON 'UNCONSCIONABILITY' IN OTHER JURISDICTIONS

Other jurisdictions have adopted a broader approach. In Australia, for example, the decision of the High Court in *Commercial Bank of Australia Ltd v Amadio*[128] formulated

---

121  Note, however, that Atiyah disputed that a distinction of this kind can be drawn with any degree of clarity: Atiyah, 1986, Chapter 11, pp 333–34.

122  Though it might be suggested that the comments of Lord Hobhouse in *Etridge (No 2)*, at [103] and by the Court of Appeal in *UCB Corporate Services Ltd v Williams* [2002] EWCA Civ 555; [2002] 3 FCR 448, at [86], as to the overlap between the concepts is a step towards recognising a unifying general principle.

123  [1978] 1 WLR 255.

124  *Fry v Lane* (1888) 40 Ch D 312, per Kay J.

125  Which, in practice, was of little value to her, unless the value of the house declined to below that of the mortgage. At the time this was highly unlikely – though there have been occasions since when the concept of 'negative equity' would have meant that the release would have been of more value.

126  See, for example, *Backhouse v Backhouse* [1978] 1 All ER 1158 (considered but not applied) and *Watkin v Watson-Smith* (1986) *The Times*, 3 July.

127  But note the comments of Nourse LJ in *Credit Lyonnais Bank Nederland NV v Burch* [1997] 1 All ER 144, p 151, where he suggests that the *Fry v Lane* principle, as applied in *Cresswell v Potter* and considered in *Backhouse v Backhouse*, indicates the possibility of a general equitable power to set aside unconscionable bargains.

128  (1983) 151 CLR 447 – discussed in some detail in Harland, 1999.

a principle of unconscionability on very similar lines to those suggested by Lord Denning in *Lloyds Bank v Bundy*, and this has been followed in later cases.[129] A similar approach has been adopted in Canada.[130] As Harland has pointed out, however, the *Amadio* approach is at least as much concerned with procedural as substantive unconscionability.[131] By contrast, s 2–302 of the United States Uniform Commercial Code states:

> If the court as a matter of law finds the contract or any clause of the contract to have been unconscionable at the time it was made the court may refuse to enforce the contract, or it may enforce the remainder of the contract without the unconscionable clause, or it may so limit the application of any unconscionable clause as to avoid any unconscionable result.

This very broadly worded provision has been used to deal with situations of both procedural and substantive unfairness.[132] The only provisions in any way comparable in English law, allowing courts to set a contract, or part of a contract, aside because its provisions are 'unfair' or 'unconscionable' operate only in much more limited areas or situations. Under the common law, there are, for example, powers to strike down clauses that are in unreasonable restraint of trade, or 'penalty' clauses.[133] Under statute, there are specific provisions to deal with unfair consumer credit transactions under the Consumer Credit Act 1974.[134] There are also the provisions of the Unfair Contract Terms Act 1977 as well as the previous provisions of the Unfair Terms in Consumer Contracts Regulations 1999 which are now largely contained in the Consumer Rights Act 2015 and which have been discussed in Chapter 7. The UCTA 1977, however, is primarily concerned with clauses limiting liability. While the CRA 2015 has wider scope, it only applies to consumer contracts and does not generally affect situations where what is involved is an overall 'bad bargain' – which may have the effect of excluding a number of situations of possible 'unconscionability'.[135] As we have seen, for example, the principle applied in *Cresswell v Potter* was designed to deal with sales at an undervalue. That kind of aspect of a contract would generally be outside the scope of the fairness provisions of the CRA 2015.

### 11.10.2 RISK OF UNCERTAINTY

One of the objections to any broad principle allowing contracts to be set aside on the basis of substantive 'unconscionability' is the uncertainty that might result.[136] Apart from anything else, it is not easy to determine whether a particular contract is fair or not simply by looking

---

129 For example, *Baburin v Baburin* [1991] 2 Qd R 240; *Louth v Diprose* (1992) 175 CLR 621; *Familiar Pty Ltd v Samarkos* (1994) 115 FLR 443; *Begbie v State Bank of New South Wales* (1994) ATPR 41–288 – all cited in Harland, 1999.

130 See Enman, 1987 and Moore, 2018.

131 Harland, 1999, p 259 – he also notes, however, the view of Chen-Wishart to the effect that the judges are in reality more concerned with substantive factors than they have generally articulated: Chen-Wishart, 1989, pp 104–09.

132 See, for example, the discussion in McLaughlin, 1992. The section applies only to 'transactions' in goods, but the Restatement (Second) of Contracts, s 208, provides a model provision in similar terms for application to any contract.

133 For discussion of penalty clauses see Chapter 15.

134 Sections 140A-140C, as added to the Consumer Credit Act 2006.

135 See s. 64 and the discussion in Chapter 7, 7.8.2.

136 This was one of the reasons for Lord Scarman's rejection of a general doctrine of inequality of bargaining power in *Pao On v Lau Yiu Long* [1980] AC 614, p 634.

at its provisions.[137] The transaction will operate within a context, and perhaps a long-term relationship, which may mean that an exchange that appears lopsided may, in fact, be based on a rational balancing that takes account of other aspects of the parties' dealings with each other. Add to this the difficulty of obtaining a uniform application of standards of fairness between different judges and different courts, and it is, perhaps, easy to see why English law has shied away from general provisions addressing substantive unfairness in favour of rules governing procedural impropriety. Where substantive unfairness is addressed, it is generally in relation to clauses or contracts of a particular type, with the decision being taken within a limiting statutory framework.[138] It is to be expected that this will continue to be the English approach. Any more general move towards control of unconscionability based on substantive unfairness was only likely as a result of a movement in this direction by European law and the future relationship of the UK and EU is, at the time of writing, uncertain.

## 11.11 SUMMARY OF KEY POINTS

- Undue influence is an equitable concept, which, if proved, makes a contract voidable (not void).

- The concept involves a person's decision to make a contract being unduly influenced by the actions of the other party particularly, although not exclusively, in the context of a pre-existing relationship of trust and confidence.

- Undue influence may be proved to have occurred in relation to a particular transaction (actual undue influence), or presumed from the parties' relationship and the nature of the transaction.

- Certain relationships will be irrebuttably presumed to involve *influence* – e.g. doctor/patient, solicitor/client (but not husband/wife).

- Other relationships may be found as a matter of fact to involve one party placing trust and confidence in the other, and thus being open to influence.

- Where a relationship of influence exists, and the transaction calls for explanation (e.g. a sale of property at a significant undervalue), *undue* influence will be presumed. The alleged influencer can attempt to rebut the presumption (e.g. by proving that the other party received independent legal advice).

- Banks and other creditors will in some circumstances be unable to enforce transactions that have been made as a result of the undue influence of a third party (e.g. a wife using her house as security for her husband's business debts as a result of the husband's undue influence).

- Wherever the relationship between a debtor and surety is non-commercial, the bank will be put on notice of the risk of undue influence of the surety.

---

137  See the comments of Collins to this effect: Collins, 1999, p 258 onwards – 'The Illusion of Unfairness'. See also Atiyah, 1986a, Chapter 11.
138  Collins (1999, p 286), on the other hand, concludes his consideration of this area by expressing the view that 'The open textured rules devised by private law appear to be the most adept at handling the complex issues which [regulating substantive unfairness in contracts] raises, though there is certainly room for specific regulation in particular market sectors'.

■ To protect itself in such a situation, the bank will need to ensure that the surety receives independent legal advice before entering into the transaction.

■ The primary remedy for undue influence in such situations is that the transaction is not enforceable. Rescission may be awarded in some cases.

■ English contract law does not recognise any general principle of 'unconscionability'.

## 11.12 FURTHER READING

### Theories of undue influence

■ Birks, P and Chin Nyuk Yin, 'On the nature of undue influence', Chapter 3 in Beatson, J and Friedmann, D (eds), *Good Faith and Fault in Contract Law*, 1995, Oxford: Clarendon Press

■ Capper, D, 'Undue influence and unconscionability: a rationalisation' (1998) 114 LQR 479

■ Cope, M, *Duress, Undue Influence and Unconscientious Bargains*, 1985, North Ryde, NSW: Lawbook Co

■ Devenney, J, & Chandler, A, 'Unconscionability and the Taxonomy of Undue Influence' [2007] JBL 269

■ Enman, S R, 'Doctrines of unconscionability in England, Canada and the Commonwealth' (1987) 16 Anglo-Am LR 191

■ Enonchong, N, *Duress, Undue Influence and Unconscionable Dealing*, 3rd edn, 2018, London: Sweet & Maxwell

■ Harland, D, 'Unconscionable and unfair contracts: an Australian perspective', Chapter 11 in Brownsword, R, Hird, N J and Howells, G (eds), *Good Faith in Contract*, 1999, Aldershot: Dartmouth

### Undue influence by third parties and vulnerable sureties

■ Auchmuty, R, 'The rhetoric of equality and the problem of heterosexuality', Chapter 3 in Mulcahy, L and Wheeler, S (eds), *Feminist Perspectives on Contract Law*, 2005, London: Glasshouse Press

■ Chen-Wishart, M, 'The *O'Brien* principle and substantive unfairness' (1997) 56 CLJ 60

■ Devenney, J, Fox-O'Mahony, L and Kenny, M, 'Standing surety in England and Wales: the sphinx of procedural protection', [2008] LMCLQ 394

■ O'Sullivan, D, 'Developing *O'Brien*' (2002) 118 LQR 337

■ Pawlowski, M and Brown, J, *Undue Influence and the Family Home*, 2002, London: Cavendish

■   Wong, S, 'Revisiting *Barclays Bank v O'Brien* and independent legal advice for vulnerable sureties' [2002] JBL 439

## COMPANION WEBSITE

*Now visit the companion website to:*

■   Revise and consolidate your knowledge of Undue Influence by tackling a series of multiple-choice questions on this chapter

■   Test your understanding of the chapter's key terms by using the flashcard glossary

■   Explore Undue Influence further by accessing a series of web links

# 12

# Illegality and public policy

**Contents**

## 12.1 OVERVIEW

This chapter deals with situations where otherwise valid contracts may be wholly or partly unenforceable because they are deemed to involve 'illegality' or are otherwise contrary to public policy (whether or not such agreements also result in criminal liability). The following issues are discussed:

- The reasons why 'illegal' contracts are potentially wholly or partially unenforceable. 'Public policy' is the central issue – but underlying reasons include 'deterrence' and maintaining the integrity of the legal process (that is, not allowing it to be used to enforce illegal arrangements).
- Categories of 'illegality':
  - Contracts to commit crimes or (intentional) torts. These are usually 'illegal'.
  - Contracts contrary to particular professional regulations (for example, Solicitors' Practice Rules). These may be unenforceable (although, as will be noted, a party may be able to claim for work actually done).
  - Contracts where *performance* involves the breach of a statute. The most difficult area is where the act itself is legal, but the manner of performance is not. The purpose of the statute and the knowledge of the parties will be relevant to the issue of enforceability.
  - Contracts to indemnify a person for breaking the law. This is generally not allowed in relation to criminal liability or intentional torts, but may be permitted in other areas.
- Effects of illegality. Two aspects need consideration:
  - Enforcement. Specific performance generally will not be available, but traditionally a legal right related to an illegal transaction may have been enforceable if the party did not need to rely on the 'illegality' to found the claim.
  - Recovery of money or property. Traditionally the general rule was that recovery was not possible, but it was sometimes allowed where:
    - the illegal purpose had not been carried out – a party was allowed time for a change of mind in relation to the illegal transaction;
    - the contract resulted from 'oppression';
    - there was no reliance on the illegal transaction;
    - the claimant was a member of the class that the statute concerned is intended to protect.
  - The Supreme Court recently considered this area in *Patel v Mirza* (2016) and, in effect, reversed the general rule.
- Agreements contrary to public policy. In this category traditionally fall:
  - Contracts related to marriage – for example:
    - for future separation (pre-nuptial agreements were traditionally caught by this);
    - imposing a liability if a person marries;
    - receiving payment for arranging a marriage.
  - Contracts promoting sexual immorality. There are old cases supporting this category but it may well be largely obsolete in the modern law.
  - Contracts to oust the jurisdiction of the courts. The parties may agree, for example, that matters of fact may be determined by other processes (for example, arbitration).
  - Contracts involving a breach of human rights. It is possible that the courts will be prepared to treat contracts that conflict with Human Rights Act obligations as unenforceable on public policy grounds.

- Normal effects of agreements contrary to public policy:
  - □ no specific performance;
  - □ property transferred can possibly be recovered.
- Wagering contracts. These have been unenforceable as a result of statutory controls, but the controls have been removed by the Gambling Act 2005. Wagers will often now be enforceable.

## 12.2 INTRODUCTION

This chapter is concerned with two (connected) situations where the courts may refuse (wholly or partly) to enforce an agreement that, on its face, has all the characteristics of a binding contract. These situations are often considered under the general heading of 'illegality';[1] equally they might also be grouped as 'contracts contrary to public policy'.[2] There are, therefore, links between these areas. It is felt, however, that they are sufficiently distinct to warrant separate treatment.[3] There will inevitably be overlaps, and some need to cross-refer, particularly in relation to remedies. The division is simply intended to clarify the discussion of the two areas; it should not be regarded as necessarily reflecting a rigid separation adopted by the courts, or as a denial that there may be significant conceptual links between topics.

In the first part of this chapter we will examine contracts that are 'illegal' in the sense that they involve, or are linked to, the commission of a legal wrong – principally, a crime or a tort (even if the agreement does not result in criminal liability). This is an area that, even under the classical law of contract, was an accepted limitation on freedom of contract. The second part of the chapter looks at contracts that, while not 'illegal', may be held to be (wholly or partly) unenforceable because they are for other reasons contrary to public policy.

## 12.3 IN FOCUS: RATIONALES FOR THE UNENFORCEABILITY OF ILLEGAL CONTRACTS

The reasons why the courts interfere to render contracts that are 'illegal' wholly or partly unenforceable, as opposed to simply leaving those who have committed a crime or a tort to the relevant procedures under those areas of law, are not often explicitly stated, other than to say that it is a matter of 'public policy'. It follows, however, from the fact that 'public policy' is the central focus, that the issue of illegality may be raised by the court of its own motion, without it needing to be pleaded by either party[4] and that the parameters of this doctrine can change over time. The law is not necessarily primarily concerned here with the protection of one party, as it is in the areas of duress or undue influence, for

---

1   See, for example, Treitel, 2015, Chapter 11.
2   'Public policy' is, of course, a difficult concept to pin down – as recognised by Burroughs J's famous reference to its being an 'unruly horse': *Richardson v Mellish* (1824) 2 Bing 229, p 252. It is possible to argue that the whole of the law of contract is simply a reflection of 'public policy' concerns about the regulation of transactions. Even a policy of encouraging market freedom is in itself a 'public policy'.
3   See Law Commission, Consultation Paper No 154, *Illegal Transactions: the Effect of Illegality on Contracts and Trusts,* 1999, para 1.11.
4   *North-Western Salt Co Ltd v Electrolytic Alkali Co Ltd* [1914] AC 461 (HL); *Edler v Auerbach* [1950] 1 KB 359 (HC) (although note the comments in *Pickering v J.A. McConville* [2003] EWCA Civ 554); *Birkett v Acorn Business Machines Ltd* (1999) *The Times,* 26 August (CA); *Pickering v J.A. McConville* [2003] EWCA Civ 554.

example, but with more general concerns of the proper scope of the law of contract and its associated remedies.

Two commentators, Atiyah and Enonchong, have attempted to explore the more specific policies that underlie the law in this area.[5] Both suggest that there are two main reasons for the law's intervention. The first is that of deterrence.[6] The law reaffirms the approach taken by the criminal law or tort, and does not allow a person to benefit from 'illegal' behaviour.[7] As Atiyah points out, the use of unenforceability may be a greater deterrent than the threat of criminal prosecution. In the area of consumer credit, for example, to make a large company liable to relatively small fines for failing to follow correct procedures in dealing with consumers may be less coercive than making the credit contracts unenforceable. This policy does not fully explain, however, why illegal contracts are in some circumstances unenforceable even by innocent parties. A person who does not realise that he or she is infringing the law by the making or performance of a contract cannot be deterred from doing so by making the transaction unenforceable.

A second suggested policy is more general. This is described by Enonchong as protecting 'the integrity of the judicial system by ensuring that the courts are not seen by law-abiding members of the community to be lending their assistance to claimants who have defied the law'.[8] Atiyah calls it 'the undesirability of jeopardising the dignity of the courts'.[9] This means that the courts do not wish to be seen to be involved in the enforcement of transactions with an 'illegal' element, since this will bring the legal process into disrepute. This provides more of a justification for refusing to assist even 'innocent' claimants in relation to 'illegal' contracts. Nevertheless, as Enonchong points out, both of the above reasons for not enforcing illegal contracts can run into conflict with the desirability of preventing injustice to a claimant or a windfall gain by a defendant. He suggests that the law has attempted to 'steer a middle course' but that, because it has developed by a process of accretion, there have been conflicts, often unacknowledged, between the above policies. For many years the result of this 'has been a baffling entanglement of rules which when brought together are, like the common law itself, "more a muddle than a system"'.[10]

The confusion arises most clearly in relation to the question of the consequences of illegality, to which we shall return in detail in due course. For the moment, two points need to be made, First, the dominant reasons for making a contract 'illegal' seem to have been those of 'deterrence' and 'maintaining the respect of the civil justice system'.[11] If the categorisation of a contract as illegal appears to serve neither of these policies, we may legitimately question whether the categorisation is justifiable. Secondly, in recent times the illegality doctrine in contract law has been considered on a number of occasions by the Supreme Court: *Allen*

---

5  See Atiyah, 1995, pp 342–44 (compare Smith, 2006, Chapter 8); Enonchong, 1998, Chapter 1, especially pp 14–20; see also Law Commission, Consultation Paper No 154, 1999, Part VI and Consultation Paper No 189, 2009, at 2,5ff.

6  To this Atiyah links the punishment of the 'offender'. See also *Patel v Mirza* [2016] UKSC 42 at [108].

7  Enonchong quotes the Lord Chancellor in *Amicable Insurance Society v Bolland* (1830) 4 Bligh (NS) 194, p 211, as saying that to allow the assignees of an insurance policy on the life of a forger who had been executed for his crimes to recover under the policy would 'take away one of those restraints operating on the minds of men against the commission of crimes'.

8  Enonchong, 1998, p 17.

9  Atiyah, 1995, p 343. Atiyah also identifies a third possible policy, i.e. 'the desirability of bringing an illegal or undesirable state of affairs to an end'. His example (a landlord wishing to evict a prostitute), however, seems more closely linked to the contracts dealt with in the second part of this chapter (12.11 onwards) and this policy will therefore be left for consideration at that point.

10 Enonchong, 1998, p 20, quoting Simpson, 1973, p 99.

11 The Law Commission has suggested two additional policies behind the illegality rules: (1) that no person should benefit from their own wrongdoing; and (2) punishment of the wrongdoer: Consultation Paper No 154, 1999, Part VI. Neither of these, however, explains why an innocent party is not allowed to enforce an illegal contract.

v Hounga;[12] *Les Laboratoires Servier v Apotex Inc*;[13] *Bilta (UK) Ltd (In Liquidation) v Nazir*;[14] and *Patel v Mirza*.[15] After *Allen v Hounga* and *Les Laboratoires Servier v Apotex Inc* it was possible to identify different approaches to the illegality doctrine within the Supreme Court:[16]

> The present appeal exposes, not for the first time, a long-standing schism between those judges and writers who regard the law of illegality as calling for the application of clear rules, and those who would wish address the equities of each case as it arises. There are recent statements of this court in support of both points of view: see *Les Laboratoires Servier v Apotex Inc* [2015] AC 340 and *Hounga v Allen* [2014] 1 WLR 2889, paras 44–45. It also raises one of the most basic problems of a system of judge-made customary law such as the common law.[17]

The approach to illegality in contract law seems to have been settled by the Supreme Court in *Patel v Mirza* in favour of a wider, underlying policy approach. The case was heard by nine Justices and Lord Toulson (with whom Lady Hale, Lord Kerr, Lord Wilson and Lord Hodge agreed) stated:

> The courts must obviously abide by the terms of any statute, but I conclude that it is right for a court which is considering the application of the common law doctrine of illegality to have regard to the policy factors involved and to the nature and circumstances of the illegal conduct in determining whether the public interest in preserving the integrity of the justice system should result in denial of the relief claimed. I put it in that way rather than whether the contract should be regarded as tainted by illegality, because the question is whether the relief claimed should be granted.[18]

Some might argue that Lord Toulson's approach introduces more uncertainty into this area of law.[19] On the other hand, it might be argued that, overall, it more accurately represents the approach taken by the courts.[20] We shall return to *Patel v Mirza* throughout this chapter.

## 12.4 CATEGORIES OF ILLEGALITY

There are two main categories of illegal contract. First, there are those contracts where the agreement itself is directly or indirectly forbidden (because, for example, it amounts to a criminal offence). Second, there are contracts which involve 'illegality' because of the way in which they are *performed;* generally this arises where the method of performance

---

12 [2014] UKSC 47.
13 [2014] UKSC 55.
14 [2015] UKSC 23.
15 [2016] UKSC 42.
16 See Buckley, 2015.
17 *Patel v Mirza* [2016] UKSC 42 at [226] *per* Lord Sumption.
18 [2016] UKSC 42 at [109].
19 See, for example, Lord Sumption in *Patel v Mirza* [2016] UKSC 42 at [263]. See also *Ronelp Marine Ltd v STX Offshore and Shipbuilding Co* [2016] EWHC 2228 (Ch). In *Gujra v Roath* [2018] EWHC 854 (QB) at [35]-[36] Martin Spencer J accepted that such an approach would often require a full trial and in *Singularis Holdings Ltd (In Liquidation) v Daiwa Capital Markets Europe Ltd* [2018] EWCA Civ 84 the Court of Appeal indicated that a court should be slow to interfere with a first instance application of the *Patel v Mirza* test.
20 Compare also *Ritz Hotel Casino Ltd v Daher* [2014] EWHC 2847 (QB) and *Gujra v Roath* [2018] EWHC 854 (QB). On some of the limits to *Patel v Mirza* see: *Rashid v Nasrullah* [2018] EWCA Civ 2685 and *RBRG Trading (UK) Ltd v Sinocore International Co Ltd* [2018] EWCA Civ 838.

contravenes a statute. There is a third, subsidiary category of contracts to indemnify a person for the consequences of unlawful behaviour, which will be discussed separately.

## 12.4.1 CONTRACTS THAT CONSTITUTE A CRIMINAL OFFENCE

In some circumstances, the making of the contract itself will be a criminal act. The most obvious example is an agreement to commit a crime, such as murder or theft. If A asks B to kill C for a payment of £5,000, and B agrees, then their agreement has all the characteristics of a binding contract in the form of offer, acceptance and consideration. But it also amounts to the criminal offence of conspiracy to murder (under the Criminal Law Act 1977), and so will be unenforceable. An agreement to commit any crime will usually be a criminal conspiracy, and treated in the same way. In addition, the Criminal Law Act 1977 preserves the common law offence of 'conspiracy to defraud'.[21] In this case the fraudulent behaviour that is agreed need not amount to a criminal offence.

Certain contracts are made illegal by statute. Under the Obscene Publications Act 1959, for example, it is illegal to sell an 'obscene article'. Here (unlike conspiracy), the offence is only committed by one party (that is, the seller).

## 12.4.2 CONTRACTS FORBIDDEN THOUGH NOT CRIMINAL

It has been confirmed in two reported cases that a contract that is forbidden by delegated legislation, in the form of the rules of a professional body can be treated as an 'illegal' contract, even though the behaviour amounts at most to a disciplinary offence under the rules of that body, rather than being criminal.

Both cases concerned the Solicitors' Practice Rules 1990, made by the Law Society under s 31 of the Solicitors Act 1974. In the first case, *Mohamed v Alaga*,[22] the defendant solicitor was engaged in asylum work. The claimant was a member of the Somali community who alleged that the defendant had agreed to pay him a share of the solicitor's fees in return for introducing asylum-seeking clients and assisting in translation work. The sharing of fees was prohibited by the Solicitors' Rules, and when the claimant sued to recover what he alleged he was owed, he was met by the defence that the agreement, even if made,[23] was illegal and unenforceable. This argument was accepted by the Court of Appeal.[24]

The second case was *Awwad v Geraghty & Co*.[25] In this case the agreement was one whereby the solicitor agreed to act on a 'conditional fee' basis. This meant that the solicitor would be entitled to a higher fee if the action was successful. After the action had been settled, the solicitor sent a bill calculated at the lower rate (because the action had been settled, rather than successfully litigated), but the client refused to pay even this amount. When the solicitor sued, the client claimed that the whole agreement was illegal, as being contrary to the Solicitors' Practice Rules,[26] and was therefore unenforceable. The Court of Appeal agreed with this analysis, and held in favour of the client.[27]

---

21  Criminal Law Act 1977, s 5, which also purports to preserve the common law offences of conspiracy to corrupt public morals or outrage public decency.

22  [1999] 3 All ER 699.

23  Which the solicitor disputed.

24  The claimant was allowed, however, to recover for the translating work that had been done on a *quantum meruit* basis: this is discussed further at 12.6, below. The case was approved by the Supreme Court in *Patel v Mirza* [2016] UKSC 42.

25  [2000] 1 All ER 608.

26  The position as regards conditional fees has now been altered as a consequence of the Access to Justice Act 1999, so that they are now lawful in certain circumstances. See also *FPH Law v Brown (t/a Integrum Law)* [2016] EWHC 1681 (QB), affirmed on appeal: [2018] EWCA Civ 1629.

27  In coming to this conclusion, the court affirmed the view taken in *Mohamed v Alaga,* despite the fact that it felt that the court in that case had not been referred to all relevant authorities: see the comments of Schiemann LJ: [2000] 1 All ER 608, p 622.

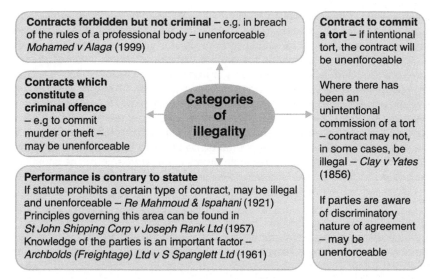

Figure 12.1

### 12.4.3 CONTRACT TO COMMIT A TORT

A contract to commit an intentional tort, such as assault or fraud, will be illegal in the same way as a contract to commit a crime.[28] On the other hand, it seems that a contract that involves the unintentional commission of a tort will not generally be illegal.[29] If, for example, there is a contract for the sale of personal property that belongs to a third party, but that both the buyer and seller believe to belong to the seller, this will involve the tort of conversion, but the contract itself will not be illegal.[30] Where only one party is innocent, it is possible that that party will be allowed to enforce the contract, though the position is uncertain.[31] There is *dicta* in *Clay v Yates*[32] that can be read to suggest that this is the case, but the point was not directly in issue and was not specifically addressed.[33]

What about a contract that would involve the commission of a 'statutory tort' under the Equality Act 2010, in that it would involve unlawful discrimination on grounds of, for example, sex, race or disability?[34] S 142(1) provides: 'A term of a contract is unenforceable against a person in so far as it constitutes, promotes or provides for treatment of that or another person that is of a description prohibited by this Act.'

---

28  *Allen v Rescous* (1676) 2 Lev 174; *Brown Jenkinson & Co Ltd v Percy Dalton (London) Ltd* [1957] 2 QB 621. Such contracts may well also involve an agreement to commit a criminal offence.

29  The Law Commission was unable to find any authority on the issue, but assumes that the position is as stated in the text: Consultation Paper No 154, para 2.23d.

30  This example is given by Treitel, 2015, p 539, noting that it is implicit in s 12 of the Sale of Goods Act 1979 that such a contract is valid.

31  See Law Commission, Consultation Paper No 154, 1999, para 2.23; Treitel, 2015, p 538.

32  (1856) 1 H & N 73, p 80, per Martin B.

33  The case concerned the publication of a book containing a libel. The printer, on discovering the defamatory nature of the passage in question, refused to print it, but was able to recover the cost of printing the rest of the book. Martin B suggests that the printer was entitled to recover for the work 'performed' and Treitel (2015, p 539) reads this as implying that he would have recovered if the libellous statement had been published unwittingly.

34  For discussion of these 'torts' see, for example, Stone, 2017, Chapter 11.

More generally a requirement to discriminate may itself be unenforceable. In *Javraj v Hashwani*,[35] the Court of Appeal held that a provision in an agreement that arbitrators were to be appointed from a particular ethnic community was void. This decision was reversed by the Supreme Court on appeal on the ground that the arbitrator was not an employee under the relevant Regulations. In any case, Lords Clarke, Phillips, Walker and Dyson felt that this stipulation, on the facts, would have been legitimate.[36] Nevertheless general principles would arguably suggest that there may be circumstances, at least where the parties are aware of the effect of the discriminatory nature of their agreement, where the agreement should be unenforceable. Even if the discrimination is unintentional[37] it may well be that the policy of not allowing the legal process to be used in a way that undermines its integrity[38] would lead a court to refuse to enforce such an agreement. The situation might also be treated as falling within the principles dealing with performance contrary to statute, as discussed in the following section.

### 12.4.4 PERFORMANCE IS CONTRARY TO STATUTE

Performance that contravenes a statute involves contracts that are *prima facie* legal, and that are concerned with the achievement of an objective that is legal, but that contravene a statute by the way in which they are performed. Thus, in relation to hire purchase agreements, the Consumer Credit Act 1974 provides that unless various formalities are complied with, the agreement may be unenforceable against the debtor. The aim of the law here is to provide protection for the debtor, and the penalty of unenforceability is used to encourage creditors to make sure that they follow the procedures that Parliament has laid down.[39]

An example of the application of this approach is to be found in *Re Mahmoud and Ispahani*.[40] The contract was to sell linseed oil. It was a statutory requirement that both seller and buyer should be licensed.[41] The seller was licensed, but the buyer was not. The buyer nevertheless told the seller that he was licensed. When the buyer refused to take delivery, the seller sued. It was held that the seller could not enforce the contract because of its illegality, despite its reasonable belief that the defendant was licensed.[42] The policy

---

35　[2010] EWCA Civ 712; [2010] 2 Lloyd's Rep 534. On appeal see [2011] UKSC 40.

36　It may be significant that the courts appeared to contemplate the possibility of intervention even before the statutory 'anti-discrimination' framework was put in place: see *Nagle v Feilden* [1966] 2 QB 633, p 655; *Edwards v SOGAT* [1971] Ch 354, p 382.

37　This might arise if an employer imposed a requirement that was *indirectly* discriminatory and unjustifiable – for example, that all candidates should have been educated in England for at least five years.

38　See above, 12.3.

39　It was argued in *Wilson v First County Trust Ltd* [2003] UKHL 40; [2003] 4 All ER 97 that some aspects of these strict rules as to enforceability were incompatible with the creditor's right to a fair trial under Art 6 of the European Convention on Human Rights, as incorporated into English law by the Human Rights Act 1998. This argument was successful in the Court of Appeal, but was rejected by the House of Lords. S 127 Consumer Credit Act 1974 was amended by the Consumer Credit Act 2006, Sched 4, para 1. This gives the courts more power to order enforcement in appropriate circumstances.

40　[1921] 2 KB 716.

41　Seeds, Oils and Fats Order 1919.

42　Could the seller in such a situation sue for misrepresentation? The court in *Mahmoud and Ispahani* refused to consider this. Whether there was such an action available would depend in part on whether the contract is void, rather than simply unenforceable. If it is void (as seems to have been the view in *Mahmoud and Ispahani*), then the seller would not have been induced to make a 'contract'. If it is simply unenforceable, then an action for misrepresentation would appear to be possible, but the courts might be unwilling to allow this to enable the seller to achieve indirectly what could not be done by a direct action on the contract: see *Awwad v Geraghty & Co* [2000] 1 All ER 608 – *quantum meruit* claim rejected on this ground. But an action based on the tort of deceit was allowed in *Saunders v Edwards* [1987] 2 All ER 651, and in *Strongman v Sincock* [1955] 2 QB 525 the Court of Appeal allowed an action based on a collateral promise that the defendant would obtain the necessary licences, even though the main contract was unenforceable. See further, 12.6, below and *Patel v Mirza* [2016] UKSC 42.

underlying the regulation was to prevent trading in linseed oil other than between those who were licensed, and the innocence of the seller was irrelevant to that policy.

In *Hughes v Asset Managers plc*,[43] by way of contrast, the Court of Appeal upheld share transactions that had been conducted by unlicensed agents. Although the Prevention of Fraud (Investments) Act 1958 imposed sanctions on those who engaged in such trading without a licence, it did not expressly, or by implication, prohibit the making of the contracts themselves. The policy of the Act could be achieved simply by penalising those who traded without a licence.

## For thought

(1)  What could the seller in Mahmoud and Ispahani have done to avoid making an unenforceable contract?
(2)  What are the practical implications of these two decisions? Is it satisfactory that parties contemplating making a contract need to consider the policy behind any legislation that may govern their transaction?

The principles that should govern this area were considered by Devlin J in St *John Shipping Corp v Joseph Rank Ltd*.[44]

## Key case St John Shipping Corp v Joseph Rank Ltd (1957)

Facts: The defendants chartered a ship from the plaintiffs to carry grain between the UK and the USA. The ship was overloaded in contravention of the Merchant Shipping Regulations. On arrival in the UK the master was convicted of the overloading offence. The defendants disputed their liability to pay the freight, because the plaintiffs had performed the contract in an illegal manner.
Held: The plaintiffs were entitled to recover. The Merchant Shipping Regulations were not intended to prohibit contracts of carriage *as such*, even if made in contravention of the Regulations.

In reaching this conclusion, Devlin J said it was necessary to ask, first, whether the statute prohibits contracts *as such*, or only penalises certain behaviour. If the answer to the first question is that it prohibits contracts, does this contract belong to the class that the statute is intended to prohibit?

In answering the first question, he suggested that it was helpful, though not conclusive, to ask whether the object of the statute was to protect the public. If so, then the contract was likely to be illegal. If, on the other hand, the purpose was to protect the revenue (as, for example, in a requirement that those who sell television sets pass the names of the purchasers to the television licensing authority), then it was likely to be legal. This test is difficult to apply, as was shown by the case itself where, despite the fact that the Merchant Shipping Regulations were clearly not designed simply to protect the revenue, the contract was held to be enforceable. It seems to have carried some weight with the Court of

---

43  [1995] 3 All ER 669.
44  [1957] 1 QB 267; [1956] 3 All ER 683.

Appeal, however, in its decision in *Skilton v Sullivan*.[45] In this case, the plaintiff entered into a contract with the defendant for the sale of koi carp. The defendant paid a deposit. Subsequently, the plaintiff issued an invoice, which described the fish as 'trout'. The defendant alleged that the plaintiff was trying to avoid paying VAT, since trout were zero-rated and koi carp were not. Thus, he argued, the contract was illegal and could not be enforced against him. The Court of Appeal considered that the plaintiff's purpose was probably to defer the payment of VAT, rather than to avoid it altogether: nevertheless, this was still an illegal purpose. The court also considered, however, that the plaintiff had formed this dishonest intention after the contract had been entered into. It was therefore not necessary for the plaintiff to rely on his unlawful act in order to establish the defendant's liability. This was the main basis for the decision, but the court also relied on the principle that illegality that has the object of protecting the revenue is less likely to render a contract unenforceable than where the object is the protection of the public.

## 12.4.5 RELEVANCE OF KNOWLEDGE

It has been suggested that the knowledge of the parties might be important, so that if both parties know that the contract can only be performed in a way that will involve the breach of the statute, then it is more likely to be illegal.

---

**Key case** *Archbolds (Freightage) Ltd v S Spanglett Ltd* (1961)[46]

Facts: The case concerned a contract for the carriage of goods. The defendants, who had licences entitling them to carry their own goods on their vans (i.e. 'C' licences), agreed to transport a quantity of whisky from London to Leeds for the plaintiffs. The plaintiffs believed that the defendants held 'A' licences for their vans, which would have entitled them to carry goods belonging to others. The whisky was stolen on the journey, owing to the negligence of the defendants' driver. The defendants sought to avoid liability on the basis that the contract was illegal. The plaintiffs succeeded at first instance and the defendants appealed.

Held: The Court of Appeal upheld the first instance decision. There was no evidence that the plaintiffs were aware or should have been aware that the defendants held only C licences. The contract was not prohibited either expressly or impliedly by the relevant statute (the Road and Rail Traffic Act 1933), and was not contrary to public policy. Pearce LJ stated, however, that:[47]

> if both parties know that though *ex facie* legal [a contract] can only be performed by illegality, or is intended to be performed illegally, the law will not help the plaintiffs in any way that is a direct or indirect enforcement of rights under the contract.

---

**For thought**

*Does this mean that if both parties are aware that a time limit stated as part of a contract of carriage can only be met by a vehicle exceeding the speed limit, the contract will be illegal and unenforceable?*

---

45  (1994) *The Times,* 25 March.
46  [1961] 1 QB 374; [1961] 1 All ER 417. See also *ParkingEye Ltd v Somerfield Stores Ltd* [2012] EWCA Civ 1338.
47  Ibid, p 384; p 422.

The issue of the knowledge of the parties has been considered further in two more recent cases concerned with employment contracts. In *Vakante v Addey & Stanhope School*,[48] the applicant was a Croatian national who was seeking asylum in the United Kingdom. He had been in the country since 1992, but was not allowed to work in the UK without permission. He nevertheless obtained a position as a graduate trainee teacher, and was employed for eight months. He was then dismissed. He brought a claim for racial discrimination and victimisation. Mummery LJ noted the test that had been laid down in *Hall v Woolston Hall Leisure Ltd*,[49] in which the Court of Appeal suggested that the proper approach in this sort of case was:

> to consider whether the applicant's claim arises out of or is so clearly connected or inextricably bound up or linked with the illegal conduct of the applicant that the court could not permit the applicant to recover compensation without appearing to condone that conduct.

In this case:

> (a) [the illegal conduct] was that of Mr Vakante; (b) it was criminal; (c) it went far beyond the manner in which one party performed what was otherwise a lawful employment contract; (d) it went to the basic content of an employment situation; (e) the duty not to discriminate arises from an employment situation which, without a permit, was unlawful from top to bottom and from beginning to end.

The Court of Appeal therefore concluded that the applicant's complaints were, applying the *Hall* test, so inextricably bound with the illegality of the relevant conduct that to allow him to recover compensation for discrimination would appear to condone his illegal conduct.

By contrast, the decision in *Wheeler v Quality Deep Trading Ltd*[50] went in favour of the applicant. She was of Thai origin and had limited knowledge of English. She was employed as a cook at a restaurant run by the defendant between November 1999 and January 2003. She was dismissed and brought an application for unfair dismissal. It transpired that she had been being paid without deduction of tax or national insurance. Inaccurate payslips were produced by the employer. The tribunal held that the applicant and her husband, who was well acquainted with the need to pay tax and national insurance and had a good grasp of English, must between them have 'known something was wrong' (para 22). It concluded that the employment contract was unlawful. On appeal, the Court of Appeal held that the tribunal had failed to apply the correct test to the situation. It did not properly distinguish between 'illegality of a contract and illegality in the performance of a legal contract' (para 26). If, as it seemed, this case fell within the second category, the test to be applied was that set out in *Hall v Woolston Hall Leisure*. It followed that:

> the employment tribunal had to be satisfied that the performance of the contract was illegal, that the employee knew of the facts which made the performance illegal and actively participated in the illegal performance.

Applying this test, the Court of Appeal noted the applicant's limited English, and the fact that it appeared that her husband had not seen her payslips until shortly before the tribunal hearing, and held that it could not be said that she had actively participated in the illegal performance.

---

48  [2004] 4 All ER 1056.
49  [2000] 4 All ER 787 (a sex discrimination case), discussed further at 12.6.
50  [2005] ICR 265.

The difference in outcome between these two decisions can be attributed to a significant extent to the court's view of the knowledge of the parties. In *Vakante* the applicant knew that he was acting illegally, whereas the employer was innocent; in *Wheeler* the situation was reversed. Vakante was not allowed to succeed in his claim, whereas Wheeler could.

A test based on the knowledge of the parties is not conclusive, as is shown by *Ailion v Spiekermann*.[51] The contract was for the assignment of a lease, for which a premium was to be paid. This was illegal under the Rent Act 1968, and both parties were aware of this. Nevertheless, the court ordered specific performance of the contract of assignment (though without the illegal premium).[52]

In *Anderson Ltd v Daniel*,[53] both the issue of the protection of the public and the knowledge of the parties were considered relevant. The contract was for the sale of artificial manure, made up of sweepings of various fertilisers from the holds of ships. Regulations required that the seller should specify the contents of the fertiliser and the proportions of each chemical it contained. This was impractical as far as sweepings were concerned. The Court of Appeal held the contract for sale to be unenforceable by the seller, because the statute was intended to protect purchasers. As Scrutton LJ put it:[54]

> When the policy of the Act in question is to protect the general public or a class of persons by requiring that a contract shall be accompanied by certain formalities or conditions, the contract and its performance without these formalities or conditions is illegal, and cannot be sued upon by the person liable to the penalties.

This seems to suggest that the answer might have been different if the purchaser had sued, rather than the seller.

The overriding questions are, therefore, first, does the statute prohibit contracts? In deciding this, it may be helpful to consider whether it is intended to protect the public, or a class of the public. Second, is this particular contract illegal? Here, it may be relevant to look at the knowledge of the parties, and the guilt or innocence of the party suing.

The second issue inevitably overlaps with the more general issue of the enforceability of illegal contracts, which is considered further below (see 12.6). Indeed the difficulties in distinguishing cases in this area provided some of the background for the Supreme Court in *Patel v Mirza* to move the wider, underlying policy approach with Lord Toulson stating:

> As to illegality in the manner of performance of a contract, Mance LJ observed in *Hall v Woolston Hall Leisure Ltd* [2001] 1 WLR 225, 246, that the conceptual basis on which a contract not illegal nor prohibited at the time of its formation may become unenforceable due to the manner of its performance is open to debate.... These and other cases led the Law Commission to describe the effect that unlawful performance has on the parties' contractual rights as very unclear. (Consultative Report on the Illegality Defence, LCCP 189 (2009), para 3.27.)[55]

---

51  [1976] Ch 158; [1976] 1 All ER 497.
52  This is probably best explained on the basis that the illegal part of the transaction, the premium, was severable from the lease itself. The result was that the purchaser of the lease got the best of both worlds – return of the premium, and enforcement of the lease. See 12.9, below, for further consideration on the power to 'sever' illegal obligations.
53  [1924] 1 KB 138.
54  [1924] 1 KB 138, p 147 – citing *Little v Poole* (1829) 9 B & C 192.
55  At [6] – [8].

## 12.5 CONTRACT TO INDEMNIFY

The parties may wish to make a type of insurance contract, whereby if one of them commits a crime or tort, the other will pay the amount of any fine or damages imposed, or otherwise provide compensation. Is such an agreement enforceable?

### 12.5.1 CRIMINAL LIABILITY

It will generally be illegal to attempt to insure against criminal liability.[56] There appears to be an exception, however, as regards strict liability offences (that is, where the prosecution does not need to prove any 'guilty mind' on the part of the defendant in order to obtain a conviction). Provided the court is satisfied that the defendant is morally innocent, then it seems the contract will be upheld. In *Osman v J Ralph Moss Ltd*,[57] the plaintiff was suing his insurance brokers who had negligently failed to keep him informed that his car insurance was no longer valid (because of the collapse of the insurance company). As a result, the plaintiff had been fined £25 for driving without insurance (an offence of strict, or absolute, liability). The Court of Appeal held that he could recover the amount of the fine from the defendants. Sachs LJ stated:[58]

> Having examined the authorities as to cases where the person fined was under an absolute liability, it appears that such fine can be recovered in circumstances such as the present as damages unless it is shown that there was on the part of the person fined a degree of *mens rea*[59] or of culpable negligence[60] in the matter which resulted in the fine.

The burden of proof was on the defendants to prove circumstances that rendered the fine irrecoverable.

An interesting more recent case is *Mulcaire v News Group Newspapers Ltd*[61] where, after a criminal action, joint tortfeasors entered into an indemnity contract under which one agreed to indemnify the other in respect of the costs etc. arising from a resulting civil action. Sir Andrew Morritt was of the opinion that such a contract of indemnity, entered into after a criminal action in respect of civil liability resulting from that criminal action, did not necessarily contravene public policy.

### 12.5.2 CIVIL LIABILITY

A contract to indemnify will be illegal as regards torts which are committed deliberately, such as deceit, or an intentional libel.[62] It is regarded as perfectly acceptable, however, to

---

56 *R Leslie Ltd v Reliable Advertising Agency Ltd* [1915] 1 KB 652. Note, however, that this case involved illegality arising from the *negligence* of the defendant; the law now seems to be prepared to allow an indemnity in such cases. In *Osman v J Ralph Moss Ltd* [1970] 1 Lloyd's Rep 313, the court preferred the earlier decision in *Cointat v Myham* [1913] 2 KB 220 to *Leslie v Reliable Advertising* on this particular point.

57 [1970] 1 Lloyd's Rep 313.

58 [1970] 1 Lloyd's Rep 313, p 316.

59 That is, intention or recklessness.

60 The case of *Askey v Golden Wine Co Ltd* [1948] 2 All ER 35 was distinguished on this basis – in that case (involving the sale of liquor not fit for public consumption) there had been 'gross negligence'.

61 [2011] EWHC 3469.

62 *WH Smith & Sons v Clinton* (1909) 99 LT 840. The action was by the printers of a magazine to recover on an indemnity given by the publishers in relation to libel. There was evidence that the printers were aware of the risk of libel, because the passage which eventually resulted in action being taken against both printers and publishers had been discussed and 'toned down' (though not sufficiently!).

have such an arrangement as regards the tort of negligence, or where a tort is committed innocently (such as an unintentional libel).[63]

Where civil liability arises out of a crime, a contract that would provide compensation may be unenforceable. Thus, in *Gray v Barr*,[64] Barr, who had been cleared of manslaughter by the criminal courts, was sued in tort by the widow of his victim. He admitted liability, but claimed that he was covered by his Prudential 'Hearth and Home' insurance policy, which covered sums he became liable to pay as damages in respect of injury caused by accidents. The Court of Appeal held (in effect ignoring the verdict in the criminal court) that Barr's actions did amount to the criminal offence of manslaughter, and that he therefore could not recover under the insurance policy.

A similar refusal to allow reliance on an insurance contract was shown in *Geismar v Sun Alliance*,[65] where the plaintiff was seeking compensation for the loss of goods that had been brought into the country without the required import duty having been paid. There was nothing illegal about the insurance contract itself, which provided standard protection against loss by, among other things, theft. The court held, however, that to allow the plaintiff to recover under the policy in relation to the smuggled goods would be assisting him to derive a profit from a deliberate breach of the law. In arriving at this decision, it was relevant that the failure to pay import duty rendered the goods liable to forfeiture at any time by Customs and Excise, and that the breach was deliberate. It was not suggested that the same approach would be taken in relation to unintentional importation or innocent possession of uncustomed goods.

Different considerations apparently apply, however, where the crime is one of strict liability, or where it arises from negligence. Thus, in *Tinline v White Cross Insurance Association Ltd*,[66] the plaintiff, who had knocked down three people while driving 'at excessive speed', was able to recover from the defendants, his insurers, the compensation he was required to pay to the victims. The exception will not apply, however, if the offence was deliberate.[67] The rules in the motoring area are, however, affected by the need to uphold the effectiveness of the system of compulsory insurance, so that the victims, and families of victims, of road accidents receive proper compensation. Thus, in *Gardner v Moore*, the House of Lords held that even though a car had been driven deliberately so as to cause injury,[68] and that therefore the driver would not be able to claim an indemnity under an insurance policy, the statutory provisions contained in the Road Traffic Acts, designed to ensure compensation for the victims of road accidents, allowed the victim to recover compensation directly from the driver's insurer.[69]

## 12.6 EFFECTS OF ILLEGALITY: ENFORCEMENT

Traditionally if an agreement was found to be tainted by illegality, it would, *prima facie*, have been unenforceable and specific performance would have been refused. This was so even if neither party had pleaded illegality.[70] Yet, in some circumstances, a court may

---

63  *Daily Mirror Newspapers Ltd v Exclusive News Agency* (1937) 81 SJ 924, where the plaintiffs recovered damages in breach of contract to cover the cost of libel damages resulting from the publication of a photograph and caption supplied by the defendant.
64  [1971] 2 QB 554; [1971] 2 All ER 949.
65  [1978] QB 383; [1977] 3 All ER 570.
66  [1921] 3 KB 327. The degree of injury caused by the negligence is irrelevant; in this case one of the victims was killed.
67  *Gardner v Moore* [1984] AC 548; [1984] 1 All ER 1100.
68  Amounting to 'grievous bodily harm' under the Offences Against the Person Act 1861, s 18.
69  In fact, in this case, the driver was uninsured, so the claim was against the Motor Insurers' Bureau.
70  See, for example, *Birkett v Acorn Business Machines* (1999) *The Times,* 25 August.

have been prepared to award damages. This may be done by allowing the action to be framed in tort, as, for example, in *Saunders v Edwards*,[71] where the plaintiff who had been party to an illegal overvaluation of furniture (for the purpose of avoiding stamp duty) in a contract for the sale of a flat was nevertheless allowed to sue for deceit on the basis of the defendant's fraudulent misrepresentation that the flat included a roof garden. The court took account of the 'relative moral culpability' of the two parties, and this question of 'guilt' or 'innocence' has always been relevant. During the 1980s, it was transformed by a number of decisions into a rather vague test of whether enforcement would offend the 'public conscience'.[72]

The House of Lords in *Tinsley v Milligan*[73] rejected this, and reasserted a test based on whether the claimant needs to rely on the illegality to found the claim. In this case, T and M had both supplied the money for the purchase of a house. It was, however, put into the name of T alone in order to facilitate the making by M of false claims to social security payments. When the parties fell out, M claimed a share of the property on the basis of a resulting trust. It was argued for T that M could not succeed because the original arrangement had been entered into in order to further an illegal purpose. The trial judge and the Court of Appeal found for M. The House of Lords also held, by a majority of 3:2, that M should succeed. In doing so, the majority rejected the approach taken by the Court of Appeal that the issue should be decided by considering whether 'the public conscience would be affronted by recognising rights created by illegal transactions'. This was too 'imponderable'. The proper test to be applied was whether the plaintiff needed to rely on the illegality in order to support her claim. In this case, the presumption of a resulting trust was raised simply by the fact that M had contributed to the purchase price of the house. It was T who had to raise the illegality in order to try to rebut that presumption. Therefore, M should succeed.[74] We have already noted[75] that the Supreme Court in *Patel v Mirza* has now adopted an underlying policy approach to questions of illegality in contract law:

> I would say that one cannot judge whether allowing a claim which is in some way tainted by illegality would be contrary to the public interest, because it would be harmful to the integrity of the legal system, without a) considering the underlying purpose of the prohibition which has been transgressed, b) considering conversely any other relevant public policies which may be rendered ineffective or less effective by denial of the claim, and c) keeping in mind the possibility of overkill unless the law is applied with a due sense of proportionality. We are, after all, in the area of public policy.[76]

Moreover *Tinsley v Milligan* was overruled by the Supreme Court in *Patel v Mirza*. Yet even before *Patel v Mirza* the situation was probably more nuanced than *Tinsley v Milligan* might have suggested. For example, in *21st Century Logistic Solutions Ltd v Madysen Ltd*,[77] the defendant resisted a claim for payment for goods delivered on the basis that the supplier had set up the transaction with the intention of carrying out a VAT fraud. The fraud was not in fact completed, because the supplier went into liquidation. The receivers sought to enforce the contract. The High Court held that the illegality was 'too remote'

71 [1987] 2 All ER 651, cited in *Hounga v Allen* [2014] UKSC 47 and *Patel v Mirza* [2016] UKSC 42.
72 See, for example, *Thackwell v Barclays Bank* [1987] 1 All ER 676; *Howard v Shirlstar Container Transport* [1990] 3 All ER 366.
73 [1994] 1 AC 340; [1993] 3 All ER 65.
74 A similar rule has been applied to the recovery of property in cases such as *Bowmakers v Barnet Instruments* [1945] KB 65; [1944] 2 All ER 579 – see below, 12.8.4.
75 At 8.3.
76 *Patel v Mirza* [2016] UKSC 42 at [101] *per* Lord Toulson.
77 [2004] EWHC 231; [2004] 2 Lloyd's Rep 92.

to prevent its enforcement. The fact that the supplier had had an illegal intention was no reason to refuse to enforce an agreement that, on its face, appeared to be a perfectly legitimate sale of goods contract.

This approach may also apply where there is illegality in performance by one side, but the illegality is ancillary to the rights being asserted by the claimant. Thus, in *Hall v Woolston Hall Leisure Ltd*,[78] the appellant was claiming compensation for sex discrimination in relation to her dismissal from employment. She was aware that the way in which the wages paid to her had been recorded by the employer was inaccurate, and that this was a deliberate attempt by the employer to defraud the Inland Revenue. Nevertheless, she was allowed to recover compensation for the fact that she had been 'dismissed' for an unlawful reason (that is, the fact that she had become pregnant). The Court of Appeal took the view that in a case of this kind:[79]

> It is the sex discrimination that is the core of the complaint, the fact of employment and dismissal being the particular factual circumstances which Parliament has prescribed for the sex discrimination complaint to be capable of being made.

The court would not, by allowing this claim, 'be seen to be condoning unlawful conduct by the employee'.[80] It might well be otherwise where the employee had been an active participant with the employer in illegal actions.[81] Here, however, there was mere passive acquiescence by the employee in what the employer was doing, and this should not preclude her discrimination action.

The same type of approach was adopted in *Mohamed v Alaga*,[82] the facts of which have been given above. Although the claimant in that case was not allowed to share in the solicitors' fees, because this was contrary to the Solicitors' Practice Rules, he was allowed to claim on a *quantum meruit* basis for the translating work that he had done (that is, he was paid a reasonable sum for the work completed). The view was taken that, although the defendant should have been aware of the Solicitors' Practice Rules, the claimant was ignorant of them, and it would not offend public policy for him to be able to recover a reasonable amount for the work actually done.

This was the basis on which *Mohamed v Alaga* was distinguished in *Awwad v Geraghty & Co*. There the claim was by the solicitor, who was taken to be aware of the rules, and a *quantum meruit* claim was rejected: 'If the court, for reasons of public policy, refuses to enforce an agreement that a solicitor should be paid, it must follow that he cannot claim on a *quantum meruit*.'[83]

Another possibility was that the court would allow the claimant to assert a 'collateral contract', which would allow for recovery without any need to rely on the illegal agreement. This approach was adopted in *Strongman (1945) Ltd v Sincock*.[84] In this case, an architect had failed to obtain the necessary licences for building work that the plaintiffs were carrying out for him. When the builders sued to recover the price of the work that had been done, they were met by a defence that the contract was illegal and that therefore

---

78 [2000] 4 All ER 787, approving *Leighton v Michael* [1996] ICR 1091 (EAT).
79 [2000] 4 All ER 787, p 799, per Peter Gibson LJ.
80 Ibid.
81 The court accepted that Scarman LJ's test of 'knowledge plus participation', as put forward in relation to a different type of contract in *Ashmore, Benson, Pease & Co Ltd v AV Dawson Ltd* [1973] 2 All ER 856, pp 862–63, was equally applicable to the employment law context.
82 [1999] 3 All ER 699. See 12.4.2.
83 [2000] 1 All ER 608 at pp 630–31.
84 [1955] 2 QB 525; [1955] 3 All ER 90 (although consider the need to use it in this context following *Patel v Mirza* [2016] UKSC 42).

they could not recover.[85] The Court of Appeal upheld the decision of the Official Referee that there was a collateral contract under which the architect had promised to obtain the licences,[86] and that the plaintiffs could recover damages under this. It was regarded as very significant that the defendants were not to blame for the fact that the work had been carried out without a licence; nor had they been negligent in leaving it to the architect to obtain the licence.[87]

---

**For thought**

*Would this approach provide a solution for the seller in Re Mahmoud and Ispahani (above, 12.4.4)? That is, could he have said to the buyer, 'if you guarantee that you have a licence then I will sell to you'? Could this then be treated as an enforceable collateral contract?*

---

The court in *Strongman v Sincock* did not make it clear what it regarded as the consideration provided by the builders for the architect's promise under this collateral contract. Presumably, it was the carrying out of the building work. The objection that the builders were already obliged to do this, so that the rule in *Stilk v Myrick* (see Chapter 3, 3.9.7) would prevent recovery, would be met by the argument that since the main agreement was illegal, the builders were in fact under no obligation to do the work. However, the contract does not really look like a 'collateral contract', since there is no main contract to which it is 'collateral'. The cynic would say that the court was here simply creating a remedy to prevent the unjust enrichment of an unmeritorious defendant.

We shall return to *Tinsley v Milligan* below at 12.8.4 where we will consider the Supreme Court decisions in *Allen v Hounga*[88] and *Patel v Mirza*.

## 12.7 EFFECTS OF ILLEGALITY: RECOVERY OF MONEY OR PROPERTY

Traditionally, in addition to illegality generally rendering a contract (partially or wholly) unenforceable, it seemed the courts would also, generally, refuse to order restitution of benefits conferred under such contracts. The general principle that applied in this area was expressed in the Latin maxim *in pari delicto potior est conditio defendentis*. This maxim, which was usually referred to in the abbreviated form *in pari delicto*, roughly translated as 'where there is equal fault, the defendant is in the stronger position'.[89] Thus, where money or other property had been transferred under an illegal contract, which was regarded as unenforceable, the court would not in general assist the claimant to recover it. However, at times, the policy against enforcing illegal contracts came into conflict with the desirability

---

85 It was accepted by all involved in the appeal proceedings, including counsel for the defendant, that the defendant had 'no merit' in raising this defence – 'justice' was clearly on the side of the plaintiffs: see Denning LJ, ibid, p 533; Birkett LJ, p 538.

86 The damages awarded by the Official Referee were equivalent to what the plaintiffs were adjudged to be owed under the building contract, had it been lawful.

87 There was evidence that it was standard practice in building contracts for the architect to obtain the necessary licences.

88 [2014] UKSC 47.

89 See Grodecki, 1955.

of preventing the defendant from being unjustly enriched at the claimant's expense. If restitution of benefits conferred under an illegal contract is not allowed, the defendant may be left with a substantial and undeserved windfall. The problems associated with a strict application of the policy against enforcing illegal contracts were recognised by Bingham LJ in *Saunders v Edwards*:[90]

> Where issues of illegality are raised, the courts have to steer a middle course between two unacceptable positions. On the one hand it is unacceptable that any court of law should aid or lend its authority to a party seeking to pursue or enforce an object or agreement which the law prohibits. On the other hand, it is unacceptable that the court should, on the first indication of unlawfulness affecting any aspect of a transaction, draw up its skirts and refuse all assistance to the plaintiff, no matter how serious his loss or how disproportionate his loss to the unlawfulness of his conduct.[91]

This area has not been fundamentally affected by the Supreme Court decision in *Patel v Mirza* (which will be discussed at 12.7.2).

### 12.7.1 TRADITIONAL RULE: NO RECOVERY
An example of the application of this traditional rule of no recovery is to be found in the following case.

---

**Key case** *Parkinson v College of Ambulance Ltd* (1925)[92]

Facts: Colonel Parkinson was approached by the secretary to the College of Ambulance who fraudulently told him that if he made a contribution to the College (a charity), it would be able to obtain a knighthood for him. Parkinson made a contribution of £3,000, but no knighthood was forthcoming. He brought an action to recover his money.
Held: The contract was illegal, as being contrary to public policy. Parkinson could not sustain his action without disclosing this, and his own complicity. The donation was on its face a gift, and therefore irrecoverable. It could only be explained as being part of a contract by disclosing the consideration alleged to have been given for it, that is, the promise of the knighthood. The plaintiff's action could only have any force as being for breach of this contract, but since the contract was illegal, the action had to fail.

---

In *Al-Kishtaini v Shanshal*,[93] the rules prohibiting the recovery of property on the basis of 'illegality' were challenged as being contrary to Art 1 of the First Protocol to the European Convention on Human Rights, as applied to English law by the Human Rights Act 1998.[94] Article 1 of the Protocol states:

---

90  [1987] 1 WLR 1116.
91  Ibid at 1134.
92  [1925] 2 KB 1.
93  [2001] 2 All ER Comm 601 (under the name *Shanshal v Al-Kishtaini*).
94  The possibility of the common law rules in this area being susceptible to such a challenge had previously been noted by the Law Commission, Consultation Paper No 154, para 1.23 – though it did not appear to regard the risk as very high.

Every natural or legal person is entitled to the peaceful enjoyment of his possessions. No one shall be deprived of his possessions except in the public interest and
subject to conditions provided for by law and by the general principles of international law.

The preceding provisions shall not, however, in any way impair the right of a
State to enforce such laws as it deems necessary to control the use of property
in accordance with the general interest or to secure the payment of taxes or other
contributions or penalties.

The courts, as public authorities under the Human Rights Act 1998, are obliged to apply
and interpret the law in a way which is compatible with the Convention.[95] It was suggested
in *Shanshal* that the rules relating to the non-recoverability of property transferred under
an illegal contract lacked the scope for the application of a test of 'proportionality' commonly applied in case law under the European Convention, by which any restriction of
rights must be 'proportionate' to the objectives that the restriction is trying to achieve.[96]
The Court of Appeal unanimously rejected this. It was not convinced that the principles
under attack engaged Art 1 at all, but if they did it was sure that in the case before it they
were justified as being in the 'public interest' within the first paragraph of Art 1 or the
'general interest' in the second paragraph.[97] The illegality in the case arose from contracts
made in breach of regulations preventing trade with Iraqi citizens,[98] passed in consequence of United Nations sanctions imposed in the aftermath of Iraq's 1990 invasion of
Kuwait. Mummery LJ noted that there was a very 'high degree' of public interest involved,
given the background to the regulations; and that, in any case, they were not absolute, in
that it was possible to obtain permission to trade with Iraqi citizens.

This decision was only concerned to deal with the Human Rights Act point as it applied
to the particular situation before the court, where the illegality arose out of a particular
set of regulations. It may be, however, that a similar approach would have been adopted
in other situations involving illegal contracts – that is, that restrictions on the recovery of
property would be held to be in the public interest. Moreover, the rules were not absolute,
as will be seen from the range of judge-created exceptions dealt with below. It is likely that
these provided for sufficient flexibility so that, in an appropriate case, a court would have
taken account of the question of whether a refusal to allow the recovery of money or other
property would be 'disproportionate', and thus achieve compatibility with the requirements of Art 1 of the First Protocol.

### 12.7.2 IMPACT OF *PATEL V MIRZA*
In *Patel v Mirza* Lord Toulson, effectively reversing the traditional rule, stated:[99]

A claimant, such as Mr Patel, who satisfies the ordinary requirements of a claim for
unjust enrichment, should not be debarred from enforcing his claim by reason only
of the fact that the money which he seeks to recover was paid for an unlawful purpose. There may be rare cases where for some particular reason the enforcement of
such a claim might be regarded as undermining the integrity of the justice system,
but there are no such circumstances in this case. I would dismiss the appeal.

---

95  Human Rights Act 1998, s 6.
96  See, for example, Stone, 2017, in particular Chapters 1 and 2.
97  See [2001] 2 All ER Comm 601, [50]–[62] (Mummery LJ); [90]–[99] (Rix LJ).
98  That is, the Control of Gold, Securities, Payments and Credits (Republic of Iraq) Directions 1990, SI
1990/1616.
99  At [121].

Moreover, doubt was cast on the overall correctness of *Parkinson v College of Ambulance Ltd*.[100]

## 12.8 TRADITIONAL EXCEPTIONS TO THE TRADITIONAL RULE

Even before the decision of the Supreme Court in *Patel v Mirza*, the no recovery rule was not always applied. In particular the courts developed and recognised a number of exceptions to this general rule, and there were therefore several situations where recovery of money or property would be allowed despite the illegality. The difficulties in distinguishing cases in this area provided some of the background for the Supreme Court in *Patel v Mirza* to move the wider, underlying policy approach.

### 12.8.1 ILLEGAL PURPOSE NOT YET CARRIED OUT

Traditionally if the contract was still executory, the claimant could have the chance to have a change of mind or heart, resile from the contract, and recover property transferred. This is sometimes referred to as the *iocus poenitentiae* ('the space for repentance'). Thus, in *Taylor v Bowers*,[101] the plaintiff had made a fictitious assignment of his goods to A as part of a scheme to defraud his creditors. Meetings of the creditors had been held, but no composition agreement had been reached. A had, in the meantime, parted with the goods to the defendant (who knew of the fraudulent scheme). The Court of Appeal held that because no creditors had actually been defrauded, the illegal purpose had not been carried out and the plaintiff could recover his goods from the defendant. This approach was applied by the Court of Appeal in *Tribe v Tribe*,[102] where shares had been transferred by father to son as a means of keeping assets out of the hands of landlords who were expected to be seeking substantial contributions towards repairs on property rented by the father. The transfer had been put in the form of a sale, but the son had never paid any money for the shares. In the event, no demands were made by the landlords, and the Court of Appeal, applying *Taylor v Bowers* and *Tinsley v Milligan*,[103] allowed the father to recover the shares. He had withdrawn from the transaction before any part of the illegal purpose had been carried into effect, and was in those circumstances allowed to use the explanation of what had been planned as a basis for undoing the apparent sale of the shares to his son.

This exception did not operate, however, where there has been substantial performance of the contract, as in *Kearley v Thomson*.[104] The plaintiff had paid money to the defendants, a firm of solicitors, in return for their agreement not to appear at the public examination of a bankrupt friend of the plaintiff, nor to oppose the order for his discharge. After the first part of the agreement had been carried out, the plaintiff changed his mind and tried to recover

---

100  At [118] Lord Toulson stated: "Bribes of all kinds are odious and corrupting, but it does not follow that it is in the public interest to prevent their repayment. There are two sides to the equation. If today it transpired that a bribe had been paid to a political party, a charity or a holder of public office, it might be regarded it as more repugnant to the public interest that the recipient should keep it than that it should be returned. We are not directly concerned with such a case but I refer to it because of the reliance placed on that line of authorities." Cf *National Iranian Oil Co v Crescent Petroleum Co International Ltd* [2016] EWHC 510 (Comm). Lord Neuberger went further and stated (at [150]): "I agree with the view that the decision in Parkinson represented "a new and regrettable extension of the scope of the maxim" of *ex turpi causa* (to quote from Professor Grodecki's article (1955) 71 LQR 254, 263), and I consider that it should be overruled."

101  (1876) 1 QBD 291.
102  [1996] Ch 107; [1995] 4 All ER 236.
103  [1994] AC 340; [1993] 3 All ER 65 – see above, 12.6.
104  (1890) 24 QBD 742.

his money. The Court of Appeal refused to allow him to do so, because there had been 'a partial carrying into effect of an illegal purpose in a substantial manner'.[105]

It was sometimes stated that the withdrawal must have been genuine: if the purpose of the contract was simply frustrated by the refusal of the other party to play his or her part, this exception would not apply.[106] However, in *Patel v Mirza*,[107] a case where an illegal agreement was frustrated before it was performed, Rimer LJ stated:

> I would regard as unattractive a distinction between cases (a) where the withdrawal is from an illegal agreement that is no longer needed for the purpose for which it was designed, and (b) where the withdrawal is from an illegal agreement that cannot be or is anyway not going to be performed. The drawing of any such distinction would, I consider, depend on holding that 'genuine repentance' on the part of the withdrawer is required. But I would take my lead from Millett LJ in *Tribe* and hold, in respectful agreement with him, that such repentance is not required. I consider that if, as in *Tribe*, voluntary withdrawal from an illegal agreement when it had ceased to be needed is sufficient to entitle the claimant to recover, it would be an odd distinction if a claimant were nevertheless not entitled to recover by relying on an illegal agreement that neither was performed nor could be performed. To recognise such a distinction would, I consider, require proof of a true sense of penitence, something that was not required or expected of the successful claimant in *Tribe*. Whether that was a correct course for this court to adopt might be a matter upon which some would have a different view. It appears to me, however, that the essence of what can be derived from *Tribe* is that, so long as the illegal agreement has not been carried into effect to any extent, the claimant can rely on it and recover. That is this case.

The majority of the Supreme Court in the same case side-stepped the issue by stating:

> It is not necessary to discuss the question of *iocus poenitentiae* which troubled the courts below, as it has troubled other courts, because it assumed importance only because of a wrong approach to the issue whether Mr Patel was prima facie entitled to the recovery of his money. In place of the basic rule and limited exceptions to which I referred at para 44 above, I would hold that a person who satisfies the ordinary requirements of a claim in unjust enrichment will not prima facie be debarred from recovering money paid or property transferred by reason of the fact that the consideration which has failed was an unlawful consideration.[108]

Presumably the issue of *locus poenitentiae* is not completely irrelevant to the underlying policy approach adopted by the majority in that case.

## 12.8.2 OPPRESSION

In the case of oppression, if the claimant was in a weak bargaining position, so that there was virtually no choice about entering into the agreement, recovery may have been

---

105 (1890) 24 QBD 742, p 747.
106 *Bigos v Bousted* [1951] 1 All ER 92 – the contract was in breach of exchange control regulations. In *Tribe v Tribe,* Millett LJ regarded this case as a dubious extension of the principle: [1996] Ch 107, p 135; [1995] 4 All ER 236, p 259.
107 [2014] EWCA Civ 1947.
108 At [116].

possible. Thus, in *Atkinson v Denby*,[109] a creditor refused to accept a composition agreement unless he was paid £50, so gaining an advantage over the other creditors. The debtor paid, but later brought an action to recover the money. It was held that the debtor could recover. Although the agreement was an illegal contract, the element of oppression meant that an exception to the general rule was justified.

The rationale of this exception was that the parties while both *in delicto* are not in fact *in pari delicto* (that is, they are not *equally* at fault). As Cockburn CJ put it in *Atkinson v Denby*:[110]

> It is true that both are *in delicto*, because the act is a fraud upon the other creditors, but it is not *pari delictum*, because the one has the power to dictate, the other no alternative but to submit.

As noted above, following *Patel v Mirza*, the supposed rule against restitution in this context has been displaced. However, that does not mean that such considerations (and those in 12.8.3) are now irrelevant to an underlying policy approach.[111]

### 12.8.3 FRAUD

If one party entered into the contract as a result of the other's fraudulent misrepresentation that it was lawful, recovery may have been allowed.[112] Again, the parties were not regarded as being equally at fault.

### 12.8.4 NO RELIANCE ON THE ILLEGAL TRANSACTION

Another exception to the traditional general rule was that if the claimant could establish a right to possession of the property without relying on the illegal contract, then recovery may have been allowed.

---

**Key case** *Bowmakers v Barnet Instruments* (1945)[113]

Facts: The defendants agreed to buy some machine tools on hire purchase terms from the plaintiffs. These agreements may well have been illegal, being in contravention of certain statutory regulations which required those disposing of machine tools to obtain a licence from the Ministry of Supply. There were three agreements. The defendants sold the machines that were the subject of two of the agreements, but kept the others. They refused to return them, or pay the hire. The plaintiffs brought one action to recover damages for conversion[114] in relation to all the machines.

Held: The Court of Appeal held that the plaintiffs could establish their rights over the goods without needing to rely on the illegal contracts. The defendants' rights as bailees had been brought to an end by their actions, and so the plaintiffs could rely on their basic rights of ownership to found their action.

---

109  (1862) 7 H & N 934; 158 ER 749.
110  Ibid, p 936; p 750.
111  Cf [2016] UKSC 42 at [67]ff.
112  *Hughes v Liverpool Victoria Legal Friendly Society* [1916] 2 KB 482.
113  [1945] KB 65; [1944] 2 All ER 579.
114  An action in conversion requires the claimant to prove a right to the goods concerned. The defendants argued that such a right could not be proved in this case without resort to the illegal transactions.

The decision in this case was not uncontroversial,[115] and is arguably inconsistent with *Taylor v Chester*,[116] where a person who had pledged a £50 bank note as security for a debauch in a brothel (an illegal contract) was held unable to recover it. The adoption, however, by the majority of the House of Lords of a similar line of argument in *Tinsley v Milligan*,[117] applying it to claims based on an equitable title (as opposed to the legal title asserted in *Bowmakers v Barnet Instruments)*, seemed to entrench this principle. However, in *Hounga v Allen*,[118] Lord Wilson (with whom Lady Hale and Lord Kerr agreed) noted that the no reliance test could operate in an arbitrary fashion.[119] He was also of the opinion that the 'no reliance' test had to be softened by reference to underlying policies, in this case balancing two competing policies: the policy behind the illegality defence and the policy of preventing human trafficking (or similar). On the facts the former gave way to the latter and so an employee could claim in tort despite the fact that she had been employed under an 'illegal' contract. In any event *Tinsley v Milligan* was overruled by the Supreme Court in *Patel v Mirza* with Lord Toulson stating:

> I agree with the criticisms made in *Nelson v Nelson* and by academic commentators of the reliance rule as laid down in *Bowmakers* and *Tinsley v Milligan*, and I would hold that it should no longer be followed. Unless a statute provides otherwise (expressly or by necessary implication), property can pass under a transaction which is illegal as a contract: *Singh v Ali* [1960] AC 167, 176, and *Sharma v Simposh Ltd* [2013] Ch 23, paras 27–44. There may be circumstances in which a court will refuse to lend its assistance to an owner to enforce his title as, for example, where to do so would be to assist the claimant in a drug trafficking operation, but the outcome should not depend on a procedural question.[120]

## 12.8.5 CLASS-PROTECTING STATUTES

In some situations, the purpose for which a statute makes an agreement illegal is to protect a particular class. For example, the provisions forbidding the taking of illegal premiums under the Rent Acts were designed to protect tenants. A member of that class may be able to recover property transferred under the agreement, notwithstanding the illegality. Many statutes of this kind have contained specific provisions for recovery.[121] Where they do not, however, the courts may apply the common law rule and allow recovery, as in *Kiriri Cotton Co Ltd v Dewani*.[122] This was a Privy Council decision concerning the payment of

---

115  See, for example, Treitel, 2015, pp 617–18, arguing that, while there was clearly a repudiatory breach in relation to the machines which had been sold, the same is not so obviously the case in relation to those retained by the defendants. Why did their rights as bailees not subsist in relation to these machines, so as to thwart the plaintiffs' claim based on ownership?

116  (1869) LR 4 QB 309.

117  [1994] AC 340; [1993] 3 All ER 65 – see above, 12.6.

118  [2014] UKSC 47.

119  At [29].

120  [2016] UKSC 42 at [110]. In relation to *Bowmakers v Barnett Instruments* Lord Toulson stated (at [111]): "The objections to the proviso have already been identified. It makes the question whether the court will refuse its assistance to the claimant to enforce his title to his property depend on a procedural question and it has led to uncertain case law about what constitutes reliance. The court ended its judgment, at p 72, by saying: "We are satisfied that no rule of law, and no considerations of public policy, compel the court to dismiss the plaintiffs' claim in the case before us, and to do so would be, in our opinion, a manifest injustice." That conclusion, rather than the answer to a procedural question, should have been the end of the illegality defence, since it is based on public policy."

121  For example, the Rent Act 1977, s 125; the Financial Services Act 1986, s 132 (now repealed).

122  [1960] AC 192; [1960] 1 All ER 177.

a premium by a tenant, which was illegal under Ugandan law. The tenant was allowed to recover the premium. As Lord Denning put it:[123]

> Thus, if as between the two of them [that is, the parties to the contract] the duty of observing the law is placed on the shoulders of one rather than the other – it being imposed on him specially for the protection of the other – then they are not in *pari delicto* and the money can be recovered back.

The underlying principle was again that in this situation the parties were not regarded as being equally at fault.[124]

## 12.9 SEVERANCE

It is likely to be the case in many illegal contracts that it is only part of the arrangement that is illegal. In some circumstances the courts will allow the contract to be split into its constituent parts, with the legal section being valid, and the illegal section unenforceable. This is what occurred, for example, in *Ailion v Spiekermann*,[125] where the contract to pay the illegal premium could be severed, because a precise amount could be assigned to the illegal part of the agreement.[126] A more recent example is to be found in *Blue Chip Trading Ltd v Helbawi*.[127] A student was studying in England on a visa that only allowed him to work for 20 hours a week in term time. He complained that he had not been paid the minimum wage. The employer defended the action on the basis that the student had worked for more than 20 hours a week and so the whole contract was unenforceable for illegality. The Employment Appeal Tribunal (EAT) held that the contract could be severed, so that the student could recover in relation to vacations (in which there was no restriction on hours) and in relation to any term-time weeks when he worked for not more than 20 hours.[128]

## 12.10 IN FOCUS: PROPOSALS FOR REFORM[129]

The Law Commission has been considering the need for reform of the law relating to the illegality defence in respect of contract, tort and restitution for some time, and in 1999 put out a Consultation Paper suggesting some possible improvements.[130] The main thrust of these proposals was that the 'technical and complex rules'[131] should be replaced by a 'structured discretion'. A further consultation paper was issued in 2009[132] and a final report

---

123  Ibid, p 204; p 181.

124  Cf *Patel v Mirza* [2016] UKSC 42 at [67]ff.

125  [1976] Ch 158; [1976] 1 All ER 497 – discussed above, 12.4.5.

126  See *Carney v Herbert* [1985] 1 All ER 438 (Privy Council), in which illegal mortgages were severed from a transaction for the purchase of shares that they were intended to guarantee.

127  [2009] IRLR 128, EAT.

128  Further discussion of the issue of severance can be found in the chapter on Restraint of Trade, which is on the companion website to this text: www.routledge.com/textbooks/stone.

129  The European Draft Common Frame of Reference deals with illegality in Articles II. – 7:301–7:304.

130  Law Commission, Consultation Paper No 154, 1999. For a broadly favourable welcome to the proposals, see Buckley, 2000.

131  Ibid, para 1.18.

132  The Illegality Defence (2009), Consultation Paper No 189.

in 2010.[133] Its conclusion was that, although the rules are 'complex and confused',[134] there should be no legislative reform in relation to contract and tort:[135]

> We have reached the conclusion that it is not possible to lay down strict rules about when the illegality defence should apply. Instead, the courts should consider the policy rationales that underlie the defence and apply them to the facts of the case.

The 'policy rationales' and the way in which the Law Commission would expect the process to operate were spelt out more fully at para 3.142 of the 2009 Consultation Paper:

> the courts should consider in each case whether the application of the illegality defence can be justified on the basis of the policies that underlie that defence. These include:
>
> (a)    furthering the purpose of the rule which the illegal conduct has infringed;
> (b)    consistency;
> (c)    that the claimant should not profit from his or her own wrong;
> (d)    deterrence; and
> (e)    maintaining the integrity of the legal system.
>
> Against those policies must be weighed the legitimate expectation of the claimant that his or her legal rights will be protected. Ultimately, a balancing exercise is called for which weighs up the application of the various policies at stake. Only when depriving the claimant of his or her rights is a proportionate response based on the relevant illegality policies, should the defence succeed. The judgment should explain the basis on which it has done so.

The Law Commission's hope is that, if the courts adopt such an approach, the law can be reformed by incremental change. No legislation in relation to the area of illegal contracts is proposed, and so no statutory reform is to be expected. Indeed, in more recent cases the courts have undertaken these balancing exercises more openly.[136]

## 12.11 AGREEMENTS CONTRARY TO PUBLIC POLICY

The second part of this chapter, like the first, is concerned with agreements that the courts traditionally refuse, wholly or partly, to enforce. In this case, however, the reason for this refusal is not that the agreements concerned amount to, or are linked to, the commission of a crime or a tort, or are forbidden by statute. Rather, they have been held to be more generally 'contrary to public policy' and, for that reason, wholly or partly unenforceable. Most of the areas dealt with here are the creation of the judges. The categories of common law public policy have been stated to be closed,[137] so that on this view the courts will not apply this approach to a type of contract to which it has not been applied previously. Such an approach perhaps has the advantage of promoting certainty, and keeping public

---

133  Law Com No 320, HC 412, 16 March 2010.
134  Ibid, Summary, para 1.3.
135  Ibid, Summary, para 1.4.
136  See, for example, *Gray v Thames Trains and others* [2009] UKHL 33 and now *Patel v Mirza* [2016] UKSC 42.
137  *Printing & Numerical Registering Co v Sampson* (1875) LR 19 Eq 462, p 465; *Janson v Driefontein Consolidated Mines Ltd* [1902] AC 484, p 491; *Fender v St John Mildmay* [1938] AC 1, p 23; *Geismar v Sun Alliance and London Assurance Ltd* [1978] QB 383, p 389; [1977] 3 All ER 570, p 575.

policy claims within limits. Whether the courts would stick to this line if faced with a novel situation that appeared to call out for intervention is another matter.[138] One area where it is possible that they might feel inclined to intervene is if a contract appeared to infringe one of the rights recognised by the Human Rights Act 1998.

One difficulty about the development of new categories of contract to be held wholly or partially unenforceable at common law on the basis of public policy is that there are no clear principles which seem to link the existing categories. At the most general level, it may be said that the argument from the 'integrity of the courts' (discussed at 12.3 in relation to illegality) will apply here as well. In other words, the courts will not wish to be seen to be being used to enforce an agreement the consequences of which are seen to be 'undesirable'. But this begs the question, since it simply moves the focus from what is contrary to public policy to what is 'undesirable'. The other main policy behind the control of illegal contracts noted earlier in this chapter, that of deterrence, has less relevance here, since the agreements concerned are not necessarily linked to an 'unlawful' act. The main conclusion that can be drawn is that the areas that currently fall within this heading are a ragbag collection of agreements, not linked by any discernible conceptual theme. This, in turn, adds to the difficulty in extending the category, since if there is no general principle linking those agreements that are currently within the category, the basis for arguing that other agreements should be included is never likely to be clear-cut. It is, of course, always open to Parliament to add to the areas that fall within the scope of 'public policy', and render further categories of contract wholly or partially unenforceable, though not illegal; but it is difficult to see this happening in practice. Where Parliament intervenes to control agreements, it usually does so through the medium of the criminal law.

## 12.12 CONTRACTS CONCERNING MARRIAGE

Traditionally the courts regarded it as being in the interests of society to preserve the status of marriage. Certain types of contract that were regarded as threatening to the institution of marriage were treated as illegal.

### 12.12.1 FUTURE SEPARATION

A contract between spouses agreeing to separate at some point in the future was traditionally invalid if it was made either before the marriage or during cohabitation.[139] This rule did not apply to an agreement that did not relate to the distant future, but is made at a time when the marriage has already broken down and in anticipation of immediate separation.[140] It was not regarded as contrary to public policy for the parties to a failed marriage to make agreements about the distribution of their property, or for the maintenance of one party or the children of the marriage by the other.[141] Nor did the rule affect arrangements

---

138  In *Lancashire County Council v Municipal Mutual Insurance Ltd* [1996] 3 All ER 545, for example, a defence based on 'public policy' was rejected, but only after careful consideration: if there were really no possibility of expanding the public policy categories, the argument would surely have been rejected out of hand. See also *Multiservice Bookbinding Ltd v Marden* [1979] Ch 84; [1978] 2 All ER 489 and *Staffordshire AHA v South Staffordshire Waterworks Co* [1978] 3 All ER 769. On the courts' changing attitudes to commercial surrogacy and family life see: *XX v Whittington Hospital NHS Trust* [2018] EWCA Civ 2832.

139  *Wilson v Wilson* (1848) 1 HL Cas 538.

140  The same exception used to apply to a promise by a married man to marry another woman: if a decree nisi had been issued in relation to the first marriage, the promise was enforceable: *Fender v St John-Mildmay* [1938] AC 1; [1937] 3 All ER 402. This is no longer of any practical significance, since the action for breach of promise of marriage was abolished by the Law Reform (Miscellaneous Provisions) Act 1970.

141  Subject to legislative provisions.

made by spouses who have been separated, and are then reconciled, since in this situation the making of the agreement may aid the reconciliation.[142]

The position has now been fundamentally altered by the Privy Council in *Macleod v Macleod*[143] (in relation to agreements during marriage) and the Supreme Court in *Granatino v Radmacher*[144] (in relation to agreements prior to marriage). In *Granatino v Radmacher* Lord Phillips stated that:[145]

> the old rule that agreements providing for future separation are contrary to public policy is obsolete and should be swept away ... If parties who have made such an agreement, whether ante-nuptial or post-nuptial, then decide to live apart, we can see no reason why they should not be entitled to enforce their agreement.

The reference to 'ante-nuptial' agreements means what are more commonly known as 'pre-nuptial' agreements, which are becoming ever more frequently used, particularly where one party is very wealthy. This type of agreement is made prior to marriage in order to avoid, or minimise, disputes about the distribution of property should the marriage break down. Following *Granatino v Radmacher*, the courts will give weight, possibly decisive weight, to such agreements. It is now possible to treat such agreements as contracts. The extent to which this will make a difference to the practical outcome of cases, however, is arguable. In dealing with disputes arising out of a failed marriage, the courts are bound by statutory provisions governing the approach to the division of property, and these give the courts the power to override any contractual agreement. The position is that there will be a presumption that the provisions of the agreement should apply, but that this presumption will be rebuttable. As Lord Phillips put it:[146]

> The court should give effect to a nuptial agreement that is freely entered into by each party with a full appreciation of its implications unless in the circumstances prevailing it would not be fair to hold the parties to their agreement.

Factors that will be relevant to 'fairness' include the welfare of children, and significant changes in circumstances subsequent to the marriage.

### 12.12.2 RESTRAINT OF MARRIAGE
A contract that imposes liability on a person if he or she marries is unenforceable. Thus, a promise by A that if he marries, he will pay a sum of money to C is unenforceable.[147] Similarly, a promise by A to make a payment if he marries anyone else other than B will also be unenforceable.[148]

### 12.12.3 MARRIAGE BROKERAGE
Marriage brokerage concerns a contract whereby A promises to procure a marriage for B. Traditionally the professional 'matchmaker' cannot make an enforceable contract for his or her services. The rule is not limited to contracts to procure marriage with a particular person. Thus, in *Hermann v Charlesworth* (discussed further below, 12.17), Miss H entered into an agreement under which, if the defendant introduced her to someone whom she

---

142 *Harrison v Harrison* [1910] 1 KB 35.
143 [2008] UKPC 64; [2010] 1 AC 298.
144 [2010] UKSC 42; [2010] 3 WLR 1367.
145 Ibid, para 52.
146 Ibid, para 75. See also Law Commission, 2014 and *Versteegh v Versteegh* [2018] EWCA Civ 1050.
147 *Baker v White* (1690) 2 Vern 215; 23 ER 740.
148 *Lowe v Peers* (1768) 4 Burr 2225.

married, Miss H would pay the defendant £250. She paid a deposit which, after several unsuccessful introductions, she sought to recover. The Court of Appeal held that the contract was illegal as being contrary to public policy. It is difficult to see, however, why such contracts are any more harmful than those between 'dating' or 'introduction' agencies and their clients, which have never been regarded as contrary to public policy. Such contracts do not, of course, depend on marriage between those introduced.

## 12.13 CONTRACTS PROMOTING SEXUAL IMMORALITY

Traditionally, contracts promoting sexual immorality will include any contract for sex outside marriage, and would presumably cover otherwise lawful homosexual, as well as heterosexual, activities. Such activities, while not constituting criminal offences or civil wrongs, may still be regarded as immoral, and contracts that involve them will be treated as contrary to public policy.

The rule may not be limited to contracts that directly concern sexual activity, as is shown by the following case.

---

**Key case** *Pearce v Brooks* (1866)[149]

Facts: There was a contract under which the plaintiffs supplied the defendant with an ornamental brougham (a type of carriage), which was to be paid for by instalments. After one instalment had been paid, the brougham was returned in a damaged condition. The plaintiffs sued for 15 guineas compensation, which was payable under the agreement if the brougham was returned early. The defendant, however, was a prostitute, and there was evidence that she intended to use the brougham to attract customers. Moreover, the jury at trial found that at least one partner in the plaintiffs' firm was aware of this.

Held: The Court of Exchequer held that this was an illegal contract, so that the plaintiffs would be unable to recover either under the contract or for the damage.

---

The knowledge of the plaintiffs was relevant here, but not every contract with a known prostitute will be illegal. In *Appleton v Campbell*[150] the action was for the recovery of board and lodging in relation to a room rented from the plaintiff. The Court held that the plaintiff could not recover if he knew that the defendant was a prostitute, and that she was using the room to entertain her clients. But:[151]

> if the defendant had her lodgings there, and received her visitors elsewhere, the plaintiff may recover, although she be a woman of the town, because persons of that description must have a place to lay their heads.

There are thus, it seems, two factors that are necessary for the contract to be unenforceable. First, there must be knowledge that the other party is a prostitute and, second, knowledge that what was supplied under the contract is to be used for the purposes of prostitution.

---

149  (1866) LR Ex 213.
150  (1826) 2 C & P 347; 172 ER 157.
151  Ibid.

The same approach will presumably apply to other 'immoral' contracts. The extent to which the other contracts are likely to be treated as 'immoral', however, must now be considered in the light of the decision in *Armhouse Lee Ltd v Chappell*.[152] In this case, the publishers of a magazine sought to recover payment for advertisements that had been placed by the defendants. The defendants resisted the claim on the basis that the content of the advertisements was illegal or immoral, since they related to telephone 'sex lines', offering pre-recorded messages, live conversations and sex dating. The trial judge found for the plaintiffs. On appeal, the Court of Appeal considered a range of ways in which the advertisements could be said to be illegal, including prostitution, obscenity and conspiracy to corrupt public morals. All were rejected. In addition, the Court refused to find that 'public policy' required the contracts to be treated as unenforceable. There was no evidence that any 'generally accepted moral code condemned these telephone sex lines'. Moreover, 'it was undesirable in such a case, involving an area regarded as the province of the criminal law, for individual judges exercising a civil jurisdiction to impose their own moral attitudes'. The decision of the trial judge was therefore upheld, and the contracts were enforceable by the plaintiffs. This case suggests that it is unlikely that there will be any significant extension of the range of contracts that will be struck down on the basis of sexual 'immorality'. In the light of the comments made by the Court of Appeal and its decision, it would seem likely that illegality will only operate to prevent the enforcement of a contract where the behaviour concerned amounts to, or involves or is linked to, a criminal offence.

### For thought

*If the law is to strike down 'immoral' contracts, why should this be limited to the area of sexual immorality? Are there other types of immoral behaviour (such as discriminating on inappropriate, though not illegal, grounds – for example, charging more to people with red hair) which should render unenforceable any contract made?*

## 12.14 CONTRACTS TO OUST THE JURISDICTION OF THE COURTS

The courts are very jealous of any attempt in a contract or other agreement to try to take away their powers to oversee the agreement, interpret it and decide on its validity. They may hold any such agreement to be unenforceable as being contrary to public policy.

### Key case *Baker v Jones* (1954)[153]

**Facts:** The rules of the British Amateur Weightlifters' Association provided that the Association's central council was to be 'the sole interpreter of the rules' of the association, and that the council's decision was in all circumstances to be final.
**Held:** Although it was perfectly in order to give a tribunal or council the power to make final decisions on questions of fact, the same could not be done as regards questions of law. These provisions in the rules were to that extent contrary to public policy, and unenforceable.

---

152  (1996) *The Times*, 7 August.
153  [1954] 2 All ER 553. See also *Lee v Showmen's Guild of Great Britain* [1952] 2 QB 329.

Figure 12.2

There are two qualifications to this general approach. First, parties may agree in their contract that disputes should be submitted to arbitration (at least as a precondition for any legal action being taken). The crucial question is the extent to which the parties may commit themselves to treat the decision of the arbitrator as binding. Under both common law and statute, the arbitrator is allowed the final say on issues of fact. As to issues of law, the common law did not allow the parties to agree to exclude the court's jurisdiction in this area. An agreement to do so was unenforceable, and a party was free to seek a ruling from the courts on the point of law at issue.[154] The statutory position is that a party may have recourse to the court on a point of law, but only with the agreement of the other side, or the leave of the court itself.[155] Such leave will only be given if the conditions set out in s 69(3) of the Arbitration Act 1996 are satisfied. These state that:

Leave to appeal shall be given only if the court is satisfied:

(a)    that the determination of the question will substantially affect the rights of one or more of the parties;
(b)    that the question is one which the tribunal was asked to determine;
(c)    that, on the basis of the findings of fact in the award:

---

154  *Czarnikow v Roth Schmidt & Co* [1922] 2 KB 478. See also *Scott v Avery* (1855) 5 HLC 811.
155  Arbitration Act 1996, s 69.

(i)    the decision of the tribunal on the question is obviously wrong; or

(ii)   the question is one of general public importance and the decision of the tribunal is at least open to serious doubt;

(d)   that, despite the agreement of the parties to resolve the matter by arbitration, it is just and proper in all the circumstances for the court to determine the question.

The jurisdiction of the court is thus retained only where it is really necessary to deal with clearly incorrect applications of the law or matters of 'general public importance'. Otherwise, the finality of arbitration and its associated benefits of reduction in costs and certainty are to be maintained.

The second qualification to the general rule against ousting the courts' jurisdiction applies to a clause in an agreement arrived at on the separation of husband and wife under which the wife, in return for a promise of maintenance, agrees not to apply to the courts. Such an agreement is unenforceable to the extent that the wife is still free to apply, but is enforceable as regards the husband's promise to pay.[156]

## 12.15 CONTRACTS IN RESTRAINT OF TRADE

A final category of contracts contrary to the public interest consists of contracts 'in restraint of trade' – in other words, contracts that restrict competition. The types of contract concerned are those that contain provisions that try to prevent one of the parties engaging in employment or business of specified kinds. For example, the owner of a hairdressing salon might try to stop employees who leave from working for a rival salon, and taking customers with them. Or the purchaser of a shop might wish to prevent the seller from opening a competing business in the next street. Or a petrol company may try to tie the owner of a petrol station to buying all its fuel from it. In all of these situations the contracts, if enforced, will have the effect of restricting trade and competition. The common law regards such provisions as *prima facie* unenforceable, as being contrary to public policy (which regards the maximisation of competition as desirable), but enforceable if the person wishing to impose the restriction can show that it is a reasonable means of protecting a legitimate interest.

This area is more appropriately dealt with by specialist texts on employment law or competition law, and so is not discussed further here. A chapter dealing with the common law approach in more detail is, however, to be found on the companion website to this text (www.routledge.com/textbooks/stone).

## 12.16 EFFECT OF CONTRACTS CONTRARY TO PUBLIC POLICY

The main consequence of a contract being contrary to public policy is that it may, depending on the precise public policy offended, be unenforceable by one or both parties.[157] In general, in this area, the contract as a whole is what offends against public policy. If, however, it is only part of the agreement that does so, then the possibility of severing the offending part arises.

As regards the recovery of money or property transferred under the agreement, the position here seemed to be different from that which applied, prior to *Patel v Mirza*, in relation to illegal contracts. In that area, as discussed above (12.7), the courts traditionally

---

156  Matrimonial Causes Act 1973, s 34.
157  See Beale, 2018, para 16–001.

started from the premise that no recovery is possible,[158] but that in certain situations there were exceptions, in particular where the parties are not equally 'at fault'.[159] In relation to contracts unenforceable as being contrary to public policy, the issue of fault may not arise in the same way: nor are they stigmatised as being improper through being illegal.[160] It seems, therefore, that even before *Patel v Mirza* the courts were probably more flexible in relation to the recovery of property transferred in relation to such contracts. Authorities are few, but this was the approach adopted in the marriage brokerage case, *Hermann v Charlesworth*.[161] The plaintiff had paid a deposit to the defendant, with the promise of further payment in the event that one of his introductions led to her getting married. She was allowed to recover the deposit, despite the fact that the contract was regarded as void. It seems likely that this would be the general approach to contracts falling within this area.

## 12.17 WAGERING CONTRACTS

Section 18 of the Gaming Act 1845 provided that:

> All contracts ... by way of gaming or wagering, shall be null and void; and no suit shall be brought or maintained in any court of law and equity for recovering any sum of money or valuable thing alleged to have been won upon any wager.

As from September 2007, however, s 334 of the Gambling Act 2005 repealed s 18 of the 1845 Act. This has the effect that gambling contracts entered into from that date are usually legally enforceable. The 1845 Act will only apply in relation to gambling contracts entered into before 1 September 2007. Its provisions are therefore not discussed further here.

## 12.18 SUMMARY OF KEY POINTS

- Contracts that constitute a criminal offence (e.g. conspiracy to commit a crime) will usually be 'illegal' for present purposes and unenforceable.
- In cases where the way in which a contract is performed involves a breach of a statute, the courts will consider:
  - whether the statute prohibits contracts as such (e.g. is it designed to protect the public or simply government revenue);
  - the knowledge of the parties as regards the illegality.

- Contracts to indemnify for penalties or damages imposed for criminal offences and deliberate torts will usually be 'illegal'; contracts to indemnify for damages payable as a result of negligence will generally be enforceable.

- Illegal contracts may be wholly or partly unenforceable as public policy demands.

- Money paid or property transferred under an 'illegal' contract can be recovered following *Patel v Mirza*.

---

158 That is, under the principle of *in pari delicto potior est conditio defendentis*.
159 See 12.8.2.
160 The concept of 'impropriety' might apply to contracts prejudicial to sexual morality but as we have seen, this is probably a very narrow range of contracts under the modern law.
161 [1905] 2 KB 123 – see above, 12.12.3.

## 12.19 FURTHER READING

### Generally

▦   Buckley, R, 'Illegal transactions: chaos or discretion' (2000) 20 LS 155

▦   Conway, H, 'Prenuptial contracts' (1995) 145 NLJ 1290

▦   Enonchong, N, *Illegal Transactions*, 1998, London: Lloyd's of London Press

▦   Goudkamp, J, 'The end of an era? Illegality in private law in the Supreme Court' (2017) 133 LQR 14

▦   Grodecki, J K, 'In *pari delicto potior est conditio defendentis'* (1955) 71 LQR 254

### Law Commission

▦   Law Commission, Consultation Paper No 189, *The Illegality Defence*, 2009

▦   Law Commission, *The Illegality Defence*, Law Com No 320, HC412, 2010

### Comparative

▦   Coote, B, 'The Illegal Contracts Act 1970', Chapter 3 in *New Zealand Law Commission, Contract Statutes Review*, 1993

## COMPANION WEBSITE

*Now visit the companion website to:*

▦   Revise and consolidate your knowledge of Illegality by tackling a series of multiple-choice questions on this chapter

▦   Test your understanding of the chapter's key terms by using the flashcard glossary

▦   Explore Illegality further by accessing a series of web links

# Frustration

**13**

## Contents

The doctrine of frustration deals with situations where circumstances change after a contract has been made and this makes performance impossible, or at least significantly different from what was intended. The following aspects need discussion:

■ The nature of the doctrine. Is the doctrine based on an implied term in the contract, or simply on a rule of law?

---

1 See, generally, Treitel, 2014; McKendrick, 1995a.

- What sort of events will lead to the frustration of a contract? Examples include:
  - ☐ destruction of the subject matter – this is the clearest example of frustration;
  - ☐ where personal performance is important, the illness of one party may frustrate the agreement;
  - ☐ where the contract presumes the occurrence of an event, its cancellation may be treated as frustration;
  - ☐ if the contract becomes illegal, or a government intervenes to prohibit it.
- Limitations on the doctrine. It will not apply where:
  - ☐ the contract simply becomes more difficult or expensive to perform;
  - ☐ the 'frustration' is attributable to the actions of one of the parties;
  - ☐ the parties have provided for the circumstances in the contract itself.
- Effects of the doctrine under the common law:
  - ☐ the contract is terminated automatically; but
  - ☐ all rights and liabilities that have already arisen remain in force; except that
  - ☐ if there is a total failure of consideration, money paid may be recovered.
- The Law Reform (Frustrated Contracts) Act 1943. This Act amends the common law, so that:
  - ☐ money paid prior to frustration can generally be recovered;
  - ☐ benefits conferred, which survive the frustrating event, can be compensated for.

## 13.2 INTRODUCTION

This chapter is concerned with the situation where, following the formation of a valid contract, an event occurs that is not the fault of either party, but that has a significant impact on the obligations contained in the contract. English law will sometimes, but not always, consider that such an event results in the 'frustration' of the contract, with the consequence that the parties are relieved from further obligations, and may be able to recover money or property transferred, and compensation for work done prior to the frustrating event.

This topic, the doctrine of frustration, has links with preceding chapters, and with the one that follows. Frustration can, from one point of view, be looked at as something that vitiates a contract, and in particular has similarities with the area of 'common mistake'.[2] Whereas vitiating factors generally relate to things that have happened, or states of affairs that exist, at or before the time when the contract is made, frustration deals with events that occur subsequent to the contract coming into existence. Since frustration has the characteristics of an event that discharges parties from their obligations under a contract, it also has links with the topics of performance and breach (see Chapter 14).

The situation with which the doctrine of frustration is concerned is where a contract, as a result of some event outside the control of the parties, becomes impossible to perform, at least in the way originally intended. What are the rights and liabilities of the parties?

### 13.2.1 ORIGINAL RULE

In *Paradine v Jane*,[3] the court took the line that obligations were not discharged by a 'frustrating' event, and that a party who failed to perform as a result of such an event -would still be in breach of contract. The justification for this harsh approach was that the parties could,

---

2   See Chapter 9, 9.4. Both frustration and common mistake can be analysed as methods by which the determination of 'risk allocation' is taken out of the hands of the parties, and dealt with by legal rules or the discretion of a judge.

3   (1647) Aleyn 26; 82 ER 897.

if they wished, have provided for the eventuality within the contract itself.[4] In commercial contracts this is in fact often done, and *force majeure* clauses are included so as to make clear where losses will fall on the occurrence of events that affect some fundamental aspect of the contract.[5] Disputes about whether a contract is frustrated are therefore less common in the commercial context than those about the interpretation of a *force majeure* clause.[6]

## 13.2.2 SUBSEQUENT MITIGATION

The *Paradine v Jane* approach, however, proved to be too strict and potentially unjust, even for the nineteenth-century courts, which were in many respects strong supporters of the concept of 'freedom of contract', taking the view that it was not for the court to interfere to remedy perceived injustice resulting from a freely negotiated bargain. The modern law has developed from the decision in *Taylor v Caldwell*.[7]

---

**Key case** *Taylor v Caldwell* (1863)

Facts: This contract, entered into in May 1861, involved the letting of the Surrey Gardens and music hall for the purposes of concerts and other events in June and August. After the agreement, but before the first concert, the hall was destroyed by fire. The fire was not the fault of either party. The concerts could not go ahead, and the plaintiffs sued for breach of contract.

Held: It was held that since performance was impossible, this event excused the parties from any further obligations under the contract. Blackburn J justified this approach on the basis that where the parties must have known from the beginning that the contract was dependent on the continued existence of a particular thing, the contract must be construed:[8]

> as subject to an implied condition that the parties shall be excused in case, before breach, performance becomes impossible from the perishing of the thing without the fault of the contractor.

---

The doctrine at this stage, then, was based on the existence of an implied term. This enabled the decision to be squared with the prevailing approach to freedom of contract, and was adopted in subsequent cases.[9] It also tied in with classical theory

---

4    Trebilcock (1993, p 136) has suggested that, in fact, the courts are unlikely to be very effective in achieving an appropriate allocation of risks in the business context, and that therefore there is an argument that 'a clear, albeit austere, rule of literal contract enforcement in most cases provides the clearest signal to parties to future contractual relationships as to when they might find it mutually advantageous to contract away from the rule'. This would support a return to the *Paradine v Jane* approach.

5    The parties may also include 'hardship clauses' (to provide for modification of the contract in the light of changed circumstances), which may also be supplemented by an 'intervener clause' (giving a third person the power to determine the appropriate modification). For further discussion of these devices, see McKendrick, 1995b, pp 327–29.

6    See the comments to this effect by McKendrick, 1995b, p 323.

7    (1863) 3 B & S 826; 122 ER 309.

8    Ibid, pp 833–34; p 312.

9    See, for example, Lord Loreburn in *FA Tamplin Steamship Co Ltd v Anglo-Mexican Petroleum Products Ltd* [1916] 2 AC 397, p 403: 'a court ... ought to examine the contract ... in order to see whether or not from the nature of it the parties must have made their bargain on the footing that a particular thing or state of things would continue to exist. And if they must have done so, then a term to that effect will be implied, though it be not expressed in the contract.'

that all is dependent on what the parties intended at the time of the contract.[10] In real-ity, of course, this is something of a fiction.[11] Some judges in more recent cases have recognised this. In particular, Lord Radcliffe in *Davis Contractors Ltd v Fareham UDC*,[12] in a passage that has often been quoted subsequently, stated that, in relation to the implied term theory:

> there is something of a logical difficulty in seeing how the parties could even impliedly have provided for something which, *ex hypothesi*, they neither expected nor foresaw; and the ascription of frustration to an implied term of the contract has been criticised as obscuring the true action of the court which consists in applying an objective rule of the law of contract to the contractual obligation which the parties have imposed on themselves.

In truth, however, the problem with the implied term theory is not one of logic. Although the parties may not have foreseen the particular event,[13] there is nothing illogical about agree-ing that, in general terms, unforeseen events affecting the nature of the parties' obligations will result in specified consequences. Indeed, most *force majeure* clauses will include a provision to this effect. And if this can be done by an express clause, there is no reason why it cannot be done by one that is implied.

The real objection to the implied term theory here, as elsewhere in the law of contract,[14] is that it obscures what the courts are actually doing – which is, in this case, deciding that certain events have such an effect on the contract that it is unfair to hold the parties to it in the absence of fault on either side, and in the absence of any clear assumption of the relevant risk by either party. That this is the basis for intervention has been recognised by some judges. In *Hirji Mulji v Cheong Yue Steamship Co Ltd*,[15] for example, Lord Sumner commented that the doctrine 'is really a device by which the rules as to absolute contracts are reconciled with a special exception which justice demands'. This line has been sup-ported by Lord Wright both judicially in *Denny, Mott and Dickson Ltd v James Fraser*[16] and, more explicitly, extra-judicially.[17] It thus forms one of the two other main theoretical bases, as alternatives to the implied term, put forward as explanations of the doctrine of frustration.[18] It is by no means universally accepted, however, perhaps because of its

---

10  Intention would, of course, generally be objectively assessed.

11  It can be said, as is the case with all terms implied by the courts on the basis of the parties' supposed inten-tions, to be based on the myth of 'presentation', exposed in particular by Macneil, which suggests that the entire future of a contract can be determined by the obligations agreed at its outset: Macneil, 1978. See also Chapter 1, 1.6.

12  [1956] 2 All ER 145, p 159.

13  This point is made by Lord Sands' hypothetical example in the Scottish case of *James Scott & Sons Ltd v Del Sel* 1922 SC 592, p 597, concerning an escaped tiger and its effect on milk deliveries – concluding that the understandable exoneration of the milk girl could not reasonably be attributed to implying a clause in the delivery contract stating 'tiger days excepted'. The example is quoted by Lord Reid in *Davis Contractors Ltd v Fareham UDC* [1956] 2 All ER 145, p 153.

14  See Chapter 6, 6.6. See also *Healthcare at Home Limited v The Common Services Agency (Scotland)* [2014] UKSC 49 at [1]-[4] per Lord Reed.

15  [1926] AC 497, p 510.

16  [1944] AC 265, pp 274–75.

17  Wright, 1939, p 258: 'The truth is that the court ... decides the question in accordance with what seems to be just and reasonable in its eyes.' See also the comments of Denning LJ in *British Movietonews Ltd v London and District Cinemas Ltd* [1951] 1 KB 190, p 200, basing the approach on what is 'just and reasonable' in the new situation – though these comments were specifically disapproved as being too broad by Viscount Simon in the House of Lords in this case: [1952] AC 166, p 183.

18  Lord Hailsham suggested in *National Carriers Ltd v Panalpina (Northern) Ltd* [1981] AC 675, p 687, that 'at least five theories for the doctrine of frustration have been put forward at various times'. Treitel (2014, p 649) has commented that the discussion of the theoretical basis of the doctrine has no practical importance. In

uncertainty, and the third theory, based on 'construction', seems to be the one that is currently favoured.[19] The most frequently cited statement of this theory is that of Lord Radcliffe in *Davis Contractors Ltd vFareham UDC*.[20] Having outlined the artificiality of the implied term approach, he commented:

> So perhaps it would be simpler to say at the outset that frustration occurs whenever the law recognises that without default of either party a contractual obligation has become incapable of being performed because the circumstance in which performance is called for would render it a thing radically different from that which was undertaken by the contract. *Non haec in foedera veni*. It was not this that I promised to do.

The approach is, therefore, to ask what the original contract required of the parties,[21] and then to decide, in the light of the alleged 'frustrating' event, whether the performance of those obligations would now be something 'radically different'. This has been subsequently endorsed as the best approach by the House of Lords in *National Carriers Ltd v Panalpina (Northern) Ltd*.[22]

The operation of this approach requires the courts to decide what situations will make performance 'radically different' – and it is to this issue that we now turn.

## 13.3 FRUSTRATING EVENTS[23]

It is clear that 'radical difference' will include, but is not limited to, situations where performance has become 'impossible'. Unfortunately, neither 'impossibility' nor 'radical difference' has a self-evident meaning in this context. Both require interpretation in their application. There is, however, guidance to be obtained from looking at the cases. Although the categories are not closed, it is possible to identify certain occurrences that have been recognised by the courts as amounting to frustration of the contract.

---

*Great Peace Shipping Ltd v Tsavliris Salvage (International) Ltd* [2003] QB 679, Lord Phillips MR regarded the doctrine of frustration as based on a 'rule of law'.

19 Though this terminology is confusing since the 'implied term' theory can also be described as being based on the 'construction' of the contract: see, for example, Atiyah, 1986a, p 272. Atiyah (1986a, p 273) also points out that it may be inaccurate to describe the various approaches as conflicting theories, since they are in fact just answers to different questions about the doctrine of frustration: the 'just solution' is the goal or objective of the doctrine; the implied term approach is a 'technique'; and what is called here the 'construction' theory (or 'change in fundamental obligation' theory) is a statement of the conditions in which the implied term approach will be applied.

20 [1956] AC 696, pp 728–29.

21 This is why the theory is sometimes referred to as the 'construction' theory: the contract has to be construed to determine the obligations that it placed on the parties. Collins 1999, pp 163–65 has criticised the heavy reliance of the courts on the formal documentation rather than the 'business deal' which underlies this: he suggests that this leads the courts, while purporting to do justice between the parties, to allocate risks in ways which do not correspond with those parties' commercial expectations.

22 [1981] AC 675.

23 On the possible effect of Brexit, which at the time of writing is subject to much uncertainty, see the discussion in *Canary Wharf (BP4) T1 Ltd v European Medicines Agency* [2019] EWHC 335 (Ch) (in that case a lease agreement in London for the headquarters of the European Medicines Agency (EMA) was held not to be frustrated by Brexit on a number of grounds including that the EMA's involuntary departure from London had been provided for in the terms of the contract).

### 13.3.1 DESTRUCTION OF THE SUBJECT MATTER

In the same way that the destruction of the subject matter prior to the formation of a contract may render it void for common mistake,[24] destruction at a later stage may fall within the doctrine of frustration, as indicated by *Taylor v Caldwell*.[25] Complete destruction is not necessary. In *Taylor v Caldwell* itself, the contract related to the use of the hall and gardens, but it was only the hall that was destroyed.[26] The contract nevertheless became impossible as regards a major element (use of the hall), and was therefore frustrated. In other words, if what is destroyed is fundamental to the performance of the obligations under the contract, then the doctrine will operate.[27]

It seems that complete physical destruction may not be necessary if the subject matter has been affected in a way which renders it practically useless. In *Asfar v Blundell*,[28] for example, a cargo of dates was being carried on a boat that sank in the Thames. The cargo was recovered, but the dates were found to be in a state of fermentation and contaminated with sewage. The judge found that they 'had been so deteriorated that they had become something which was not merchantable as dates'.[29] On that basis, there was a total loss of the dates, and the contract was frustrated.

### 13.3.2 PERSONAL SERVICES – SUPERVENING INCAPACITY

If a contract envisages performance by a particular individual, as in a contract to paint a portrait, and no substitute is likely to be satisfactory, then the contract will generally be frustrated by the incapacity of the person concerned.

**Key case** *Condor v Barron Knights* (1966)[30]

Facts: The drummer with a pop group was taken ill. Medical opinion was that he would only be fit to work three or four nights a week, whereas the group had engagements for seven nights a week.
Held: His contract of employment was discharged by frustration. He was incapable of performing his contract in the way intended.

In many cases, of course, the identity of the person who is to perform the contract will not be significant. Suppose, for example, a garage agrees to service a car on a particular day, but on that day, as a result of illness, it is short-staffed and cannot carry out the service. This will be treated as a breach of contract, rather than frustration. The contract is simply to carry out the service, and the car owner is unlikely to be concerned about the identity of the particular individual who performs the contract, so long as he or she is competent.[31]

---

24  As in *Couturier v Hastie* (1856) 5 HLC 673: see Chapter 9, 9.4.
25  (1863) 3 B & S 826; 122 ER 309.
26  Indeed, it seems that the defendant continued to be able to use the gardens and to charge for admission to them despite the fire: see Treitel, 2014, p 207.
27  See also Sale of Goods Act 1979, s 7: see 13.6 below.
28  [1896] 1 QB 123.
29  [1896] 1 QB 123, p 128.
30  [1966] 1 WLR 87. Note, however, *Blankley v Central Manchester & Manchester Children's University Hospitals NHS Trust* [2014] EWHC 168 and [2015] EWCA Civ 18 where a solicitor's retainer was not frustrated by the client's fluctuating capacity. On the relevance of disability law, see *Warner v Armfield* [2014] ICR 239.
31  Cf the cases on mistaken identity – discussed above, Chapter 9, 9.5.5 and 9.5.6.

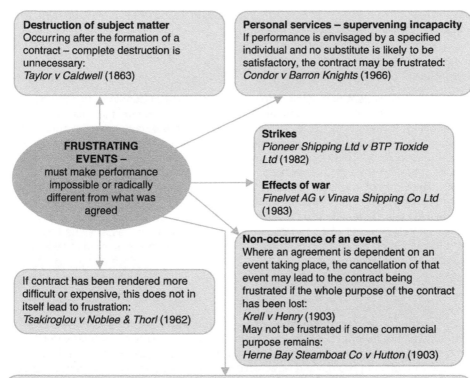

Figure 13.1

---

**For thought**

*Do you think the position would be the same if there was a flu epidemic, and the garage had no mechanics available at all?*

---

In *Atwal v Rochester*[32] a building contract with a sole trader was held to be frustrated when the sole trader suffered a heart attack. HHJ Kirkham stressed the personal relationship between the parties.

### 13.3.3 NON-OCCURRENCE OF AN EVENT

If the parties reach an agreement that is dependent on a particular event taking place, the cancellation of that event may well lead to the contract being frustrated. This situation

---

32  [2010] EWHC 2338.

arose in relation to a number of contracts surrounding the coronation of Edward VII, which was postponed owing to the king's illness.

> **Key case** *Krell v Henry* (1903)[33]
>
> Facts: The defendant had made a contract for the use of certain rooms in Pall Mall owned by the plaintiff for the purpose of watching the coronation procession. He paid a deposit of £25 and was to pay the balance of £50 on the day before the coronation. Before this day arrived, the king was taken ill, and the procession was postponed. The plaintiff sued for the payment of the £50, and the defendant counterclaimed for the return of the £25 (though this claim was later dropped).
>
> Held: The Court of Appeal held that the postponement of the procession frustrated the contract. Although literal performance was possible, in that the room could have been made available to the defendant at the appropriate time, and the defendant could have sat in it and looked out of the window, in the absence of the procession it had no point, and the whole purpose of the contract had vanished. The decision of the trial judge in favour of the defendant was upheld.

By contrast in another 'coronation case', *Herne Bay Steamboat Co v Hutton*,[34] the contract was not frustrated. Here, the contract was that the plaintiff's boat should be 'at the disposal of' the defendant on 25 June to take passengers from Herne Bay for the purpose of watching the naval review, which the king was to conduct, and for a day's cruise round the fleet. The king's illness led to the review being cancelled. In this case, however, the Court of Appeal held that the contract was not frustrated. The distinction from *Krell v Henry* is generally explained on the basis that the contract in *Herne Bay* was still regarded as having some purpose. The fleet was still in place (as Stirling LJ pointed out), and so the tour of it could go ahead, even if the review by the king had been cancelled. The effect on the contract was not sufficiently fundamental to lead to it being regarded as frustrated.

### 13.3.4 IN FOCUS: ANOTHER INTERPRETATION OF *HERNE BAY V HUTTON*

Brownsword has taken a different view of the *Herne Bay* case. He has argued that the contract would not have been frustrated even if the fleet had sailed away.[35] In his view the distinction between the cases is that Hutton, the hirer of the boat, was engaged in a purely commercial enterprise, intending to make money out of carrying passengers around the bay, whereas Henry was in effect a 'consumer', whose only interest was in getting a good view of the coronation procession. This approach also emphasises that it is important to determine exactly what the parties had agreed. As Vaughan Williams LJ suggested in *Krell v Henry*,[36] if there was a contract to hire a taxi to take a person to Epsom on Derby Day, and the Derby was subsequently cancelled, this would not affect the contract for the hire of the taxi; the hirer would be entitled to be driven to Epsom, but would also be liable for the fare if he chose not to go.

---

33 [1903] 2 KB 740. Cited in *Durkin v DSG Retail Ltd* [2014] UKSC 21 at [25] per Lord Hodge JSC.
34 [1903] 2 KB 683. Compare also *Flying Music Co Ltd v Theater Entertainment SA* [2017] EWHC 3192 (QB) where a contract for theatre performances was not frustrated by civil unrest in Greece as the civil unrest was present at the time the contract was signed and had not got worse.
35 Brownsword, 1993, pp 246–47.
36 [1903] 2 KB 740, pp 751–52.

## 13.3.5 GOVERNMENT INTERVENTION

If a contract is made, and there is then a declaration of war that turns one of the parties into an enemy alien, then the contract will be frustrated.[37] Similarly, the requisitioning of property for use by the government can have a similar effect, as in *Metropolitan Water Board v Dick Kerr*.[38] In this case, a contract for the construction of a reservoir was frustrated by an order by the Minister of Munitions, during the First World War, that the defendant should cease work, and disperse and sell the plant.

Here, as is the case in relation to the non-occurrence of an event, it must be clear that the interference radically or fundamentally alters the contract. In *FA Tamplin v Anglo-Mexican Petroleum*,[39] a ship that was subject to a five-year charter was requisitioned for use as a troopship. It was held by the House of Lords that the charter was not frustrated, since judging it at the time of the requisition, the interference was not sufficiently serious.[40] There might have been many months during which the ship would have been available for commercial purposes before the expiry of the contract.

Similarly, the fact that the contract has been rendered more difficult, or more expensive, does not frustrate it.

---

**Key case** *Tsakiroglou & Co v Noblee and Thorl* (1962)[41]

Facts: The appellants agreed to sell groundnuts to the respondents to be shipped from Port Sudan to Hamburg. Both parties expected that the shipment would be made via the Suez Canal, but this was not specified in the contract. The Suez Canal was closed by the Egyptian government, and this meant that the goods would have had to be shipped via the Cape of Good Hope, extending the time for delivery by about four weeks. The appellants failed to ship the goods and the respondents sued for non performance. The appellants argued that the contract had been frustrated.

Held: The House of Lords held that this was not frustration. The route for shipment had not been specified in the contract, nor was any precise delivery date agreed. The fact that the rerouting would cost more was regarded as irrelevant. The appellants were in breach of contract and the respondents were entitled to succeed in their action.

---

The government intervention need not relate to war or international relations. In *Gamerco SA v ICM/Fair Warning Agency*,[42] the Spanish government's closure of a stadium for safety reasons was held to frustrate a contract to hold a pop concert there.

An unsuccessful attempt was made in *Amalgamated Investment and Property Co Ltd v John Walker & Sons*[43] to base frustration on a different type of government interference, namely the 'listing' of a building as being of architectural and historic interest, and therefore subject to strict planning conditions. Despite the fact that this was estimated as having the effect of reducing the market value of the building to £200,000

---

37 *Fibrosa Spolka Ackyjna v Fairbairn Lawson Combe Barbour Ltd* [1943] AC 32.
38 [1918] AC 119. See also *Bank Line v Arthur Capel Ltd* [1919] AC 435 – requisition of a ship which was the subject of a 12-month time charter. When the ship was released some six months after the expected start date, an action for non-delivery (brought on the basis that the charter could have run for 12 months from that date) failed: the charter was held to be frustrated.
39 [1916] 2 AC 397.
40 This was a majority view, with two of the members of the House dissenting.
41 [1962] AC 93; [1961] 2 All ER 179.
42 [1995] 1 WLR 1126.
43 [1976] 3 All ER 509.

(the contract price was £1,700,000), the Court of Appeal held that the contract was not frustrated. It was not part of the contract that the building should not be listed, and the change in the market value of the property could not in itself amount to frustration. The decision presumably leaves open the possibility that if the non-listing of a building was stated as being a crucial element in the contract, then frustration could follow from such a listing.

An interesting contrast is the Court of Appeal's later decision in the case of *Bromarin AB v 1MB Investments Ltd*.[44] In this case, a contract for the purchase of the share capital of two companies had been set up with the main purpose of enabling the buyer to be able to set off losses against gains, as was at that time allowed by tax law. Subsequently, the law changed, so that such losses could no longer be set off. The seller sought to enforce the agreement but, at first instance, it was held that the contract had been frustrated by the change in the law. On appeal, however, the Court of Appeal ruled that frustration could not be used where, as a result of a change in the law, a bargain turned out to be less advantageous than had been hoped.

### 13.3.6 SUPERVENING ILLEGALITY

If, after a contract has been made, its purpose becomes illegal, this may be regarded as a frustrating event. In *Denny, Mott and Dickson v James Fraser*,[45] there was an agreement for the sale of timber over a number of years. It provided that the buyer should let a timber yard to the seller, and give him an option to purchase it. In 1939, further dealings in timber were made illegal. The House of Lords held that not only the trading contract, but also the option on the timber yard, was frustrated. The main object of the contract was trading in timber and, once this was frustrated, the whole agreement was radically altered.

### 13.3.7 OTHER FRUSTRATING EVENTS

Other types of event that have been held to lead to frustration include industrial action, particularly if in the form of a strike, and the effects of war. For example, in *Pioneer Shipping Ltd v BTP Tioxide Ltd*,[46] the House of Lords upheld an arbitrator's view that a time charter was frustrated when strikes meant that only two out of the anticipated six or seven voyages would be able to be made. As regards the effects of war, in *Finelvet AG v Vinava Shipping Co Ltd*,[47] a time-chartered ship was trapped by the continuing Gulf War between Iran and Iraq. Again, the court upheld the view of an arbitrator that this was sufficiently serious to mean that the contract was frustrated.

Note that in the former case, it was the *extent* of the effect of the strike that was important. In the latter case, it was made clear that the outbreak of war did not necessarily frustrate a contract on which it had a bearing; it was only when it became clear that the war would be protracted that the contract was frustrated. This again emphasises the point that, whatever the frustrating event (and the categories are never likely to be closed), it is the *effect* of that event on the contract, and what the parties have agreed, that is the most important consideration, and not the *nature* of the event itself.[48] Only if its effect is to change fundamentally the conditions of the contract, and to make performance radically different from what the parties had agreed, will frustration take place.

---

44  [1999] STC 301.
45  [1944] AC 265; [1944] 1 All ER 678.
46  [1982] AC 724; [1981] 2 All ER 1030.
47  [1983] 2 All ER 658.
48  See also *Edwinton Commercial Corp v Tsavliris Russ Worldwide Salvage & Towage) Ltd* [2007] EWCA Civ 547 at [112].

## 13.4 LIMITATIONS ON THE DOCTRINE

The general limitations on the availability of a plea of frustration, in terms of the seriousness of the event and its effect on what the parties have agreed, have been discussed above. In this section, three more specific limitations are noted.

### 13.4.1 SELF-INDUCED FRUSTRATION

If it is the behaviour of one of the parties that, while not necessarily in itself amounting to a breach of contract, has brought about the circumstances that are alleged to frustrate the contract, this will be regarded as 'self-induced frustration', and the contract will not be discharged. For example, if the fire that caused the destruction of the music hall in *Taylor v Caldwell*[49] had been the result of negligence by one of the parties, the contract probably would not have been frustrated. This is an obvious restriction, but it may not always be easy to determine the type of behaviour that should fall within its scope. An example of its application is *Maritime National Fish Ltd v Ocean Trawlers Ltd*.[50] The appellants chartered a trawler from the respondents. The trawler was fitted with an 'otter' trawl, which it was illegal to use without a licence, as both parties were aware. The appellants applied for five licences to operate otter trawls, but were only granted three. They decided to use these for boats other than the one chartered from the respondents. They claimed that this contract was therefore frustrated, since the trawler could not legally be used. The Privy Council held that the appellants were not discharged. It was their own election to use the licences with the other boats that had led to the illegality of using the respondents' trawler.

This decision seems fair where it is the case, as it was here, that the party exercising the choice could have done so without breaking any contract (since the trawlers to which the licences were assigned all belonged to the appellants).[51] It may not be so fair, however, if a person is put in a position where there is no choice but to break one of two contracts. Nevertheless, when this situation arose in *Lauritzen (J) AS v Wijsmuller BV, The Super Servant Two*,[52] the Court of Appeal applied the concept of self-induced frustration strictly.

---

**Key case** *Lauritzen (J) AS v Wijsmuller BV, The Super Servant Two* (1990)

Facts: The parties had made a contract for the transportation of a drilling rig, which, as they both knew, could only be carried out by one of two vessels owned by the defendants, namely, *Super Servant One* and *Super Servant Two*. The contract referred to both vessels, but did not specify which one would be used. The defendants, intending to use *Super Servant Two*, allocated *Super Servant One* to other contracts. *Super Servant Two* then sank. The defendants claimed that the contract was frustrated, but the plaintiffs alleged that the impossibility of performance arose from the defendants' own acts,[53] and that they should not therefore be discharged from performance.
Held: The Court of Appeal held that, even though the defendants were neither negligent nor in breach of contract in the way in which they had allocated the vessels, the

---

49  See above, 13.2.2.
50  [1935] AC 524.
51  Treitel (2015, p 1082) has argued that this element should be treated as an important part of the decision in *Maritime National Fish v Ocean Trawlers*.
52  [1990] 1 Lloyd's Rep 1.
53  That is, the contract was not automatically made impossible by the sinking of the *Super Servant Two,* which would have amounted to frustration, but only by the subsequent decision of the defendants not to use the *Super Servant One* for this contract.

doctrine of frustration did not operate to remove their liability under the contract with the plaintiffs.[54] Bingham LJ felt that it was:

> inconsistent with the doctrine of frustration as previously understood on high authority that its application should depend on any decision, however reasonable and commercial, of the party seeking to rely on it.

It seems then that any exercise of choice by one of the parties that contributes to a situation where the contract becomes impossible, or radically different, will prevent the doctrine of frustration from applying.

The *Super Servant Two* decision has been strongly criticised by Treitel. In his view, the situation was distinguishable from that in the *Maritime National Fish* case, because there the defendant had a choice about whether any contracts were broken or not. Moreover, to the extent that the basis of the decision in *Super Servant Two* is that it was within the shipowners' control as to what contracts were made and what risks were undertaken, this 'seems to undermine the whole basis of the doctrine of frustration: it has just as much force where the promisor enters into a single contract as where he enters into two or more, with different contracting parties'.[55]

Despite these criticisms, the decision in *Super Servant Two* has not been the subject of any reported challenge so perhaps it is not such a difficult decision for the commercial world to cope with as might appear at first sight.

### 13.4.2 EVENTS FORESEEN AND PROVIDED FOR[56]

One way in which the parties can avoid the situation discussed in the previous subsection, and its perceived unfairness, is by including specific provision in the contract to deal with that situation. Indeed, in *Super Servant Two*, it was held that the defendants could take advantage of a specific *force majeure* clause, provided that the sinking of the vessel was not due to their negligence, even though the contract was not frustrated as far as the common law was concerned. As was noted at the start of this chapter, a *force majeure* clause is one that the parties have inserted to cover various eventualities outside their control, which may affect the contract. It will provide the way in which risks and consequential losses are to be distributed in such circumstances. The existence of such a clause, covering the facts that have arisen, will often prevent the contract from being frustrated. It will not inevitably do so, however, as is shown by *Jackson v Union Marine Insurance Co Ltd*.[57] A ship was chartered in November 1871 to proceed with all possible dispatch 'damages and accidents of navigation excepted' from Liverpool to Newport and there to

---

54  The court did hold, however, that the defendants could rely on a *force majeure* clause included in the contract, provided that the sinking of the *Super Servant Two* did not result from their negligence (or that of their employees). For discussion of this aspect of the case, see McKendrick, 1995b, pp 323–27.

55  Treitel, 2014, pp 537–40; Treitel, 2015, p 1082. McKendrick (1995b, pp 323–27) considers, but rejects, an alternative argument that allowing greater scope to frustration than was the case in *Super Servant Two* would decrease transaction costs, in that it would reduce the need for the negotiation of complex *force majeure* clauses: such a move would increase uncertainty, and a wider legal rule enforced by the courts would not provide the flexible outcomes that parties can devise for themselves by specially constructed clauses.

56  On events foreseen and not provided for, see *The Eugenia* [1964] 2 QB 226 at 239 per Lord Denning MR, *Edwinton Commercial Corp v Tsavliris Russ Worldwide Salvage & Towage Ltd* [2007] EWCA Civ 547 at [127] and *Armchair Answercall Limited v People in Mind Limited* [2016] EWCA Civ 1039 at [30].

57  (1874) LR 10 CP 125.

load a cargo for carriage to San Francisco. She sailed on 2 January but, before reaching Newport, ran aground off the Welsh coast. On 15 February, the charterers abandoned the charter and found another ship. On 18 February, the ship got off, but repairs were not finished until August. The shipowner brought an action against the charterers for failure to load. It was held by the Exchequer Chamber that the exception in the contract absolved the shipowner from liability in the event of delay, but did not give him the right to sue if the delay was bad enough to frustrate the contract. This was the situation here, and so the shipowner's action failed.

---

**For thought**

*Do you think the answer in this case would have been the same if the ship had been ready to load on 18 February?*

---

A similar conclusion was reached in *Metropolitan Water Board v Dick Kerr*,[58] where the contract contained a provision for extension of the time for performance in the event of delays 'howsoever caused'. It was held by the House of Lords that this provision was only meant to deal with temporary delays, and did not:[59]

cover the case in which the interruption is of such a character and duration that it vitally and fundamentally changes the conditions of the contract, and could not possibly have been in the contemplation of the parties to the contract when it was made.

This suggests that the parties need to be very specific if they intend a clause to deal with circumstances that would otherwise amount to frustration. It is likely, however, that in modern circumstances, the courts will have regard to the fact that *force majeure* clauses are a common feature of commercial contracts and will attempt to interpret them in the light of the purposes that such clauses are intended to fulfil.[60]

### 13.4.3 LAND

A contract for the sale of land can apparently be frustrated. This must have been assumed to be the case in *Amalgamated Investment and Property Co Ltd v John Walker & Sons Ltd*,[61] since otherwise there would have been no need to consider whether the listing of a building could have such an effect. In practice, the buyer of land will virtually always insure it from the point of exchange of contracts, and so the issue of frustration will be unlikely to arise.

In relation to leases, at one time it seemed as though frustration was not possible. Although it is clear that the doctrine of frustration can apply to contracts to use property on the basis of a licence, as in *Taylor v Caldwell*[62] and *Krell v Henry*,[63] this was not necessarily the case with a lease, which involves the tenant taking a legal interest in the land itself

---

58 [1918] AC 119 – see above, 13.3.5.
59 [1918] AC 119, p 126.
60 There is, however, an argument that *force majeure* clauses are in effect exclusion clauses falling within the scope of the UCTA 1977 (see Wheeler and Shaw, 1994, p 760).
61 [1983] QB 84; [1981] 3 All ER 577 – see above, 13.3.5.
62 (1863) 3 B & S 826; 122 ER 309 – see above, 13.2.2.
63 [1903] 2 KB 740 – see above, 13.3.3.

(rather than the contractual right to use the land which is involved in a licence). The issue was raised in *Cricklewood Property Investment Trust v Leighton's Investment Trusts Ltd*.[64] This concerned a building lease, which was expressed to last for 99 years from May 1936. Following the outbreak of the Second World War in 1939, legislation was passed that prohibited building. The tenant claimed that the lease was frustrated. Two members of the House of Lords expressed the view that a lease could never be frustrated, while two others thought that it could if, for example, the land were washed into the sea, or became subject to a permanent ban on building. The fifth member of the panel refused to express a view on this issue, but agreed with the decision that on the facts there was in any case no frustration, because there were still 90 years left on the lease once the wartime restrictions were lifted.

The matter did not arise for decision again until 1981, and the case of *National Carriers Ltd v Panalpina (Northern) Ltd*.[65] This contract concerned a ten-year lease of a warehouse. After five years, the local authority closed the street, preventing access, because of problems with another (listed) building in the street. The closure was likely to last for about 18 months. There would, therefore, have been some three years of the lease to run after the street reopened. The tenants, however, stopped paying rent, on the basis that the contract had been frustrated. The House of Lords took the view (Lord Russell dissenting) that there was no reason in logic or law why a lease should not be frustrated in a situation where no substantial use of a kind permitted by the lease and contemplated by the parties remained possible for the lessee. Thus, even where the land itself remained available, rather than slipping into the sea or being covered by sand, the lease could be frustrated if its purpose had been frustrated. On the facts of the case, however, the interruption to the availability of the premises was not sufficient to amount to frustration, and the landlords' action for the rent therefore succeeded.

## 13.5 EFFECTS OF FRUSTRATION: COMMON LAW

The effects of a frustrating event are dealt with both by common law rules and the provisions of the Law Reform (Frustrated Contracts) Act 1943. This section deals with the common law, and section 13.6 with the Act. It is in this context that the objectives of the doctrine become particularly important. Why are contracts held to be 'frustrated'? Is it simply to relieve one or other of the parties of the unfair burden of continuing obligations which have become impossible? Or is it to attempt to make a fair distribution of the losses that have arisen from an unpredictable event that was not the fault of either party?[66] As will be seen, the common law tends to take the first view, while the statutory intervention may be seen as a move towards the second. A further possibility, not so far adopted by English law but suggested by the proposed European Draft Common Frame of Reference,[67] is that the frustrating event should lead to renegotiation of the contract, to take account of the changed circumstances.

### 13.5.1 AUTOMATIC TERMINATION

The first point to note is that the common law regards the frustrating event as automatically bringing the contract to an end. It is not a situation such as that which arises in relation to (some types of) mistake, misrepresentation or breach of contract, where one party can decide, notwithstanding what has happened, that the contract should continue. The

---

64  [1945] AC 221; [1945] 1 All ER 252.
65  [1981] AC 675; [1981] 1 All ER 161.
66  Or, to put it in other words, to decide upon the appropriate allocation of risks in relation to such an event.
67  Art III. – 1:110(3)(d). See generally Unberath and McKendrick, 2013.

application of this rule can be seen in *Hirji Mulji v Cheong Yue Steamship*.[68] By a charter-party entered into in November 1916, shipowners agreed that their ship, the *Singaporean*, should be placed at the charterers' disposal on 17 March 1917 for ten months. Shortly before this date, the ship was requisitioned by the government. The shipowners thought the ship would soon be released, and asked the charterers if they would still be willing to take up the charter when this happened. The charterers said that they would. In fact, the ship was not released until February 1919, at which point the charterers refused to accept it. The shipowners argued that the charterers had affirmed the contract after the frustrating event, and were therefore still bound. The House of Lords held that affirmation was not possible. The frustrating event automatically brought the contract to an end, and discharged both the shipowners and the charterers from their obligations.

### 13.5.2 FUTURE OBLIGATIONS ONLY DISCHARGED

It is important to note that frustration, unlike an operative common law mistake, does not render a contract void *ab initio*. Its effect is to bring the contract to an end prematurely, but all existing obligations at the time of the contract remain unaffected, as far as the common law is concerned. If money has been paid or property transferred, it cannot generally be recovered, and if valuable services have been provided, compensation cannot be claimed.

Thus, in *Krell v Henry*,[69] the hirer of the room had paid a deposit, which was irrecoverable. On the other hand, the obligation to pay the balance did not, under the terms of the contract, arise until after the date on which the coronation procession was cancelled. This, therefore, was also irrecoverable by the owner of the room. By contrast, in *Chandler v Webster*[70] (another case on the hiring of a room to view the coronation), under the terms of the contract, the obligation to pay arose before the frustrating event occurred. In this case, it was held that not only could money paid not be recovered, but the obligation to pay money due (but not in fact paid) before the event was cancelled remained. Because frustration only discharged the contract from the point when the event occurred, the court refused to regard this as a case where there was a total failure of consideration, which might have justified recovery on a restitutionary basis.[71]

This aspect of Chandler v Webster was, however, overruled by the House of Lords in *Fibrosa Spolka Ackyjna v Fairbairn Lawson Combe Barbour Ltd*.[72]

---

**Key case** *Fibrosa Spolka Ackyjna v Fairbairn Lawson Combe Barbour Ltd* (1942)

Facts: An English company (the respondents) had made a contract to supply machinery to a Polish company (the appellants). The appellants had paid £1,000 towards this contract. It was then frustrated by the German invasion of Poland in 1939. The appellants sought to recover the £1,000.

Held: The House of Lords held that since they had received nothing at all under the contract, there had been a total failure of consideration and recovery was therefore possible.

---

This decision, that in cases of total failure of consideration, money can be recovered, is probably an improvement on *Chandler v Webster*, but it still leaves two areas of difficulty

---

68 [1926] AC 497. On the relevance of the subsequent actions of the parties see *Armchair Answercall Limited v People in Mind Limited* [2016] EWCA Civ 1039 at [51].

69 [1903] 2 KB 740 – see above, 13.3.3.

70 [1904] 1 KB 493.

71 The area of restitution is considered in Chapter 15, 15.8.

72 [1943] AC 32; [1942] 2 All ER 122.

and potential injustice. First, it can only apply where the failure of consideration is total. If the other party has provided something, no matter how little, no recovery will be possible. Second, it takes no account of the fact that the party who has received the money may well have incurred expenses in relation to the contract, and so will end up out of pocket if the entire sum has to be refunded. Both of these difficulties are addressed to some extent by the Law Reform (Frustrated Contracts) Act 1943.[73]

This Act also attempts to tackle another limitation of the common law, which is exemplified by *Appleby v Myers*.[74] In this case, the contract was for the erection of machinery on the defendant's premises. Payment was to be made on completion of the work. When the work was nearly finished, the whole premises, including the machinery, were destroyed by fire. The contract was undoubtedly frustrated, but the question was whether the plaintiffs could recover any compensation for the work they had done. The answer was no. The obligation to pay had not arisen at the time the contract was frustrated, and therefore the plaintiffs were entitled to nothing.

The common law approach, based on relieving from future obligations, thus led to the potential injustices outlined above. More fundamentally, the result in a particular case would depend entirely on the timing of obligations under the contract. Thus, the distinction between *Krell v Henry* and *Chandler v Webster* arose purely from the fact that in the former case payment was to be paid in two instalments, while in the latter the entire payment was due at the start of the contract. It is clearly unsatisfactory, and serves no discernible policy,[75] that the same factual situation should give rise to such different results simply on this basis. The courts proved incapable, however, of developing a more satisfactory set of rules,[76] and eventually statutory reform was put in place.

## 13.6 EFFECTS OF FRUSTRATION: THE LAW REFORM (FRUSTRATED CONTRACTS) ACT 1943

Before considering the provisions of s 1(2) and (3), which contain the most significant provisions of the Law Reform (Frustrated Contracts) Act (LR(FC)A) 1943, it must be noted that not all contracts are within its scope. Section 2(5) indicates that the Act does not apply:

(a)    to any charterparty, except a time charterparty or a charterparty by way of demise,[77] or to any contract (other than a charterparty) for the carriage of goods by sea;[78] or

(b)    to any contract of insurance,[79] save as is provided by sub-section (5) of the foregoing section;[80] or

---

73   See below, 13.6.

74   (1867) LR 2 CP 651.

75   Other than possibly that of 'freedom of contract': but if this is to be the governing principle, then why not return to *Paradine v Jane* (1647) Aleyn 26; 82 ER 897 – above, 13.2.1?

76   Other than the relatively minor development as regards 'total failure of consideration' in the *Fibrosa* case. This occurred just before the statutory reform: it is arguable, therefore, that the courts would in time have built on the *Fibrosa* decision to produce a more flexible set of remedies for frustration.

77   The effect of this is basically that the Act does not apply to charterparties for a particular voyage (voyage charterparties), but does apply to all other charterparties.

78   This exclusion is apparently based on the fact that established rules in shipping law dealing with the loss or misdelivery of freight should be allowed to stand: see Treitel, 2015, p 1094.

79   This obviously complies with the normal view of an insurance contract as representing in itself the parties' decision as to the allocation of risk. Its effect is that if, for example, goods are destroyed in a way not covered by the insurance policy, the owner is not allowed to claim a return of the premiums paid.

80   Section 1(5) provides that in deciding on the distribution of losses under s 1(2) or (3) (which is discussed below at 13.6.1 and 13.6.2), the court should ignore any contract of insurance, unless there was an express obligation to insure.

(c)    to any contract to which [section 7 of the Sale of Goods Act 1979] ... applies, or to any other contract for the sale, or the sale and delivery, of specific goods, where the contract is frustrated by reason of the fact that the goods have perished.

Section 7 of the Sale of Goods Act (SGA) 1979 provides that:

> where there is an agreement to sell specific goods, and subsequently the goods, without any fault on the part of the seller or buyer, perish before the risk passes to the buyer, the agreement is thereby avoided.

An 'agreement to sell' is a contract under which ownership has not yet passed to the buyer. 'Risk' will normally pass at the same time as 'ownership',[81] though the parties may make a different agreement if they so wish. 'Specific goods' are those that are identified at the time of the agreement, as opposed to generic goods, which are sold by description. Thus, a contract to buy 'all the grain currently in X warehouse' would be a contract for specific goods; a contract to buy 'five tonnes of grain' (which can come from any source) would be a contract for generic goods. The former contract would fall within the scope of s 7 of the SGA 1979, and would therefore not be subject to the 1943 Act if X warehouse burnt down, destroying all the grain before the risk had passed to the buyer. The contract would be 'avoided' by s 7, and the common law rules on the effects of frustration would apply.[82] The latter contract would not generally be capable of being frustrated, since the buyer is not concerned with where the seller obtains the grain; but if the contract specified a particular source for the grain (for example, 'five tonnes of the 100 tonnes currently held in X warehouse'), then the contract could be frustrated by the total destruction of the source.[83] In that case, the 1943 Act would apply to the contract rather than the common law rules. There seems to be no good reason for these distinctions, which seem to serve no sensible policy. It would surely be preferable for all sale of goods contracts to be treated in the same way.

Section 2(3) of the LR(FC)A 1943 states:

> Where any contract to which this Act applies contains any provision which, upon the true construction of the contract, is intended to have effect in the event of circumstances arising which operate, or would but for the said provision operate, to frustrate the contract, or is intended to have effect whether such circumstances arise or not, the court shall give effect to the said provision and shall only give effect to the foregoing section of this Act to such extent, if any, as appears to the court to be consistent with the said provision.

This makes it clear that the parties may reach their own agreement as to what the effects of frustration are going to be. In this situation, again, the LR(FC)A 1943 may have no application. The parties are deemed to be best placed to decide where the risks should lie, and it is only by default that the court will intervene.

---

81  Sale of Goods Act 1979, s 20. Contrast Consumer Rights Act 2015, s 29. On the changes to the law relating to the sale of goods made by the Consumer Rights Act 2015 see, in particular, above at 6.7.

82  Thus, if the buyer had made a payment, this may be recoverable on the basis of a total failure of consideration on the *Fibrosa* principle.

83  See *Howell v Coupland* (1876) 1 QBD 258 – contract for 200 tons of potatoes to be grown on a specified piece of land. Failure of the crop led to the frustration of the contract. See also *CTI Group Inc v Transclear SA* [2008] EWCA Civ 856 at [23].

## 13.6.1 SECTION 1(2): MONEY PAID OR PAYABLE PRIOR TO FRUSTRATION

Section 1(2) of the LR(FC)A 1943 deals with the *Chandler v Webster*, or *Fibrosa*, type of situation – that is, where money has been paid or is owed under the contract before the frustrating event takes place. It states:

> All sums paid or payable to any party in pursuance of the contract before the time when the parties were so discharged [that is, by frustration] ... shall, in the case of sums so paid, be recoverable from him as money received by him for the use of the party by whom the sums were paid, and, in the case of sums so payable, cease to be so payable.

In other words, in such a situation, money paid is recoverable, and money owed ceases to be payable. To that extent the section adopts and extends the *Fibrosa* decision, in that the rule now applies even where there is not a total failure of consideration. Subject to the provisions of s 1(3),[84] concerning the conferring of valuable benefits, there can be recovery of sums paid even where there has been partial performance by the other side.

There is, however, a proviso to s 1(2),[85] which is designed to limit the potential injustice in the *Fibrosa* decision, that is, even where there is a total failure of consideration, the other party may have incurred expenses in getting ready to perform. The section accordingly provides that if the party to whom sums were paid or payable:

> incurred expenses before the time of discharge in, or for the purposes of, the performance of the contract, the court may, if it considers it just to do so having regard to all the circumstances of the case, allow him to retain or, as the case may be, recover the whole of the sums paid or payable, not being an amount in excess of the expenses so incurred.

It is important to note two limitations on this attempt to spread the losses of frustration between the parties.[86] First, the recovery of expenses can only take place where there was an obligation to pay some money prior to the frustrating event. If the contract provided for the entire payment to become due only on completion of the contract, then there will be no scope for the recovery of expenses under s 1(2). Second, even if some money was paid or payable, it is possible that the expenses will exceed this amount, and so will not be fully recoverable. For example, if on a contract worth £5,000 a deposit of £500 has been paid, but the other party has incurred expenses of £750, the maximum that can be retained under s 1(2) is £500. The remaining £250 is irrecoverable, unless s 1(3)[87] can be brought into play.[88]

Finally, even if expenses have been incurred that could be compensated by money paid or payable, this cannot be claimed as of right. It is at the court's discretion to decide whether or not there should be any recovery of expenses, depending on its view as to whether this would be just in all the circumstances.

---

84  See below, 13.6.2.

85  See above, 13.5.2.

86  Goff J, however, stated in *BP Exploration Co (Libya) Ltd v Hunt (No 2)* [1982] 1 All ER 925 that the purpose of the 1943 Act was not to apportion losses, but to prevent unjust enrichment.

87  Below, 13.6.2.

88  Campbell has argued that the effect of the proviso contained in s 1(2) is to confuse the restitution and reliance interests, and, in effect, that the job that the proviso is intended to do would have been better left to s 1(3). In particular, the cap on the recovery of expenses is 'a limit alien to the reliance interest with no clear justification'. The result is 'a curious hybrid unknown to reliance or restitution' with 'no sound foundation in either principle': Harris, Campbell and Halson, 2002, Chapter 16, p 248.

**Key case** *Gamerco SA v ICM/Fair Warning Agency* (1995)[89]

Facts: The plaintiffs were claiming the repayment of $412,500 paid in connection with a pop concert, which could not take place because the government had, on safety grounds, closed the stadium at which it was to be held. The defendants wished to retain an amount to cover their expenses. On the facts, there were considerable difficulties in calculating the defendants' expenses, but the judge estimated that they might have amounted to $50,000.

Held: The court confirmed that the use of a broad discretion, rather than any other particular formula (for example, sharing losses equally) was the correct approach to the application of the proviso under s 1(2). In all the circumstances, and taking account of the plaintiffs' loss (around $450,000), the judge concluded that justice would be done if the money paid by the plaintiffs (that is, the $412,500) was returned without deduction.

**For thought**

*Is this the best approach, or does it leave matters too vague and uncertain? Would it be better simply to try to share the losses equally between the parties, given that the contract has come to an end without any fault on the part of either party to the contract? If the courts adopted such an approach, would it encourage parties to settle rather than litigate in relation to frustrated contracts?*

The decision emphasises the very broad power that the court has in relation to the proviso to s 1(2).

### 13.6.2 SECTION 1(3): COMPENSATION FOR A 'VALUABLE BENEFIT'

Section 1(3) of the LR(FC)A 1943 provides that where a party to a contract has obtained a 'valuable benefit' (other than money) before the time of discharge, the other party can obtain compensation for having provided this. Suppose, then, that D has contracted to hire C's hall for a series of ten concerts, with the entire fee to be payable at the end of the contract. If after one concert the hall is destroyed by fire, under the common law, C would not be able to recover anything from D. By virtue of s 1(3), however, C would be entitled to seek compensation from D in relation to the use of the hall for the one concert that took place. D would have received a 'valuable benefit' in the use of the hall for one concert. As with s 1(2), recovery is not available as of right, but is in the discretion of the court, which can award what it considers just in all the circumstances, up to the value of the benefit to the party obtaining it. In particular, the court is directed to take into account, by virtue of s 1(3)(a), any expenses incurred by the party obtaining the benefit, and also, by virtue of s 1(3)(b), the effect, in relation to the benefit, of the circumstances that frustrated the contract.

This provision would seem at first sight to provide a more satisfactory outcome to the case of *Appleby v Myers*,[90] in that it might allow the supplier of the machinery to recover compensation for the work that had been done. This depends, however, on whether the 'valuable benefit' has to be judged before or after the frustrating event has occurred. If it is the former, then some compensation may be possible; if it is the latter, then the other party

---

89  [1995] 1 WLR 1126.
90  (1867) LR 2 CP 651 – above, 13.5.2.

may well argue that no benefit has in the end been received, since the machinery was not completed, and was in any case destroyed by the fire.

These issues were considered in some detail by Goff J, as he then was, in the key case on s 1(3) of the LR(FC)A 1943, *BP Exploration Co (Libya) Ltd v Hunt (No 2)*.[91] The case concerned oil concessions that had been frustrated by expropriation by the Libyan government. Goff J started by stating that the underlying principle of the Act was not the apportionment of losses, but the prevention of the 'unjust enrichment' of one party to a frustrated contract at the expense of the other. He then approached s 1(3) on the basis that it involves two tasks: first, the identification of the 'valuable benefit'[92] and, second, the determination of the 'just sum' to be awarded, the amount of which is capped by the 'valuable benefit'. In relation to the first task, he noted that s 1(3)(b) of the Act states that the court should take into account 'the effect, in relation to the said benefit, of the circumstances giving rise to the frustration of the contract'. He therefore came to the conclusion that 'benefit' means the 'end product' of what the plaintiff has provided, not the value of the work that has been done. Thus, he concluded:[93]

Suppose that a contract for work on a building is frustrated by fire which destroys the building and which, therefore, also destroys a substantial amount of work already done by the plaintiff. Although it might be thought just to award the plaintiff a sum assessed on a *quantum meruit* basis ... in respect of the work he has done, the effect of s 1(3)(b) will be to reduce the award to nil, because of the effect, in relation to the defendant's benefit, of the circumstances giving rise to the frustration of the contract.

In other words, he adopted the second of the approaches outlined in the previous paragraph as regards the assessment of the benefit.

### 13.6.3 IN FOCUS: CRITICISM OF GOFF J'S ANALYSIS

Goff J's analysis is not accepted as correct by all commentators. Treitel and Peel, for example, argue that although the Act makes reference to the relevance of the effect of the frustrating circumstances, this should be interpreted as applying to the assessment of the 'just sum' to be awarded (as discussed below), rather than the valuation of the benefit itself.[94] Goff J's judgment, however, having been upheld by the Court of Appeal and the House of Lords,[95] must be taken to represent the current law on this issue. As a result, it is clear that in a case such as *Appleby v Myers*, the answer given by the LR(FC)A 1943 is the same as that under the common law, and that no compensation will be recoverable for the work that has been done, because, once the frustrating event has occurred, it is of no value to the other party.

As has been noted, Goff J's conclusion as to the effect of s 1(3) has been criticised, but much of this criticism has been directed at the poor drafting of the section rather than his analysis of it.[96] Goff J himself clearly had sympathy with the argument that the provision of services should in itself be regarded as a 'benefit' even if those services lost their value as a result of the frustrating event.[97] But he felt obliged to find that the true construction of the Act led to the opposite conclusion.

---

91  [1982] 1 All ER 925. The Court of Appeal and the House of Lords dismissed appeals against the first instance decision, but without any detailed consideration of Goff's analysis of the 1943 Act: [1983] 2 AC 352.
92  Ibid, p 939.
93  See, generally, Treitel, 2015, p 1091.
94  Though without any detailed consideration of the operation of s 1(3).
95  See, generally, *Benedetti v Sawiris* [2013] UKSC 50.
96  But see Haycroft and Waksman, 1984 for criticism of the judgment itself.
97  [1982] 1 All ER 925, p 940.

## 13.6.4 CALCULATING THE 'JUST SUM'

The second element in the process under s 1(3), once the valuable benefit has been determined, is the calculation of the 'just sum' to be awarded. Goff J took the view that the basic measure of recovery should be:[98]

> the reasonable value of the plaintiff's performance: in case of services, a *quantum meruit* or reasonable remuneration, and in the case of goods, a *quantum valebat* or reasonable price.[99]

This, however, is subject to the limitation that the amount awarded cannot exceed the 'valuable benefit' that the defendant has received. If, therefore, as a consequence of the frustrating event, the valuable benefit is nil, then the just sum will also, inevitably, be nil.

The facts of *BP v Hunt* were concerned with the value of the exploitation by BP of oil concessions granted to Hunt by the Libyan government. These concessions had later been withdrawn by a subsequent government, with the proceeds being expropriated. BP were seeking compensation for the work done in exploiting the concessions. Applying the approach outlined above, Goff J found that the eventual benefit to Hunt, following the frustration, consisted of the value of the oil that he had received, plus the compensation from the Libyan government.[100] This produced a 'benefit' of £85m. The 'just sum' was, on the other hand, based on the value of the services that BP had provided to Hunt, less the value of the oil which BP had itself received under the contract. This produced a figure of £35m which, being less than the 'valuable benefit', was awarded in full.

## 13.6.5 CONCLUSIONS ON THE LAW REFORM (FRUSTRATED CONTRACTS) ACT 1943

The 1943 Act has been the subject of strong criticism. McKendrick has noted that it 'suffers from a number of deficiencies' and agrees with the view of the British Columbia Law Commission that it 'was not well thought out or drafted'.[101] Campbell comments:[102]

> As there are but a handful of Acts of Parliament which affect the basic structure of remedies for breach of contract, it is rather dismal to note that this one is so poorly drafted that it has given rise to problems of interpretation out of all proportion to its short length, and has brought very limited improvement to the common law.

Some of the criticism pulls in opposite directions, however. McKendrick is unhappy that so much discretion is left to trial judges, and suggests that it is 'regrettable that the Court of Appeal [in *BP v Hunt*] did not establish guidelines to assist ... and to ensure a measure of consistency'.[103] Campbell, on the contrary, sees this 'abhorrence of discretion' as 'misguided':[104]

> Dispute resolution in this area is, *ex hypothesi*, highly contingent upon the unforeseen empirical circumstances of each case, and therefore it is pointless to regret that the law cannot develop detailed rules. The pursuit of such rules continues to

---

98 [1982] 1 All ER 925, p 942.

99 Campbell argues that this approach to the just sum, equating it with the value of the services provided, effectively reduces the two-stage process to one: Harris, Campbell and Halson, 2002, p 250.

100 The enhanced value of the concession resulting from BP's work could not be included as part of the benefit, because this had been lost as a result of the frustrating event.

101 McKendrick, 1995a, p 243. See also Stewart and Carter, 1992.

102 Harris, Campbell and Halson, 2002, p 252.

103 McKendrick, 1995a, p 238.

104 Harris, Campbell and Halson, 2002, pp 252–53.

hinder explicit recognition of the use of discretion which the nature of the case and not the shortcomings of the statute make necessary.

There is nothing wrong, in his view, with giving the trial judge discretion, as long as this is not 'unbridled', and is focused on achieving 'rescission'.[105]

While Campbell's criticisms of the 1943 Act may be over-harsh (it is hard to see that it is not an improvement on the common law), his view on the role of discretion is to be preferred to McKendrick's in this situation. If the parties want certainty, which is one of the reasons for having clear legal rules, then they can achieve this through a *force majeure* clause, as we have seen that commercial contractors generally do. The point where frustration becomes important is exactly where what has happened was unpredictable. There is therefore little point in suggesting that contractual planning can be made more efficient in this area by the adoption of fixed rules. A discretion that enables a judge to take account of the context of the contract, and in particular the business context (where relevant), in deciding where losses should fall, is to be preferred. The problem with the 1943 Act is not that it allows for too much discretion, but that it constrains that discretion in the wrong ways.[106]

There has been very little case law on the 1943 Act, and this might be thought to indicate that it is in practice a successful piece of legislation. Campbell, however, suggests that the more likely explanation is that 'competent commercial parties' will have included provisions in their contracts to allow for alternative dispute resolution or arbitration, which will give them 'far more flexibility to apportion loss than any conceivable restitutionary recasting of the frustration rules might do'.[107] This again supports the view that a flexible rather than a rigid law on the effects of frustration would be more likely to meet the needs of the business world.

## 13.7 SUMMARY OF KEY POINTS

- A contract is frustrated when an event beyond the control of either party makes continued performance impossible or radically different from what was agreed. It is not enough that the contract is made more difficult or expensive.

- Types of frustrating event include:
  - □ destruction of the subject matter;
  - □ personal incapacity;
  - □ government action;
  - □ non-occurrence of event;
  - □ effects of war.

- If a decision of the party unable to perform has contributed to the frustration, it may be regarded as 'self-induced', and the doctrine of frustration will not apply.

- The parties may have provided for the circumstances that have occurred by contractual terms. If so, the doctrine of frustration will not generally apply.

---

105 By which Campbell means returning the parties to their positions prior to the agreement.
106 As is demonstrated by Goff J's judgment in *BP v Hunt*.
107 Harris, Campbell and Halson, 2002, p 253. Campbell cites in support of this the empirical evidence of the non-use of contract by business people provided by the work of Macaulay and others – see Macaulay, 1963; Beale and Dugdale, 1975.

■  At common law the effect of frustration is to terminate the contract and absolve
   the parties from all future obligations, but:

   □  obligations that had arisen prior to the frustrating event subsist, except that
      if there is a total failure of consideration, money paid can be recovered;

   □  there can be no compensation for work done prior to the frustrating event
      for which payment was not due until after the event.

■  The Law Reform (Frustrated Contracts) Act 1943 provides that:

   □  money paid prior to a frustrating event can be recovered, subject to the
      deduction of expenses (as approved by the court);

   □  compensation (to the extent considered just by the court) can be provided
      for benefits from the contractual performance which survive the frustrating
      event.

■  The 1943 Act does not apply to all contracts.


## 13.8 FURTHER READING

### Generally

■  Harris, D, Campbell, D and Halson, R, *Remedies in Contract and Tort*, 2nd edn,
   2002, London: Butterworths, Chapter 16

■  Hedley, S, 'Carriage by sea: frustration and *force majeure*' (1990) 49 CLJ 209

■  McKendrick, E (ed), *Force Majeure*, 2nd edn, 1995a, London: Lloyd's of London
   Press

■  McKendrick, E, 'The regulation of long-term contracts in English law' (1995b),
   Chapter 12 in Beatson, J and Friedmann, D (eds), *Good Faith and Fault in
   Contract Law*, Oxford: Clarendon Press

■  Treitel, G H, *Frustration and Force Majeure*, 3rd edn, 2014, London: Sweet & Maxwell

### Effects

■  Haycroft, A M and Waksman, D M, 'Frustration and restitution' [1984] JBL 207

■  Stewart, A and Carter, J W, 'Frustrated contracts and statutory adjustment: the
   case for a reappraisal' [1992] CLJ 66


## COMPANION WEBSITE

*Now visit the companion website to:*

■  Revise and consolidate your knowledge of Frustration by tackling a series of
   multiple-choice questions on this chapter

■  Test your understanding of the chapter's key terms by using the flashcard glossary

■  Explore Frustration further by accessing a series of web links

# Discharge by performance or breach

## Contents

### 14.1 OVERVIEW

This chapter examines the discharge of a contract by either performance or breach. The most significant issues are as follows:

◼ Discharge by performance. The general rule is that performance must be precise and exact to discharge a contractor's obligations. This has the following consequences:

- ☐ In an 'entire' contract (where payment only becomes due on complete performance), payment only has to be made when performance is fully completed – there is generally no payment for partial performance, unless:
  - ☐ the other party has prevented completion of performance; or
  - ☐ the partial performance has been accepted; or
  - ☐ the court deems there to have been 'substantial performance'.
- ☐ In a 'divisible' contract a party may be entitled to payment for completion of particular stages.
- ◼ Time of performance. If performance is offered late, is the other party obliged to accept it? The general rule is that time is not 'of the essence' unless the parties have made it so. In particular:
  - ☐ under s 10 of the Sale of Goods Act 1979, time for payment is *prima facie* not 'of the essence' and so late payment is *prima facie* not a ground for rejection; but
  - ☐ the House of Lords did suggest that in *commercial* contracts, time is often of the essence.
- ◼ Where time is of the essence, even a very short delay will entitle the other party to terminate.
- ◼ Discharge by breach. Breach, however serious, does not necessarily create an entitlement to terminate a contract – a key question is when a breach entitles the other party to terminate ('repudiatory' breach). The answer, generally, depends on the type of term breached. The courts divide contractual terms into the following:
  - ☐ Conditions. Breach of a condition entitles the other party to terminate the contract (as well as claiming damages).
  - ☐ Warranties. Breach of warranty only entitles the other party to claim damages, not to terminate.
  - ☐ Innominate terms. The consequences of breach of an innominate term depend on the seriousness of the breach. If it deprives the other party of the main benefit of the contract, it will allow that party to terminate.
- ◼ Problem areas.
  - ☐ Long-term contracts. It may be difficult in a long-term contract to determine what level of breach will be repudiatory.
  - ☐ Instalment contracts. Similarly, there may be difficulties in determining how many instalments need to be defective to constitute a repudiatory breach.
- ◼ Anticipatory breach. If a party indicates in advance that it is not going to perform, the other party may elect to terminate immediately, rather than waiting for the date for performance to arrive.

## 14.2 INTRODUCTION

This chapter is concerned with ways in which contractual obligations may be discharged. We have already discussed one way in which this can happen in the previous chapter, under the doctrine of frustration. Contracts may also be discharged by express agreement. If both parties decide that neither of them wishes to carry on with a contract that contains continuing obligations, or in relation to which some parts are still executory, they may agree to bring it to an end early. The main problem that arises here is where the executory obligations are all on one side, so that the party who has completed performance *prima facie* receives no consideration for promising not to enforce the other party's obligations. This issue has already been dealt with in Chapter 3, in connection with the doctrine of consideration and, in particular, the concept of promissory estoppel, and so is not discussed further here.[1] The focus in this chapter is on discharge by performance or by breach: discharge in this context means (in broad terms) that all further obligations of either or both of the parties are at an end.

## 14.3 DISCHARGE BY PERFORMANCE

Once the parties have done all that they are bound to do under a contract, all 'primary' obligations will cease.[2] There may, of course, be some continuing 'secondary' obligations, such as the obligation to pay compensation if goods turn out to be defective at some point after sale and delivery.

The problem that concerns us here is what constitutes satisfactory performance. If there is some minor defect, does this negative discharge by performance? The practical importance of this relates primarily to the situation where performance by one side gives rise to the right to demand performance from the other. Most typically, this will occur where payment for goods or services is only to be made once the goods have been supplied or the services have been completed. Suppose there is some minor defect in what has been supplied – does this entitle the other party to withhold its own performance by refusing payment?

### 14.3.1 PERFORMANCE MUST BE PRECISE AND EXACT

The general rule under the classical law of contract is that performance must be precise and exact; and the courts have at times applied this very strictly. Consider, for example, two cases under the Sale of Goods Act 1893. In *Re Moore & Co and Landauer & Co*,[3] the defendants agreed to buy from the plaintiffs 3,000 tins of canned fruit. The fruit was to be packed in cases of 30 tins. When the goods were delivered, a substantial part of the consignment was packed in cases of 24 tins. It was held that this did not constitute satisfactory performance and the defendants were entitled to reject the whole consignment. Similarly, in *Arcos Ltd v EA Ronaasen & Son*,[4] the buyer had ordered timber staves for the purpose of making barrels. The contract description said that they should be ½ inch thick. Most of the consignment consisted of staves that were in fact *9/16* inch thick. They were still perfectly usable for making barrels. Nevertheless, it was held that this did not constitute satisfactory performance and the buyer was entitled to reject all the staves. In other words, in both these cases, the seller had not performed satisfactorily and so had not discharged his obligations under the contract.[5]

Both of these cases turned in part on the interpretation of s 13 of the Sale of Goods Act 1893, which implied an obligation to supply goods that matched their contract description. This obligation is now contained in s 13 of the Sale of Goods Act (SGA) 1979.[6] In recent years, the courts have been more generous in the application of this section (although it is not yet clear what approach the courts will adopt under s 11 of the Consumer Rights

---

1  See 3.10.1, 3.11.
2  For the distinction between primary and secondary obligations, see Lord Diplock in *Photo Production Ltd v Securicor Transport Ltd* [1980] AC 827, pp 848–49; [1980] 1 All ER 556, pp 565–66.
3  [1921] 2 KB 519.
4  [1933] AC 470.
5  Beale, Bishop and Furmston (2007, p 429) suggest that the reason for the courts' strict approach may have been that in many cases 'the goods were being bought for resale and the exact description might be important to some other buyer further down the chain'. The suspicion must be, however, that in at least some of these cases the buyer was simply trying to find a reason to escape from a bad bargain.
6  See Chapter 6, 6.6.12. Chapter 6 also discusses the recent reform of that part of the law.

Act 2015), and s 15A of the 1979 Act now prevents a business purchaser from unreasonably rejecting goods that are only slightly different from the contract description. A similar approach had previously been taken by the House of Lords in *Reardon Smith Line Ltd v Hansen-Tangen*,[7] where a tanker was built at a different yard to that specified in the contract, but in all other respects met the purchaser's requirements. The House of Lords refused to accept that, by analogy with s 13 of the SGA 1979, the tanker could be rejected for non-compliance with its contractual description. Lord Wilberforce commented that some of the cases on the Act were 'excessively technical and due for fresh examination'.[8]

The principle that in general each party is entitled to expect the other to perform to the letter of their agreement remains, however. This was confirmed by the Privy Council in *Union Eagle Ltd v Golden Achievement Ltd*,[9] which concerned a contract for the sale of a flat. Time for performance had been made 'of the essence', and under the contract the purchase price was to be tendered by 5 pm on a particular day. In fact, it was tendered at 5.10 pm. The Privy Council confirmed that this entitled the seller to repudiate the agreement and retain the deposit that had been paid. The interests of certainty meant that the court should, in this type of situation, strictly enforce what the parties had agreed.

This approach makes it imperative for the parties to be careful in making their contract to ensure that they allow for flexibility in their performance if that is likely to be a problem for them.[10]

### 14.3.2  PARTIAL PROVISION OF SERVICES

In the sale of goods cases, a failure to meet the terms of the contract often prevented the seller from claiming any compensation, even in relation to any goods supplied that did match the contract description. The buyer was often entitled to withhold performance (the payment of the price) because the seller had failed in its obligations. The same approach is applied to the provision of services. Here a person may have done a certain amount of work towards a contract and the question is whether there is any right to claim payment under the contract for what has been done if it does not amount to complete performance.

The starting point for the consideration of this issue is a case that is regarded as the classic example of the common law's insistence on complete performance.

---

**Key case** *Cutter v Powell* (1785)[11]

Facts: The defendant agreed to pay Cutter 30 guineas provided that he served as second mate on a voyage from Jamaica to Liverpool. The voyage began on 2 August. Cutter died on 20 September, when the ship was 19 days short of Liverpool. Cutter's widow brought an action to recover a proportion of the 30 guineas.
Held: The widow's action failed. The contract was interpreted as being an 'entire' contract for a lump sum and nothing was payable until it was completed. Thus, even though the defendant had had the benefit of Cutter's labour for a substantial part of the voyage, no compensation for this was recoverable.

---

7  [1976] 3 All ER 570.
8  Ibid, p 576. He made particular reference to *Re Moore & Co and Landauer & Co* in this context.
9  [1997] AC 514; [1997] 2 All ER 215.
10 As Collins (2003, p 293) points out in relation to the courts' general refusal to grant relief for change of circumstances making a contract more onerous (for which see Chapter 13), a strict liability rule 'provides an incentive for the parties to plan for risks and contingencies'.
11 (1785) 6 Term Rep 320; [1775–1802] All ER Rep 159. For the full background to the case, and the somewhat fortuitous route by which it has become a 'leading case', see Dockray, 2001.

One reason for this rather harsh decision seems to have been that the 30 guineas was about four times the normal wage for such a voyage. The court therefore looked on it as something of a gamble.[12] Cutter had agreed to take the chance of a larger lump sum at the end of the voyage, rather than to take wages paid on a weekly basis. This element of the decision was not picked up in later cases, however, and *Cutter v Powell* was taken to lay down a general rule that in 'entire' contracts (that is, where various obligations are to be performed in return for a lump sum payment at the end), nothing is payable until the contract has been fully completed.

### 14.3.3 DIVISIBLE CONTRACTS OR OBLIGATIONS[13]

One way to mitigate this rule, which has the potential to operate very harshly, is to find that the contract is not entire but divisible into sections, with the completion of each section giving rise to a right to some payment. Thus, if Cutter had been engaged at a certain rate per week, instead of for a lump sum for the whole voyage, his widow would probably have been able to recover for the time he had actually served.[14] This is now the standard position in relation to employment contracts: although a salary may be stated on an annual basis, a person who leaves part way through the year will expect to be paid *pro rata*, even if the contract was for a particular project that has not been completed, or for a fixed period of time that has not expired.[15]

This will also apply if there are concurrent but independent obligations. In *Bolton v Mahadeva*,[16] there was a contract to (a) install a central heating system, and (b) supply a bathroom suite. The central heating system turned out to be defective and there was no obligation to pay for this, but the supply of the bathroom suite was severable, and an appropriate proportion of the contract price was recoverable in relation to this obligation.[17]

### 14.3.4 NON PERFORMANCE DUE TO OTHER PARTY

If one party prevents the other from completing their obligations under an entire contract, the latter party (if they have performed) may be able to recover on a *quantum meruit* basis for the work already done. Thus, in *Planché v Colburn*,[18] the plaintiff recovered £50 towards the work that he had done in writing a book for a series that had then been cancelled by the defendants. The contract price had been £100 but the plaintiff had not completed the book at the time that the defendants brought the contract to an end. A claimant in this situation may also be able to recover damages for consequential losses.

### 14.3.5 ACCEPTANCE OF PARTIAL PERFORMANCE

If a party accepts partial performance, this may be sufficient in certain circumstances to discharge the other party's further obligations under the contract and moreover allow

12 Dockray (2001, p 673) suggests that the court may have misunderstood the factual background on this issue, in that Cutter's skill as a carpenter would be likely to have been of special value to Powell, making the rate of pay less extraordinary than it appeared.

13 It is common to refer to entire or divisible *contracts:* as Treitel (2015, pp 919–20) has pointed out, it would be more accurate to refer to entire or divisible *obligations*. See further below, 14.3.6.

14 See *Taylor v Laird* (1856) 25 LJ Ex 329: a plaintiff was employed to command a steamer at £50 per month for a particular voyage but subsequently abandoned the command. It was held that he could recover for the months for which he had served.

15 See also the Apportionment Act 1870, ss 2 and 5, which state that salaries shall be treated as 'accruing from day to day'.

16 [1972] 2 All ER 1322.

17 For further discussion of this case, see below, 14.3.6.

18 (1831) 8 Bing 14; [1824–34] All ER Rep 94. This case is discussed further in the context of 'restitution' in Chapter 15, 15.8.7.

that party to sue on a *quantum meruit* for the work already done. For example, suppose that goods are to be transported from London to Hull and the van breaks down en route. If the recipient of the goods agrees to take delivery at Doncaster, the carrier will be able to sue for a proportion of the carriage. In *Christy v Row*,[19] this rule was said to be based on a fresh agreement involving an implied promise to pay for the benefit received. In this case, there was a contract of carriage in relation to seven keels of coal, to be taken from Shields to Hamburg. Seven keels were delivered at Gluckstadt by arrangement with the consignee. It was held that the carrier was entitled to recover freight at the contract rate of £20 per keel.

This exception will not apply, however, if the party effectively has no option but to accept the performance.

---

**Key case** *Sumpter v Hedges* (1898)[20]

Facts: The plaintiff, a builder, contracted to build two houses and stables on the defendant's land for £565. The plaintiff did work to the value of £333 and then abandoned the contract because he had no money. The defendant finished the buildings himself, using building materials left by the plaintiff. The plaintiff brought an action to recover the value of the work he had done on the buildings.

Held: The Court of Appeal held that the plaintiff could not recover. Collins LJ pointed out, although in some circumstances an agreement to pay might be inferred from the acceptance of a benefit, nevertheless:[21]

> in order that that may be done, the circumstances must be such as to give an option to the defendant to take or not to take the benefit of the work done.

---

It would not be reasonable to expect the defendant to keep on his land a building that was in an incomplete state, and would constitute a nuisance.

### 14.3.6 SUBSTANTIAL PERFORMANCE

The principle of 'substantial performance' has the potential to constitute a more general exception.[22] It is based on the idea that where there is only a minor variation from the terms of the contract, the other party cannot claim to be discharged, but must rely on an action for damages for breach. The origins of it can be traced to *Boone v Eyre*,[23] a case concerning the sale of a plantation, together with its slaves. It was suggested by Lord Mansfield CJ that the fact that the seller could not establish ownership of every single slave stated to be included in the contract would not prevent him from recovering payment from the buyer under the agreement. The principle is, however, stated most clearly in *Dakin v Lee*[24] and *Hoenig v Isaacs*.[25]

---

19 (1808) 1 Taunt 300.
20 [1898] 1 QB 673.
21 Ibid, p 676.
22 It is argued by Treitel and Campbell that the doctrine of substantial performance can only apply to a severable obligation, since the claim that there can be substantial performance of an entire obligation is contradictory: see Treitel, 2015–1, p 922; Harris, Campbell and Halson, 2002, p 46.
23 (1779) 1 Hy Bl 273.
24 [1916] 1 KB 566.
25 [1952] 2 All ER 176.

**Key case** *Dakin v Lee* (1916)

Facts: The contract was for the repair of a house. The work was not done in accordance with the contract. In particular, the concrete underpinning was only half the contract depth; the columns to support a bay window were of 4 inch diameter solid iron, instead of 5 inch diameter hollow; and the joists over the bay window were not cleated at the angles or bolted to caps and to each other. The official referee found that the plaintiffs had not performed the contract, and therefore could not claim for any payment in respect of it. The plaintiff appealed.

Held: The Court of Appeal noted that there was a distinction between failing to complete[26] and completing badly. Here, the contract had been performed, though badly performed, and the plaintiff could recover for the work done, less deductions for the fact that it did not conform to the contract requirements.

A similar approach was taken in *Hoenig v Isaacs*, where there were found to be defects (which would cost £55 to repair) in work done in redecorating a flat. The total contract price was £750. It was held that there was substantial performance, and that the plaintiff could recover the contract price, less the cost of repairs.[27]

**For thought**

*If the repairs in Hoenig v Isaacs had cost £255 rather than £55, do you think this would have made a difference to the decision? If so, where would the 'tipping point' be between substantial and non-substantial performance as regards the cost of repairs?*

The Court of Appeal refused to apply substantial performance in *Bolton v Mahadeva*,[28] as regards the obligation to install a central heating system. The system as fitted gave out much less heat than it should have done and caused fumes in one of the rooms. Although the complete system had been fitted, it did not fulfil its primary function of heating the house, and so the installer was not allowed to recover.

The doctrine of substantial performance appears to be infrequently used and may not be of great significance in practice. That it is still available, however, was confirmed by the Court of Appeal in *Young v Thames Properties Ltd*.[29] The contract was for the construction of a car park. The main complaints of the defendant (the car park owner), who was resisting paying for the work, were that the sub-base consisted of limestone scalpings 30mm

---

26  As in *Sumpter v Hedges*; see 14.3.5 above.

27  Treitel (2015, p 922) explains *Hoenig v Isaacs* (and by implication *Dakin v Lee*) on the basis that the obligations as to the *quantity* of work to be done were severable from the obligations as to the *quality* of the work. The obligation as to quantity was entire; the obligation as to quality was not. There was no substantial failure of this obligation, so the plaintiff was entitled to recover. This analysis has some force, but it should be noted that in *Dakin v Lee* Pickford LJ specifically included the situation where the contractor is in breach by 'omitting some small portion of' the work as amounting to possible 'substantial performance', in addition to breach through 'doing his work badly': [1916] 1 KB 566, p 580. Similarly Lord Cozens-Hardy's example of a painter putting on two coats of paint rather than the specified three could be argued to go to 'quantity' rather than 'quality': ibid, p 579. Compare also *Foxholes Nursing Home Ltd v Accora Ltd* [2013] EWHC 3712.

28  [1972] 2 All ER 1322.

29  [1999] EWCA Civ 629.

**Performance generally must be precise and exact:**
*Arcos Ltd v EA Ronaasen & Son* (1933)
S 13 Sale of Goods Act 1979
Qualified for business purchaser – s 15A prevents rejection of goods which are only slightly different from description

**Partial provision of services:**
In entire contracts, nothing is payable until the contract has been fully completed (the 'entire obligation' rule):
*Cutter v Powell* (1785)

**Divisible contracts or obligations:**
Mitigates the entire obligation rule
Contract is divisible into sections – payment on discharge of each section:
*Bolton v Mahadeva* (1972)

**Discharge by performance**

**Non-performance due to other party:**
Can recover on a *quantum meruit* basis for work completed:
*Planche v Colburn* (1831)

**Acceptance of part performance:**
Operates to discharge the contract, unless party has no option but to accept:
*Sumpter v Hedges* (1898)

**Substantial performance:**
Where there is only a minor variation from contract terms, the other party cannot withhold payment, but must take action for damages:
*Hoenig v Isaacs* (1952)

Figure 14.1

deep when, according to the contract, they should have been 100mm deep, and that the wrong grade of tarmacadam had been used as the top surface. The judge accepted evidence that these defects made little practical difference to the quality of the car park and that the cost of remedying them (which would have involved taking up and relaying the whole area) would have been disproportionate. He held that the plaintiff was entitled to the contract price, less the amount that he had saved through the various failures to comply with the specifications. The Court of Appeal confirmed that the doctrine of substantial performance should be applied as laid down in *Dakin v Lee* and that, in particular, there was a difference between work that was abandoned and work that was completed and done badly. Approval was given to the following statement in the headnote to *Dakin v Lee*:[30]

> Where a builder has supplied work and labour for the creation or repair of a house under a lump sum contract, but has departed from the terms of the contract, he is entitled to recover for his services, unless: (1) the work that he has done has been of no benefit to the owner; (2) the work he has done is entirely different from the work which he has contracted to do; or (3) he has abandoned the work and left it unfinished.

In the end, however, 'the essence of the doctrine of substantial performance is that it depends on the nature of the contract and all the circumstances which arise in the present case'. The question of whether there had been substantial performance was one of fact and degree and, therefore, essentially an issue for the trial judge. On the facts, the judge had been entitled to conclude that the various defects that had been identified did not prevent a finding that there had been substantial performance; nor was there anything wrong with his approach to the calculation of the damages.

30 [1916] 1 KB 566.

The same approach was adopted by the Court of Appeal in *Williams v Roffey Bros & Nicholls (Contractors) Ltd*.[31] Applying *Hoenig v Isaacs*, it held that the trial judge had been entitled to find that there had been substantial completion of the work on eight flats, entitling the plaintiffs to payment.

## 14.4 TENDER OF PERFORMANCE

Being ready to perform a contract ('tender of performance') may be treated as equivalent to performance in the sense that, if it is rejected, it will lead to a discharge of the tenderer's liabilities. Thus, as s 28 of the SGA 1979 puts it, where the expectation is that goods will be paid for on delivery:

> the seller must be ready and willing to give possession of the goods to the buyer in exchange for the price and the buyer must be ready and willing to pay the price in exchange for the possession of the goods.

### 14.4.1 DEFINITION OF TENDER

What amounts to satisfactory 'tender', so as to bring the above principle into play? This will largely depend on the terms of the contract, but something of the approach of the courts can be seen from *Startup v Macdonald*.[32] The plaintiff agreed to sell 10 tons of oil to the defendant. Delivery was to be 'within the last 14 days of March'. Delivery was in fact tendered at 8.30 pm on 31 March, which was a Saturday. The defendant refused to accept or pay for the goods. It was held that, provided that the seller had actually found the other party and that there was time to examine the goods to check compliance with the contract, this was a satisfactory tender.

From this it will be seen that the requirements are that the tender should meet the strict terms of the contract and that it should be brought to the attention of the other party in time for any rights which might arise on tender to be exercised.

### 14.4.2 TENDER OF MONEY

If a debtor tenders payment, and this is not accepted, this does not cancel the obligation to pay. The debtor, however, is not obliged to attempt to pay again, but can wait until the creditor calls for payment.

The exact amount must be tendered. There is no legal obligation to give change, though of course in the majority of situations the creditor will be quite happy to do so.

There are particular statutory rules as to the maximum amounts of particular types of coin that will constitute 'legal tender'.[33]

## 14.5 TIME FOR PERFORMANCE

Is the time for performance important? Is time, as the courts put it, 'of the essence'? The common law said that it was, unless the parties had expressed a contrary intention. Equity took the opposite view, so that time was not of the essence unless the parties had specifically made it so. The equitable rule was given precedence in s 41 of the Law of Property

---

31  [1991] 1 QB 1; [1990] 1 All ER 512. The facts of this case are dealt with in Chapter 3, 3.9.9.
32  (1843) 6 Man & G 593.
33  Coinage Act 1971, s 2.

Act 1925, so that where under equity time is not of the essence, contractual provisions dealing with time should be interpreted in the same way at common law. Note also that s 10(1) of the SGA 1979 states that:

> Unless a different intention appears from the terms of the contract, stipulations as to time of payment are not of the essence of a contract of sale.[34]

The reference to the intention of the parties that appears in this section is of general application, as was confirmed by the House of Lords in *United Scientific Holdings Ltd v Burnley Borough Council*.[35] Refusing to be bound by the position as regards the common law and equitable rules prior to 1873, the House preferred to look at the nature of the contract itself. The dispute concerned the operation of a rent review clause within a 99-year lease. The House held that time was not of the essence as far as the activation of the review machinery was concerned, so that the landlord was able to put it in motion even though he had just missed the ten-year deadline specified in the lease itself. In coming to this conclusion, the House expressed approval for the following statement in *Halsbury's Laws of England*:[36]

> Time will not be considered to be of the essence unless: (1) the parties expressly stipulate that conditions as to time must be strictly complied with; or (2) the nature of the subject matter of the contract or the surrounding circumstances show that time should be considered to be of the essence.

The first element of this paragraph is unproblematic. As regards the second category, however, it is unclear whether commercial contracts should be regarded as always falling within its scope. In *Bunge Corp v Tradax SA*,[37] there are statements in both the Court of Appeal and the House of Lords that, in commercial contracts, stipulations as to time are usually to be treated as being 'of the essence'.[38] This seems to suggest a *prima facie* rule, which is contrary to the presumption in *Halsbury* that time is not usually of the essence. The statements in *Bunge v Tradax* are somewhat diffident, however, and the House at the same time gave approval to the statement in *Halsbury*.[39] The best approach is probably that the issue should be determined on the basis of the commercial context of the particular contract under consideration rather than being subject to any specific presumption. The judicial statements are sufficiently vague to allow such an approach.[40]

Where time is not initially of the essence, it seems that it may become so by one party giving notice. This is what happened in *Charles Rickards Ltd v Oppenheim*,[41] the facts of

---

34  Note that this only specifically deals with time of payment: it says nothing about any other obligation which may arise under the contract, such as the time for delivery. Note also the reform of the Sale of Goods Act 1979 noted in Chapter 6. Compare s 28 of the Consumer Rights Act 2015.

35  [1978] AC 904; [1977] 2 All ER 62.

36  Volume 9, para 481. See Viscount Dilhorne, p 937; p 78; Lord Simon, p 944; p 83. Lord Fraser also approved the third limb of the paragraph from *Halsbury,* which reads '(3) a party who has been subjected to unreasonable delay gives notice to the party in default making time of the essence': ibid, p 958; p 94.

37  [1981] 2 All ER 540.

38  Ibid, p 535, per Megaw LJ; p 542, *per* Lord Wilberforce.

39  Ibid, p 542.

40  See Treitel's comments to this effect: Treitel, 2015, p 1026. Compare *Kuwait Rocks Co v AMN Bulkcarriers Inc* [2013] EWHC 865 at [110] (time generally of the essence in mercantile contracts), a case explicitly not followed in *Spar Shipping AS v Grand China Logistics Holding (Group) Co Ltd* [2015] EWHC 718 (Comm). The approach at first instance in *Spar Shipping AS v Grand China Logistics Holding (Group) Co Ltd* was approved on appeal ([2016] EWCA Civ 982) with *Kuwait Rocks Co v AMN Bulkcarriers Inc* being overruled on this point.

41  [1950] 1 KB 616; [1950] 1 All ER 420.

which are given in Chapter 3.[42] This possibility appears to arise as soon as the contractual date for performance has passed. This was the view taken by the Court of Appeal in *Behzadi v Shaftesbury Hotels Ltd*,[43] which was a contract for land. The court held that if the contract contained a specific date for performance, even though this was not of the essence, there was nevertheless a breach of contract as soon as that date had passed, and the party not in breach was entitled to serve a notice immediately making time of the essence. As Purchas LJ put it:[44]

> I see no reason for the imposition of any further period of delay after the breach of contract has been established by non-performance in accordance with its terms before it is open to a party to serve such a notice. The important matter is that the notice must in all the circumstances of the case give a reasonable opportunity for the other party to perform his part of the contract.

Only after that period had expired would the party who has issued the notice be entitled to treat the contract as repudiated by the other side's failure to perform. In coming to this conclusion, the court disapproved *dicta* in *British and Commonwealth Holdings plc v Quadrex Holdings Inc*,[45] which suggested that there must be an unreasonable delay before the right to give notice making time of the essence arises. Since both these cases are Court of Appeal decisions, the latter one, *Behzadi v Shaftesbury Hotels Ltd*, should be taken to prevail, pending a ruling by the Supreme Court.

## 14.6 DISCHARGE BY BREACH

A breach of contract may have a range of consequences. It may entitle the innocent party to seek an order for performance of the contract, to claim damages, or to terminate the contract, or some combination of these. It is termination that we are concerned with in this chapter,[46] since this will also entail the discharge of many future obligations. Where the innocent party terminates a contract as a result of a breach by the other side, it is in fact likely to be indicating three things: (1) that it will not perform any of its outstanding obligations under the contract; (2) that it will not expect the other party to perform any of its outstanding obligations, and will reject performance if it is tendered; and (3) that it may seek financial compensation (damages) for losses resulting from the other party's breach.[47]

### 14.6.1 EFFECT OF BREACH

There have at various times been suggestions that a breach of contract, if sufficiently serious, amounting to what is often called a 'repudiatory' breach, might bring a contract to an

---

42  See 3.10.2. See also the passage from *Halsbury* approved by Lord Fraser in *United Scientific Holdings v Burnley*, above. The theory behind making time of the essence was discussed by the Chancellor (Sir Terrence Etherton) in *Urban I (Block Street) Ltd v Ayres* [2013] EWCA Civ 816 at [42]-[44].

43  [1992] Ch 1; [1991] 2 All ER 477.

44  Ibid, p 24; p 496.

45  [1989] QB 842; [1989] 3 All ER 492. Mentioned in *Goldman Sachs International v Videocon Global Ltd* [2016] EWCA Civ 130.

46  The other two are dealt with in Chapter 15.

47  In some cases damages will not be sought if, for example, defective goods are supplied under a sale of goods contract. The buyer may be satisfied simply by the return of any money paid, in exchange for the rejection of the goods.

end automatically, irrespective of the wishes of the parties.[48] The current view, however, is that a breach only ever has the effect of allowing the innocent party the choice of whether to terminate the agreement or allow it to continue.[49] This was confirmed by the House of Lords in *Photo Production v Securicor*.[50] In all cases, therefore, the innocent party will have the possibility of electing either to treat the contract as repudiated and therefore to terminate it or to affirm it (and possibly claim damages).

Termination for repudiatory breach is not the same thing as 'rescission', though the courts do not always distinguish between them and in certain circumstances the effects are similar. In a simple sale of goods transaction, for example, if there is a repudiatory breach in relation to the quality of the goods, the effect may well be that the buyer will return the goods and reclaim the price. This is similar to if there had been rescission for misrepresentation. There are differences, however. First, there will always be a right to claim damages for a repudiatory breach, whereas rescission (for example, in relation to a totally innocent misrepresentation) may be the only remedy.[51] Second, in a complex or continuing contract, whereas rescission requires the whole transaction to be undone, termination may leave intact obligations that have arisen prior to the breach – although in a simple transaction the effects may be the same.

As Lord Wilberforce explained in *Johnson v Agnew*,[52] where there is reference to 'rescission' for breach of contract:[53]

> this so-called 'rescission' is quite different from rescission *ab initio*, such as may arise, for example, in cases of mistake, fraud or lack of consent. In those cases, the contract is treated in law as never having come into existence ... In the case of repudiatory breach, the contract has come into existence but has been put to an end or discharged. Whatever contrary indications may be disinterred from old authorities, it is now quite clear, under the general law of contract, that acceptance of a repudiatory breach does not bring about 'rescission *ab initio*'.

This meant that if there had been a repudiatory breach and the claimant had been granted an order of specific performance, but such performance became impossible, a court would have the power to discharge the order and award damages for the original breach.

### 14.6.2 NATURE OF REPUDIATORY BREACH

What types of breach of contract will give rise to the right to treat the agreement as repudiated and therefore to terminate it? There are a number of ways of approaching this issue. It could be said that this is a matter for the parties to determine and that they should agree in their contract whether a particular type of breach is to be repudiatory or not. Second, it could be argued that the issue can only be determined when the consequences of an actual breach are known. Third, it might be thought best to have specific legal rules which state that particular contractual obligations fall into one category or the other. English law, as we shall see, uses a mixture of all three approaches. It will be convenient, however, to start with the third, and look at a situation where a statute determines the consequences of particular breaches.

---

48  See, for example, Lord Denning's judgment in the Court of Appeal in *Harbutt's Plasticine v Wayne Tank and Pump* [1970] 1 QB 447; [1970] 1 All ER 225 or, in the employment law context, *Hill v CA Parsons* [1972] 1 Ch 305; [1971] 3 All ER 1345 and *Sanders v Neale* [1974] 3 All ER 327.

49  In effect, the right to terminate is a kind of 'self-help' remedy – see Harris, Campbell and Halson, 2002, pp 51–7.

50  [1980] AC 827; [1980] 1 All ER 556. In the employment context, see now *Geys v Société Générale, London Branch* [2012] UKSC 63.

51  See Chapter 8, 8.4.1.

52  [1980] AC 367; [1979] 1 All ER 883.

53  Ibid, pp 392–93; p 889.

### 14.6.3 THE SALE OF GOODS ACT 1979: IMPLIED CONDITIONS AND WARRANTIES

The implied terms under the SGA 1979 are labelled as being either 'conditions' or 'warranties'. The consequences of this are spelled out in s 11(3), which indicates that a 'condition' is a stipulation the breach of which may give rise to a right to treat the contract as repudiated, whereas a breach of 'warranty' may give rise to a claim for damages, but not to a right to treat the contract as repudiated.

The SGA 1979 thus uses the terminology of condition and warranty to distinguish between repudiatory and other breaches. Only if the term broken is a condition will the breach be repudiatory. The question then arises as to which terms are conditions and which are warranties. As far as the implied terms under the SGA 1979 are concerned, the Act itself provides the answer, by labelling them as one or the other. In relation to other provisions in a sale of goods contract, however, the question is, as s 11(3) makes clear, one of the 'constructions of the contract'. This is the position in relation to most other contracts as well, and so we need to consider this next.[54]

### 14.6.4 IN FOCUS: POSSIBLE AMBIGUITY IN TERMINOLOGY

Before considering the construction of the contract, it is important to note that both 'condition' and 'warranty' are, at times, used in other senses than the ones under consideration here. 'Condition' is used, for example, in relation to a 'condition precedent' or 'condition subsequent', or very generally to mean the provisions of a contract, as in 'terms and conditions'. 'Warranty' on the other hand can mean simply a 'promise' or a 'guarantee'. Care is needed, therefore, in looking at discussions of contractual terms, particularly by judges, in order to be sure that the meaning that is being attached to a particular word is clear.

### 14.6.5 CATEGORISATION OF TERMS: THE COURTS' APPROACH

Where a term is not labelled by statute, the courts themselves have to decide whether it is a condition, breach of which will be repudiatory and give the other party the right to terminate, or a warranty, breach of which will only give rise to a right to damages. The main factor will be the importance of the term in the context of the contract. Is it of major significance in relation to the purpose of the contract, or is its role only minor?

The traditional approach of the courts under the classical law of contract can be seen in the contrasting cases of *Bettini v Gye*[55] and *Poussard v Spiers*.[56] Both cases concerned singers.

---

**Key case** *Poussard v Spiers* (1876)

Facts: The plaintiff singer was contracted to play a part in an operetta, starting in November. The first performance was announced for 28 November. The plaintiff attended several rehearsals but then was taken ill. She missed the remaining rehearsals and the first four performances of the operetta. By this time a substitute had been employed and the plaintiff's failure to appear was treated as a repudiatory breach.

---

54 For recent changes to, for example, the law relating to the sale of goods, see the discussion of the Consumer Rights Act 2015 in Chapter 6. Note that the Consumer Rights Act 2015, unlike under the Sale of Goods Act 1979, does not classify terms as conditions or warranties with the associated impact on available remedies. Instead the Consumer Rights Act 2015 expressly sets out the remedies for breach of these statutory terms. At one level this, as was the intention, simplifies this area of law: there is no need for businesses or consumers to understand the significance of the distinction between conditions and warranties. Yet any such gains need to be set against the complexity of the (partial) remedial framework under the Act.
55 (1876) 1 QBD 183.
56 (1876) 1 QBD 410.

Held: The failure to perform on the opening night and at the early performances went to the root of the contract and was a breach of condition, justifying the defendant's termination of her contract.

### Key case *Bettini v Gye* (1876)

Facts: The singer had agreed to sing a lead part in the defendant's opera. Under the contract he was required to be present for rehearsals six days before the start of the performance. As a result of illness, he was delayed and arrived three days late. The defendant purported to terminate the contract.

Held: The court treated the failure to appear for the rehearsals as a breach that was not repudiatory. As Blackburn J said, the classification of terms 'depends on the true construction of the contract as a whole'[57] and here the breach did not go to the root of a contract that was scheduled to last for several months.

In *Poussard v Spiers*, the failure to meet the obligation to be present for a performance was treated as much more serious than Bettini's failure to meet the obligation to be present for a rehearsal. The former breach had a much more significant impact on the main purpose of the contract than the latter.

### For thought

*If Bettini had missed all the rehearsals, do you think the outcome would have been the same? If not, what precisely was the term that amounted to a condition of the contract that Bettini would have broken (in contrast to the position on the facts as they actually occurred)?*

In some cases, the courts will not look so much to the interpretation of the individual contract but to the expectations of parties who regularly include clauses of a particular type in their agreements. In *Bunge Corp v Tradax Export SA*,[58] as we have seen,[59] it was stated that time clauses in mercantile contracts should usually be treated as conditions. As Lord Wilberforce explained, to treat such terms as 'innominate'[60] would be commercially 'most undesirable':[61]

It would expose the parties, after a breach of one, two, three, seven and other numbers of days, to an argument whether this delay would have left the seller time to provide the goods. It would make it, at the time, at least difficult, and sometimes impossible, for the supplier to know whether he could do so. It would fatally remove

---

57  (1876) 1 QBD 183, p 187.
58  [1981] 2 All ER 513.
59  Above, 14.5.
60  This meaning that the right to repudiate would depend on the seriousness of the breach – see below, 14.6.8.
61  [1981] 2 All ER 513, p 541.

from a vital provision in the contract that certainty which is the most indispensable quality of mercantile contracts, and lead to a large increase in arbitrations.

Applying this approach to the facts, a four-day delay in giving notice of the readiness of a vessel to receive a cargo was a breach of a condition in the shipment contract, entitling the sellers to treat the contract as repudiated.

A similar approach to a clause relating to time was taken by the Privy Council in *Union Eagle Ltd v Golden Achievement Ltd*,[62] as noted above at 14.3.1.

## 14.6.6 CATEGORISATION OF TERMS: LABELLING BY THE PARTIES

One way in which the courts may be able to determine the parties' intentions as regards the effect of breaking particular terms is where they have been labelled. If they have gone through the contract and referred to certain terms as conditions, and the rest as warranties, then it may be presumed that this was intended to have the same significance as the labels used in the SGA 1979. The use of labels will not be conclusive, however, as is shown by *Schuler AG v Wickman Tools Sales Ltd*.[63] The defendants were under an obligation to make weekly visits to six named firms, over a period of four and a half years, in connection with a contract under which they were given the sole selling rights of the plaintiffs' panel presses. This obligation was referred to as a 'condition', and none of the other 19 clauses in the contract was described in this way. This would seem to suggest that the parties intended that any breach of it would be repudiatory. The majority of the House of Lords refused to interpret it in this way, however. Noting that the contract required in total some 1,400 visits to be made and that it was likely that in a few cases a visit would be impossible, Lord Reid pointed out that:

> if Schuler's contention is right failure to make even one visit entitles them to terminate the contract, however blameless Wickman might be. This is so unreasonable that it must make me search for some other possible meaning of the contract.

This 'other possible meaning' the House found by treating a breach of the visits clause as being a 'material breach' sufficient to bring into play other termination procedures under another clause.

A similar approach is to be found in *Rice v Great Yarmouth Borough Council*.[64] In this case the 'labelling' did not refer to conditions or warranties, but directly to the circumstances in which the right to terminate for breach would arise. The contract was for provision of leisure management and grounds maintenance services to the council for a four-year period. After seven months the council purported to terminate the agreement for breach of contract. The council relied on cl 23 of the contract, which stated:

> If the contractor … commits a breach of any of its obligations under the contract … the council may, without prejudice to any accrued right or remedies under the contract, terminate the contractor's employment under the contract by notice in writing having immediate effect.

The trial judge held that this clause should not be applied literally and that there should be a right to terminate only where the breach was serious enough to be treated as repudiatory. The Court of Appeal upheld this conclusion. First, in the context of a four-year contract involving

---

62 [1997] 2 All ER 215.
63 [1974] AC 235; [1973] 2 All ER 39. See also *Process Components Ltd v Kason Kek-Gardner Ltd* [2016] EWHC 2198 (Ch) and [2017] EWCA Civ 2132.
64 [2001] 3 LGLR 4.

substantial financial obligations and 'a myriad of obligations of differing importance and varying frequency', a common sense interpretation should be placed on the strict words of the contract. Clause 23 did not characterise any term as a 'condition' or 'indicate which terms were to be considered so important that any breach would justify termination'. It was only where there was a repudiatory breach or an accumulation of breaches that could be said to be repudiatory that the right to terminate under cl 23 would arise.[65] As noted above, in contrast to *Schuler v Wickman*, the clause was not concerned with the labelling of obligations but the process for termination, but the approach is similar: the court refuses to give the words of the contract their literal meaning. In this case, the literal wording would have allowed termination for any breach, however minor, but the Court of Appeal insisted that it must be interpreted in the overall context of the contract and in line with 'common sense'.[66] The same line was taken in *Dominion Corporate Trustees Ltd v Dominion Trust Ltd*.[67] The words:

> If ... either party shall in any respect fail or neglect to observe or perform any of the provisions of this Agreement ... then either party may by notice to the defaulting party any time after such occurrence terminate this Agreement

were taken to mean:[68]

> if either party shall in any respect fail or neglect to observe or perform any provision of the Agreement in a way that amounts to a repudiatory breach, or if an insolvency event arises, then the innocent party may terminate by giving notice.

Taking into account the context of the contract, and the many ways in which it would have been possible to breach it, this is what 'a reasonable commercial person would understand' the clause to mean.

The decisions in these cases do not mean that the parties' own labelling of terms is to be ignored, simply that it is not conclusive of the issue. In other cases the courts have shown themselves to be willing to give effect to clearly stated provisions as to the consequences of a breach. In *Awilco A/S v Fulvia SpA di Navigazione, The Chikuma*,[69] for example, in discussing a clause giving a right to withdraw a ship for late payment of hire, Lord Bridge said that where parties bargaining at arm's length use 'common form' clauses, it is very important that their meaning and legal effect should be certain:[70]

> The ideal at which the courts should aim, in construing such clauses, is to produce a result such that in any given situation both parties seeking legal advice as to their rights and obligations can expect the same clear and confident answer from their advisers and neither will be tempted to embark on long and expensive litigation in the belief that victory depends on winning the sympathy of the court.

Similarly, in *Lombard North Central plc v Butterworth*,[71] the Court of Appeal upheld the parties' own express provisions as to the consequences of breach of terms as to payment in a contract of hire, even though they were not happy about the justice of the overall result.

---

65 That is, the approach should be that adopted in *Hong Kong Fir Shipping Co v Kawasaki Kisen Kaisha* – discussed below, 14.6.8.
66 Which presumably means what the court thinks reasonable parties would be taken to have intended by the clause at the time of contracting. If so, this becomes another example of the courts' assumption that all incidents of a long-term (or 'relational') contract are capable of 'presentation' – see Macneil, 1978, and Chapter 1, 1.6.
67 [2010] EWHC 1193.
68 Ibid, para 32.
69 [1981] 1 All ER 652.
70 Ibid, p 659.
71 [1987] QB 527; [1987] 1 All ER 267.

### 14.6.7 IN FOCUS: CONSEQUENCES OF CATEGORISATION

The categorisation of terms as either conditions or warranties implies that the actual consequence of a particular breach is not a relevant factor. Once a term is a 'condition', any breach of it will be repudiatory, no matter that it can be easily remedied or has on this occasion caused no substantial loss to the other party. Similarly, whatever the consequences of a breach of warranty, and however great the losses it causes, it will never give rise to the right to terminate the contract. This approach is therefore rigid, and may appear to cause injustice in some cases, but it has the merit of certainty in that the parties can be aware in advance what the legal consequences of any particular breach will be.[72]

### 14.6.8 INTERMEDIATE TERMS

There are times when the categorisation of terms in the way outlined in the previous sections does not work and, at least since 1962, the courts have recognised that it is necessary to have an intermediate category. The leading case is *Hong Kong Fir Shipping Co v Kawasaki Kisen Kaisha Ltd*,[73] though some would argue that earlier decisions were, in fact, based on the same considerations.

---

**Key case** *Hong Kong Fir Shipping Co v Kawasaki Kisen Kaisha Ltd* (1962)

Facts: The contract concerned a 24-month time charter of a ship. One of the terms effectively required the ship to be 'seaworthy'. It was not in such a condition on delivery, on account of the state of the engines. Repairs were required and delays resulted. Four months into the contract the charterers purported to terminate the charter. The owners sued for wrongful repudiation. The trial judge held in favour of the owners. The charterers appealed.

Held: The Court of Appeal agreed with the trial judge that the breach did not go to the root of the contract. The charterers had not been deprived of substantially the whole benefit of the contract and did not have the right to terminate it for breach.

---

Diplock LJ admitted that some terms may be classifiable as conditions or warranties, but felt that there are many contractual undertakings of a more complex nature that cannot be classified in that way. The obligation as to seaworthiness, for example, could be broken in any number of ways. For example, the failure to have the correct number of lifejackets on board could render a ship 'unseaworthy' just as much as a major defect in the hull. In such a case, it was not possible to determine beforehand the consequences of a breach, in terms of whether it would be repudiatory or not. Rather, what a judge had to do was to:[74]

> look at the events which had occurred as a result of the breach at the time when the charterers purported to rescind the charterparty and to decide whether the occurrence of those events deprived the charterers of substantially the whole benefit which it was the intention of the parties as expressed in the charterparty that the charterers should obtain from the further performance of their own contractual undertakings.

---

72  See the comments of Lord Bridge in *The Chikuma* (see above, 14.6.6).
73  [1962] 2 QB 26; [1962] 1 All ER 474.
74  Ibid, p 72; pp 488–89.

Figure 14.2

So, on this analysis, the focus is not on the parties' intentions at the time of the contract, but on the effect of the actual breach that has occurred: that is, the second of the approaches outlined at the start of this section.[75] If the breach is so serious as to strike fundamentally at the purpose of the contract, then it will be treated as repudiatory, in the same way as if it was a breach of condition; if it is less serious, it will give rise only to a remedy in damages, like a warranty.

### 14.6.9 EFFECTS OF *HONG KONG FIR*

The courts have never doubted, since the decision in *Hong Kong Fir*, that there are three categories of term, namely conditions, warranties and 'innominate' or intermediate terms.[76] An approach based on the consequences of breach has even been adopted, perhaps somewhat surprisingly, in relation to sale of goods contracts, in *Cehave NV v Bremer Handelsgesellschaft mbH, The Hansa Nord*.[77] Lord Denning, in this case, was concerned with the definition of 'merchantable quality'[78] under the SGA 1893, the obligation to supply goods of such quality being a term labelled as a 'condition' by the statute itself. In determining whether the goods are 'merchantable', however, Lord Denning suggested that:[79]

---

75 See above, 14.6.2.

76 Reynolds (1981, pp 548–49), following the argument of Upjohn LJ in *Hong Kong Fir*, has argued that in effect there are only two types of term: those where any breach will give rise to the right to terminate, and those where the right to terminate will depend on the consequences of the breach (that is, conflating 'warranties' with 'innominate terms'). But this analysis has not found favour in subsequent cases. See also Treitel, 2015, p 987. See also the detailed analysis by Lewison LJ in *Ampurius Nu Homes Holdings Ltd v Telford Homes (Creekside) Ltd* [2013] EWCA Civ 577 at [38] – [53].

77 [1976] QB 44.

78 Now 'satisfactory quality' – see above, Chapter 6, 6.6.13.

79 [1976] QB 44, p 62.

In these circumstances, I should have thought a fair way of testing merchantability would be to ask a commercial man: was the breach such that the buyer should be able to reject the goods ...?

In other words, the consequences of breach were used to determine merchantable quality and therefore, indirectly, whether or not a breach of condition has occurred. On the facts, since the goods, though damaged, had been used for their intended purpose as animal feed, there was not a breach that would have entitled the buyer to reject, and the goods were thus 'merchantable'. This ingenious incorporation of a *Hong Kong Fir* approach into the area of the statutorily labelled implied terms was not adopted by the other members of the Court of Appeal, although they agreed that the pellets were 'merchantable' and so cannot be regarded as authoritative. It has, in any case, probably been superseded by the much more specific statutory definitions of quality to be found in the current SGA 1979.[80] The court was, however, unanimous that the *Hong Kong Fir* approach could be applied to express obligations in a sale of goods contract. In this case, the obligation that the goods should be 'shipped in good condition' was treated as an innominate term. Since the pellets had been able to be used, it could not be said that there was a breach of sufficient seriousness to justify repudiation.

In other areas, however, the attraction of the flexibility of Diplock LJ's analysis in *Hong Kong Fir* has frequently bowed to considerations of the desirability of commercial certainty, spelled out in the quotation from Lord Bridge in *The Chikuma*.[81] Thus, in *Maradelanto Cia Naviera SA v Bergbau-Handel GmbH, The Mihalis Angelos*,[82] the obligation of being 'expected ready to load' at a particular time, a clause that clearly could be broken with varying degrees of seriousness, was treated as a condition, irrespective of the consequences of the particular breach. And as we have seen, a similar view was taken of time clauses in mercantile contracts in *Bunge Corp v Tradax* SA.[83] It will continue to be important, therefore, to ask the question 'is this a condition or a warranty?', before considering the consequences of the breach of contract. The answer to that question may render such consideration unnecessary.

## 14.7 SOME SPECIAL TYPES OF BREACH

There are three particular situations that call for some special consideration. The first is where the contract involves the performance of services over a period of time. In what circumstances will the breach of an innominate term be regarded as repudiatory? The second situation is where the contract is divided into instalments. What is the position if the breach relates to only a small proportion of those instalments? Finally, what is the position where the consequences of the breach do not affect the possibilities of the physical performance of the contract, but affect its commercial viability?

### 14.7.1 LONG-TERM CONTRACTS

This issue was considered by the Court of Appeal in *Rice v Great Yarmouth BC*.[84] The contract was for the provision of leisure management and grounds maintenance services

---

80  See above, 6.6.13.
81  See above, 14.6.6.
82  [1971] 1 QB 164; [1970] 3 All ER 125.
83  [1981] 2 All ER 513 – see above, 14.6.4. A similar view was also taken by the Court of Appeal in *BS & N Ltd v Micado Shipping Ltd (Malta) (No 2)* [2001] 1 All ER Comm 240.
84  [2001] 3 LGLR 4. See also above, 14.6.5. On relational contracts, see also *Bristol Groundschool Ltd v Intelligent Data Capture Ltd* [2014] EWHC 2145 discussed above at 1.11. See also Mouzas & Furmston, 2008.

to the council for a four-year period. After seven months the council purported to termi-nate the agreement for breach of contract. The Court of Appeal, as noted above,[85] held that the clause in the contract on which the council relied did not give a right to terminate for every breach. This meant that it then had to consider the question of what, in this type of long-running contract for the provision of public services, would amount to a repudia-tory breach. The Court of Appeal could find no direct authority on the issue, though there were some parallels with charterparties or building contracts. It was accepted that it was relevant to look at the contractor's performance over a full year and to ask whether the council was deprived of the whole benefit of what it had contracted for over that period. As in building contracts, past breaches were relevant not only for their own sake, but also for what they showed about the future. It was right to ask whether the accumulation of breaches was such as to justify an inference that the contractor would continue to deliver a sub-standard performance, thus leading to the council being deprived of 'a substantial part of the totality of that which it had contracted for that year'.[86]

Subject to the possibility that there were some aspects of the contract that were so impor-tant 'that the parties were to be taken to have intended that depriving the council of that part of the contract would be sufficient in itself' to justify termination, this was the approach to be adopted. The judge had dealt with the issues appropriately and there was no need to interfere with his decision, which was that the council did not have the right to terminate.

This case shows that deciding what is, on the *Hong Kong Fir* approach, a repudiatory breach in a long-term contract can be tricky. Here the Court of Appeal seems to have started from the point that deprivation of at least 25 per cent of the overall benefit of the contract (that is, performance over one year out of four) would be necessary (other than in relation to breach of any terms that might be of particular importance). The decision is understandable, but it does not particularly assist parties who may be looking for certainty as to the consequences of particular actions on their part (that is, as to if and when the other party will be entitled to treat their actions as repudiatory).

### For thought

*Would it be more satisfactory in this type of situation if the courts laid down a general rule that the breach must affect 30 per cent of the contract, for example, in order for it to be considered repudiatory? What difficulties might that give rise to?*

In *Force India Formula One Team Ltd v Etihad Airways PJSC*,[87] the Court of Appeal held that an accumulation of breaches over a period of time could amount to a repudiatory breach, entitling the other party to terminate the contract.[88]

### 14.7.2 INSTALMENT CONTRACTS

A similar problem to that just considered arises here. In a contract that is to be performed by instalments, will the breach of one of them ever amount to a repudiatory breach? If so,

---

85  See above, 14.6.6.
86  Cf *Decro-Wall International SA v Practitioners in Marketing Ltd* [1971] 2 All ER 216 – regular late payment for goods received under a continuing contract did not amount to a repudiatory breach. The consequences of late payment could be adequately compensated by recovering extra interest. See also *Valilas v Januzaj* [2014] EWCA Civ 436.
87  [2010] EWCA Civ 1051.
88  Ibid, para 99.

then the contract can be brought to an end as soon as that one breach has occurred and there will be no further obligations as regards the rest of the instalments. On the other hand, if the innocent party allows the contract to continue, could that amount to affirmation of the contract, so that the breach could not subsequently be relied on as being repudiatory?

The resolution of these issues may, of course, be determined by what the parties have themselves agreed in the contract. This is supported by s 31(2) of the Sale of Goods Act 1979, which, where applicable, states that in cases of defective delivery, or a refusal to accept delivery:

> it is a question in each case depending on the terms of the contract and the circumstances of the case whether the breach of contract is a repudiation of the whole contract or whether it is a severable breach giving rise to a claim in compensation but not to a right to treat the whole contract as repudiated.

An example of the application of this is to be seen in *Maple Flock Co Ltd v Universal Furniture Products (Wembley) Ltd*.[89] The sellers had contracted to sell 100 tons of rag flock to the buyers. Out of the first 20 loads delivered, one, the 16th, was defective. The Court of Appeal held that this was not a repudiatory breach, since it related only to one instalment, and therefore only one and a half tons out of the whole contract. In contrast, in *RA Munro & Co Ltd v Meyer*,[90] 1,500 tons of meat and bone meal were to be delivered in 12 instalments of 125 tons. After 768 tons had been delivered, it was discovered that all were adulterated and did not match the contract description. It was held that this was sufficient to amount to a repudiatory breach.

The proportion of the instalments involved in the breach is not the only issue, however, as is shown by the House of Lords' decision in *Mersey Steel and Iron Co v Naylor, Benzon & Co*.[91] The contract was for the sale of 5,000 tons of steel, to be delivered at the rate of 1,000 tons per month, with payment within three days of receipt of the shipping documents. The sellers delivered only part of the first instalment, but delivered the second complete. Shortly before payment was due, the sellers were the subject of a petition for winding up and, as a result, the buyers (acting on inaccurate legal advice) withheld payment. The sellers sought to treat this as a repudiatory breach. The House of Lords noted that the buyers had indicated a continuing willingness to pay as soon as any legal difficulties had been resolved, and therefore held that this was not a repudiatory breach. The context was important in determining the effect of a breach in relation to one instalment.

As well as illustrating the courts' approach to instalment contracts, this case shows that the intention of the party in breach, and the reasons for the breach, may be important factors in determining whether it is repudiatory. The fact that the buyers had no intention to repudiate, but were acting under a bona fide mistake of law, was a very relevant consideration.

### 14.7.3 COMMERCIAL DESTRUCTION

In most cases of repudiatory breach, there is some act or omission that means that the obligations under the contract have only partially been fulfilled. Goods do not match their description, or are supplied in insufficient quality; services are not supplied, or do not meet contractual standards; money owed is paid late or not at all. In all these situations the innocent party is being deprived of the benefit of the contract. It is possible, however, for a party to complete his or her major obligations, but for the consequences of some minor breach to be such that, although it does not affect the practical possibility of continuing

---

89 [1934] 1 KB 148.
90 [1930] 2 KB 312.
91 (1884) 9 App Cas 434.

with the contract, commercially it would be unreasonable to do so. This is exemplified by *Aerial Advertising Co v Batchelors Peas*.[92] The contract was for the towing of an advertising banner on daily flights by an aeroplane. The pilot was supposed to clear his flight plan each day, but on one occasion he failed to do so. He flew over Salford and saw a large crowd assembled in the main square. He flew close to it displaying the sign 'Eat Batchelors Peas'. Unfortunately, the date was 11 November and the crowd had assembled to keep the traditional two minutes' silence on Remembrance Day. The actions of the pilot led to much criticism of Batchelors. The judge held that it was 'commercially wholly unreasonable to carry on with the contract' and that, in the circumstances, the consequences of the breach (that is, the failure to clear the flight plan) meant that Batchelors were entitled to treat the contract as repudiated.

## 14.8 ANTICIPATORY BREACH

While there are obligations still to be performed, one party may indicate in advance that he or she intends to break the contract.[93] This is known as an 'anticipatory breach' and will generally give the other party the right to treat the contract as repudiated, and to sue at once for damages. For example, in *Hochster v De La Tour*,[94] the defendant engaged the plaintiff on 12 April to enter his service as a courier and accompany him on a foreign tour. This employment was to start on 1 June. On 11 May, the defendant wrote to the plaintiff to inform him that his services would no longer be required. It was held that the plaintiff was entitled to bring an action for damages immediately, without waiting for 1 June.

The reason for allowing this type of action, rather than making the plaintiff wait until performance is due, was given by Cockburn CJ in *Frost v Knight*.[95] He held that it involves a breach of a right to have the contract kept open as a subsisting and effective contract. It, of course, also has the practical benefit of enabling the innocent party to obtain compensation for any damage speedily.

As will be seen in the next section, however, the innocent party does not have to accept the anticipatory breach as repudiating the contract. He or she may wait until performance is due, and then seek damages for non performance at that stage. It has even been held in one case that the innocent party can legitimately incur expenses towards his or her own performance even after a clear indication of an intention to break the contract has been given by the other side. These may then be claimed as damages once the contract date for performance has passed.[96]

---

92  [1938] 2 All ER 788.

93  In *Geden Operations Ltd v Dry Bulkhandy Holidays Inc* [2014] EWHC 885, at [15] Popplewell J stated: 'Anticipatory breach is the name given to conduct of one party to a contract before the time for performance of his obligations has arrived which is sufficient to entitle the other contracting party to treat himself as discharged from further performance. It may consist of one or both of two kinds of conduct. The first, renunciation, comprises words or conduct which evince an intention by the contracting party no longer to be bound by his contractual obligations. The second, self-induced impossibility, comprises conduct by the contracting party which puts it out of his power to perform his contractual obligations. In each case the anticipatory breach must be repudiatory in character. That is to say that the breach of contractual obligations, which the party's conduct anticipates that he cannot or will not perform, must be of the same character as would entitle the other party to treat himself as discharged from future performance if it occurred after the time for performance had arisen. So the anticipated breach must be breach of a condition, or breach of an innominate term which goes to the root of the contract or deprives the innocent party of substantially the whole benefit of the contract.'

94  (1853) 2 E & B 678; [1843–60] All ER Rep 12.

95  (1872) LR 7 Exch 111.

96  See generally *White and Carter (Councils) Ltd v McGregor* [1962] AC 413; [1961] 3 All ER 1178. This case will be discussed further in detail at 15.6.6.

## 14.9 EFFECT OF BREACH: RIGHT OF ELECTION

In relation to all repudiatory breaches, the innocent party has the right to elect to treat the contract as discharged and claim for damages or to affirm the contract, notwithstanding the breach. The latter course will prevent the contract from being discharged, but damages may still be recovered.

### 14.9.1 NEED FOR COMMUNICATION

Where the innocent party elects to treat the breach as repudiatory, this decision will normally only be effective if communicated to the other party.[97] However, this statement needs to be read in the light of the House of Lords' decision in *Vitol SA v Norelf Ltd, The Santa Clara*.[98]

---

**Key case** *Vitol SA v Norelf Ltd, The Santa Clara* (1996)

Facts: V and N had entered into a contract on 11 February 1991 for the purchase of a cargo of propane. On 8 March, V sent a telex to N repudiating the contract. This was subsequently agreed to amount to an anticipatory breach which, if accepted by N, would bring the contract to an end immediately. N did not communicate with V but, on 12 March, started to try to find an alternative buyer and, on 15 March, sold the cargo to X. V challenged the arbitrator's decision that these actions by N amounted to an acceptance of the anticipatory breach. Phillips J upheld the decision of the arbitrator. The Court of Appeal, however, reversed this decision. There was a further appeal to the House of Lords.

Held: The House of Lords restored the decision of the arbitrator and the trial judge, and held that N's actions constituted acceptance of V's anticipatory breach.

---

The difference between the Court of Appeal and House of Lords in this case merits further consideration. In the Court of Appeal, the view was taken that since the differing consequences following from acceptance of repudiation on the one hand or affirmation of the contract on the other were immediate and serious, it was essential that the choice of repudiation should be clear and unequivocal. It needed to be manifested by word or deed. As Nourse LJ put it:[99]

> A choice, however resolute, which gains no expression outside the bosom of the chooser cannot be clear and unequivocal in the sense that the law requires. Silence and inaction, being in the generality of cases equally consistent with an affirmation of the contract, cannot constitute acceptance of a repudiation.

What if the innocent party has failed to perform his or her obligations under the contract, as had happened here? Is this sufficient to indicate acceptance of repudiation? The Court of Appeal thought not. The failure to perform was equally consistent with a misunderstanding by the innocent party of his or her rights under the contract, or indecision, or even inadvertence. The House of Lords, however, rejected the view of the Court of Appeal

---

97  See the European Draft Common Frame of Reference, which suggests that notice of termination should be given 'within a reasonable time': Art III. – 3:508(1). See also Chen-Wishart and Magnus, 2013.

98  [1996] AC 800; [1996] 3 All ER 193.

99  [1996] QB 108, p 114.

and restored the decision of the arbitrator and the judge at first instance. Lord Steyn set out three principles that apply to acceptance of a repudiatory breach:

(a)    Where a party has repudiated a contract, the aggrieved party has an election whether to accept the repudiation or affirm the contract.
(b)    An act of acceptance of a repudiation requires no particular form: a communication does not have to be couched in the language of acceptance. It is sufficient that the communication or conduct clearly and unequivocally conveys to the repudiating party that the aggrieved party is treating the contract as at an end.
(c)    The aggrieved party need not personally, or by an agent, notify the repudiating party of his election to treat the contract as at an end. It is sufficient that the fact of the election comes to the repudiating party's attention; for example, notification by an unauthorised broker or other intermediary may be sufficient.

In applying these principles to the case, Lord Steyn noted that the specific issue before the House was 'whether non-performance of an obligation is ever *as a matter of law* capable of constituting acceptance'.[100] Their Lordships answered this question in the affirmative, stating that whether there is acceptance in a particular case 'all depends on the particular contractual relationship and the particular circumstances of the case'.[101] These were issues of fact, which the arbitrator was in the best position to decide. Lord Steyn was quite prepared to accept, however, that the failure of the seller (N) to take the next stephat would have been required if the contract was to continue (that is, submitting the bill of lading to the buyer (V)), could be found to amount to an unequivocal notification to V of N's acceptance of V's repudiation. The arbitrator was entitled to come to that conclusion on the facts, and his decision should be restored.

Despite this decision, which opens up the possibility of acceptance by inaction, the safest course for a party who intends to accept a repudiatory breach, and therefore terminate the contract, is to do so specifically, by communicating this to the other party. This will remove any danger that the behaviour of the party not in breach will be deemed 'equivocal', and therefore not sufficient to constitute a valid acceptance.

## 14.9.2 RISKS OF ACCEPTANCE

There are, of course, dangers in treating an action by the other party as repudiatory, if it turns out to be viewed otherwise by the court. The party purporting to accept a repudiatory breach may well take action (as was the case in *Vitol v Norelf*) that itself involves a breach of obligations under the contract. If this turns out not to be justified by what the other party has done, then the party who thought it was acting in response to a repudiatory breach may find the tables turned, and that that party itself is now liable to damages for its own breach of the contract. In *Federal Commerce and Navigation Co Ltd v Molena Alpha Inc, The Nanfri*,[102] which concerned the operation of three time charterparties, the charterers deducted various amounts from the hire, which they paid to the owners. The owners objected and issued instructions to the masters of the vessels concerned to, *inter alia*, withdraw all authority to the charterers or their agents to sign bills of lading. This action was held to amount to a repudiatory breach, which entitled the charterers to terminate the charterparties.

In *Woodar Investment Development Ltd v Wimpey Construction UK Ltd*,[103] the majority of the House of Lords seemed to take the view that this consequence would not necessarily

---

100  [1996] AC 800, p 811 (emphasis added).
101  Ibid.
102  [1979] AC 757; [1979] 1 All ER 307.
103  [1980] 1 All ER 571. See also *Eminence Property Developments Ltd v Heaney* [2010] EWCA Civ 1168.

follow if the party purporting to accept the repudiation was acting as a result of a mistake made in good faith as to his or her rights. Many commentators regard this aspect of the *Woodar v Wimpey* decision as dubious, and prefer the view that an unjustified failure to meet contractual obligations is itself a repudiatory breach, even if it is a response to action from the other party that is mistakenly thought to be repudiatory.

### 14.9.3 RISKS OF AFFIRMATION

An election to affirm the contract carries risks as well, as is shown by the following case.

---

**Key case** *Avery v Bowden* (1855)[104]

Facts: The plaintiff chartered his ship to the defendant. The ship was to sail to Odessa, and there to take a cargo from the defendant's agent, which was to be loaded within a certain number of days. The vessel reached Odessa, but the agent was unable to supply a cargo. The ship remained at Odessa, with the master continuing to demand a cargo. Before the period specified in the contract had elapsed, war broke out between England and Russia, and the performance of the contract became legally impossible. The plaintiff sued for breach.

Held: Even if the original action of the agent constituted a repudiatory breach, the contract had been affirmed by the fact that the ship remained at Odessa awaiting a cargo. The contract was then frustrated, and it was too late at that stage for the plaintiff to claim for breach. The defendant was not liable.

---

Similarly, in *Fercometal Sarl v Mediterranean Shipping Co SA*,[105] it was held that a party that had affirmed a contract following an anticipatory breach could not subsequently rely on that breach to justify its own failure to fulfil its obligations under the contract.

---

### 14.10 SUMMARY OF KEY POINTS

- Performance must generally be precise and exact, though the modern approach may be to avoid excessive technicality in interpreting obligations.

- If an obligation (or contract) is 'entire' (with payment due after complete performance), no payment can be claimed for incomplete performance, unless the partial performance is accepted, or what has been done amounts to 'substantial performance'.

- In relation to divisible obligations (or contracts), payment may be recoverable for partial performance.

- Time is not generally 'of the essence' unless made so by the parties. In mercantile contracts, some cases suggest that obligations as to time are usually of the essence.

---

104 (1855) 5 E & B 714.
105 [1989] AC 788; [1988] 2 All ER 742.

- The effect of a breach will depend on the type of breach:
  - if it is a breach of condition, the claimant will be able to repudiate the contract and claim damages;
  - if it is a breach of warranty, the claimant will only be able to claim damages;
  - if it is a breach of an intermediate ('innominate') term, the right to repudiate the contract will depend on the effect of the breach.

- The Sale of Goods Act 1979 implied terms are labelled as 'conditions' or 'warranties'. In relation to other contracts, the courts often decide. Labelling by the parties is not conclusive.

- Advance notice of an intention to break a contract ('anticipatory breach') will generally give the other party the right to terminate immediately.

- Even a repudiatory breach does not terminate a contract automatically: the other party always has the right to elect to affirm the contract, rather than accepting the repudiation. This right exists even in relation to anticipatory breach.

## 14.11 FURTHER READING

### Generally
- Dockray, M, *'Cutter v Powell:* a trip outside the text' (2001) 117 LQR 664

- Harris, D, Campbell, D and Halson, R, *Remedies in Contract and Tort*, 2nd edn, 2002, London: Butterworths

### Types of term
- Treitel, G H, 'Types of contractual terms', Chapter 3 in *Some Landmarks of Twentieth Century Contract Law*, 2002, Oxford: Clarendon Press

### Breach and consequences
- Andrews, N, 'Breach of contract: a plea for clarity and discipline' (2018) 134 LQR 117

- Brownsword, R, 'Retrieving reasons, retrieving rationality? A new look at the right to withdraw for breach of contract' (1992) JCL 83

- Reynolds, F M B, 'Discharge of contract by breach' (1981) 97 LQR 541

- Treitel, G H, 'Affirmation after repudiatory breach' (1998) 114 LQR 22

## COMPANION WEBSITE

*Now visit the companion website to:*

- Revise and consolidate your knowledge of Discharge by tackling a series of multiple-choice questions on this chapter

- Test your understanding of the chapter's key terms by using the flashcard glossary

- Explore Discharge further by accessing a series of web links

# Remedies and restitution

## Contents

### 15.1 OVERVIEW

The main remedies for breach of contract in the law of England and Wales are damages and, to a lesser extent, specific performance. These provide the focus for this chapter. The following issues are discussed:

- Purpose of damages. The general rule is that damages are compensatory, rather than punitive, and are intended to put claimants in the position they would have been in had the contract been performed properly.
- Measure of damages. There are several methods of calculating damages:
  - Expectation measure. This is the usual measure. It allows the claimant to recover particular lost benefits, such as lost profits that would have been made had the contract been properly performed. Problems can arise where:
    - the benefits were not certain – the claimant may be compensated for the loss of a chance to obtain the benefit;
    - the costs of providing the benefit following a breach are out of proportion to the value of the benefit itself – the court may refuse to allow full recovery in these circumstances.
  - Reliance measure. The claimant may choose to seek damages on this basis – compensating for expenses incurred in relation to the contract – where, for example, the expectation interest is difficult to calculate (though not where the claimant has simply made a bad bargain).
- Non-pecuniary losses. The claimant can exceptionally recover for loss of enjoyment or mental distress caused by a breach of contract. Generally, either the contract must be one that has the provision of non-pecuniary benefits as an important objective, or the breach must have caused physical discomfort that has led to the distress.
- Non-compensatory damages. In limited circumstances a claimant may be allowed to recover the benefit that the defendant has obtained through breaking a contract (as opposed to the claimant's own loss), but this is exceptional.
- Limitations on recovery. The claimant's right to damages is limited by:
  - the rules of remoteness – the claimant can generally recover only those losses that were normally to be expected, or, if unusual, were in the reasonable contemplation of the parties at the time of the contract;
  - mitigation – the claimant must take reasonable steps to prevent the losses increasing.
- Liquidated damages clauses are enforceable; penalty clauses, aiming to 'terrorise' the defendant into performance, are not.
- Restitution. The principles of 'restitution' are designed to prevent 'unjust enrichment'. They may require the return of money or property transferred under a contract that has been terminated, or in a situation where a contract has never come into existence.
- Specific performance. This equitable remedy will only be available where damages would be inadequate. The order will not normally be made where:
  - it would need continuous supervision;
  - it relates to personal services;
  - it would cause undue hardship to the defendant;
  - the claimant has not acted equitably.
- Injunctions. These can be used to prevent a breach of contract, but not as a means of indirectly obtaining specific performance where this remedy would not be permitted.

## 15.2 INTRODUCTION[1]

At various points during earlier chapters, remedies of one kind or another have been considered. For example, rescission and damages for misrepresentation were

---

1    See, generally, Beale, 1980; Harris, Campbell and Halson, 2002; Burrows, 2004.

discussed in Chapter 8 and rescission for mistake in Chapter 9. The 'self-help' remedies of withholding performance and terminating on the basis of repudiatory breach were dealt with in Chapter 14.[2] Here, we will consider more generally the award of damages for breach of contract and the order of 'specific performance', which will instruct a party to perform its obligations under an agreement. Some discussion of injunctions will also be necessary.[3]

In general, as we shall see, the common law aims to put the parties into the position they would have been in had the contract been performed, by ordering one party to pay money to the other. Where one of the parties has performed its side of the bargain and is awaiting payment from the other party, this can sometimes be achieved by the 'action for an agreed sum', or in sale of goods contracts the 'action for the price'.[4] In other words, the party who has promised to pay for goods, or services, which have been transferred or performed by the other party, can be required to make good that promise. This was, for example, the form of action taken by Mrs Carlill to compel the Carbolic Smoke Ball Co to pay her the £100,[5] and it is in practice probably the most frequently used action following a breach of contract.[6] In other situations, the normal requirement will be for the payment of compensatory damages. An order to perform part of the contract, other than paying money that is owed, is much more unusual.

We start, therefore, by considering the remedy of 'damages', and will then look at specific performance and injunctions.

## 15.3 DAMAGES: PURPOSE

The aim of contractual damages is, generally, to put the innocent party, so far as money can, into the position it would have been in had the contract been performed. This principle can be traced back to *Robinson v Harman*,[7] and was more recently restated by Lord Scott in *Farley v Skinner*:[8]

> The basic principle of damages for breach of contract is that the injured party is entitled, so far as money can do it, to be put in the position he would have been in if the contractual obligation had been properly performed. He is entitled, that is to say, to the benefit of his bargain.

---

2 Rescission for mistake or misrepresentation can also be regarded as 'self-help', in that there is no necessity for the court's involvement. Compare also the Consumer Protection (Amendment) Regulations 2014, SI 2014/870.

3 'Specific performance' is a type of injunction, which requires a person to act in a particular way; injunctions are also used to *prohibit* a person from carrying out some action. Note also that under the Consumer Rights Act 2015 a consumer may be able to choose remedies such as repair or replacement when a trader delivers goods that do not conform with the contract (see s 23) or the remedy of repeat performance where a trader performs a service that does not conform with the contract (see s 55).

4 See the Sale of Goods Act 1979, s 49. See full discussion in *FG Wilson (Engineering) Ltd v John Holt & Co. (Liverpool) Ltd* [2013] EWCA Civ 1232 although the Supreme Court in *PST Energy 7 Shipping LLC and another v O W Bunker Malta Limited* [2016] UKSC 23 doubted this case preferring the view that s 49 was not a complete code.

5 See *Carlill v Carbolic Smoke Ball Co* [1893] 1 QB 256 – discussed in Chapter 2, 2.7.8.

6 See, for example, Collins, 1999, pp 324–25; Harris, Campbell and Halson, 2002, p 160, n 12.

7 (1848) 1 Exch 850, p 855.

8 [2001] UKHL 49, [76]; [2001] 4 All ER 801, pp 826–27.

The main objective of contract damages is therefore compensation, not punishment.[9] Although, of course, in some situations, a party thinking about breaking an agreement may be deterred by the prospect of having to pay damages, or a party who has broken an agreement may suffer considerably from having to pay compensation, nevertheless these consequences are not the purpose of the award. This is shown by the fact that if the party not in breach has suffered no quantifiable loss, usually only nominal damages will be awarded. If, for example, there is a failure to deliver goods, and the buyer is able to obtain an alternative supply without a problem, and at a price that is the same or lower than the contract price, no substantial damages will be recoverable.[10]

### 15.3.1 IN FOCUS: THE CONCEPT OF 'EFFICIENT BREACH'

In relation to the fact that damages will generally only be awarded where the claimant has suffered a quantifiable loss, it is important to note the concept of the 'efficient breach'. Looking at the law of contract from the economic point of view, as a means of wealth maximisation,[11] it may sometimes make sense for a party to break a contract. The typical example[12] given is where a seller (S) has contracted to sell an item to a buyer (B1) for £100. Before the transaction takes place a second potential buyer (B2) offers S £200 for the item. If S sells to B2, S will receive £200, but may have to pay compensation to B1 for not fulfilling the original contract. But as long as that compensation is below £100, S will still have made a profit. All parties are in theory happy. S has sold the item at a higher price to B2, to whom the item is obviously more valuable than it would be to B1. B1 has not received the item, but has received damages that fully compensate for any losses.

The concept of 'efficient breach' is most commonly discussed in terms of the advantage to the party breaking the contract in 'maximising gain'. As Campbell has pointed out, however, it should also be recognised as encompassing the situation where the party in breach acts to 'minimise loss'.[13] This may arise, for example, where circumstances change in a way that increases the costs of performance to an extent that the increase exceeds the damages that would be payable to the other party. Here again, the economic answer is that the efficient result is not to enforce the contract, but to allow the party whose costs have increased to escape from it by paying appropriate compensation.

The concept of efficient breach goes some way to explaining why the law of contract is generally more disposed to award damages than to insist on performance.[14] The analysis works best, however, in relation to discrete business contracts that are fully executory. Once the parties are in a long-term relationship, either in respect of the contract under consideration or as regards a series of contracts, the economic analysis of the possible advantages of breach becomes much more complex. The risks of endangering the future

---

9 See, for example, Lord Lloyd in *Ruxley Electronics and Construction Ltd v Forsyth* [1996] AC 344, p 365; [1995] 3 All ER 268, p 282: 'It is first necessary to ascertain the loss the plaintiff has suffered by reason of the breach. If he suffered no loss, as sometimes happens, he can recover no more than nominal damages. For the object of damages is always to compensate the plaintiff, not to punish the defendant.' This principle was recently underlined by the Supreme Court in *Morris-Garner v One Step (Support) Ltd* [2018] UKSC 20 although the Supreme Court did note that the law is tolerant of some imprecision where the loss cannot be precisely measured. See also *Aarons v Brocket Hall (Jersey) Ltd* [2018] EWHC 222 (QB) on the general non-availability of exemplary damages. For a contrary view, see Cunnington, 2006.
10 This is the effect of s 51(3) of the Sale of Goods Act 1979.
11 See Chapter 1.
12 See, for example, Atiyah, 1995, p 428.
13 Harris, Campbell and Halson, 2002, pp 13–21.
14 As Campbell comments, 'In this sense, the function of the law of contract is to allow breach, but on the right occasions and on the right terms': ibid, p 17.

**Damages:**

Principle of damages – *compensation* of the claimant, not *punishment* of the defendant (*Robinson v Harman* (1848)) – so if breach causes no loss, only nominal damages are recoverable

Normal measure is based on putting the claimant into the position he or she would have been in had the contract been performed – the **'expectation interest'**

Where the profit from the contract is uncertain, the claimant may seek compensation for expenses incurred – the **'reliance interest'** – *Anglia Television v Reed* (1972)

**Specific performance:**

An order directing one of the parties to perform his/her contractual obligations

Equitable (and so discretionary) remedy – generally only available where damages would be an inadequate remedy

Usually available in relation to contracts for sale/purchase of land

Not usually available:

- if supervision required: *Co-operative Insurance Society Ltd v Argyll Stores (Holdings) Ltd* (1998)
- for contracts involving personal services or employment: *Hill v CA Parsons & Co Ltd* (1972)

**REMEDIES**

**Injunction:**

An order directing a party not to act in a way which will amount to a breach of contract

Equitable (and so discretionary) remedy – infrequently used

Will not be granted if it amounts to an indirect enforcement of a contract for personal services: *Page One Records v Britton* (1967)

Figure 15.1

relationship need to be added in to the equation. Similarly, if one party has already performed part of its obligations (particularly if these are in the form of services, rather than goods or money, thus making restitution difficult), allowing breach plus compensation may not be straightforward. Finally, in relation to consumer transactions, it may well be felt that the need to protect the consumer means that the economically efficient answer is not the one that the courts should support.[15] In addition, consumers may well place a value on what they are seeking to receive under the contract, which is higher than the market value -thus giving rise to the concept of what has been called the 'consumer surplus'.[16] It is also important to remember that parties will not always act in the most economically efficient way in relation to a particular transaction: for example, being seen as a firm that honours its contracts may be more 'valuable' (though difficult to quantify) than making a bigger profit on a particular deal. Nevertheless, provided that its limitations are recognised, the concept of the efficient breach is a useful tool to apply in the analysis of the law on damages for breach of contract.[17]

### 15.3.2 NON-COMPENSATORY DAMAGES?

As stated at the beginning of this section, the purpose of contract damages is generally accepted to be to compensate the claimant. It should be noted, however, that a possibly significant exception to the solely compensatory nature of contract damages has been opened up by the decision of the House of Lords in *Attorney General v Blake*.[18] It was held there that a defendant could, in certain circumstances, be required to hand over to the claimant a benefit acquired by breaking a contract, even where there is no corresponding loss to the claimant. This decision and its implications are discussed fully below (see 15.5).

## 15.4 DAMAGES: MEASURE

Within the overall principle of compensation, there are two basic methods by which damages may be calculated. These can be conveniently labelled as the 'expectation' measure and the 'reliance' measure. Some consideration also needs to be given to consequential losses and non-pecuniary losses. Note also that in some situations the court may order the return of money or property that has been transferred. This is known as 'restitution' and is dealt with at 15.8.

### 15.4.1 EXPECTATION MEASURE

This is the approach that most clearly relates to putting the innocent party into the position he or she would have been in had the contract been properly performed. It is concerned with fulfilling the expectations of that party, so far as money can, as to the anticipated benefits that would have flowed from the successful completion of the contract.[19] In particular, where the innocent party, as will commonly be the case, was expecting to

---

15  See Collins, 2003, pp 401–02 for the impact of considerations of the 'social market' on the concept of 'efficient breach'.

16  The phrase was coined by Harris, Ogus and Phillips, 1979. See also Harris, Campbell and Halson, 2002, p 168. The existence of the concept has now been recognised by several members of the House of Lords – see Lord Mustill in *Ruxley Electronics and Construction Ltd v Forsyth* [1996] AC 344, p 360; [1995] 3 All ER 268, p 277, and Lords Steyn (somewhat diffidently) and Scott (in fact, though not in name) in *Farley v Skinner* [2001] UKHL 49, [21] and [79]; [2001] 4 All ER 801, pp 810 and 828.

17  Macneil, however, suggests that, outside of 'futures' contracts, the opportunities for gain through 'efficient breach' are in reality so rare as to be almost non-existent, so that 'general propositions about remedies based on them tell singularly little about efficiency in the real world': Macneil, 1988, p 15. See also Macneil, 1980 and Macneil, 1982. These three articles are all extracted in Campbell, 2001, Chapter 7. See also Harris, Campbell and Halson, 2002, pp 19–20, for a response to some of Macneil's criticisms.

18  [2001] 1 AC 268; [2000] 4 All ER 385.

19  In contrast to the standard measure of damages in tort, which aims to compensate for losses arising from the wrongful action by putting the claimant back into the position he or she was in prior to the tort being committed.

make a profit as a result of the contract, this will generally be recoverable,[20] as well as any other consequential losses flowing from the breach. Suppose, for example, A has a piece of machinery that needs repair and he engages B to carry out the work. A tells B that the work must be done on 1 November because A has an order for which he needs the machine on 2 November, and which he will lose if it is unavailable. If B, in breach of contract, fails to carry out the work, A will probably be able to claim the lost profit on the 2 November contract. If B had performed the contract properly, A would have made the profit, and therefore it should be recoverable.

In general, the calculation of the expectation interest involves looking at where the claimant would have ended up if the contract had been performed properly. In making that calculation, account must of course be taken of any costs that the claimant may have saved by the defendant's non performance. It is the claimant's *profit* on the contract that is recoverable, which will not necessarily involve the defendant in paying the full price of the missing performance. If, for example, in the situation described in the previous paragraph, the non-availability of the machine has meant that A has employed fewer staff and therefore has a reduced wage bill, this might be taken into account in assessing the profit that has been lost. It also follows that if A would not in fact have made any profit from the transaction, only nominal damages will be recoverable.

There are two situations that may cause particular difficulty for calculation of the expectation interest and that accordingly merit further consideration: first, where the profit was not certain and, second, where after breach the cost of fulfilling the claimant's full expectation may be disproportionate to the eventual benefit.

In the situation where the profit was not certain to be made, there may be a partial recovery on the basis that the claimant has lost the chance to make it. In *Chaplin v Hicks*,[21] for example, the breach of contract prevented the plaintiff from taking part in an audition.[22] She was allowed to recover a proportion of what she might have earned had she been successful in the audition. Similarly, in *Simpson v London and North Western Railway Co*,[23] the defendant failed to deliver some specimens to a trade fair by the specified date. The plaintiff was allowed to recover compensation for the loss of sales he might have made had the specimens arrived on time. In these cases, it should be noted that the claimant may do better than would have been the case if the contract had not been broken. Ms Chaplin might not have been selected at the audition, and Mr Simpson might not have made any sales. The court may be said in fact to be placing a monetary value on what is essentially a non-pecuniary loss – that is, the loss of a chance. Alternatively, it might be said that in this situation the compensatory aspects of contract damages are tinged with a punitive element, in that the defendant is made to pay in order to show that his or her behaviour fell below an acceptable level.[24] Another area of uncertainty may arise where

---

20  Subject to the rules of remoteness, mitigation, etc., dealt with below, 15.5.
21  [1911] 2 KB 786. See also Reece, 1996. Compare *Chweidan v Mishcon de Reya (A Firm)* [2014] EWHC 2685 (QB). In *Britned Development Ltd v ABB AB* [2018] EWHC 2616 (Ch) at [12] Smith J stated: "A good example is the case of *Chaplin v Hicks* [1911] 2 KB 786, where the claimant lost the chance of participating in the final of a competition. Damages were assessed according to the claimant's chance of winning (i.e. one in 10). This level of compensation is, in one sense, wrong, in that either the claimant would have won the competition (in which case one in 10 under-compensates) or the claimant would not have won (in which case one in 10 over-compensates), but it achieves a proper outcome by navigating between these extremes."
22  The case is often referred to as involving a 'beauty contest' (see Treitel, 2015, p 1145; Harris, Campbell and Halson, 2002, p 81; Halson, 2013, p 463), but this is clearly wrong.
23  (1876) 1 QBD 274. For other examples of this type of situation, see *Manubens v Leon* [1919] 1 KB 208 (opportunity for hairdresser to earn tips); *Joseph v National Magazine Co* [1959] 1 Ch 14 (opportunity to enhance reputation by publishing a book).
24  See, for example, the comment by Vaughan Williams LJ: 'But the fact that damages cannot be assessed with certainty does not relieve the wrongdoer of the necessity of paying damages for his breach of contract':

the party in breach had a discretion as to how exactly to perform the contract. The Court of Appeal held, in *Durham Tees Valley Airport Ltd*,[25] that in such a situation the court should base damages on the probable level of performance, not on the minimum level that the defendant could provide under the contract. The court was entitled to assume that the defendant would have operated the contract in line with its own best interests.

### 15.4.2 WHAT IF THE COST OF COMPENSATING THE CLAIMANT IS DISPROPORTIONATE TO THE COST OF THE CONTRACT?

The second area of difficulty in finding the appropriate award to meet the claimant's expectations arises in connection with the situation (usually occurring in construction contracts) where the cost, following a breach, of providing the claimant with exactly what was bargained for may be out of all proportion to the benefit that would thereby be obtained. This problem was given full consideration by the House of Lords in *Ruxley Electronics and Construction Ltd v Forsyth*.[26]

The position under previous case law on this type of situation involving building contracts was that the court would normally allow the recovery of the 'cost of cure' – that is, putting the building into the condition it should have been in if the breach had not occurred. This is subject to the limitation that if the cost of cure is significantly greater than the reduction in value of the property concerned, then the court may refuse to allow it.[27] This limitation did not, however, normally apply to the situation where the 'cure' relates to the defendant providing something that was specifically promised in the contract. Thus, in *Radford v De Froberville*,[28] the plaintiff was allowed to recover for the cost of building a brick wall, because this is what had been contracted for, even though a cheaper fence would have served the purpose (which was simply to mark a boundary).

This aspect of the courts' approach must now be considered in the light of *Ruxley Electronics and Construction Ltd v Forsyth*.[29]

---

**Key case** *Ruxley Electronics and Construction Ltd v Forsyth* (1996)

Facts: The defendant in this case entered into a contract for the construction of a swimming pool and building to enclose it, at a cost of £70,000. The depth of this pool at one end was to be 7ft 6in. After the work was completed, the depth of the pool was discovered to be only 6ft 9in. The plaintiff sought to recover payment for the installation of the pool. The defendant counterclaimed that the pool did not meet its specification and sought compensation for this. It was not possible for the pool to be adapted and the only way to produce a pool with a depth of 7ft 6in would have been by total reconstruction. This would have cost over £20,000.

The trial judge found that the pool was entirely suitable for the purpose for which the defendant wished to use it and, given the very high cost of reconstruction, held that the measure of damages should be the difference in value between the pool as supplied, and a pool that met the contract specification. He assessed this difference as nil, but awarded the defendant £2,500 for 'loss of amenity'. The defendant appealed, and the Court of Appeal held that he was entitled to have a pool that met the contract

---

[1911] 2 KB 786, p 792. Bridge (1995, p 445) suggests that the award of damages in this area is simply a result of the courts' unwillingness to limit the claimant to nominal damages.

25 [2010] EWCA Civ 485. See also *Jet2.com Ltd v SC Compan’a Netionala de Transporturi Aeriene Romane Tarom SA* [2014] EWCA Civ 87.

26 [1996] AC 344; [1995] 3 All ER 268. A very helpful analysis of this case is to be found in O'Sullivan, 1997.

27 *Watts v Morrow* [1991] 4 All ER 937 – cost of repairing house £34,000, diminution in value £15,000.

28 [1978] 1 All ER 33.

29 [1996] AC 344; [1995] 3 All ER 268.

specification. It awarded him damages of over £20,000 to meet the cost of reconstruction. The customer appealed.

Held: The House of Lords restored the trial judge's decision. It confirmed that in building contracts there are two principal measures of damages, namely the difference in
value and the cost of reinstatement. Where it would be unreasonable to award the cost
of reinstatement (because, for example, the expense would be totally out of proportion
to the benefit to be obtained), the court should award the difference in value. As Lord
Jauncey put it:[30]

> Damages are designed to compensate for an established loss and not to provide
> a gratuitous benefit to the aggrieved party.

Given that the defendant had a perfectly serviceable swimming pool, 'were he to receive
the cost of building a new one and retain the existing one he would have recovered
not compensation for loss but a very substantial gratuitous benefit'.[31] The appropriate
measure here was therefore the difference in value, which (given the judge's finding)
meant that only nominal damages were recoverable under this head. The House of
Lords was, however, prepared to allow the judge's award of £2,500 for 'loss of amenity'
to stand.

The precise nature of the award for loss of amenity is considered further, below.

## For thought

*What do you think the outcome of Ruxley Electronics and Construction Ltd v Forsyth
would have been if the swimming pool had been too shallow to allow the claimant to
carry out some activity, such as diving? Would the claimant then have been able to
claim the cost of having the pool rebuilt?*

### 15.4.3 IN FOCUS: HOW FAR DOES THE *RUXLEY* DECISION GO?

The House of Lords' decision in this case appears quite sensible on the facts. Nevertheless, it leaves open the problem that an unscrupulous contractor may be able to play fast
and loose with the contract specifications in a construction contract, provided perhaps
that the final product is fit for the purposes for which the other party wishes to use it. If it
is so fit, then significant reconstruction costs needed to meet the contract specification
may be considered unreasonable, and there may well be little or no difference in the market value of the relevant construction. The innocent party is largely left without a remedy,
despite the fact that what has been provided is not what he or she wanted. Comparison
can be made with the position as regards commercial sales of goods, where a purchaser
may still have a remedy, even if goods are 'fit for their purpose', if they do not match the
contract description. By virtue of s 13 of the Sale of Goods Act 1979, the purchaser will
generally be able to reject such goods. The person who contracts for the construction of a
building now seems to be in a much weaker position. Much will depend on just how far the
courts are prepared to go. Suppose, for example, I contract for a house to be built with a

---

30  [1996] AC 344, p 357; [1995] 3 All ER 268, p 274.
31  Ibid, p 358; p 275.

special warm air heating system that has to be built into the walls during construction. The builder constructs a house with a conventional gas-fired central heating system and radiators. The house is perfectly fit to be lived in, and its value is not significantly different from the house with a warm air system (indeed, it may have a higher market value). Am I really to be left without any effective remedy against the builder? The principles applied by the House of Lords in *Ruxley Electronics v Forsyth* would arguably seem to suggest so. This is a situation that might have been dealt with by the restitutionary approach suggested by the Court of Appeal in *Attorney General v Blake*.[32] The constructors of the swimming pool had delivered a 'skimped performance' and the Court of Appeal's approach would have allowed the court to award to the customer the money that had been saved in not building the swimming pool to the contract specification.[33] This aspect of the Court of Appeal's judgment in *Blake* was, however, specifically rejected by the House of Lords in that case.[34]

### 15.4.4 WHAT IS 'LOSS OF AMENITY'?

As was noted above, the only award which the plaintiff received in *Ruxley Electronics v Forsyth* was for 'loss of amenity'. What is the precise nature of this award? There are two possible answers. One is that it is based on the concept of the 'consumer surplus' – that it compensates the claimant for something that has been contracted for going beyond the market value of what is to be provided. The expectation interest must therefore be increased to take account of this. The second possibility is that it is an example of one of the limited range of cases where the courts are prepared to award damages for 'distress and inconvenience' arising as a consequence of a breach of contract. This area is discussed further below (see 15.4.5) where we will explore the House of Lords' decision in *Farley v Skinner*.[35] *Farley v Skinner* concerned a contract for the survey of a house, where the surveyor had been specifically asked by the prospective purchaser to check on aircraft noise. The surveyor failed to do this properly and the purchaser, having moved in, sought compensation for the fact that his enjoyment of the property was reduced, though there was no reduction in its market value. The House of Lords approved an award of £10,000 for disappointment and distress (see further 15.4.8 below). In so doing *Ruxley Electronics v Forsyth* was discussed. There was, however, disagreement in their Lordships' speeches as to the correct basis of the award in *Ruxley*. Lords Steyn and Hutton, as well as Lord Clyde on slightly different grounds, leant towards the second possible basis outlined above. By contrast, Lord Scott felt that an award for 'loss of amenity' is a separate element in the expectation interest that, in appropriate cases, will be awarded in addition to any other elements (for example, reduction in the market value of what has been supplied).[36] The calculation of the value of a 'loss of amenity' is always going to be difficult, since it is by its nature 'non-pecuniary' loss. In both *Ruxley Electronics* and *Farley v Skinner*, the House of Lords clearly took the view that the amounts should be modest,[37] and that the awards in both cases were generous to the claimant. No satisfactory method of calculating what should be awarded is put forward, however, and it seems to be left to the virtually unfettered discretion of the trial judge as to how much should be given under

---

32  [1998] Ch 439; [1998] 1 All ER 833. See below, 15.5.

33  Though, on the facts, the constructors do not seem to have saved any significant sum on the work.

34  [2000] 1 AC 268; [2000] 4 All ER 385.

35  [2001] UKHL 49; [2001] 4 All ER 801. See also *Newman v Framewood Manor Management Co Ltd* [2012] EWCA Civ 159 at [48]-[54] *per* Arden LJ.

36  See O'Sullivan, 1997, pp 14–6. This would also seem to be implicit in Lord Scott's comment in *Farley v Skinner* to the effect that damages for discomfort (as opposed to loss of amenity) would not be recoverable in addition to a reduction in market value: [2001] UKHL 49, para 109; [2001] 4 All ER 801, p 833.

37  See also *Freeman v Niroomand* [1996] 52 Con LR 116, discussed in O'Sullivan, 1997, p 16. See also *Harrison v Shepherd Homes Ltd* [2011] EWHC 1811 at [264] on claiming 'loss of amenity' with other heads of loss; for the appeal see [2012] EWCA Civ 964.

this head. This is clearly unsatisfactory, as O'Sullivan has pointed out,[38] but it is difficult to find a solution. The value of the benefit lost is by definition something personal to the claimant, yet the claimant's subjective view cannot be allowed to be the determining factor. It may be that all that can be done is to wait for practice to develop (as it has done in other areas of non-pecuniary loss) so that a standard level for this type of award gradually becomes established.

Finally, it should be noted that the award for loss of amenity is most likely to arise in nonbusiness contracts. It seems likely that if the swimming pool in *Ruxley Electronics* had been built for a developer who was going to sell the property once it was completed, then probably no damages at all would have been recoverable for the failure to build it to the specified depth.

## 15.4.5 RELIANCE MEASURE[39]

In some situations, it may not be easy for the claimant to prove the profits that would have been made if the contract had been properly performed. Here it may sometimes be more sensible to abandon the attempt and, instead, to seek recovery of expenditure that has been incurred in anticipation of the contract. This is what is referred to as the 'reliance' measure. The general result of this type of award is that the claimant is put back to the position he or she occupied prior to the contract being made, rather than in the position if the contract had been performed properly.[40]

An example of this type of situation is *Anglia Television Ltd v Reed*.[41]

**Key case** *Anglia Television Ltd v Reed* (1972)

Facts: Reed was an actor who was under contract to play a leading role in a television film. At a late stage, Reed withdrew and the project was unable to go ahead. In suing Reed for breach of contract, Anglia did not seek their lost profits. It would have been very difficult to estimate exactly what these would have been, given the uncertainties of the entertainment industry. Instead, they sought compensation for all the expenses incurred towards setting up the film.

Held: The company was entitled to all its expenses, including, somewhat surprisingly, expenditure incurred *before* the contract with Reed was entered into (provided that these fell within the rule of remoteness).[42] The basis for this was that at the time the contract was entered into, the defendant must have been aware of the expenditure that had already taken place and that therefore this would be wasted if the project collapsed.

The decision as to whether to seek expectation or reliance damages will generally lie with the claimant (as was made clear in *Anglia Television Ltd v Reed*). There have been examples, however, of the court deciding that reliance is the appropriate measure. This occurred in the Australian case of *McRae v Commonwealth Disposals Commission*,[43] in

---

38 O'Sullivan, 1997, pp 17–8. See also Harris, Ogus and Phillips, 1979.
39 See Fuller and Perdue, 1936 – the classic article analysing the reliance interest. Compare Campbell, 2015.
40 The measure is thus much closer to the normal tort measure of damages.
41 [1972] 1 QB 60; [1971] 3 All ER 690.
42 See below, 15.6.1.
43 (1951) 84 CLR 377 – loss of profits rejected as too speculative. For other aspects of this case, see Chapter 9, 9.4.1.

relation to the contract to salvage a non-existent ship. In some situations, on the other hand, the court may say that the reliance measure should not be available. This will be the case, for instance, where the difficulty in identifying profits results primarily from the fact that the claimant has made a bad bargain so that even if the contract had been properly performed, the claimant would not have covered his or her expenses.[44] In *C and P Haulage v Middleton*,[45] some of the plaintiff's costs were in fact reduced as a result of the breach and the plaintiff's loss of equipment (which had to be handed over to the defendant) was an integral part of the original contract. In that situation, the plaintiff was only allowed to sue for the expectation interest. The burden of proving that the bargain was 'bad' in this sense often falls on the defendant.[46] The claimant does not have to prove that sufficient profit would have been made on the contract to cover the expenses incurred.

Although in general a choice must be made as to which measure of damages is being sought, in certain circumstances it may be possible to recover both expectation and reliance losses, as long as this does not lead to double recovery. Thus, in *Naughton v O'Callaghan*,[47] which concerned a racehorse that turned out not to have the pedigree contracted for, the buyer recovered the difference in value resulting from this breach (expectation loss) and the costs of training and stabling (reliance loss). Where lost profits are claimed, however, it is only if net profits are claimed that reliance damages may also be available. If *gross* profits are recovered, the claimant cannot also recover the money spent in generating these profits. In the case of *Cullinane v British 'Rema' Manufacturing Co Ltd*,[48] there appears to have been some confusion between gross and net profits, and the case is sometimes cited as authority for the proposition that expectation and reliance damages can never be recovered together.[49] It is submitted, however, that the better view is that outlined above, which distinguishes between gross and net profits.[50]

### 15.4.6 CONSEQUENTIAL LOSSES

There are some losses that flow from the breach, but that cannot be put into the category of 'expenses' (that is, reliance) or thwarted expectations. Provided the causal link can be established, and they are not too remote,[51] then they may be recoverable. If there is a contract for the purchase of a piece of machinery, for example, and it is defective, then the expectation interest may allow the recovery of lost profits that would have been gained by using the machine. If, however, the defect causes the machine to explode, which results in damage to the buyer's premises, or personal injury to the buyer, compensation in relation to these consequential losses can also be recovered.

---

44  See *Omak Maritime Ltd v Mamola Challenger Shipping Co* [2010] EWHC 2026 (Comm).

45  [1983] 3 All ER 94.

46  In *Dataliner Ltd v Vehicle Builders and Repairers Association* (1995), *The Independent,* 30 August 1995, it was held that the burden of proof is ordinarily on the claimant. However, certainly if the nature of the breach is such that it is impossible for the claimant to discharge this burden the burden seems to shift to the defendant: *CCC Films (London) Ltd v Impact Quadrant Films Ltd* [1985] QB 16; [1984] 3 All ER 298 and *Omak Maritime Ltd v Mamola Challenger Shipping Co* [2010] EWHC 2026 (Comm). However, more recent authority suggests that the burden is generally on the defendant *(Grange v Quinn* [2013] EWCA Civ 24 and *Thai Airways International Public Company Ltd v KI Holdings Co Ltd* [2015] EWHC 1250 (Comm)). See also the Australian case of *The Commonwealth of Australia v Amann Aviation Pty Ltd* [1991] 174 CLR 64, discussed in this context by Bridge, 1995, p 468.

47  [1990] 3 All ER 191.

48  [1954] 1 QB 292; [1953] 2 All ER 1257.

49  See, for example, Lord Denning in *Anglia Television Ltd v Reed* [1972] 1 QB 60, pp 63–4; [1971] 3 All ER 690, p 692.

50  See also MacLeod, 1970; Harris, Campbell and Halson, 2002, pp 130–32; Beale, 1980, p 156.

51  See below, 15.6.1.

## 15.4.7 SUPERVENING EVENTS

The issue of the measure of damages when supervening events have increased the claimant's loss was considered by the Court of Appeal in *Beoco Ltd v Alfa Laval*.[52] The first defendants had installed a heat exchanger at the plaintiffs' works. A leak was discovered and a repair attempted by the second defendants. The plaintiffs put the heat exchanger back in use without carrying out proper tests. In fact, the defects in the exchanger were more extensive than had been realised and shortly afterwards it exploded. The plaintiffs sought to recover from the first defendants an amount relating to the loss of profits they would have suffered as a result of the need to further repair or replace the exchanger had it not exploded. Their action was based on the defendants' breach of contract in their initially having supplied a defective exchanger. The Court of Appeal held that the measure of damages for hypothetical losses should be the same in contract as in tort.[53] Thus, where a supervening event causes greater damage than the original breach of contract, the claimant cannot recover losses that would have been suffered had the event not occurred. Since the explosion was caused by the negligence of the plaintiffs' employees, they could not recover the lost profits that they might otherwise have suffered as a result of the first defendants' breach of contract. This conclusion is, in one sense, out of line with the normal approach to the assessment of contractual damages, which requires the issues to be looked at in the light of the parties' knowledge *at the time of the contract*. This is the way in which the question of 'remoteness' is dealt with.[54] Taking account of later events, as in this case, means that they may well have the effect of reducing the defendants' liability. If, however, the event does not occur until after the damages have been assessed, then this will not apply. Thus, if in this case the explosion had not occurred until after trial, the plaintiffs would probably have been able to claim the lost profits they were seeking. This runs the risk of making the assessment of damages dependent on rather arbitrary factors, such as when exactly a particular event occurs.

A different approach to a particular type of supervening event was taken by the House of Lords in *South Australia Asset Management Corp v York Montague Ltd*.[55] This was concerned with cases where there had been a negligent overvaluation of a property, which has been used as security for a loan. The question at issue was to what extent should the negligent valuer be liable for the fact that the property has reduced in value because of a fall in the market. Suppose, for example, that the property is valued at £15m when its true value is £10m. The lender lends £12m. When the borrower defaults, the property is sold but, because of a fall in market values, only realises £5m. Should the valuer be liable for the full loss that the lender has suffered (that is, £7m) or only the difference between the valuation and the actual value at the time of the contract (£5m)? The House of Lords, with reference to the relevant duty of care, took the view that the valuer should only be liable for those losses that are properly attributable to having given wrong information. It held that the lender's loss in this situation is having less security for the loan than was thought. The correct measure of damages was therefore the difference between the actual and true valuations – in the example given above, £5m. The decision, which reversed the judgment of the Court of Appeal, is not uncontroversial. There is some strength in the Court of Appeal's view that if the valuer had given correct information, the lender would not have entered into the transaction at all, and that therefore the full losses should be recoverable. The House of Lords has, however, settled this issue for the time being.[56]

---

52 [1994] 4 All ER 464.
53 *Carslogie Steamship Co Ltd v Royal Norwegian Government* [1952] AC 292; [1952] 1 All ER 20 was applied.
54 See below, 15.6.1.
55 [1997] AC 191; [1996] 3 All ER 365.
56 In *Hughes-Holland v BPE Solicitors* [2017] UKSC 21 at [34]-[36] Lord Sumption (with whom Lords Neuberger, Mance, Clarke and Hodge agreed) provided some clarification of this case when stating: "The decision

The effect of a supervening event foreseen by the parties was considered by the House of Lords in *Golden Strait Corporation v Nippon Yusen Kubishika Kaisa*.[57] The contract between the parties had provided that it could be determined by either party in the event of war breaking out between, for example, the United States and Iraq. In 2001 the defendants repudiated the contract. This breach was accepted by the claimants, who sued for damages. In 2003 war broke out between the United States and Iraq. The question was whether this event, which would have entitled the defendants to terminate the contract without being in breach, put a cap on the claimants' damages. The House of Lords, by a majority of 3:2, held that it did. In deciding on an award of damages a judge or arbitrator was entitled to take account of possible future events that would have an impact on the amount of such an award. If the damages had been assessed in 2001, the award would have appropriately taken account of the possibility of a future war, which

---

in *SAAMCO* has often been misunderstood, not least by the writers who have criticised it. The misunderstanding arises, I think, from a tendency to overlook two fundamental features of the reasoning…The first is that where the contribution of the defendant is to supply material which the client will take into account in making his own decision on the basis of a broader assessment of the risks, the defendant has no legal responsibility for his decision…This is why in *SAAMCO* itself Lord Hoffmann had rejected the distinction made by the Court of Appeal between "no transaction" and "successful transaction" cases. It was "irrelevant to the scope of the duty of care"…The second fundamental feature of the reasoning follows from the first. It is that the principle has nothing to do with the causation of loss as that expression is usually understood in the law."

57   [2007] UKHL 12; [2007] 3 All ER 1. See also *Ageas (UK) Ltd vKwik-Fit (GB) Ltd* [2014] EWHC 2178 and *Flame SA v Glory Wealth Shipping Pte Ltd* [2013] EWHC 3153 (Comm). In *Bunge SA v Nidera BV (formerly Nidera Handelscompagnie BV)* [2013] 1 CLC 325, at [54] Hamblen J stated: "I would not accept that it is settled law that *The Golden Victory* approach applies to a one-off sale of goods contract such as this. The majority in *The Golden Victory* recognised that they were departing from the general rule that damages in respect of a marketable commodity fall to be assessed by reference to the available market price at the date of breach, but considered that the compensatory principle justified them so doing in the circumstances. However, *The Golden Victory* concerned a period contract and the departure from the general rule was only adopted in relation to the period element of the damages claim, not the applicable hire rate. Further, as the Board observed, Lord Scott at para 34 recognised that the assessment at the date of breach rule "is particularly apt" in sale of goods cases, as is reflected in the Sale of Goods Act. At para 35 he drew a distinction between a one-off sale and "a contract for the supply of goods over some specified period". It is also to be noted that *Benjamin* treats *The Golden Victory* as being relevant to sale of goods cases because its 'reasoning could apply to long term contracts for the sale of goods' (para 19–170)." The case involved a contract for the sale of Russian milling wheat which was, prior to the shipping period and in breach of contract, cancelled. It transpired that the contract could, subsequently, have been legitimately cancelled, within the shipping period and under the terms of the contact, following a Russian embargo on the export of wheat. To what extent, if at all, could the subsequent ability to legitimately cancel the contract be taken into account in calculating damages? This required a consideration of *The Golden Victory* and the Supreme Court in *Bunge SA v Nidera BV(formerly Nidera Handelscompagnie BV)* [2015] UKSC 43 clarified the scope of the decision in *The Golden Victory*. Lord Sumption (with whom Lord Neuberger, Lord Mance, Lord Clarke and Lord Toulson (who delivered a separate speech)) stated: "The leading speech for the majority, which was delivered by Lord Scott of Foscote, contains dicta which have sometimes been taken to suggest a distinction between a contract for a one-off sale and a contract for the supply of goods or services over a period of time: see paras 34–35. These dicta influenced both the Appeal Board and Hamblen J in the present case. But I do not think that Lord Scott was suggesting that the underlying principle was any different in the case of a one-off sale. Where the only question is the relevant date for taking the market price, the financial consequences of the breach may be said to "crystallise" at that date. But where, after that date, some supervening event occurs which shows that that neither the original contract (had it continued) nor the notional substitute contract at the market price would ever have been performed, the concept of "crystallising" the assessment of damages at that price is unhelpful. The occurrence of the supervening event would have reduced the value of performance, possibly to nothing, even if the contract had not been wrongfully terminated and whatever the relevant market price. The nature of that problem does not differ according to whether the contract provides for a single act of performance or several successive ones. Nor, as it seems to me, is there any principled reason why the majority's solution should be any different in the two cases."

Accordingly only nominal damages were awarded.

would have allowed termination. The chance of this occurring, which could range from extremely unlikely to virtual certainty, would have had to have been assessed. If, however, the assessment was being made, as was the case here, after the event justifying termination had occurred, it was appropriate for it to be fully taken into account in assessing the claimants' losses.

### 15.4.8 NON-PECUNIARY LOSSES

Damages for breach of contract are primarily concerned with economic losses of one kind or another (pecuniary loss). In some situations, however, non-pecuniary losses will be caused by a breach of contract. If, for example, a defective product results in personal injury to the purchaser, there is no reason in principle why damages should not be recovered in relation to the pain and suffering so caused. Of course, third parties who are injured will have to rely on tortious remedies at common law or under the Consumer Protection Act 1987.

A more difficult question arises in relation to any mental distress, anguish or annoyance caused by a breach of contract. The courts have tended to be wary of awarding compensation under this heading but the whole area was fairly recently reconsidered in a number of House of Lords' decisions.[58] The traditional view is that expressed in *Addis v Gramophone Co Ltd*.[59] The House of Lords refused to uphold an award that had been made in relation to the 'harsh and humiliating' way in which the plaintiff had been dismissed from his job in breach of contract. This line was followed in a more recent dismissal case, *Bliss v South East Thames RHA*,[60] where a surgeon had sued the health authority by which he was employed. The authority had, following a dispute between the surgeon and a colleague, required him to undergo a psychiatric examination. The surgeon refused and was suspended. The surgeon treated this as a repudiatory breach and sued for breach of contract. He succeeded at first instance, and was awarded £2,000 for mental distress. The Court of Appeal held, however, that it was bound by *Addis v Gramophone*, and held that it was not possible to recover damages for mental distress in an action for wrongful dismissal.

In coming to this conclusion, it disapproved the decision in *Cox v Phillips Industries Ltd*,[61] where damages were recovered for distress and anxiety resulting from a demotion. Some doubts about *Addis v Gramophone* were raised by the decision of the House of Lords in *Malik v BCCI*,[62] the facts of which have been given in Chapter 6, 6.6.7. The House took the view that where there was a breach of the implied term of trust and confidence in an employment contract, *Addis* should not always be regarded as precluding an award of damages for loss of reputation or difficulty in obtaining future employment. The House was not, however, dealing with the manner of dismissal in this case and was not concerned with 'injury to feelings'. The House of Lords subsequently confirmed in *Johnson v Unisys Ltd*[63] that *Addis* should not be regarded as having been overruled in *Malik v BCCI*. Damages for distress and injury to feelings resulting from the manner of a dismissal are still unavailable in an action for breach of contract.[64] The Supreme Court, in *Edwards v*

---

58 *Johnson v Gore Wood & Co* [2001] 1 All ER 481 *Johnson v Unisys Ltd* [2001] UKHL 13; [2001] 2 All ER 801; *Farley v Skinner* [2001] UKHL 49; [2001] 4 All ER 801. Compare the position in relation to psychiatric injury on which see *Yapp v Foreign and Commonwealth Office* [2014] EWCA Civ 1512.

59 [1909] AC 488.

60 [1985] IRLR 308.

61 [1976] 3 All ER 161.

62 [1998] AC 20; [1997] 3 All ER 1. In *Oraki v Bramston* [2015] EWHC 2046 Proudman J considered, without fully deciding, whether a claimant could bring a claim for mental distress against their trustee in bankruptcy.

63 [2001] UKHL 13; [2001] 2 All ER 801.

64 Lord Hoffmann in *Johnson v Unisys* suggested that non-pecuniary losses could be recovered under the statutory regime governing 'unfair dismissal', and used this as part of the argument for rejecting a common law action. This suggestion was rejected by the House of Lords in *Dunnachie v Kingston-upon-Hull City*

*Chesterfield Royal Hospital NHS Foundation Trust*, has also now ruled that the *Johnson* approach applies to breach of an express term of a contract relating to dismissal proce-dures, as well as to an implied term.[65] Exceptionally, however, it may be possible to claim damages for non-pecuniary loss in relation to a breach of contract that is constituted by treatment leading up to a dismissal. This was the view of the House of Lords in *Eastwood v Magnox Electric*.[66]

On the other hand, it has been held that where one of the purposes of the contract is to provide pleasure or enjoyment, damages for distress and disappointment caused by a breach may be recovered. Thus, in *Jarvis v Swan's Tours Ltd*,[67] such damages were awarded in relation to breach of contract in the provision of a holiday that had promised to provide 'a great time'.[68] Where, however, the contract is a purely commercial one, dam-ages for anguish and vexation will not generally be allowed. Thus, in *Hayes v James and Charles Dodd*,[69] the plaintiffs were suing their solicitors for breach of contract.

The solicitors had given an assurance that a right of way existed in relation to access to a property that the plaintiffs were purchasing for their business. This turned out to be untrue, and the plaintiffs' business failed as a result. The trial judge awarded damages of £1,500 to each plaintiff for anguish and vexation. The Court of Appeal, however, applied the same approach as in *Bliss v South East Thames RHA*. This meant that, as Staughton LJ held:[70]

> damages for mental distress in contract are, as a matter of policy, limited to certain classes of case. I would broadly follow the classification by Dillon LJ in *Bliss v South East Thames RHA*: '... where the contract which has been broken was itself a con-tract to provide peace of mind or freedom from distress'. It may be that the class is somewhat wider than that. But it should not, in my judgment, include any case where the object of the contract was not comfort or pleasure, or the relief of discom-fort, but simply carrying on a commercial activity with a view to profit.

Subsequent cases have taken a similar line. In *Watts v Morrow*, the general rule and its exceptions were restated by Bingham LJ, in a passage that has subsequently been approved by the House of Lords:[71]

> A contract-breaker is not in general liable for any distress, frustration, anxiety, dis-pleasure, vexation, tension or aggravation which his breach of contract may cause to the innocent party ... But the rule is not absolute. Where the *very object* of the contract is to provide pleasure, relaxation, peace of mind or freedom from molesta-tion, damages will be awarded if the fruit of the contract is not provided or if the contrary result is procured instead ... A contract to survey a house for a prospec-tive purchaser does not fall within this exceptional category. In cases not falling within this exceptional category, damages are in my view recoverable for *physical*

---

*Council* [2004] UKHL 36; [2004] 3 All ER 1011. Damages under s 123(1) of the Employment Rights Act 1996 do not extend to non-pecuniary loss. See also *Santos Gomes v Higher Level Care Ltd* [2018] EWCA Civ 418 (in relation to a breach of the Working Time Regulations 1998).

65  [2011] UKSC 58.

66  [2004] UKHL 35; [2004] 3 All ER 991.

67  [1973] QB 233; [1973] 1 All ER 71.

68  A similar approach can be seen in *Jackson v Horizon Holidays* [1975] 3 All ER 92 – discussed in Chapter 5, 5.7.

69  [1990] 2 All ER 815.

70  Ibid, p 824.

71  [1991] 4 All ER 937, pp 959–60 (emphasis added). Approved in *Johnson v Gore Wood & Co* [2001] 1 All ER 481 and in *Farley v Skinner* [2001] UKHL 49; [2001] 4 All ER 801.

*inconvenience* and discomfort caused by the breach and mental suffering directly related to that inconvenience and discomfort.

Bingham LJ's analysis allows for two categories of case where non-pecuniary losses may be recoverable. The first is where the 'very object' of the contract is to provide pleasure, etc. This will include contracts for holidays, wedding photographs, etc.[72] It will not include cases where disappointment is merely an incidental consequence of a breach. Thus, in *Alexander v Rolls-Royce Motor Cars Ltd*,[73] the Court of Appeal refused to award damages for disappointment, loss of enjoyment or distress resulting from a breach of a contract to repair the plaintiff's motor car. The second of Bingham's categories is where the breach of contract has caused 'physical inconvenience and discomfort'. These two categories have now been fully reviewed by the House of Lords in *Farley v Skinner*.[74]

> **Key case** *Farley v Skinner* (2001)
>
> **Facts:** The claimant was seeking damages from a surveyor who had inspected and reported on a house that the claimant had then bought. Specific instructions had been given to the surveyor to check and report on any problems with aircraft noise.[75] The surveyor failed to mention in his report that the house was near an aircraft navigation beacon, around which aircraft were often 'stacked' waiting to land, so that the use and enjoyment of the property was affected by aircraft noise (particularly at weekends). The county court judge found that the defendant was in breach. He held that the value of the house was not affected by the breach, but awarded the claimant £10,000 for non-pecuniary damage. The Court of Appeal overturned the award on the basis that, applying the *Watts v Morrow* tests, this was not a case where the 'very object' of the contract was to provide pleasure,[76] nor could the annoyance caused by the aircraft noise be considered to amount to 'physical inconvenience'.
>
> **Held:** The House of Lords restored the judge's award, holding that this was a situation where non-pecuniary loss was recoverable, given that the specific obligation to check for aircraft noise was designed to enhance the claimant's enjoyment.

The four speeches delivered in the House of Lords differ in some respects in their reasoning,[77] but there is a fair degree of similarity between the positions of Lord Steyn and Lord Scott. Since Lord Browne-Wilkinson in concurring expressed agreement with both their speeches, their conclusions will be taken as representing the *ratio* of the case.

In analysing Bingham LJ's first category (in *Watts v Morrow*), where the 'very object' of the contract is to provide pleasure, etc., the view was taken that this should not be confined too narrowly. It did not mean that the overall contract had to be one concerned with

---

72  See *Diesen v Samson* 1971 SLT (Sh Ct) 49 (a Scottish case dealing with wedding photographs); *Heywood v Wellers* [1976] QB 446; [1976] 1 All ER 300 (solicitor's failure to take action to protect the plaintiff from 'molestation'). See also *Halcyon House Ltd v Baines* [2014] EWHC 2216.

73  [1996] RTR 95.

74  [2001] UKHL 49; [2001] 4 All ER 801.

75  The house was situated near to Gatwick Airport, so this was clearly likely to be an issue.

76  In this the Court was influenced by the fact that *Watts v Morrow* was itself a case of a negligent survey, and damages for non-pecuniary loss had been refused.

77  For a full discussion, see McKendrick and Graham, 2002. On the difficulties of classifying this type of loss see *Moorjani v Durban Estates Ltd* [2015] EWCA Civ 1252.

the provision of pleasure. Lord Steyn said: 'It is sufficient if a major or important object of the contract is to give pleasure, relaxation or peace of mind.'[78] Lord Scott went even further. Relying on *Ruxley Electronics and Construction Ltd v Forsyth*,[79] he concluded that:[80]

> if a party's contractual performance has failed to provide to the other contracting party something to which that other was, under the contract, entitled, and which, if provided, would have been of value to that party, then, if there is no other way of compensating the injured party, the injured party should be compensated in damages to the extent of that value.

The question for Lord Scott is therefore simply whether there is an obligation of the relevant type within the contract; it does not necessarily have to be a major part of the contract.[81]

The statements of Lord Steyn and Lord Scott clearly apply where there is a positive obligation to bring about such a result – for example, to provide a holiday of the right quality, or (possibly, see 15.4.4) a swimming pool of a specified depth. In *Farley v Skinner*, the obligation was not of this kind. The surveyor did not undertake to guarantee that the property was unaffected by aircraft noise, but simply to take reasonable care in checking whether it was so affected. It was partly on this basis that the Court of Appeal had distinguished *Farley v Skinner* from *Ruxley Electronics v Forsyth*. Lord Steyn, however, refused to accept that this made any difference. He could not see, for example, that there was any difference between a travel agent who guarantees that there is a golf course next to a hotel and one who negligently advises that all hotels in a particular chain have golf courses nearby. In both cases the holidaymaker's holiday may be spoilt by the breach of contract.[82] It was therefore 'difficult to see why in principle only those plaintiffs [sic] who negotiate guarantees may recover non-pecuniary damages for a breach of contract'.[83] Any distinction between obligations of 'guarantee' and those to take reasonable care should therefore be rejected. Lord Scott did not specifically deal with this point, but it is implicit in his conclusions that he agreed with the line taken by Lord Steyn. The conclusion of the House was, therefore, that the buyer could in this case recover damages under Bingham LJ's first category, as applied in *Ruxley Electronics v Forsyth*.

Both Lord Steyn and Lord Scott, however, also took the view that there could be recovery under Bingham LJ's second category. The Court of Appeal had felt that the aircraft noise did not constitute 'physical inconvenience'. The House disagreed. Their view is most clearly stated by Lord Scott. Noting that the distinction between 'physical' and 'non-physical' may be unclear (for example, is being awoken at night by aircraft noise 'physical'?), he concluded:[84]

---

78  [2001] UKHL 49, para 24; [2001] 4 All ER 801, p 812 – disapproving the Court of Appeal's decision in *Knott v Bolton* (1995) 45 Con LR 127, in which non-pecuniary damages were refused for an architect's failure to provide a wide staircase for a gallery and impressive entrance hall. Compare *Khan v University of Leeds* [2018] EWHC 912 (Ch) where damages for mental distress would have been refused if there had been liability as the claim was in relation to a matter peripheral to the main educational purpose of the contract.

79  [1996] AC 344; [1995] 3 All ER 268. The case is fully discussed above, 15.4.2.

80  [2001] UKHL 49, [79]; [2001] 4 All ER 801, p 828.

81  Campbell, however, regards the treatment of Bingham's first category in *Farley v Skinner* as 'a most regrettable muddying of a pool which had begun to clear': Harris, Campbell and Halson, 2002, p 599. See also *Glen Haysman v Mrs Rogers Films Ltd* [2008] EWHC 2494 (QB) and *Herrmann v Withers LLP* [2012] EWHC 1492.

82  See, also, the similar example given by Lord Clyde at [2001] UKHL 49, [43]; [2001] 4 All ER 801, p 818.

83  [2001] UKHL 49, [25]; [2001] 4 All ER 801, p 812.

84  Ibid, [85]; p 829. See also Lord Hutton, [57] – [60]; pp 824–25.

In my opinion, the critical distinction to be drawn is not a distinction between the different types of inconvenience or discomfort of which complaint may be made, but a distinction based on the cause of the inconvenience or discomfort. If the cause is no more than disappointment that the contractual obligation has been broken, damages are not recoverable even if the disappointment has led to a complete mental breakdown. But, if the cause of the inconvenience or discomfort is a sensory (sight, touch, hearing, smell etc.) experience, damages can, subject to the remoteness rules, be recovered.

Since in this case it was clear that the effect was 'physical' in this sense, the buyer was entitled to damages under this heading, as an alternative to those under the first category.

As to the amount that should be awarded, the House of Lords was clearly of the view that the judge's £10,000 was on the high side, but did not interfere with it, nor give any clear guidance on how judges should approach this issue in the future. The problem is the same as that which has been discussed above in relation to *Ruxley Electronics v Forsyth*,[85] and the only answer is probably to wait for case law to establish a 'going rate' for particular types of non-pecuniary loss.

In *Hamilton Jones v David Snape*,[86] the principles set out in *Farley v Skinner* were applied to a contract with a solicitor, where the solicitor had negligently failed to prevent the claimant's children being removed from the jurisdiction by their father. The High Court held that damages for the consequent distress to the claimant were recoverable in an action for breach of contract. A significant purpose of the contract was to ensure that the claimant retained custody of her children and the pleasure and peace of mind that would result from this. On the basis of *Watts v Morrow*, as interpreted in *Farley v Skinner*, the claimant was awarded damages of £20,000 for mental distress. This fairly substantial award suggests that the courts may be prepared to move beyond the very cautious approach to the issue of the appropriate level of damages in this area taken in *Farley v Skinner*.

*Farley v Skinner* has clearly expanded the scope for recovery for non-pecuniary losses. Exactly how far remains to be seen. The High Court decision in *Wiseman v Virgin Atlantic Airways Ltd*[87] suggests that the courts will remain reluctant to allow compensation in this area. The claimant had been refused access to a flight by the defendant's staff, in breach of contract. He had also been falsely accused of having a false passport, and claimed to have been ridiculed by the defendant's staff and called a criminal. The court held that there could be no recovery for any of these non-pecuniary losses (though without making any reference to *Farley v Skinner*). The court clearly did not regard a normal flight from Nigeria to England as being a contract for which enjoyment was a main objective. As regards the claimant's mental distress, there was limited medical evidence, and in any case it was not linked to 'physical inconvenience or discomfort' as required by the *Watts v Morrow* test. As this case shows, the courts are likely to continue to adopt a restrictive line towards claims for non-pecuniary loss.

## For thought

*Do you think the outcome would have been the same if the claimant had been returning from holiday, and had booked the flight as part of that contract?*

---

85  15.4.2. See also *Milner v Carnival Plc* [2010] EWCA Civ 389.
86  [2003] EWHC 3147 (Ch)
87  [2006] EWHC 1566; 103 LSG 29.

As regards the long-term influence of *Farley v Skinner*, one of the most interesting developments is Lord Scott's interpretation of *Ruxley Electronics v Forsyth* as establishing a general right to damages in relation to the 'consumer surplus',[88] as expressed in this passage:[89]

> In summary, the principle expressed in the *Ruxley Electronics* case should be used to provide damages for deprivation of a contractual benefit where it is apparent that the injured party has been deprived of something of value but the ordinary means of measuring the recoverable damages are inapplicable. The principle expressed in *Watts v Morrow* should be used to determine whether and when contractual damages for inconvenience or discomfort can be recovered.

If these categories of damages do expand as a result of this decision, this will place more weight on the rule of remoteness, to be discussed in the next section, as a means of keeping the floodgates closed.

## 15.5 NON-COMPENSATORY DAMAGES

The methods of calculating damages dealt with in the previous section are all focused on compensating the claimant for losses, rather than (otherwise than indirectly) requiring the defendant to hand over any benefits obtained. This is in line with the general principles of contractual damages as stated in cases such as *Robinson v Harman*.[90] In other words, the purpose of contract damages is not the punishment of the defendant, but the compensation of the claimant. If the defendant has happened to gain a benefit from breaking the contract, this is irrelevant as long as all the claimant's losses are fully compensated. The idea that there could be recovery not only for the claimant's loss but also for the defendant's gain was specifically rejected by the Court of Appeal in *Surrey CC v Bredero Homes Ltd*.[91] Here a developer deliberately built more houses on a piece of land than it was entitled to under its contract with the local authority from which the land was acquired. The Court of Appeal held that the damages would only be nominal because the local authority had suffered no loss. The case of *Attorney General v Blake*,[92] however, re-opened this issue.

---

**Key case** *Attorney General v Blake* (2001)

Facts: The case concerned the notorious spy George Blake, who had been a member of the British secret service. He was convicted in 1961 of spying for Russia and sentenced to a total of 42 years' imprisonment. In 1966 he escaped and fled to Moscow where he continued to live. While there, he wrote his autobiography, which was published in 1990. The book included descriptions of his life as a member of the secret service. He was to be paid £50,000 on the signing of the contract, £50,000 on the delivery of the manuscript and £50,000 on publication. At the time of the legal action, £90,000 remained payable by the publishers. The Attorney General brought an action to prevent Blake receiving any further benefit from the book.

---

88  See above, 15.4.2. See also the comments of Lord Steyn at [2001] UKHL 49, [21]; p 810.
89  Ibid, [86]; p 829.
90  See above, 15.3.
91  [1993] 3 All ER 705.
92  [2001] 1 AC 268; [2000] 4 All ER 385. In *Morris-Garner v One Step (Support) Ltd* [2018] UKSC 20 Lord Reed stressed at [82] that the correctness of the *Blake* decision was not in question in that appeal.

Held: The House of Lords held that in exceptional circumstances a claimant could recover an account of profits in an action for breach of contract. Here the government had a legitimate interest in preventing the disclosure of official information by current or former members of the security services. On that basis, the Attorney General's action was successful.

This decision requires further analysis. The Court of Appeal had held that the Attorney General could succeed in that, in his role as guardian of the public interest, he could obtain an injunction to prevent a person benefiting from criminal activity (the disclosures made by Blake in the book amounting to offences under the Official Secrets Act 1989). However, the court, in addition, considered the situation as regards contract law. Blake was in breach of contract since, when he joined the secret service, he undertook a lifelong contractual obligation not to disclose anything about his work. The problem was to establish any loss for which compensation could be awarded to the Crown. If no such loss existed, then the damages could only be nominal on traditional principles. The Court of Appeal, however, felt that although the Attorney General at that stage had declined to argue the point, this was a situation where an exception to the general compensatory rule might be made. It suggested that the law was 'now sufficiently mature to recognise a restitutionary claim for profits made from a breach of contract in appropriate circumstances'. What were the 'appropriate circumstances'? The Court of Appeal suggested two. First, in relation to 'skimped performance':[93]

This is where the defendant fails to provide the full extent of the services which he has contracted to provide and for which he has charged the plaintiff.

The example given is of a fire service that did not provide the contracted number of firemen, horses or length of hosepipe.[94] The fire service had saved expenses, but had not failed to put out any fires. Nevertheless, it was suggested by Lord Woolf that it would be just to allow the other contracting party to recover damages based on the amount that the fire service had saved by this 'skimped' performance.[95]

The second situation in which the court suggested that damages based on the defendant's gain might be appropriate is where the defendant has obtained a profit 'by doing the very thing which he contracted not to do'.[96] This was exactly Blake's situation. He had promised not to disclose information about his work, but this was precisely what he had done in writing and publishing the book. It is clear that, had the Attorney General pursued this issue, the Court of Appeal would have been prepared to award damages for breach of contract on this basis. It reconciled this approach with that taken in *Surrey CC v Bredero Homes Ltd* on the basis that that decision should be regarded as allowing restitutionary damages to be available in exceptional cases.

When the case reached the House of Lords, the contractual basis of the claim was fully argued. The House reached the same effective result as the Court of Appeal by rejecting

93 [1998] Ch 439, p 458; [1998] 1 All ER 833, p 845.

94 As in the American case of *City of New Orleans v Firemen's Charitable Association* (1891) 9 So 486 – though no recovery was, in fact, allowed in this case.

95 A major objection to this example is, as pointed out by Campbell, that if the fire service had not failed in its duties under the contract (i.e. to put out fires), in what sense could its performance be said to be 'skimped'?: Harris, Campbell and Halson, 2002, pp 277–78. Indeed, it would not appear that there was any breach of contract at all.

96 [1998] Ch 439, p 458; [1998] 1 All ER 833, p 846.

the public law claim, but allowing the Attorney General to recover the money due to Blake on the basis of breach of contract. Lord Nicholls, who delivered the main speech on behalf of the majority,[97] found support for such an approach in a first instance decision that preceded *Surrey v Bredero Homes*, but was approved in it, namely *Wrotham Park Estate Co Ltd v Parkside Homes Ltd*.[98] In that case houses had been built on land in breach of a restrictive covenant and the plaintiff sought an injunction which would have led to their demolition. The court was reluctant, 'for social and economic reasons',[99] to grant such an injunction. Instead the judge awarded damages based on an estimate of what the defendant would have had to pay to obtain a release from the restrictive covenant. This he valued at 5 per cent of the profit that the defendants had made on the development. This decision is difficult to reconcile with *Surrey v Bredero*, though it is true that in the latter case no injunction was sought, so the earlier case may be thought to be based on the power to award damages in lieu of an injunction.[100] This analysis was not accepted by the Court of Appeal, however, in *Jaggard v Sawyer*.[101]

In *Blake*, Lord Nicholls did not attempt to achieve a reconciliation of these issues. His conclusion was simply that 'in so far as the *Bredero Homes Ltd* decision is inconsistent with the approach adopted in the *Wrotham Park* case, the latter approach is to be preferred'.[102] He went on to declare that *Wrotham Park* stood as a 'solitary beacon' showing that contract damages are not always confined to the recovery of financial losses.[103] Damages on the *Wrotham Park* basis were not, however, what the Attorney General was seeking in *Blake*. He was not asking for a sum by which Blake could have bought his release from the restrictive provision in his contract of employment; on the facts, the Crown would not have agreed to such a release on any terms. The Attorney General was, therefore, seeking a full 'account of profits' made by Blake from the breach. Lord Nicholls, despite the assistance of counsel, was unable to find any cases in which the courts had made such an order in a contract case,[104] but noted that there is a 'light sprinkling' of cases in which an order to the same effect as an account of profits has been made, but not with that label.[105] From here he jumped to the somewhat surprising general conclusion

---

97  Lord Hobhouse dissented, on the basis that he could see no grounds for the Crown recovering substantial damages for Blake's breach of contract.

98  [1974] 2 All ER 321. Note that in *Morris-Garner v One Step (Support) Ltd* [2018] UKSC 20 at [3] Lord Reed (with whom Lady Hale, Lord Wilson and Lord Carnwath agreed) stated: "This judgment will abjure the use of the term "Wrotham Park damages". Although it will be necessary to consider the case of *Wrotham Park*, it is a source of potential confusion because of the opacity of its reasoning, and it can now be regarded as being of little more than historical interest. Instead, this judgment will use the expression "negotiating damages", introduced by Neuberger LJ in *Lunn Poly Ltd v Liverpool & Lancashire Properties Ltd* [2006] EWCA Civ 430; [2006] 2 EGLR 29, para 22."

99  Lord Nicholls in *Attorney General v Blake* [2001] 1 AC 268, p 282; [2000] 4 All ER 385, p 395.

100  As now provided by the Senior Courts Act 1981, s 50. The power was originally given by the Chancery Amendment Act 1858, s 2, commonly known as Lord Cairns' Act.

101  [1995] 2 All ER 189. See also *Morris-Garner v One Step (Support) Ltd* [2018] UKSC 20 at [113] *per* Lord Sumption. Until recently it was also often thought that the House of Lords in *Johnson v Agnew* [1980] AC 367; [1979] 1 All ER 883 had held that the damages awarded in relation to a breach of contract should be the same whether awarded in equity (as would be the case if given in substitution for an equitable remedy such as an injunction) or under common law. However, such a view was doubted in *Morris-Garner v One Step (Support) Ltd* [2018] UKSC 20 at [47].

102  [2001] 1 AC 268, p 283; [2000] 4 All ER 385, p 396.

103  Note, however, that in *Morris-Garner v One Step (Support) Ltd* [2018] UKSC 20 the Supreme Court regarded the damages in *Wrotham Park* as compensatory in nature.

104  Though he noted that such an approach was rejected in *Tito v Waddell (No 2)* [1977] Ch 106; [1977] 3 All ER 129 by Megarry J, and even more forcefully by Kerr J in *Occidental Worldwide Investment Corp v Skibs, The Siboen and the Sibotre* [1976] 1 Lloyd's Rep 293.

105  The cases cited were *Lake v Bayliss* [1974] 2 All ER 1114; *Reid-Newfoundland Co v Anglo-American Telegraph Co Ltd* [1912] AC 555 and *British Motor Trade Association v Gilbert* [1951] 2 All ER 641.

that 'there seems to be no reason, in principle, why the court must in all circumstances rule out an account of profits as a remedy for breach of contract'.[106]

Having opened this box, however, the difficulty is to find a way to keep the remedy within bounds and in particular to avoid it disrupting the normal expectations of commercial contracts.[107] Lord Nicholls' response to this was to state that the remedy of an account of profits will only be available 'in exceptional circumstances'.[108] What then will constitute exceptional circumstances? On this question Lord Nicholls' speech is unhelpfully vague. It seems that exceptional cases will arise where normal damages are 'inadequate',[109] and that all the circumstances must be taken into account. Beyond this, however, the only guidance given is that a relevant question is 'whether the [claimant] had a legitimate interest in preventing the defendant's profit-making activity and, hence, in depriving him of his profit'.[110] The problem with this is that it is capable of a very broad or a very narrow interpretation: in one sense, the claimant will always have a 'legitimate interest' in preventing a breach of contract, and thus preventing the defendant's consequent profit-making activity; in the narrow sense, this will only arise where the claimant has a non-commercial interest in preventing the actions that constitute the breach.[111] It is to be suspected that the latter is what Lord Nicholls means, but the language used does not make this clear. On the facts of *Blake*, the case was 'exceptional', and an account of profits appropriate, because 'the Crown had and has a legitimate interest in preventing Blake profiting from the disclosure of official information, whether classified or not, while a member of the service or thereafter'.[112] Moreover, the obligation being broken was 'closely akin to a fiduciary obligation, where an account of profits is a standard remedy in the event of breach'.[113]

## For thought

*If Blake is applied more generally, would it mean that a former employee who breaks a restrictive covenant in relation to future employment could be made to hand over the wages earned from doing so?[114]*

---

106 [2001] 1 AC 268, p 284; [2000] 4 All ER 385, p 397. Lord Nicholls objects to the label 'restitutionary damages'; but if the point of an account of profits is the prevention of the unjust enrichment of the defendant, which is the basis of restitutionary remedies, his objection would be without merit.

107 It causes particular problems for the concept of the 'efficient breach' which, it has been suggested above (15.3), is an important element in the standard English law approach to contract damages.

108 [2001] 1 AC 268, p 285; [2000] 4 All ER 385, p 398.

109 In *Abbar v Saudi Economic & Development Co (SEDCO) Real Estate Ltd* [2013] EWHC 1414 (Ch) at [226] David Richards J rejected the submission that a 'lack of an identifiable financial loss was not a precondition' to *Wrotham Park-type* damages (see Chapter 15, 15.5.1).' However, the Court of Appeal in *One Step (Support) Ltd v Morris-Garner* [2016] EWCA Civ 180 explicitly disagreed with the view of David Richards J in *Abbar v Saudi Economic & Development Co (SEDCO) Real Estate Ltd. Abbar* was cited in argument in the Supreme Court in *Morris-Garner v One Step (Support) Ltd* [2018] UKSC 20 but was not discussed in the judgments although it would seem that the Supreme Court would not approve the approach of David Richards J: see for example [2018] UKSC 20 at [95].

110 [2001] 1 AC 268, p 285; [2000] 4 All ER 385, p 398.

111 See also *Marathon Asset Management LLP & Anor v Seddon & Ors* [2017] EWHC 300 (Comm) at [216] where Leggatt J stated: "Under an ordinary commercial contract the claimant's legitimate interest in performance of the contract is limited to its 'expectation' interest – that is to say its interest in receiving the profit it expects to make from performance. Hence the normal measure of damages for breach seeks to place the claimant in the same financial position as if the contract had been performed. In general, the claimant has no legitimate interest in preventing the contract-breaker from making a profit which is not reflected in any loss which the claimant has suffered."

112 [2001] 1 AC 268, p 287; [2000] 4 All ER 385, p 399.

113 Ibid, p 287; p 400.

114 Compare *One Step (Support) Ltd v Morris Garner* [2014] EWHC 2213 (High Court), [2016] EWCA Civ 180 (CA) and [2018] UKSC 20 (SC).

### 15.5.1 CASE LAW POST-SLAKE

It remains to be fully seen whether *Blake* will turn out to be a major development in the law relating to damages for breach of contract, or simply an interesting, but anomalous, side note. The decision has been the subject of severe criticism,[115] and it is difficult not to have sympathy with Lord Hobhouse's dissenting view that the majority had departed from principle in order to stop Blake benefiting from 'his past deplorable criminal conduct'.[116] If that is true, the effect of the case should be regarded as being limited by its own particular and exceptional facts, and therefore not indicating a new path for the development of restitutionary, as opposed to compensatory, damages for breach of contract.

Subsequent case law has been equivocal as to how far courts will find situations sufficiently 'exceptional' to justify using the *Blake* approach. In *Esso Petroleum Co Ltd v Niad Ltd*,[117] the breach of contract was committed by a petrol manager, who failed to pass on to his customers discounts given by his supplier. It would clearly be difficult for the supplier in this situation to prove its loss on an expectation measure.[118] The judge at first instance, however, thought that there were two other bases on which the supplier might recover.

First, he suggested that there could be an account of profits derived from the defendant's breach of contract. The judge referred to the fact that in *Attorney General v Blake* such a remedy was regarded as 'exceptional'. Nevertheless, he thought that this case was exceptional because:[119]

(a)    damages were an inadequate remedy;
(b)    the obligation to implement and maintain recommended pump prices was fundamental to the contract;
(c)    the defendant's breach was much more extensive than previously thought and continued after it had been pointed out; and
(d)    the supplier had a legitimate interest in preventing the defendant from profiting from its breach of obligation.

This appears to be adopting a very broad approach to exceptional circumstances. Many of these factors would apply to ordinary commercial disputes and it is difficult to see them as rendering the case 'exceptional' in the way that *Attorney General v Blake* was exceptional.

The other possible approach that the judge suggested was the 'restitutionary' remedy of requiring the defendant to pay back to the supplier the amount by which the actual prices charged to customers exceeded the recommended prices. The judge cited no authority in support of such a course, but it might be thought also to follow from *Attorney General v Blake*. Once again, however, the problem is whether this case was truly 'exceptional', thus justifying such a departure from the normal approach to compensatory damages.

It is to be hoped that this case is not an example of a trend towards extensive use of the *Blake* 'exception', which it seems unlikely that the House of Lords intended should apply to straightforward commercial disputes.[120]

The second major case to consider *Blake* was a Court of Appeal decision, *Experience Hendrix LLC v PPX Enterprises*.[121] The dispute arose out of a settlement of an earlier case between the parties, under which the defendant had agreed not to grant further licences

---

115  See, for example, Hedley, 2000; Harris, Campbell and Halson, 2002, Chapter 17.
116  [2001] 1 AC 268, p 299; [2000] 4 All ER 385, p 411.
117  [2001] EWHC 458 (Ch).
118  Compare *Morris-Garner v One Step (Support) Ltd* [2018] UKSC 20 at [95] although *Niad* was not cited and, of course, *Blake* was not directly at issue.
119  [2001] EWHC 458 (Ch), para 63.
120  For further criticism of this case, see Sandy, 2003.
121  [2003] EWCA Civ 323; [2003] 1 All ER Comm 830.

in relation to recordings made by the guitarist Jimi Hendrix. The defendant did issue such licences and the claimant sought compensation. The judge at first instance granted an injunction but no compensation. The Court of Appeal considered whether it would be appropriate in this case to award an account of profits, on the basis of *Blake*. It decided, however, that this was not an 'exceptional' case within the meaning of *Blake*. In particular, Mance LJ pointed out:[122]

> We are not concerned with a subject anything like as special or sensitive as national security. The State's special interest in preventing a spy benefiting by breaches of his contractual duty of secrecy, and so removing at least part of the financial attraction of such breaches, has no parallel in this case. Secondly, the notoriety which accounted for the magnitude of Blake's royalty earning capacity derived from his prior breaches of secrecy, and that too has no present parallel. Thirdly, there is no direct analogy between [the defendant's] position and that of a fiduciary.

This approach seems much more satisfactory than that adopted in the *Niad* case (to which the Court of Appeal in *Hendrix* referred, but without expressing a view on its correctness or otherwise).

The Court of Appeal did, however, hold that damages were recoverable on a different basis. This it did by drawing on the decision in *Wrotham Park Estate Ltd v Parkside Homes Ltd*,[123] and holding that the plaintiff could recover a sum that it might have demanded from the defendant as the price of relaxing the terms of the previous settlement and allowing the defendant to issue the licences.[124]

A similar approach was taken by the Court of Appeal in *WWF-World Wide Fund for Nature v World Wrestling Federation Entertainment* Inc,[125] which confirmed the exceptional nature of the remedy of account of profits in a contract action. The parties had been in dispute about the use of the initials 'WWF' but had reached a compromise agreement. The claimants then sued for breach of this agreement. They sought a remedy on the basis of an account of profits, as awarded in *Attorney General v Blake*, but this was rejected by the trial judge on the basis that the case was not sufficiently 'exceptional'. This view was not challenged in the Court of Appeal, where the claimants were in fact seeking a different remedy, based on *Wrotham Park*. As far as the *Blake* claim was concerned, the Court of Appeal was clearly of the view that the relevant issues had been appropriately addressed in *Experience Hendrix LLC v PPX Enterprises*. It seems that the narrow approach in the *Hendrix* case to the account of profits remedy, rather than the broader view taken in *Esso Petroleum Co Ltd v Niad*, is likely to be followed in future. In coming to its conclusion, the Court of Appeal held that damages on the *Wrotham Park* basis were 'compensatory' rather than 'gain-based'.[126] A decision that damages were not available on the *Blake* basis did not preclude a *Wrotham Park* claim. On the facts, however, the claimant had raised this basis for a claim too late to be allowed to succeed.[127]

---

122 [2003] EWCA Civ 323; [2003] 1 All ER Comm 830, para 37. See also *Force India Formula One Team Limited v Aerolab SRL* [2013] EWCA Civ 780.
123 [1974] 2 All ER 321 – see above.
124 On the difficulties in assessing such a sum see *CF Partners (UK) LLP v Barclays Bank plc* [2014] EWHC 3049 (Ch).
125 [2007] EWCA Civ 286; [2008] 1 All ER 74.
126 Any suggestion that the award in *Blake* was compensatory in nature has been dispelled by *Morris-Garner v One Step (Support) Ltd* [2018] UKSC 20 where Lord Reed (with whom Lady Hale, Lord Wilson and Lord Carnwath agreed) was of the opinion that the award in *Blake* was not compensatory in nature.
127 Recent cases have confirmed the exceptional nature of the *Blake* remedy, and refused to apply it. See, e.g., *Vercoe v Rutland Fund Management Ltd* [2010] EWHC 424; *Luxe Holding Ltd v Midland Resources Holding Ltd* [2010] EWHC 1908.

Damages on the *Wrotham Park* basis were recently considered by the Supreme Court in *Morris-Garner v One Step (Support) Ltd.*[128] The claimant was a company which provided care for vulnerable adults and children and the defendants were a former director/shareholder of the company and a former manager of the company. The defendants were bound, for a period of time, by certain covenants not to: compete with the claimant company; solicit the claimant company's clients; nor use the claimant company's confidential information. Ultimately the claimant company alleged these covenants had been breached. The judge found that there had been some breaches of the covenants and, therefore, the issue became the measure of damages. Moreover the judge held that, as the loss was difficult to assess, the claimant could, if it wished, instead claim hypothetical release damages. The Court of Appeal rejected the appeal but subsequently the Supreme Court allowed an appeal.

Lord Reed (with whom Lady Hale, Lord Wilson and Lord Carnwath agreed) was of the opinion that the award in *Wrotham Park* was compensatory in nature.[129] That award was made in lieu of an injunction (as permitted under Lord Cairns' Act) and, as such, one "possible method of quantifying damages under this head is on the basis of the economic value of the right which the court has declined to enforce, and which it has consequently rendered worthless."[130] In valuing such a right a court might use "…the amount which the claimant might reasonably have demanded as a quid pro quo for the relaxation of the obligation in question" (so-called 'negotiating damages').[131] Moreover, Lord Reed recognised that negotiating damages might also be awarded at common law in appropriate circumstances. In particular, such damages might be awarded where the breach of contract results in the "loss of a valuable asset created or protected by the right which was infringed."[132] Examples might include the breach of a restrictive covenant over land, the breach of an intellectual property agreement or the breach of a confidentiality agreement.[133] In such cases, the imaginary negotiation is merely a tool for determining the value of the relevant asset.[134] Crucially Lord Reed was of the opinion that not all contract rights were to be considered as an asset in this sense[135] although it is, perhaps, not clear how the distinction will be made. Moreover, Lord Reed disagreed with some of the wider statements in *Hendrix* that negotiating damages could be used more widely to achieve 'practical justice'. Nevertheless Lord Reed agreed with the decision in the case on the basis, essentially, that it involved the breach of an intellectual property agreement.[136]

### 15.5.2 IN FOCUS: ACADEMIC VIEWS OF *ATTORNEY GENERAL V BLAKE*

In terms of academic commentary on *Blake*, there is further interesting and critical discussion of the implications of this decision by Campbell and Harris (2002). They argue that the implication of the *Blake* decision is that all breaches should be penalised. This, they say, is misguided, because not all breaches are 'wrongs' that should be deterred:

> Breach has a positive, indeed essential, role in the operation of the law of contract as the legal institution regulating economic exchange and pursuit of its general prevention is inconsistent with the operation of a market economy.

---

128 [2018] UKSC 20.
129 Ibid at [95].
130 [2018] UKSC 20 at [95]
131 Ibid.
132 Ibid.
133 [2018] UKSC 20 at [92].
134 [2018] UKSC 20 at [91].
135 [2018] UKSC 20 at [93].
136 [2018] UKSC 20 at [89].

A response to Campbell and Harris is to be found in Jaffey (2002), who argues that a general rule that only 'punishes' non performance where losses are caused to the other party, and an exceptional rule punishing non performance itself (as in *Blake)*, can both be accommodated within a particular version of the 'reliance' theory of contract. Under this theory, parties contract on the basis of 'assumptions of responsibility for reliance' by the other party. Generally, such reliance, if disappointed, can be compensated by ensuring that the innocent party is not 'worse off' as a result of having entered into the contract. In exceptional cases, however, reliance can only be compensated by actual performance – for example, where the contractual obligation is not to disclose confidential information. In such cases:[137]

> Non-performance is wrongful, and performance should be compelled by order of specific performance if possible, and if not the law should respond with disgorgement or even punitive damages.

Jaffey sees his reliance-based approach as capable of accommodating both the general economic arguments of Campbell and Harris relating to 'efficient breach' and the possibility of restitutionary remedies in exceptional cases, such as *Blake*.

## 15.6 LIMITATIONS ON RECOVERY

There are two further main limitations on the amount of damages that can be recovered for a breach of contract, namely the rules on remoteness and the requirement of mitigation. The issue of contributory negligence will also be considered below (see 15.6.7).

### 15.6.1 THE RULE OF REMOTENESS

At various points in this chapter, it has been mentioned that the award of damages under a particular head will be subject to the rules of remoteness. This is a rule that basically prevents recoverable losses from extending too far and placing unreasonable burdens on the defendant. It should also be recalled that in Chapter 8 it was noted that there are no remoteness rules in relation to the tort of deceit or, it seems, the remedy for negligent misrepresentation under s 2(1) of the Misrepresentation Act 1967.[138] This is exceptional, however, and in general, in both tort and contract, damages are only recoverable in relation to losses that are not too remote.

The type of recovery this rule is designed to prevent is as follows. Suppose that a contract for the hire of a car is broken in that the one supplied is unfit for its purpose and breaks down. The hirer may as a result fail to arrive at a sale where he would have been able to buy a valuable painting, which he could have resold for a £100,000 profit. Should the hire company be liable for the £100,000? English law will *normally* regard this loss as too remote from the breach to be recoverable. To take a recent example from a decided case, in *Wiseman v Virgin Atlantic Airways Ltd*[139] the claimant had been delayed for some days in catching a flight as a result of the defendant's breach of contract. While he was waiting for a replacement flight he was attacked by robbers. It was held that this was too remote from the breach of contract to give rise to any compensation from the airline company. This approach ties in with the view of contract law as a mechanism by which the parties to an exchange transaction allocate the risks of their enterprise. In order to be

---

137  Jaffey, 2002, p 576. Compare *Vercoe v Rutland Fund Management Ltd* [2010] EWHC 424 and *Morris-Garner v One Step (Support) Ltd* [2018] UKSC 20 at [84].
138  See Chapter 8, 8.4.6.
139  [2006] EWHC 1566; 103 LSG 29.

able to do this properly, they must be aware of the risks at the time of contracting, so that they can be properly catered for in the contract price, exclusion clauses or other terms of the contract. If unforeseen losses were recoverable, this would arguably unbalance the contractual relationship.[140]

## 15.6.2 THE RULE IN *HADLEY V BAXENDALE*

In contract, the starting point for the rule of remoteness is *Hadley v Baxendale*.[141]

---

**Key case** *Hadley v Baxendale* (1854)

Facts: The plaintiff, the owner of a flour mill, contracted with the defendant, a carrier, for the transport of a broken mill-shaft to an engineer who was to use it as a pattern for a new mill-shaft. There was a delay in the delivery to the engineer, which constituted a breach of contract by the carrier. The plaintiff received the new shaft five days late, which resulted in considerable losses to his business because no spare shaft was available and the mill was shut for longer than expected. The plaintiff sued for lost profits. Held: The Exchequer Court held that the lost profits could not be recovered because they were too remote. In this case, there was delay in the transport of a broken mill-shaft, which resulted in considerable losses for the mill owner, because no spare shaft was available. The court stated the rule as being that the defendant will only be liable for losses:[142]

> either arising naturally, that is, according to the usual course of things, from such breach of contract itself, or such as may reasonably be supposed to have been in the contemplation of both parties at the time they made the contract as the probable result of the breach of it.

Applying this to the facts of the case, the court held that in most cases of a breach of this kind, no such losses would have followed (as there would have been a spare mill-shaft), so that it could not be said that the losses followed naturally from the breach. Nor were the defendants aware, at the time of the contract, of the circumstances that meant that the mill would not be able to function at all without this particular shaft. Therefore, the losses were not recoverable.

---

## 15.6.3 RELEVANCE OF KNOWLEDGE

There are two aspects of this test that should be noted. First, it is clear that the remoteness rule has to be assessed on the basis of the parties' knowledge *at the time the contract is made*. The House of Lords in *Jackson v Royal Bank of Scotland*[143] confirmed that this was so, even if the time between formation and breach was short. The reason for this is that, as indicated above, awareness of a particular risk may affect the terms of the contract. If, to use the example given above, the firm hiring out a car is aware that the customer is using it

---

140 This explanation cannot, of course, apply to the rules which operates in the law of tort. It may be, therefore, that the contractual rules of remoteness also have a basis in ideas of 'fairness'. For discussion of the justification of the differences between the contract and tort approaches from an economic perspective, see Bishop, 1983.

141 (1854) 9 Exch 341; 156 ER 145. For consideration of the commercial and industrial context in which the case was decided, see Danzig, 1975.

142 (1854) 9 Exch 341, p 354; 156 ER 145, p 151.

143 [2005] UKHL 3; [2005] 2 All ER 71.

to attend a sale in order to buy a rare painting, the firm may want to (a) increase the price, (b) insert an exclusion clause, (c) seek insurance of the risk, or (d) refuse to enter into the contract at all. Knowledge that the defendant acquired after the formation of the contract is therefore irrelevant to the rule of remoteness.

It should be noted that it seems that 'knowledge' here means more than simply 'awareness': the relevant information must be given in a context where it is clear that the information giver is expecting the other party to assume the relevant risk. The casual mention of a particular fact will not be sufficient.[144]

### 15.6.4 'REASONABLE CONTEMPLATION' TEST

Second, the rule as stated in *Hadley v Baxendale* appears to have two parts, the first relating to the natural consequences of breach and the second to the contemplation of the parties. As interpreted in the later cases of *Victoria Laundry (Windsor) Ltd v Newman Industries*[145] and *Koufos v C Czarnikow Ltd, The Heron* II,[146] however, the two limbs are really just aspects of one general principle. As Lord Walker commented in *Jackson v Royal Bank of Scotland plc*,[147] the test 'cannot be construed and applied as if it were a statutory test, nor are its two limbs mutually exclusive'. The situation should be looked at through the eyes of the reasonable defendant, who will be presumed to have in contemplation the normal types of loss that would follow from a particular breach. As regards anything more unusual, it will have to be established that the particular defendant had sufficient actual knowledge to be aware of the risk. The test is thus, simply, can this defendant, bearing in mind his or her state of knowledge at the time of the contract, be reasonably presumed to have expected the consequence of the breach of contract that occurred (and, possibly, to have assumed responsibility for it, see below at 15.6.5)?

In *Victoria Laundry (Windsor) v Newman*, the breach of contract was a lengthy delay in the delivery of a boiler that the plaintiffs (as the defendants were aware) wished to use in their laundry and dyeing business. The Court of Appeal held that the plaintiffs could recover lost profits at a level reasonably to be anticipated from a business of this type. They could not recover, however, in relation to some particularly lucrative dyeing contracts with the Ministry of Defence, of which the defendants were unaware.

### 15.6.5 DEGREE OF RISK

The degree of risk that has to be contemplated before a loss is not too remote is difficult to pin down and there is no clear, single phrase that is used to express it. The issue was considered in the following case.

---

**Key case** *The Heron II* (1969)

Facts: The plaintiff charterers lost money when the ship they had chartered to carry a cargo of sugar deviated from its route and arrived late at the port of destination. The sugar was sold immediately, as had always been the plaintiffs' intention, but the market price had fallen significantly as compared with the date on which the ship should have arrived. The issue was whether the defendant shipowners were liable for this loss, since

---

144 *Kemp v Intasun Holidays* [1987] BTLC 353 – mention of the plaintiff's medical condition when booking a holiday was insufficient to make the defendant liable for losses resulting from it. For discussion of the practical problems in communicating special circumstances to large, fragmented organisations, see Danzig, 1975, pp 279–80.
145 [1949] 2 KB 528; [1949] 1 All ER 997.
146 [1969] 1 AC 350; [1967] 3 All ER 686.
147 [2005] UKHL 3; [2005] 2 All ER 71, [46] – [49].

they were not specifically aware of the charterers' intentions in relation to the sale of the cargo. The court therefore had to consider the degree of risk that had to be contemplated before a loss was not too remote.

Held: The House agreed that the test in contract was distinguishable from that in tort, which is based on 'reasonable foreseeability'. The contract test was stricter than that, and depended on the loss being contemplated as 'not unlikely', or 'liable to result'. Lord Reid put it this way:[148]

> The crucial question is whether, on the information available to the defendant when the contract was made, he should, or the reasonable man in his position would, have realised that such loss was sufficiently likely to result from the breach of contract to make it proper to hold that the loss flowed naturally from the breach or that loss of that kind should have been within his contemplation.

Applying this approach, it was held that the defendants should have known that it was not unlikely that the sugar would be sold as soon as it arrived at its destination. They must also have been aware that the price of sugar fluctuates, and that there was a risk that a delay would mean that the plaintiffs would suffer a loss on the sale. The plaintiffs were entitled to recover their loss.

It seemed that it is the *type* of loss, rather than the precise way in which it occurs, or its extent, that must be contemplated. In *Parsons (Livestock) Ltd v Uttley Ingham & Co Ltd*,[149] the defective installation of a hopper used for storing pig food led to the death of a large number of the plaintiff's pigs as a result of the food going mouldy. The defendants were held liable for this loss because some harm to the pigs was within the reasonable contemplation of the parties as something that would result from a defective installation, even though the particular disease was not. As Lord Scarman put it:[150]

> While, on [the judge's] finding, nobody at the time of contract could have expected *E coli* to ensue from eating mouldy nuts, he is clearly, and as a matter of common sense, rightly, saying that people would contemplate ... the serious possibility of injury and even death among the pigs.

Where a particularly unusual aspect of the claimant's activity has increased the loss caused by the defendant's breach, the defendant will normally only be liable if he had actual knowledge. Thus, in *Balfour Beatty Construction (Scotland) Ltd v Scottish Power plc*,[151] the House of Lords held that a supplier of electricity who was in breach of contract because of an interruption in the supply was not liable for the full losses suffered by the plaintiff. The interruption had occurred while the plaintiff was in the middle of a construction project that required a 'continuous pour' of concrete. The break in supply meant that the work that had been done was worthless and had to be demolished. There was no evidence, however, that the defendants were aware of the need for a continuous pour and there was no presumption that a supplier of a commodity should be taken to be aware of all the techniques involved in the other party's business.

---

148  [1969] 1 AC 350, p 385; [1967] 3 All ER 686, p 691.
149  [1978] QB 791; [1978] 1 All ER 525.
150  Ibid, p 812; p 541.
151  1994 SC 20.

In two later decisions, the House of Lords gave further considerations to the exact scope of the rules of remoteness in contract. In *Jackson v Royal Bank of Scotland*, the Bank had, in connection with the supply of letters of credit, allowed a customer of the claimant to discover the amount of the claimant's mark-up on goods it was supplying. The customer therefore took its business elsewhere. The Bank had broken its contractual duty of confidence. The House, applying the *Hadley v Baxendale* test, held that it was within the reasonable contemplation of the parties at the time of the contract that a breach of this term would lead to some loss. The contract had no cut-off point, so the only limit was when the loss became too speculative. The House was happy to accept the quantification of the loss which had been arrived at by the trial judge, based on a four-year period of lost sales. The Court of Appeal, which had limited the loss to one year, had erred in taking into account the knowledge of the parties at the time of the breach – this was not relevant to the application of the remoteness rules.

The second decision is *Transfield Shipping Inc v Mercator Shipping Inc, The Achilleas*.[152] This involved a charter of a ship at a time when the market rates for charters were extremely volatile. Under an extension to the original charter, the rate of which was $16,750 per day, the defendant charterers were obliged to return the ship to the owners not later than 2 May. In anticipation of this, the owners took advantage of the increase in the market rates to negotiate a six-month charter with a third party, starting on 8 May at a rate of $39,500 per day. In breach of their agreement, the defendants failed to return the ship on 2 May. On 5 May it became clear that the ship would not be available for the new charter on 8 May. By this time the rates for charters had fallen again, and the third party was only prepared to agree to late delivery of the ship if the charter rate was reduced to £31,500 for the whole of their charter. The ship was eventually made available on 11 May. The owners claimed from the defendants' damages for breach of contract based on their full losses on the charter with the third party ($8,000 for 191 days with some adjustments). This amounted to $1,364,584.37. The defendants claimed that they were only liable for the difference between their charter rate and the market rate for the period between 2 May and 11 May. This amounted to $158,301.17. The arbitrators, the trial judge and the Court of Appeal all found in favour of the owners, on the basis that the loss was of a type that was foreseeable and that the defendants should be liable for the full extent of the actual loss suffered.

The House of Lords disagreed. The rationale for its decision is not that easy to determine, however, since there was some disagreement between their Lordships as to the precise basis for this view. The more orthodox approach adopted by Lord Rodger and Lord Walker, with tentative support from Lady Hale, was that the loss went beyond what would have been in the reasonable contemplation of the parties at the time of the original contract, or its extension, because no one could have predicted the extreme volatility in the market that actually occurred. In other words, it did not follow in the natural course of events (under the first limb of *Hadley v Baxendale*) and the parties did not have the required knowledge at the relevant time to fall within the second limb of *Hadley v Baxendale*. On this basis the case seems to follow from *Victoria Laundries v Newman* where some losses were foreseeable, but not the losses based on the particularly lucrative contracts that the plaintiffs had negotiated in that case. Lord Hoffmann and Lord Hope relied on a slightly different analysis. They suggested that the loss was not recoverable because the defendants could not be taken to have assumed this liability at the time when they entered into the agreement. In other words, they found an absence of assumption of responsibility, drawing analogies with *South Australia Asset Management Corp v York Montague Ltd*.[153] This analysis took account of the evidence that it was common in shipping cases for the

---

152 [2008] UKHL 48; [2008] 4 All ER 159.
153 Discussed above at 15.4.7.

losses on delayed return under a charter to be calculated on the difference between the contract rate and the market rate for the period of delay. This suggests that the test of remoteness should take account of the commercial expectations of the parties at the time of the contract, and not simply the types of losses that could be contemplated as likely (or not unlikely) to occur.

The view of Lords Hoffmann and Hope in this case clearly raised the possibility of a change in the way in which the remoteness rules should be applied in contract cases. Whether it would lead to such a development, and whether such a development would be desirable, would have to wait to be explored, as Lady Hale commented, 'in another case and another context'.[154] In *Supershield Ltd v Siemens Building Technologies FE Ltd*,[155] the Court of Appeal suggested that while *Hadley v Baxendale* remains the standard rule:[156]

> there may be cases where the court, on examining the contract and the commercial background, decides that the standard approach would not reflect the expectation or intention reasonably to be imputed to the parties.

In that situation, the court, on the basis of the *Transfield v Mercator* approach, could take account of whether the loss that occurred was one for which the charterer assumed contractual responsibility, taking account of the nature and object of their business transaction. The court also pointed out that, while in *Transfield v Mercator* the effect of this approach was exclusionary, in that it reduced the losses that were recoverable, there was no logical reason why it should not have the opposite effect. Thus if, on analysis of the contract against its commercial background, the loss was within the scope of an assumed duty, the loss could not be regarded as too remote, even if it would not have occurred in ordinary circumstances.[157]

### 15.6.6 MITIGATION

Once a breach of contract has occurred, in general terms the claimant is not entitled to sit back and do nothing while losses accumulate. There is an obligation to take reasonable steps to mitigate losses that was laid down by, for example, the House of Lords in *British Westinghouse Electric and Manufacturing Co v Underground Electric Railways Co of London*.[158] Viscount Haldane LC explained that this obligation:[159]

> imposes on a plaintiff the duty of taking all reasonable steps to mitigate the loss consequent on the breach, and debars him from claiming any part of the damage which is due to his neglect to take such steps.

Furthermore:

> this ... principle does not impose on the plaintiff an obligation to take any step which a reasonable and prudent man would not ordinarily take in the course of his

---

154  [2008] UKHL 48, at [93].
155  [2010] EWCA Civ 7; [2010] 1 CLC 241. See also *ASM Shipping Ltd of India v TTMI Ltd of England* [2009] 1 Lloyd's Rep 293.
156  Ibid, at [43]. Compare *Saipol SA v Inerco Trade SA* [2014] EWHC 2211 and *Swynson Limited v Lowick Rose LLP* [2014] EWHC 2085 (although ultimately the decision in that case was reversed: [2017] UKSC 32).
157  Ibid.
158  [1912] AC 673. For a discussion of the role of the claimant's knowledge see *Secretary of State for Health v Servier Laboratories Ltd* [2016] EWHC 2381 (Ch). The burden of proof is on the defendant to show that the claimant's loss was fully or partially mitigated (see *Thai Airways International Public Co Ltd v KI Holdings Co Ltd* [2015] EWHC 1250 (Comm)).
159  Ibid, p 689.

business. But when in the course of his business he has taken action arising out of the transaction, which action has diminished his loss, the effect in actual diminution of the loss he has suffered may be taken into account even though there was no duty on him to act.

The court will look at what the claimant's actual losses are, rather than what they might hypothetically have been had the claimant not acted, even if the claimant's actions in reducing the loss have gone beyond what might reasonably have been required. If the claimant has done nothing, however, the court will consider what steps might reasonably have been taken to reduce the losses. The claimant will be debarred from claiming any part of the damage that would have been avoided by such steps. So, if the seller fails to deliver in a sale of goods contract, usually the buyer will be expected to go into the market and attempt to obtain equivalent goods. If such are available at or below the market price, then only nominal damages will be recoverable. If the buyer fails to enter the market until the price has risen, or pays over the odds, these increased losses may not be recoverable. Similarly, a reasonable offer of performance following a breach should not be spurned. In *Payzu Ltd v Saunders*,[160] the plaintiffs had failed to make prompt payment for an instalment of goods. The defendants had, in breach of contract, then refused to deliver any more goods but did offer to deliver more goods if the plaintiffs agreed to pay cash with each order. It was held that the plaintiffs should have accepted this offer, which would have reduced their loss (since the market value of the goods in question was rising above the contract price).

Mitigation only requires the claimant to act 'reasonably' in all the circumstances. In *Wroth v Tyler*,[161] the plaintiff's lack of resources was considered a reasonable ground for a failure to go into the market and make an alternative purchase. Similarly, in *Lagden v O'Connor*,[162] a claimant who was unable to pay for a hire car, and therefore had to obtain one on credit, which was more expensive, was allowed to recover the full loss. As Lord Nicholls put it:[163]

[I]n measuring the loss suffered by an impecunious plaintiff *[sic]* by loss of use of his own car the law will recognise that, because of his lack of financial means, the timely provision of a replacement vehicle for him costs more than it does for his affluent neighbour.

In *Fulton Shipping Inc of Panama v Globalia Business Travel S.A.U.*[164] the owners of a ship claimed damages from the charterers of the ship who had repudiated the contract. Following the breach the owners had terminated the contract and sold the ship for $23.7m before the world financial crisis. At the time of the trial the ship would only have been worth $7m. The charterers claimed that the shipowners should give them credit for the difference between the price of the ship sold and the price it would have sold for in 2009 (approximately $17m). Popplewell J disagreed.[165] The charterers' breach had not caused this benefit – it merely provided the shipowners with an

---

160 [1919] 2 KB 581. See also *Gul Bottlers (PVT) Ltd v Nichols Plc* [2014] EWHC 2173.
161 [1974] Ch 30; [1973] 1 All ER 897.
162 [2003] UKHL 64; [2004] 1 All ER 277. This case concerned a negligence claim in tort, but the mitigation principles were the same as for a contractual action. Reference, of course, would also need to be made to the relevant remoteness rules in contract. See also *Nautical Challenge Ltd v Evergreen Marine (UK) Ltd* [2019] EWHC 163 (Admlty).
163 [2003] UKHL 64, at [7]. Note that two members of the House of Lords dissented from the conclusion.
164 ([2017] UKSC 43.
165 [2014] 2 Lloyd's Rep 230.

opportunity to sell the ship. However the Court of Appeal[166] reversed the decision of Popplewell J. In so doing it was influenced by the fact that the principles of mitigation might sometimes require a shipowner to sell a ship and, if so, relevant benefits (such as the additional amount received on an earlier sale) so received would need to be taken into account. On a further appeal to the Supreme Court, Lord Clarke (with whom Lord Neuberger, Lord Mance, Lord Sumption, and Lord Hodge agreed) allowed the appeal, preferring the view of Popplewell J:

> That difference or loss was, in my opinion, not on the face of it caused by the repudiation of the charterparty. The repudiation resulted in a prospective loss of income for a period of about two years. Yet, there was nothing about the premature termination of the charterparty which made it necessary to sell the vessel, either at all or at any particular time. Indeed, it could have been sold during the term of the charterparty. If the owners decide to sell the vessel, whether before or after termination of the charterparty, they are making a commercial decision at their own risk about the disposal of an interest in the vessel which was no part of the subject matter of the charterparty and had nothing to do with the charterers.[167]

The principle of mitigation raises particular issues in cases of anticipatory breach. If the claimant accepts the breach and the contract terminates immediately, then the normal rules will apply. If, however, the claimant does not accept the breach but elects to affirm the contract and wait for the other party to perform, it seems that there will not be any duty at that stage to reduce losses. This is illustrated by the following case.

---

**Key case** *White and Carter (Councils) Ltd v McGregor* (1962)[168]

Facts: The defendants had contracted to buy advertising space on litter bins owned by the plaintiffs. This contract was wrongfully cancelled by the defendants before any work had been done. The plaintiffs refused to accept this anticipatory breach and went ahead with the production and display of the advertisements over the full three years of the contract. They then sued for the full sum due under the contract.[169]
Held: The House of Lords, by a majority of 3:2, held that there was no obligation on the claimant in such a situation to mitigate the losses and full recovery is possible. The plaintiffs were entitled to recover the sum agreed as payment for the work done.

---

The decision has been regarded as harsh on the defendant, and involving an unnecessary waste of resources. It has been widely criticised,[170] but it still stands as the leading authority on this issue. Lord Reid, however, identified two limitations, one practical and one legal, which exist in relation to the situations where a *White and Carter* response to anticipatory breach will be acceptable. The practical limitation is that the claimant will not be able to act in this way where the performance of the contractual obligations requires

---

166  [2015] EWCA Civ 1299
167  [2017] UKSC 43 at [32].
168  [1962] AC 413; [1961] 3 All ER 1178.
169  In other words, this was an action for an agreed sum, rather than for compensatory damages: see above, 15.2.
170  See Furmston, 1962; Goodhart, 1962; Harris, Campbell and Halson, 2002, pp 161–65; Burrows, 2004.

the co-operation of the defendant, as will often be the case.[171] As regards the legal limitation, Lord Reid suggested that:[172]

> It may well be that, if it can be shown that a person has no legitimate interest, financial or otherwise, in performing the contract rather than claiming damages, he ought not to be allowed to saddle the other party with an additional burden with no benefit to himself.

Lord Reid clearly felt that the burden of proving the absence of any such 'legitimate interest' rested on the defendants and in this case they had not attempted to establish it.[173] Lord Reid does not specify what might constitute a 'legitimate interest' but clearly this might arise where failing to continue with the contract might involve the 'innocent' party in breach of other obligations owed to third parties.[174] This type of interest was found to exist by Kerr J in *Gator Shipping Corp v Trans-Asiatic Oil Ltd SA, The Odenfeld*,[175] in holding that the owners of a vessel were not obliged to accept the repudiatory breach of a time charter. In other cases, however, the 'no legitimate interest' restriction has been used to distinguish *White and Carter*. Thus, in *Attica Sea Carriers Corp v Ferrostaal Poseidon Bulk Reederei GmbH, The Puerto Buitrago*,[176] the Court of Appeal considered a case where the charterers of a ship had a repair obligation. The repairs would have cost twice the value of the ship, and the charterers tried to return it unrepaired (which involved a breach of the charter). The owners refused to accept this breach and insisted that the charterers should continue to pay the charter hire until the ship was repaired. The Court of Appeal held for the charterers. Orr LJ (with whom Browne LJ agreed) based this in part on the fact that the charterers had here shown that the shipowners had no legitimate interest in continuing the charter.[177] A similar line was taken by Lloyd J in *Clea Shipping Corp v Bulk Oil International Ltd, The Alaskan Trader*,[178] where, after 12 months of a two-year charter, the charterers indicated that they did not wish to continue with the contract, following the breakdown of the ship. The owners, however, repaired the ship and kept it crewed and ready for the remainder of the charter period. It was held that the owners did not have a legitimate interest in continuing with the contract as opposed to claiming damages.

---

171 This limitation was applied by Megarry J in *Hounslow LBC v Twickenham Garden Developments Ltd* [1971] Ch 233 – work to be done on property owned by the other party. The need for 'passive co-operation' was sufficient to exclude the *White and Carter* approach.

172 [1962] AC 413, p 481; [1961] 3 All ER 1178, p 1183.

173 Though this may surely have been because they did not realise that they needed to. In *MSC Mediterranean Shipping Co SA v Cottonex Anstalt* [2015] EWHC 283 (Comm) Leggatt J linked this principle to a concept of good faith. In that case, Leggatt J held that the carriers had no legitimate interest in continuing (rather than terminating and claiming damages) with a contract which required the shippers to pay demurrage for a delay in returning containers which had been used to ship goods. On appeal ([2016] EWCA Civ 789) Moore-Bick LJ appeared in agreement on the no legitimate interest point (see [43]) but held, on the facts, that it did not arise as the purpose of the adventure had been commercially frustrated. Moore-Bick LJ had less sympathy with the attempt by Leggatt J to link legitimate interest to a concept of good faith (see [45]) and to the clause being penal in nature (see [46]).

174 Friedmann (1995) has suggested that this limitation indicates that 'the right to keep the contract open, coupled with the right to claim the agreed sum, are not absolute but in fact subject to a requirement of good faith'.

175 [1978] 2 Lloyd's Rep 357.

176 [1976] 1 Lloyd's Rep 250.

177 Lord Denning agreed, but more generally on the basis that *White and Carter* ought not to be used as a form of disguised 'specific performance' where damages would be an adequate remedy.

178 [1984] 1 All ER 129.

The position is, therefore, that *White and Carter (Councils) v McGregor* remains good law, but the two restrictions set out in Lord Reid's speech may be used to avoid its being applied in inappropriate and unreasonable circumstances.

### 15.6.7 CONTRIBUTORY NEGLIGENCE

In tort, it is well established that the damages recoverable may be reduced by contributory negligence on the part of the claimant.[179] Does the same principle apply in contract? The issue was considered by Hobhouse J and the Court of Appeal in *Forsikringsaktieselskapet Vesta v Butcher*,[180] where it was stated that the Law Reform (Contributory Negligence) Act 1945 did apply where there was concurrent liability in tort and contract (that is, where there is a breach of a contractual duty to use reasonable care and skill, in a situation where there was also a tortious duty of care). This has subsequently been accepted as correct by the House of Lords in *Platform Home Loans Ltd v Oyston Shipways*.[181] Where, on the other hand, the breach of contract is based on strict liability, there is no scope for contributory negligence, and the 1945 Act is irrelevant. This was confirmed by the Court of Appeal in *Barclays Bank plc v Fairclough Building Ltd*,[182] which concerned a breach of strict obligations arising under a building contract. The judge had held that the plaintiffs had failed to supervise the work properly and therefore reduced the damages. The Court of Appeal reversed this decision. Where contractual liability was strict, it was inappropriate to apportion losses, even if the defendant might also be said to have been negligent. Simon Brown LJ explained his reasons for coming to this conclusion in this way:[183]

> The very imposition of a strict liability upon the defendant is to my mind inconsistent with an apportionment of the loss. And not least because of the absurdities that the contrary approach carries in its wake. Assume a defendant, clearly liable under a strict contractual duty. Is his position to be improved by demonstrating that besides breaching that duty he was in addition negligent?

Where, however, the contractual liability is based on 'negligence' but there is no concurrent tortious duty, there is no clear authority. There is some suggestion from the case of *De Meza v Apple*[184] that the Act does apply in such a case, but this was not supported by *dicta* in *Forsikringsaktieselskapet Vesta v Butcher*. And although losses were apportioned in *Tenant Radiant Heat Ltd v Warrington Development Corp*,[185] this was on the basis of one side having broken the contract, and the other being independently liable in tort. The area is thus in some confusion, and a clear ruling from the Supreme Court would be helpful. The Law Commission has recommended that contributory negligence should always be available to apportion losses where there has been breach of a contractual duty to take reasonable care,[186] whether or not there is an overlap with tort, and this seems the most sensible solution.

One issue that has been considered by the House of Lords is the way in which contributory negligence should be dealt with in cases of overvaluation of property. The general rule for calculating damages in such cases has been established in *South Australia Asset Management Corp v York Montague Ltd*,[187] discussed above (see 15.4.7). The issue

---

179  See, in particular, the Law Reform (Contributory Negligence) Act 1945.
180  [1986] 2 All ER 488 and [1988] 3 WLR 565. Affirmed on other grounds: [1989] AC 852; [1988] 2 All ER 43.
181  [2000] 2 AC 190; [1999] 1 All ER 833.
182  [1995] QB 214; [1995] 1 All ER 289.
183  Ibid, p 233; p 306.
184  [1974] 1 Lloyd's Rep. 508 (affirmed on appeal without reference to this point: [1975] 1 Lloyd's Rep 498).
185  [1988] EGLR 41.
186  Law Commission, 1993, para 4.7.
187  [1997] AC 191; [1996] 3 All ER 365.

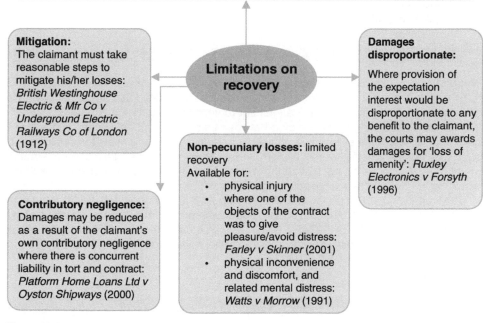

**Rules of remoteness:**

Rules which prevents recoverable losses from extending too far:
*Hadley v Baxendale* (1854):
Two types of recoverable loss:
1. losses arising as a natural consequence of the breach
2. losses in the contemplation of the parties when the agreement is formed

Court will look at whether the reasonable person would have realised, at the time the contract was made, that such loss was likely to result from the breach: *Victoria Laundries v Newman* (1949); *Koufos v C Czamikow Ltd, The Heron II* (1969)

It is the type of loss, rather than the precise way in which it occurs, or its extent which must be contemplated: *Parsons (Livestock) Ltd v Uttley Ingham & Co Ltd* (1978)

**Limitations on recovery**

**Mitigation:**
The claimant must take reasonable steps to mitigate his/her losses: *British Westinghouse Electric & Mfr Co v Underground Electric Railways Co of London* (1912)

**Contributory negligence:**
Damages may be reduced as a result of the claimant's own contributory negligence where there is concurrent liability in tort and contract: *Platform Home Loans Ltd v Oyston Shipways* (2000)

**Non-pecuniary losses:** limited recovery
Available for:
- physical injury
- where one of the objects of the contract was to give pleasure/avoid distress: *Farley v Skinner* (2001)
- physical inconvenience and discomfort, and related mental distress: *Watts v Morrow* (1991)

**Damages disproportionate:**
Where provision of the expectation interest would be disproportionate to any benefit to the claimant, the courts may awards damages for 'loss of amenity': *Ruxley Electronics v Forsyth* (1996)

Figure 15.2

in *Platform Home Loans Ltd v Oyston Shipways Ltd*[188] was, first, whether contributory negligence applies where the claimant's 'negligence' is different from the defendant's negligence; and, second, if it does, to what sum any reduction should be applied. On the first question, the Court of Appeal held that the fact that the lender had an imprudent lending policy could operate as contributory negligence to reduce damages, even though this had nothing to do with the defendant's negligent overvaluation of the property. The analogy was used of the seat belt cases in tort: not wearing a seat belt will not contribute to the negligence of the driver but it can be used as a reason for reducing the claimant's damages. The House of Lords upheld the Court of Appeal on this issue. It disagreed, however, on the second issue, that is, the way in which the reduction should be calculated. The Court of Appeal had held that the percentage reduction suggested by the trial

---

188 [2000] AC 190; [1999] 1 All ER 833.

judge should be applied to the lender's loss as established by the *South Australia Asset Management Corp* approach. This limited the loss to the difference between the overvaluation and the true valuation at the time of the contract. Thus, in this case, the difference in the valuations was £500,000 and the judge had found the lender to be 20 per cent contributorily negligent. The Court of Appeal therefore awarded damages of £400,000. The House of Lords, however, held that the reduction should be applied to the lender's full loss, which had been increased by the fall in market values. In this case, the property had been resold for only £435,000, and the trial judge had found that the lender's full loss was £611,748. It was to this figure that the 20 per cent reduction should be applied. Only if the resulting amount was higher than the figure arrived at on the *South Australia Asset Management Corp* calculation should it be capped at that level. In this case, the 20 per cent reduction produced a figure of £489,398. Since this was below the figure of £500,000, the lender was entitled to recover this amount, rather than the £400,000 awarded by the Court of Appeal.

## 15.7 LIQUIDATED DAMAGES AND PENALTY CLAUSES

The parties to a contract may decide to include provision as to the compensation that is to be paid in the event of a breach. This is known as a 'liquidated damages' clause and is generally a perfectly acceptable arrangement to which the courts will happily give effect. It is an example of the parties deciding between themselves not only where some of the risks should lie but the extent of such risks. Economic analysis is likely to conclude that such clauses are an efficient mechanism, in that they reduce the transaction costs that might otherwise follow a breach of contract in terms of negotiating compensation or, in the worst case, having to take legal action to recover it.[189]

The limitation that English law traditionally imposed on this approach was that the sum specified in the contract must have been a 'genuine pre-estimate' of the claimant's loss and not a 'penalty'. If it was the latter, then it would be unenforceable. This distinction was insisted upon by the House of Lords in *Dunlop Pneumatic Tyre Co Ltd v New Garage and Motor Co Ltd*.[190]

---

**Key case** *Dunlop Pneumatic Tyre Co Ltd v New Garage and Motor Co Ltd* (1915)

Facts: This concerned a contract for the supply of car tyres to the respondents, who would sell them to their customers. The contract contained a clause stating that a sum of £5 was stated to be payable 'by way of liquidated damages and not as a penalty' in relation to any breaches of this contract. The respondents sold tyres below the list price, which constituted a breach of contract. The appellants brought an action for the specified sum of £5 per breach. At trial they succeeded, but the Court of Appeal held that the relevant clause was a penalty clause and unenforceable. The appellants appealed.

Held: The House of Lords held that the clause was enforceable. The losses against which the appellants were trying to protect themselves were indirect and difficult to calculate. Even though the clause could apply to a variety of breaches, there was no reason to hold that it was not a genuine attempt to estimate the appellants' likely losses.

---

189  See Harris, Campbell and Halson, 2002, pp 139–42, and in particular the articles cited at p 142, nn 13 and 14.
190  [1915] AC 79. It has more recently been approved by the Privy Council in *Philips Hong Kong Ltd v Attorney General of Hong Kong* (1993) 61 BLR 41. See also *Murray v Leisureplay* [2005] EWCA Civ 963.

In coming to this conclusion, the House noted that the parties' own statement as to the effect of the clause was not conclusive. A sum payable could constitute a penalty not only if it was excessive in comparison to the loss, but also if it was payable on the occurrence of a range of events, *and in relation to at least one of these* the sum would be clearly excessive. Although in the case before it, a range of breaches may have been covered, the House nevertheless felt that on balance the £5 should not be regarded as a penalty since it was not likely to be excessive in relation to any of the potential breaches. On this approach it may therefore be acceptable to use a single figure for compensation as a type of 'averaging' of the likely losses resulting from a range of breaches, the precise effects of which may be difficult to quantify.

### 15.7.1 APPLICATION OF *DUNLOP* PRINCIPLES

The principles in this area are reasonably clear. The difficulty comes in applying them to particular provisions. The area was reconsidered by the Privy Council in *Philips Hong Kong Ltd v Attorney General of Hong Kong*.[191] The case concerned a claim by Philips that they were not liable to pay the Hong Kong government liquidated damages for delay in completion of contract works because these amounted to a penalty. The Court of Appeal of Hong Kong allowed an appeal from a first instance decision upholding Philips' claim. Philips appealed to the Privy Council. The Privy Council stated that in deciding whether a clause was a penalty clause, or a genuine pre-estimate of damages, the court was not helped by the use in argument of unlikely hypothetical examples of situations where the sums payable under the liquidated damages clause would be wholly out of proportion to any loss. Although the clause must be judged objectively, at the date on which the contract was made, what happened subsequently could provide valuable evidence of what could reasonably be expected to be the loss at the time the contract was made. The appeal was dismissed. In reaching its conclusions, the Privy Council accepted Lord Dunedin's statement in *Dunlop Pneumatic Tyre Co Ltd v New Garage and Motor Co* that:[192]

> The question whether a sum stipulated is penalty or liquidated damages is a question of construction to be decided upon the terms and inherent circumstances of each particular contract, judged as at the time of the contract not as at the time of the breach.

Nevertheless, as noted above, it was felt that what had actually happened might provide a better guide than hypothetical examples thought up by counsel. Furthermore, where the range of possible losses was broad, the better approach might be simply to say that the clause was not intended to apply to breaches where the liquidated damages would be totally out of proportion to the loss, rather than to strike the clause down in its entirety. The court was clearly influenced by the fact that this was a commercial contract where what the parties had agreed should normally be upheld. The decision suggests a flexible, but to some extent unpredictable, approach to the effect of such clauses.

In *Duffen v Fra Bo SpA*,[193] the Court of Appeal considered a term in an agency contract that provided that on termination by the agent the principal should immediately pay the agent £100,000. This was stated in the contract to be 'liquidated damages' with the sum being 'agreed by the parties to be a reasonable pre-estimate of the loss and damage which the agent will suffer on termination of the agreement'. Nevertheless, the court held that it was a penalty clause and thus unenforceable. It was not a genuine attempt to estimate the loss that the agent would suffer following breach by the principal, nor

191 (1993) 61 BLR 41.
192 [1915] AC 79, pp 86–7.
193 [2000] 1 Lloyd's Rep 180.

was it graduated in relation to the unexpired term of the agent's contract. Enforcing it would give the agent a substantial windfall, which would be both 'extravagant and unconscionable'.

### 15.7.2 RECASTING THE PENALTY RULE

In *Makdessi v Cavendish Square Holdings BV* and *ParkingEye Ltd v Beavis*[194] the Supreme Court considered, in detail, the operation of the penalty rule, the first time the Supreme Court (or House of Lords) had done so for a century.[195] In so doing the Supreme Court resisted calls for both the abolition and extension of the penalty rule in relation to contracts.

---

**Key case** *Makdessi v Cavendish Square Holdings BV; ParkingEye Ltd v Beavis* (2015)

Facts: There were two conjoined appeals. The first case *(Makdessi)* concerned a share purchase contract, in respect of a marketing company, between commercial parties. Under the agreement the seller agreed not to compete with the marketing company. The contract provided that if the non-competition stipulation was breached (a) no further instalments would be payable under the contract (clause 5.1) and (b) the buyer would have an option to buy the seller's remaining shares at a reduced price (as it would disregard goodwill, clause 5.6). The seller breached the non-competition stipulation and the buyer sought to exercise clauses 5.1 and 5.6. The seller claimed that these clauses were unenforceable on the ground that they were penalty clauses. This claim was rejected at first instance but accepted by the Court of Appeal. The second case *(ParkingEye)* involved a car park where parking was free for the first two hours but, if that period was exceeded, a fee of £85 was payable. The defendant parked his car for almost three hours and subsequently refused to pay the £85 fee on the ground that it was a penalty clause. At first instance and in the Court of Appeal the defendant's argument failed.

Held: The law relating to penalty clauses needed to be recast. More specifically a penalty clause is a secondary obligation that bears no proportion to the legitimate interest, if any, that the innocent party has in the enforcement of the primary obligation(s). Applying this to the facts of *Makdessi* the Supreme Court held that relevant clauses were not penal. The buyer had a legitimate interest in the compliance with non-competition stipulations that were crucial to the health of the company. Moreover both parties were experienced commercial parties with the benefit of legal advice. As regards *ParkingEye* the Supreme Court also held that the fee was not penal in nature. Although it did not represent the loss that the claimant would suffer as a result of the defendant staying beyond two hours, the claimant had a legitimate interest in the efficient functioning of the car park and was comparable to charges in the locality.

---

Anchoring of the test for a penalty clause to the vague concept of the legitimate interest of the innocent party may fuel further litigation. It should also be noted that a clause that imposes an obligation on a consumer to pay a 'disproportionately high sum' for failure to fulfil an obligation may well be unenforceable by virtue of the Consumer Rights Act 2015.[196] This Act is discussed in more detail in Chapter 7.[197]

---

194  [2015] UKSC 67.
195  See [1] per Lord Neuberger and Lord Sumption.
196  See Sched 2, Part 1, para 6.
197  See above, 7.8.

## 15.8 RESTITUTION AND UNJUST ENRICHMENT

'Restitution' in relation to remedies for breach of contract may refer to the return of money paid under a contract following, and as a corollary of, termination for a repudiatory breach.[198] If such a breach has been accepted, then the claimant may also be entitled to claim the restitution of anything that has been given to the defendant. The easiest example is the situation of defective goods. The buyer returns the goods and expects a refund of the price. In many situations, and in particular in relation to consumer contracts, that may be all that can be recovered. The buyer may not have been expecting to make a profit out of the use or resale of the goods, and there may be no other losses resulting from the breach. In appropriate circumstances, however, it is possible to combine a claim for restitution with one for reliance or expectation damages. In *Millar Machinery Co Ltd v David Way & Son*,[199] the plaintiff recovered all three. The contract involved the purchase of a machine that proved to be defective on delivery and so was rejected. The disappointed buyer had spent money on installation costs and had lost profits from the use of the machine. He was able to recover the price (restitution), the installation costs (reliance) and the lost profits (expectation).[200]

Restitution also has a more general role to play in relation to contracts that are void, or rescinded (for example, for mistake or misrepresentation), or where no contract has ever come into existence. In this context, 'restitutionary' remedies are part of a more general concept developed by the courts to prevent the defendant being 'unjustly enriched'. As Lord Wright put it in *Fibrosa Spolka Ackyjna v Fairbairn Lawson Combe Barbour Ltd*:[201]

> It is clear that any civilised system of law is bound to provide remedies for what has been called unjust enrichment, or unjust benefit, that is, to prevent a man from retaining the money of, or some benefit derived from, another which it is against his conscience he should keep.

It is the law of England and Wales' response to this requirement in situations that are closely related to contract that we are concerned with in this part of this chapter. There are two main topics to consider: the recovery of money and the payment for work which has been done.

### 15.8.1 RECOVERY OF MONEY

The transfer of money outside a contractual relationship raises particular problems. If I give you possession of my car in connection with a contract that turns out to be void, I can maintain an action for the recovery of it relying on my continuing rights of ownership, but with the transfer of money the position is more complicated. There may not be any possibility of identifying the particular notes or coins which have been transferred, or of 'unmixing' funds from a bank account into which they have been paid. In other words, the money itself may become the property of the person to whom it has been transferred and the most that is left is the obligation to repay an equivalent sum. There are four situations where the possibility of such recovery is clearly recognised: (1) where there is a total failure of consideration; (2) where the money was transferred under a mistake of fact; (3) where the money was transferred under a mistake of law; and sometimes (4) where money has been paid to a third party for the benefit of the defendant.

---

198 For which, see Chapter 14, 14.6.2.
199 (1935) 40 Com Cas 204.
200 Only net profits were recoverable.
201 [1943] AC 32; [1942] 2 All ER 122.

### 15.8.2 TOTAL FAILURE OF CONSIDERATION (FAILURE OF BASIS)

One example of this situation has already been discussed in Chapter 13, in relation to the doctrine of frustration. As we saw there, the House of Lords, in *Fibrosa Spolka Ackyjna v Fairbairn Lawson Combe Barbour Ltd*,[202] accepted that if a party who had paid money under a frustrated contract had received nothing in return, the money could be recovered. The rule is thus that the claimant must have received nothing of what had been contracted for or, rather, that the defendant has not performed any part of the contractual duties in respect of which payment is due.[203] If there has been partial performance of any kind, this remedy will usually not be available.

The action based on a total failure of consideration has also been used, not without controversy, in the sale of goods area. In the cases of *Rowland v Divall*[204] and *Butterworth v Kingsway Motors*,[205] discussed in Chapter 6,[206] it was used to allow the recovery of the full purchase price from the sellers of cars who, unwittingly, did not have the right to sell at the relevant time, even though the buyer had had some use of the car. The fact that transfer of ownership, the main object of a contract for the sale of goods, had not taken place meant that there was a 'total failure of consideration'.

In a contract to design and construct an object, and then to transfer it to the buyer, as opposed to simply a contract of sale, the failure to transfer ownership may not amount to a total failure of consideration. This was confirmed by the House of Lords in *Stocznia Gdanska SA v Latvian Shipping Co*,[207] applying *Hyundai Heavy Industries Co Ltd v Papadopoulos*.[208] The contract was for the construction and supply of a number of ships, and payments were made in instalments. The ships were never completed or transferred, but it was held by the House of Lords that the shipyard was entitled to resist a claim by the buyers, based on a total failure of consideration, for recovery of the instalment payments.

In cases outside the sale of goods area, the fact that property has been used by the claimant (for example, by his or her going into residence under a tenancy) may well prevent a claim based on a total failure of consideration.[209]

### 15.8.3 MISTAKE OF FACT

Money paid under a mistake of fact will be recoverable, provided that the mistake is as to a fact that, if true, would have legally,[210] or morally,[211] obliged the claimant to pay the money or, at least, is sufficiently serious to justify the requirement of repayment. Where a contract is void as a result of being based on a common mistake of fact (such as a false belief in the existence of the subject matter), then recovery will certainly be possible. Other situations where recovery has been held to be possible include mistaken payments under insurance policies. Thus, in *Norwich Union Fire Insurance Society Ltd v Price Ltd*,[212] payment was made on the basis that a cargo of fruit had been destroyed, whereas in fact it had been resold because it was becoming overripe. Recovery of the payment was allowed.

Lord Goff has suggested that recovery under this head will not be possible if the payer intended the payee to benefit in any event; or there is good consideration from the payee

---

202  [1943] AC 32; [1942] 2 All ER 122. See 13.5.2.
203  See the comments of Lord Goff in *Stocznia Gdanska SA v Latvian Shipping Co* [1998] 1 All ER 883.
204  [1923] 2 KB 500.
205  [1954] 1 WLR 1286.
206  See 6.6.11.
207  [1998] 1 All ER 883.
208  [1980] 2 All ER 29.
209  *Hunt v Silk* (1804) 5 East 449; 102 ER 1142. Compare *Marks & Spencer Plc v BNP Paribas Securities Services Trust Co (Jersey) Ltd* [2014] EWCA Civ 603 and [2015] UKSC 72.
210  *Aiken v Short* (1856) 1 H & N 210; 156 ER 1180.
211  *Larner v LCC* [1949] 2 KB 683.
212  [1934] AC 455.

(such as the discharge of a debt); or the payee has changed his or her position in good faith as a result of the payment.[213] As far as payment to discharge an existing debt is concerned, it was confirmed by the Court of Appeal in *Lloyds Bank plc v Independent Insurance Co Ltd*[214] that such a change of position would constitute a good defence to a claim for restitution based on a mistake of fact.

### 15.8.4 MISTAKE OF LAW

Until 1998, it was generally accepted that it was not possible to reclaim money paid under a mistake of law. This was based on the maxim that 'ignorance of the law is no excuse', as applied in this situation in *Bilbie v Lumley*.[215] However, in *Kleinwort Benson Ltd v Lincoln City Council*,[216] the House of Lords overturned this rule, and held that, in certain circumstances, money paid under a mistake of law could be recovered. In coming to this conclusion, it was following developments that had taken place in other parts of the common law world and recommendations for change from the Law Commission.[217]

---

**Key case** *Kleinwort Benson Ltd v Lincoln City Council* (1999)

Facts: The factual background to this decision was 'interest rate swap' agreements entered into by various local authorities during the 1980s as a means of raising money. The agreements involved the advance of a capital sum by the lending bank, coupled with an agreement for mutual payment of interest on a notional sum, one side paying at a fixed rate, the other at a market rate. A balancing of liabilities was to take place at various points. Clearly, the arrangement involved a prediction (almost a 'gamble') as to how market rates would change vis-à-vis the fixed rate. In *Hazell v Hammersmith and Fulham LBC*,[218] it was held by the House of Lords that agreements of this kind were *ultra vires* as regards the local authorities and therefore unlawful and void. In this action Kleinwort Benson sought to recover the money it had lent to Lincoln City Council. The council denied any liability to repay on the basis that the money had been paid under a mistake of law and was therefore irrecoverable. The preliminary issue as to whether there could ever be recovery of money paid under a mistake of law was eventually appealed to the House of Lords.

Held: The House of Lords held that it was time to recognise that there could be recovery of money paid under a mistake of law, where this would otherwise lead to the unjust enrichment of the recipient.

---

In coming to this decision, Lord Goff, who delivered the main speech, made it clear that the recipient's honest belief in his entitlement to the money would not in itself provide a defence. The fact that the recipient had changed his position in reliance on the payment might do so. The test is whether it would be unjust to allow the recipient to retain the benefit of the money paid.

---

213 *Barclays Bank Ltd v Simms and Cooke (Southern) Ltd* [1980] QB 677; [1979] 3 All ER 522. See also *Leslie v Farrar Construction Ltd* [2016] EWCA Civ 1041.
214 [1999] 2 WLR 986.
215 (1802) 2 East 469; 102 ER 448.
216 [1999] 2 AC 349; [1998] 4 All ER 513. Compare *Prudential Assurance Co Ltd v Revenue and Customs Commissioners* [2018] UKSC 39 on some of the issues created by this case.
217 Law Commission, 1994.
218 [1992] 2 AC 1; [1991] 1 All ER 545.

The decision in *Kleinwort Benson* is clearly a very significant addition to the law of restitution. The precise way in which it will operate in practice remains to be seen. The House of Lords was only concerned with the preliminary issue of whether an action for recovery based on mistake of law was possible, not with how this should apply to the particular transactions entered into by the local authorities. An interesting case in which the principle has been applied was *Nurdin and Peacock plc v DB Ramsden & Co Ltd*.[219] This concerned overpayments made under a lease. After these had been made for some months, the plaintiffs discovered that they had been paying too much. Up to that point, the payments were made under a mistake of fact. The final payment, however, was made with full knowledge of the situation but on the basis of incorrect legal advice to the effect that it would automatically be repayable if proceedings being taken against the defendant were successful. This was therefore made under a mistake of law. The court held that recovery for mistake of law did not depend on a belief on the part of the payer that there was a liability to make the payment. The final payment was recoverable as having been made on the basis of a mistake of law.

### 15.8.5 PAYMENT TO A THIRD PARTY

What is the position in respect of money that has been paid by the claimant to a third party but which benefits the defendant? Can the claimant recover this money from the defendant? One major limitation on this is that the claimant must have been acting not purely as a volunteer but under some constraint. A mother who decides, out of the goodness of her heart, to settle her son's debts, cannot then claim restitution from the son.

This rule was applied in a commercial context in *Macclesfield Corp v Great Central Railway*,[220] where the plaintiffs carried out repairs on a bridge that the defendants were legally obliged (but had refused) to maintain. The plaintiffs were regarded as acting purely as volunteers, and so could not recover from the defendants the money spent on the work. An example of a situation where recovery was allowed is *Exall v Partridge*.[221] The plaintiff in this case paid off arrears of rent owed by the defendant. The reason for doing this was to avoid the seizure by bailiffs of a carriage belonging to the plaintiff that had been left on the defendant's premises. The plaintiff was thus acting under a constraint, and not simply as a volunteer, and could recover his money.

A second limitation is that the *defendant* must have been under a legal obligation to pay the money. In *Exall v Partridge*, for example, the obligation on the defendant was to pay his rent. In *Metropolitan Police District Receiver v Croydon Corp*,[222] however, the plaintiffs failed to satisfy this requirement. A policeman had been injured and could not work, but the plaintiffs, the police authority, were obliged to continue to pay his wages. The policeman sued the defendants for negligence and recovered compensation. This did not, however, contain any element for loss of wages, since the policeman was still being paid by the plaintiffs. The plaintiffs sought to recover the cost of the policeman's wages from the defendants. Their argument was that they had made payments to the policeman that were the responsibility of the defendants, since it was their negligence that had caused the policeman to be off work. Their payment of the policeman's wages was thus a benefit to the defendants. The court, however, took the view that the defendants had no legal obligation to pay the policeman's wages. Their only obligation was to compensate him for his losses. Since he had lost no wages, there was no legal obligation in this respect, and therefore the plaintiffs could not recover.

---

219 [1999] 1 All ER 941.
220 [1911] 2 KB 528.
221 (1799) 8 TR 308; 101 ER 1405.
222 [1957] 2 QB 154; [1957] 1 All ER 78.

**For thought**

*Would the outcome of this case have been different if the police authority had not been obliged to continue to pay the wages, but had done so as a gesture of goodwill to a valued employee?*

## 15.8.6 RECOVERY OF COMPENSATION FOR A BENEFIT

The claimant, rather than paying money to the defendant, may have done work for or provided some other benefit to the defendant. Since, by definition, any compensation for such a benefit is not defined by any agreement between the parties (because we are concerned with the situation where there is no contract), the claimant will be seeking compensation on, for example, a *quantum meruit* basis.[223] There are three situations to consider, namely: (1) where a contract has been broken; (2) where it is void; and (3) where agreement is never reached.

## 15.8.7 CONTRACT BROKEN

A broken contract will not usually give rise to consideration of a *quantum meruit* remedy, but an example of how it can be appropriate can be seen in the following case.

**Key case** *Planché v Colburn* (1831)[224]

Facts: The plaintiff had been engaged to write a book on costume and ancient armour. He carried out research and did some of the writing. The defendants then abandoned the project. There were some further negotiations to try to renew the contract but these failed and the plaintiff then sued for breach of contract and for a *quantum meruit*. The action for breach of contract would have been unlikely to succeed because it appears that the original contract was 'entire',[225] with a specific sum payable on completion of the book. Held: The court held that the plaintiff could recover on a *quantum meruit* basis and awarded him 50 guineas.

This type of action is likely to be unusual but is clearly available in appropriate circumstances where a contract has come to an end and the claimant would otherwise be without a remedy. It is difficult to see, however, that in *Planché v Colburn* the defendant had received any benefit from the plaintiff's work, since a half-finished book was of no use to him. This also makes it difficult to fit this case within the general principle of 'unjust enrichment', since the defendant had not in fact been 'enriched'.[226]

## 15.8.8 CONTRACT VOID

We have seen that money paid under a void contract is recoverable. Equally, work that has been done may be compensated on a *quantum meruit* basis. In *Craven-Ellis v Canons Ltd*,[227] for example, the proper procedures were not followed in appointing the plaintiff as managing director. As a result, his appointment was a nullity. Before this was discovered,

---

223  That is, the payment of an amount equivalent to the value of the benefit conferred.
224  (1831) 8 Bing 14; 131 ER 305.
225  See Chapter 14, 14.3.4, above.
226  See the criticism of this case in Harris, Campbell and Halson, 2002, pp 236–37.
227  [1936] 2 KB 403.

however, the plaintiff rendered services for the company in accordance with the agreement that he thought had been entered into. Since the company had benefited from this work, he was allowed to recover on a *quantum meruit* claim. This enabled him to claim reasonable remuneration for the work that he had done. Similarly, in *Mohammed v Alaga*,[228] the Court of Appeal held that a person who had provided translation services under an illegal, and therefore void, fee-sharing agreement with a firm of solicitors could claim on a *quantum meruit* basis for the work actually done.[229]

### 15.8.9 AGREEMENT NEVER REACHED

It is not uncommon in relation to complex contracts, such as those entered into in the building or engineering industries, for work to be done on a project prior to the formalisation of a contract. Although an 'agreement to agree' will not be enforced,[230] no particular problem arises with this as long as a contract does materialise at some point. The Court of Appeal's decision in *Trentham Ltd v Archital Luxfer*[231] confirms that in such a situation the courts will be happy to allow the eventual contract to act retrospectively and govern the work that has been done. Moreover, that decision has also relaxed to some extent the rules concerning formation, making it more likely that a binding contract will be found. Nevertheless, there will still be situations where no contract exists, and it becomes necessary to decide whether, and if so on what basis, compensation can be recovered for work that has been done.[232]

Two principles seem to govern this area. First, recovery will be allowed where the work has been requested by the defendant. Second, if the work has been done without a request, but has been 'freely accepted', it seems likely that the defendant will be expected to pay something for it. In *William Lacey (Hounslow) Ltd v Davis*,[233] the plaintiffs had submitted the lowest tender for a building contract and had been led to believe that they would be awarded it. At the defendant's request, they prepared various plans and estimates. The defendants then decided not to proceed. The court argued by analogy from *Craven-Ellis v Canons*.[234] If it was possible to recover in relation to work done on a void contract, Barry J thought that the same should be true of:[235]

> work done which was to be paid for out of the proceeds of a contract which both parties erroneously believed was about to be made. In neither case was the work done gratuitously, and in both cases the party from whom the payment was sought requested the work and obtained the benefit of it.

The plaintiffs were therefore allowed to recover a reasonable sum for the work done. This line was followed in the following case.

**Key case** *British Steel Corp v Cleveland Bridge and Engineering Co Ltd* (1984)[236]

Facts: The project in this case was for the construction and delivery of a set of cast steel nodes. A 'letter of intent' was issued by the defendants, indicating that they

---

228  [1999] 3 All ER 699. See also *Patel v Mirza* [2016] UKSC 42 at [119].
229  See further Chapter 12, 12.6.
230  *Courtney and Fairbairn v Tolaini Bros (Hotels) Ltd* [1975] 1 WLR 297.
231  [1993] 1 Lloyd's Rep 25 – discussed above, Chapter 2, 2.11.5.
232  The position as regards money paid will be governed by the rules discussed above, 15.4.
233  [1957] 2 All ER 712.
234  [1936] 2 KB 403 – see above, 15.8.8.
235  [1957] 2 All ER 712, p 719.
236  [1984] 1 All ER 504.

intended to enter into the contract with the plaintiffs. The defendants then requested the plaintiffs to start work on the construction of the nodes. It proved impossible to reach agreement, however, on a number of major terms, including the price. Despite this, all the nodes were eventually constructed and delivered, though some were delivered late. The plaintiffs claimed for the value of the nodes. It was clear that there was no contract. On the other hand, the defendants had requested the work to be done, and had freely accepted the nodes when they were delivered.

Held: The plaintiffs were able to succeed in a restitutionary claim for the value of what had been supplied. It should be noted, however, that the defendants' counterclaim for compensation for late delivery failed. Since there was no contract, there could be no obligation concerning the date for delivery and therefore there was no basis on which such a claim could succeed.

This indicates that although the remedy of restitution does allow the courts to avoid unjust enrichment, it may not be sufficiently flexible as yet to allow the courts to take into consideration all the circumstances, and distribute losses and benefits between the parties accordingly.

## 15.9 SPECIFIC PERFORMANCE

As noted at the beginning of this chapter, the only situation where the common law required performance of a contractual obligation was in relation to the action for an agreed sum. Another aspect of what some commentators refer to as 'literal enforcement',[237] that is, the power to order a party to perform a non-monetary obligation, was left to the Chancery courts. The remedy of specific performance involves the court in issuing an order directing one of the parties to a contract to carry out his or her obligations. The sanction for a failure to comply is that the person concerned will be in contempt of court, and liable to fines and even imprisonment as a consequence. Since the remedy is an equitable one, developed by the Chancery courts, it is discretionary, unlike damages, which are available as of right.[238] This means that a claimant is not entitled to the order simply as a result of proving that the other party is in breach of its obligations. Once this has been established, the court will then decide whether it is appropriate in the particular case that the order should be made. For example, as we saw in Chapter 9, one way in which the courts will allow a party to escape the consequences of a mistake concerning the terms of the contract is by refusing to order specific performance.[239] Similarly, the order may not be granted if the claimant has taken advantage of the defendant, for example because he or she was drunk.[240]

Although this discretionary element inevitably attaches a degree of uncertainty to the remedy, in fact the courts have developed a number of rules about its use which mean that in many cases it will be fairly easy to determine whether or not the order is likely to be granted. The rest of this section looks at these.

---

237 See, for example, Beale, Bishop and Furmston, 2007, Chapter 23; Harris, Campbell and Halson, 2002, Chapter 9. Other forms of specific relief may also be available. For example, under s 19 of the Consumer Rights Act 2015 a consumer might have a right of repair or replacement in relation to defective goods, or under s 54 a consumer may have the right to request repeat performance in relation to services.

238 That is, once the claimant has proved a breach of contract the court must award some damages, even if they are only nominal.

239 See above, Chapter 9, 9.7.1.

240 *Malins v Freeman* (1837) 2 Keen 25.

## 15.9.1 ADEQUACY OF DAMAGES

One of the reasons why the remedy of specific performance developed is that, in certain situations, damages will be an inadequate remedy. If no pecuniary loss can be established, or if it is impossible to quantify, this may mean that there would be no effective sanction for a breach of contract, in the absence of the order for specific performance. In *Harnett v Yielding*, for example, Lord Redesdale said:[241]

> Unquestionably, the original foundation of these decrees was simply this, that damages would not give the party the compensation to which he was entitled; that is, it would not put him in a situation as beneficial to him as if the agreement were specifically performed.

Thus, as Kindersley VC explains in *Falcke v Gray*,[242] the Courts of Equity would not allow an injustice to stand, but intervened to order performance of the obligations. Now, of course, the remedy is available in all courts, and the question to be asked is: when will damages not be regarded as an adequate remedy?

If there is a contract for the sale of goods in which there is an active market, then it is very unlikely that an order for specific performance will be granted.[243] The party not in breach can buy or sell in the market, and be compensated by way of damages for any financial loss resulting from a difference between the contract and market prices.[244] If, on the other hand, what is being sold is a valuable antique, or some other item that is not generally available, specific performance may well be the appropriate remedy. This distinction is supported by s 52 of the Sale of Goods Act 1979, which allows for specific performance in relation to 'specific' or 'ascertained' goods, but not 'generic' goods. Even where the goods are 'specific', however, the discretion to order performance will not be exercised unless they are something out of the ordinary. It is not appropriate to order performance where the goods in question are 'ordinary articles of commerce and of no special value or interest'.[245]

Similarly, it is normally the case that the order will be available to enforce contracts for the sale of land, since every piece of land is regarded as unique. This applies in favour of the seller as well as the buyer because it is a general principle that there should be mutuality in the availability of the remedy.[246]

---

**For thought**

*Is it true that every piece of land is unique? If you are buying a new house on a housing estate, on which the houses are of identical design, does it really matter which one you end up with? Or, if you are buying a terraced house to let out to students, are you concerned with precisely which property you acquire, as long as it is of an equivalent value?*

---

241  (1805) 2 Sch & Lef 549.

242  (1859) 4 Drew 651; 62 ER 250.

243  If the market is affected by unusual circumstances, the courts may well be more prepared to grant a remedy that effectively requires performance. See, for example, *Sky Petroleum Ltd v VIP Petroleum Ltd* [1974] 1 WLR 576, where at the time of an 'oil crisis' the court was prepared to grant an injunction restraining an oil company from withholding supplies to filling stations.

244  Insisting on performance in this situation would interfere with the concept of the 'efficient breach', which suggests that allowing a party to breach may in fact increase 'wealth'. See above, 15.3.

245  *Cohen v Roche* [1927] 1 KB 169, p 181. The goods in this case were a set of eight Hepplewhite chairs, which were sold for £60 and valued by the court at £70–80.

246  See below, 15.9.4.

In *Behnke v Bede Shipping Co Ltd*,[247] a 'unique' ship was held to be capable of being subject to an order for specific performance, but in *The Stena Nautica (No 2)*[248] the decision went the other way. The Court of Appeal accepted that as a matter of law a ship could, in appropriate circumstances, be the subject of an order for specific performance. On the facts, however, it was felt that the judge had been wrong to make such an order relating to the plaintiffs' option to purchase a vessel. A factor that had apparently weighed heavily with the judge was that the ship concerned was a sister ship of other vessels operated by the plaintiffs. On the other hand, he had made the order subject to another charter with a third party that was to operate for the next two years. The Court of Appeal found these two elements in the judge's decision to be inconsistent. As May LJ commented:[249]

> If the sister ship point was relevant and indeed vital, in deciding whether the [plaintiffs] should be limited to their remedy in damages, it is I think somewhat surprising that the learned judge went on in effect to deprive them of the use of the sister ship over the next two years, in imposing the condition that he did on the order for specific performance which he made.

Indeed, it is always likely to raise a question as to whether such an order is necessary, on the basis that damages are inadequate, if it is made subject to a delay in its operation.

In some cases, it seems that if damages would only be nominal, then the order may be made. Thus, in *Beswick v Beswick*,[250] the fact that the deceased's estate suffered no direct loss from the failure of the nephew to pay his aunt meant that only nominal damages would be recoverable in an action by the estate. Justice clearly demanded, however, that the contract should be enforced and so the order was granted. It will not always be the case that the fact that damages would be nominal will allow specific performance to be ordered. If that were so it would include all the cases of sale of goods where there is an available market offering a price more attractive than the contract one. There must be some other factor that will persuade the court to make the order, but it is difficult to predict what this will be, or to make a list of the appropriate circumstances.

### 15.9.2 NEED FOR SUPERVISION

A court will be reluctant to order specific performance where it would have to supervise the parties over a period of time to ensure compliance. In *Ryan v Mutual Tontine Westminster Chambers Association*,[251] for example, the court refused to grant specific performance of a landlord's obligation to have a resident porter 'constantly in attendance'. It appears, however, to be only where the supervision would need to concern the detail of performance that this limitation applies. In *Wolverhampton Corp v Emmons*,[252] the contract concerned a building contract for some new houses, which would obviously take time to complete. The court was prepared to order specific performance because the obligations of the defendant were clearly defined by the building plans and so there would be no need for detailed supervision while the work was being done.

---

247 [1927] 1 KB 649.
248 [1982] 2 Lloyd's Rep 336.
249 [1982] 2 Lloyd's Rep 336, p 349.
250 [1968] AC 58; [1967] 2 All ER 1197. The facts of this case are given above, Chapter 5, 5.4.1. Moreover in *Evans Marshall & Co. Ltd. v Bertola S.A. and Another* [1973] 1 WLR 349 at 379 Kerr J stated 'The standard question in relation to the grant of an injunction, "Are damages an adequate remedy?", might perhaps, in the light of the authorities of recent years, be rewritten: "Is it just, in all the circumstances, that a plaintiff should be confined to his remedy in damages?"' See also *Alstom Transport UK Ltd v London Underground Ltd* [2017] EWHC 1521.
251 [1893] 1 Ch 116.
252 [1901] 1 KB 515.

A more recent example of the application of this principle is to be found in the follow-ing case.

---

**Key case** *Co-operative Insurance Society Ltd v Argyll Stores (Holdings) Ltd* (1998)[253]

Facts: The plaintiffs were seeking specific performance of a covenant in a lease of retail premises to keep them open for business during particular hours. The defendants had closed the supermarket that had been run at the premises. The trial judge refused specific performance, but this ruling was overturned by the Court of Appeal.
Held: The House of Lords restored the ruling of the trial judge. It held that it was not usu-ally appropriate to give an order for specific performance requiring someone to carry on a business. One of the main reasons for this was the prospect of the court having to make a series of orders over a period of time, backed up by the heavy-handed remedy of contempt of court, in order to ensure compliance. This was not appropriate, not least in terms of likely cost to the parties and the resources of the judicial system. A one-off award of damages would be much more satisfactory. The trial judge's decision should therefore be restored.

---

### 15.9.3 PERSONAL SERVICES

The courts will be reluctant to grant an order for specific performance in relation to employ-ment or other contracts for personal services. The fact that the matter has come to court almost certainly shows that relations between the parties have broken down and it would be undesirable to try to force them to work together. Where, however, it can be demonstrated that mutual trust and respect do still exist, then the order may be available. In *Hill v CA Parsons & Co Ltd*,[254] for example, a dismissal had resulted from union pressure, rather than a dispute between employer and employee. This limitation on the general rule as regards personal ser-vices was also recognised in *Powell v Brent London Borough Council*,[255] where an injunction was granted. The problem in this case had arisen simply because the employer had appointed the employee after a process that did not comply with the requirements of its equal opportuni-ties procedures. The subsequent dismissal of the employee was a result of this rather than any dissatisfaction with the employee's work. Of course, most disputes about employment will nowadays fall to be considered under the employment protection legislation, which specifi-cally provides for 'reinstatement' as one of the remedies for unfair dismissal.

### 15.9.4 NEED FOR MUTUALITY

A court will generally not order specific performance unless it would also be available against the party seeking it. If, however, unenforceable obligations have in fact already been performed, the court may order the other side to go through with the contract. The time to assess the issue is at the date of trial, rather than the date of contract, as is shown by the following case.

---

**Key case** *Price v Strange* (1978)[256]

Facts: The defendant had granted the plaintiff the continuation of an underlease of a flat, at an increased rent, in consideration for his agreeing to carry out certain internal and

---

253 [1998] AC 1; [1997] 3 All ER 297.
254 [1972] 1 Ch 305; [1971] 3 All ER 1345. Compare *Ashworth v Royal National Theatre* [2014] EWHC 1176.
255 [1986] ICR 176.
256 [1978] Ch 337; [1977] 3 All ER 371.

external repairs. The agreement started to operate and the plaintiff carried out the interior repairs. At that point, the defendant purported to terminate the agreement. She then had the exterior repairs completed at her own expense. The plaintiff sought an order for specific performance, but the trial judge rejected this. His reason was that, at the time of the contract, the plaintiff's obligations to carry out the repairs would not have been specifically enforceable, so that there was a lack of mutuality. The plaintiff appealed.

Held: The Court of Appeal disagreed with the trial judge. By the time of the trial, all the repair work had been completed and the defendant was not in danger of being forced to grant the underlease without being able to enforce the obligation to carry out the repairs. The court felt that the time of trial was the correct point at which to decide the issue, and therefore granted the order sought by the plaintiff.

### 15.9.5 HARDSHIP

If the granting of an order, which on other grounds would seem to be available, will cause disproportionate hardship to the defendant, the court may refuse it. This is an aspect of the general 'equitable' nature of the remedy, which requires the court always to have in mind the need to achieve justice between the parties. In *Denne v Light*,[257] for example, specific performance of a contract for the sale of land would have left the defendant with a plot surrounded by land owned by others and with no point of access. The order was not granted. Even straightforward financial hardship, if sufficiently severe, may be enough, particularly if it was unforeseeable at the time of the contract. In *Patel v Ali*,[258] the defendant had become disabled, and relied greatly on a network of support from neighbours. This network would have been lost if she had been forced to move and it would have been very expensive to have to pay for equivalent help. The order for specific performance was not granted.

### 15.9.6 CLAIMANT MUST HAVE ACTED EQUITABLY

Since specific performance is an equitable remedy, the courts will apply the general equitable maxims that 'he who seeks equity must do equity' and 'he who comes to equity must come with clean hands'. In other words, the claimant will not be granted the remedy unless he or she, in the eyes of the court, has also acted equitably. For example, the remedy was refused in *Walters v Morgan*,[259] where the plaintiff had taken advantage of the defendant's ignorance as to the true value of property over which a mining lease had been granted. Similarly, in *Shell UK Ltd v Lostock Garage Ltd*,[260] the Court of Appeal refused to grant an injunction that would have in effect compelled the defendants to go through with a contract. The plaintiff's discriminatory pricing policy was regarded as unfair, and a basis for refusing the order.

## 15.10 INJUNCTIONS

In some situations, the courts may be prepared to grant an injunction restraining a person from acting in a way that would amount to a breach of contract. The injunction may be interim in nature, that is temporary pending a full trial, or permanent. One example of a situation where this may be a valuable remedy is in relation to restrictive covenants relating to the sale of a business, or competing employment. In any contract in which a party promises *not* to do something, there will be potential scope for the use of an injunction. An

---

257  (1857) 8 DM & G 774; 44 ER 588.
258  [1984] Ch 283; [1984] 1 All ER 978.
259  (1861) 3 De GF & J 718; 45 ER 1056.
260  [1977] 1 All ER 481. See also Chapter 6, 6.6.7.

injunction, however, like the order for specific performance, is an equitable remedy, and thus subject to the discretion of the court.

The courts will not allow an injunction to be used as an indirect means of specifically enforcing a contract for which a direct order to perform would not be granted. Thus, in *Page One Records v Britton*,[261] the court refused an injunction that would have restrained a pop group from employing anyone as their manager other than the plaintiff, with whom they had fallen out. This was regarded as effectively forcing the group to employ the manager, and would amount to an indirect enforcement of a contract for personal services. Earlier decisions, however, had shown the courts being more willing to act in this area. In *Lumley v Wagner*,[262] for example, a singer had been restrained from singing in other theatres,[263] and in *Warner Bros v Nelson*,[264] the actress Bette Davis had been restrained from working in films or theatre for any other company. The court in this case felt that she was not being compelled to work for Warner Bros because she could have found employment other than as an actress, a conclusion which was technically correct, but practically very unrealistic. It may be that the *Page One* decision represents the more likely approach of a modern court to these issues.

## 15.11 SUMMARY OF KEY POINTS

- The main remedy for breach of contract is damages, though the courts will sometimes be prepared to award specific performance, or an injunction.

- The normal purpose of damages is compensatory; they are normally intended to put the claimant in the position he or she would have been in had the contract been performed properly.

- The alternative measures of damages are:
  - □ expectation interest (including lost profits);
  - □ reliance interest (compensating for lost expenditure).

- Consequential losses can generally be recovered.

- Non-pecuniary losses in the form of personal injury may be recoverable.
  - □ Other types of non-pecuniary loss, such as mental distress or disappointment, are only recoverable in exceptional cases (such as where the purpose of the contract was to provide pleasure).

- Non-compensatory damages, based on the benefit that the defendant has gained through breaking a contract, are only available in exceptional circumstances.

- Recovery of damages is limited by the rules of remoteness and mitigation.

- Liquidated damages clauses are enforceable; penalties are not.

- Restitution. In some situations the courts will require the return of money or property, in order to prevent 'unjust enrichment'. This can arise as a result of a

---

261  [1967] 3 All ER 822.
262  (1852) 1 De GM & G 604; 42 ER 687. See Waddams, 2001 for the background to this case.
263  Cf *Lumley v Gye* (1853) 2 E & B 216; 118 ER 749 – discussed in Chapter 5, 5.14.
264  [1937] 1 KB 209; [1936] 3 All ER 160.

> breach of contract, where a contract is declared void or where the parties have failed to make a contract.
>
> ■ Specific performance is generally only available where damages would be an inadequate remedy.
>
> ■ Injunctions can be used to prevent a breach of contract, but not as a means of obtaining specific performance when that remedy would not normally be available.

## 15.12 FURTHER READING

### Generally

■ Burrows, A, *Remedies for Torts and Breach of Contract*, 3rd edn, 2004, Oxford: Oxford University Press

■ Friedmann, D, 'Good faith and remedies for breach of contract', Chapter 16 in Beatson, J and Friedmann, D (eds), *Good Faith and Fault in Contract Law*, 1995, Oxford: Clarendon Press

■ Fuller, L and Perdue, W, 'The reliance interest in contract damages' (1936) 46 Yale LJ 52

■ Harris, D, Campbell, D and Halson, R, *Remedies in Contract and Tort*, 2nd edn, 2002, London: Butterworths

### Unjust enrichment

■ Birks, P, *Unjust Enrichment*, 2nd edn, 2005, Oxford: Clarendon

■ Burrows, A, *The Law of Restitution*, 3rd edn, 2010, Oxford: Oxford University Press

■ R. Havelock, 'A taxonomic approach to quantum meruit' (2016) 132 LQR 470

■ Mitchell, C, Mitchell, P and Watterson, S, *Goff & Jones: The Law of Unjust Enrichment*, 9th edn, 2016, London: Sweet & Maxwell

■ Law Commission, Restitution: Mistakes of Law and Ultra Vires Public Authority Receipts and Payments, Report No 227, 1994

■ Rose, F (ed), Failure of Contracts, Contractual Restitutionary and Proprietary Consequences, 1997, Oxford: Hart Publishing

### Measure of contractual damages

■ Bridge, M G, 'Expectation damages and uncertain future losses', Chapter 17 in Beatson, J and Friedmann, D (eds), *Good Faith and Fault in Contract Law*, 1995, Oxford: Clarendon Press

■ Burrows, A, 'Limitations on compensation', in Burrows, A and Peel, E (eds), *Commercial Remedies: Current Issues and Problems*, 2003, Oxford: Oxford University Press

■ Cartwright, J, 'Remoteness of damage in contract and tort: a reconsideration' [1996] CLJ 488

- Chandler, A, and Devenney, J, 'Breach of contract and the expectation deficit: inconvenience and disappointment' (2007) 27 LS 126

- Coote, B, 'The performance interest, *Panatown*, and the problem of loss' (2001) 117 LQR 81

- Cunnington, R, 'Should punitive damages be part of the judicial arsenal in contract cases?' (2006) 26 LS 369

- Cunnington, R, 'A lost opportunity to clarify' (2007) 123 LQR 48

- Davies, P, 'One step backwards: restricting negotiating damages for breach of contract.' [2018] L.M.C.L.Q. 433

- Harris, D, Ogus, A and Phillips, J, 'Contract remedies and the consumer surplus' (1979) 95 LQR 581

- Hedley, S, ' "Very much the wrong people": the House of Lords and publication of spy memoirs' [2000] Web JCLI

- Kramer, A, 'An agreement-centred approach to remoteness and contract damages', in Cohen, N and McKendrick, E (eds), *Comparative Remedies for Breach of Contract*, 2004, Oxford: Hart Publishing

- McKendrick, E and Graham, M, 'The sky's the limit: contractual damages for non-pecuniary loss' [2002] LMCLQ 161

- O'Sullivan, J, 'Loss and gain at greater depth: the implications of the *Ruxley* decision', Chapter 1 in Rose, F (ed), *Failure of Contracts, Contractual Restitutionary and Proprietary Consequences*, 1997, Oxford: Hart Publishing

- Peel, E, 'Remoteness re-visited' (2009) 125 LQR 6, 7–12

- Reece, H, 'Loss of chances in the law' (1996) 59 MLR 188

- Sandy, D, 'Spies, rock stars and restitutionary damages' (2003) 153 NLJ 723

**Specific performance**
- Harris, D, 'Specific performance – a regular remedy for consumers' (2003) 119 LQR 541

## COMPANION WEBSITE

*Now visit the companion website to:*

- Revise and consolidate your knowledge of Remedies by tackling a series of multiple-choice questions on this chapter

- Test your understanding of the chapter's key terms by using the flashcard glossary

- Fine-tune your legal skills by reading our tips and suggestions for Remedies problem questions

- Explore Remedies further by accessing a series of web links

# Bibliography

Adams, J, Beyleveld, D and Brownsword, R, 'Privity of contract – the benefits and burdens of law reform' (1997) 60 MLR 238

Adams, J and Brownsword, R, 'The Unfair Contract Terms Act: a decade of discretion' (1988) 104 LQR 94

Adams, J and Brownsword, R, 'Contract, consideration and the critical path' (1990a) 53 MLR 536

Adams, J and Brownsword, R, 'Privity and the concept of a network contract' (1990b) 10 Legal Studies 12

Adams, J and Brownsword, R, *Key Issues in Contract*, 1995, London: Butterworths

Adams, J and Brownsword, R, *Understanding Contract Law*, 5th edn, 2007, London: Sweet & Maxwell

Allen, D, *Misrepresentation*, 1988, London: Sweet & Maxwell

Allen, D, 'The gentleman's agreement in legal theory and in modern practice' [2000] Anglo-American Law Review 204

Atiyah, P S, '*Couturier v Hastie* and the sale of non-existent goods' (1957) 73 LQR 340

Atiyah, P S, 'Contracts, promises and the law of obligations' (1978) 94 LQR 193

Atiyah, P S, *The Rise and Fall of Freedom of Contract*, 1979, Oxford: Clarendon Press

Atiyah, P S, 'Economic duress and the overborne will' (1982) 98 LQR 197

Atiyah, P S, *Essays on Contract*, 1986a, Oxford: Clarendon Press

Atiyah, P S, 'Consideration: a re-statement', Chapter 8 in Atiyah, P S, *Essays on Contract*, 1986b, Oxford: Clarendon Press

Atiyah, P S, *An Introduction to the Law of Contract*, 5th edn, 1995, Oxford: Clarendon Press

Auchmuty, R, 'The rhetoric of equality and the problem of heterosexuality', Chapter 3 in Mulcahy, L and Wheeler, S (eds), *Feminist Perspectives on Contract Law*, 2005, London: Glasshouse Press

Austen-Baker, R, 'A strange sort of survival for *Pinnel's case: Collier v P & MJ Wright (Holdings) Ltd*' (2008) 71 MLR 611

Baker, J H, 'From sanctity of contract to reasonable expectation' [1979] 32 Current Legal Problems 17

Barendt, E, 'Exclusion clauses: incorporation and interpretation' (1972) 35 MLR 644

Beale, H, *Remedies for Breach of Contract*, 1980, London: Sweet & Maxwell

Beale, H, 'Penalties in termination provisions' (1988) 104 LQR 355

Beale, H, 'Unfair contracts in Britain and Europe' [1989] Current Legal Problems 197

Beale, H, 'Damages in lieu of rescission for misrepresentation' (1995a) 111 LQR 60

Beale, H, 'Points on misrepresentation' (1995b) 111 LQR 385

Beale, H, 'Legislative control of fairness: the Directive on Unfair Terms in Consumer Contracts', in Beatson J and Friedmann, D (eds), *Good Faith and Fault in Contract Law*, 1995c, Oxford: Clarendon Press

Beale, H (ed), *Chitty on Contracts*, 33rd edn, 2018, London: Sweet & Maxwell

Beale, H, Bishop, W and Furmston, M, *Contract Cases and Materials*, 5th edn, 2007, London: Butterworths

Beale, H and Dugdale, T, 'Contracts between businessmen' (1975) 2 Brit J Law & Society 45

Beatson, J, 'Reforming the law of contracts for the benefit of third parties: a second bite at the cherry' [1992] Current Legal Problems 1

Beatson, J, Burrows, A and Cartwright, J (eds), *Anson's Law of Contract*, 30th edn, 2016, Oxford: Oxford University Press

Beatson, J and Friedmann, D (eds), *Good Faith and Fault in Contract Law*, 1995, Oxford: Clarendon Press

Bennett, H N, 'Statements of fact and statements of belief in insurance contract law and general contract law' (1998) 61 MLR 886

Beyleveld, D and Brownsword, R, 'Privity, transitivity and rationality' (1991) 54 MLR 48

Bigwood, R, 'Pre-contractual misrepresentation and the limits of the principle in *With v O'Flanagan*' [2005] CLJ 94

Birks, P, *An Introduction to the Law of Restitution*, 1989, Oxford: Clarendon Press

Birks, P and Chin Nyuk Yin, 'On the nature of undue influence', Chapter 3 in Beatson, J and Friedmann, D (eds), *Good Faith and Fault in Contract Law*, 1995, Oxford: Clarendon Press

Bishop, W D, 'The contract-tort boundary and the economics of insurance' (1983) 12 JLS 241

Bradgate, R, 'Unreasonable standard terms' (1997) 60 MLR 582

Bridge, M G, 'Expectation damages and uncertain future losses', Chapter 17 in Beatson, J and Friedmann, D (eds), *Good Faith and Fault in Contract Law*, 1995, Oxford: Clarendon Press

Bridge, M G, 'Good faith in commercial contracts', Chapter 7 in Brownsword, R, Hird, NJ and Howells, G (eds), *Good Faith in Contract*, 1999, Aldershot: Dartmouth

Bridge, M G, *The Sale of Goods*, 2nd edn, 2009, Oxford: Oxford University Press

Bright, S, 'Winning the battle against unfair contract terms' (2000) 20 LS 331

Brown, I, 'The letter of comfort: placebo or promise?' [1990] JBL 281

Brown, I, 'The contract to negotiate: a thing writ in water?' [1992] JBL 353

Brownsword, R, 'Retrieving reasons, retrieving rationality? A new look at the right to withdraw for breach of contract' (1992) Journal of Contract Law 83

Brownsword, R, 'Towards a rational law of contract', in Willhelmson, T (ed), *Perspectives of Critical Contract Law*, 1993, Aldershot: Dartmouth

Brownsword, R, 'Individualism, cooperativism, and an ethic for European contract law' (2001) 64 MLR 628

Brownsword, R, 'After *Investors*: interpretation, expectation and the implicit dimension of the "new contextualism"?', Chapter 4 in Campbell, D, Collins, H and Wightman, J (eds), *Implicit Dimensions of Contract*, 2003, Oxford: Hart Publishing

Brownsword, R, *Contract Law: Themes for the Twenty-First Century*, 2nd edn, 2006, London: Butterworths

Brownsword, R, Hird, N J and Howells, G (eds), *Good Faith in Contract*, 1999, Aldershot: Dartmouth

Buckley, R, '*Walford v Miles*: false certainty about uncertainty – an Australian perspective' (1993) JCL 58

Buckley, R, 'Illegal transactions: chaos or discretion' (2000) 20 LS 155

Buckley, R, 'Illegality in the Supreme Court' (2015) 131 LQR 341

Burrows, A S, 'Specific performance at the crossroads' (1984) 4 LS 102

Burrows, A S, *The Law of Restitution*, 1993, London: Butterworths

Burrows, A S, *Understanding the Law of Obligations*, 1998, Oxford: Hart Publishing

Burrows, A S, 'The Contracts (Rights of Third Parties) Act and its implications for commercial contracts' [2000] LMCLQ 540

Burrows, A S, *Remedies for Torts and Breach of Contract*, 3rd edn, 2004, Oxford: Oxford University Press

Buxton, R, 'The HRA and private law' (2000) 116 LQR 48

Campbell, D, 'The relational constitution of the discrete contract', Chapter 3 in Campbell, D and Vincent-Jones, P (eds), *Contract and Economic Organisation*, 1996, Aldershot: Dartmouth

Campbell, D (ed), *The Relational Theory of Contract: Selected Works of Ian Macneil*, 2001, London: Sweet & Maxwell

Campbell, D, 'Good faith and the ubiquity of the relational contract' (2014) 77 MLR 475

Campbell, D, 'Better than Fuller: a two interest model of remedies for breach of contract' (2015) 78 MLR 296

Campbell, D, Collins, H and Wightman, J (eds), *Implicit Dimensions of Contract*, 2003, Oxford: Hart Publishing

Campbell, D and Harris, D, 'Flexibility in long term contractual relationships: the role of cooperation' (1993) 20 J of Law and Soc 166

Campbell, D and Harris, D, 'In defence of breach: a critique of restitution and the performance interest' (2002) 22 LS 208

Campbell, D and Vincent-Jones, P (eds), *Contract and Economic Organisation*, 1996, Aldershot: Dartmouth

Cartwright, J, 'Damages for misrepresentation' [1987a] Conv 423

Cartwright, J, '*Solle v Butcher* and the doctrine of mistake in contract' (1987b) 103 LQR 584

Cartwright, J, *Unequal Bargaining*, 1991, Oxford: Oxford University Press

Cartwright, J, 'Remoteness of damage in contract and tort: a reconsideration' (1996) 55 CLJ 488

Cartwright, J and Schmidt-Kessel, M, 'Defects in consent: mistake, fraud, threats, unfair exploitation' in Dannemann, G and Vogenauer, S (eds), *The Common European Sales Law in Context: Interactions with English and German Law*, 2013, Oxford: Oxford University Press

Chandler, A, 'Self-induced frustration, foreseeability and risk' [1990] NILQ 362

Chandler, A and Devenney, J, 'Breach of contract and the expectation deficit: inconvenience and disappointment' (2007) 27 LS 126

Chandler, A, Devenney, J and Poole, J, 'Common mistake: theoretical justification and remedial inflexibility' [2004] JBL 34

Chen-Wishart, M, *Unconscionable Bargains*, 1989, Wellington: Butterworths

Chen-Wishart, M, 'The *O'Brien* principle and substantive unfairness' (1997) 56 CLJ 60

Chen-Wishart, M and Magnus, U, 'Termination, price reduction and damages', in Dannemann, G and Vogenauer, S (eds), *The Common European Sales Law in Context: Interactions with English and German Law*, 2013, Oxford: Oxford University Press

Collins, H, *The Law of Contract*, 1st edn, 1986, London: Weidenfeld & Nicolson

Collins, H, 'Good faith in European contract law' (1994) 14 OJLS 229

Collins, H, 'Competing norms of contractual behaviour', Chapter 4 in Campbell, D and Vincent-Jones, P (eds), *Contract and Economic Organisation*, 1996, Aldershot: Dartmouth

Collins, H, *Regulating Contracts*, 1999, Oxford: Oxford University Press

Collins, H, *The Law of Contract*, 4th edn, 2003, London: Butterworths

Conway, H, 'Prenuptial contracts' (1995) 145 NLJ 1290

Cooke, R, review of *Consensus ad Idem: Essays in the Law of Contract in Honour of Guenter Treitel* (1998) 114 LQR 505

Coote, B, *Exception Clauses*, 1964, London: Sweet & Maxwell

Coote, B, 'Validation under the Illegal Contracts Act' (1992) 15 NZULR 80

Coote, B, 'The Illegal Contracts Act 1970', Chapter 3 in *New Zealand Law Commission, Contract Statutes Review*, 1993

Coote, B, '*Dunlop v Lambert:* the search for a rationale' (1998) JCL 91

Coote, B, 'Consideration and variations: a different solution' (2004) 120 LQR 19

Cope, M, *Duress, Undue Influence and Unconscientious Bargains*, 1985, North Ryde, NSW: Lawbook Co

Cretney, S, 'The little woman and the big bad bank' (1992) 108 LQR 534

Cumberbatch, J, 'In freedom's cause: the contract to negotiate' (1992) 12 OJLS 586

Cunnington, R, 'Should punitive damages be part of the judicial arsenal in contract cases?' (2006) 26 LS 369

Cunnington, R, 'A lost opportunity to clarify' (2007) 123 LQR 48

Dalton, C, 'An essay in the deconstruction of contract doctrine' (1985) 94 Yale LJ 997

Danzig, R, *'Hadley v Baxendale:* a study of the industrialisation of the law' (1975) 4 J Leg St 249

Davies, PS, 'Rectification versus interpretation: the nature and scope of the equitable jurisdiction' (2016) 75 CLJ 62

Dean, M, 'Unfair contract terms: the European approach' (1993) 56 MLR 581

Denning, A, *The Discipline of Law*, 1979, London: Butterworths

Department for Business, Innovation and Skills, *Draft Consumer Rights Bill: Government Response to Consultations on Consumer Rights*, June 2013 (BIS/13/916)

Devenney, J, 'Gordian knots in Europeanised private law: unfair terms, bank charges and political compromises' [2011] 62 NILQ 33

Devenney, J and Kenny, M, 'Unfair terms, surety transactions and European harmonisation: a crucible of Europeanised private law?' [2009] Conv 295

Devenney, J, 'Re-Examining Damages for Fraudulent Misrepresentation: Towards a More Measured Response to Compensation and Deterrence', in Di Matteo, L, Rowley, K, Zhou, Q & Santier, S, *Current Issues in Commercial Contracts: Transatlantic Perspectives*, 2013, Cambridge: Cambridge University Press

Devenney, J and Kenny, M, 'The omission of personal property law from the proposed common European sales law: the Hamlet syndrome ... without the prince?' [2015] JBL 607

Devenney, J, 'Private Redress Mechanisms in England and Wales for Unfair Commercial Practices' (2016) 5 EuCML 100

Dockray, M, *'Cutter v Powell:* a trip outside the text' (2001) 117 LQR 664

Eisenberg, M A, 'Relational contracts', Chapter 11 in Beatson, J and Friedmann, D (eds), *Good Faith and Fault in Contract Law*, 1995, Oxford: Clarendon Press

Enman, S R, 'Doctrines of unconscionability in England, Canada and the Commonwealth' (1987) 16 Anglo-Am LR 191

Enonchong, N, *Illegal Transactions*, 1998, London: Lloyd's of London Press

Evans, D M, 'The Anglo-American mailing rule' (1966) 15 ICLQ 553

Fehlberg, B, 'The husband, the bank, the wife and her signature' (1994) 57 MLR 467

Flannigan, R, 'Privity – the end of an era (error)' (1987) LQR 564

Freeman, M, 'Contracting in the haven: *Balfour v Balfour* revisited', in Halson, R (ed), *Exploring the Boundaries of Contract*, 1996, London: Dartmouth

Fried, C, *Contract as Promise*, 2nd edn, 2015, Oxford: Oxford University Press

Friedmann, D, 'Good faith and remedies for breach of contract', Chapter 16 in Beatson, J and Friedmann, D (eds), *Good Faith and Fault in Contract Law*, 1995, Oxford: Clarendon Press

Fuller, L and Perdue, W, 'The reliance interest in contract damages' (1936) 46 Yale LJ 52

Furmston, M P, 'The case of the insistent performer' (1962) 25 MLR 364

Furmston, M P, 'The analysis of illegal contracts' (1966) 16 Univ of Toronto LJ 267

Furmston, M P, 'The Illegal Contracts Act 1970 – an English view' (1972–73) 5 NZULR 151

Furmston, M P, *Cheshire, Fifoot and Furmston's Law of Contract*, 17th edn, 2017, London: Oxford University Press

Furmston, M P, *The Law of Contract*, 6th edn, 2017, London: Lexis Nexis

Gardner, S, 'Trashing with Trollope: a deconstruction of the postal rules' (1992) 12 OJLS 170

Gee, S, 'The interpretation of commercial contracts' (2001) 117 LQR 358

Gilmore, G, *The Death of Contract*, 1974, Columbus: Ohio State University Press

Goff, R and Jones, G, *The Law of Restitution*, 4th edn, 1993, London: Sweet & Maxwell

Goodhart, A L, 'Measure of damages when a contract is repudiated' (1962) 78 LQR 263

Goodrich, P, 'The posthumous life of the postal rule: requiem and revival of *Adams v Lindsell*', Chapter 4 in Mulcahy, L and Wheeler, S, *Feminist Perspectives on Contract Law*, 2005, London: Glasshouse Press

Griffith, J A G, *Politics of the Judiciary*, 5th edn, 2010, London: Fontana

Grodecki, J K, 'In *pari delicto potior est conditio defendentis*' (1955) 71 LQR 254

Halson, R, 'Sailors, sub-contractors and consideration' (1990) 106 LQR 183

Halson, R, 'Opportunism, economic duress and contractual modifications' (1991) 107 LQR 649

Halson, R, 'The offensive limits of promissory estoppel' [1999] LMCLQ 256

Halson, R, *Contract Law*, 2nd edn, 2013, Harlow: Pearson Education

Hamson, C J, 'The reform of consideration' (1938) 54 LQR 233

Handley, K R, 'Exclusion clauses for fraud' (2003) 119 LQR 537

Hare, C, 'Identity mistakes: a missed opportunity' (2004) 67 MLR 993

Harland, D, 'Unconscionable and unfair contracts: an Australian perspective', Chapter 11 in Brownsword, R, Hird, N J and Howells, G (eds), *Good Faith in Contract*, 1999, Aldershot: Dartmouth

Harris, D, 'Penalties and forfeiture: contractual remedies specified by the parties' [1990] LCMLQ 158

Harris, D, 'Incentives to perform, or break contracts' [1992] Current Legal Problems 29

Harris, D, 'Specific performance – a regular remedy for consumers' (2003) 119 LQR 541

Harris, D, Campbell, D and Halson, R, *Remedies in Contract and Tort*, 2nd edn, 2002, London: Butterworths

Harris, D, Ogus, A and Phillips, J, 'Contract remedies and the consumer surplus' (1979) 95 LQR 581

Haycroft, A M and Waksman, D M, 'Frustration and restitution' [1984] JBL 207

Hedley, S, 'Keeping contract in its place: *Balfour v Balfour* and the enforceability of informal agreements' (1985) 5 OJLS 391

Hedley, S, 'Carriage by sea: frustration and *force majeure*' (1990) 49 CLJ 209

Hedley, S, ' "Very much the wrong people": the House of Lords and publication of spy memoirs' [2000] 4 Web JCLI

Hepple, B, 'Intention to create legal relations' (1970) CLJ 122

Hird, N J and Blair, A, 'Minding your own business – *Williams v Roffey* revisited' [1996] JBL 254

Hooley, R, 'Damages and the Misrepresentation Act 1967' (1991) 107 LQR 547

Horwitz, M, 'The historical foundations of modern contract law' (1974) 87 Harv LR 917

Howarth, W, 'The meaning of objectivity in contract' (1984) 100 LQR 205

Hudson, A H, 'Retraction of letters of acceptance' (1966) 82 LQR 169

Hudson, A H, 'Mental incapacity revisited' [1986] Conveyancer and Property Lawyer 178

Hunt, M, 'The horizontal effect of the HRA' [1998] PL 423

Jackson, B, *Law, Fact and Narrative Coherence*, 1988, Liverpool: Deborah Charles

Jaffey, P, 'Efficiency, disgorgement and reliance in contract: a comment on Campbell and Harris' (2002) 22 LS 570

Kramer, A, 'An agreement-centred approach to remoteness and contract damages', in Cohen, N and McKendrick, E (eds), *Comparative Remedies for Breach of Contract*, 2004, Oxford: Hart Publishing

Kronman, A, 'Mistake disclosure, information and the law of contracts' (1978) 7 J Leg Stud 1

Kronman, A, 'Paternalism and the law of contract' (1983) Yale LJ 763

Kronman, A and Posner, R, *The Economics of Contract Law*, 1979, Boston, MA: Little, Brown

Lando, O and Beale, H (eds), *The Principles of European Contract Law*, Parts I and II, 2000, The Hague: Kluwer Law International

Law Commission, *Transfer of Land: Formalities for Deeds and Escrows*, Working Paper No 93, 1985

Law Commission, *Law of Contract: the Parol Evidence Rule*, Report No 154, Cmd 9700, 1986

Law Commission, *Deeds and Escrows*, Report No 163, HC1, 1987

Law Commission, *Privity of Contract: Contracts for the benefit of third parties*, Consultation Paper No 121, 1991

Law Commission, *Contributory Negligence as a Defence in Contract Law*, Report No 219, 1993

Law Commission, *Restitution: Mistakes of Law and* Ultra Vires *Public Authority Receipts and Payments*, Report No 227, 1994

Law Commission, *Illegal Transactions: the Effect of Illegality on Contracts and Trusts*, Consultation Paper No 154, 1999

Law Commission, *Unfair Terms in Contracts*, Law Com No 292, Scot Law Com No 199, Cm 6464, 2005

Law Commission, *The Illegality Defence*, Consultation Paper No 189, 2009

Law Commission, *The Illegality Defence*, Law Com No 320, HC412, 2010

Law Commission, *Matrimonial Property, Needs and Agreements*, Law Com No 343, 2014

Law Reform Committee, *Transfer of Title to Chattels*, Twelfth Report, Cmd 2958, 1966

Law Revision Committee, Sixth Interim Report, Cmd 5449, 1937

Leff, A, 'Economic analysis of law: some realism about nominalism' (1974) 60 Virginia LR 451

Lewis, R, 'Contracts between businessmen: reform of the law of firm offers' (1982) 9 Brit J Law & Society 153

Luther, P, 'Campbell, Espinasse and the sailors: text and context in the common law' (1999) 19 LS 526

Macaulay, S, 'Non-contractual relations in business' (1963) 28 Am Sociological Rev 35

Macdonald, E, 'Incorporation of contract terms by a consistent course of dealing' (1988) 8 LS 48

Macdonald, E, 'Exclusion clauses: the ambit of s 13(1) of the Unfair Contract Terms Act 1977' (1992) 12 LS 277

Macdonald, E, 'Unifying unfair terms legislation' (2004) 67 MLR 69

Macdonald, E, 'Dispatching the dispatch rule? The postal rule, email, revocation and implied terms' (2013) 19(2) WebJCLI

MacLeod, J K, 'Damages: reliance or expectancy interest' [1970] JBL 19

MacMillan, C, 'The end of the exception in *Dunlop v Lambert?*' [2001] LMCLQ 338

MacMillan, C, 'How temptation led to mistake: an explanation of *Bell v Lever Bros Ltd*' (2003) 119 LQR 625

MacMillan, C, 'Mistake as to identity clarified?' (2004) 120 LQR 369

MacMillan, C, *Mistakes in Contract Law*, 2010, Oxford: Hart Publishing

Macneil, I R, 'Restatement (second) of contracts and presentiation' (1974) 60 Virginia LR 589

Macneil, I R, 'Contracts: adjustments of long term economic relations under classical, neo classical and relational contract law' (1978) 72 Northwestern UL Rev 854

Macneil, I R, 'Essays on the nature of contract' (1980) 10 South Carolina Central LJ 159

Macneil, I R, 'Efficient breach: circles in the sky' (1982) 68 Virginia LR 947

Macneil, I R, 'Relational contract theory as sociology: a reply to Professors Lindenberg and de Vos' (1987) 143 Journal of Institutional and Theoretical Economics 272

Macneil, I R, 'Contract remedies: a need for a better efficiency analysis' (1988) 144 Journal of Institutional and Theoretical Economics 6

Macneil, I R, 'Relational contract theory: challenges and queries' (2000) 94 Northwestern UL Rev 877

McClintock, R, 'Objectivity in contract' (1988–91) 6 Auckland UL Rev 317

McKendrick, E, 'The battle of the forms and the law of restitution' (1988) 8 OJLS 197

McKendrick, E (ed), *Force Majeure*, 2nd edn, 1995a, London: Lloyd's of London Press

McKendrick, E, 'The regulation of long term contracts in English law' (1995b), Chapter 12 in Beatson, J and Friedmann, D (eds), *Good Faith and Fault in Contract Law*, 1995, Oxford: Clarendon Press

McKendrick, E, 'The interpretation of contracts: Lord Hoffmann's re-statement' Chapter 6 in Worthington, S (ed), *Commercial Law and Commercial Practice*, 2003, Oxford: Hart Publishing

McKendrick, E and Graham, M, 'The sky's the limit: contractual damages for non-pecuniary loss' [2002] LMCLQ 161

McLaughlan, D W, 'Contract and commercial law reform in New Zealand' (1984–85) 11 NZULR 36

McLaughlin, G, 'Unconscionability and impracticality: reflections on two UCC indeterminacy principles' (1992) 14 Loyola Int & Comp LJ 439

McMeel, G, 'The rise of commercial construction in contract law' [1998] LMCLQ 382

Miller, C J, *'Felthouse v Bindley* re-visited' (1972) 35 MLR 489

Mitchell, C, 'Leading a life of its own? The roles of reasonable expectation in contract law' (2003) 23 OJLS 639

Mitchell, C, 'Contracts and contract law: challenging the distinction between the "real" and "paper" deal' (2009) 29 OJLS 675

Mitchell, C, Mitchell, P and Watterson, S, *Goff & Jones: The Law of Unjust Enrichment*, 9th edn, 2016, London: Sweet & Maxwell

Mitchell, P and Phillips, J, 'The contractual nexus: is reliance essential?' (2002) 22 OJLS 115

Monopolies Commission, *Report on the supply of petrol to retailers in the United Kingdom*, HC 265, 1965

Montrose, J L, 'The contract of sale in self-service stores' (1955) 4 Am J Comp Law 235

Mouzas, S & Furmston, M, 'From contract to umbrella agreement' (2008) 67(1) Cambridge Law Journal 37.

Mulcahy, L and Wheeler, S, *Feminist Perspectives on Contract Law*, 2005, London: Glasshouse Press

Murdoch, J R, 'The nature of estate agency' (1975) 91 LQR 357

Neill, P, 'A key to lock-out agreements?' (1992) 108 LQR 405

Ogus, A, *The Law of Damages*, 1973, London: Butterworths

O'Sullivan, J, 'In defence of *Foakes v Beer*' (1996) 55 CLJ 219

O'Sullivan, J, 'Loss and gain at greater depth: the implications of the *Ruxley* decision', Chapter 1 in Rose, F (ed), *Failure of Contracts, Contractual Restitutionary and Proprietary Consequences*, 1997, Oxford: Hart Publishing

O'Sullivan, D, 'Developing *O'Brien*' (2002) 118 LQR 337

Palmer, N and Yates, D, 'The future of the Unfair Contract Terms Act 1977' (1981) 40 CLJ 108

Peden, E and Carter, J W, 'Incorporation of terms by signature: L'Estrange Rules!' (2005) 21 JCL 96

Peel, E, 'Remoteness re-visited' (2009) 125 LQR 6

Peel, E, *Treitel: The Law of Contract*, 14th edn, 2015, London: Sweet & Maxwell

Phang, A, 'Common mistake in English law: the proposed merger of common law and equity' (1989) 9 LS 291

Phang, A, 'Implied terms revisited' [1990] JBL 394

Phang, A, 'Implied terms in English law: some recent developments' [1993] JBL 242

Phang, A, 'Specific performance – exploring the roots of settled practice' (1998a) 61 MLR 421

Phang, A, 'Implied terms, business efficacy and the officious bystander – a modern history' [1998b] JBL 1

Phang, A and Tjio, H, 'The uncertain boundaries of undue influence' [2002] LMCLQ 231

Pollock, F, *Principles of Contract Law*, 7th edn, 1902, London: Stevens

Poole, J, 'Damages for breach of contract – compensation and personal preferences: *Ruxley Electronics and Construction Ltd v Forsyth* (1996) 59 MLR 272

Poole, J and Devenney, J, 'Reforming Damages for Misrepresentation: The Case for Coherent Aims and Principles' [2007] Journal of Business Law 269

Posner, R, 'Gratuitous promises in economics and law' (1977) 6 J Leg St 411

Posner, R, *The Economic Analysis of Law*, 4th edn, 1992, Boston, MA: Little, Brown

Powell, J, *Essay upon the Law of Contracts and Agreements*, 1790, London: details unknown

Rawlings, R, 'The battle of the forms' (1979) 42 MLR 715

Reece, H, 'Loss of chances in the law' (1996) 59 MLR 188

Reynolds, F M B, 'Discharge of contract by breach' (1981) 97 LQR 541

Reynolds, F M B, 'Unfair contract terms' (1994) 110 LQR 3

Reynolds, F M B (ed), *Bowstead and Reynolds on Agency*, 18th edn, 2005, London: Sweet & Maxwell

Robertson, A (ed), *The Law of Obligations: Connections and Boundaries*, 2004, London: UCL Press

Rose, F (ed), *Failure of Contracts, Contractual Restitutionary and Proprietary Consequences*, 1997, Oxford: Hart Publishing

Ross, J, 'Setting the standards' (2001) 145 Sol Jo 650

Samuel, G, 'Failure of long term contracts and the duty to re-negotiate – a comment', Chapter 11 in Rose, F (ed), *Failure of Contracts, Contractual Restitutionary and Proprietary Consequences*, 1997, Oxford: Hart Publishing

Sands, D, 'With this contract I thee wed' [1991] LSG 15 May, p 2

Sandy, D, 'Spies, rock stars and restitutionary damages' (2003) 153 NLJ 723

Schanze, E, 'Failure of long term contracts and the duty to re-negotiate', Chapter 10 in Rose, F (ed), *Failure of Contracts, Contractual Restitutionary and Proprietary Consequences*, 1997, Oxford: Hart Publishing

Shea, A, 'Discharge from performance of contracts by failure of condition' (1979) 42 MLR 623

Simpson, A W B (ed), *Oxford Essays in Jurisprudence*, 1973, Oxford: Oxford University Press

Simpson, A W B, *A History of the Common Law of Contract*, 1975a, Oxford: Clarendon Press

Simpson, A W B, 'Innovation in nineteenth century contract law' (1975b) 91 LQR 247

Simpson, A W B, 'The Horwitz thesis and the history of contracts' (1979) 46 U Chic LR 533

Simpson, A W B, 'The rise and fall of the legal treatise: legal principles and the forms of legal literature' (1981) 48 U Chic LR 632

Simpson, A W B, 'Quackery and contract law: the case of the Carbolic Smoke Ball' (1985) 14 J Leg St 345

Simpson, A W B, 'Contracts for cotton to arrive: the case of the two ships *Peerless*' (1989) 11 Cardozo L Rev 287

Smith, J C, 'Civil concepts in the criminal law' [1972] CLJ 197

Smith, J C, 'Contracts – mistake, frustration and implied terms' (1994) 110 LQR 400

Smith, S A, 'Reconstructing restraint of trade' (1995) OJLS 565

Smith, S A, 'In defence of substantive fairness' (1996) 112 LQR 138

Smith, S A, 'Contracting under pressure: a theory of duress' [1997a] CLJ 343

Smith, S A, 'Performance, punishment and the nature of contractual obligations' (1997b) 60 MLR 360

Smith, S A, 'Contracts for the benefit of third parties: in defence of the Third-Party Rule' (1997c) OJLS 643

Smith, S A, *Contract Theory*, 2004, Oxford: Clarendon Press

Smith, S A, *Atiyah's Introduction to the Law of Contract*, 6th edn, 2006, Oxford: Clarendon Press

Spencer, J, 'Signature, consent and the rule in *L'Estrange v Graucob*' (1973) 32 CLJ 104

Staughton, C, 'How do the courts interpret commercial contracts?' [1999] CLJ 303

Stevens, R, 'The Contracts (Rights of Third Parties) Act 1999' (2004) 120 LQR 292

Stewart, A and Carter, J W, 'Frustrated contracts and statutory adjustment: the case for a reappraisal' [1992] CLJ 66

Steyn, J, 'Contract law: fulfilling the reasonable expectations of honest men' (1997) 113 LQR 433

Stone, R, 'Usual or ostensible authority: one concept or two?' [1993] JBL 325

Stone, R, *Law of Agency*, 1996, London: Cavendish Publishing

Stone, R, 'Withdrawal of offer to settle – Pt 36 of the Civil Procedure Rules 1998' (2001) 33 SLR 23

Stone, R, *Textbook on Civil Liberties and Human Rights*, 11th edn, 2017, Oxford: Oxford University Press

Stone, R, 'Forming contracts without offer and acceptance, Lord Denning and the harmonisation of English contract law' [2012] 4 WebJCLI

Swain, W, 'The classical model of contract: the product of a revolution in legal thought?' (2010) 30 Legal Studies 513

Tan, Cheng-Han, 'Undisclosed principals and contract' (2004) 120 LQR 480

Tettenborn, A, 'Of FOB sales, sellers' obligations and disclaimers' [2009] LMCLQ 417

Thompson, M P, 'Representation to expectation: estoppel as a cause of action' (1983) 42 CLJ 257

Tiplady, M, 'The limits of undue influence' (1985) 48 MLR 579

Tjio, H, *'O'Brien* and unconscionability' (1997) 113 LQR 10

Trakman, L, 'Frustrated contracts and legal fictions' (1983) 46 MLR 39

Trebilcock, M J, *The Common Law of Restraint of Trade*, 1986, London: Sweet & Maxwell

Trebilcock, M J, *The Limits of Freedom of Contract*, 1993, Cambridge, MA: Harvard University Press

Treitel, G H, 'Consideration: a critical analysis of Professor Atiyah's fundamental restatement' (1976) 50 Australian LJ 439

Treitel, G H, 'Damages on rescission for breach of contract' [1987] LCMLQ 143

Treitel, G H, 'Mistake in contract' (1988) 104 LQR 501

Treitel, G H, 'Affirmation after repudiatory breach' (1998a) 114 LQR 22

Treitel, G H, 'Damages in respect of a third party's loss' (1998b) 114 LQR 527

Treitel, G H, 'Types of contractual terms', Chapter 3 in *Some Landmarks of Twentieth Century Contract Law*, 2002, Oxford: Clarendon Press

Treitel (2015) – See Peel, E.

Treitel, G H, *Frustration and Force Majeure*, 3rd edn, 2014, London: Sweet & Maxwell

Twigg-Flesner C, Canavan, R, and MacQueen, H, *Atiyah and Adams' Sale of Goods*, 13th edn, 2016, Harlow: Pearson

Unberath, H, 'Third party losses and black holes: another view' (1999) 115 LQR 535

Unberath, H and McKendrick, E, 'Supervening events' in Dannemann, G and Vogenauer, S (eds), *The Common European Sales Law in Context: Interactions with English and German Law*, 2013, Oxford: Oxford University Press

Unger, J, 'Self-service shops and the law of contract' (1953) 16 MLR 369

Unger, R, *The Critical Legal Studies Movement*, 1983, Cambridge, MA: Harvard University Press

Vincent-Jones, P, 'The reception of Ian Macneil's work on contract in the UK', Chapter 3 in Campbell, D (ed), *The Relational Theory of Contract: Selected Works of Ian Macneil*, 2001, London: Sweet & Maxwell

Vogenauer, S and Weatherill, S, *The Harmonisation of European Contract Law*, 2006, Oxford: Hart Publishing

Von Bar, C, Clive, E and Schulte Nölke, H (eds), *Principles, Definitions and Model Rules of European Private Law. Draft Common Frame of Reference (DCFR)*, 2009, Munich, Sellier

von Mehren, A, 'General limits on the use of contract', Vol vii, *International Encyclopaedia of Comparative Law*, 1982, The Hague: Mohr/Nijhoff

Waddams, S, 'Johanna Wagner and the rival opera houses' (2001) 117 LQR 431

Wade, H R W, 'Horizons of horizontally' (2000) 116 LQR 217

Wallace, D, 'Third party damage: no legal black hole' (1999) 115 LQR 394

Warwick, M, 'Misuse of the matrix' (2003) 153 NLJ 1579

Weatherill, S, 'The Consumer Rights Directive: how and why a quest for "coherence" has (largely) failed' (2012) 49 CML Rev 1279

Wedderburn, K W, 'Collateral contracts' [1959] CLJ 58

Wheeler, S and Shaw, J, *Contract Law Cases, Materials and Commentary*, 1994, Oxford: Clarendon Press

Whish, R, *Competition Law*, 5th edn, 2003, London: Butterworths

Wightman, J, *Contract: A Critical Commentary*, 1996, London: Pluto Press

Wightman, J, 'Negligent valuations and a drop in the property market: the limits of the expectation loss principle' (1998) 61 MLR 68

Wilhelmsson, T (ed), *Perspectives of Critical Contract Law*, 1993, Aldershot: Dartmouth

Wilkinson, H W, 'Unfair contract terms – not again?' (2000) 150 NLJ 1778

Williams, D C, 'A survey of recent case law' (1953) 10 NILQ 117

Williston, S, *Williston on Contracts*, 4th edn (edited by Lord, RA), 1990, New York: Lawyers Co-operative Publishing

Wilson, S and Woodley, M, 'Restraint, drafting and the rule in General Billposting' [1998] JBL 272

Wright, R A, *Legal Essays and Addresses*, 1939, Cambridge: Cambridge University Press

Yates, D, *Exclusion Clauses in Contracts*, 2nd edn, 1982, London: Sweet & Maxwell

Yates, D, 'Drafting *force majeure* and related clauses' (1991) 3 J of Cont L 186

# Index